D0141883

# A Guide
## to
# Folktales
## in the
# English Language

**Recent Titles in**
**Bibliographies and Indexes in World Literature**

Psychocriticism: An Annotated Bibliography
*Joseph P. Natoli and Frederik L. Rusch, compilers*

Olaf Stapledon: A Bibliography
*Harvey J. Satty and Curtis C. Smith, compilers*

Spanish Literature, 1500-1700: A Bibliography of Golden Age
Studies in Spanish and English, 1925-1980
*William W. Moseley, Glenroy Emmons, and Marilyn C. Emmons, compilers*

Monthly Terrors: An Index to the Weird Fantasy Magazines
Published in the United States and Great Britain
*Frank H. Parnell, compiler, with the assistance of Mike Ashley*

The Independent Monologue in Latin American Theater:
A Primary Bibliography with Selective Secondary Sources
*Duane Rhoades, compiler*

J.R.R. Tolkien: Six Decades of Criticism
*Judith A. Johnson*

Bibliographic Guide to Gabriel García Márquez, 1979-1985
*Margaret Eustella Fau and Nelly Sfeir de Gonzalez, compilers*

Eastern Europe in Children's Literature: An Annotated Bibliography
of English-language Books
*Frances F. Povsic*

The Literary Universe of Jorge Luis Borges: An Index to References
and Allusions to Persons, Titles, and Places in His Writings
*Daniel Balderston, compiler*

Film as Literature, Literature as Film:
An Introduction to and Bibliography of Film's Relationship to Literature
*Harris Ross*

# A Guide
## to
# Folktales
## in the
# English Language

*Based on the Aarne-Thompson*
*Classification System*

## D. L. Ashliman

WITHDRAWAL

Bibliographies and Indexes in World Literature, Number 11

**Greenwood Press**
New York • Westport, Connecticut • London

**Library of Congress Cataloging-in-Publication Data**

Ashliman, D. L.
  A guide to folktales in the English language.

  (Bibliographies and indexes in world literature,
ISSN 0742-6801 ; no. 11)
  Bibliography: p.
  Includes index.
  1. Tales—Classification—Bibliography.   2. Tales—
Themes, motives—Bibliography.   I. Title.   II. Series.
Z5983.F17A83   1987   [GR74.6]     016.3982'012     87-15017
ISBN 0-313-25961-5 (lib. bdg. : alk. paper)

British Library Cataloguing in Publication Data is available.

Copyright © 1987 by D. L. Ashliman

All rights reserved. No portion of this book may be
reproduced, by any process or technique, without the
express written consent of the publisher.

Library of Congress Catalog Card Number: 87-15017
ISBN: 0-313-25961-5
ISSN: 0742-6801

First published in 1987

Greenwood Press, Inc.
88 Post Road West, Westport, Connecticut 06881

Printed in the United States of America

The paper used in this book complies with the
Permanent Paper Standard issued by the National
Information Standards Organization (Z39.48-1984).

10 9 8 7 6 5 4 3 2 1

To
Elgarda Zobell Ashliman
Storyteller

# Contents

# Introduction

**STORIES BY NUMBER.** Everyone knows the story about the visitor to an asylum who observed the inmates taking turns calling out numbers, upon which the others would all laugh, sometimes a polite chuckle, sometimes a roar. As the host explained, the residents—for reasons of economy—had assigned a number to every joke known to the group. That done, they needed only to call out a story's number to entertain one another. The visitor decided to test the scheme and called out a number of his own, but his contribution was met with stoney silence. The host explained: "Some can tell a joke, and some can't." Others give the tale a different ending, in which the visitor's number is received with uncontrolled laughter. The host, in this version, responds: "They hadn't heard that one yet!"

Assigning numbers to stories is not exclusively the province of asylum jokes. Folklorists have long used numerical systems to identify and analyze the motifs and plots that serve as the building blocks of folktales. The following *Guide to Folktales* is based on the oldest and most widely used of these systems, *The Types of the Folktale,* first published in German in 1910 by the Finnish scholar Antti Aarne, revised in 1928, then translated into English and substantially enlarged by the American folklorist Stith Thompson in 1961.

The Aarne-Thompson system catalogs some 2500 basic plots from which, for countless generations, European and Near Eastern storytellers have built their tales. It also includes, but only parenthetically, literary stories that have an independent oral tradition. As Europeans and Near Easterners traveled to the New World, the Far East, Africa, and other distant places, their tales migrated as well, often flourishing in their new environments. Hence the Aarne-Thompson system encompasses tales found around the world, although it excludes, except for a few coincidental items, stories not indigenous to Europe or the Near East.

In selecting entries for the following *Guide to Folktales,* I have, in the main, followed Aarne's and Thompson's geographic limits. Thus, I include non-European stories only if they have European counterparts. However, my listing of any particular African, American, or Asian tale should not be interpreted as a claim for European origins, although given the travel patterns of the past few centuries, this will more often than not be the case. Tale migration toward Europe has also taken place, especially from India and the Arabic world, cultures with rich heritages in storytelling. Further, there is always the possibility that stories with similar plots evolved independently in two or more regions.

Given the evolution of the Aarne-Thompson catalog and the complexity and magnitude of its subject, it should come as no surprise that the work displays inconsistencies, for example, the sometimes confusing usage of letters and asterisks in its numbering scheme. Every serious user soon develops a list of proposed adjustments to the system as a whole, but its use by several generations of scholars, archivists, and librarians around the world dictates that the old numbers not be tampered with lightly, although categories can be added as new stories come to light. Anticipating this need, Aarne and Thompson left numerous gaps between their numbers. New type numbers that I myself suggest include 171 (The Three Bears), 504 (The Changeling), 776 (The Goose That Laid Golden Eggs), 1215A (The Man with Two Wives), and 1500 (The Old Woman's Cure). Additionally, I have incorporated several new numbers proposed by other scholars and collectors.

Although my listings, with few exceptions, follow the Aarne-Thompson numbers I have thoroughly revised Thompson's verbal descriptions of the types, in part for stylistic reasons, but more often to better describe the variants that are currently available in English.

I have made no attempt to include all printed sources of a given variant, limiting myself instead to a few reliable editions. Favorite stories from the Grimms' collection, for example, are reprinted in countless editions, but I have given only one or two listings for each tale. In general I follow the judgment of individual editors, where they provide type listings of stories in their collections. Editions not including type listings (for example, those by Afanasyev, Asbjørnsen and Moe, Bushnaq, Calvino, Crane, Jacobs, Lang, Opie, Perrault, Pourrat, Sampson, Straparola, and Thomas) were type-analyzed by me, as were the Grimms' tales (existing type analyses of this most important collection are inaccurate and incomplete). Because of the Grimms' centrality in folktale research, I include a complete listing of their tales, including type classifications, as an appendix.

**KINDS OF FOLKTALES.** The larger divisions in the Aarne-Thompson classification scheme correspond to folktale genres. Although based primarily on plot, traditional differentiation of folktale genres is also related to the tales' social and psychological functions.

Their first group (types 1-299) consists primarily of fables: succinct stories featuring animals and inanimate objects as characters. Recognized as fiction by teller and listener alike, fables are nonetheless perceived as carriers of truth in the form of didactic lessons, psychological observations, or social commentary. The fable's obvious literary and philosophical potential has attracted writers and thinkers for many centuries. The resulting inter-play between folkloristic and literary traditions has benefited both.

Tales of magic (types 300-749), also known as "wonder tales," or "Zaubermärchen," constitute one of the largest, and probably the most mem-orable of all folktale genres. Although frequently referred to as "fairy tales," a term borrowed in the mid eighteenth century from the French "contes des fées," these stories rarely deal with fairies *per se,* but they do rely on magic for the fantasy solutions to seemingly insurmountable problems. By any name, these stories, told for pure entertainment, are rich expressions of human fantasy. The elaborate imagery typical of the genre often elicits symbolic and psychological interpretations.

One person's magic is another's religion, and religious tales also consti-tute an important part of folklore. Types 750-849 are, for the most part, stories of divine rewards and punishments told within the framework of es-tablished European religions (generally Roman Catholicism), but lacking details of time and place. Similar stories that specify time, place, or partici-pants, and that are accepted as fact by storyteller and audience, are classified as legends, and generally are not included in the Aarne-Thompson catalog, in spite of their obvious importance in folklore.

As a rule, Aarne and Thompson include legends (i.e., believed tales) in their catalog only to the extent that they are similar to obviously fictitious tales, for example, accounts of dragon killers (type 300). However, scattered throughout their system are stories that in times past certainly were accepted as truth. There are accounts of vampires (types 307, 363), blue-bearded wife killers (types 312, 955), grave robbers (type 326B*), specter bridegrooms returning for their fiancées (type 365), prankster elves (type 503), Saint Christopher and the Christ Child (type 768), and the Wandering Jew (type 777), to mention but a few prominent examples.

Another folklore genre built on belief is the myth. Although in popular usage any fanciful or untrue story can be called a myth, folklorists assign more dignity to the term. Myths, in this sense, are serious stories of explana-tion (for example, accounts of creation) that were, or still are, accepted as truth by both teller and listener. Typically, myths invoke powers that tran-scend the earth. The magic of mythology is not the "ordinary" magic that turns a frog into a prince or lets a donkey drop gold pellets. It rather in-volves the omnipotence of such world creators and arbiters of justice and wisdom as Zeus, Odin, and Yahweh. Stories from mythology, as a rule, are not included in the Aarne-Thompson index.

Romantic tales (types 850-999), also known as novelle (plural, from the Italian "novella"), are compact stories with pointed plots. They usually have a literary heritage, with parallel printed and oral forms mutually contribut-ing to each other's evolution. These accounts typically depict acts of great patience, wisdom, courage, selflessness, and the like, and they seldom rely on magic solutions. Their didactic intent is usually self evident.

Anecdotes and jests (types 1000-1999) open a peep hole onto the back room stage of human comedy. There is no magic here, no subtle symbolism, and no sophisticated moral reasoning. Told, more often than not, with crude humor, these tales depict struggles for the basics: food, sex, power, and revenge. The trickster steals food from his companion, sleeps with his master's wife or daughter (or both!), then gives his competitor a beating, and we laugh at his exploits.

Formula tales (types 2000-2399) are told for the sheer pleasure of hearing fanciful words: "This is the farmer sowing his corn, that kept the cock that crow'd in the morn, that waked the priest all shaven and shorn, that married the man all tatter'd and torn, that kissed the maiden all forlorn, that milk'd the cow with the crumpled horn, that tossed the dog, that worried the cat, that kill'd the rat, that ate the malt, that lay in the house that Jack built." Some delight in contradiction: "One dark night, in the middle of the day. . . ." Others serve as signals, for example the brief tale that my mother used to mark the end of story time: "I'll tell you a story about Jack O'Nory, and now my story's begun; I'll tell you another about Jack and his brother, and now my story is done."

**THE LEGACY OF FOLKTALES.** The motifs and themes of traditional folktales still permeate twentieth century life. We meet them in children's literature, journalism, advertising, and everyday conversation. Names and concepts such as the golden goose, Cinderella, Hansel and Gretel, Bluebeard, sour grapes, or the lion's share elicit emotional responses in us all, whether or not we know the "original" tales. For good reason, folktales continue to provide raw material for scholarly discourse not only among folklorists, but also in such fields as psychology, anthropology, sociology, and literary criticism.

Folktales, of one sort or another, have always been with us, and their themes and motifs have been adopted and re-formed by literary artists throughout the ages. Aesop (if he existed), Apuleius, the poet of the *Nibelungenlied,* Boccaccio, Chaucer, Poggio, Pauli, Straparola, Basile, the makers of countless chapbooks, Shakespeare, Grimmelshausen, Perrault, and Andersen—the list could be extended—all are literary artists of greater or lesser stature who made liberal use of traditional folktale materials.

In many instances their formulations then returned to the illiterate world, which until the mid nineteenth century was larger than the world of readers, even in enlightened Europe and America. European popular tales thus have a mixed heritage, a fact often overlooked both by folklorists, many of whom despise printed sources, and by historians of literature, who all too frequently are blissfully ignorant of oral traditions.

Folklore as an intellectual and artistic pursuit received its greatest infusion of energy and respectability during the late eighteenth and early nineteenth centuries. In part as a reaction against the more sterile aspects of the Enlightenment, numerous events from about 1750 onward paved the way for

increased appreciation of folklore, not only as raw material for artistic re-
finement, but also as an art form in its own right.

A seminal work in this development was Jean Jacques Rousseau's essay
*Discours sur les Arts et Sciences* (1750), which praised the values and life-
styles of primitive cultures. Equally sensational, the purported poetry of the
third-century Gaelic poet Ossian, published in 1762 and 1763 by the Scottish
schoolmaster James Macpherson, was greatly admired by Goethe and other
influential literary figures. Although these "translations," as soon became
evident, were forgeries, they helped prepare for an acceptance of the naïve
art of folklore.

Thomas Percy's *Reliques of Ancient English Poetry* (1765), ballads
based on the manuscript collection of a sixteenth-century performer, had a
similar—but longer lasting—influence on Europe's literary establishment.
The folk-like ballad became a respected literary form, especially in Germany. Such poets as Herder, Bürger, Schiller, and Goethe enthusiastically
contributed to the genre, openly praising its folk origins and natural
qualities.

It was only a question of time before a "German Percy" would emerge,
and he came as a team, when Achim von Arnim and Clemens Brentano published their two-volume collection *Des Knaben Wunderhorn* in 1806 and
1808. It contained folk and folk-like poetry of every description: ballads,
love songs, church hymns, fairy tales in verse, working songs, and children's
rhymes. Their sources were equally varied: books, manuscripts, printed
broadsides, translations, old hymnals, and even poetry composed by the editors. The enterprise was immensely successful, and a third volume, to be
dedicated to folktales, was announced. The editors solicited contributions
from friends and associates throughout Germany.

**THE GRIMM BROTHERS.** In December 1810, two brothers, Jacob and
Wilhelm Grimm, answered von Arnim's and Brentano's call and submitted a
manuscript containing fifty-three stories, some written out in detail, others
sketched in brief outline form. Volume three of *Des Knaben Wunderhorn,*
the fairy-tale volume, never materialized, but the Grimms' interest in col-
lecting and editing folklore did not die. In 1812 they published their own
collection of eighty-six tales, entitled *Kinder- und Hausmärchen, (Children's
and Household Tales),* an unpretentious volume that was destined to become
the most widely read, most frequently imitated, and most influential book
ever created in the German language. A second volume appeared in 1814
(dated 1815), adding seventy stories. Revisions and new printings followed,
until the seventh edition of 1857, the last to appear during the Grimms' life-
time. Their final version contained two hundred numbered tales and an appendix of ten "Children's Legends."

Some twentieth-century writers have criticized the process of evolution to
which the Grimms subjected their tales during their half century of collect-
ing, editing, and publishing. The Grimms did claim that the stories were

authentic folk material, and that they had done little more than to filter out offensive expressions and to translate local dialects into standard German (although a number of tales were left in Low German and other dialects). In truth they took substantial editorial liberties, especially between the manuscript collection of 1810 and the first published edition of 1812, and again between the first edition and the second one, which appeared in 1819.

The Grimms and many of their champions in later years overstated the simple folk origins of their work. As emerging scholars of philology, medieval literature, and ancient Germanic civilization, the Grimms made substantial, but not slavish, use of printed sources in their selection and editing process, and they did receive their tales primarily by word of mouth. But even in this, some modern critics grumble about their choice of informants, who for the most part were women from the literate middle class, including members of their own circle of intellectual friends. Dorothea Wild, one of their most prolific informants, married Wilhelm in 1825.

It is unfair and misleading to belittle the Grimms' *Kinder- und Hausmärchen* on these grounds. Granted, illiterate informants, relatively untouched by formal learning, would have provided invaluable folkloristic, sociological and psychological insights, but this is not to suggest that the Grimms' versions—admittedly influenced by the world of books—are not authentic folklore. They were, in fact, both accepted and denigrated as such by contemporary critics, many of whom found the collection too unpolished, too common, and too vulgar for use in respectable homes.

We need only compare the Grimms' work with "folktales" of their immediate forebears and contemporaries (for example, Musäus, Tieck, and Bechstein) to appreciate the folkloristic qualities of their versions. They were pioneers in the science of folklore, and it is unrealistic to hold them to the standards expected of twentieth-century practitioners, just as it would be unfair to criticize Joseph Priestley for not following modern laboratory practices in his pioneering experiments with oxygen.

The best argument for the authenticity of the *Kinder- und Hausmärchen* emerges from the research that followed their efforts. Subsequent folklorists, working in every corner of Europe and beyond, have independently discovered, in readily recognizable variants, nearly all of the Grimms' two hundred tales. Moreover, the versions discovered by later collectors demonstrate that in most instances the Grimms' poetic license in no way compromised their tales' folkloristic qualities and functions.

I offer, as one of numerous examples, the Grimms' "All-Kinds-of-Fur" (no. 65, type 510B), whose central theme, as in most variants, is a king's attempt to enter into a sexual relationship with his own daughter. The Grimms make minor adjustments to the text from one edition to the next. They omit a scene in which the heroine is forced to delouse her future husband (not her father, but a similarly abusive man), and they soften an episode in which this man throws his boots at her head. However, the text's main interest, and certainly its traditional *raison d'être,* a father's sexual exploitation of his daughter, is faithfully recorded, although the theme undoubtedly offended many contemporary readers. At least one English translation alters the Grimms' text, making the king's minister, not the king himself, pursue the princess. Similarly, the Grimms' popular contemporary Ludwig Bechstein completely suppressed the incest motif in his telling of the story ("Aschenpüster mit der Wünschelgerte"), although in so doing he destroyed the plot's logic.

The Grimms' versions, then, are not perfect in their folkloristic authenticity. However, given the substantial breadth of their collection and the editorial practices of their contemporaries, their *Kinder- und Hausmärchen* remains the most significant collection of European folktales ever published. Without their efforts, there still would be stories of Cinderellas, Hansels and Gretels, Frog Kings, Sleeping Beauties, and Kings Who Wanted to Marry Their Daughters, but no one can say to what remote corners one would have to travel in order to find them.

**HOW TO USE THIS BOOK.** The first aim of *A Guide to Folktales in the English Language* is to help readers find reliable texts of any given folktale, not only in its best-known version, but also in less familiar variants. Those who do not know the Aarne-Thompson type number of a tale can begin their search in the index at the end of the book, where the titles of the best-known tales and key words from typical plots are located. The index does not attempt to list all stories by title, but does include entries by title, subject matter, and character for representative tales of every type.

The type numbers in the index refer to the book's main section. Many stories consist of multiple episodes, each with its own type number. I include such tales in each relevant group. I have placed many tales in groups where they fit only marginally, or where the connection is one of function rather than of plot. As a rule, adjacent numbers in the Aarne-Thompson system represent stories with similar plots. Thus, readers often can locate related tales by browsing within a range of type numbers. Each entry in the main section gives a tale's published title and a short reference to the collection where it can be found. Full information about the sources is contained in the bibliography of folktale collections beginning on page 335.

For further study, I also include a bibliography of selected books about folklore and folktales (see page 328). Many of these books also contain folktale texts. Moreover, many of the collections, notably the *Dictionary of British Folk-Tales* by Katharine M. Briggs, the entire series *Folktales of the World* under the general editorship of Richard M. Dorson, and individual works edited by Roger D. Abrahams, Jan Harold Brunvand, Atelia Clarkson, Gilbert B. Cross, and Susie Hoogasian Villa, contain copious notes and references to variants. In addition, Aarne's and Thompson's *The Types of the Folktale,* with its detailed descriptions and prolific source listings, remains an indispensable tool for folktale research. Ernest W. Baughman's *Type and Motif Index of the Folktales of England and North America* lists tales originating in England and America, and is especially useful for locating variants published only in folklore journals.

**HOW THIS BOOK WAS MADE.** The genesis of *A Guide to Folktales* began with a box of index cards cross-referencing international folktales with similar themes. When the box became too small, it was replaced by a Radio Shack® computer and a data base program named Profile. When the data base, which included tales both in the English and German languages, outgrew the small computer, it was transferred to a DEC® mainframe computer, where it grew to well over 10,000 records. A grant to the University of Pittsburgh from the Apple Corporation gave me easy access to a Macintosh® computer and a LaserWriter®. The bibliographic entries that constitute this book were transferred from the mainframe data base to micro disks, edited with Microsoft® Word, and printed on the laser printer.

In truth though, this description of my book's production has little to do with its genesis. My involvement with folktales began well before the computer age, even—for me personally—before the age of index cards and filing boxes. I was not introduced to folktales through the "authoritative" texts of scholarly editions, but rather through the magic of a gifted storyteller, my mother. To her I dedicate this book.

# Animal Tales

1 **A FOX STEALS FISH BY PLAYING DEAD.** A fox played dead by the side of the road, and a man with a load of fish picked him up, praising his luck for the beautiful pelt. But the clever fox stole the fish and escaped. (Lang)

> Brother Rabbit Outdoes Mister Man. Harris, *Nights with Uncle Remus,* no. 52.
> Buh Fox's Number Nine Shoes (USA, Black). Clarkson and Cross, *World Folktales,* no. 21.
> Fish Thief, The. Seki, *Folktales of Japan,* no. 1.
> Fox and the Lapp, The (Lapland). Lang, *Brown Fairy Book,* p. 245.
> Fox Eats the Arab's Chickens, The. Arewa, *Northern East Africa,* p. 139.
> Fox in Inishkea, The. O'Sullivan, *Folktales of Ireland,* no. 3.
> Foxes, the Fisherman, and the Horse, The. Campbell, *West Highlands,* v. 1, p. 286.
> How Brother Fox Was Too Smart. Harris, *Nights with Uncle Remus,* no. 4.
> Little Sister Fox and the Wolf. Afanasyev, *Russian Fairy Tales,* p. 371.
> Reynard and Bruin. Jacobs, *European Folk and Fairy Tales,* no. 6.
> Tub of Butter, The (Canada). Dorson, *Folktales around the World,* p. 445.
> Wolf and the Fox, The. Massignon, Folktales of France, no. 54.

1* **THE FOX AND THE RABBIT STEAL A BASKET.** The fox and the rabbit entered a partnership. The rabbit pretended to be hurt by the side of the road, and a woman set down her basket of eggs and tried to capture him. The fox made off with the eggs, but he did not give his partner the rabbit his promised share. (Ranke)

> Fox and the Hare in Winter, The. Ranke, *Folktales of Germany,* no. 1.
> Fox and the Magpie, The. Briggs, *DBF,* pt. A, v. 1, p. 109.
> Hare, Badger, Monkey, and Otter, The. Seki, *Folktales of Japan,* no. 2.

2 **HOW THE BEAR LOST HIS TAIL.** The bear met the fox, who was carrying a string of stolen fish. The fox claimed he had caught them through a hole in the ice, and he showed the bear how to use his long tail for a line. The bear sat on the ice until the hole froze shut, and he had to pull off his tail to escape. (Asbjørnsen and Moe)

Crafty Wolf, The. Grimm, *Other Tales*, p. 49.
Fish Thief, The. Seki, *Folktales of Japan,* no. 1.
Fox and the Hare in Winter, The. Ranke, *Folktales of Germany,* no. 1.
Fox and the Lapp, The (Lapland). Lang, *Brown Fairy Book,* p. 245.
Fox and the Magpie, The. Briggs, *DBF,* pt. A, v. 1, p. 109.
How Mister Rabbit Lost His Fine Bushy Tail. Harris, *Uncle Remus,* no. 25.
How the Wolf Lost His Tail. Campbell, *West Highlands,* v. 1, p. 280.
Little Sister Fox and the Wolf. Afanasyev, *Russian Fairy Tales,* p. 371.
Rabbit and Fox Go Fishing. Dorson, *Negro Tales,* p. 28.
Reynard and Bruin. Jacobs, *European Folk and Fairy Tales,* no. 6.
Why the Bear is Stumpy-Tailed. Asbjørnsen and Moe, *East o' the Sun,* p. 172
Wolf and the Fox, The. Massignon, *Folktales of France,* no. 54.

**2A    CAUGHT BY THE TAIL.** Brer Rabbit offered to help Brer Fox repair his roof, but while they were working, he nailed Brer Fox's tail to the shingles. He then ate Brer Fox's dinner and escaped.

Brother Rabbit Gets Brother.Fox's Dinner. Harris, *Nights with Uncle Remus,* no. 59.

**2B    THE TRICKSTER DROWNS HIS FISHING PARTNER.** The fox presented the wolf with a plan to catch fish. They tied a pot around the wolf's neck and swam into the water, but the pot filled with water, and the wolf drowned.

Fox and the Wolf Go a-Fishing, The. Megas, *Folktales of Greece,* no. 1.

**3    SHAM BLOOD AND BRAINS.** See type 4.

**4    GETTING A RIDE BY PRETENDING TO BE INJURED.** Sister Fox smeared herself with dough and told the wolf she had had her brains beaten out. Feeling pity, the wolf carried her home. (Afanasyev)

Bear and the Squirrel, The. Lindell, II, no. 9.
Fox and His Cousin, The. Grimm, *Tales,* no. 74.
Fox and the Crocodile, The. Thundy, *South Indian Folktales,* no. 40.
Fox, the Lion, and the Smith, The. Arewa, *Northern East Africa,* p. 94.
Little Sister Fox and the Wolf. Afanasyev, *Russian Fairy Tales,* p. 371.
Mister Rabbit Grossly Deceives Mister Fox. Harris, *Uncle Remus,* no. 6.
Reynard and Bruin. Jacobs, *European Folk and Fairy Tales,* no. 6.
Tiger Becomes a Riding Horse. Abrahams, *Afro-American Folktales,* no. 25.
Vixen, The. Pino-Saavedra, *Folktales of Chile,* no. 1.

**5    BITING THE ROOT.** The bear chased the fox into a briar bush and caught the fox's leg in his mouth. The fox cried out: "You fool, you're biting a root." So the bear relaxed his grip and snapped again. This time he did bite into a root. "That's my leg! Don't hurt me!" shouted the fox. The bear bit down harder, and the fox escaped. (Jacobs)

Fox and the Crocodile, The. Thundy, *South Indian Folktales,* no. 40.
Hare Escapes, The (3 variants). Arewa, *Northern East Africa,* p. 115.

How Brer Rabbit Saved Brer B'ar's Life. Harris, *Uncle Remus and the Little Boy,* no. 4.

Mister Fox Tackles Old Man Tarrypin. Harris, *Uncle Remus,* no. 12.

Reynard and Bruin. Jacobs, *European Folk and Fairy Tales,* no. 6.

**6      OPEN YOUR MOUTH AND LOSE YOUR MEAL.** A fox captured a cock and was carrying him between his teeth. "He's mine!" cried the hen. "Tell her that I belong to you," said the cock to his captor. The fox opened his mouth to do so, and the cock escaped. (Campbell)

Cock and the Fox, The. Asbjørnsen and Moe, *Norwegian Folktales,* p. 135.

Fox, the Cock, and Their Tricks, The. Campbell, *West Highlands,* v. 1, p. 279.

Liar Mvkang and the Water Snake (Burma). Dorson, *Folktales around the World,* p. 282.

Raven and the Lobster, The. Afanasyev, *Russian Fairy Tales,* p. 612.

**7      A CONTEST TO NAME THREE TREES.** A bear and a fox entered into a contest to see who could name three trees first. The bear called out "spruce, fir, and pine," but the fox claimed that these were merely different names for the same tree. The fox then shouted "ash, aspen, oak!" and declared himself the winner.

Bear and the Fox Who Made a Bet, The. Asbjørnsen and Moe, *Norwegian Folktales,* p. 120.

**8      PAINTING THE BEAR RED.** The fox told the envious bear that he had acquired his beautiful coat by having his old one burned red, and he offered to help the bear do the same thing. Thus the bear lay down on a stack of hay, which the fox set afire. The bear nearly died in the flames and ended up with badly singed fur. (Boss)

Brother Fox Smells Smoke. Harris, *Uncle Remus and His Friends,* no. 8.

Fox and the Lapp, The (Lapland). Lang, *Brown Fairy Book,* p. 245.

Vain Bear, The (Finland). Booss, *Scandinavian Tales,* p. 591.

**8A    CURLY HAIR FROM BOILING WATER.** A bear captured a beautiful girl and was envious of her curly hair. Her brother tracked them to his lair and told the bear that the only way to curl hair would be to stick one's head in boiling water. The bear fell for the trick, and the children escaped.

Little Boy and His Dogs, The. Harris, *Daddy Jake,* no. 3.

**9      THE UNJUST PARTNER.** A dove and a fox became farming partners, but every time there was a job to do, the fox made an excuse and the dove had to work alone. But after the harvest, the fox took charge of the crop division, giving himself the grain and the dove the straw. (Dorson)

Dove and the Fox, The (Italy). Dorson, *Folktales around the World,* p. 74.
Farmers Three (Finland). Booss, *Scandinavian Tales,* p. 590.
Fox and the Heron, The. O'Sullivan, *Folktales of Ireland,* no. 1.
Monkey and the Crab, The. Seki, *Folktales of Japan,* no. 5.

**9B   DIVIDING THE HARVEST.** The fox and the wolf divided their crop, the fox taking the smaller pile, containing the corn, and the wolf taking the larger pile, containing nothing but chaff. (Ranke)

Farmers Three (Finland). Booss, *Scandinavian Tales,* p. 590.
Fox and the Wolf, The. Ranke, *Folktales of Germany,* no. 2.
How the Ewe Outwitted the Jackal. Bushnaq, *Arab Folktales,* p. 236.

**15   STEALING THE PARTNER'S BUTTER.** The cat and the mouse set up housekeeping together, and they bought a pot of fat to share during the coming winter. But the cat, on three occasions, told the mouse he was going to a christening, and sneaked to the hiding place and ate part of the fat. The mouse discovered the fraud and confronted her partner. The cat replied by eating her up. (Grimm)

Biyera Well, The. El-Shamy, *Folktales of Egypt,* no. 51.
Brer Goat. Saucier, *French Louisiana,* no. 30.
Bruin and Reynard. Asbjørnsen and Moe, *East o' the Sun,* p. 409.
Cat and Mouse in Partnership. Grimm, *Tales,* no. 2.
Fox and the Heron, The. O'Sullivan, *Folktales of Ireland,* no. 1.
Fox as Midwife, The. Afanasyev, *Russian Fairy Tales,* p. 191.
Hare, the Leopard, and the Cow, The. Arewa, *Northern East Africa,* p. 38.
Little Hen and the Little Cock, The. Ranke, *Folktales of Germany,* no. 3.
Mister Rabbit Nibbles Up the Butter. Harris, *Uncle Remus,* no. 17.
Mrs. Fox and Mister Wolf. Calvino, *Italian Folktales,* no. 125.
Possum He Didn't Eat, The. Randolph, *Hot Springs and Hell,* no. 314.
Rabbit Fool the Panther. Dorson, *Negro Tales,* p. 160.
Reynard and Bruin. Jacobs, *European Folk and Fairy Tales,* no. 6.
Stealing the Butter, Hiding in the Log. Dorson, *Negro Tales,* p. 13.
Stealing the Butter. Dorson, *Negro Tales,* p. 11.
Tub of Butter, The (Canada). Dorson, *Folktales around the World,* p. 445.
Why Dawg Hate Puss. Dance, *Folklore from Contemporary Jamaicans,* no. 13.
Wolf and the Fox, The. Massignon, *Folktales of France,* no. 54.

**20   EAT THE SMALLEST ONE FIRST.** A squirrel, a hare, a marten, a fox, a wolf, and a bear were starving, so the bear decreed that they must eat each other, starting with the smallest one. Hearing this, the squirrel, the hare, and the marten ran away. The fox was now the smallest, and he persuaded the wolf, the next in line, that they should give up the plan and work together as partners. (Lang)

End of the World, The (Finland). Booss, *Scandinavian Folk Tales,* p. 589.
Lion in the Well, The. Abrahams, *Afro-American Folktales,* no. 61.
Six Hungry Beasts (Finland). Lang, *Crimson Fairy Book,* p. 233.

**20A  ANIMALS IN A PIT.** A pig, a wolf, a fox, a hare, and a squirrel fell into a pit. They had no choice but to eat each other. Following the fox's plan, they ate first the one with the thinnest voice and then the one with the roughest voice, until only the fox and the pig were left. —Continues as type 21. (Afanesyev)

> Beasts in a Pit. Afanasyev, *Russian Fairy Tales,* p. 498.

**20B  A MAN IS CAUGHT IN HIS OWN TRAP.** A man was caught in his own trap and died. Wild animals worked together to drag him into the forest, where they devoured him. —Continues as type 20. (Lang)

> Six Hungry Beasts (Finland). Lang, *Crimson Fairy Book,* p. 233.

**20C  THAT THE WORLD NOT COME TO AN END.** Henny-Penny dreamed that unless she got to the Dovrefell the world would come to an end. Cocky-Locky, Ducky-Lucky and Goosy-Poosey joined the pilgrimage. An adventure with Foxy-Cocksy took the life of the duck and the goose, but Cocky-Locky and Henny-Penny made it to the Dovrefell, and the world did not come to an end. (Asbjørnsen and Moe) Cf. type 2033.

> Cock and Hen That Went to the Dovrefell, The. Asbjørnsen and Moe, *East o' the Sun,* p. 353.

**20D\*  THE COCK THAT WANTED TO BE POPE.** A cock and a hen decided to go to Rome and become pope and popess. Upon their arrival, they entered an open church, but the sexton caught them, wrung their necks, and served them to his friends. (Crane, no. 88)

> Cock That Wished to Become Pope, The. Crane, *Italian Popular Tales,* no. 88.
> Cock, The. Crane, *Italian Popular Tales,* no. 87.
> Nun Vixen, The. Megas, *Folktales of Greece,* no. 2.

**21  EATING ONE'S OWN ENTRAILS.** A fox and a pig were caught in a pit. The fox pretended to tear himself open and to eat his own bowels. "You do it too," he told the pig, so the pig tore open his own belly, and the fox ate him for dinner. (Afanasyev)

> Beasts in a Pit. Afanasyev, *Russian Fairy Tales,* p. 498.

**30  THE FOX LEADS THE WOLF INTO A PIT.** The fox plotted to destroy his enemy the wolf. Declaring friendship, he led the wolf into a vineyard where he knew there was a pitfall. As planned, the wolf fell into the hole. The fox then showered him with abuse, and watched from the distance as the farmers stoned the entrapped wolf to death. *(1001 Nights)*

> Brer Rabbit. Saucier, *French Louisiana,* no. 33.

Little Sister Fox and the Wolf. Afanasyev, *Russian Fairy Tales,* p. 371.
Mangoose and Mangoes. Thundy, *South Indian Folktales,* no. 34.
Piti Bonhomme Godron (Tar Baby). Saucier, *French Louisiana,* no. 33A.
Wolf and the Fox, The. Mathers, *1001 Nights,* v. 1, p. 597.

**31    ESCAPE FROM A PIT ON ANOTHER'S BACK.** A fox fell into a pit and could not get out. He caught the attention of a passing goat, claiming that he had jumped into the pit to get water for the coming drought. The goat, not wanting to be without water, jumped into the pit herself, whereupon the fox escaped, using her back and horns as a ladder. (Aesop)

Fox and the Goat, The. Jacobs, *Aesop,* no. 82.
Look Before You Leap. Handford, *Aesop,* no. 7.
Old Mister Rabbit, He's a Good Fisherman. Harris, *Uncle Remus,* no. 16.

**32    ONE BUCKET DOWN; ONE BUCKET UP.** One dry summer Brer Rabbit let himself down a two-bucket well to get water, but he couldn't get back out. He shouted to Brer Terrapin, that he too should come down for a drink. Brer Terrapin let himself down in the top bucket, thus pulling Brer Rabbit to freedom. In parting, the rabbit said: "Some are up and some are down." (Abrahams)

Fox and Rabbit in the Well. Dorson, *Negro Tales,* p. 167.
Fox and the Wolf, The (de Trueba). Lang, *Orange Fairy Book,* p. 56.
Some Are Up and Some Are Down. Abrahams, *Afro-American Folktales,* p. 33.
Wolf and the Fox in the Well, The. Massignon, *Folktales of France,* no. 55.

**33    THE FOX PLAYS DEAD AND ESCAPES FROM THE PIT.**

Lachmidasi and the Parrot-King. Thundy, *South Indian Folktales,* no. 36.
Mongooses Escape from a Pit-Trap. Arewa, *Northern East Africa,* p. 96.

**33\*    ESCAPE BY PLAYING DEAD.** A jackal jumped into a grain silo and ate until he was so heavy that he could no longer reach the opening. Hearing some one approaching, he played dead. The farmer slung the supposedly dead animal out of his silo, and the jackal escaped. Cf. type 41.

Father of a Hundred Tricks. Bushnaq, *Arab Folktales,* p. 239.

**33\*\*    THE FOX PLAYS DEAD FOR A BOAT RIDE.** A fox decided he would sooner live on an island than on the mainland, so he lay down, as though dead, near the boat landing. The boatmen, wanting his pelt, put him aboard, and as soon as they arrived on the island, the fox came to life and ran off.

Fox in Inishkea, The. O'Sullivan, *Folktales of Ireland,* no. 3.

**34**   **DIVING FOR THE MOON.** The rabbit and the coyote saw the moon's reflection on a lake. Thinking it was cheese, the wolf jumped into the water, but could not get to it. "You'll have to dive deeper," prompted the rabbit, and to help he tied a stone around the coyote's neck. The coyote went to the bottom and never came out again. (Paredes)

> Fox and the Wolf, The (de Trueba). Lang, *Orange Fairy Book,* p. 56.
> Golden-Crested Bird in the Water Tank (India). Clouston, *Book of Noodles,*
>    p. 44.
> Gothamite and the Green Cheese, The. Clouston, *Book of Noodles,* p. 44.
> How the Wolf Lost His Tail. Campbell, *West Highlands,* v. 1, p. 280.
> Rabbit and the Coyote, The. Parades, *Folktales of Mexico,* no. 26.
> Wolf and the Fox in the Well, The. Massignon, *Folktales of France,* no. 55.
> Wolf, the Laborer, the Fox and the Cheese, The. Briggs, *DBF,* pt. A, v. 1, p.
>    125.

**34A**   **THE MEAT IN THE WATER.** A dog with a piece of meat in his mouth crossed a brook on a plank. Seeing his reflection in the water, he thought it was another dog with another piece of meat. "I'll have that piece too!" he thought, and snapped at the reflection. But the meat fell from his mouth, and he had nothing. (Aesop)

> Dog and the Shadow, The. Jacobs, *Aesop,* no. 3.
> Dog Carrying Meat, The. Daly, *Aesop,* no. 133.
> Substance and Shadow. Handford, *Aesop,* no. 118.

**34C**   **THE FOX IN THE PIT** (new classification). A hungry fox was prowling about the forest, wishing that God had made him a bird instead of a fox. Suddenly he fell into a pit, whereupon he said, "If there were water in here, I would drown. To think that I was complaining the way God made me!"

> Fox in the Pit, The. Megas, *Folktales of Greece,* no. 7.

**36**   **THE HARE TAKES ADVANTAGE OF MRS. FOX.** The hare tried repeatedly to seduce Mrs. Fox. One day while chasing the persistent hare away, she followed him between two trees. She became stuck, and the shameless hare made a quick circle and took his pleasure on the defenseless fox. (Afanasyev)

> Fox and the Hare, The. Afanasyev, *Erotic Tales,* p. 87.
> Rabbit and the Fox, The. Parades, *Folktales of Mexico,* no. 24.
> Vixen and the Hare, The. Afanasyev, *Secret Tales,* p. 1.

**37**   **THE NURSEMAID EATS THE CHILDREN.** A mother alligator caught Little Boy-Bear and was about to eat him up, but the bear saved himself by offering to be the nursemaid for her seven children. Little Boy-Bear, working as nursemaid, ate the baby alligators, until there was only one left. When mother alligator wanted to see her seven children, Little Boy-Bear showed her the one child seven times. Finally he ate the last one as well and made his escape. (Abrahams)

> How the Bear Nursed the Little Alligator. Harris, *Nights with Uncle Remus,* no. 60.
> Hyena Eats the Lion's Children, The (10 variants). Arewa, *Northern East Africa,* p. 53.
> Little Boy-Bear Nurses the Alligator Children. Abrahams, *Afro-American Folktales,* no. 54.
> Mangoose and Mangoes. Thundy, *South Indian Folktales,* no. 34.
> Mother-in-Law and the Clear Water, The. Postma, *Tales from the Basotho,* no. 14.
> Six Hungry Beasts (Finland). Lang, *Crimson Fairy Book,* p. 233.

**37*  THE FOX AS HERDSMAN.** A woman hired a fox to be her herdsman, but he ate up all of her goats, sheep, and cows. When she went out to see how things were, he ate the cream that was in her churn. In a rage, she threw the last bit of cream at the fleeing fox. A dab stuck to his tail, and the fox has had a white tip on his tail ever since. (Asbjørnsen and Moe)

> Fox as Herdsman, The. Asbjørnsen and Moe, *East o' the Sun,* p. 69.
> Fox as Shepherd, The. Asbjørnsen and Moe, *Norwegian Folktales,* p. 106.

**40   A BEAR BELLS ITSELF BY EATING A BELLED HORSE.**

> Hyena Is Belled, The. Arewa, *Northern East Africa,* p. 41.

**41   OVEREATING IN THE PANTRY.** The wolf and the fox knew where a wedding feast was being prepared, and they squeezed between the bars of the pantry window. After each few mouthfuls the fox tried his size at the bars, but the wolf gorged himself without care. When the guests arrived, the fox could still squeeze between the bars, and he escaped, but the wolf was too swollen to fit, and he received a terrible beating. (Massignon) Cf. types 33*, 33**.

> Bouki and Lapin in the Smokehouse. Dorson, *Buying the Wind,* p. 246.
> Struggle between the Wolf and the Fox, The. Ranke, *Folktales of Germany,* no. 4.
> Wolf and the Fox, The. Grimm, *Tales,* no. 73.
> Wolf and the Fox, The. Massignon, *Folktales of France,* no. 54.

**41*  OVEREATING IN A HOLLOW TREE.** A half-starved fox found some bread and meat hidden in a hollow tree. He squeezed in and ate it, but then found himself too swollen to escape. Another fox came by and offered advice: "Stay there until you are as thin as you were when you went in, and you will get out quite easily."

> Case for Patience, A. Handford, *Aesop,* no. 1.

**43  A HOUSE OF WOOD AND A HOUSE OF ICE.** One winter the fox made a hut for himself from linden bark, while the wolf made one for himself from ice. In the spring the fox's hut was still good, but the wolf's soon melted away. (Afanasyev, p. 371) Cf. type 1097.

> Ewe, the Goat, and the Lion, The. Sabar, *Kurdistani Jews,* p. 163.
> Fox, the Hare, and the Cock, The. Afanasyev, *Russian Fairy Tales,* p. 192.
> Little Sister Fox and the Wolf. Afanasyev, *Russian Fairy Tales,* p. 371.

**44  THE OATH ON A TRAP.** A sheep, a wolf, and a fox were walking along when the wolf said to the sheep: "You are wearing my coat." The fox countered: "Will you swear to that?" "I will take a solemn oath," answered the wolf. Now the fox knew where some peasants had set a trap, and he pointed to the spot, saying, "Step there to take your oath." The wolf was caught in the trap, and the fox and the sheep left him for good. (Afanasyev)

> Sheep, the Fox, and the Wolf, The. Afanasyev, *Russian Fairy Tales,* p. 275.

**47A  CATCHING A HORSE BY THE TAIL.** Brer Rabbit came to Brer Fox with a plan to catch a horse. They approached a sleeping horse, and the fox allowed himself to be tied to its tail. "Just pull him down when he tries to get up," advised Brer Rabbit. But when the horse awoke and started jumping about, Brer Fox could not pull him down, and he barely escaped with his life. (Harris, no. 2)

> Brother Fox Catches Mister Horse. Harris, *Nights with Uncle Remus,* no. 2.
> Brother Wolf Falls a Victim. Harris, *Nights with Uncle Remus,* no. 36.
> Fox and the Horse, The. Grimm, *Tales,* no. 132.

**47E  THE MESSAGE ON THE HORSESHOE.** A big fox and a little fox saw a horse with some writing on his shoe. "I will see what is written there," said the big fox, but when he lifted the hoof, the horse kicked out his brains. "No scholar me, nor wish I to be," concluded the little fox.

> Foxes, the Fisherman, and the Horse, The. Campbell, *West Highlands,* v. 1, p. 286.

**49  THE FOX, THE BEAR, AND THE WASPS' NEST.** The fox offered to share his honey tree with the bear, but he led him to a nest with no honey. It was a wasps' nest, and the bear was badly stung. (Asbjørnsen and Moe)

> Bear and Fox Who Made a Bet. Asbjørnsen and Moe, *Norwegian Folktales,* p. 120.
> Brer Rabbit's Riddle. Abrahams, *Afro-American Folktales,* no. 68.
> Brother Rabbit's Laughing-Place. Harris, *Told by Uncle Remus,* no. 4.
> Brother Rabbit's Riddle. Harris, *Nights with Uncle Remus,* no. 10.
> End of Mister Bear, The. Harris, *Uncle Remus,* no. 28.

How Brother Fox Failed to Get His Grapes.  Harris, *Nights with Uncle Remus,* no. 16.

Man, Bear, and Dog.  Thundy, *South Indian Folktales,* no. 61.

**49A  THE SCHOOL IN A WASPS' NEST.** The rabbit, standing next to a wasps' nest, told the coyote that he was being paid generously to be a schoolmaster.  The coyote asked to take the rabbit's place, and the rabbit agreed, instructing him to whip the students two or three times to make them study.  When the coyote struck the nest with his stick, out flew the wasps and stung him horribly.  (Paredes)

Rabbit and the Coyote, The.  Parades, *Folktales of Mexico,* no. 26.

**50    CURING A SICK LION.** The king of beasts lay ill.  The arrogant fox delayed paying him a visit, but the wolf went promptly, commenting that the absent fox showed little respect to his king.  At that moment the fox appeared, claiming that he had just learned from from a famous physician that the lion's only cure would be for him to wrap himself in the skin of a freshly killed wolf.  The lion immediately had the wolf killed and flayed.  (Megas)

Brer Rabbit Causes Brer Fox to Lose His Hide.  Harris, *Uncle Remus and the Little Boy,* no. 3.

Hoist with Her Own Petard.  Handford, *Aesop,* no. 99.

How Brother Rabbit Brought Family Trouble on Brother Fox.  Harris, *Uncle Remus Returns,* no. 5.

Lion Eats the Hyena's Liver, The.  Arewa, *Northern East Africa,* p. 41.

Lion, Wolf, and Fox.  Megas, *Folktales of Greece,* no. 3.

Liver of the Wise and the Liver of the Foolish, The.  El-Shamy, *Folktales of Egypt,* no. 10.

Plotter Out-Plotted, A.  Handford, *Aesop,* no. 26.

**50A  TRACKS INTO THE LION'S DEN.** The lion made it known that he was sick unto death and summoned all animals to hear his last will.  Many animals did so, but not the fox, who waited safely outside.  Why do you not come in to pay your respects, called the lion.  "Because," replied the fox, "I see many tracks going into your den, but none coming out again."

Lion, the Fox, and the Beasts, The.  Jacobs, *Aesop,* no. 73.

Old Lion and the Fox, The.  Daly, *Aesop,* no. 142.

One-Way Traffic.  Handford, *Aesop,* no. 11.

**50C  KICKING THE DYING LION.** A lion was mortally ill, and his subjects, seeing his helplessness, came to settle old grudges.  Even the cowardly ass kicked at him.  "This is a double death," growled the lion.

Mighty Fallen, The.  Handford, *Aesop,* no. 23.

Sick Lion, The.  Jacobs, *Aesop,* no. 9.

**51    THE LION'S SHARE.** The jackal, the fox, and the lion went hunting together, and they killed a bear, a partridge, and a hare. The jackal divided the prey: the hare for the lion, the partridge for the fox, and the bear for himself. The lion responded with a blow that nearly killed the jackal. Then the fox divided the prey: the bear for the lion's breakfast, the hare for the lion's dinner, and the partridge for the lion's snacks between meals. The jackal's bleeding scalp had taught him well the art of just division. (Bushnaq)

> Division of the Prey. Bushnaq, *Arab Folktales,* p. 241.
> Lion's Share, The. Arewa, *Northern East Africa,* p. 49.
> Lion's Share, The. Handford, *Aesop,* no. 21.
> Lion's Share, The. Jacobs, *Aesop,* no. 4.
> Mangoose and Mangoes. Thundy, *South Indian Folktales,* no. 34.
> Origin of the Ocean, The. Harris, *Nights with Uncle Remus,* no. 58.
> Taught by Experience. Handford, *Aesop,* no. 13.

**52    THE BRAINLESS ASS.** The lion sent the ass a message, proposing an alliance, but when the ass arrived for their meeting, the lion killed him. He then asked the fox to guard the prey while he slept. The fox took advantage of the situation and ate the ass's brains. The lion, upon his return, noticed the loss immediately, roaring: "What have you done with the brains?" "Brains?" responded the fox. The ass had none, or he never would have fallen into your trap."

> Ass's Brains, The. Jacobs, *Aesop,* no. 74.
> Bitten But Not Shy. Handford, *Aesop,* no. 61.

**55    KEEPING THE LAZY ANIMAL FROM THE WELL.** During a time of drought the animals dug a community well. Only the lazy jackal refused to help. Upon completing the well, the animals took turns standing watch to keep the jackal from drinking. Twice the jackal succeeded in tricking the guard and getting a drink. Finally the tortoise was chosen as guard. When the jackal approached him, the tortoise seized him by the leg, and he barely escaped with his life. (Lang)

> Brother Rabbit Secures a Mansion. Harris, *Nights with Uncle Remus,* no. 6.
> Hare Escapes Enemies by Pretending to Help Them, The. Arewa, *Northern East Africa,* p. 102.
> Jackal and the Spring, The (Africa). Lang, *Grey Fairy Book,* p. 265.

**56    THE JACKAL STEALS A BABY BIRD.** The jackal called to a mother dove: "Throw me one of your children or I will eat all of you up." In desperation, the dove threw down one of her young ones. Then the heron came to her and said: "The jackal could never jump this high; you are safe in your nest." So when the jackal returned with the same threat, the dove gave him nothing. Robbed of a meal, the jackal was determined to take revenge against the heron. —Continues as type 56D. (Lang)

Crazy Sue's Story. Harris, *Daddy Jake*, no. 1.
Fox and the Blackbird, The. Massignon, *Folktales of France*, no. 68.
Fox and the Wrens, The. Campbell, *West Highlands*, v. 1, p. 279.
Jackal, the Dove, and the Panther, The (Africa). Lang, *Pink Fairy Book*, p. 315.
Mountain Hen and the Fox, The. Ranke, *Folktales of Germany*, no. 5.

**56A  THE FOX THREATENS TO CUT DOWN THE BIRD'S TREE.** The fox stood beneath the tall tree where the magpie had her nest, and said aloud: "This is the right wood for my snowshoes." "No," begged the mother bird, and the fox agreed to seek another tree only if she would throw down one of her little ones. A few days later the trick worked again, and the fox got another baby magpie, but then the crow saw what had happened and told the magpie that the fox had neither a knife nor an ax and could not cut down the tree, so when he tried the ploy again, he received only scorn from the magpie. (Lang)

Fox and the Woodpecker, The. Afanasyev, *Russian Fairy Tales*, p. 199.
Six Hungry Beasts (Finland). Lang, *Crimson Fairy Book*, p. 233.

**56C  THE JACKAL AS SCHOOLMASTER.** The jackal offered to take the panther's ten children into his school, but one after the other, he ate them all. When the mother panther demanded to see her children, the jackal led her to a beehive, and claimed that the buzzing was the children's singing. While the panther was listening to their song, the baboon took a stick and stirred up the bees. To escape the stings, the panther flung herself in a lake, and she drowned.

Father of a Hundred Tricks. Bushnaq, *Arab Folktales*, p. 239.
Jackal, the Dove, and the Panther, The (Africa). Lang, *Pink Fairy Book*, p. 315.

**56D  WHAT DOES A BIRD DO WHEN IT RAINS?** The jackal asked the heron: "What do you do when it rains?" The heron demonstrated by covering his head with his wings, and the jackal seized him. (Lang)

Dove, the Heron, and Jackal, The. Postma, *Tales from the Basotho*, no. 13.
Jackal, the Dove, and the Panther, The (Africa). Lang, *Pink Fairy Book*, p. 315.

**57  THE SINGING CROW LOSES HER CHEESE.** A crow with a piece of cheese in her beak sat in a tree. "Your voice must be even more beautiful than your body," said the fox below. "If only I could hear you sing!" The flattered crow opened her beak in song, and the cheese fell into the waiting fox's mouth.

Fox and the Crow, The. Jacobs, *Aesop*, no. 8.

Lesson for Fools, A. Handford, *Aesop,* no. 57.

**59    THE FOX AND THE GRAPES.** A fox saw a bunch of grapes just beyond his reach in a vineyard. He could not jump the wall, so he walked away saying: "I am sure they are sour." (Aesop)

> Fox and the Grapes (Aesop). Cole, *Folktales,* no. 40.
> Fox and the Grapes, The. Jacobs, *Aesop,* no. 31.
> Signifying Monkey, The. Abrahams, *Afro-American Folktales,* no. 29.
> Sour Grapes. Handford, *Aesop,* no. 3.

**60    THE FOX AND THE STORK EXCHANGE INVITATIONS.** A stork invited a fox to dinner, and served milk in a deep pitcher. The fox got only the few drops that fell from the stork's long beak. The fox returned the invitation, and served milk on a flat stone. This time the stork's beak was useless, but the fox lapped up all he wanted. (Megas)

> Fox and Stork. Megas, *Folktales of Greece,* no. 4.
> Fox and the Crane, The. Afanasyev, *Russian Fairy Tales,* p. 171.
> Fox and the Crane, The. Daly, *Aesop,* no. 426.
> Fox and the Stork, The. Jacobs, *Aesop,* no. 19.
> Hospitality of Abu L'Hssein, The. Bushnaq, *Arab Folktales,* p. 219.
> Husband's and the Wife's Chamberpots, The. Legman, *Rationale of the Dirty Joke,* vol. 1, p. 336.
> Macaque and the Turtle, The (4 variants). Arewa, *Northern East Africa,* p. 66.
> Tit for Tat. Handford, *Aesop,* no. 77.

**61    THE COCK THAT CLOSED AN EYE ON THE FOX.** The fox once boasted to the cock that his grandfather could shut one eye and shout. "I can do that too," replied the cock, closed one eye and began to crow. But the eye he closed was the one next to the fox, and the fox seized him at once. —Continues as type 6. (Campbell)

> Fox, the Cock, and Their Tricks, The. Campbell, *West Highlands,* v. 1, p. 279.
> Nun's Priest's Tale, The. Chaucer, *The Canterbury Tales,* p. 232.

**61A  THE FOX AS CONFESSOR.** A fox decided to become a nun. A rooster, a pigeon, and a skylark agreed to join her on her trip to the nunnery, for she had vowed never to eat meat again. The nun-to-be heard confessions from the rooster and the pigeon, and ate them both up. But the skylark escaped and led a hunter to the fox, and that was the end of the fox. (Megas)

> Fox Confessor, The. Afanasyev, *Russian Fairy Tales,* p. 72.
> Little Sister Fox and the Wolf. Afanasyev, *Russian Fairy Tales,* p. 371.
> Nun Vixen, The. Megas, *Folktales of Greece,* no. 2.

**61B  THE CAT, THE COCK, AND THE FOX.** An old man had a cat and a cock. One day while the man and the cat were out, the fox came to the house and tricked the cock into opening the window, then seized him and carried him away. The cat heard the cock's cries and rescued him. The fox came a second time, and once again the cat rescued the cock. But the third time the fox was successful; the cock was careless once again, and the fox ate him up.

Cat, the Cock, and the Fox, The. Afanasyev, *Russian Fairy Tales,* p. 86.

**62 UNIVERSAL PEACE.** A fox approached a cock roosting above his reach and told him that the king had declared universal peace. Henceforth no animal need fear another, so the cock could safely fly down from his perch. But at that moment they saw a dog running toward them, and the fox turned and fled. "I fear," he explained in retreating, "that the dog has not yet heard the good news." (Aesop)

Fox, the Chickens, and the Dogs, The. Campbell, *West Highlands,* v. 1, p. 277.
Fox, the Cock, and the Dog, The. Jacobs, *Aesop,* no. 59.
Invitation to Universal Peace, The. Mathers, *1001 Nights,* v. 3, p. 515.
Jackal and Hen. Postma, *Tales from the Basotho,* no. 16.
Rabbit and the Dog, The. Dorson, *Negro Tales,* p. 165.
Rooster, Fox, and Dog. Megas, *Folktales of Greece,* no. 5.

**62\* THE LAW AGAINST SITTING IN TREES.** A fox came to a bird sitting in a tree and reported that a new law prohibited birds from sitting in trees. But hearing the sound of horses and dogs, he suddenly decided that he had more urgent business at home.

Fox and the Woodcock, The. Afanasyev, *Russian Fairy Tales,* p. 171.

**63 THE FOX WITH FLEAS.** A fox rids himself of fleas by taking a piece of wool in his mouth and wading into water. As the water gets deeper, the fleas run toward his head and finally onto the dry wool. Finally the fox dips his nose under water and lets the flea-laden wool float away.

Fox and the Fleas, The. Campbell, *West Highlands,* v. 1, p. 276.

**64 THE FOX WITHOUT A TAIL.** A fox lost his tail in a trap. At first he was ashamed of the stump, but then he began to propose that all foxes cut off their tails, pointing out their many inconveniences. "That is all very well," said an older fox, "but I hardly think you would be giving this advice if you hadn't lost your own tail." (Aesop)

Cut Off Your Tails to Save My Face! Handford, *Aesop,* no. 8.
Fox without a Tail, The. Jacobs, *Aesop,* no. 65.
Knotter of Tails, The. Bushnaq, *Arab Folktales,* p. 234.
Reward of the Wicked, The. Handford, *Aesop,* no. 67.

**65    MRS. FOX'S SUITORS.** An old fox with nine tails put his wife to the test by playing dead. New suitors soon arrived, one with one tail, one with two tails, and so forth. Mrs. Fox turned them all away, until one came with nine tails. Him she accepted. But just as the wedding was to take place, old Mr. Fox jumped up and drove Mrs. Fox and everyone else out of the house. Cf. types 1350, 1510.

> Mrs. Fox's Wedding (two tales). Grimm, *Tales,* no. 38.

**66A   HELLO, HOUSE!** Brer Wolf sneaked into Brer Rabbit's house, hoping to catch him. But when Brer Rabbit came home, he noticed that the door was open a crack, so he didn't go in. Instead, he called out: "Hello, house!" After a short silence he called again: "Hello, house! Why don't you answer the way you usually do?" This fooled the hiding wolf, and he called back like he thought a house might: "Hello yourself!" But that revealed Brer Wolf's ambush, and he didn't catch Brer Rabbit. (Harris)

> Hare Escapes from the Lion, The. Arewa, *Northern East Africa,* p. 112.
> Heyo, House! Harris, *Uncle Remus and His Friends,* no. 19.
> Rabbit and the Coyote, The. Parades, *Folktales of Mexico,* no. 26.

**66B   THE DEAD TRICKSTER SHOWS SIGNS OF LIFE.** Anansi and his wife were starving, so Anansi played dead while his wife mourned loudly. Many different animals came to see the dead Anansi, and his wife killed them, one at a time. The dove came by too, but he didn't think Anansi was really dead. "If he is really dead, then why doesn't he fart?" he asked. "I've always heard that dead men fart." Hearing that, Anansi let go with a fart, and the dove made his escape. (Abrahams)

> Anansi Plays Dead. Abrahams, *Afro-American Folktales,* no. 70.
> Brother Wolf and the Horned Cattle. Harris, *Nights with Uncle Remus,* no. 62.
> Mister Wolf Makes a Failure. Harris, *Uncle Remus,* no. 11.

**67    THE DROWNING FOX PRETENDS TO BE SWIMMING.** A fox was caught by a raging river's current. As she was being carried away, she called to her friends on the bank: "I am taking a message down to Miletus."

> Foxes on the Meander River, The. Daly, *Aesop,* no. 232.

**67**   THE FOX, THE MAN, AND THE FIRE.** The audacious fox slipped into the man's house and sat down by the fire. The man came home and saw him there. "I'll stand guard by the door so he can't escape, and whistle up the dogs to catch him," said the man. Then the fox took the man's shoes, one at a time, and dropped them into the fire. Not even this drew the man from the doorway, so the fox picked a burning stick from the fire and headed for the man's bed. To save his bed (and hence his house) from the fox's torch, the man jumped from the doorway, and the fox quickly bolted for freedom. (Glassie)

> Fox and the Fox-Hunter, The. Campbell, West Highlands, v. 1, p. 277.
> Fox and the Ranger, The. Glassie, *Irish Folktales*, no. 37.

**68**  **EATING AN ANIMAL FROM THE INSIDE.** Every night Anansi would creep into a sleeping elephant's body, chop off a little piece of meat, and carry it home. One night he took his friend Yawarri with him. Yawarri was greedy; he stayed inside the elephant cutting and eating meat, until the elephant died. The next day the king's men cut open the dead elephant and killed Yawarri. (Abrahams)

> Crawling into the Elephant's Belly. Abrahams, *Afro-American Folktales*, no. 64.
> Hare Kills the Elephant by Pretending to Be a Doctor, The. Arewa, *Northern East Africa*, p. 115.
> Sad Fate of Mister Fox, The. Harris, *Uncle Remus*, no. 34.

**68A**  **TRAPPED IN A JUG.** The mouse found a clay pot filled with sweetened meal, and ate up what he could. On his way home, the fox grabbed him by the neck. "Don't eat me!" pleaded the mouse, "and I'll show you a jug of sweetened meal." The fox ate the meal until his entire head was in the jug, and he could not get it out again. He was trapped.

> Mouse and the Fox, The (Peru). Dorson, *Folktales around the World*, p. 527.

**70**  **MORE COWARDLY THAN A HARE.** The hares were afraid of every animal, but one time, as they approached a lake, a troop of frogs took fright and jumped into the water. "Things are not so bad as they seem," said one of the hares.

> Hares and the Frogs, The. Jacobs, *Aesop*, no. 15.
> Second Thoughts. Handford, *Aesop*, no. 37.

**72**  **GOING COURTING ON THE COMPETITOR'S BACK.** Anansi and the tiger were both courting the same girl, and Anansi tried to discredit his competitor by saying: "He's nothing but a riding horse." The angry tiger insisted that Anansi take this back, but Anansi claimed he was too sick to walk to the girl's house. The tiger would have to carry him. As they approached the girl's house, Anansi suddenly became well and shouted: "See, he's nothing but a riding horse!" The tiger galloped away in shame and never returned. (Abrahams) Cf. type 4.

Anancy Is Riding-Horse. Dance, *Folklore from Contemporary Jamaicans,* no. 19.

Fox, the Lion, and the Smith, The. Arewa, *Northern East Africa,* p. 94.

Mister Rabbit and Mister Frog Make Mister Fox and Mister Bear Their Riding Horses. Dorson, *Negro Tales,* p. 26.

Riding-Horse. Dorson, *Negro Tales,* p. 161.

Tiger Becomes a Riding Horse. Abrahams, *Afro-American Folktales,* no. 25.

Wolf and Jackal and the Beautiful Girl. Postma, *Tales from the Basotho,* no. 2.

**72\*   TEACHING YOUNG ANIMALS TO OBSERVE.** The fox was teaching a youngster to fend for himself. Stopping outside a noisy house he asked: "Who is inside?" "Either two women or twelve men," answered the young one. "You'll do well in the world," concluded father fox.

Two Women or Twelve Men. O'Sullivan, *Folktales of Ireland,* no. 5.

**73   BLINDING THE GUARD.** The tiger cornered the rabbit in a hollow tree, but when he put his head up to the hole, the rabbit blew pepper into his eyes. The tiger ran away, and the rabbit laughed until his sides hurt. (Abrahams, "Trouble Coming Down the Road")

Brother Rabbit Lays in His Beef Supply. Harris, *Nights with Uncle Remus,* no. 47.

Fox and the Lapp, The (Lapland). Lang, *Brown Fairy Book,* p. 245.

Hare Blinds His Guard and Escapes (7 variants). Arewa, *Northern East Africa,* p. 108.

Hare Escapes by Blinding the Lion, The. Arewa, *Northern East Africa,* p. 101.

Mister Fox Is Again Victimized. Harris, *Uncle Remus,* no. 7.

Mister Terrapin Appears upon the Scene. Harris, *Uncle Remus,* no. 10.

Sad Fate of Mister Fox, The. Harris, *Uncle Remus,* no. 34.

Tricking All the Kings. Abrahams, *Afro-American Folktales,* no. 43.

Trouble Coming Down the Road. Abrahams, *Afro-American Folktales,* no. 73.

**74B\*   THE PANTHER GIVES A PARTY.** A panther invited seven children to a party. They brought rice and other good things for him to cook,  but he cooked them as well, and ate them all up.

Trust Not the Panther. Thundy, *South Indian Folktales,* no. 35.

**75   THE MOUSE RESCUES THE LION.** A lion captured a mouse, but spared his life. Later the lion was captured in a trap. The mouse happened by, and he rescued the lion by gnawing away the ropes that held him. (Aesop)

As Good as His Word. Handford, *Aesop,* no. 39.

Lion and the Mouse, The. Jacobs, *Aesop,* no. 11.

Son-of-Adam and the Lion. El-Shamy, *Folktales of Egypt,* no. 48.

**75\*   THE NURSE, THE CHILD, AND THE WOLF.** The wolf overheard the nurse say to the child: "Be good, or I will throw you to the wolf." The wolf positioned himself by the window and waited for the promised child. But when the nurse saw him, she called the dogs, and he had to run for his life.

> Nurse and the Wolf, The. Jacobs, *Aesop,* no. 46.

**76   THE WOLF AND THE CRANE.** A wolf had a bone stuck in his throat. He convinced the crane to remove it with his long beak. When the crane asked for a reward, the wolf replied: "You've had your head inside a wolf's mouth and are still alive. That's reward enough." (Aesop)

> Kindness Ill Requited. Handford, *Aesop,* no. 29.
> Lion and the Crane, The. Jacobs, *Indian Fairy Tales,* p. 1.
> Wolf and the Crane, The. Jacobs, *Aesop,* no. 5.

**77   THE STAG IS CAPTURED BY HIS ANTLERS.** A stag stood by a pool, admiring the reflection of his great antlers, but bemoaning the size of his thin legs. At that moment a hunter approached, and the stag bolted. His legs served him well, but his antlers became entangled in some branches, and that was his end. (Aesop)

> Hart and the Hunter, The. Jacobs, *Aesop,* no. 25.
> Irony of Fate, The. Handford, *Aesop,* no. 63.

**78   TIED TOGETHER IN LIFE AND IN DEATH.** A rat and a frog tied their feet to each other's. But the frog dived into a pond, and the rat drowned. Then a hawk seized the rat's floating body, and carried the frog away as well. (Aesop)

> Fox, Dog, Monkey, and Tiger, The. Thundy, *South Indian Folktales,* no. 39.
> Making the Punishment Fit the Crime. Handford, *Aesop,* no. 45.

**78A   TIED UP AGAINST A STORM.** Brer Rabbit claimed a hurricane was coming, and he offered to tie Mr. Lion to a tree. After securely binding Mr. Lion, Brer Rabbit sat by his side and abused the helpless beast, in full view of all the other animals. (Harris)

> Brother Bear and the Honey Orchard. Harris, *Uncle Remus and His Friends,*
>     no. 2.
> Brother Rabbit Ties Mister Lion. Harris, *Nights with Uncle Remus,* no. 56.
> Mouse and the Fox, The (Peru). Dorson, *Folktales around the World,* p. 527.
> Peasant, the Bear, and the Fox, The. Afanasyev, *Russian Fairy Tales,* p. 288.

**85   THE MOUSE, THE BIRD, AND THE SAUSAGE.** The mouse, the bird, and the sausage kept house together. Each had his or her job, and everything went well, until one day they decided to trade tasks. The sausage, on her way to gather wood, was eaten by a dog; the mouse scalded herself in the stew; and the bird fell into the well and drowned. (Grimm)

> Little Sausage and the Little Mouse, The. Ranke, *Folktales of Germany,* no. 6.
> Mouse, the Bird, and the Sausage, The. Grimm, *Tales,* no. 23.
> Mouse, the Sausage, and the Bird, The. Dorson, *Buying the Wind,* p. 258.

**91    THE MONKEY'S HEART.** The monkey and the shark became friends. One day, while the monkey was riding on the his back, the shark announced that the sultan was ill and that the only cure was a monkey's heart. The monkey responded that it was a pity he hadn't known this earlier, for he had left his heart at home for safekeeping. He offered to fetch it. The shark took him to shore, but the monkey never came back. (Lang)

> Brother Rabbit and the Gizzard-Eater. Harris, *Told by Uncle Remus,* no. 15.
> Heart of a Monkey, The (Swahili). Lang, *Lilac Fairy Book,* p. 42.
> Monkey and the Crocodile, The (India). Cole, *Folktales,* no. 146.
> Monkey and the Jelly-Fish, The (Japan). Lang, *Violet Fairy Book,* p. 275.
> Monkey Escapes from the Shark by Returning for His Heart, The (3 variants).
>   Arewa, *Northern East Africa,* p.97.
> Monkey's Liver, The. Seki, *Folktales of Japan,* no. 11.
> Woodcutter without a Brain, The. Bushnaq, *Arab Folktales,* p. 217.

**92    THE LION IN THE WATER.** Brer Rabbit told Brer Lion about a ferocious beast. The proud lion wanted to see the animal for himself, so Brer Rabbit led him to a deep spring. Seeing his own reflection in the water, Brer Lion became enraged at the threatening beast, and leaped upon him. He could not escape from the pool, and he drowned. (Harris)

> Brother Rabbit Conquers Brother Lion. Harris, *Uncle Remus and His Friends,*
>   no. 18.
> Lion in the Well, The. Abrahams, *Afro-American Folktales,* no. 61.

**93    WHEN A THREAT IS TO BE TAKEN SERIOUSLY.** A lark had a nest in a cornfield. One day the farmer said: "It's time to call my friends to help with the harvest," but as yet the lark felt no threat to her nest. Later he came again and said: "I will hire workers, so we can begin the harvest." The lark knew he was now serious, so she took her babies from the nest and left the field. (Aesop)

> When a Magyar Gets Really Angry. Dégh, *Folktales of Hungary,* no. 24.
> When a Man Means Business. Handford, *Aesop,* no. 79.

**96\*   GOOD NEWS AND BAD NEWS ABOUT THE HARE'S MARRIAGE.** The hare's marriage was not all good, for his wife could be a devil, but there was good news: she had a good dowry and a house of her own. But there was bad news too, for the house burned down. But the news wasn't all bad, because his wife burned up with it. Cf. type 2014A.

> Hare Who Had Been Married, The. Asbjørnsen and Moe, *Norwegian Folktales,* p. 115.

**100  THE WOLF, A GUEST OF THE DOG, SINGS.** The wolf, while visiting the dog, heard musicians and sang along, in spite of the dog's warning. The men heard him and drove both animals away with sticks.

> Dog and Wolf. Carpenter, *A Latvian Storyteller,* p. 206.

**100\*  THE PARROT AND THE HAWK.** A hawk seized a parrot. When the hawk began to eat him, he called out: "You rascal!" frightening the hawk. He released his grip, and the parrot escaped. (Briggs, "The Scottish Parrot")

> Hawk and the Parrot, The. Briggs, *DBF,* pt. A, v. 2, p. 114.
> Scottish Parrot, The. Briggs, *DBF,* pt. A, v. 2, p. 228.

**101  THE OLD DOG RESCUES THE CHILD.** A farmer intended to shoot a faithful dog, now too old to be of use. But the dog's friend the wolf had a plan. Accordingly, he seized the master's child; the dog pursued and with a pretended struggle rescued the child. The grateful farmer now promised to keep the old dog as long as he lived. (Grimm)

> Bear, the Dog, and the Cat, The. Afanasyev, *Russian Fairy Tales,* p. 453.
> Old Sultan. Grimm, *Tales,* no. 48.

**102  THE FOX MAKES CLOTHES FOR THE WOLF.** The fox offered to make a fine garment for the wolf. For raw materials he required many lambs, which the wolf brought him. However, the fox ate the lambs, and the wolf never received his new clothes.

> Fox as Tailor and Weaver, The. Sabar, *Kurdistani Jews,* p. 166.

**103A  THE CAT AND THE FOX GET MARRIED.** An abandoned tomcat and a wild she-fox decided to get married. The cat mounted his new mate and cried out: "Again, again!" "He never has enough," said the she-fox.

> Cat and the Vixen, The. Afanasyev, *Russian Secret Tales,* p. 9.

**103A\*  THE CAT AS KING OF BEASTS.** A cat frightened all other animals into submission, and they held a feast for him. But the bear tried to seize him, so the cat climbed a tree. The other animals pursued, climbing on one another to reach the cat. Then the cat sneezed, and they all fell down.

Cecus-Becus Berneusz. Dégh, *Folktales of Hungary*, no. 25.

**104  WAR BETWEEN THE VILLAGE ANIMALS AND THE FOREST ANIMALS.** The fox and the wolf declared war against each other and selected allies for a battle. The boar and the bear went with the wolf, and the village animals with the fox. The wolf's friends thought the cat's tail was a lance and the goat's horns a pitchfork, and they fled in fear. (Ranke, "The Struggle between the Wolf and the Fox")

> Bear, Fox, and Man. Ranke, *Folktales of Germany*, no. 7.
> Old Sultan. Grimm, *Tales*, no. 48.
> Struggle between the Wolf and the Fox, The. Ranke, *Folktales of Germany*, no. 4.

**105  THE CAT'S ONLY TRICK.** A fox boasted to a cat that he possessed a sackful of tricks. The cat admitted that she had only one: climbing trees. At that moment a hunter with dogs came by. The cat rescued herself in the nearest tree, but the fox was killed. (Grimm)

> Fox and the Cat, The. Grimm, *Tales*, no. 75.
> Fox and the Cat, The. Jacobs, *Aesop*, no. 38.

**105\*  THE HEDGEHOG'S ONLY TRICK.** A hedgehog took shelter in a fox's hole. The fox, afraid of his quills, had no choice but to abandon the den. (Megas)

> Father of a Hundred Tricks. Bushnaq, *Arab Folktales*, p. 239.
> Hedgehog and Fox. Megas, *Folktales of Greece*, no. 8.

**106  TALKING LIKE AN ANIMAL.** A mother sow, having been chased by a dog, grunted: "We won't go there any more, more, more." Her piglets squealed their reply: "You say that always, always, always."

> Sow and Her Banbh, The. O'Sullivan, *Folktales of Ireland*, no. 9.

**110  BELLING THE CAT.** The mice convened to discuss their enemy, the cat. A young mouse proposed that a bell be placed around the cat's neck, so they could always hear her coming. Everyone agreed, until an old mouse said: "That is all very well, but who will bell the cat?" (Aesop)

> Belling the Cat. Briggs, *DBF*, pt. A, v. 1, p. 104.
> Belling the Cat. Jacobs, *Aesop*, no. 67.
> Brother Rabbit Takes a Walk. Abrahams, *Afro-American Folktales*, no. 60.
> Brother Rabbit Takes a Walk. Harris, *Nights with Uncle Remus*, no. 53.

**111   THE CAT AND THE MOUSE CONVERSE.** Two sentences from a long conversation: Mouse: "I bought me a pudding, my lady, my lady." Cat: "And I'll eat you, good body, good body." (Jacobs)

> Cattie Sits in the Kiln-Ring Spinning, The. Briggs, *DBF,* pt. A, v. 2, p. 513.
> Mouse and Mouser. Jacobs, *English Fairy Tales,* p. 48.

**111A  THE WOLF AND THE LAMB.** "How dare you muddy my water?" said the wolf to a lamb drinking at a spring. She replied that she was drinking downstream from him. Then the wolf said: "Why did you call me bad names a year ago?" She answered that she was even now only six months old. "Then it was your father!" snarled the wolf, and he ate her up.

> Always in the Wrong. Handford, *Aesop,* no. 28.
> Feline Sophistry. Handford, *Aesop,* no. 93.
> Wolf and the Lamb, The. Jacobs, *Aesop,* no. 2.

**111A\*  A DRUNKARD'S PROMISE.** A mouse fell into a cask of ale. She called to a passing cat: "Save me from drowning, and you can have me." The cat pulled her out, and she immediately darted for her hole. "Wait!" cried the cat, "you promised I could have you." "Yes," said the mouse, "folks'll say anything when they're in liquor."

> Dutch Courage. Briggs, *DBF,* pt. A, v. 2, p. 66.
> Mouse in the Ale-Cask, The. Briggs, *DBF,* pt. A, v. 2, p. 194.

**112   THE TOWN MOUSE AND THE COUNTRY MOUSE.** A country mouse visited her cousin in the city. The food was good, but they had just begun their meal when the house dogs attacked them. She cut her visit short and returned to the simpler, but safer life in the country. (Aesop)

> Dog and the Jackal, The. (2 variants). Arewa, *Northern East Africa,* p. 68.
> House Mouse and the Country Mouse, The. Asbjørnsen and Moe, *Norwegian Folktales,* p. 116.
> Mouse in the Hill and the Mouse in a Farm, The. Campbell, *West Highlands,* v. 1, p. 287.
> Palace Mouse and the Garden Mouse, The. Calvino, *Italian Folktales,* no. 120.
> Town Mouse and Country Mouse (Horace). Handford, *Aesop,* Notes, p. 218.
> Town Mouse and Country Mouse. Handford, *Aesop,* no. 41.
> Town Mouse and the Country Mouse, The. Jacobs, *Aesop,* no. 7.

**113A  THE KING O' THE CATS.** A sexton returned from the graveyard to his wife and their black cat, Tom, and reported a strange funeral. Nine black cats had buried a coffin, and one of the group had said to him: "Tell Tom that Tildrum Tim Toldrum is dead." Upon hearing this, Tom shrieked out: "Tim is dead! Then I'm the King o' the Cats!" With that he rushed up the chimney and was never seen again. (Jacobs) Cf. Christiansen, *Migratory Legends,* type 6070B.

Cats Are Queer Articles. Glassie, *Irish Folktales,* no. 83.
Dildrum, King of Cats. Briggs, *DBF,* pt. B, v. 1, p. 206.
King o' Cats, The (I, II). Briggs, *DBF,* pt. B, v. 1, p. 294.
King o' the Cats, The (England). Clarkson and Cross, *World Folktales,* no. 33.
King o' the Cats, The. Jacobs, *More English Fairy Tales,* p. 169.
Mally Dixon. Briggs, *DBF,* pt. B, v. 1, p. 309.
Mányó Is Dead. Dégh, *Folktales of Hungary,* no. 26.
Sennentunscheli on the Wyssenboden (Switzerland). Dorson, *Folktales around the World,* p. 83.
We Had One of Them in the House for a While. Glassie, *Irish Folktales,* no. 64.

**113B THE CAT AS A HOLY MAN.** The cat went on a pilgrimage to Mecca. The king of the mice felt obliged to congratulate him on his safe return. He found him in a white cap saying prayers, but when the cat saw the mouse, he sprang at him and nearly bit off his tail. "The cat may pray like a holy man," reported the king of the mice to his subjects, "but he still pounces like a cat." (Bushnaq)

Cat Who Went to Mecca. Bushnaq, *Arab Folktales,* p. 216.
Harnit and the Bittle, The. Briggs, *DBF,* pt. A, v. 1, p. 115.

**119B\* UNITED WE STAND, DIVIDED WE FALL.** Four oxen protected themselves by standing in a close circle, their tails inward. If a the lion attacked them, he was turned away by their horns. Then they had a dispute, and each went to a separate corner of the field. Now the lion could attack them one at a time, and soon they were all dead.

Four Oxen and the Lion, The. Jacobs, *Aesop,* no. 52.

**120 THE WAGER TO SEE THE SUNRISE FIRST.** The fox and the crow made a wager as to who would be first to see the sunrise. The next morning the fox shouted at his first glimpse of the rising sun. But the crow, from her nest high in a tree, was already bathed in sunlight, and she won the wager. (Campbell)

Hoodie and the Fox, The. Campbell, *West Highlands,* v. 3, p. 134.
Why the Hawk Catches Chickens. Harris, *Uncle Remus and His Friends,* no. 1.

**121 THE LADDER OF WOLVES.** A woodcutter's wife once scalded a wolf with hot soup. Later the scalded wolf attacked the woodcutter. The man escaped up a tree, but the wolf called his brothers, and they made a ladder of wolves reaching up the tree. Just before he was caught, the woodcutter shouted: "Pour away, Jeanette!" The scalded wolf, who was at the bottom of the ladder, feared another shower of hot soup, and bolted. The column of wolves crashed to the ground, and they all limped away. The woodcutter walked home safely. (Massignon)

> Scalded Wolf, The (France). Dorson, *Folktales around the World*, p. 59.
> Scalded Wolf, The. Massignon, *Folktales of France*, no. 61.
> Son-of-Adam and the Lion. El-Shamy, *Folktales of Egypt*, no. 48.

**122  THE TRICKSTER ESCAPES.** Brer Fox invited Brer Rabbit to chicken dinner. When the rabbit arrived he saw only a pan and a carving knife, but no food. Not letting his suspicions show he said: "You don't have calamus root? I'll run and get some." With that he leaped out of the door, but he didn't come back with the calamus root. (Harris, "Uncle Remus Initiates the Little Boy")

> Brer Rabbit and the Gold Mine. Harris, *Uncle Remus and Brer Rabbit*, no. 5.
> Dancing to the River. Abrahams, *Afro-American Folktales*, no. 72.
> Dove, the Heron, and Jackal, The. Postma, *Tales from the Basotho*, no. 13.
> Mister Bear Catches Old Mister Bull-Frog. Harris, *Uncle Remus*, no. 24.
> Mister Hawk and Brother Rabbit. Harris, *Nights with Uncle Remus*, no. 65.
> No Chicken Tonight. Abrahams, *Afro-American Folktales*, no. 74.
> Uncle Remus Initiates the Little Boy. Harris, *Uncle Remus*, no. 1.

**122A  DON'T EAT AN UNBAPTIZED PIG!** The wolf captured a pig and her newborn piglets. Before he could eat them the mother said: "You can't eat the piglets yet; they haven't been baptized." So they went to the mill stream, and the fox agreed to stand as godfather, thinking how good each little one would taste. However, the cunning pig opened the watergate, and the wolf was carried away in the flood. (Afanasyev)

> Foolish Wolf, The. Afanasyev, *Russian Fairy Tales*, p. 450.

**122B\*  PRAY BEFORE YOU EAT, AND LOSE YOUR MEAL.** The cat caught a rat. Before devouring him, he allowed the rat to say one last prayer. The pious cat joined in prayer, but as he raised his paws, the rat scampered to safety. (Bushnaq)

> Brother Wolf Says Grace. Harris, *Nights with Uncle Remus*, no. 27.
> Fox and the Goose, The. Campbell, *West Highlands*, v. 1, p. 275.
> Mountain Hen and the Fox, The. Ranke, *Folktales of Germany*, no. 5.
> Pious Cat, The. Bushnaq, *Arab Folktales*, p. 222.
> Ungrateful Lion Loses His Prey, The. Arewa, *Northern East Africa*, p. 136.

**122C  MUSIC BEFORE DINNER, BUT NO DINNER.** A wolf captured a goat. "Let me die with ceremony," asked the goat. "You play the flute, and I will dance." The wolf agreed, but the music attracted the dogs, and the wolf had to run for his life.

> One Thing at a Time. Handford, *Aesop*, no. 101.

**122D  I'LL BRING YOU BETTER GAME.**  Mr. Wildcat seized Brer Rabbit and was set to eat him, when the rabbit said: "I can hear wild turkeys out there. Let me help you catch some. You play dead and I'll call the turkeys up close to you where you can grab all you want." So Mr. Wildcat let Brer Rabbit go, but he didn't catch any turkeys that day. (Harris)

> Brother Rabbit and Mister Wildcat. Harris, *Nights with Uncle Remus,* no. 48.
> Hare Escapes from the Lion, The. Arewa, *Northern East Africa,* p. 65.
> Roaqo, the Woman Who Ate People. Postma, *Tales from the Basotho,* no. 6.

**122E  WAIT FOR THE BIGGER GOAT.**  A troll stopped the youngest Billy-Goat Gruff on the bridge. "Wait for the next goat, he's bigger," said the little goat, and the troll let him pass. Hoping for a still larger meal, the troll let the second goat pass as well. He tried to stop the third Billy-Goat Gruff, but this giant goat charged at the troll and crushed him with his horns. (Asbjørnsen and Moe)  Cf. types 2027, 2028.

> Little Mangy One. Bushnaq, *Arab Folktales,* p. 233.
> Three Billy-Goats Gruff, The (Norway). Clarkson and Cross, *World Folktales,* no. 22.
> Three Billy-Goats Gruff, The (Norway). Thompson, *100 Favorite Folktales,* no. 1.
> Three Billy-Goats Gruff, The. Asbjørnsen and Moe, *East o' the Sun,* p. 264.
> Three Kids, the Billy Goat, and the Wolf. Dégh, *Folktales of Hungary,* no. 28.

**122F  EAT ME WHEN I'M FATTER.**  A little lamb was on his way to visit his granny when he was caught by a jackal. Before the jackal could eat him, the lamb said: "To Granny's house I go, where I shall fatter grow, then you can eat me so." The jackal thought this reasonable, and he let the lamb go. (Jacobs)

> Fisher and the Little Fish, The. Jacobs, *Aesop,* no. 53.
> Fisherman and the Minnow, The. Daly, *Aesop,* no. 18.
> Foolish Wolf, The. Afanasyev, *Russian Fairy Tales,* p. 450.
> Fox and the Wolf, The (de Trueba). Lang, *Orange Fairy Book,* p. 56.
> Halfman. Lang, *Violet Fairy Book,* p. 345.
> Lambikin, The. Jacobs, *Indian Fairy Tales,* p. 17.
> Mister Hawk and Brother Rabbit. Harris, *Nights with Uncle Remus,* no. 65.
> Profitting by Experience. Handford, *Aesop,* no. 117.
> Sleeping Dog and the Wolf, The. Daly, *Aesop,* no. 134.

**122G  SOAKING OFF THE TURTLE'S SHELL.**  Brer Fox captured Brer Mud Turtle, but he couldn't open up the shell. "Claws and teeth won't work," said the turtle from inside his enclosure. "You'll have to soak it off with mud." But when the fox put him in the mud, the turtle sunk out of sight and escaped.

> Brother Mud Turtle's Trickery. Harris, *Uncle Remus and His Friends,* no. 23.

Lovely Dream and a Fateful Journey, A. Delarue, *French Folktales,* p. 309.

**122J  THE WOLF AND THE ASS WITH A THORN IN HIS FOOT.**
An ass, about to be eaten by a wolf, pretended to have a thorn in his
foot. "You had better pull it out before you eat me," said the ass, "or
you will prick your mouth." The wolf accordingly lifted the ass's foot,
but received such a blow that it knocked out all of his teeth. (Aesop)

> Every Man to His Own Trade. Handford, *Aesop,* no. 111.
> Wolf, Fox, and Ass. Megas, *Folktales of Greece,* no. 9.

**122M\*  THE GOAT RUNS INTO THE WOLF'S STOMACH.** The
wolf captured a big billy goat, who said: "Why should you break your
teeth on me?   Open your mouth, and I'll jump right into your
stomach." The foolish wolf did what the goat said, and the goat gave
him such a blow with his horns that it knocked him senseless.

> Foolish Wolf, The. Afanasyev, *Russian Fairy Tales,* p. 450.

**122Z  ESCAPING FROM A CAPTOR**  —Miscellaneous tricks.

> Brother Rabbit and the Little Girl. Harris, *Nights with Uncle Remus,* no. 3.
> License to Steal, A. Abrahams, *Afro-American Folktales,* no. 62.

**123  THE WOLF AND THE KIDS.** One day when mother goat was
away, the wolf came to her house and ate her kids. The mother found
the villain asleep in the meadow and cut open his belly. Out sprang the
kids, for the wolf had swallowed them whole. The mother filled the
his belly with stones and sewed him shut. When he awoke he went to a
well to drink. The stones made him fall in, and he drowned. (Grimm)
Cf. type 333.

> Calf and a Girl Are Born from a Man's Knee, A. Arewa, *Northern East Africa,*
>     p. 223.
> Cunning Snake, The. Harris, *Nights with Uncle Remus,* no. 43.
> Cutta Cord-La. Abrahams, *Afro-American Folktales,* no. 47.
> Ewe, the Goat, and the Lion, The. Sabar, *Kurdistani Jews,* p. 163.
> Fire-Test, The. Harris, *Nights with Uncle Remus,* no. 42.
> Goat and Her Kids, The. Delarue, *French Folktales,* p. 300.
> Goat Who Lied, The. Massignon, *Folktales of France,* no. 15.
> Goat, the Kids, and the Wolf, The. Massignon, *Folktales of France,* no. 36.
> Golden Chain from Heaven, The. Seki, *Folktales of Japan,* no. 21.
> Granny Who Had Many Children. Fowke, *Folklore of Canada,* p. 291.
> How the Fox Took a Turn Out of the Goat. Campbell, *West Highlands,* v. 3,
>     p. 103.
> Trust Not the Panther. Thundy, *South Indian Folktales,* no. 35.
> Wolf and the Goat, The. Afanasyev, *Russian Fairy Tales,* p. 249.
> Wolf and the Seven Young Kids, The. Grimm, *Tales,* no. 5.

**123B   THE WOLF IN SHEEP'S CLOTHING.** A wolf found a sheep's pelt. He put it over his own coat and mingled freely among the sheep. For some time he deceived the sheep and enjoyed many good meals.

> Case of Mistaken Identity, A. Handford, *Aesop,* no. 36.
> Wolf in Sheep's Clothing, The. Jacobs, *Aesop,* no. 39.

**124   BLOWING THE HOUSE IN.** Three little pigs set out on their own. The first built a house of straw, but the wolf blew that house in and ate the pig. The second built a house of twigs, but the wolf blew that house in and ate the second pig as well. The third built a house of bricks. The wolf could not blow this house in, so he came down the chimney after the pig, but the pig caught him in a pot of boiling water and ate him for supper. (Jacobs)

> Awful Fate of Mister Wolf, The. Harris, *Uncle Remus,* no. 13.
> Fox and the Geese, The. Briggs, *DBF,* pt. A, v. 2, p. 524.
> Fox and the Pixies, The. Briggs, *DBF,* pt. A, v. 2, p. 528.
> Fox and the Pixies, The. Whitlock, *Folklore of Devon,* p. 39.
> Little Blue Bonnet, The. Gmelch and Kroup, *To Shorten the Road,* p. 177.
> Little Geese, The. Calvino, *Italian Folktales,* no. 94.
> Old Sow and the Three Shoats. Chase, *Grandfather Tales,* no. 8.
> Pigs, The. Harris, *Nights with Uncle Remus,* no. 8.
> Sow and the Wolf, The. Delarue, *French Folktales,* p. 292.
> Three Cottages, The. Calvino, *Italian Folktales,* no. 24.
> Three Goslings, The. Crane, *Italian Popular Tales,* no. 86.
> Three Hares, The (Turkey). Clarkson and Cross, *World Folktales,* no. 24.
> Three Hares, The (Turkey). Cole, *Best-Loved Folktales,* no. 113.
> Three Little Pigs, The (I, II). Briggs, *DBF,* pt. A, v. 2, p. 568.
> Three Little Pigs, The. Jacobs, *English Fairy Tales,* p. 68.
> Three Little Pigs, The. Lang, *Green Fairy Book,* p. 100.
> Three Little Pigs. Randolph, *Who Blowed Up the Church House?,* p. 84.
> Three Pullets, The. Delarue, *French Folktales,* p. 297.
> Three Wee Pigs, The. Briggs, *DBF,* pt. A, v. 2, p. 572.

**125   FRIGHTENING WOLVES WITH A WOLF'S HEAD.** A ram and a cat decided to run away. They found a wolf's head and carried it along. They came to a fire where twelve wolves were warming themselves. "Choose the fattest of our wolf's heads for supper," said the cat, and the ram held up the head for all to see. "No, choose a better one," said the cat, and the ram held up the same head again. This show of heads so frightened the wolves that they all ran away. (Afanasyev)

> Lion and the Cock, The. Arewa, *Northern East Africa,* p. 30.
> Lion and the Cow, The. Arewa, *Northern East Africa,* p. 30.
> Ram, the Cat, and the Twelve Wolves, The. Afanasyev, *Russian Fairy Tales,* p. 196.

**126   A GOAT FRIGHTENS A LION.** A goat came face to face with a lion. Thinking quickly, he said: "I have been sent by the Lord of

Creation to kill seven lions. Let me see if you are one that must die. No, praise destiny, you are not among the unlucky seven. Go your way." The lion thanked fate for his narrow escape and left. (Bushnaq)

> Brother Rabbit Frightens Brother Tiger. Harris, *Uncle Remus and His Friends,* no. 13.
> Mister Benjamin Ram and His Wonderful Fiddle. Harris, *Nights with Uncle Remus,* no. 9.
> Mister Benjamin Ram Defends Himself. Harris, *Nights with Uncle Remus,* no. 49.
> Two Close Calls. Bushnaq, *Arab Folktales,* p. 238.

**127A\* A KID ON THE ROOF; A WOLF ON THE GROUND.** A kid atop a house shouted insults to the wolf below. "Curse away, my friend," said the wolf.

> Wolf and the Kid, The. Jacobs, *Aesop,* no. 16.

**130 OUTCAST ANIMALS FIND A NEW HOME.** A donkey, a dog, a cat, and a rooster had all grown old and feared for their lives, so they set out for Bremen, where they hoped to become town musicians. That night they came to a house in the woods. Seeing a band of robbers inside, they devised a plan to drive the villains away. The donkey placed his forefeet on the window ledge, the dog mounted the donkey, the cat climbed on the dog's back, and the rooster perched on the cat's head. Then each began to sing. The terrified robbers fled, and the four musicians stayed there from then on. (Grimm) Cf. type 1653.

> Animals and the Robbers, The. Roberts, *South from Hell,* no. 1.
> Bremen Town Musicians, The. Grimm, *Tales,* no. 27.
> Bull, the Tup, The Cock and the Steg, The. Briggs, *DBF,* pt. A, v. 1, p. 174.
> Cat That Went a-Traveling, The (USA). Clarkson and Cross, *World Folktales,* no. 23.
> Cat That Went a-Traveling, The. Campbell, *Cloudwalking Country,* p. 226.
> Four Friends, The. Massignon, *Folktales of France,* no. 52.
> Goat and the Fox, The. Crane, *Italian Popular Tales,* no. 89.
> How Jack Went to Seek His Fortune. Briggs, *DBF,* pt. A, v. 1, p. 313.
> How Jack Went to Seek His Fortune. Jacobs, *English Fairy Tales,* p. 24.
> How the Animals Kept the Lions Away. Bushnaq, *Arab Folktales,* p. 242.
> Jack and His Comrades. Jacobs, *Celtic Fairy Tales,* p. 112.
> Jack and the Robbers. Chase, *The Jack Tales,* no. 4.
> Journey to Toulouse of the Animals That Had Colds, The. Delarue, *French Folktales,* p. 285.
> Little John and His Animals. Thomas, *It's Good to Tell You,* no. 1.
> Michel Michelkleiner's Good Luck (Luxembourg). Bødker, *European Folk Tales,* p. 98.
> Mister Korbes the Fox. Briggs, *DBF,* pt. A, v. 2, p. 543.
> Nung-Kua-Ma. Eberhard, *Folktales of China,* no. 63.
> Ram and the Pig Who Went into the Woods to Live by Themselves, The. Asbjørnsen and Moe, *Norwegian Folktales,* p. 102.
> Struggle between the Wolf and the Fox, The. Ranke, *Folktales of Germany,* no. 4.
> White Pet, The. Campbell, *West Highlands,* v. 1, p. 199.

**130A OUTCAST ANIMALS BUILD A NEW HOME.** An ox, a sheep, and a cock—all threatened with slaughter—joined company and ran off into the woods where they built themselves a hut. A bear wanted to eat them, but they raised a great din and frightened him away. (Afanasyev)

> Bear and the Cock, The. Afanasyev, *Russian Fairy Tales,* p. 455.
> Brother Rabbit Secures a Mansion. Harris, *Nights with Uncle Remus,* no. 6.
> Ram Who Lost Half His Skin, The. Afanasyev, *Russian Fairy Tales,* p. 188.

**136A\* THE GUILTY ANIMAL FALLS INTO THE WELL.** A donkey, a goat, and a duck and planted a field of clover in partnership. One night the greedy donkey devoured the entire patch. No one would admit to the crime, so to find the truth they went to the Biyera Well. Each partner swore his innocence and jumped across the well. The duck and the goat made it safely, but the donkey fell in.

> Biyera Well, The. El-Shamy, *Folktales of Egypt,* no. 51.

**150 A CAPTURED BIRD BUYS FREEDOM WITH ADVICE.** A man trapped a nightingale, but the bird talked him into freeing him in exchange for three pieces of advice. These were the bird's counsels: "First, never believe the impossible; second, guard what is yours; and third, do not grieve for that which you have lost and cannot recover." With that the nightingale flew to freedom.

> Laborer and the Nightingale, The. Briggs, *DBF,* pt. A, v. 1, p. 119.

**151 MUSIC LESSONS FOR WILD ANIMALS.** A fiddler played so well that many animals asked for lessons. He agreed, but tricked them cruelly. The wolf ended his first lesson with his paws wedged in a tree. Similarly, the fiddler strung the fox between two saplings and tied the hare by his neck to a tree. (Grimm) Cf. types 1159, 1160.

> Cat, Lion, and Man. Megas, *Folktales of Greece,* no. 11.
> Lion That Learned to Swing, The. Delarue, *French Folktales,* p. 288.
> Strange Musician, The. Grimm, *Tales,* no. 8.

**152A\* THE SCALDED WOLF.** A wolf crept toward a farmyard, hoping to steal a sheep, but the peasants threw boiling wash water on it. (Grimm)

> Fox and His Cousin, The. Grimm, *Tales,* no. 74.
> Scalded Wolf, The (France). Dorson, *Folktales around the World,* p. 59.
> Scalded Wolf, The. Massignon, *Folktales of France,* no. 61.
> Son-of-Adam and the Lion. El-Shamy, *Folktales of Egypt,* no. 48.

**154 A SACKFUL OF DOGS.** A bear threatened to destroy a peasant's flock if he didn't give him a horse. A fox offered to help the man, in return for a fat sheep. Thus, when the bear came for the horse, the fox made a noise like a hunter. The bear, to save himself, pretended to be a log, and let the man tie him onto his sledge. The peasant quickly killed the now helpless bear with his ax. The fox came for his promised reward, and the peasant gave him a large sack. But when the fox opened it, two fierce dogs jumped out, and he had to run for his life. (Asbjørnsen and Moe)

> Fox as Mourner, The. Afanasyev, *Russian Fairy Tales*, p. 437.
> Fox Loses His Promised Reward, The. Arewa, *Northern East Africa*, p. 137.
> How the Ewe Outwitted the Jackal. Bushnaq, *Arab Folktales*, p. 236.
> Man, Snake, and Fox. Megas, *Folktales of Greece*, no. 10.
> Parson and the Poor Man, The. Dégh, *Folktales of Hungary*, no. 10.
> Peasant, the Bear, and the Fox, The. Afanasyev, *Russian Fairy Tales*, p. 288.
> Reynard and Bruin. Jacobs, *European Folk and Fairy Tales*, no. 6.
> Snow White and the Fox. Afanasyev, *Russian Fairy Tales*, p. 283.
> Well Done and Ill Paid. Asbjørnsen and Moe, *East o' the Sun*, p. 266.

**155 THE TIGER IS TRICKED BACK INTO CAPTIVITY.** A Brahman came upon a trapped tiger and, trusting the beast's promise not to hurt him, set him free. But the ungrateful tiger seized the man and was about to eat him, when a jackal came upon the scene. The jackal agreed to serve as judge, but he would have to see how it all began. He convinced the tiger to reenter the cage, so he could determine exactly what had happened. With the tiger inside, the jackal quickly locked the door, concluding: "Let matters remain as they were." (Jacobs, *Indian Fairy Tales* )

> Brother Wolf Still in Trouble. Harris, *Nights with Uncle Remus*, no. 46.
> Good is Repaid with Evil. Parades, *Folktales of Mexico*, no. 25.
> Great Flood, The. Eberhard, *Folktales of China*, no. 67.
> Ingrates, The (Italy). Thompson, *100 Favorite Folktales*, no. 2.
> Ingrates, The. Crane, *Italian Popular Tales*, no. 38.
> Inside Again. Jacobs, *European Folk and Fairy Tales*, no. 20.
> Man Who Knew How to Cure a Snakebite, The (Cambodia). Clarkson and Cross, *World Folktales*, no. 52.
> Man, Snake, and Fox. Megas, *Folktales of Greece*, no. 10.
> Man, the Serpent, and the Fox, The. Crane, *Italian Popular Tales*, no. 49.
> Old Favors Are Soon Forgotten. Afanasyev, *Russian Fairy Tales*, p. 273.
> Son-of-Adam and the Crocodile. El-Shamy, *Folktales of Egypt*, no. 47.
> Tiger, the Brahman, and the Jackal, The (India). Cole, *Best-Loved Folktales*, no. 143.
> Tiger, the Brahman, and the Jackal, The. Jacobs, *Indian Fairy Tales*, p. 66.
> Trouble with Helping Out, The. Abrahams, *Afro-American Folktales*, no. 57.
> Ungrateful Animals (12 variants). Arewa, *Northern East Africa*, p. 130.
> Ungrateful Serpent, The. Clouston, *Popular Tales*, v. 1, p. 262.
> Ungrateful Snake, the Fox, and the Man, The. Dawkins, *More Greek Folktales*, no. 3.
> Who is Blessed with the Realm, Riches, and Honor? Noy, *Folktales of Israel*, no. 57.

**156  ANDROCLES AND THE LION.** An escaped slave named Androcles came upon a lion with a thorn in its paw, and removed the thorn. Later both the slave and the lion were captured, and Androcles was to be fed to the wild beast in the emperor's arena. But the lion recognized his friend and licked his hands like a friendly dog. The emperor was so impressed that he freed them both. (Aesop)

> Androcles and the Lion. Jacobs, *European Folk and Fairy Tales,* no. 13.
> Androcles. Jacobs, *Aesop,* no. 23.
> Wolf's Reward, The. Seki, *Folktales of Japan,* no. 7.

**156A THE FAITHFUL LION.** Duke Henry came to the aid of a lion about to be overcome by a dragon. The dragon was killed, and the lion became Henry's lifelong companion. When Henry finally died at a ripe old age, the lion laid himself on his master's tomb and refused to move. (Grimm)

> Henry the Lion. Grimm, *German Legends,* no. 526.
> Man Helps a Lion, The. Arewa, *Northern East Africa,* p. 121.

**157  LEARNING TO FEAR MAN.** A wolf boasted that he was stronger than a man. To let him prove his claim, the fox directed him to a hunter carrying a gun and a sword. After their confrontation, the shattered wolf reported to the fox: "He blew into a stick and lightning and hail flew up my nose. Then he drew a rib from his body and slashed me with it until I was nearly dead." (Grimm, no. 72)

> Bear, Fox, and Man. Ranke, *Folktales of Germany,* no. 7.
> Cat, Lion, and Man. Megas, *Folktales of Greece,* no. 11.
> Goose, the Peacock and the Peahen, The. Mathers, *1001 Nights,* v. 1, p. 583.
> Meeting Man. Dorson, *Negro Tales,* p. 34.
> Mister Lion Hunts for Mister Man. Harris, *Nights with Uncle Remus,* no. 7.
> Mister Lion's Sad Predicament. Harris, *Nights with Uncle Remus,* no. 57.
> Son-of-Adam and the Lion. El-Shamy, *Folktales of Egypt,* no. 48.
> Sparrow and His Four Children, The. Grimm, *Tales,* no. 157.
> Trouble Coming Down the Road. Abrahams, *Afro-American Folktales,* no. 73.
> Why the Buzzard Is Bald. Dorson, *Negro Tales,* p. 158.
> Wolf and the Man, The. Grimm, *Tales,* no. 72.
> Wolf and the Soldier, The. Massignon, *Folktales of France,* no. 21.

**157A THE LION IN SEARCH OF THE MAN.** Mr. Lion, eager to prove his strength, was in search of Mr. Man. He came to a woodcutter splitting rails. "Do you know Mr. Man?" the lion asked. "Yes, I'll fetch him if you'll hold this log open until I get back." The lion put his paw in the crack, and the man knocked out the wedge, trapping the beast. Then he cut a stick and beat the lion half to death. (Harris) Cf. types 151, 1085, 1160.

> Mister Lion Hunts for Mister Man. Harris, *Nights with Uncle Remus,* no. 7.
> Power of Man, The. Sabar, *Kurdistani Jews,* p. 161.

**159A THE ANIMALS AND THE CHARCOAL BURNER.** One cold day some wild animals came to a charcoal burner's hut and asked if they could warm themselves. He let them in. After they were warm, they decided to put together a meal, and they brought back a calf, a lamb, chickens, and a cabbage. Then they fell asleep by the fire. The charcoal burner heated his hammer red hot and beat the animals until they ran away, leaving behind their food, and he had enough to eat for a whole year. (Massignon)

> Charcoal Burner, The. Massignon, *Folktales of France,* no. 64.
> Father Mazaraud. Delarue, *French Folktales,* p. 304.

**159B WHY THE LION HATES THE MAN.** Formerly the man and the lion were friends. One day the man said: "You have many virtues, but your breath stinks." At this the lion got up and asked the man to hit him on the neck with his ax. The man did not understand, but he did what he was asked. Sometime later the lion asked the man to look at his neck. "It is completely healed," said the man. "Yes, answered the lion, but what you said about my breath still hurts, and if you ever come to this place again, I'll eat you up."

> Old Woodcutter and the Lion, The. Megas, *Folktales of Greece,* no. 12.

**160 GRATEFUL ANIMALS AND AN UNGRATEFUL MAN ARE RESCUED FROM A PIT.** A wealthy man once fell into a pit where a lion and a serpent had already been trapped. A poor woodcutter heard their cries and helped them out, after receiving the promise of a generous reward from the rich man. Later the grateful lion brought the woodcutter a goat and the serpent brought him a precious stone. When the woodcutter reminded the rich man about the promised reward, he threw the poor man into prison, but the judges heard of this injustice, and they forced the rich man to compensate the woodcutter. (Briggs)

> Grateful Animals (4 variants). Arewa, *Northern East Africa,* p. 125.
> Grateful Beasts, The. Briggs, *DBF,* pt. A, v. 1, p. 111.
> How a Dove and a Snake Took Pity on a Man. Noy, *Folktales of Israel,* no. 29.
> Thankful Beasts, The. Clouston, *Popular Tales,* v. 1, p. 223.
> Treachery of Man, The. Bushnaq, *Arab Folktales,* p. 246.

**161 BETRAYED BY A POINTING FINGER.** A woodcutter hid a fox that was being pursued by hunters. When the hunters asked if the woodcutter had seen the fox, he said "No," but as he spoke he pointed toward the fox's hiding place. However, the hunters missed the cue, and went away. As the fox took his leave of the woodcutter he said: "I would thank you, but your actions did not agree with your words."

Actions Speak Louder Than Words. Handford, *Aesop*, no. 4.
Fox and the Woodcutter, The. Daly, *Aesop*, no. 22.

**161A\*   THE BEAR WITH THE WOODEN PAW.** A bear challenged an old man to a fight, and the man cut off his paw with his ax. The bear made himself a paw of wood and hobbled to the old man's house, where he ate up the old man and his wife.

Bear, The. Afanasyev, *Russian Fairy Tales*, p. 74.

**162   THE MASTER SEES THE HIDDEN STAG.** A stag pursued by hunters buried itself under the hay in a stall. Neither the hunters nor the stable boys could see the hidden prey, but the master immediately noticed the horns protruding from the hay, and they made a quick end of the stag.

Hart in the Ox-Stall, The. Jacobs, *Aesop*, no. 30.

**163   THE SINGING WOLF.** An old man and his old wife had five sheep, a colt, and a calf. A wolf came to them and sang such a fine song that the woman said to the man: "Give him a sheep." This happened again and again until the wolf had eaten all the animals. Then he ate the woman, and the old man was all alone.

Wolf, The. Afanasyev, *Russian Fairy Tales*, p. 312.

**166A\*   THE WOLF LOSES HIS TAIL IN A PIGSTY.** A wolf was catching baby pigs by putting his tail through a hole in a pigsty. When a little pig would come to sniff his tail, he would turn around, snatch the pig, and run away. The peasant discovered what was happening, and hid in the pigsty. When the wolf put his tail through the hole, the peasant held it fast. To escape, the wolf pulled his tail off, but he ran only a short distance before dying from the loss of blood.

Wolf, The. Afanasyev, *Russian Secret Tales*, p. 7.

**170A THE CLEVER ANIMAL TRADES WISELY.** A little rooster had a thorn in his foot. His mother removed it and threw it on the fire. "I want my thorn back," demanded the rooster, and his mother had to give him a loaf of bread in compensation. A farmer ate his bread and had to give him a lamb. A wedding party ate his lamb, so they had to give him the bride. The bride's brothers were thieves, but they were soon captured, so the little rooster and his bride carried their treasure back to his mother, and they lived with her happily ever after. (Villa) Cf. types 1415, 1655.

It Started with a Thorn. Villa, *100 Armenian Tales*, no. 96.
Sparrow, The. El-Shamy, *Folktales of Egypt*, no. 50.
Travels of a Fox, The (USA). Clarkson and Cross, *World Folktales*, no. 41.

**171  THE THREE BEARS**  (new classification).  Three bears lived
together in a house in a wood.  One day, while the bears were out, a
little old woman came to their house.  She walked right in and tasted
their porridge, sat in their chairs, and fell asleep in the little bear's bed.
When the bears returned, they found her there.  She awoke with a start
and jumped out the window, and the three bears never saw her again.
(Jacobs, *English Fairy Tales*)

> Scrapefoot (summary). Briggs, *DBF,* pt. A, v. 2, p. 557.
> Scrapefoot. Jacobs, *More English Fairy Tales,* p. 94.
> Three Bears, The (England). Opie, *Classic Fairy Tales,* p. 264.
> Three Bears, The. Briggs, *DBF,* pt. A, v. 2, p. 564.
> Three Bears, The. Jacobs, *English Fairy Tales,* p. 93.
> Three Bears, The. Lang, *Green Fairy Book,* p. 234.

**173  MEN, ANIMALS, AND THE SPAN OF LIFE.**  When God
created the world he offered thirty years of life each to the donkey, the
dog, the monkey, and the man.  The first three thought it was too
much, and the man·thought it was too little, so God gave man part of
the animals' years.  Thus man lives seventy years.  His first thirty are
his human years, and they pass quickly; then follow eighteen
burdensome years from the donkey, when he carries the grain that
feed others and is rewarded by blows; then come twelve years from the
dog, when he lies growling in the corner.  His last ten years are from
the monkey; then he becomes foolish and silly minded, and children
laugh at him.  (Grimm)  —Note: Aarne and Thompson also categorize
this tale as type 828.

> Ages of Man, The (Poland). Dorson, *Folktales around the World,* p. 106.
> Duration of Life, The. Grimm, *Tales,* no. 176.
> Man's Years. Daly, *Aesop,* no. 105.
> Span of Man's Life, The. Noy, *Folktales of Israel,* no. 26.

**175  THE TARBABY AND THE RABBIT.**  Brer Fox hit upon a plan
to catch Brer Rabbit.  He made a doll of sticky tar and set it at the side
of the road.  When Brer Rabbit came by, he greeted the figure, but it
didn't answer.  He soon grew impatient and popped the tarbaby on the
head.  His hand stuck fast, and he fought back with his free hand and
with his feet until he was completely stuck.  The fox stepped from his
hiding place and claimed his prize.  —Continues as type 1310A.
(Harris)

> Anansi Plays Dead (Africa). Clarkson and Cross, *World Folktales,* no. 42.
> Bouki and the Rabbit and the Well. Dorson, *Buying the Wind,* p. 248.
> Brer Turtle. Saucier, *French Louisiana,* no. 31.
> Demon with the Matted Hair, The. Jacobs, *Indian Fairy Tales,* p. 194.  ·
> Hare Sticks to the Bird Lime, The (7 variants). Arewa, *Northern East Africa,*
>     p. 46.
> Mouse and the Fox, The (Peru). Dorson, *Folktales around the World,* p. 527.

Ploughboy Kills a Dragon with a Wooden Man. A. Simpson, *Folklore of the Welsh Border*, p. 47.
Rabbit and the Coyote, The. Parades, *Folktales of Mexico*, no. 26.
Tar Baby. Dorson, *Negro Tales*, p. 16.
Tar Banana Tree. Dance, *Folklore from Contemporary Jamaicans*, no. 17.
Tarbaby, The. Pino-Saavedra, *Folktales of Chile*, no. 2.
Tortoise and a Mischievous Monkey, A (Brazil). Lang, *Brown Fairy Book*, p. 327.
Tricking All the Kings. Abrahams, *Afro-American Folktales*, no. 43.
Wonderful Tar-Baby Story, The. Harris, *Uncle Remus*, no. 2.

**176\*  DRAGGING THE MEAT BY A STRING.** Brer Rabbit joined Mr. Man, who was carrying a piece of meat. The rabbit complained about a bad smell, concluding: "It must be the meat." "But," he added, "you can bring back its freshness by dragging it on a line." So the man tied his meat to a line and pulled it along behind. Brer Rabbit offered to brush the flies from the meat as they walked, but he replaced the meat with a stone, and disappeared. (Harris, "Mr. Man Has Some Meat")

How Brother Rabbit Got the Meat. Harris, *Nights with Uncle Remus*, no. 24.
Mister Man Has Some Meat. Harris, *Nights with Uncle Remus*, no. 23.

**178  KILLING THE ANIMAL THAT HAS SAVED YOUR LIFE.** A king wanted to drink from a spring, but as he brought the cup to his lips, his falcon beat it from his hands. This happened a second and a third time, and the king killed the bird. Then a servant ran up, saying: "There is a serpent in the spring. The water is poisonous." Now the king knew that he had killed the falcon for saving his life. (Tolstoy)

King and the Falcon, The. Tolstoy, *Fables and Fairy Tales*, p. 24.
Traveler Kills His Donkey, A. Arewa, *Northern East Africa*, p. 176.

**178A  LLEWELLYN AND HIS DOG GELLERT.** During his absence, Prince Llewellyn's dog Gellert would watch his baby son. One day the prince returned to see the dog covered with blood. Presuming Gellert had killed the child, the prince slew the dog. The next instant he saw the baby, safe and sound. Nearby was the mangled body of a huge wolf that had been killed by the brave and faithful Gellert. (Baring-Gould)

Choking Doberman and Its Ancestors, The (examples and commentary). Brunvand, *The Choking Doberman*, ch. 1.
Dog Gellert, The. Baring-Gould, *Curious Myths of the Middle Ages*, no. 6.
Llewellyn and His Dog Gellert. Clouston, *Popular Tales*, v. 2, p. 166.

**179  WHAT THE BEAR WHISPERED.** Two men were accosted by a bear. One climbed a tree, but the other had no other option but to play dead. The bear sniffed about his head, then finally lumbered away. Coming down from the tree, his comrade laughed and said: "What did the bear whisper in your ear?" The man replied: "He said to never trust a friend who deserts you in need."

Friend in Need Is a Friend Indeed, A. Handford, *Aesop,* no. 176.
Two Fellows and the Bear, The. Jacobs, *Aesop,* no. 50.

**200  WHY DOGS DISLIKE CATS.**  A dog received a patent of nobility, drawn up on parchment, which he entrusted to the cat for safekeeping.  But a hungry mouse discovered the cat's hiding place, and nibbled the parchment to pieces.  The cat declared everlasting war on the mouse and the dog likewise on the cat.

Why Dogs Dislike Cats and Cats Dislike Mice. Grimm, *Other Tales,* p. 139.

**200A  THE DOG WITH THE LETTER UNDER HIS TAIL.**  The dogs wrote a letter to St. Peter, complaining that they received only bones without any meat.  The greyhound was to deliver the letter, which was tied beneath his tail for the journey.  But he lost the letter, and from that time forth dogs have sniffed at each other's tails in search of the lost letter.

Why the Dogs Sniff at Each Other. Ranke, *Folktales of Germany,* no. 8.

**200B  THE DOG WITH THE PEPPER UNDER HIS TAIL.**  The lion gave a feast, but there was no pepper, so he sent a dog to the next town to fetch some.  Vexed at the lion, the dog did not return, but ran off with the pepper.  The lion sent the other dogs to punish the runaway, saying that until they found him they would get only bones and no meat.  From that day, dogs sniff at one another, trying to find the dog with the pepper.  (Grimm)

When Brother Rabbit Was King. Harris, *Told by Uncle Remus,* no. 7.
Why Dogs Sniff One Another. Grimm, *Other Tales,* p. 140.

**200C\*  WHY DOGS CHASE HARES.**  A dog and a hare became partners and went to the sea to swim.  "May I try on your socks?" asked the hare.  The dog agreed, but the hare ran away with them.  Ever since, hares have worn socks, and dogs chase hares whenever they see them.

Why the Dog Chases the Hare. Megas, *Folktales of Greece,* no. 13.

**200D\*  WHY CATS STAY INSIDE AND DOGS OUTSIDE.**  The dog and the cat had a race to determine who would live in the master's house and who would have to stay outside.  The dog was ahead, running with his mouth open, when he approached a beggar.  The beggar thought the dog was attacking him, and struck him with a stick, so the dog stopped to take his revenge on the beggar.  This delay cost him the race, and since that day cats have lived indoors and dogs outside.

> Cat and the Dog, The. O'Sullivan, *Folktales of Ireland,* no. 8.

**201   THE DOG AND THE WOLF.** A hungry wolf was at first envious of his well-fed cousin the dog. But noticing that a collar and chain had worn away the hair on the dog's neck, he said: "It is better to starve in freedom than to live as a fat slave."

> Counting the Cost. Handford, *Aesop,* no. 105.
> Dog and the Wolf, The. Jacobs, *Aesop,* no. 28.

**201E\*   THE DOG SACRIFICES HERSELF FOR MAN.** In a certain village there was a wonder dog called El Rabo. Whatever house she lived in had good luck. After one litter of pups she died, but one female pup looked exactly like the mother, and she too brought good fortune to the family she chose. And so it went for many years, until a selfish man stole El Rabo, wanting to bring good luck to his house. She escaped, but on her way back to the home from which she had been taken she was caught in a fox trap and died. There was never again another El Rabo.

> El Rabo (The Tail). Musick, *Green Hills of Magic,* no. 78.

**202   TWO STUBBORN GOATS.** Two goats met on a bridge and neither would give way. They butted at each other until their horns locked, and then they both fell into the water.

> Two Billygoats. Carpenter, *A Latvian Storyteller,* p. 208.

**207A   THE ASS PERSUADES THE OX TO PLAY SICK.** Upon hearing the ox's complaints of burdensome work, the ass advised his friend to pretend to be sick. The ox followed this advice, so the next day the ass was harnessed to the plow and had to do the ox's work. At the day's end he reported to the ox: "The master says that if you don't recover soon, he'll have to slaughter you." The ox recovered at once and returned to his work the very next morning. (Megas)

> Donkey Who Gave Advice, the Ox Who Became Sick, and the Rooster Who Was Clever, The. Sabar, *Kurdistani Jews,* p. 181.
> Fable of the Ass, the Bull and the Husbandman, The. Mathers, *1001 Nights,* v. 1, p. 6.
> Ox and Ass. Megas, *Folktales of Greece,* no. 14.

**207B   THE HARD-HEARTED HORSE AND THE ASS.** An ass, ill with fatigue, begged the horse to take part of his load, but the hard-hearted horse refused. The ass fell down and died, so the master put his entire load, including the ass's skin, on the horse.

Punishment of Selfishness, The. Handford, *Aesop,* no. 90.

**207C  THE BELL OF JUSTICE.**  A blind prince proclaimed that anyone suffering from injustice should ring a certain bell. A snake had a nest beneath the bell, and one day a toad lay claim to the nest. Unable to drive away the toad, the snake rang the bell, and the prince had the toad killed. Later the snake came to the prince's bedroom with a precious stone in its mouth. It laid the stone on the prince's eyes, and his blindness was cured.

> Bell of Justice, The. Musick, *Green Hills of Magic,* no. 35.
> Tantony Pig, The. Briggs, *DBF,* pt. B, v. 2, p. 771.

**210  THE TRAVELING ANIMALS AND THE WICKED MAN.**  A cock and a hen harnessed four mice to their carriage and started out for the house of Herr Korbes. On their way they were joined by a cat, a millstone, an egg, a duck, a pin, and a needle. Herr Korbes was not home when they arrived, so they hid themselves in his house. When he came in, the cat threw ashes in his face, the duck splashed water on him, the egg glued his eyes shut, the pin and the needle pricked him, and the millstone fell on him and struck him dead. Herr Korbes must have been a very wicked man! (Grimm, no. 41)

> Herr Korbes. Grimm, *Tales,* no. 41.
> Little Hen and the Little Cock, The. Ranke, *Folktales of Germany,* no. 3.
> Little Old Grandmother Who Lived at the Edge of the Forest, The. Fowke, *Folklore of Canada,* p. 293.
> Little, Little Woman, The. El-Shamy, *Folktales of Egypt,* no. 52.
> Monkey and the Crab, The. Seki, *Folktales of Japan,* no. 5.
> Monkey and the Pheasant, The. Seki, *Folktales of Japan,* no. 6.
> Nung-Kua-Ma. Eberhard, *Folktales of China,* no. 63.
> Pack of Ragamuffins, The. Grimm, *Tales,* no. 10.

**211  THE ASS WITH HIS LOAD OF SALT AND OF SPONGES.**  An ass loaded with salt slipped while crossing a river, and much of his burden dissolved in the water. On another trip, he decided to lighten his load in the same manner, and he purposely dropped into the water. But this time he was loaded with sponges, which became so heavy with water, that the ass could not pull himself back up, and he drowned.

> Ass Carrying Salt, The. Daly, *Aesop,* no. 180.
> Too Clever by Half. Handford, *Aesop,* no. 106.

**212  THE GOAT THAT LIED.**  A tailor sent his eldest son to graze their goat. He did not bring her home until she had eaten her fill of fine grass, but the goat claimed that she had not found a single leaf to eat. The tailor drove his son out of the house with blows. The story repeated itself twice more, and the man drove away his second and third sons, because of what the goat said. Now the tailor himself had to take the goat to pasture. He soon discovered how she had lied, so he shaved her head clean and drove her away with a whip. —Continues as type 563. (Grimm) Cf. type 2015.

> Goat That Lost Half his Skin, The. Dégh, *Folktales of Hungary,* no. 29.
> Goat Who Lied, The. Massignon, *Folktales of France,* no. 15.
> Skinned Goat, The. Ranke, *Folktales of Germany,* no. 9.
> Table-Be-Set, Gold-Donkey, and Cudgel-out-of-the-Sack. Grimm, *Tales,* no. 36.

## 214 THE ASS THAT BEHAVED LIKE A LAP DOG.
An ass, noticing the favored treatment the master gave to his lap dog, tried to imitate the little animal. He tried to climb into his master's lap, but the master's servants drove him away with sticks.

> Ass and the Lap-Dog, The. Jacobs, *Aesop,* no. 10.
> Know Your Limitations. Handford, *Aesop,* no. 110.

## 214A THE SINGING ASS AND THE DANCING CAMEL.
An ass and a camel were eating cabbages in a garden when the ass said: "Friend, I've a mind to sing," and although the camel begged him to be still, he began to bray. The gardener heard the noise and came after the pair with a stick. The ass managed to escape, but the camel received a terrible beating. Later the camel suggested that they cross a river to eat some plants on the other side, and offered to carry the ass on his back. In mid stream, the camel said: "I've a mind to dance." And dance he did, until the ass fell from his back and drowned.

> Ass and Camel. Megas, *Folktales of Greece,* no. 15.

## 214B THE ASS IN A LION'S SKIN.
An ass found a lion's skin that hunters had left out to dry. Putting it on, he went toward his village. Everyone who saw him fled in fear, and he was so proud that he brayed with delight. But then everyone recognized him, and his master gave him a beating for the trouble he had caused. (Aesop)

> Ass in a Lion's Skin, An (2 variants). Handford, *Aesop,* nos. 108, 109.
> Ass in the Lion's Skin, The. Jacobs, *Aesop,* no. 49.
> Ass in the Lion's Skin, The. Jacobs, *Indian Fairy Tales,* p. 150.

## 221 THE WREN BECOMES KING OF THE BIRDS.
The wren and the eagle had a contest who could fly the highest. The victor would be king of the birds. The eagle flew higher in great circles, with the wren riding on his back. When the eagle could fly no higher, he called out: "Where art thou, wren?" "Here above thee!" came the answer. Thus the wren won the crown. (Campbell)

> Eagle and the Wren, The. Campbell, *West Highlands,* v. 1, p. 285.
> King of Birds, The (2 tales). Briggs, *DBF,* pt. A, v. 1, p. 117.
> Willow Wren, The. Grimm, *Other Tales,* p. 109.

Wren the King of the Birds, The. Briggs, *DBF,* pt. A, v. 1, p. 128.
Wren, The. Grimm, *Tales,* no. 171.

**222  THE WAR BETWEEN BIRDS AND BEASTS.** The bear
wanted to see the wren, king of birds, in his royal palace, but when he
found it was only a simple nest, he said bad things about the wren. So
the wren and all other flying things declared war against the bear and
all other four-legged creatures. The animals chose the fox as their
general. They were to attack when he held his tail high and to retreat
when he dropped it. The animals advanced to battle, but a hornet stung
the fox beneath his tail. The fox put his tail between his legs and
retreated. All the other animals ran to their holes, and the birds were
declared the victors. (Grimm)

Bear and The Beetle, The. Massignon, *Folktales of France,* no. 49.
Cricket and the Lion, The. Espinosa, *Folklore of Spain in the American
    Southwest,* p. 184.
Hungry Bear, The. Saucier, *French Louisiana,* no. 32.
King of Birds. Bushnaq, *Arab Folktales,* p. 228.
Wren and the Bear, The. Grimm, *Tales,* no. 102.

**222A  THE BAT IN THE WAR BETWEEN BIRDS AND BEASTS.**
At the time of the great conflict between the birds and the beasts the bat
could not decide which side to join. When the war was over, neither
side would accept him.

Bat, the Birds, and the Beasts, The. Jacobs, *Aesop,* no. 24.

**225  A GROUND ANIMAL LEARNS TO FLY.** Brer Terrapin asked
Brer Buzzard to teach him to fly. The buzzard advised against the
enterprise, but finally gave in to his friend's pleas, and carried him
into the air. Slipping from the bird's back, the terrapin flapped his feet
and wagged his tail, but still he crashed to the earth. If it hadn't been
for his hard shell, he would have been killed. (Harris)

Bird Cherry Island. Dance, *Folklore from Contemporary Jamaicans,* no. 12A.
How the Terrapin Was Taught to Fly. Harris, *Daddy Jake,* no. 6.
Waste of Good Counsel, A. Handford, *Aesop,* no. 65.

**225A  THE TORTOISE FLIES TO A NEW HOME.** Two wild ducks
offered to fly a tortoise to another country. The tortoise bit onto a
stick which they carried between them. All went well until the tortoise
heard some villagers far below shouting about the tortoise being
carried on a stick. "If my friends choose to carry me in this manner, it
is none of your affair," he started to say, but the instant he opened his
mouth he lost his grip on the stick and fell to the earth and split in two.
(Jacobs, "The Talkative Tortoise")

Angel Wedding, The. Bushnaq, *Arab Folktales,* p. 245.
Fate of the Turtle, The (India). Lang, *Olive Fairy Book,* p. 242.

Talkative Tortoise, The. Jacobs, *Indian Fairy Tales,* p. 100.
Tortoise and the Birds, The. Jacobs, *Aesop,* no. 47.
Tortoise and the Osprey, The (Africa). Clarkson and Cross, *World Folktales,*
    no. 59.

**227 THE GEESE'S ETERNAL PRAYER.** A fox captured some geese, but he showed pity and allowed them a final prayer before eating them. "Ga! Ga!" they prayed, and they are still praying. Cf. types 1199B, 1376A*, 2013, 2300, 2320..

Fox and the Geese, The. Grimm, *Tales,* no. 86.

**228 THE CRICKET IN THE ELEPHANT'S EAR.** The elephant, the lion, and the tiger were boasting of their strength when the cricket said: "I can make you run your heads off." They all laughed at the little fellow. Later, one after the other, he crept into each one's ear and made such a chirping sound that they ran in fright. (Harris)

Greedy Hawk, The. Seki, *Folktales of Japan,* no. 8.
Little Mister Cricket and the Other Creatures. Harris, *Told by Uncle Remus,*
    no. 6.
Rhinoceros and the Bees, The. Arewa, *Northern East Africa,* p. 29.

**231 THE CRANE, THE FISH, AND THE CRAB.** A crane once offered to carry some fish from their own small pond to a larger, better pond. The fish foolishly agreed, and the crane carried them away one at a time, and ate them. His last passenger was a crab, but the crab sensed his danger, and as they lit, he cut through the crane's neck with his claws and escaped.

Cruel Crane Outwitted, The. Jacobs, *Indian Fairy Tales,* p. 46.

**232D\* THE CROW AND THE PITCHER.** A thirsty crow came upon a pitcher half filled with water. He could not reach the water, so he dropped pebbles into the pitcher until the water reached the top, and he could quench his thirst.

Crow and the Pitcher, The. Jacobs, *Aesop,* no. 55.

**233 THE BIRDS IN A NET.** A hunter caught a great many birds in his net, but they flew off together, carrying the net with them. When evening approached, each bird tried to fly toward its own nest. Pulling in different directions, they fell to the earth, and the hunter captured them.

Birds in a Net. Tolstoy, *Fables and Fairy Tales,* p. 44.

**233C THE BIRDS AND THE HEMP SEEDS.** A swallow and other birds were eating some recently sown hemp seeds. "Be careful to pick up every seed," warned the swallow, but the other birds paid no heed.

Later the hemp was harvested and made into cord, and the cord into nets. Many of the birds that ignored the swallow's advice were caught in these very nets.

Swallow and the Other Birds, The. Jacobs, *Aesop,* no. 12.

**234   THE NIGHTINGALE BORROWS THE BLINDWORM'S EYE.** Formerly the nightingale and the blindworm had one eye apiece. The nightingale was invited to a wedding and borrowed the worm's eye for the occasion, but he liked having two eyes so well that he refused to give it back. Ever since, nightingales have two eyes and the blindworm none.

Nightingale and the Slow-Worm, The. Grimm, *Other Tales,* p. 19.

**234A\*   A BIRD BREWS BEER.** A crow, having learned that beer is made from barley, dropped a grain of barley into a lake. She then took a drink, and said: "It is indeed better now."

Water Is Better Now, The. Carpenter, *A Latvian Storyteller,* p. 202.

**235   THE BIRDS' BEAUTY CONTEST.** The birds had a contest to determine which was the most beautiful. Miss Cuckoo came dressed in feathers borrowed from Miss Ostrich and was declared the winner. Then she slipped away from the others, and never returned Miss Ostrich's feathers.

Most Beautiful Bird in the World, The. Harris, *Uncle Remus Returns,* no. 6.

**236   THE MAGPIE TEACHES NEST BUILDING.** All the birds asked the magpie to teach them to build nests. She started with some mud and formed it into a round cake. "I can do that!" said the thrush and flew away. Then the magpie arranged twigs around the mud. "So that's how it's done!" said the blackbird, and off he flew. And so it continued: each bird learned one of the magpie's tricks and flew away to build its own nest. And that is why there are so many kinds of bird's nests. (Jacobs)

Magpie's Nest, The. Briggs, *DBF,* pt. A, v. 1, p. 123.
Magpie's Nest, The. Briggs, *DBF,* pt. B, v. 2, p. 405.
Magpie's Nest, The. Jacobs, *English Fairy Tales,* p. 195.
Wood-Pigeon's Nest, The. Briggs, *DBF,* pt. A, v. 1, p. 126.
Wood-Pigeon's Nest, The. Briggs, *DBF,* pt. B, v. 2, p. 406.

**236\*   IMITATING BIRD SOUNDS** —Miscellaneous tales.  Cf. type 2075.

Bittern and Hoopoe, The. Grimm, Tales, no. 173.
Cock, the Cuckoo, and the Blackcock, The. Asbjørnsen and Moe, *East o' the Sun,* p. 198.

Crow Talks with the Frog, The. Campbell, *West Highlands,* v. 1, p. 283.
Grouse Cock and His Wife, The. Campbell, *West Highlands,* v. 1, p. 284.
The Crumbs on the Table. Grimm, *Tales,* no. 190.

**237   THE PARROT IS PUNISHED FOR TELLING THE TRUTH.**
A grocer's parrot observed his master mixing lard with the butter.
When a customer asked for butter, the parrot cried out: "Lard in the
butter!"   The grocer wrung the bird's neck and cast her into the
garbage pit.  The parrot, not quite dead, saw a dead cat lying next to
her.  "Poor Tom," she sighed, "he too loved truth."  (Briggs, "The
Grocer and the Parrot")  Cf. types 243, 1352A, 1422.

Angry Mistress, The. Briggs, *DBF,* pt. A, v. 2, p. 225.
Grocer and the Parrot, The.  Briggs, *DBF,* pt. A, v. 2, p. 225.
Parrot, The. Briggs, *DBF,* pt. A, v. 2, p. 226.
Parrot, The. Briggs, *DBF,* pt. A, v. 2, p. 228.
Parrots and Other Fowl (commentary and examples). Legman, *Rationale of the
   Dirty Joke,* v. 1, p. 199.

**240A\***  **A DOVE SAVES A DROWNING ANT.** An ant was carried
away by a stream.  A dove dropped him a twig, and he rescued himself.
Later, a hunter came with a trap to capture the dove.  The ant stung his
foot, making him drop his trap, and the dove was saved.

One Good Turn Deserves Another. Handford, *Aesop,* no. 139.

**242   THE CROW CAPTURES THE FROG WITH KIND WORDS.**
A crow, with flattering words and promises, invited a frog to join him
at a dance, but when the frog emerged from his hole, the crow ate him
up.

Frog and the Crow, The. Briggs, *DBF,* pt. A, v. 1, p. 110.

**243   TEACHING A PARROT TO TALK.**  A man tried to teach his
parrot to say uncle, but the parrot refused.  In anger he beat the parrot
with a stick and threw him outside for dead.  The next morning he saw
the parrot, now recovered, with a stick in his hand chasing a rooster
about the chicken run while shouting: "Say uncle, say uncle."  (Briggs,
"Say Uncle")  Cf. types 237, 1352A, 1422.

Appy Boswell's Monkey. Briggs, *DBF,* pt. A, v. 2, p. 8.
Lachmidasi and the Parrot-King. Thundy, *South Indian Folktales,* no. 36.
Man Tried to Teach His Parrot to Talk, A. Briggs, *DBF,* pt. A, v. 2, p. 228.
Smart Parrot, The (Puerto Rico). Cole, *Best-Loved Folktales,* no. 193.

**244   BORROWED FEATHERS.**  A jay found some peacock feathers
and afixed them to his tail.  He strutted toward the peacocks, but they
saw the fraud and plucked out the plumes.  So he returned to his fellow
jays, but having observed his failure from the distance, they too
rejected him.

Borrowed Plumes. Handford, *Aesop,* no. 72.
Crow, The. Thundy, *South Indian Folktales,* no. 30.
Getting the Worst of Both Worlds. Handford, *Aesop,* no. 71.
Jay and the Peacock, The. Jacobs, *Aesop,* no. 21.
Raven, the Fox, and the Rabbit, The. Sabar, *Kurdistani Jews,* p. 167.

**244A\* THE CRANE AND THE HERON WOO EACH OTHER.**
The crane proposed marriage to the heron, but she rejected him
because of his spindly legs. But she reconsidered and went to the crane
with her own proposal, and this time he rejected her. And so it has
continued to the present time; every day they go to each other to
propose, but they never get married.

Crane and the Heron, The. Afanasyev, *Russian Fairy Tales,* p. 66.

**244C\* A RAVEN KILLS THE YOUNG WHO PROMISE TOO
MUCH.** A raven was carrying his young, one at a time, from an
island to the mainland. In flight, he asked the first: "When I am weak
and you are strong will you carry me?" The youngster answered
"yes," but the father did not believe him, and dropped him in the sea.
The same thing happened with his second son. But the third son
answered the question: "No, when you are old and I am grown, I will
have my own young to feed and carry." "He speaks the truth," said the
father bird, and carried this son to safety.

Raven and His Young, The. Tolstoy, *Fables and Fairy Tales,* p. 35.

**244D\* THE BIRD AND THE HUNTER'S SKULL.** A hunter
pursued a yellow bird, but he could never shoot it. Finally he died,
alone in the forest, and there was no one to bury him. His skull lay on
the ground and filled with rainwater. The yellow bird came to drink,
but she got caught inside the skull. Then the yellow bird sang: "Now
that you are dead you've finally caught me. But what use is that to
you?"

Yellow Bird, The. Dégh, *Folktales of Hungary,* no. 30.

**247 EACH BIRD'S CHILD IS THE PRETTIEST.** The partridge
asked the owl to take lunch to her child at school. "But I don't know
which one your child is," said the owl. "He's easy to find," answered
the partridge. "He's the prettiest one there." The owl took the bread,
but she could not find the baby partridge, because, as she told the
mother owl, "in the whole school there is no prettier child than my
own." (Megas)

One's Own Children Are Always Prettiest. Asbjørnsen and Moe, *East o' the
Sun,* p. 180.
Owl and Partridge. Megas, *Folktales of Greece,* no. 17.

**248  THE MAN, THE DOG, AND THE BIRD.** A man driving a cart ran over a dog sleeping in the road, and killed it. The dog's friend, the sparrow, took revenge. He pecked out the horse's eyes, and when the man tried to hit the bird with his ax, he killed his own horse. Then he flew to the waggoner's house and broke all of his windows and furniture. At last the man caught the bird, and to punish it, swallowed it whole, but the sparrow only fluttered up into his mouth and stuck out his head. The man's wife tried to kill the bird with an ax, but she struck her husband dead instead. Then the sparrow flew away. (Grimm)

Dog and the Sparrow, The. Grimm, *Tales,* no. 58.
Dog and the Woodpecker, The. Afanasyev, *Erotic Tales,* p. 89.
Dog and the Woodpecker, The. Afanasyev, *Russian Fairy Tales,* p. 499.
Wood-Pecker, The (shortened). Afanasyev, *Russian Secret Tales,* p. 11.

**250A THE FLOUNDER'S CROOKED MOUTH.** The fish had a race to select their king, and the herring won. The envious flounder challenged the results with the insult: "The naked herring?" Since that time the flounder has been cursed with a crooked mouth.

Flounder, The. Grimm, *Tales,* no. 172.

**253  THE LITTLE FISH ESCAPE THROUGH THE NET.** A fisherman pulled his catch ashore. He had a number of big fish, but the little ones had escaped through the meshes of the net.

Big and Little Fish. Handford, *Aesop,* no. 204.

**275  THE RACE BETWEEN THE FOX AND THE LOBSTER.** A fox and a lobster agreed to a race. The lobster took hold of the fox's tail, and when the fox reached the goal, the lobster jumped off, saying: "I have been here a long time." (Afanasyev)

Brer Fox and Little Mister Cricket. Harris, *Uncle Remus and the Little Boy,* no. 6.
Cat and the Crab, The. Seki, *Folktales of Japan,* no. 10.
Fox and the Lobster, The. Afanasyev, *Russian Fairy Tales,* p. 310.
Race between the Turtle and the Lion, The. Arewa, *Northern East Africa,* p. 74.
Whale and the Sea Slug, The. Seki, *Folktales of Japan,* no. 9.

**275A THE RACE BETWEEN THE TORTOISE AND THE HARE.** The tortoise accepted the hare's challenge to race. The hare darted far ahead, then to show his contempt for the tortoise, he lay down to have a nap. However, he slept too long, and the tortoise plodded past him and won the race. (Aesop)

Devil and Rabbit. Carpenter, A Latvian Storyteller, p. 179.

Hare and the Tortoise, The (Aesop). Cole, *Best-Loved Folktales,* no. 39.
Hare and the Tortoise, The. Clouston, *Popular Tales,* v. 1, p. 266.
Hare and the Tortoise, The. Jacobs, *Aesop,* no. 68.
Slow but Sure. Handford, *Aesop,* no. 66.

**275A\* THE RACE BETWEEN THE HEDGEHOG AND THE HARE.** The hedgehog challenged the hare to a race. The hedgehog hid his wife, who looked exactly like him, at the end of the course. The race began, and the hare quickly arrived at the goal, but a hedgehog was already there claiming victory. Beside himself, the hare insisted that they run back as well, but at the other end the first hedgehog jumped out, shouting: "I'm here already." And so it went, back and forth, until the hare dropped to the ground from sheer exhaustion. (Grimm) Cf. type 1074.

Fox and the Hedgehog, The. Briggs, *DBF,* pt. A, v. 1, p. 108.
Hare and the Hedgehog, The (England). Clarkson and Cross, *World Folktales,* no. 25.
Hare and the Hedgehog, The. Grimm, *Tales,* no. 187.
Hare and the Prickly-Backed Urchin, The. Briggs, *DBF,* pt. A, v. 1, p. 113.
Hedgehog and the Hare, The. Ranke, *Folktales of Germany,* no. 10.
Hedgehog and the Hare, The. Tolstoy, *Fables and Fairy Tales,* p. 46.
Mister Rabbit Finds His Match at Last. Harris, *Uncle Remus,* no. 18.
Partnership between Wolf and Mouse. El-Shamy, *Folktales of Egypt,* no. 49.
Rabbit and Hedgehog. Dorson, *Negro Tales,* p. 24.
Race between the Tortoise and the Hare, The. Arewa, *Northern East Africa,* p. 72.
Race between Toad and Donkey, The. Abrahams, *Afro-American Folktales,* no. 63.
Tortoise and a Mischievous Monkey, A (Brazil). Lang, *Brown Fairy Book,* p. 327.

**276   THE CRAB THAT WALKED SIDEWAYS.** A crab scolded her child for walking sideways. He responded: "I follow your example."

Example Is Better Than Precept. Handford, *Aesop,* no. 131.
Two Crabs, The. Jacobs, *Aesop,* no. 48.

**277   THE FROGS AND THEIR TWO KINGS.** The frogs prayed for a king, and jokingly Jove dropped a log into their swamp. But the frogs were not happy with this king, so they asked for a more powerful one. This time Jove sent them a stork, who immediately began to eat them up. The frogs then repented of their dissatisfaction, but it was too late.

Frogs Desiring a King, The. Jacobs, *Aesop,* no. 13.
We Get the Rulers We Deserve. Handford, *Aesop,* no. 42.

**277A THE FROG THAT WANTED TO BE AS LARGE AS AN OX.** A young frog was telling an old frog about a monster he had seen. "It was only an ox," said the old frog, inflating himself as he spoke, "and not much larger than I." "No, much larger!" answered the young one. "Larger than this?" challenged the old frog, and he blew and swelled until he burst.

Frog and the Ox, The. Jacobs, *Aesop,* no. 22.
Too Big for Her Skin. Handford, *Aesop,* no. 46.

**278A\*  THE FROGS DECIDE NOT TO JUMP INTO A WELL.** Their pond dried up, so two frogs set out to find water. Finding a well, the one wanted to jump in at once, but the other warned: "If the well dries up as our pond did, how will we get out?"

Frogs Hunting Water, The. Daly, *Aesop,* no. 43.

**279\*  THE SNAKE EMBRACES THE CRAB.** A snake and a crab became friends, and to show his affection, the snake wrapped himself around the crab. "Too tight!" complained the crab. The snake paid no heed, so the desperate crab gripped his neck with his claws until he straightened out. (Megas)

Crab and Snake. Megas, *Folktales of Greece,* no. 18.
Snake and the Crab, The. Daly, *Aesop,* no. 196.

**280A  THE ANT AND THE GRASSHOPPER.** The ant spent its summer days gathering food, but the grasshopper wanted only to sing. Winter arrived, and the grasshopper learned the value of the ant's toil, but now it was too late. (Aesop)

Ant and the Grasshopper, The. Jacobs, *Aesop,* no. 36.
Ant and the Tumblebug, The. Daly, *Aesop,* no. 112.
Bum Bee, The. Briggs, *DBF,* pt. A, v. 1, p. 104.
Go to the Ant, Thou Sluggard (2 variants). Handford, *Aesop,* nos. 137, 138.
Why Mister Cricket Has Elbows on His Legs. Harris, *Told by Uncle Remus,* no. 2.

**281  THE GNAT AND THE BULL.** A gnat lit on a bull's horn. Before flying off, he thought he should take leave. The bull replied: "I didn't notice when you came, nor will I notice when you go."

Beneath Notice. Handford, *Aesop,* no. 134.

**281A\*  THE GNAT AND THE LION.** A gnat challenged a lion to a fight, biting him about the face until the lion gave in. Flying away in triumph, he became entangled in a spider's web and perished.

Bearding the Lion. Handford, *Aesop,* no. 133.

**285  THE CHILD AND THE SNAKE.** A little boy always took his bread and milk outside to eat. One day his mother noticed that he was sharing it with a rattlesnake. In fear and anger, she killed the snake. A short time later the boy took ill and died. (Randolph)

Child and Snake. Briggs, *DBF,* pt. B, v. 2, p. 765.
Girl with the Golden Hair, The. Thundy, *South Indian Folktales,* no. 54.
Little Boy and the Snake. Randolph, *Who Blowed Up the Church House?,* p. 87.
Snake and Baby. Dorson, *Negro Tales,* p. 220.
Tales of the Toad (I). Grimm, *Tales,* no. 105.

### 285B* THE WOMAN WHO SWALLOWED A SNAKE. A woman fell asleep in a field, and a snake ran down her throat. A doctor cured her by having her lie on her side with a saucer of milk near her mouth. The snake came out for the milk, and the doctor killed it. (Campbell)

Bosom-Serpent Legends (examples and commentary). Brunvand, *The Choking Doberman,* p. 107.
Man Who Swallowed the Mouse, The. O'Sullivan, *Folktales of Ireland,* no. 7.
Seven Giant Brothers, The. Villa *100 Armenian Tales,* no. 7.
Woman Who Swallowed a Serpent, The. (Norway) Campbell, *West Highlands,* v. 2, p. 382.
Woman Who Swallowed a Toad, The. Campbell, *West Highlands,* v. 2, p. 382.

### 285D THE MAN AND THE SNAKE BECOME ENEMIES. A man and a snake entered into an agreement. The man was to bring the snake milk every day, in return for which the snake would cause the man to prosper. One day, fearing the serpent's power, the man struck at him with his ax. The snake escaped and took revenge by killing the man's baby. Seeing the snake's power, the man asked the snake to return to their old arrangement. "That is not possible," replied the snake, for I will always remember your ax, and you will always remember your empty cradle." (Aesop)

Blood Feud, A. Handford, *Aesop,* no. 52.
Gold-Giving Serpent, The (Indian, Greek, and Latin variants compared). Jacobs, *Indian Fairy Tales,* p. 247.
Gold-Giving Serpent, The. Jacobs, *Indian Fairy Tales,* p. 112.
Man and the Serpent, The. Jacobs, *Aesop,* no. 6.
Pain from a Blow Heals, The; the Pain from a Word Does Not. Sabar, *Folk Literature of the Kurdistani Jews,* p. 169.
Serpent and the Poor Man, The. Sabar, *Folk Literature of the Kurdistani Jews,* p. 168.
Shepherd and Snake. Megas, *Folktales of Greece,* no. 19.
Snake Who Brought Wealth, The. Daly, *Aesop,* no. 573A.

### 289 BAT, BRAMBLE, AND COOT ARE SHIPWRECKED. A bat, a bramble, and a coot became business partners. The bat borrowed money, the coot contributed bronze, and the bramble brought clothing. They put it all aboard a ship, but they lost everything in a storm. Since then the coot has been diving, looking for her sunken

bronze, the bramble attaches herself to every garment looking for her lost clothing, and the bat—afraid of his creditors—comes out only at night.

Bat, the Bramble, and the Coot, The. Daly, *Aesop,* no. 171.

**291   A DECEPTIVE TUG-OF-WAR.** Brer Terrapin challenged Brer Bear to a pulling contest. The terrapin secretly tied his end of the rope to a tree. The bear pulled until he was exhausted, but he could not wrest the rope away from the terrapin, so he lost the contest. (Harris)

How Wattle Weasel Was Caught. Harris, *Nights with Uncle Remus,* no. 55.
Mister Terrapin Shows His Strength. Harris, *Uncle Remus,* no. 26.
Tortoise and a Mischievous Monkey, A (Brazil). Lang, *Brown Fairy Book,* p. 327.
Tug-of-War between the Hare, the Elephant, and the Hippopotamus. Arewa, *Northern East Africa,* p. 72.

**292   LOCUSTS TEACH THE ASS TO SING.** The ass, fond of the locusts' singing, asked for their secret. They said it was a diet of dew, so the ass went on such a diet, but he died of starvation.

Ass and the Locusts, The. Daly, *Aesop,* no. 184.

**293   THE BODY PARTS DEBATE.** The various parts of the body went on strike against the belly, because he got all the food and none of the work. The hands would not pick up food, and so forth. But soon they all became weak and ill, and they learned that they had to all work together or perish.

Belly and the Feet, The. Daly, *Aesop,* no. 130.
Belly and the Limbs, The. Handford, *Aesop,* Notes, p. 224.
Belly and the Members, The. Jacobs, *Aesop,* no. 29.
Body Is Not One Member, The. Bible: 1 Corinthians 12:14-27.
Marching on the Stomach. Handford, *Aesop,* no. 146.
Senor Coyote and the Dogs (Mexico). Cole, *Best-Loved Folktales,* no. 177.
Vagina and the A..e. Afanasyev, *Russian Secret Tales,* p. 13.

**294   MONTHS AND SEASONS.** A shepherd received favorable weather from January, February, and March. With only one day of the month left, he said: "March, who's afraid of you now?" In response, March borrowed three days from April, and during these three stormy days, the shepherd lost his entire flock.

March and the Shepherd. Calvino, *Italian Folktales,* no. 198.

**295   THE STRAW, THE COAL, AND THE BEAN.** A bean, a straw, and a glowing coal set forth for distant parts. They came to a brook, and the straw stretched himself across to form a bridge. The coal went first, but burned the straw in two, and they both fell into the water.

The bean, from the safety of the shore, laughed until it split. A passing tailor sewed it together, and since that day, all beans have had a seam. (Grimm)

> Bladder, the Straw, and the Shoe, The. Afanasyev, *Russian Fairy Tales,* p. 590.
> Straw, Bean, and Coal. Ranke, *Folktales of Germany,* no. 12.
> Straw, Coal, and Bean. Grimm, *Tales,* no. 18.

**298  THE CONTEST BETWEEN THE WIND AND THE SUN.** The wind and the sun wagered as to which could make a traveler take off his cloak. The wind tried first, but the harder he blew the tighter the man pulled his cloak around him, and finally the wind gave up. Then the sun came out and warmed the traveler, who soon found it too hot to continue without removing his cloak. (Aesop)

> Brer Rabbit Treats the Creeturs to a Race. Harris, Uncle Remus and Brer Rabbit, no. 4.
> Gentle Art of Persuasion, The. Handford, *Aesop,* no. 143.
> Wind and the Sun, The. Jacobs, *Aesop,* no. 60.

**298C\*  A REED BENDS, BUT A TREE IS UPROOTED BY A STORM.** A tree boasted to a reed about its great height and strength, but a great storm arose, uprooting the tree and casting it on the ground. The reed gave with the wind and stood upright again when the storm had passed.

> Bowing before the Storm. Handford, *Aesop,* no. 141.
> Tree and the Reed, The. Jacobs, *Aesop,* no. 37.

# Magic Tales

**300**  **THE DRAGON SLAYER.** A princess was held captive by a seven-headed serpent, and the king promised her in marriage to the man who could free her. A fisherman's son killed the serpent, and cut out the seven tongues. But another man found the dead serpent, cut off its heads, and claimed the princess as a bride. At the celebration before the wedding, the real hero asked the king to examine the serpent's heads, and everyone saw that the tongues were missing. The hero then pulled them from his bag as proof that he had rescued the king's daughter. They threw the other man out of the palace, and the fisherman's son married the princess. (One episode from Thompson, "The Castle of No Return," type 303) —Note: Killing dragons and other ogres is an integral part of many different folktales. Cf. types 301, 303, 305*, 315, 466, 466*, 466**, 502, 530, 532, 553.

Abandoned Child, The. Lindell, *Folk Tales from Kammu,* II, no. 11.
Anthousa the Fair with Golden Hair. Megas, *Folktales of Greece,* no. 22.
Assipattle and the Mester Stoorworm. Briggs, *DBF,* pt. A, v. 1, p. 144.
Assipattle and the Muckle Mester Stoor Worm. Marwick, *Folklore of Orkney and Shetland,* p. 139.
Assipattle Slays the Stoor Worm. Marwick, *Folklore of Orkney and Shetland,* p. 20.
Bad Boy Who Became a Knight, The. Musick, *Green Hills of Magic,* no. 24.
Birth of Finn MacCumhail, The. Glassie, *Irish Folktales,* no. 109.
Black Crow and the White Cheese, The. El-Shamy, *Folktales of Egypt,* no. 2.
Castle of No Return, The (Spain). Thompson, *100 Folktales,* no. 5.
Cockatrice of Hampshire, The. Boase, *Folklore of Hampshire,* p. 110.
Cold Feet and the Lonesome Queen. Campbell, *Cloudwalking Country,* p. 106.
Connal. Campbell, *West Highlands,* v. 1, p. 147.
Dragon, The. Gottfried von Strassburg, *Tristan,* ch. 12-14.
Dragon and the Snake, The. Thundy, *South Indian Folktales,* no. 44.
Dragon of the North, The (Estonia). Lang, *Yellow Fairy Book,* p. 9.
Dragons and Monstrous Birds. Clouston, *Popular Tales,* v. 1, p. 155.
Dragon, The (Spain). Bødker, *European Folk Tales,* p. 174.
Fiery Dragon, The. Sampson, *Gypsy Folk Tales,* p. 1.
Firey Dragon, The. Gmelch and Kroup, *To Shorten the Road,* p. 88.
Five Counsels, The. Paredes, *Folktales of Mexico,* no. 43.

Flea, The. Basile, *Pentamerone*, Day 1, Tale 5.
Flower Queen's Daughter, The (Bukovina). Lang, *Yellow Fairy Book*, p. 192.
Gallant Szérus. Dégh, *Folktales of Hungary*, no. 8.
Gashany Bull. Dance, *Folklore from Contemporary Jamaicans*, no. 21.
Hedgy. Musick, *Green Hills of Magic*, no. 23.
Horns. Afanasyev, *Russian Fairy Tales*, p. 292.
How Geirald the Coward Was Punished (Iceland). Lang, *Brown Fairy Book*,
   p. 114.
Ilya Muromets and the Dragon. Afanasyev, *Russian Fairy Tales*, p. 569.
Jack and Bill. Glassie, *Irish Folktales*, no. 115.
Jack and the Gower. Randolph, *The Talking Turtle*, p. 55.
Jack and the King's Daughter. Briggs, *DBF*, pt. A, v. 1, p. 333.
Jack the Giant-Killer (I, II). Briggs, *DBF*, pt. A, v. 1, p. 329.
Jack the Giant-Killer. Lang, *Blue Fairy Book*, p. 374.
Janni and the Draken. Lang, *Grey Fairy Book*, p. 61.
Jay Bird That Had a Fight with a Rattle Snake,The. Campbell, *Cloudwalking
   Country,* p. 132.
Lambton Worm, The. Briggs, *DBF*, pt. A, v. 1, p. 373.
Lambton Worm, The. Jacobs, *More English Fairy Tales*, p. 215.
Little Bull-Calf, de Three Giants, and de Fiery Dragon, De. Briggs, *DBF*, pt.
   A, v. 1, p. 382.
Little Bull-Calf, De. Briggs, *DBF*, pt. A, v. 1, p. 380.
Little Bull-Calf, The. Jacobs, *More English Fairy Tales*, p. 186.
Lyminster Knucker, The (several variants). Simpson, *Folklore of Sussex*, p.
   39.
Merchant's Two Sons, The. Basile, *Pentamerone*, Day 1, Tale 7.
Monster's Hairs, The. Villa, *100 Armenian Tales*, no. 22.
Nikita the Tanner. Afanasyev, *Russian Fairy Tales*, p. 310.
Piers Shonks Slays a Dragon. Jones-Baker, *Folklore of Hertfordshire*, p. 60.
Pretty Goldilocks (d'Aulnoy). Lang, *Blue Fairy Book*, p. 193.
Red Etin, The. Briggs, *DBF*, pt. A, v. 1, p. 463.
Red Etin, The. Lang, *Blue Fairy Book*, p. 385.
Red Ettin, The. Jacobs, *English Fairy Tales*, p. 131.
Saint George and the Dragon. Dawkins, *More Greek Folktales*, no. 21.
Saint George for Merry England. Briggs, *DBF*, pt. A, v. 1, p. 474.
Saint George. Baring-Gould, *Curious Myths of the Middle Ages*, no. 13.
Saint George. Briggs, *DBF*, pt. B, v. 2, p. 442.
Schippeitaro (Japan). Lang, *Violet Fairy Book*, p. 36.
Seven-Headed Animal; or, Fearless John. Saucier, *French Louisiana*, no. 4.
Seven-Headed Monster, The. Massignon, *Folktales of France*, no. 8.
Seven-Headed Serpent, The (Greece). Lang, *Yellow Fairy Book*, p. 60.
Shippei Taro. Seki, *Folktales of Japan*, no. 15.
Shortshanks. Asbjørnsen and Moe, *East o' the Sun*, p. 131.
Sir Maurice Berkeley Kills the Dragon at Bisterne. Boase, *Folklore of
   Hampshire,* p. 110.
Smith's Son, The. Campbell, *West Highlands*, v. 1, p. 100.
Thirteenth Son of the King of Erin, The (Ireland). Cole, *Folktales*, no. 61.
Three Brothers and the Fig Tree, The. Mathias and Raspa, *Italian Folktales in
   America,* no. 12.
Three Brothers and the Three Tasks, The. Briggs, *DBF*, pt. A, v. 1, p. 507.
Three Brothers, The. Ranke, *Folktales of Germany*, no. 29.
Three Dogs and the Dragon, The. Delarue, *French Folktales*, p. 147.
Three Dogs, The. Calvino, *Italian Folktales*, no. 48.
Three Dogs, The. Espinosa, *Folklore of Spain in the American Southwest*, p.
   181.
Three Dogs, The. Lang, *Green Fairy Book*, p. 360.
Trip to Wag-El-Wag, The. El-Shamy, *Folktales of Egypt*, no. 1.

**300A THE BATTLE ON THE BRIDGE.** Ivan, a poor peasant's son, stood watch with six men at a bridge to prevent a dragon from capturing the king's daughter. His companions all got drunk, so Ivan alone killed the three dragons that crossed the river. Other adventures followed, and in the end, Ivan married the princess. (Afanasyev)

**300B ABDUCTED BY A SNAKE.** After threatening to destroy an entire village, a big snake was given a girl as wife. Later the snake's wife hid herself and her child in a box. He tried to get at them, but in his fury hit his head and killed himself; the girl returned home safely with her child.

**301 RESCUING THREE UNDERGROUND PRINCESSES.** Ivashko's two older brothers lowered him into an underground realm, where he discovered three kingdoms. In each kingdom he found a beautiful maiden, and together they returned to the entrance where the brothers were waiting. They pulled up the three maidens, but let Ivashko fall back into the cavern and deserted him. But Ivashko found his way back home, took his bride from his brothers, and married her. (Afanasyev, "The Three Kingdoms")

John the Bear (France). Thompson, *100 Folktales,* no. 3.
Juan Oso. Paredes, *Folktales of Mexico,* no. 29.
King of Lochlin's Three Daughters, The. Campbell, *West Highlands,* v. 1, p. 244.
Little Gray Man, The (Germany). Lang, *Grey Fairy Book,* p. 129.
Norka, The. Lang, *Red Fairy Book,* p. 116.
Oni's Laughter, The. Seki, *Folktales of Japan,* no. 16.
Prince Ivan and Byely Polyanin. Afanasyev, *Russian Fairy Tales,* p. 475.
Princess in the Underworld, The (Germany). Bødker, *European Folk Tales,* p. 90.
Shepherd Paul (Hungary). Lang, *Crimson Fairy Book,* p. 295.
Terrible Valley, The. Campbell, *Cloudwalking Country,* p. 89.
Three Brothers, The (Poland). Lang, *Yellow Fairy Book,* p. 134.
Three Kingdoms, The. Afanasyev, *Russian Fairy Tales,* p. 49.
Three Princesses in the Mountain-in-the-Blue. Asbjørnsen and Moe, *Norwegian Folktales,* p. 31.
Three Stolen Princesses, The. Pino-Saavedra, *Folktales of Chile,* no. 3.
Tobe Killed a Bear. Randolph, *Sticks in the Knapsack,* p. 17.
Twopence Halfpenny. Sampson, *Gypsy Folk Tales,* p. 37.

**301A  THE QUEST FOR THE VANISHED PRINCESSES.** Three princesses disappeared, and the king proclaimed that the man who returned them should have one of them in marriage. Three huntsmen took on the task. Each day one remained behind and cooked, while the other two sought the missing girls. One day a gnome came begging for food, but he tricked the huntsman and gave him a beating. The same thing happened the next day, but when he tried to trick the youngest huntsman, he failed, and the huntsman forced him to tell where the king's daughters were. So the three huntsmen were able to rescue the princesses. (Grimm, "The Gnome")

Big Bird Dan, The. Asbjørnsen and Moe, *East o' the Sun,* p. 382.
Bird Dam. Christiansen, *Folktales of Norway,* p. 243.
Blue Mountains, The. Lang, *Yellow Fairy Book,* p. 256.
Dirtybeard. Roberts, *South from Hell,* no. 2.
Flowers That Vanished in the Night. Bushnaq, *Arab Folktales,* p. 104.
Four Kings of Ireland, The. Gmelch and Kroup, *To Shorten the Road,* p. 168.
Gnome, The. Grimm, *Tales,* no. 91.
Golden Ball, The. Calvino, *Italian Folktales,* no. 78.
Little Red Hairy Man, The. Briggs, *DBF,* pt. A, v. 1, p. 391.
Little Redman, The. Briggs, *DBF,* pt. A, v. 1, p. 393.
Man Wreathed in Seaweed, The. Calvino, *Italian Folktales,* no. 2.
Old Fire Dragaman. Chase, *The Jack Tales,* no. 2.
Princess and the Elephant, The. Thundy, *South Indian Folktales,* no. 45.
Rübezahl (Musäus). Lang, *Brown Fairy Book,* p. 283.
Sister of the Sun, The (Lapland). Lang, *Brown Fairy Book,* p. 215.
Strong Hans. Grimm, *Tales,* no. 166.
Three Boys and the Three Girls, The. Dawkins, *Modern Greek Folktales,* no. 26.
Three Fairies of Sandy Batoum, The. Dawkins, *More Greek Folktales,* no. 2.
World Below, The. Villa, *100 Armenian Tales,* no. 34.

**301B  A STRONG MAN AND HIS COMPANIONS RESCUE PRINCESSES.** A strong boy set forth into the world. He met a man who twisted oak trees into binding hoops, and a man who broke large boulders with a pair of pincers. They continued together until they came to an empty castle in the woods. —Continues in the manner of types 301 and 301A. (Delarue)

> Ivan the Peasant's Son and the Thumb-Sized Man. Afanasyev, *Russian Fairy Tales*, p. 262.
> John the Bear. Thomas, *It's Good to Tell You*, no. 3.
> John-of-the-Bear. Delarue, *French Folktales*, p. 45.
> Son of the Cow with a Broken Horn, The. Dégh, *Folktales of Hungary*, no. 1.
> Son of the Gray Horse. Villa, *100 Armenian Tales*, no. 35.

**301B\* A STRONG MAN AND HIS COMPANIONS KILL A GIANT.** A woman had a son who became very strong, but he ate so much that she had to send him away. He became partners with two strong men. Following an adventure with trolls (similar to the episode in type 301A), the three were engaged by the king to get the giant Asterekjempen's sword. They sailed to the giant's farm, killed his son, stole his sword, and rowed away. Asterekjempen tried to stop them by drinking the ocean dry, but his attempt failed, and he died.

> Strong Peter and His Men (Norway). Bødker, *European Folk Tales*, p. 43.

**302 THE GIANT WHOSE HEART WAS IN AN EGG.** Jack set forth into the world. He came to four animals quarreling over the division of their prey, and he settled their dispute. In return, they made it possible for him to take on different forms himself. Using this gift, Jack found his way to the king's daughter, who was being held by the sorcerer Body-without-Soul, and he discovered that the sorcerer kept his heart in a black egg, in the craw of a black eagle. Jack brought the egg to the imprisoned princess, and she broke it on her captor's head, killing him. Jack then took her back home, and they were married forthwith. (Calvino, "Body-without-Soul")

> Body-without-Soul. Calvino, *Italian Folktales*, no. 6.
> Crystal Ball, The. Grimm, *Tales*, no. 197.
> Crystal Mountain, The. Afanasyev, *Russian Fairy Tales*, p. 482.
> Giant Who Had No Heart in His Body (Norway). Thompson, *100 Folktales*, no. 4.
> Giant Who Had No Heart in his Body. Asbjørnsen and Moe, *East o' the Sun*, p. 59.
> Juan Oso. Paredes, *Folktales of Mexico*, no. 29.
> King of the Animals, The. Calvino, *Italian Folktales*, no. 52.
> Koshchey the Deathless. Afanasyev, *Russian Fairy Tales*, p. 485.
> Maria Morevna. Afanasyev, *Russian Fairy Tales*, p. 553.
> Mermaid and the Poor Fisherman, The. Pino-Saavedra, *Folktales of Chile*, no. 4.
> Ogre with No Soul, The. Thomas, *It's Good to Tell You*, no. 4.
> Ogre's Soul, The. Villa, *100 Armenian Tales*, no. 1.
> Prezzemolina. Calvino, *Italian Folktales*, no. 86.
> Prince and the Dragon, The (Serbia). Lang, *Crimson Fairy Book*, p. 80.

Punchkin. Jacobs, *Indian Fairy Tales*, p. 21.
Seven-Headed Animal; or, Fearless John. Saucier, *French Louisiana*, no. 4.
Son of the Gray Horse. Villa, *100 Armenian Tales*, no. 35.
Sultan's Forty Sons, The. Walker and Uysal, *Tales in Turkey*, p. 77.
Trip to Wag-El-Wag, The. El-Shamy, *Folktales of Egypt*, no. 1.
Troll's Daughter, The (Denmark). Lang, *Pink Fairy Book*, p. 247.
Weaver's Boy, The. Campbell, *Cloudwalking Country*, p. 85.
Widow's Son and an Old Man, The. Briggs, *DBF*, pt. A, v. 1, p. 573.

**302A   IN THE LAND OF THE OGRES.** Prince Sigurd was kidnapped
by his stepmother's sister, a giantess, and taken to the land of the ogres.
After many adventures he escaped, returning home just in time to save
his stepmother, who was under suspicion of having killed him. (Lang)

Horse Gullfaxi and the Sword Gunnföder, The (Iceland). Lang, *Crimson Fairy
Book*, p. 314.
Kadar and Cannibals. Thundy, *South Indian Folktales*, no. 49.

**302B   THE HERO WHOSE LIFE IN HIS SWORD.** Following a long
quest, the hero found the most beautiful girl in the world and married
her. A witch discovered that the hero's life force was in his sword, and
she threw it in the sea. He was about to die, but his blood friend
discovered the danger (in a manner similar to type 303) and recovered
the sword, saving the hero's life.

Hüsnügüzel. Walker and Uysal, *Tales in Turkey*, p. 34.

**303   THE BLOOD BROTHERS.** A man gave his wife two pieces of
magic fish, and within a year she gave birth to twins. When it came
time for them to leave home, the elder departed first, leaving a bottle
of water that would would become cloudy if he needed help. The elder
twin then killed a seven-headed serpent and married the princess (see
type 300). Some time afterward he grew restless and sought out the
castle of no return, where he was placed under a spell by a witch. The
bottle of water he had left with his brother showed his danger, and the
younger twin set forth to find him. When he reached the palace, the
princess took him for her husband. They slept together, but he placed
a sword between himself and her. The next day he found the castle of
no return and rescued his brother. In relating his adventures, he
started to tell how he had slept with the princess, but before he could
finish, the older twin drew his sword and killed him. Upon his return
to the palace, he learned of his brother's loyalty, and with a magic cure
he brought the dead twin back to life. (Thompson)

Alice and Ben. Roberts, *South from Hell*, no. 3A.
All-Black and All-White. Christiansen, *Folktales of Norway*, p. 175.
Black Jack and White Jack. Abrahams, *Afro-American Folktales*, no. 98.
Cannelora. Calvino, *Italian Folktales*, no. 135.
Castle of No Return, The (Spain). Thompson, *100 Folktales*, no. 5.
Child Rowland. Briggs, *DBF*, pt. A, v. 1, p. 180.

Cloud, The. Crane, *Italian Popular Tales,* no. 6.
Crab with the Golden Eggs. Calvino, *Italian Folktales,* no. 146.
Cutthroat, Chawfine, and Suckblood. Dance, *Folklore from Contemporary Jamaicans,* no. 109.
Draglin' Hogney, The. Briggs, *DBF,* pt. A, v. 1, p. 216.
Dragon with the Seven Heads. Calvino, *Italian Folktales,* no. 58.
Enchanted Hind, The. Basile, *Pentamerone,* Day 1, Tale 9.
Fish of Gold, The. Briggs, *DBF,* pt. A, v. 1, p. 324.
Fisher in Skye, The. Campbell, *West Highlands,* v. 1, p. 95.
Fisherman, The. Pino-Saavedra, *Folktales of Chile,* no. 5.
Gold-Children, The. Grimm, *Tales,* no. 85.
Golden Children, The. Campbell, *Cloudwalking Country,* p. 36.
Horse, Hound and Hawk. Gmelch and Kroup, *To Shorten the Road,* p. 138.
Ivan the Cow's Son. Afanasyev, *Russian Fairy Tales,* p. 234.
Jack and Bill. Glassie, *Irish Folktales,* no. 115.
Johnnie and His Younger Brother. Dawkins, *More Greek Folktales,* no. 6.
King of England, The (Scotland). Dorson, *Folktales around the World,* p. 10.
King of England, The. Briggs, *DBF,* pt. A, v. 1, p. 351.
King of the Fishes, The. Jacobs, *European Folk and Fairy Tales,* no. 3.
Knights of the Fish, The. Lang, *Brown Fairy Book,* p. 342.
Merchant's Two Sons, The. Basile, *Pentamerone,* Day 1, Tale 7.
Miller's Three Sons, The. Delarue, *French Folktales,* p. 187.
Minnikin. Lang, *Red Fairy Book,* p. 307.
Nine-Seeded Apple, The. Villa, *100 Armenian Tales,* no. 27.
Nyange and Katumi. Arewa, *Northern East Africa,* p. 233.
Once In, Never Out Again (Austria). Bødker, *European Folk Tales,* p. 92.
Prince and the Fakir, The. Jacobs, *Indian Fairy Tales,* p. 179.
Red Etin, The. Briggs, *DBF,* pt. A, v. 1, p. 463.
Red Etin, The. Lang, *Blue Fairy Book,* p. 385.
Red Ettin, The. Jacobs, *English Fairy Tales,* p. 131.
Sea-Maiden, The. Campbell, *West Highlands,* v. 1, p. 72.
Shippei Taro. Seki, *Folktales of Japan,* no. 15.
Shortshanks. Asbjørnsen and Moe, *East o' the Sun,* p. 131.
Three Brothers, The. Ranke, *Folktales of Germany,* no. 29.
Three Princes and Their Beasts, The (Lithuania). Lang, *Violet Fairy Book,* p. 41.
Three-Legged Hare, The. Briggs, *DBF,* pt. A, v. 1, p. 520.
Twin Brothers, The. Lang, *Grey Fairy Book,* p. 322.
Twin Brothers, The. Megas, *Folktales of Greece,* no. 21.
Two Brothers, The (Italy). Lang, *Pink Fairy Book,* p. 209.
Two Brothers, The. Grimm, *Tales,* no. 60.
Two Brothers, The. Musick, *Green Hills of Magic,* no. 25.
Two Brothers, The. Tolstoy, *Fables and Fairy Tales,* p. 64.
Two Ivans, Solder's Sons. Afanasyev, *Russian Fairy Tales,* p. 463.
Who Eats My Heart. Clouston, *Popular Tales,* v. 1, p. 462.
Younger Brother Rescues the Elder, The. Dawkins, *Modern Greek Folktales,* no. 38.

**303A SEVEN BRIDES FOR SEVEN BROTHERS.** Six brothers set forth to find brides for themselves and for their youngest brother, who stayed at home to tend the house. They found seven beautiful sisters, but on their return a sorcerer turned the six brothers and their six brides into stone, keeping the youngest bride for himself. Some time later the brother who had stayed at home set out to find his lost ones. He killed the sorcerer and broke the spell holding his brothers and their brides. Then the seven brothers married the seven sisters, and they lived many years happily together. (Lang)

> Eleven Brothers and Eleven Sisters. Musick, *Green Hills of Magic,* no. 43.
> Man without a Heart, The. Lang, *Pink Fairy Book,* p. 200.
> Trip to Wag-El-Wag, The. El-Shamy, *Folktales of Egypt,* no. 1.

**304   THE HUNTSMAN.** A huntsman killed three giants who were about to attack a sleeping princess. Then he cut out the giants' tongues and took one of the princess's slippers. The king's captain claimed to have killed the giants, but the huntsman showed the tongues and the slipper, proving that he was the rescuer. The captain was put to death, and the huntsman married the princess. (Grimm)

> Clever Daniel. Villa, *100 Armenian Tales,* no. 4.
> Cold Feet and the Lonesome Queen. Campbell, *Cloudwalking Country,* p. 106.
> Giant-Slayer, The. Villa, *100 Armenian Tales,* no. 5.
> Jack Outwits the Giants. Roberts, *South from Hell,* no. 4.
> Monk, The. Megas, *Folktales of Greece,* no. 20.
> Niels and the Giants. Lang, *Crimson Fairy Book,* p. 284.
> Of Tigers and a Hunter. Thundy, *South Indian Folktales,* no. 66.
> Ogre's Soul, The. Villa, *100 Armenian Tales,* no. 1.
> Sharpshooter, The. Delarue, *French Folktales,* p. 233.
> Three Brothers, The. Ranke, *Folktales of Germany,* no. 29.
> Trained Huntsman, The. Grimm, *Tales,* no. 111.
> White-Milk Deer, The. Briggs, *DBF,* pt. A, v. 1, p. 565.

**305A   THE SWORD OF WISDOM** (new classification). A boy lost at cards with a man who called himself Death of the State. The winner demanded the Sword of Wisdom in payment. When Death of the State came to collect the sword, the boy held it out for him, but as he approached, the boy cut off his head and was rid of him.

> Sword of Wisdom, The (Canada). Dorson, *Folktales around the World,* p. 455.

**306   THE SHOES THAT WERE DANCED TO PIECES.** A king had twelve daughters who mysteriously danced their shoes to pieces every night. With the help of a magic cloak, a soldier discovered how every night the twelve were entering an underground realm to dance with bewitched princes. His reward was the hand in marriage of one of the twelve. (Grimm)

> Danced-Out Shoes, The (Russia). Thompson, *100 Folktales,* no. 6.
> Elena the Wise. Afanasyev, *Russian Fairy Tales,* p. 545.
> Giant-Slayer, The. Villa, *100 Armenian Tales,* no. 5.
> Hild, Queen of the Elves. Simpson, *Icelandic Folktales and Legends,* p. 43.
> Secret Ball, The. Afanasyev, *Russian Fairy Tales,* p. 224.
> Shoes That Were Danced to Pieces, The. Grimm, *Tales,* no. 133.
> Twelve Dancing Princesses, The (France). Lang, *Red Fairy Book,* p. 1.
> Twelve Dancing Princesses, The (Grimm). Opie, *Classic Fairy Tales,* p. 248.

**306A THE PRINCESS WHO DANCED IN HEAVEN.** A prince found a lock of hair floating in the river and would marry only the girl from whose head it had been cut. He found her, and she married him, but only under the condition that she be allowed to return home every night. The prince discovered that she was flying on a magic chair to the Rajah Indra, before whom she danced and sang. When confronted, she agreed to give up her nightly flights, and she promised never to leave her husband again. (Lang)

> Dorani (India). Lang, *Olive Fairy Book*, p. 188.
> Girl on the Island, The. O'Flaherty, *Tales of Sex and Violence*, p. 95.
> Invisible Woman, The. Thundy, *South Indian Folktales*, no. 57.

**307 THE VAMPIRE PRINCESS.** A priest's son sat watch by a princess's coffin. At the stroke of midnight she emerged, threatening the boy with great terrors, but she could not harm him. In the morning the king saw the open coffin, and learned what had happened. He ordered that a wooden stake be driven through her heart before she was buried. (Afanasyev)

> Enchanted Princess, The. Ranke, *Folktales of Germany*, no. 23.
> Jacques (Belgium). Bødker, *European Folk Tales*, p. 155.
> Jean of Bordeaux. Massignon, *Folktales of France*, no. 28.
> La Ramée and the Phantom. Delarue, *French Folktales*, p. 252.
> Princess in the Chest (Denmark). Lang, *Pink Fairy Book*, p. 57.
> Sentry and the Princess in the Coffin, The. Grimm, *Other Tales*, p. 131.
> Son of the Gray Horse. Villa, *100 Armenian Tales*, no. 35.
> Sorceress, The. Afanasyev, *Russian Fairy Tales*, p. 567.

**310 RAPUNZEL, THE MAIDEN IN THE TOWER.** A man gathering rampion (rapunzel) for his wife was caught by the witch who owned the garden; he gained his freedom only by promising her his next child. The child was a girl named Rapunzel, and when she was twelve years old the sorceress locked her in a tower. Some time later a prince discovered her. She let down her hair, allowing him to climb up. Discovering the visits, the sorceress sent Rapunzel into a wilderness and caused the prince to go blind. He wandered about for years, finally arriving in the wilderness where Rapunzel and the twins to which she had given birth lived in misery. Upon seeing him, Rapunzel broke into tears. Two of the tears fell into his eyes, bringing back his sight. He then took her to his kingdom where they lived long and happy lives. (Grimm) Cf. type 891A.

> Anthousa the Fair with Golden Hair. Megas, *Folktales of Greece*, no. 22.
> Beautiful Catharinella. Grimm, *Other Tales*, p. 20.
> Canary Prince, The. Calvino, *Italian Folktales*, no. 18.
> Fair Angiola, The. Crane, *Italian Popular Tales*, no. 5.
> Fated Marriage, The. Dawkins, *More Greek Folktales*, no. 18.
> Garden Witch, The. Calvino, *Italian Folktales*, no. 181.

Girl on the Island, The. O'Flaherty, *Tales of Sex and Violence,* p. 95.
Godchild of the Fairy in the Tower, The. Delarue, *French Folktales,* p. 103.
Golden Hair; or, the Little Frog. Massignon, *Folktales of France,* no. 29.
King of Denmark's Son. Calvino, *Italian Folktales,* no. 36.
Louliyya, Daughter of Morgan. El-Shamy, *Folktales of Egypt,* no. 8.
Maiden in the Tower, The (France). Thompson, *100 Folktales,* no. 7.
Petrosinella. Basile, *Pentamerone,* Day 2, Tale 1.
Prezzemolina. Calvino, *Italian Folktales,* no. 86.
Princess, The; or, Fair One of the World. Dawkins, *Modern Greek Folktales,* no. 6.
Prunella. Lang, *Grey Fairy Book,* p. 382.
Rapunzel. Grimm, *Tales,* no. 12.
Reptensil. Roberts, *South from Hell,* no. 5.

## 311 THE HEROINE RESCUES HERSELF AND HER SISTERS.

A wizard captured a girl and took her to his house. Later he went on a journey, leaving her with an egg, a ring of keys, and a strict warning to not enter one forbidden room. But she did enter the room, finding there blood and body parts. Terrified, she dropped the egg into the gore. Upon his return, the man saw the stained egg and killed the girl. He then captured her sister, and the entire story repeated itself. He captured the third sister as well. She too opened the forbidden door, but she had placed her egg in a safe place, so the man did not discover her disobedience, and she gained power over him. She magically brought her sisters back to life, and all three made their escape. Their brothers returned and burned down the wizard's house with him inside. (Grimm, "Fitcher's Bird") Cf. types 312, 955.

Beggar with the Baskets, The. Campbell, *Cloudwalking Country,* p. 200.
Captain Murderer. Briggs, *DBF,* pt. A, v. 1, p. 175.
Devil Gets Tricked. Mathias and Raspa, *Italian Folktales in America,* no. 4.
Fäderäwisch, The. Ranke, *Folktales of Germany,* no. 24.
Fellow That Married a Dozen Times, The. Campbell, *Cloudwalking Country,* p. 246.
Fitcher's Bird. Grimm, *Tales,* no. 46.
Giant, the Princesses, and Peerie-Fool, The. Marwick, *Folklore of Orkney and Shetland,* p. 144.
Girl Who Married a Ghost, The (American Indian). Cole, *Folktales,* no. 181.
Hare's Bride, The. Grimm, *Tales,* no. 66.
Hen Is Tripping in the Mountain, The. Christiansen, *Folktales of Norway,* p. 228.
How the Devil Married Three Sisters (Italy). Thompson, *100 Folktales,* no. 8.
Jurma and the Sea God (Finland). Booss, *Scandinavian Tales,* p. 554.
Little Blue Ball, The. Randolph, *Who Blowed Up the Church House?,* p. 59.
Little Blue Ball, The. Roberts, *South from Hell,* no. 6A.
Lord of the World Below, The. Dawkins, *Modern Greek Folktales,* no. 17.
Merchant and his Three Daughters, The (Spain). Bødker, *European Folk Tales,* p. 173.
Old Dame and Her Hen, The. Asbjørnsen and Moe, *East o' the Sun,* p. 14.
Old Rinkrank. Grimm, *Tales,* no. 196.
Peerifool. Briggs, *DBF,* pt. A, v. 1, p. 446.
Poor Woman and Her Three Daughters, The. Campbell, *West Highlands,* v. 2, p. 288.

Seven Cauldrons Bubbling. Bushnaq, *Arab Folktales,* p. 315.
Silver Nose. Calvino, *Italian Folktales,* no. 9.
Three Chicory Gatherers, The. Calvino, *Italian Folktales,* no. 142.
Three Sisters, The. Sampson, *Gypsy Folk Tales,* p. 24.
Widow and Her Daughters, The. Campbell, *West Highlands,* v. 2, p. 279.

**312  BLUEBEARD.** A girl married a mysterious man with a blue beard. He gave her the keys to the house, but warned her that she must not enter one particular room. She could not resist the temptation, and behind the forbidden door she saw the bodies of several dead women. Bluebeard discovered that she had entered the forbidden room, and told her that she would have to die, granting her only a short respite to say her prayers. She called for help from the window, and at the last moment her brothers burst into the house and killed Bluebeard. (Perrault)  Cf. types 311, 955.

Bloody House, The. Roberts, *South from Hell,* no. 7B.
Blue Beard (France). Cole, *Folktales,* no. 4.
Blue Beard, The (Perrault). Opie, *Classic Fairy Tales,* p. 137.
Blue-Beard (France). Bødker, *European Folk Tales,* p. 158.
Bluebeard. Grimm, *Other Tales,* p. 135.
Bluebeard. Perrault, *Fairy Tales* (trans. Carter), p. 29.
Don Firriulieddu. Crane, *Italian Popular Tales,* no. 76.
Fitcher's Bird. Grimm, *Tales,* no. 46.
Girl Who Married the Devil, The. Ranke, *Folktales of Germany,* no. 25.
How the Devil Married Three Sisters. Crane, *Italian Popular Tales,* no. 16.
How Toodie Fixed Old Grunt. Randolph, *The Devil's Pretty Daughter,* p. 63.
Leopard and the Girl, The. Arewa, *Northern East Africa,* p. 207.
Little Boy and His Dogs, The. Harris, *Daddy Jake,* no. 3.
White Dove, The. Delarue, *French Folktales,* p. 36.

**312B  THE TWO GIRLS AND THE DEVIL.** Two little girls, Marie and Marguerite, got lost in the woods. An old woman offered them aid, but she was the devil's wife, and she locked them up. When the devil came home, he began taking off Marie's clothes, throwing them into the stove. Marguerite stood in the doorway, and in the distance she saw a man and a woman on a silver road. The devil continued to undress Marie, and when she had nothing left on but her shift, in came the man and the woman from the silver road. They were the Good Lord and the Holy Virgin. They threw the devil and his wife into the fire. Then they dressed Marie and took the two sisters back to their parents. (Delarue)

Child Rowland. Briggs, *DBF,* pt. A, v. 1, p. 180.
Clever Little Tailor, The. Briggs, *DBF,* pt. A, v. 1, p. 190.
Devil and the Two Little Girls, The. Delarue, *French Folktales,* p. 42.

**312D  THE HERO RESCUES HIS BROTHERS AND SISTER.**
Burd Ellen was carried off by the fairies. Her two elder brothers attempted to bring her back, but they too were captured. Childe Rowland, the youngest brother, set forth too, stopping first for

instructions from Warlock Merlin. "Once in Elfland," Merlin said, "strike off the head of anyone who speaks to you, and neither eat nor drink until you return to Middle Earth." Childe Rowland thus was able to defeat the king of the elves and rescue his brothers and Burd Ellen. (Jacobs)

> Born of His Mother's Tears. Dawkins, *Modern Greek Folktales,* no. 10.
> Child Rowland. Briggs, *DBF,* pt. A, v. 1, p. 180.
> Childe Rowland. Jacobs, *English Fairy Tales,* p. 117.
> Clever Little Tailor, The. Briggs, *DBF,* pt. A, v. 1, p. 190.

**313 THE GIRL HELPS THE HERO FLEE.** A giant offered to carry a king across a dangerous river in return for Nix Naught Nothing. The king agreed, but upon arriving home, he discovered that his wife had given birth to a son, and had called him Nix Naught Nothing. So they were forced to surrender the young prince to the giant. The giant gave the hero impossible tasks: to clean a monstrous stable, to drain a huge lake, and to climb a gigantic tree. The giant's beautiful daughter helped the hero perform these tasks, then the two ran away. The giant pursued them, but they threw down the girl's comb, and it became a briar patch in the giant's way. Her hair pin became a hedge of razors, and her magic flask released a flood that drowned the giant. The prince went on alone to inquire about lodging, and a wicked woman put a spell on him. The king promised that any maiden who could break the spell should marry him. A gardener's daughter knew the charm, but before the prince married this false bride, the giant's daughter found him, and he claimed her for his true bride. (Jacobs) —Note: Tales of this type beginning with the episode of the hero promised to an ogre are often categorized under number 313A. Those ending with the episode of the false bride are often classified as type 313C.

> Abo Beckeer. Villa, *100 Armenian Tales,* no. 8.
> Adventures of Simon and Susanna, The. Harris, *Daddy Jake,* no. 12.
> Ann Gej and Visivej (Denmark). Bødker, *European Folk Tales,* p. 70.
> Anthousa the Fair with Golden Hair. Megas, *Folktales of Greece,* no. 22.
> Battle of the Birds, The. Campbell, *West Highlands,* v. 1, p. 25.
> Becket's Parents. Briggs, *DBF,* pt. B, v. 2, p. 4.
> Billiards Player, The. Calvino, *Italian Folktales,* no. 22.
> Black Cloak, The. Briggs, *DBF,* pt. A, v. 1, p. 160.
> Black Dog of the Wild Forest, The. Briggs, *DBF,* pt. A, v. 1, p. 161.
> Blancaflor. Paredes, *Folktales of Mexico,* no. 30.
> Clever Pat. Briggs, *DBF,* pt. A, v. 1, p. 191.
> Daughter Greengown. Briggs, *DBF,* pt. A, v. 1, p. 202.
> Daughter of Black-White Red, The. Campbell, *West Highlands,* v. 1, p. 59.
> Devil and His Three Daughters, The. Massignon, *Folktales of France,* no. 6.
> Devil's Pretty Daughter, The. Randolph, *The Devil's Pretty Daughter,* p. 3.
> Dove, The. Basile, *Pentamerone,* Day 2, Tale 7.
> Drummer, The. Grimm, *Tales,* no. 193.
> Dschemil and Dschemila (Tripoli). Lang, *Grey Fairy Book,* p. 38.

Widow's Son, The. Campbell, *West Highlands,* v. 1, p. 48.
Witch's Daughter, The. Eberhard, *Folktales of China,* no. 27.
Woman Who Came Down from Heaven, The. Seki, *Folktales of Japan,* no. 23.
Wren, The. Campbell, *West Highlands,* v. 1, p. 49.
Young Bekie. Briggs, *DBF,* pt. A, v. 1, p. 579.

### 313E* THE GIRL WHOSE BROTHER WANTS TO MARRY HER.

A prince had a ring, and he had been told that he should marry only the woman whom it fitted. He tried the ring on many women, but it fitted only his sister. He made preparations for their wedding, but the earth opened, and she fell inside. Underground, she was captured by Baba Yaga, but Baba Yaga's daughter helped her escape, and together they returned to the earth. The brother married Baba Yaga's daughter, whose finger the ring fitted perfectly, and the heroine married another good man.

Prince Danila Govorila. Afanasyev, *Russian Fairy Tales,* p. 351.

### 313H* THE GIRL ESCAPES FROM A WITCH.

An evil woman sent her stepdaughter to the girl's aunt to borrow a needle and thread. The aunt was Baba Yaga, and she made preparations to eat the girl, but the girl took a towel and a comb and ran away. Baba Yaga pursued, but the girl threw down the towel and the comb, and they turned into a wide river and a thick forest in Baba Yaga's way. The girl arrived home and told her father where the stepmother had sent her; he became very angry and killed his wife. (Afanasyev)

Baba Yaga. Afanasyev, Russian Fairy Tales, p. 363.
Baba Yaga (Russia). Clarkson and Cross, *World Folktales,* no. 27.

### 314 THE GOLDEN-HAIRED BOY AND HIS MAGIC HORSE.

A boy was placed in the care of his godfather, a magician. The boy gave special care to the magician's mare, and she helped him escape. Together they went to the king's castle, where the boy worked as a gardner. When war was declared against the king, the garden boy volunteered to go to battle, but the king gave him only a three-legged horse and a gun that didn't shoot. However, the magician's mare brought him handsome clothes and a magic sword, and together they fought in three battles, winning splendid victories. Later the court learned that the garden boy and the three valiant knights were one and the same, and he married the princess. (Thomas) Cf. types 502, 530, 531.

Boy Whose Mother Wanted to Throw Him in Boiling Water, The. Massignon, *Folktales of France,* no. 7.
Cannetella. Basile, *Pentamerone,* Day 3, Tale 1.
Cruel Stepmother, The. Villa, *100 Armenian Tales,* p. 499.
Eleventh Captain's Tale, The. Mathers, *1001 Nights,* v. 4, p. 397.

Fire Boy, The. Seki, *Folktales of Japan,* no. 24.
Handsome András. Dégh, *Folktales of Hungary,* no. 3.
Jay Bird That Had a Fight with a Rattle Snake, The. Campbell, *Cloudwalking Country,* p. 132.
King of the Herrings. Sampson, *Gypsy Folk Tales,* p. 9.
Little Gardener with Golden Hair, The (France). Thompson, *100 Folktales,* no. 10.
Little John ('Tit Jean). Saucier, *French Louisiana,* no. 18.
Little Johnny Sheep-Dung. Delarue, *French Folktales,* p. 140.
Magic Filly, The. El-Shamy, *Folktales of Egypt,* no. 4.
Magician's Horse, The. Lang, *Grey Fairy Book,* p. 116.
Mangy One, The. Calvino, *Italian Folktales,* no. 110.
Monster's Hairs, The. Villa, *100 Armenian Tales,* no. 22.
Paperarello (Sicily). Lang, *Crimson Fairy Book,* p. 122.
Pigskin (Finland). Bødker, *European Folk Tales,* p. 10.
Prince and the Water of Life, The. Dawkins, *Modern Greek Folktales,* no. 39.
Prince of the Sword, The. Pino-Saavedra, *Folktales of Chile,* no. 6.
Seven Foals, The. Asbjørnsen and Moe, *East o' the Sun,* p. 302.
Teigneux. Thomas, *It's Good to Tell You,* no. 5.
Tree That Reached Up to the Sky, The. Dégh, *Folktales of Hungary,* no. 6.
Turkey Raiser, The. Saucier, *French Louisiana,* no. 6.
Widow's Son, The. Asbjørnsen and Moe, *East o' the Sun,* p. 311.

**314A  THE POOR BOY AND THE GIANTS.** A poor boy left home riding on a sheep and wearing pants patched with so many pieces that they called him Seven Colors. He worked for the king herding cattle and killed three giants who threatened him. Further, he broke the spell that had transformed a princess into a frog (see type 402) and married her. (Pino-Saavedra)

Little Blacksmith, The. Delarue, *French Folktales,* p. 249.
Seven Colors. Pino-Saavedra, *Folktales of Chile,* no. 7.

**314A\*  THE BULLOCK SAVIOR.** A bear with iron fur was ravaging the kingdom. Prince Ivan and Elena the Fair escaped by mounting a bullock and crossing a river. The pursuing bear sank and drowned. The bullock then asked them to kill him and eat his flesh. But they should keep the bones, for these would form a man who would come to their aid in time of need. —Continues as type 315.

Milk of Wild Beasts, The. Afanasyev, *Russian Fairy Tales,* p. 304.

**315  THE TREACHEROUS SISTER.** Elena the Fair fell in love with a robber chieftain, and together they plotted to kill her brother Prince Ivan. But at Little Fist's command (see type 314A\*), wild animals tore the chieftain to pieces, and Elana was tied naked to a tree, so that the mosquitoes might devour her. (Afanasyev)

Clever Daniel. Villa, *100 Armenian Tales,* no. 4.
Faithless Sister, The. Pino-Saavedra, *Folktales of Chile,* no. 8.
Jeweled Cage and the Evil Sister, The. Walker and Uysal, *Tales in Turkey,* p. 90.

Milk of Wild Beasts, The.  Afanasyev, *Russian Fairy Tales,* p. 304.

**315A  THE CANNIBAL SISTER.**  A woman gave birth to a girl with a head as big as a caldron and teeth like axes.  While still a baby, she would kill and eat whole sheep.  Later, she tried to eat her brother, but he escaped and killed her.  (Walker and Uysal, "The Caldron-Headed, Ax-Toothed Sister")

> Caldron-Headed, Ax-Toothed Sister, The.  Walker and Uysal, *Tales in Turkey,* p. 86.
> Jeweled Cage and the Evil Sister, The.  Walker and Uysal, *Tales in Turkey,* p. 90.
> Strigla, The (The Gelló).  Dawkins, *Modern Greek Folktales,* no. 27.

**316  THE NIXIE IN THE POND.**  A nixie promised a miller great wealth in return for that which had just been born at his house.  Thinking it was a puppy, he agreed, but his wife had just given birth to a baby boy.  The boy grew up and married.  One day the nixie pulled him into the pond, and he disappeared.  His faithful wife, after repeated tries, broke the nixie's spell, and the two were happily reunited on dry land.  (Grimm)

> Golden Comb, The.  Campbell, *Cloudwalking Country,* p. 40.
> Jack the Fisherman.  Gmelch and Kroup, *To Shorten the Road,* p. 97.
> Mermaid and the Poor Fisherman, The.  Pino-Saavedra, *Folktales of Chile,* no. 4.
> Nixie in the Pond, The.  Grimm, *Tales,* no. 181.
> Witch from the Ocean Waters, The.  Campbell, *Cloudwalking Country,* p. 216.
> Yara, The (Brazil).  Lang, *Brown Fairy Book,* p. 88.

**317A\*  THE PEASANT GIRL RESCUES THE PRINCE.**  A prince disappeared, and the king promised half the kingdom to whoever would return him.  A peasant's daughter discovered that two troll-wives were keeping him prisoner.  She helped him escape on the troll-wives' flying bed; they returned to the king and were married forthwith.

> Prince Hlini (Iceland).  Bødker, *European Folk Tales,* p. 50.

**318  THE FAITHLESS WIFE.**  Anpu lived in the same house with his wife and his younger brother Bata.  One day the wife asked Bata to lie with her, but he rejected her.  The wife later told her husband that Bata had beaten her when she had refused to lie with him.  Bata had to flee for his life.  Anpu learned the truth, and he killed his wife and threw her body to the dogs.  (Thompson)  Cf. type 884A.

> Anpu and Bata (Egypt).  Thompson, *100 Folktales,* no. 11.
> Anup and Bata (Balkan Variants).  Dégh, *Studies,* p. 231f.
> Joseph and Potiphar's Wife.  Bible: Genesis 39:7-23.

**321  EYES RECOVERED FROM A WITCH.**  A king who had seven wives was hunting in the forest, where he encountered a mysterious maiden.  She asked him to give her the eyes of his seven wives, and he was so bewitched by her beauty that he did so.  Later one of the blind queens bore a son, and when he had matured, he recovered the fourteen eyes from the mysterious maiden, who was wearing them on a string as a necklace.

> Son of Seven Queens, The. Jacobs, *Indian Fairy Tales,* p. 115.

**325  THE MAGICIAN AND HIS PUPIL.**  A poor boy was apprenticed to a magician and learned many skills.  When the boy returned to his father, he transformed himself into a horse, which the father sold at market; the boy then changed back to his human form and returned home.  The master discovered what was happening and pursued the boy by transforming himself into various animals.  But the pupil outwitted the magician.  He changed into grains of wheat, whereupon the master turned into a rooster to pick them up, but the wheat became a fox and ate the rooster. (Delarue)  Cf. Christiansen, *Migratory Legends,* type 3000.

> Black King of Morocco, The. Briggs, *DBF,* pt. A, v. 1, p. 162.
> Boy Magician, The. Bushnaq, *Arab Folktales,* p. 166.
> Changeable Man, The. Campbell, *Cloudwalking Country,* p. 243.
> Doctor and His Pupil, The (France). Cole, *Folktales,* no. 7.
> Doctor and His Pupil, The (France). Thompson, *100 Folktales,* no. 12.
> Doctor and His Pupil, The. Delarue, *French Folktales,* p. 135.
> Farmer Weathersky. Asbjørnsen and Moe, *East o' the Sun,* p. 285.
> Fisherman's Son and the Gruagach of Tricks, The (Ireland). Cole, *Folktales,* no. 60.
> Fisherman's Son, The. Campbell, *Cloudwalking Country,* p. 92.
> Horse, Hound and Hawk. Gmelch and Kroup, *To Shorten the Road,* p. 138.
> King of the Black Art, The (Scotland). Bødker, *European Folk Tales,* p. 122.
> King of the Black Art, The. Briggs, *DBF,* pt. A, v. 1, p. 347.
> Maghrabi's Apprentice, The. El-Shamy, *Folktales of Egypt,* no. 6.
> Magic Book, The (Denmark). Lang, *Orange Fairy Book,* p. 349.
> Magical Transformations. Clouston, *Popular Tales,* v. 1, p. 413, 482.
> Magician's Pupil, The (Denmark). Booss, *Scandinavian Tales,* p. 485.
> Man and His Son, The. Saucier, *French Louisiana,* no. 8.
> Master and Pupil (Denmark). Lang, *Pink Fairy Book,* p. 220.
> Master and Pupil. Dawkins, *Modern Greek Folktales,* no. 24.
> Pupil Who Excelled His Master, The. Noy, *Folktales of Israel,* no. 55.
> School of Salamanca, The. Calvino, *Italian Folktales,* no. 128.
> Sorcerer and His Apprentice (Russia). Dorson, *Folktales around the World,* p. 119.
> Thief and His Master, The. Grimm, *Tales,* no. 68.
> Twelfth Captain's Tale, The. Mathers, *1001 Nights,* v. 4, p. 400.
> Two Witches, The. Dorson, *Buying the Wind,* p. 434.

**325\*  THE SORCERER'S APPRENTICE AND THE DEMON.**  A sorcerer's apprentice, when his master was away, conjured up a demon.  At the boy's command, the demon began carrying water, but the apprentice did not know how to reverse the charm, and the demon fetched water until the room was flooded. Finally the master returned and spoke the words that sent the demon away. (Jacobs) Cf. type 1174 and Christiansen, *Migratory Legends,* type 3020.

Auld Scairie and the Black Airt. Briggs, *DBF,* pt. B, v. 2, p. 614.
Black Hen and the Vicar's Servant, The. Whitlock, *Folklore of Devon,* p. 62.
Black Hen, The. Briggs, *DBF,* pt. B, v. 2, p. 622.
Do-All Ax, The (USA, Black). Clarkson and Cross, *World Folktales,* no. 5.
Mass John Scott. Briggs, *DBF,* pt. B, v. 1, p. 534.
Master and His Pupil, The. Briggs, *DBF,* pt. A, v. 1, p. 411.
Master and His Pupil, The. Jacobs, *English Fairy Tales,* p. 73.
Schoolboys Raise the Devil. Simpson, *Folklore of the Welsh Border,* p. 184.
Schoolmaster of Bury, The. Briggs, *DBF,* pt. B, v. 1, p. 135.
Wizard of Abergavenny and His Servant, The. Simpson, *Folklore of the Welsh Border,* p. 62.

**326   THE BOY WHO SET OUT TO LEARN FEAR.** A boy set out to learn how to shudder. He responded to the king's promise to give his daughter in marriage to anyone who could spend three nights in a haunted castle. Each night terrible apparitions tormented him, but he overcame them all, and won the princess. Still he did not know fear, but his new wife taught him to shudder by pouring a bucket of minnows over him in bed. (Grimm, no. 4)

Ashypelt. Briggs, *DBF,* pt. A, v. 1, p. 140.
Big Black Booger, The. Randolph, *The Talking Turtle,* p. 22.
Boy That Never Seen a Fraid, The (4 tales). Roberts, *South from Hell,* no. 9.
Boy Who Did Not Know Fear, The (Iceland). Booss, *Scandinavian Tales,* p. 646.
Boy Who Feared Nothing, The. Briggs, *DBF,* pt. A, v. 2, p. 29.
Boy Who Found Fear at Last, The (Turkey). Lang, *Olive Fairy Book,* p. 279.
Boy Who Knew No Fear, The. Simpson, *Icelandic Folktales and Legends,* p. 122.
Boy Who Set Out to Learn Fear, A (Germany). Thompson, *100 Folktales,* no. 13.
Dauntless Girl, The. Briggs, *DBF,* pt. A, v. 1, p. 204.
Dauntless Girl, The. Porter, *Folklore of East Anglia,* p. 170.
Dauntless Little John. Calvino, *Italian Folktales,* no. 1.
Dean Man's Arm, The. Calvino, *Italian Folktales,* no. 43.
Fearless Simpleton. Calvino, *Italian Folktales,* no. 80.
Good Fortune Kettle, The. Seki, *Folktales of Japan,* no. 31.
Headless Dwarfs, The (Estonia). Lang, *Violet Fairy Book,* p. 281.
I'm Going to Fall. Dorson, *Negro Tales,* p. 76.
Jack the Ghost. Gmelch and Kroup, *To Shorten the Road,* p. 71.
Make-Me-Shudder. Grimm, *Other Tales,* p. 13.
Man Who Did Not Know Fear, The. Afanasyev, *Russian Fairy Tales,* p. 325.
Man Who Didn't Believe in Ghosts and 'Chantments, The. Briggs, *DBF,* pt. A, v. 1, p. 404.
Man Who Went to Find Fear (commentary). Dawkins, *Modern Greek Folktales,* no. 78.
Queen of the Three Mountains of Gold. Calvino, *Italian Folktales,* no. 55.
Seven-Headed Animal. Saucier, *French Louisiana,* no. 4.
Soldier, The. Campbell, *West Highlands,* v. 2, p. 290.

That's a Lie; You Never Had Two Heads. Porter, *Folklore of East Anglia,* p. 108.
Wager Won, A. Briggs, *DBF,* pt. A, v. 2, p. 343.
Waiting for Martin. Dorson, *Negro Tales,* p. 78.
Yann the Fearless. Massignon, *Folktales of France,* no. 1.
Youth Who Went Forth to Learn What Fear Was, The. Grimm, *Tales,* no. 4.

**326A\* RELEASING A SOUL FROM TORMENT.** A soldier spent the night in a haunted building. During the night a ghost appeared, but the soldier remained undaunted. In the morning the ghost gave him three crocks of gold: two for himself, and one to say masses for the ghost. (Glassie) Cf. Christiansen, *Migratory Legends,* type 4020.

Beausoleil. Thomas, *It's Good to Tell You,* no. 18.
Black Cat, The. Briggs, *DBF,* pt. A, v. 1, p. 159.
Cutler and the Tinker, The. Briggs, *DBF,* pt. A, v. 1, p. 200.
Death Bree, The. Briggs, *DBF,* pt. B, v. 1, p. 434.
Golden Ball, The. Briggs, *DBF,* pt. A, v. 1, p. 280.
Golden Ball, The. Jacobs, *More English Fairy Tales,* p. 12.
Grey Castle, The. Briggs, *DBF,* pt. A, v. 1, p. 298.
Haunted Castle, The. Briggs, *DBF,* pt. A, v. 1, p. 308.
King of the Cats, The. Briggs, *DBF,* pt. A, v. 1, p. 350.
Lousy Jack and His Eleven Brothers. Briggs, *DBF,* pt. A, v. 1, p. 395.
Soldier in the Haunted House, The. Glassie, *Irish Folktales,* no. 53.
Three Golden Balls, The. Briggs, *DBF,* pt. A, v. 2, p. 567.
Tinker and the Ghost, The (Spain). Clarkson and Cross, *World Folktales,* no. 29.
Twopenny Priss. Briggs, *DBF,* pt. A, v. 1, p. 545.
Wee Tailor, The. Briggs, *DBF,* pt. B, v. 1, p. 597.

**326B\* ROBBERS FRIGHTENED BY A CORPSE.** Having no better place, a poor boy slept near his mother's grave. Two men with a horse came to rob a grave, but when the boy stood up and greeted them, they fled, leaving their horse behind. (Briggs, "Resurrection Men") Cf. type 1318.

Burke and Hare. Briggs, *DBF,* pt. B, v. 2, p. 11.
Dead Man Who Was Warm, The. Pourrat, *French Tales,* p. 37.
Down the Rotten Row. Briggs, *DBF,* pt. A, v. 2, p. 63.
Grave Robbers. Randolph, *The Devil's Pretty Daughter,* p. 24.
Resurrection Men. Briggs, *DBF,* pt. A, v. 2, p. 249.

**327 THE CHILDREN AND THE OGRE.** A man and a woman had more children than they could support, so they abandoned the three youngest girls in the woods. A giant's wife took them in. At bedtime the giant placed gold chains around his own daughters' necks and straw chains around the poor girls' necks. Molly Whuppie, the youngest of the poor girls, secretly exchanged the necklaces. In the night the giant felt for the necks with the straw, and clubbed his own daughters to death. Thus the three sisters made their escape. —Continues as type 328. (Jacobs, "Molly Whuppie") Cf. type 1119.

Black Brottie. Briggs, *DBF,* pt. A, v. 1, p. 153.
Brother and Sister Are Abandoned by Their Parents. Arewa, *Northern East Africa,* p. 229.
Jean and Jeannette. Massignon, *Folktales of France,* no. 50.
Little Girl and the Giant, The. Roberts, *South from Hell,* no. 10C.
Little Guava, The. Paredes, *Folktales of Mexico,* no. 31.
Little Peter. Mathias and Raspa, *Italian Folktales in America,* no. 11.
Luckie Minnie and the Little Boy. Marwick, *Folklore of Orkney and Shetland,* p. 163.
Mally Whuppie. Briggs, *DBF,* pt. A, v. 1, p. 400.
Man and Woman with Too Many Children. Sampson, *Gypsy Folk Tales,* p. 89.
Merrywise. Roberts, *South from Hell,* no. 10A.
Mister Miacca. Briggs, *DBF,* pt. A, v. 2, p. 546.
Mister Miacca. Jacobs, *English Fairy Tales,* p. 164.
Molly Whuppie (England). Clarkson and Cross, *World Folktales,* no. 6.
Molly Whuppie. Jacobs, *English Fairy Tales,* p. 125.
Ninnillo and Nennella. Basile, *Pentamerone,* Day 5, Tale 8.
Witch, The (Russia). Lang, *Yellow Fairy Book,* p. 216.
Woodcutter's Wealthy Sister, The. Bushnaq, *Arab Folktales,* p. 137.

## 327A HANSEL AND GRETEL.

**327A  HANSEL AND GRETEL.**  Abandoned by their parents, Hansel and Gretel found refuge with an old woman in a gingerbread house. They soon discovered that she intended to eat them, but Gretel pushed her into her own oven, and the two escaped, taking with them the witch's gold and gems. They returned to their father, who greeted them with joy. (Grimm) Cf. type 1121.

Chick. Calvino, *Italian Folktales,* no. 130.
Deserted Children, The (American Indian). Cole, *Folktales,* no. 180.
Grumbling Old Woman, The. Afanasyev, *Russian Fairy Tales,* p. 340.
Haensel and Gretel (Germany). Thompson, *100 Folktales,* no. 14.
Hansel and Gretel (Grimm). Opie, *Classic Fairy Tales,* p. 312.
Hansel and Gretel. Grimm, *Tales,* no. 15.
Johnnie and Grizzle. Jacobs, *European Folk and Fairy Tales,* no. 22.
Kadar and Cannibals. Thundy, *South Indian Folktales,* no. 49.
Lost Children, The. Delarue, *French Folktales,* p. 97.
Oni and the Three Children, The. Seki, *Folktales of Japan,* no. 20.
Two Lost Babes, The. Chase, *Grandfather Tales,* no. 19.

**327B  THE SMALL BOY DEFEATS THE OGRE.**  A poor woodcutter and his wife had seven sons, the youngest of whom was so tiny that they called him "Hop-o'-My-Thumb." No longer able to feed them, the father abandoned the children in the woods. They found refuge with an ogre and his family, and were given a bed in the same room with the ogre's daughters, who went to sleep wearing golden crowns.   In the night, Hop-o'-My-Thumb exchanged the golden crowns for his and his brothers' nightcaps. In the dark, the ogre felt for the nightcaps and killed his own daughters. The brothers escaped, and Hop-o'-My-Thumb also stole the ogre's seven-league boots and his treasure. (Perrault) Cf. types 700, 1119.

Clever Little Tailor, The. Briggs, *DBF,* pt. A, v. 1, p. 190.
Esben and the Witch (Denmark). Lang, *Pink Fairy Book,* p. 258.
Hop o' My Thumb. Perrault, *Fairy Tales* (trans. Carter), p. 111.
Little Poucet (Hop o' My Thumb, Perrault). Opie, *Classic Fairy Tales,* p. 170.
Maol a Chliobain. Campbell, *West Highlands,* v. 1, p. 259.
Mutsmag. Chase, *Grandfather Tales,* no. 4.
Ogre, The. Grimm, *Other Tales,* p. 47.
Poucette (Tom Thumb). Saucier, *French Louisiana,* no. 13.

**327C  THE WITCH CARRIES THE BOY HOME IN A SACK.** The witch caught Petie Pete and put him in a sack. On her way home, she stopped to relieve herself, and Petie Pete escaped, placing a stone in her sack. The witch captured him again, and again she stopped to relieve herself. This time Petie Pete put a dog in the sack. She captured him again, and this time she carried him home without stopping. At the witch's house, Petie Pete jumped onto the hood over the fireplace. The witch made a ladder of pots to go after him, but they came crashing down, and she fell into the fire and burned to ashes. (Calvino)

Buchettino. Crane, *Italian Popular Tales,* no. 85.
Butter Ball Spa (Norway). Bødker, *European Folk Tales,* p. 47.
Butterball. Asbjørnsen and Moe, *Norwegian Folktales,* p. 97.
Buttercup. Asbjørnsen and Moe, *East o' the Sun,* p. 124.
Enchanted Mountain, The. Briggs, *DBF,* pt. A, v. 1, p. 224.
Fairy Jip and Witch One-Eye. Briggs, *DBF,* pt. A, v. 1, p. 228.
Jack the Buttermilk. Briggs, *DBF,* pt. A, v. 1, p. 322.
Petie Pete versus Witch Bea-Witch. Calvino, *Italian Folktales,* no. 37.
Tib and the Old Witch. Briggs, *DBF,* pt. A, v. 1, p. 522.

**327G  THE BOY KILLS THE OGRE'S DAUGHTER.** A boy, to please his king, stole silver ducks and a quilt from a troll. He returned for the troll's gold harp, but was captured this time. When the troll's daughter came to prepare him for dinner, the boy tricked her and cut off her head. He then changed clothes with her, cooked her for the troll's dinner, took the gold harp, and escaped.

Boots and the Troll. Asbjørnsen and Moe, *East o' the Sun,* p. 215.

**328  THE BOY STEALS THE OGRE'S TREASURES.** A poor widow sent her son Jack to market to sell their only cow, but Jack traded the cow for a handful of beans. His mother, in anger, threw the beans out the window. During the night they grew into a beanstalk that reached the sky. Jack climbed the beanstalk into a realm where a giant lived. He stole a bag of gold from the giant and climbed back to earth. He returned twice more, stealing a hen that laid golden eggs and a magic harp. On the final trip, the giant pursued him onto the beanstalk. Jack reached the ground safely, then chopped the beanstalk in two, and the giant fell to his death. (Jacobs, "Jack and the

Beanstalk") —Note: For other tales with plants reaching to heaven see types 468, 804A, 1960G.

Adventures with Giants. Clouston, *Popular Tales,* v. 1, p. 133, 466.
Big Old Giant, The. Randolph, *Who Blowed Up the Church House?,* p. 48.
Boots and the Troll (Norway). Thompson, *100 Folktales,* no. 15.
Boy Called Thirteen, The. Dawkins, *Modern Greek Folktales,* no. 3.
Cock and the Hand Mill, The. Afanasyev, *Russian Fairy Tales,* p. 387.
Esben and the Witch (Denmark). Lang, *Pink Fairy Book,* p. 258.
Gallant Szérus, The. Dégh, *Folktales of Hungary,* no. 8.
Giant Goulaffre, The. Delarue, *French Folktales,* p. 20.
Giant's Treasure, The (Sweden). Bødker, *European Folk Tales,* p. 33.
How the Dragon Was Tricked (Greece). Lang, *Pink Fairy Book,* p. 6.
How the Stalos Were Tricked. Lang, *Orange Fairy Book,* p. 319.
Jack and the Bean Tree. Chase, *The Jack Tales,* no. 3.
Jack and the Bean-Stalk (England). Opie, *Classic Fairy Tales,* p. 214.
Jack and the Beanstalk (I-III). Briggs, *DBF,* pt. A, v. 1, p. 316.
Jack and the Beanstalk. Jacobs, *English Fairy Tales,* p. 59.
Jack and the Beanstalk. Lang, *Red Fairy Book,* p. 133.
Jack and the Giants (England). Opie, *Classic Fairy Tales,* p. 64.
Jack and the Giants. Briggs, *DBF,* pt. A, v. 1, p. 326.
Jack in the Giants' Newground (USA). Cole, *Folktales,* no. 176.
Jack in the Giants' Newground. Chase, *The Jack Tales,* no. 1.
Jack the Giant-Killer (II). Briggs, *DBF,* pt. A, v. 1, p. 331.
Jack the Giant-Killer (several variants). Deane and Shaw, *Folklore of Cornwall,* p. 98.
Jack the Giant-Killer. Jacobs, *English Fairy Tales,* p. 99.
Jack the Giant-Killer. Lang, *Blue Fairy Book,* p. 374.
Little Bull with the Golden Horns, The. Thomas, *It's Good to Tell You,* no. 6.
Lost Prince, The. Pino-Saavedra, *Folktales of Chile,* no. 9.
Mally Whuppie. Briggs, *DBF,* pt. A, v. 1, p. 400.
Molly Whuppie (England). Clarkson and Cross, *World Folktales,* no. 6.
Molly Whuppie. Jacobs, *English Fairy Tales,* p. 125.
Nippy. Roberts, *South from Hell,* no. 11A.
Rooster-Brother. Villa, *100 Armenian Tales,* no. 76.
Tabagnino the Hunchback. Calvino, *Italian Folktales,* no. 51.
Thirteenth. Crane, *Italian Popular Tales,* no. 18.
Wang-Liang's Magic Cap, The. Eberhard, *Folktales of China,* no. 43.

**328A\* THREE BROTHERS RESTORE SUN, MOON, AND STARS.** The sky was dark, and the king offered a great reward to anyone who could afix the sun and the moon in the sky. Three Gypsy boys, the youngest of whom had magic powers, answered the call, and after many adventures they successfully placed the sun and moon in the sky.

Csucskári. Dégh, *Folktales of Hungary,* no. 2.

**329 HIDING FROM THE PRINCESS.** A princess made it known that she would marry only the man who could hide himself so well that she could not find him within three days. Every man who tried failed. One day a man rescued an ant from drowning, and in gratitude, the ant gave him the power to turn into an ant. The man presented himself before the princess and declared that he would hide himself. He then turned into an ant and climbed into her garter. When the three days were up, he turned himself back into a man, and she had to marry him. (Massignon) —Note: In some versions, the hero wins a wager by hiding from an ogre.

Horse, Hound and Hawk. Gmelch and Kroup, *To Shorten the Road*, p. 138.
King of Ireland's Son, The. Glassie, *Irish Folktales*, no. 117.
Mule, The. Glassie, *Irish Folktales*, no. 116.
Princess Elisa. Massignon, *Folktales of France*, no. 62.
Wandering Soldier, The. Pino-Saavedra, *Folktales of Chile*, no. 10.

**329A\* THE MAN WHO SOLD HIS SHADOW.** A stranger offered a poor man a purse that would never run out of money in exchange for his shadow. The poor man agreed and became wealthy. However, people began to ask questions about his wealth and about his shadow. They accused him of robberies and sent him to prison, where he died.

Man Who Sold His Shadow, The. Musick, *Green Hills of Magic*, no. 2.

**330 THE SMITH OUTWITS THE DEVIL.** —Note: Type 330 tales contain one or more episodes summarized below under types 330*-330D.

Blacksmith Who Sold Himself to the Devil, The. Briggs, *DBF*, pt. A, v. 1, p. 167.
Contracts with the Evil One. Clouston, *Popular Tales*, v. 1, p. 387.
Death Corked in the Bottle. Calvino, *Italian Folktales*, no. 165.4.
Devil's Whetstone, The. Briggs, *DBF*, pt. B, v. 1, p. 92.
Devil, Death, and Simon Greene, The. Musick, *Green Hills of Magic*, no. 8.
Dule upon Dun. Briggs, *DBF*, pt. A, v. 1, p. 221.
Giufà's Exploits. Crane, *Italian Popular Tales*, no. 103.
Jacky-My-Lantern. Harris, *Uncle Remus*, no. 32.
Jay Caught the Devil. Randolph, *Who Blowed Up the Church House?*, p. 54.
Jump into My Sack. Calvino, *Italian Folktales*, no. 200.
Legend of Twardowski, The. Musick, *Green Hills of Magic*, no. 1.
Man Who Wouldn't Go Out at Night, The. Briggs, *DBF*, pt. A, v. 1, p. 407.
Master-Smith, The (Norway). Thompson, *100 Folktales*, no. 16.
Master-Smith, The. Asbjørnsen and Moe, *East o' the Sun*, p. 105.
Misery and His Dog Poverty. Pourrat, *French Tales*, p. 85.
My Jon's Soul. Simpson, *Icelandic Folktales and Legends*, p. 196.
Old Smith, The. Briggs, *DBF*, pt. A, v. 1, p. 428.
Pedro de Ordimalas. Dorson, *Buying the Wind*, p. 429.
Saint Dunstan and the Devil. Briggs, *DBF*, pt. B, v. 2, p. 438.
Saint Dunstan and the Devil. Palmer, *Folklore of Somerset*, p. 39.
Shepherd of Bidlip Hill and Old Nick, The. Briggs, *Folklore of the Cotswolds*, p. 75.
Smith and the Devil, The. Briggs, *DBF*, pt. A, v. 1, p. 493.
Soldier Jack. Chase, *The Jack Tales*, no. 18.
Three Wishes, The. Glassie, *Irish Folktales*, no. 119.
Will the Smith. Briggs, *DBF*, pt. A, v. 1, p. 574.
Willy the Wisp. Glassie, *Irish Folktales*, no. 120.

**330\*  HEAVEN ENTERED BY A TRICK.** Pedro Urdimale squeezed into the gate of heaven as far as his waist before St. Peter slammed the door shut, cutting him in two. God passed by and asked why the lower half of his body was outside. Pedro answered: "That's the part with the sins." Then God joined the two halves together, and Pedro lived on in heaven.

Abbé Chanut. Pourrat, *French Tales*, p. 217.
Beppo Pipetta. Crane, *Italian Popular Tales*, no. 66.
Brother Merry. Grimm, *Tales*, no. 81.
Pedro Urdimale Gets into Heaven. Pino-Saavedra, *Folktales of Chile*, no. 12.
Peter the Rogue. Espinosa, *Folklore of Spain in the American Southwest*, p. 182.

**330A  THE SMITH'S THREE WISHES.** Gambling Hansel gave shelter to the Lord and St. Peter, in return for which he was granted three wishes. He requested cards and dice that would always win and a fruit tree that would capture anyone who climbed it. When it was time for Death to claim Gambling Hansel, he caught him in his tree and held him there for seven years. Finally, because no one on earth was dying, the Lord made Gambling Hansel release Death. Death took Gambling Hansel first to heaven, but they would have nothing to do with him, so he went to hell. He freed himself from there with the magic cards. Because he was neither in heaven nor in hell, the Lord threw him back to earth; his soul broke into pieces and entered those who live for gambling. (Grimm)

Gambling Hansel. Grimm, *Tales*, no. 82.
Occasion. Crane, *Italian Popular Tales*, no. 63.
Pedro the Blacksmith. Pino-Saavedra, *Folktales of Chile*, no. 11.
Wicked John and the Devil. Chase, *Grandfather Tales*, no. 3.

**330B  THE DEVIL IN THE SACK.** The Lord granted a good monk his wish that anyone he commanded would have to get into his sack. When he died, there was no room for him in heaven, so he went to the gates of hell, and captured Lucifer and his devils in his sack. He then took the sack to a smith, who pounded it until the devils were mangled. Again he went to the doorway of heaven, but was denied entrance, so he captured all heaven-bound souls in his sack. To save these souls, St. Peter pulled the sack inside. The monk immediately wished himself into the sack as well, thus tricking his way into heaven. (Crane, "Brother Giovannone")

Beppo Pipetta. Crane, *Italian Popular Tales*, no. 66.
Brother Giovannone. Crane, *Italian Popular Tales*, no. 64.
Brother Merry. Grimm, *Tales*, no. 81.
Impty-Umpty and the Blacksmith. Harris, *Uncle Remus Returns*, no. 2.
Lad and the Deil, The. Asbjørnsen and Moe, *East o' the Sun*, p. 377.
Legend of Twardowski, The. Musick, *Green Hills of Magic*, no. 1.

**330C  THE WINNING CARDS.** Jolly Hans gave St. Peter and our Lord shelter, and they in return granted him three wishes. He chose cards and dice that would always win plus a fiddle that would make everything stick where it was. When he died he escaped from hell and made his way into heaven with the help of his magic gifts.

> Jolly Hans. Grimm, *Other Tales*, p. 119.

**330D  MISERY STUCK ON EARTH.** Godfather Misery captured Death in his magic fig tree (in a manner similar to type 330A), thus tricking him into not taking him. Hence, Misery still lives on earth.

> Godfather Misery. Crane, *Italian Popular Tales*, no. 65.

**331  THE DEMON IN THE BOTTLE.** A fisherman found a bottle in his net. He removed the stopper and a huge genie emerged, announcing that he was going to kill the fisherman. Thinking fast, the threatened man asked him how a person of such great size could fit in a small bottle. To show him, the genie reduced himself to smoke and re-entered the vessel, whereupon the the fisherman pushed the stopper back into place, locking him inside. *(1001 Nights)*

> Child Sold to the Devil, The (France). Thompson, *100 Folktales*, no. 17.
> Demon Enclosed in a Bottle, The. Clouston, *Popular Tales*, v. 1, p. 381.
> Fisherman and the Genie, The (Arabian Nights). Cole, *Folktales*, no. 109.
> Fisherman and the Jinni, The. Mathers, *1001 Nights*, v. 1, p. 19.
> Old Man Who Cheated the Devil, The (Greece). Bødker, *European Folk Tales*, p. 195.
> Spirit in the Bottle, The. Grimm, *Tales*, no. 99.
> Virgilius the Sorcerer. Lang, *Violet Fairy Book*, p. 364.
> Yallery Brown. Briggs, *DBF*, pt. A, v. 1, p. 577.
> Yallery Brown. Jacobs, *More English Fairy Tales*, p. 28.

**332  GODFATHER DEATH.** A poor man with a large family could find no one to be godfather for his latest son. Finally Death appeared, and the poor man chose him, saying: "You make no distinction between high and low." Years later, on the godson's wedding night, Death called him from his bed and took him to a cave where countless candles were burning. "Whose light is that?" asked the godson, pointing to a candle that was flickering out. "Your own," answered the godfather, and with that the light went out and the godson fell down dead. (Thompson) Cf. type 532*.

> Boy with the Beer Keg, The. Asbjørnsen and Moe, *Norwegian Folktales*, p. 131.
> Contract with Azrael, The. El-Shamy, *Folktales of Egypt*, no. 17.
> Doctor That Acted a Partner with Death. Campbell, *Cloudwalking Country*, p. 185.
> Godfather Death (Sweden). Thompson, *100 Folktales*, no. 18.
> Godfather Death. Grimm, *Tales*, no. 44.

Godfather, The. Grimm, *Tales,* no. 42.
Godmother, The. Musick, *Green Hills of Magic,* no. 7.
Just Man for a Godfather, A. Dawkins, *Modern Greek Folktales,* no. 80.
Just Man, The. Crane, *Italian Popular Tales,* no. 67.
Shepherd and the Three Diseases, The. Megas, *Folktales of Greece,* no. 23.
Soldier Jack. Chase, *The Jack Tales,* no. 18.
Soul-Taking Angel, The. Villa, *100 Armenian Tales,* no. 45.
Town That Had Faith in God, The. Noy, *Folktales of Israel,* no. 8.

**333 RED RIDING HOOD.** On her way through the woods to visit her grandmother, Red-Cap met a wolf. Not knowing he was a dangerous animal, she told him where she was headed. The wolf ran ahead and ate the grandmother alive. When Red-Cap arrived, he ate her as well, and then fell asleep. A hunter heard him snoring and cut open his belly. Out popped Little Red-Cap and the grandmother. Little Red-Cap then filled him with stones and sewed him shut. When he awoke, he felt the stones inside in his belly, went into a convulsion, and died. (Grimm) Cf. types 123, 2028. —Note: Some versions, notably Perrault's, end with the girl's death. See Zipes, *The Trials and Tribulations of Little Red Riding Hood,* and Ritz, *Streit um Rotkäppchen.*

Bear Ate Them Up, The. Randolph, *Sticks in the Knapsack,* p. 59.
Boudin-Boudine. Massignon, *Folktales of France,* no. 16.
False Grandmother, The. Calvino, *Italian Folktales,* no. 116.
Finn and the Dragon. Briggs, *DBF,* pt. A, v. 1, p. 234.
Golden Chain from Heaven, The. Seki, *Folktales of Japan,* no. 21.
Grandmother, The. Delarue, *French Folktales,* p. 230.
Gunny Wolf, The. Botkin, *American Folklore,* p. 681.
Little Red Riding Hood. Falassi, *Folklore by the Fireside,* p. 68.
Little Red Riding Hood. Perrault, *Fairy Tales* (trans. Carter), p. 21.
Little Red Riding-Hood (France). Thompson, *100 Folktales,* no. 19.
Little Red Riding-Hood, The (Perrault). Opie, *Classic Fairy Tales,* p. 122.
Little Red-Cap. Grimm, *Tales,* no. 26.
True History of Little Goldenhood, The (France). Lang, *Red Fairy Book,* p. 215.
Wolf and the Three Girls, The. Calvino, *Italian Folktales,* no. 26.

**333A THE WOLF AND THE GREEDY GIRL.** A little girl borrowed a skillet from Uncle Wolf, who asked that it be returned full of pancakes. However, the greedy girl ate the wolf's pancakes, and filled the skillet with donkey dung before returning it. Uncle Wolf tasted the pancake and said: "Uck, this is donkey dung! I am coming to eat you." And that is just what he did.

Uncle Wolf. Calvino, *Italian Folktales,* no. 49.

**334 AT THE WITCH'S HOUSE.** A little girl went to see Frau Trude, although her parents told her not to. On the steps she saw a black man. Frau Trude said it was a charcoal burner. Then she saw a green man. "He was a hunter," said Frau Trude. Then there was a blood-red man.

"He was a butcher," was the explanation. Finally the girl said, "When I saw you through the window, it looked like the devil with a head of fire." Frau Trude answered by turning the girl into a block of wood, which she threw into the fire. (Grimm)

> Devil's Wife as Godmother, The. Ranke, *Folktales of Germany,* no. 26.
> Frau Trude. Grimm, *Tales,* no. 43.

**335 DEATH'S MESSENGERS.** Death promised a young man that he would not claim him without first sending messengers. The man's youth soon passed, and he became miserable. One day Death arrived to take him, but he complained that the messengers had not yet appeared. Death responded: "Were you not sick? Have you not experienced dizziness, ringing in your ears, toothache, and blurred vision? These were my messengers." The man yielded and went away quietly. (Grimm)

> Death's Messengers. Grimm, *Tales,* no. 177.
> Speaking Animals. Thundy, *South Indian Folktales,* no. 24.

**360 THE THREE APPRENTICES AND THE DEVIL.** Three apprentices, in return for wealth, they agreed with the devil to answer every question: "The three of us," "For money," and "Quite right, too!" Later their innkeeper murdered a wealthy guest, and the three apprentices were accused. Their answers were interpreted as confessions, and they were about to be hanged, but in the last minute, the devil, dressed as a nobleman, arrived with their pardon. The innkeeper was found guilty, and the devil secured his soul. (Grimm) Cf. types 821, 1697

> Three Journeymen, The. Grimm, *Tales,* no. 120.
> Three Traveling Artisans, The. Ranke, *Folktales of Germany,* no. 28.

**361 THE MAN WHO DID NOT WASH FOR SEVEN YEARS.** A recently discharged soldier agreed to not wash himself for seven years. In return the devil gave him a purse that would never run out of money. With this wealth he helped a poor man, who promised him one of his daughters in marriage. But only the youngest girl would have him. When his seven years were up, dressed now as a magnificent nobleman, he returned for his bride. Seeing what they had rejected, the two older sisters killed themselves. (Grimm)

> Bearskin. Grimm, *Tales,* no. 101.
> Coat or the Task, The. Briggs, *DBF,* pt. A, v. 1, p. 194.
> Devil's Breeches, The. Calvino, *Italian Folktales,* no. 53.
> Don Giovanni de la Fortuna (Sicily). Lang, *Pink Fairy Book,* p. 356.
> First of the Bearskins, The (Grimmelshausen). David and Meek, *Twelve Dancing Princesses,* p. 171.

Good Bear and the Orphan Girls, The. Thundy, *South Indian Folktales,* no. 41.
Licentiate of Saint Andrews, The. Briggs, *DBF,* pt. B, v. 1, p. 111.
Man That Never Washed for Seven Years. Campbell, *Cloudwalking Country,* p. 193.
Road to Hell, The. Ranke, *Folktales of Germany,* no. 58.
Soldier and the Bad Man, The (Finland). Bødker, *European Folk Tales,* p. 1.
Three Traveling Artisans, The. Ranke, *Folktales of Germany,* no. 28.

**363  THE VAMPIRE SUITOR.** A girl had a mysterious suitor, and she followed him one night to a churchyard, where she saw him eat a corpse. He asked her if she had seen him, and she said no. Soon thereafter her mother and father died. When the vampire threatened her again, she threw holy water on him, and he turned into dust. (Afanasyev) Cf. type 1476B and Christiansen, *Migratory Legends,* type 4005.

> Coffin-Lid, The (Russia). Clarkson and Cross, *World Folktales,* no. 31.
> Vampire, The. Afanasyev, *Russian Fairy Tales,* p. 593.
> Wanted, A Husband. Briggs, *DBF,* pt. A, v. 1, p. 553.

**365  THE DEAD BRIDEGROOM CLAIMS HIS BRIDE.** A girl had promised to marry a man who went off to war. When he did come back, seven years later, he pulled her onto his horse and rode off furiously. He was dead, and wanted to take her to his grave, but she escaped by hiding in an open tomb. (Lindow)

> Deacon of Myrka, The. Simpson, *Icelandic Folktales and Legends,* p. 132.
> Dead Bridegroom, The. Lindow, *Swedish Legends and Folktales,* no. 98.
> Drowned Sailor of Saint Levan. Deane and Shaw, *Folklore of Cornwall,* p. 108.
> Fair Maid of Clifton. Briggs, *DBF,* pt. B, v. 1, p. 449.
> Lovers of Porthangwartha, The. Briggs, *DBF,* pt. B, v. 1, p. 526.
> Pleasant and Delightful. Deane and Shaw, *Folklore of Cornwall,* p. 81.
> Seven Bones. Musick, *Green Hills of Magic,* no. 20.
> Spectre Bridegroom, The. Briggs, *DBF,* pt. B, v. 1, p. 577.
> Suffolk Miracle, The. Briggs, *DBF,* pt. B, v. 1, p. 586.
> Yorkshire Jack. Briggs, *DBF,* pt. B, v. 1, p. 603.

**366  THE CORPSE CLAIMS ITS PROPERTY.** A man married a woman who had an arm of gold. She died, and following the funeral the man dug up her body and cut off the golden arm. The next night his wife's ghost came to him and demanded the return of her golden arm. (Jacobs)

> Big Black Toe. Roberts, *South from Hell,* no. 12C.
> Bone, The. Briggs, *DBF,* pt. A, v. 2, p. 512.
> Chunk o' Meat. Chase, *Grandfather Tales,* no. 25.
> Ghost Story, A. Harris, *Nights with Uncle Remus,* no. 29.
> Give Me My Bone, Gunna! Simpson, *Icelandic Folktales and Legends,* p. 111.
> Golden Arm, The (England). Clarkson and Cross, *World Folktales,* no. 30.

Golden Arm, The. Briggs, *DBF,* pt. A, v. 2, p. 530.
Golden Arm, The. Campbell, *Cloudwalking Country,* p. 175.
Golden Arm, The. Jacobs, *English Fairy Tales,* p. 138.
Golden Arm, The. Roberts, *South from Hell,* no. 12A.
Grandfather's Liver, The. Fowke, *Folklore of Canada,* p. 267.
Lady That Went to Church, The. Briggs, *DBF,* pt. A, v. 2, p. 539.
Lady with the Golden Arm, The. Fowke, *Folklore of Canada,* p. 267.
Lazy Maiden, The. Afanasyev, *Russian Fairy Tales,* p. 423.
Liver, The. Briggs, *DBF,* pt. A, v. 2, p. 541.
Ma Uncle Sandy. Briggs, *DBF,* pt. A, v. 2, p. 542.
My Jawbones! Simpson, *Icelandic Folktales and Legends,* p. 112.
Old Man at the White House, The. Briggs, *DBF,* pt. A, v. 2, p. 550.
Peggy with the Wooden Leggy. Briggs, *DBF,* pt. A, v. 2, p. 555.
Saddaedda. Crane, *Italian Popular Tales,* no. 73.
Shroud, The. Grimm, *Other Tales,* p. 121.
Strange Visitor, The. Briggs, *DBF,* pt. A, v. 2, p. 506.
Strange Visitor, The. Jacobs, *English Fairy Tales,* p. 179.
Taily-po. Harris, *Uncle Remus Returns,* no. 3.
Tailypo. Botkin, *American Folklore,* p. 679.
Teeny-Tiny (I, II). Briggs, *DBF,* pt. A, v. 2, p. 561.
Teeny-Tiny. Jacobs, *English Fairy Tales,* p. 57.
Young Rake, The. Pourrat, *French Tales,* p. 186.

**400  THE QUEST FOR A LOST BRIDE.** Esben Ash-Rake observed three girls dressed like swans soar through the air and land. Taking off their feathers, they danced about the meadow. He silently took their feathery robes, and then told the girls that he would return them only if one of them would marry him. The youngest, Maid Lena, agreed. Then the swan-girls disappeared into the air. Esben made preparations for his wedding, but he soon learned that he would have to fetch his bride from a castle located south of the sun, west of the moon, and in the center of the earth. Undaunted, he set forth. On the way he came into the possession of a hat that made him invisible, boots that would carry him a hundred miles with each step, and a knife that would kill any enemy. With the help of these magic items, Esben found his bride and killed the witch. (Thompson, "Maid Lena") Cf. type 413.

Adventures of Hasan of Basrah, The. Mathers, *1001 Nights,* v. 3, p. 170.
Bird Maiden, The. Lindell, *Folk Tales from Kammu,* II, no. 2.
Country of the Beautiful Gardens, The. Villa, *100 Armenian Tales,* no. 18.
Dove Girl, The. Calvino, *Italian Folktales,* no. 164.
Drummer, The. Grimm, *Tales,* no. 193.
Enchanted Palace, The. Calvino, *Italian Folktales,* no. 66.
Gallant Szérus, The. Dégh, *Folktales of Hungary,* no. 8.
Grey Castle, The. Briggs, *DBF,* pt. A, v. 1, p. 298.
Handsome András. Dégh, *Folktales of Hungary,* no. 3.
Iron Pestle and the Girl with the Donkey's Head. Bushnaq, *Arab Folktales,* p. 158.
Iron Pot, The. Massignon, *Folktales of France,* no. 17.
José Guerné. Pino-Saavedra, *Folktales of Chile,* no. 13.
Maid Lena (Denmark). Cole, *Best-Loved Folktales,* no. 83.
Maid Lena (Denmark). Thompson, *100 Favorite Folktales,* no. 20.

Maiden Tsar, The. Afanasyev, *Russian Fairy Tales*, p. 229.

Nine Pea-Hens and the Golden Apples, The (Serbia). Lang, *Violet Fairy Book*, p. 55.

Old Witch, The. Grimm, *Other Tales*, p. 146.

Princess of the Blue Mountains, The. Briggs, *DBF*, pt. A, v. 1, p. 448.

Seal's Skin, The. Simpson, *Icelandic Folktales and Legends*, p. 100.

Seven Young Sky Women (Philippines). Dorson, *Folktales around the World*, p. 259.

Slim Yellow Catfish, A. Randolph, *The Devil's Pretty Daughter*, p. 9.

Snake Princess, The. Campbell, *Cloudwalking Country*, p. 151.

Son of the Widow, The. Dawkins, *Modern Greek Folktales*, no. 19.

Soria Moria Castle. Asbjørnsen and Moe, *East o' the Sun*, p. 396.

Soria Moria Castle. Asbjørnsen and Moe, *Norwegian Folktales*, p. 67.

Swan Maidens, The. Jacobs, *European Folk and Fairy Tales*, no. 12.

Three Princesses in Whittenland, The. Christiansen, *Folktales of Norway*, p. 153.

Three Princesses of Whiteland, The (Norway). Thompson, *100 Folktales*, no. 21.

Three Princesses of Whiteland, The. Asbjørnsen and Moe, *East o' the Sun, p. 181.*

Twelve Doves on the Mountain of the Sun, The. Mathias and Raspa, *Italian Folktales in America*, no. 13.

Wild Edric. Briggs, *DBF*, pt. A, v. 1, p. 574.

Wild Edric. Briggs, *DBF*, pt. B, v. 1, p. 405.

Woman Who Came Down from Heaven, The. Seki, *Folktales of Japan*, no. 23.

**400*   THE SWAN MAIDEN.** A young hunter saw three swans alight, cast off their feathery attire, and then swim about in the sound as beautiful maidens. He stole one of their feathery garbs. Soon thereafter two of them put on their feathers and flew off. Ignoring her pleas to return her attire, the youth put his cloak about the third maiden and took her home. They were soon married. Seven years later he brought the swan feathers from their hiding place and showed them to his wife. She had scarcely touched them when she once again turned into a swan and took flight through an open window, never to return. (Booss) Cf. type 413 and Cf. Christiansen, *Migratory Legends,* type 4080.

Adventures of Hasan of Basrah, The. Mathers, *1001 Nights*, v. 3, p. 170.

Bird-Maidens. Clouston, *Popular Tales*, v. 1, p. 182.

Gwraig and the Three Blows, The (Wales). Bødker, *European Folk Tales*, p. 120.

Seal's Skin, The (Iceland). Cole, *Best-Loved Folktales*, no. 86.

Shemsi Bani, Padishah of Pigeons. Walker and Uysal, *Tales in Turkey*, p. 104.

Swan Maiden, The (Sweden). Booss, *Scandinavian Tales*, p. 248.

Swan-Maidens. Baring-Gould, *Curious Myths of the Middle Ages*, no. 21.

**401   THE GIRL TRANSFORMED INTO AN ANIMAL.** A mother said to a naughty little girl: "I wish you were a raven." In that instant, she turned into a raven and flew away. One day a man was in the forest, and the raven told him her story, begging him to set her free.

To do so, the man would have to come to the golden castle of Stromberg. Undaunted, the man set forth. —Continues as type 400. (Grimm)

Beauty and the Beast. Saucier, *French Louisiana,* no. 5.
Cat 'n Mouse! Chase, *The Jack Tales,* no. 14.
Enchanted Man, The. Briggs, *DBF,* pt. A, v. 1, p. 222.
Jack and the Old Witch. Randolph, *The Talking Turtle,* p. 130.
Raven, The. Grimm, *Tales,* no. 93.
Singing Bride, The. Briggs, *DBF,* pt. A, v. 1, p. 486.

**401A THE ENCHANTED PRINCESS IN HER CASTLE.** To free a princess from evil spirits, Ivan subjected himself to three nights of torment in her castle. (Afanasyev)

Enchanted Princess, The. Afanasyev, *Russian Fairy Tales,* p. 600.
King of the Golden Mountain, The. Grimm, *Tales,* no. 92.
King's Son Who Is Afraid of Nothing, The. Grimm, *Tales,* no. 121.
Princess; or, The Fair One of the World. Dawkins, *Modern Greek Folktales,* no. 6.
Queen of the Three Mountains of Gold. Calvino, *Italian Folktales,* no. 55.
Soria Moria Castle. Asbjørnsen and Moe, *East o' the Sun,* p. 396.
Soria Moria Castle. Asbjørnsen and Moe, *Norwegian Folktales,* p. 67.
Three Black Princesses, The. Grimm, *Tales,* no. 137.
Tritill, Litill, and the Birds (Hungary). Lang, *Crimson Fairy Book,* p. 213.
Two Sea Merchants, The. Calvino, *Italian Folktales,* no. 171.

**402 THE ANIMAL BRIDE.** A king with three sons decreed that the one who brought home the most beautiful wife should inherit his kingdom. Then he blew three feathers into the air to determine which way they should go. The youngest boy's feather lead him to a toad, who changed into a beautiful woman. He married her and inherited the kingdom. (Grimm, no. 63)

Animal Wife, The. Dawkins, *Modern Greek Folktales,* no. 18A.
Doll i' the Grass. Asbjørnsen and Moe, *East o' the Sun,* p. 374.
Enchanted Lake, The. Megas, *Folktales of Greece,* no. 24.
Forest Bride, The (Finland). Cole, *Best-Loved Folktales,* no. 88.
Fresh Loaf, The; or, The Three-Legged Lamb. Gmelch and Kroup, *To Shorten the Road,* p. 83.
Frog Princess, The (Russia). Thompson, *100 Favorite Folktales,* no. 22.
Frog Princess, The. Afanasyev, *Russian Fairy Tales,* p. 119.
Frog, The (Italy). Lang, *Violet Fairy Book,* p. 311.
Golden Hair; or, The Little Frog. Massignon, *Folktales of France,* no. 29.
Little Frog, The. Pino-Saavedra, *Folktales of Chile,* no. 14.
Little Frog, The. Pourrat, *Treasury of French Tales,* p. 19.
Monkey Palace. Calvino, *Italian Folktales,* no. 63.
Mouse Bride, The (Finland). Booss, *Scandinavian Tales,* p. 541.
Petit Jean and the Frog. Delarue, *French Folktales,* p. 108.
Piece of Cloth, The. Massignon, *Folktales of France,* no. 23.
Poor Miller's Boy and the Cat, The. Grimm, *Tales,* no. 106.
Prince and the Tortoise, The. Mathers, *1001 Nights,* v. 4, p. 202.
Prince Who Married a Frog, The. Calvino, *Italian Folktales,* no. 14.
Puddocky (Germany). Lang, *Green Fairy Book,* p. 222.

Rat, The (Sweden). Bødker, *European Folk Tales*, p. 23.
Sea Tortoise, The. Dawkins, *Modern Greek Folktales*, no. 18B.
Seven Colors. Pino-Saavedra, *Folktales of Chile*, no. 7.
Three Feathers; or, Jack and the Puddock (I, II). Briggs, *DBF*, pt. A, v. 1, p.
   513.
Three Feathers, The. Grimm, *Tales*, no. 63.
Ti-Jean and the Big White Cat. Fowke, *Folklore of Canada*, p. 53.
Turtle Skin, The. Villa, *100 Armenian Tales*, no. 23.
White Cat, The (France). Cole, *Best-Loved Folktales*, no. 5.

**402A\* THE SERPENT PRINCESS.** King Arthur promised Sir
   Gawain in marriage to a hideously ugly woman. When they were in
   bed together she turned into a beautiful girl. She had been cursed by a
   jealous stepmother, but Gawain's acceptance of her broke the spell.
   (Briggs)

   Bewitched Princess, The. Musick, *Green Hills of Magic*, no. 32.
   Laidley Worm of Spindleston Heughs, The. Briggs, *DBF*, pt. A, v. 1, p. 371.
   Laidly Worm of Spindleston Heugh, The. Jacobs, *English Fairy Tales*, p. 183.
   Marriage of Sir Gawain, The. Briggs, *DBF*, pt. A, v. 1, p. 409.
   Marriage of Sir Gawain, The. Rowling, *Folklore of the Lake District*, p. 48.

**403 THE BLACK AND THE WHITE BRIDE.** The Lord asked two
   stepsisters the way to the village. One refused to help, and the Lord
   cursed her with black skin. The other was helpful, and the Lord
   granted her three wishes: beauty, a purse that would never grow
   empty, and the promise of heaven. The fair girl had a brother who
   worked for the king. The king saw the girl's picture and fell in love.
   A wedding was planned as soon as the bride could come. On the way to
   the castle, the stepmother and the black girl pushed the beautiful girl
   from a bridge. A white duck emerged from the water. The black girl
   put on the bride's clothes and married the king, whose sight had been
   clouded by the stepmother's magic arts. The white duck revealed
   herself to the king, ultimately changing back to the white bride. Now
   knowing what had happened, the king had the witch and her black
   daughter put to death, and he married the white bride. (Grimm)
   —Note: Tales of this type introduced with the episode of the wishes (as
   above) are classified 403A. Those introduced with an episode of a
   woman sending her stepdaughter to find strawberries under the snow
   (for example: Grimm, "The Three Little Men in the Forest" and
   Campbell, "A Queen That Got Her Just Deserts") are classified 403B.
   Cf. types 533, 450.

   Beautiful Stepdaughter, The. Dawkins, *Modern Greek Folktales*, no. 11.
   Belmiele and Belsole. Calvino, *Italian Folktales*, no. 101.
   Black Bride and the White Bride, The (Italy). Bødker, *European Folk Tales*, p.
      176.
   Brother and Sister. Megas, *Folktales of Greece*, no. 25.
   Bushy Bride. Asbjørnsen and Moe, *East o' the Sun*, p. 322.
   Delgadina and the Snake. Pino-Saavedra, *Folktales of Chile*, no. 15.

**405 JORINDE AND JORINGEL.** A witch turned Jorinde into a bird, and locked her in a cage. Her beloved, Joringel, dreamed of a blood-red flower that could break the witch's spell. He searched until he found such a flower, and took it to the witch's castle. She had no power over him. Inside he found thousands of birds in cages and touched them with the flower, whereupon they turned back into maidens. He took Jorinde back home, and they lived happily together. (Grimm)

**405A\* THE ENCHANTED GIRL SAVED BY VARIOUS MEANS.** A man and his wife left their seven daughters at home with instructions to not open the door. The six older girls disobeyed, and a witch ate them. The youngest escaped, making her way to the house of an ogre, who kept her as a daughter. A neighboring prince saw her at the window and asked for her hand in marriage. The ogre agreed, but he commanded the girl to speak to the prince only if he swore by the head of Buk Ettemsuch. The wedding followed, but soon the prince grew suspicious of his wife who refused to speak, so he threatened to get a new wife. In the end, however, he learned of the oath, asked his wife to speak to him by the head of Buk Ettemsuch, and the curse was broken. (Lang)

> Daughter of Buk Ettemsuch (Tripoli). Lang, *Grey Fairy Book,* p. 280.
> Fair Foster Child of the Ghoul, The. Bushnaq, *Arab Folktales,* p. 174.
> Sheikh of the Lamps. Bushnaq, *Arab Folktales,* p. 201.

**407   THE GIRL AS A FLOWER.** A woman was a flower by day and a woman by night. Her husband set her free by picking her while she was in the form of a flower. (Grimm)

> Girl That Changed into a Flower Bloom. Campbell, *Cloudwalking Country,* p. 247.
> Golden Girl, The. Thundy, *South Indian Folktales,* no. 42.
> Riddling Tale, A. Grimm, *Tales,* no. 160.
> Water-Lily, The. Lang, *Blue Fairy Book,* p. 174.

**407A   THE MYRTLE CHILD.** A woman bemoaned her childlessness, stating: "If I could only bring something into the world, even a sprig of myrtle." And she did indeed give birth to a myrtle branch, which she tended in a flower pot. A prince became enamored of the plant and took it into his chamber. At night a beautiful girl emerged from the plant, and the prince married her. (Basile) —Note: Aarne and Thompson also use number 652A to classify tales of this type.

> Apple Girl. Calvino, *Italian Folktales,* no. 85.
> Girl in the Bay-Tree. Dawkins, *Modern Greek Folktales,* no. 25.
> Myrtle, The. Basile, *Pentamerone,* Day 1, Tale 2.
> Rosemary. Calvino, *Italian Folktales,* no. 161.

**407B   THE WOMAN WHO MARRIED DEATH.** A spinster, sick of life, uttered the curse: "I wish Death would marry me!" Shortly thereafter a pale man began to court her. She followed him one night and observed him eating children with his comrades. Later he asked her what she had seen, and she replied, "nothing." That night her father died. A week later he returned, and she again denied having seen anything. Then her mother died. The third time she also denied having seen anything, and she herself died. A marvelous blood-red rose grew from her grave; a prince plucked it and took it home. The flower became a beautiful girl, and the prince married her. (Ranke) Cf. type 363.

> Mrizala and Her Bridegroom, Death. Ranke, *Folktales of Germany,* no. 27.
> Pretty-Maid Ibronka. Dégh, *Folktales of Hungary,* no. 4.
> Vampire, The. Afanasyev, *Russian Fairy Tales,* p. 593.

**408   THE LOVE OF THREE ORANGES.** A prince broke an old woman's pot while playing ball, and she angrily cursed: "You will not be happy until you have found the love of three oranges." In despair the prince set out in search of the three oranges. Finally he found them. Opening the first, he saw a beautiful princess inside who asked for water. But he had none, and the princess died. The same thing happened with the second orange, so before opening the third orange, he found a fountain. Inside the third orange was the most beautiful woman. He gave her the water she asked for, and they rode away together. Before he could take her to his castle, he wanted to bring her jewels and clothing worthy of a princess. During the prince's absence, a false bride took the place of the princess from the orange, who flew away as a dove. The false bride blamed her ugliness on the sun, claiming that her former beauty would return. The dove came to the prince, and then changed back to his beautiful bride. The false bride was put to death, and the prince married the woman from the orange. (Delarue)

Bad Negress, The. Paredes, *Folktales of Mexico,* no. 33.
Girl Bare in Her Shift, The. Dawkins, *Modern Greek Folktales,* no. 1.
Girl Out of the Egg, The. Ranke, *Folktales of Germany,* no. 30.
Little Shepherd, The. Calvino, *Italian Folktales,* no. 8.
Love of the Three Oranges, The. Crane, *Italian Popular Tales,* no. 24.
Love of the Three Pomegranates, The. Calvino, *Italian Folktales,* no. 107.
Love of Three Oranges, The. Delarue, *French Folktales,* p. 126.
Lovely Ilonka (Hungary). Lang, *Crimson Fairy Book,* p. 1.
Maiden of the Tree of Raranj and Taranj, The. Bushnaq, *Arab Folktales,* p. 109.
Three Citrons, The (Italy). Thompson, *100 Favorite Folktales,* no. 24.
Three Citrons, The. Basile, *Pentamerone,* Day 5, Tale 9.
Three Magic Oranges (Costa Rica). Cole, *Best-Loved Folktales,* no. 195.
Three Oranges, The (Italy). Bødker, *European Folk Tales,* p. 178.
Young Lord and the Cucumber Girl, The. Walker and Uysal, *Tales in Turkey,* p. 64.

**409A   THE CHICKEN BRIDE.** A childless woman gave birth to a chicken. One day the chicken laid a cloth on the ground, and it turned into a palace, and she herself became a beautiful lady. A prince saw her and fell in love, but in that instant the palace became a cloth and the lady became a hen. So the prince carried the chicken into his room and made a nest for her beside his bed. When she next turned into a beautiful woman, the prince threw her chicken feathers into the fire. The spell was broken, and the two were married.

Chicken Laundress, The. Calvino, *Italian Folktales,* no. 122.

**410   SLEEPING BEAUTY.** A jealous fairy's curse caused a princess to fall into a hundred-year sleep. When the hundred years had passed, a prince awoke her with a kiss, and they were married the same day. (Grimm)

Glass Coffin, The. Grimm, *Tales,* no. 163.
Little Briar-Rose. Grimm, *Tales,* no. 50.
Neapolitan Soldier, The. Calvino, *Italian Folktales,* no. 100.
Ninth Captain's Tale, The. Mathers, *1001 Nights,* v. 4, p. 390.
Sleeping Beauty and Her Children. Calvino, *Italian Folktales,* no. 139.
Sleeping Beauty in the Wood, The (Perrault). Opie, *Classic Fairy Tales,* p. 108.
Sleeping Beauty in the Wood, The. Lang, *Blue Fairy Book,* p. 54.
Sleeping Beauty in the Wood, The. Perrault, *Fairy Tales* (trans. Carter), p. 55.
Sleeping Beauty (Sweden). Thompson, *100 Favorite Folktales,* no. 25.
Sleeping Beauty, The. Massignon, *Folktales of France,* no. 37.
Sleeping Beauty. Pino-Saavedra, *Folktales of Chile,* no. 16.
Sleeping Beauty. Roberts, *South from Hell,* no. 14.
Sun, Moon, and Talia. Basile, *Pentamerone,* Day 5, Tale 5.
Young Slave, The. Basile, *Pentamerone,* Day 2, Tale 8.

**412  THE GIRL WHOSE SOUL WAS IN HER NECKLACE.** An angel gave a necklace to a newborn baby, explaining that the girl would die if the necklace were removed from her neck. When she came of age, a prince declared his intention to marry her, but her wicked aunts tore out her eyes and put one of their daughters in her place. The heroine recovered her eyes, but then the false queen stole her necklace of life. The prince discovered his true bride near death and brought her back to life with the necklace. The wicked aunts and the false bride were put to death, and the prince married the heroine.

Fairy Child, The. Villa, *100 Armenian Tales,* no. 3.

**413  MARRIAGE BY STEALING CLOTHING.** The son of a virgin, saw a beautiful girl swimming in the river. He stole her clothes, and would not return them until she promised to marry him. Cf. types 400, 400*.

Divine Couple, A. Thundy, *South Indian Folktales,* no. 6.

**425  THE SEARCH FOR THE LOST HUSBAND.** A princess made herself a suitor from flour and sugar, with a pepper for a nose. She named him King Pepper, and sang to him until he came to life. Shortly after their marriage a queen named Turk-Dog carried King Pepper away. The princess set out to find him. On her way she acquired three magic nuts. Arriving at Turk-Dog's castle, she opened the first nut. Inside was a golden loom, which she offered to the queen, if she could spend one night with her husband. The queen agreed, but drugged King Pepper's wine, so he did not recognize his true bride. Similar gifts from the second and third nuts bought the princess more nights with King Pepper, and finally he recognized his true wife. Together they escaped to their own country. When Queen Turk-Dog discovered her loss she tore off her own head and perished. (Calvino, "The Handmade King") —Note: Convention differs in distinguishing between types 425 and 425A. Many of the tales listed below could also be categorized under type 425A.

Barbarina and the Black Snake. Mathias and Raspa, *Italian Folktales in America*, no. 1.
Beast, The. Massignon, *Folktales of France*, no. 9.
Bully Bornes. Roberts, *South from Hell*, no. 15A.
Dough Prince, The. Musick, *Green Hills of Magic*, no. 36.
Fair as the Sun. Dawkins, *More Greek Folktales*, no. 8.
Feather of Finist, the Bright Falcon, The. Afanasyev, *Russian Fairy Tales*, p. 580.
Gold Ball, The. Massignon, *Folktales of France*, no. 40.
Greenish Bird, The. Paredes, *Folktales of Mexico*, no. 34.
Handmade King, The. Calvino, *Italian Folktales*, no. 140.
Khastakhumar and Bibinagar (Afghanistan). Dorson, *Folktales around the World*, p. 230.
Magic Box, The. Villa, *100 Armenian Tales*, no. 25.
Man Who Came Out Only at Night, The. Calvino, *Italian Folktales*, no. 4.
Mountains of Mogollón, The. Espinosa, *Folklore of Spain in the American Southwest*, p. 180.
Pinto Smalto. Basile, *Pentamerone*, Day 5, Tale 3.
Serpent and the Grape-Grower's Daughter, The. Delarue, *French Folktales*, p. 177.
Snail Choja, The. Seki, *Folktales of Japan*, no. 27.
Speckled Bull, The. O'Sullivan, *Folktales of Ireland*, no. 19.
Tamlane. Jacobs, *More English Fairy Tales*, p. 172.
Ten Serpents, The. Noy, *Folktales of Israel*, no. 58.
Three Daughters of King O'Hara. Curtin, *Myths and Folktales of Ireland*, p. 15.

**425A THE ANIMAL BRIDEGROOM.** A poor farmer was approached by a bear, who offered him great wealth in return for his daughter. The man talked his daughter into the match, and she rode away astride the beast. At the bear's castle, she learned that her husband was a bear only by day; at night he turned into a handsome man. They lived together happily, but with time she became homesick. The bear gave her leave to visit her family, but she had to promise not to talk alone with her mother. She failed to keep this promise, and the mother told her she should light a candle and look at her husband in his sleep. She did this, and drops of tallow awakened her sleeping husband. He told her that because of a spell cast on him by his stepmother, he would now have to go to a castle east of the sun and west of the moon and marry a woman with a nose three ells long. With that he disappeared. Undaunted, his true wife set out to find him. —Continues as type 425. (Asbjørnsen and Moe)

Beauty and the Beast. Saucier, *French Louisiana*, no. 5.
Beauty and the Beast. Thundy, *South Indian Folktales*, no. 51.
Black Bull of Norroway, The. Briggs, *DBF*, pt. A, v. 1, p. 155.
Black Bull of Norroway, The. Jacobs, *More English Fairy Tales*, p. 20.

Black Bull of Norroway, The. Lang, *Blue Fairy Book,* p. 380.
Brown Bear of Norway (England). Lang, *Lilac Fairy Book,* p. 118.
Crab, The. Dawkins, *Modern Greek Folktales,* no. 12.
Cupid and Psyche Legends. Clouston, *Popular Tales,* v. 1, p. 205, 469.
Cupid and Psyche. Apuleius, *The Golden Ass,* pp. 105-142.
Daughter of the Skies, The. Campbell, *West Highlands,* v. 1, p. 208.
East o' the Sun and West o' the Moon (Norway). Thompson, *100 Folktales,*
    no. 26.
East o' the Sun and West o' the Moon. Asbjørnsen and Moe, *East o' the Sun,*
    p. 22.
Enchanted Pig, The (Romania). Lang, *Red Fairy Book,* p. 104.
Enchanted Snake, The. Lang, *Green Fairy Book,* p. 186.
Eros and Psyche (Greece). Cole, *Best-Loved Folktales,* no. 43.
Filo d'Oro and Filomena. Calvino, *Italian Folktales,* no. 136.
Girl That Married a Flop-Eared Hound Dog. Campbell, *Cloudwalking
    Country,* p. 147.
Glass Mountain, The. Briggs, *DBF,* pt. A, v. 1, p. 271.
Glass Mountains, The. Briggs, *DBF,* pt. A, v. 1, p. 274.
He-Goat and the King's Daughter, The. Mathers, *1001 Nights,* v. 4, p. 194.
Hoodie-Crow, The (Scotland). Lang, *Lilac Fairy Book,* p. 336.
Hoodie, The. Campbell, *West Highlands,* v. 1, p. 64.
Hurleburlebutz. Grimm, *Other Tales,* p. 91.
Iron Stove, The. Grimm, *Tales,* no. 127.
King of Love, The. Crane, *Italian Popular Tales,* no. 1.
King's Son in the Henhouse, The. Calvino, *Italian Folktales,* no. 174.
Little Old Rusty Cook Stove in the Woods. Campbell, *Cloudwalking Country,*
    p. 59.
Master Semolina. Megas, *Folktales of Greece,* no. 27.
Monkeys and Men. Thundy, South Indian Folktales, no. 37.
Mouse with the Long Tail. Calvino, *Italian Folktales,* no. 182.
Musk and Amber. Dawkins, *Modern Greek Folktales,* no. 13.
Padlock, The. Basile, *Pentamerone,* Day 2, Tale 9.
Prince Swan. Grimm, *Other Tales,* p. 85.
Prince White Hog. Thomas, *It's Good to Tell You,* no. 7.
Prince Who Was Bewitched, The. Grimm, *Other Tales,* p. 99.
Red Bull of Norroway, The. Briggs, *DBF,* pt. A, v. 1, p. 458.
Roarin' Bull of Orange. Gmelch and Kroup, *To Shorten the Road,* p. 147.
Serpent, The. Basile, *Pentamerone,* Day 2, Tale 5.
Seven Bits of Bacon-Rind, The. Basile, *Pentamerone,* Day 4, Tale 4.
Sir Fiorante, Magician. Crane, *Italian Popular Tales,* no. 20.
Snake Prince, The (India). Lang, *Olive Fairy Book,* p. 247.
Snake, The. Tolstoy, *Fables and Fairy Tales,* p. 55.
Snotty Goat, The. Afanasyev, *Russian Fairy Tales,* p. 200.
Sprig of Rosemary, The (Spain). Lang, *Pink Fairy Book,* p. 230.
Ten Serpents, The. Noy, *Folktales of Israel,* no. 58.
Three Feathers. Jacobs, *More English Fairy Tales,* p. 37.
Unseen Bridegroom, The. Jacobs, *European Folk and Fairy Tales,* no. 17.
White Wolf, The. Lang, *Grey Fairy Book,* p. 168.
White-Bear Whittington. Randolph, *Who Blowed Up the Church House?,* p.
    173.
White-Bear-King-Valemon. Asbjørnsen and Moe, *Norwegian Folktales,* p.
    150.

**425C  BEAUTY AND THE BEAST.** A merchant stopped at a garden,
and seeing no one, plucked a rose for his daughter. A huge beast
appeared and declared that for the stolen rose the merchant must either

forfeit his life or surrender his daughter. So the girl went to live with the beast. He treated her well, and with time she even came to like him. One day she found him lying motionless. Throwing herself at him, she said: "Why did you have to die? I love you." With that a handsome prince emerged. A magician had caused him to become an ugly beast until a girl, of her own accord, should say that she loved him. The enchantment was now broken, and they married and lived happily ever after. (Jacobs)

Beauty and the Beast (de Beaumont). Opie, *Classic Fairy Tales,* p. 182.
Beauty and the Beast (de Villeneuve). Lang, *Blue Fairy Book,* p. 100.
Beauty and the Beast (France). Cole, *Best-Loved Folktales,* no. 2.
Beauty and the Beast. Jacobs, *European Folk and Fairy Tales,* no. 5.
Belle-Rose. Pourrat, *Treasury of French Tales,* p. 220.
Bellinda and the Monster. Calvino, *Italian Folktales,* no. 59.
Bunch of Laurela Blooms for a Present, A. Campbell, *Cloudwalking Country,* p. 228.
Gift to the Youngest Daughter, The. Dawkins, *Modern Greek Folktales,* no. 15.
Singing, Springing Lark, The. Grimm, *Tales,* no. 88.
Small-Tooth Dog, The (England). Bødker, *European Folk Tales,* p. 114.
Small-Tooth Dog, The. Briggs and Tongue, *Folktales of England,* no. 1.
Small-Tooth Dog, The. Briggs, *DBF,* pt. A, v. 1, p. 487.
Sorrow and Love. Briggs, *DBF,* pt. A, v. 1, p. 495.
Three Feathers, The. Briggs, *DBF,* pt. A, v. 1, p. 511.
Whitebear Whittington. Chase, *Grandfather Tales,* no. 5.
Zelinda and the Monster. Crane, *Italian Popular Tales,* no. 2.

## 425D  A WIFE FINDS HER LOST HUSBAND BY KEEPING AN INN.
A princess's husband was a crab by day and a man by night. She revealed this secret to her mother, and her husband disappeared. After a long search for him, she opened an inn by a crossroads, so she could ask all travelers if they had seen her husband. Finally a traveler told her about a mysterious underground castle. She found the place and broke her husband's enchantment. (Megas)

Amorous Prince Outwitted. Thundy, *South Indian Folktales,* no. 55.
Crab, The. Megas, *Folktales of Greece,* no. 28.
Shemsi Bani, Padishah of Pigeons. Walker and Uysal, *Tales in Turkey,* p. 104.

## 425F  THE THIEVING BIRD.
A dove stole a princess's comb, her hair clasp, and her scarf. She followed him, and he turned into a handsome youth, who told her that he could only be disenchanted if she would sit in a certain hut and keep her eyes trained on a distant mountain without a break for a year, a month, and a day. She did this, and when his enchantment was broken, the two were married. (Calvino)

Princess's Kerchief, The. Dawkins, *Modern Greek Folktales,* no. 16.
Serpent Son, The (Italy). Bødker, *European Folk Tales,* p. 182.

Shemsi Bani, Padishah of Pigeons. Walker and Uysal, *Tales in Turkey,* p. 104.
Thieving Dove, The. Calvino, *Italian Folktales,* no. 153.

**425G A SERVANT TAKES THE SLEEPING HEROINE'S PLACE.** A princess was promised marriage to a king if she would keep watch over his body a year, three months, and a week. She watched faithfully until only one week was left. Then she decided to sleep a little, instructing her slave girl to watch carefully and to awaken her on the fourth day. But the slave let her sleep the whole week. When the king came to life, the slave claimed that she herself had watched the entire time, so he married her. However, he discovered the truth, had the deceitful girl burned to death, and married the deserving bride. (Calvino)

Dead Man's Palace, The. Calvino, *Italian Folktales,* no. 32.
Nourie Hadig. Villa, *100 Armenian Tales,* no. 2.
Prince in a Swoon, The. Dawkins, *Modern Greek Folktales,* no. 32.
Prince in a Swoon, The. Dawkins, *More Greek Folktales,* no. 5.
Princess Zoza Restores Prince Taddeo to Life. Basile, *Pentamerone,* Frame-Story.
Sleeping Prince, The. Megas, *Folktales of Greece,* no. 29.

**425J THE HEROINE SERVES IN HELL FOR HER BRIDEGROOM.** A woman fell in love with a man who had temporarily escaped from hell. She volunteered to serve his penance for him, and spent seven years of torment in hell. Then she returned to him, and they married. (O'Sullivan)

Man Who Was Rescued from Hell, The. O'Sullivan, *Folktales of Ireland,* no. 24.
Woman Who Went to Hell, The (Ireland). Bødker, *European Folk Tales,* p. 136.

**425L THE HUSBAND WITH A LOCK IN HIS NAVEL.** A girl married the Lord of the World Below. Her sister told her that her husband had a key in his navel, and that by turning it she could see the whole world. She did this, but it nearly killed her husband, and the next day he put her out. After many adventures she returned, and he accepted her again as his wife. (Dawkins)

Lord of the World Below, The. Dawkins, *Modern Greek Folktales,* no. 17.
Padlock, The. Basile, *Pentamerone,* Day 2, Tale 9.
Sun and His Wife, The. Megas, *Folktales of Greece,* no. 26.

**425N THE BIRD HUSBAND.** A crow told a princess that he was a prince under enchantment, and that she could help him by being his companion in a haunted castle. By silently enduring the torments of the evil spirits in the castle she freed the prince from his spell, and they lived happily together for a hundred years.

Crow, The (Poland). Lang, *Yellow Fairy Book,* p. 92.

**426 THE TWO GIRLS, THE BEAR, AND THE DWARF.** One wintry day a bear came to the house of Snow-White and Rose-Red, wanting to warm himself. He was so kind and gentle that they became quite attached to him. One day the sisters came upon a dwarf with a bag of gems. The bear suddenly appeared and struck him dead, whereupon his bearskin fell off, and a handsome prince emerged. He said: "I was bewitched by that dwarf, who also stole my treasures. But I am now free." The prince married Snow-White and his brother married Rose-Red, and they lived together happily. (Grimm)

Lion and the Frog, The. Grimm, *Other Tales,* p. 93.
Snow-White and Rose-Red. Grimm, *Tales,* no. 161.

**430 THE DONKEY BRIDEGROOM.** A woman gave birth to a donkey. But it was no ordinary donkey, for he learned to play the lute so marvelously, that the king offered him his daughter in marriage. On their wedding night the donkey took off his rough skin and turned into a man before going to bed. The king's servants threw the donkey skin in the fire, and his transformation into a man was complete. (Grimm)

Camel Husband, The. Bushnaq, *Arab Folktales,* p. 188.
Donkey That Was a Boy, The. Campbell, *Cloudwalking Country,* p. 158.
Little Donkey, The. Grimm, *Tales,* no. 144.

**431 THE HOUSE IN THE FOREST.** A girl became lost and asked for shelter at a house in the woods, where an old man lived with a cock, a hen, and a cow. She failed to feed the three animals, and that night the man opened a trap door, and dropped her into the cellar. The next day the same experiences befell her sister. The third day the youngest sister arrived at the house, but she fed the three animals before going to bed. That night the little house changed into a palace and the old man into a handsome young prince. The girl's kindness had broken a spell placed on him by a witch, and he married her forthwith. (Grimm)

Hut in the Forest, The. Grimm, *Tales,* no. 169.
Leaves That Hung but Never Grew. Sampson, *Gypsy Folk Tales,* p. 33.

**432 THE PRINCE AS A BIRD.** A girl had an enchanted bean. When she opened it, a king, in the form of a bird would fly to her, bathe himself in a bath that she had prepared, and then, now a handsome man, would make love to her. The heroine's suspicious sisters secretly placed broken glass in the bath. When the bird next arrived, the glass cut him badly, and he flew away to die. The girl followed him and healed him with a magic cure. (Thompson)

Earl Mar's Daughter. Briggs, *DBF*, pt. A, v. 1, p. 221.
Earl Mar's Daughter. Jacobs, *English Fairy Tales*, p. 159.
Enchanted Prince. Espinosa, *Folklore of Spain in the American Southwest*, p. 191.
Greenish Bird, The. Paredes, *Folktales of Mexico*, no. 34.
King Bean (Italy). Thompson, *100 Favorite Folktales*, no. 27.
King Bean. Crane, *Italian Popular Tales*, no. 3.
Little Orphan Girl, The. Pino-Saavedra, *Folktales of Chile*, no. 17.
Prince Verdeprato. Basile, *Pentamerone*, Day 2. Tale 2.
Shemsi Bani, Padishah of Pigeons. Walker and Uysal, *Tales in Turkey*, p. 104.

**433A    A SERPENT CARRIES HIS BRIDE TO HIS CASTLE.** A snake came down from the hills looking for a bride. The Prophet Muhammad vouched for him, so the daughter of Omar returned with him to his palace. Later Omar visited his daughter and learned that she was living happily with her husband. (El-Shamy)

Beast That Took a Wife, The. El-Shamy, *Folktales of Egypt*, no. 20.
Crab Prince, The. Calvino, *Italian Folktales*, no. 30.
Tortoise, The. Lindell, *Folk Tales from Kammu*, II, no. 12.
Turtle and His Bride, The. Lang, *Brown Fairy Book*, p. 106.
Woman, Snake, and Sex. Thundy, *South Indian Folktales*, no. 56.

**433B    KING LINDORM.** A girl found a white snake on her father's coat. It said to her: "Climb on my back," and they set forth on a journey. At the snake's request, she cut off his head, and he turned into a prince. (Thompson) Cf. type 533*.

Girl Thrice Accursed, The. Dawkins, *Modern Greek Folktales*, no. 14.
Golden Crab (Greece). Lang, *Yellow Fairy Book*, p. 26.
King Lindorm (Sweden). Lang, *Pink Fairy Book*, p. 301.
King Lindorm (Sweden). Thompson, *100 Favorite Folktales*, no. 28.
King of Snakes, The. Villa, *100 Armenian Tales*, no. 26.
King Wivern (Denmark). Bødker, *European Folk Tales*, p. 64.
Serpent King. Calvino, *Italian Folktales*, no. 144.
Wicked Stepmother, The. Villa, *100 Armenian Tales*, p. 533.

**440    THE FROG KING.** A princess lost her golden ball in a well. A frog recovered it for her on the promise  that she would eat and sleep with him. She resisted when he came to collect his reward, but her father forced her to do what she had promised. They ate together, but instead of taking him to bed, she threw him against the wall. He fell down as a handsome prince, and the two fell asleep with pleasure. (Grimm, "The Frog King") —Note: A parallel tradition describes the frog turning into a man after the princess has slept with him for three nights. (Grimm, "The Frog Prince")

Bunch of Laurela Blooms for a Present, A. Campbell, *Cloudwalking Country,*
   p. 228.
Frog and the Princess, The. Dorson, *Buying the Wind,* p. 256.
Frog King, The; or, Iron Henry. Grimm, *Tales,* no. 1.
Frog King, The (Germany). Thompson, *100 Favorite Folktales,* no. 29.
Frog Prince, The. Briggs, *DBF,* pt. A, v. 1, p. 259.
Frog Prince, The. Grimm, *Other Tales,* p. 16.
Frog Sweetheart, The. Briggs, *DBF,* pt. A, v. 1, p. 260.
Frog-Prince, The (Grimm, Altered). Opie, *Classic Fairy Tales,* p. 241.
Frog, The. Briggs, *DBF,* pt. A, v. 1, p. 258.
Frog, The. Hyde-Chambers, *Tibetan Folk Tales,* p. 169.
Marriage, A. Thundy, *South Indian Folktales,* no. 59.
Mountains of Mogollón, The. Espinosa, *Folklore of Spain in the American
   Southwest,* p. 180.
Paddo, The. Briggs, *DBF,* pt. A, v. 1, p. 443.
Princess and the Frog, The. Falassi, *Folklore by the Fireside,* p. 39.
Queen Who Sought a Drink from a Certain Well, The. Campbell, *West
   Highlands,* v. 2, p. 141.
Toad Frog, The. Randolph, *The Devil's Pretty Daughter,* p. 91.
Toad-Bridegroom, The (Korea). Clarkson and Cross, *World Folktales,* no. 7.
Well of the World's End, The. Briggs, *DBF,* pt. A, v. 1, p. 563.
You'd Be Surprised the Trouble She Had Making Her Mother Believe It.
   Legman, *Rationale of the Dirty Joke,* vol. 1, p. 443.

**441  HANS-MY-HEDGEHOG.**  A boy who was half human and half
hedgehog herded animals in the forest.  On two occasions he showed a
lost king the way out of the woods in return for a promise of marriage
with his daughter.  He received a hostile reception at the first king's
castle, so he pricked the princess with his quills until she was bloody
and went to the second castle.  There he received a friendly welcome,
and he married this princess.  At night he took off his spiny coat, and
the king's men threw it into the fire, ending his curse.  (Grimm)

Galeotto, King of Anglia, Has a Son Who Is Born in the Shape of a Pig.
   Straparola, *Facetious Nights,* Night 2, Tale 1.
Hans-My-Hedgehog. Grimm, *Tales,* no. 108.
King Crin. Calvino, *Italian Folktales,* no. 19.
Prince Hedgehog (Russia). Cole, *Best-Loved Folktales,* no. 95.
Valiant Chanticleer, The (Sweden). Booss, *Scandinavian Tales,* p. 194.

**442  THE OLD WOMAN IN THE FOREST.**  A girl was alone in the
woods.  A dove gave her a key that opened a tree full of food.  At
nightfall the dove brought her another key that opened a tree
containing a bed.  One day the dove asked her to go to the house of an
old woman and bring back a ring that she would find there.  When the
dove touched the ring, he turned into a prince.

Old Woman in the Forest, The. Grimm, *Tales,* no. 123.

**444D\*  THE CAT HUSBAND.**  A girl discovered an underground
mansion that was occupied by a large cat.  She came to him every day,
returning to her own room at night.  One time she came after dark as

well, and discovered that by night the cat was a handsome prince. The next day she told her stepsister about the cat. The jealous stepsister killed the girl.

Enchanted Cat, The. Roberts, *South from Hell,* no. 15B.

**444\*   ENCHANTED PRINCES.** —Miscellaneous tales.

Enchanted Head, The (Asia Minor). Lang, *Brown Fairy Book,* p. 205.
Hábogi (Iceland). Lang, *Brown Fairy Book,* p. 126.
Old Witch, The. Grimm, *Other Tales,* p. 146.
Prince Ring (Iceland). Lang, *Yellow Fairy Book,* p. 237.
Wounded Lionk, The (Spain). Lang, *Pink Fairy Book,* p. 191.

**449   THE QUEEN'S DOG.** A king followed his wife to an underground palace and saw her make love with a black man. After she left, the king killed the black man, and the next morning he gave his wife her lover's head on a plate. Upon seeing the head the queen turned her husband into a dog. A merchant's daughter bathed the dog, changing him back into a man. She then gave him a magic pin with which he transformed the queen into a donkey. He made her carry heavy loads until she died. (Noy) Cf. type 871A.

Master of the White Mare, The. Mathers, *1001 Nights,* v. 4, p. 127.
Queen Who Was a Witch, The. Noy, *Folktales of Israel,* no. 51.
Sure News Is Up Ahead (Egypt). Dorson, *Folktales around the World,* p. 149.
Young Man and the Fishes, The. Mathers, *1001 Nights,* v. 1, p. 42.

**450   LITTLE BROTHER, LITTLE SISTER.** A brother and a sister ran away from their cruel stepmother into the forest. The boy drank from an enchanted spring and turned into a deer. Later a king found the girl and took her as his bride. They lived happily, together with the deer, until the wicked stepmother killed the young queen and put her own daughter in her place. The true bride returned every night to nurse her child. The king saw her and took her into his arms, bringing her back to life. The false bride and the stepmother were put to death, and the brother regained his human form. (Grimm, no. 11) Cf. types 403, 533.

Brother Who Was a Lamb, The. Massignon, *Folktales of France,* no. 41.
Cruel Stepmother, The. Ranke, *Folktales of Germany,* no. 31.
Little Boy and His Elder Sister. Dawkins, *More Greek Folktales,* no. 1.
Little Brother and Little Sister. Grimm, *Tales,* no. 11.
Little Lamb and the Little Fish, The. Grimm, *Tales,* no. 141.
My Favoritest Olden Tale. Campbell, *Cloudwalking Country,* p. 230.
Ninnillo and Nennella. Basile, *Pentamerone,* Day 5, Tale 8.
Pleiad and Star of Dawn. Dawkins, *Modern Greek Folktales,* no. 2.
Seven Oxen, The. Espinosa, *Folklore of Spain in the American Southwest,* p. 183.
Sister Alionushka, Brother Ivanushka (Russia). Thompson, *100 Folktales,* no. 30.

Sister Alionushka, Brother Ivanushka. Afanasyev, *Russian Fairy Tales*, p. 406.
Stepmother, The. Crane, *Italian Popular Tales*, no. 22.
Three Stags, The. Delarue, *French Folktales*, p. 182.
Yeghnig Aghpar. Villa, *100 Armenian Tales*, no. 33.

## 450A  THE BROTHER WHO WAS TURNED INTO A SNAKE. A
witch changed a man into a snake after he refused to become her lover.
His sister tended him until one Halloween the Fairy Queen broke the
spell, restoring the youth to his own shape.

Allison Gross. Briggs, *DBF*, pt. A, v. 1, p. 135.

## 451  THE BROTHERS WHO WERE TURNED INTO BIRDS.
Twelve princes fled at the birth of their sister, because their father had
threatened to put them to death in order to guarantee her inheritance.
Years later the princess found her brothers in their forest cottage, but
by picking twelve flowers, she turned them into ravens. This curse
could be broken only if she would remain silent for seven years. A
king married her. His mother accused her of many wicked deeds, but
because of the oath of silence she could not defend herself. Finally the
king agreed to have his wife burned at the stake. The flames were just
reaching her clothes when the seven years expired, and her brothers
returned. Now she could explain everything, and the wicked mother
was put to death. (Grimm, no. 9)

Calf with the Golden Horns, The. Calvino, *Italian Folktales*, no. 178.
Curse of the Seven Children, The. Crane, *Italian Popular Tales*, no. 11.
Girl Who Banished Seven Youths, The. Bushnaq, *Arab Folktales*, p. 119.
Magic Swan Geese, The. Afanasyev, *Russian Fairy Tales*, p. 349.
Ogre, The. Massignon, *Folktales of France*, no. 42.
Seven Brothers, The. Briggs, *DBF*, pt. A, v. 1, p. 477.
Seven Doves, The. Basile, *Pentamerone*, Day 4, Tale 8.
Seven Giant Brothers, The. Villa, *100 Armenian Tales*, no. 7.
Seven Ravens, The. Grimm, *Tales*, no. 25.
Seven Ravens, The. Megas, *Folktales of Greece*, no. 31.
Silent for Seven Years. Calvino, *Italian Folktales*, no. 31.
Six Brothers, The. Ranke, *Folktales of Germany*, no. 32.
Six Swans, The (Sweden). Thompson, *100 Folktales*, no. 31.
Six Swans, The. Grimm, *Tales*, no. 49.
Six Swans, The. Lang, *Yellow Fairy Book*, p. 4.
Strigla, The (The Gelló). Dawkins, *Modern Greek Folktales*, no. 27.
Three Shirts and a Golden Finger Ring. Campbell, *Cloudwalking Country*, p. 34.
Twelve Brothers, The. Grimm, *Tales*, no. 9.
Twelve Oxen, The. Calvino, *Italian Folktales*, no. 16.
Twelve Wild Ducks, The. Asbjørnsen and Moe, *East o' the Sun*, p. 51.
Twelve Wild Ducks, The. Asbjørnsen and Moe, *Norwegian Folktales*, p. 182.
Udea and Her Seven Brothers (Libya). Lang, *Grey Fairy Book*, p. 153.
Wild Swans, The. Andersen, *Complete Fairy Tales*, no. 13.

**460B  THE JOURNEY IN SEARCH OF LUCK.**  A poor man set forth to find God.  A wolf, a girl, and a tree asked him to find answers to their problems as well.  The wolf was always hungry, the girl unhappy, and the tree parched.  The man found God, who promised him luck and also gave him answers for the others.  The tree was parched because of a treasure buried at its roots, but the man would not take time to dig it up; instead, he wanted to find the luck promised him. The girl was advised to seek a man's love, but the traveler hurried on to find his luck.  God's message for the wolf was that he could still his hunger by eating a foolish man.  And that is what he did.  (Clarkson and Cross)  Cf. type 461.

Blocked Up. Dawkins, *Modern Greek Folktales,* no. 79A.
Chance and the Poor Man. Megas, *Folktales of Greece,* no. 46.
Foolish Man, The (Armenia). Clarkson and Cross, *World Folktales,* no. 54.
Invisible Woman, The. Thundy, *South Indian Folktales,* no. 57.
Lucky Luck (Hungary). Lang, *Crimson Fairy Book,* p. 8.
Moustafat. Saucier, *French Louisiana,* no. 12.
Search for Luck, The (2 tales). Dawkins, *Modern Greek Folktales,* no. 79.
Undying Sun, The. Dawkins, *Modern Greek Folktales,* no. 79B.

**461  THREE HAIRS FROM THE DEVIL.**  A king proclaimed that the man who brought him three hairs from the devil should marry his daughter.  A youth set out for hell, and on the way others asked him to find help for them as well.  In one town there was a tree that no longer bore golden fruit; in another there was a well of wine that had gone dry; and there was a ferryman who was weary of his endless task.  In hell, the devil's grandmother helped him find answers to his questions, and plucked three hairs from the devil for him.  On his return he told the owners of the well that they must kill a toad now living in their well; they rewarded him with gold.  He told the villagers with the tree to kill the mouse gnawing at its roots, and they too gave him gold. After the ferryman had taken him across the river, the youth told him that anyone who took hold of his oar would have to take his place. When the king saw the youth's gold, he too set forth for hell, hoping for the same fortune.  When he came to the river, the ferryman put an oar in his hand.  Since that time, the king has had to ferry.  (Grimm, no. 29)  Cf. type 460B.

Antti and the Wizard's Prophecy (Finland). Booss, *Scandinavian Tales,* p. 547.
Devil with the Three Golden Hairs, The. Grimm, *Tales,* no. 29.
Feathered Ogre, The. Calvino, *Italian Folktales,* no. 57.
Feathers from the Bird Venus, The. Ranke, *Folktales of Germany,* no. 33.
Griffin, The. Grimm, *Tales,* no. 165.
Marco the Rich and Vasily the Luckless. Afanasyev, *Russian Fairy Tales,* p. 213.
Mason Wins the Prize, The. Eberhard, *Folktales of China,* no. 20.
Phoenix, The. Grimm, *Other Tales,* p. 27.
Queen of the Planets, The. O'Sullivan, *Folktales of Ireland,* no. 37.

Rich Man and His Son-in-Law, The (Sweden). Thompson, *100 Folktales*, no. 32.

Rich Peter the Pedlar. Asbjørnsen and Moe, *East o' the Sun*, p. 199.

Seven Doves, The. Basile, *Pentamerone*, Day 4, Tale 8.

Three Gold Hairs from The Devil, The. Massignon, *Folktales of France*, no. 24.

Three Wonderful Beggars, The (Serbia). Lang, *Violet Fairy Book*, p. 23.

Wife of the Gandharva in the Waters. O'Flaherty, *Tales of Sex and Violence*, p. 87.

## 461A  A MAN JOURNEYS TO GOD SEEKING ADVICE.

An old couple had no children, so the man set forth to find God and ask for a child. On the way he met others who also wanted advice from God: a young woman who had no suitors, a stream with bitter water, and a tree that bore only bad apples. Finally he came to an aged dervish who told him what the others should do and gave him an apple, promising that if he shared it with his wife, she would bare him a child. He helped the young woman, the stream, and the tree, but he ate the apple himself. Some time later a small box came out of his throat, and a voice came from the box, asking for the hand of the princess. —Continues as type 425. (Villa)

Magic Box, The. Villa, *100 Armenian Tales*, no. 25.

Prince Who Would Seek Immortality (Hungary). Lang, *Crimson Fairy Book*, p. 178.

## 463A*  A PRINCE SEEKS HIS FATHER'S LOST FRIEND.

Prince, a King, and a Horse, A. Dégh, *Folktales of Hungary*, no. 5.

## 465  A KING TRIES TO STEAL A POOR MAN'S WIFE.

A king desired a fisherman's beautiful wife. Calling the poor man to the palace, he commanded him to produce twelve fierce lions or to forfeit his wife. The wife gave her husband a seal, which he was to strike on a certain rock. He followed her instructions, and the twelve fierce lions appeared. The king gave him other difficult tasks as well, but the magic seal always came to his aid. Finally the king commanded him to capture the sister of the seven giants. The fisherman succeeded in this task too, and upon their return, the giantess killed the king. Then the fisherman became king, and no one tried to take his beautiful wife from him again. (Walker and Uysal) —Note: Many tales listed under type 465A also contain the motif of the man persecuted because of his beautiful wife. Cf. type 571B.

Emelyan and the Empty Drum. Tolstoy, *Fables and Fairy Tales*, p. 89.

Huntsman, The. Villa, *100 Armenian Tales*, no. 15.

Mason Wins the Prize, The. Eberhard, *Folktales of China*, no. 20.

One Sesame Seed, The. El-Shamy, *Folktales of Egypt*, no. 3.

Pig That Warms the Ocean, The. Eberhard, *Folktales of China*, no. 25.

Son of the Fisherman, The. Walker and Uysal, *Tales in Turkey*, p. 55.

Third Captain's Tale, The. Mathers, *1001 Nights,* v. 4, p. 354.
Turtle Skin, The. Villa, *100 Armenian Tales,* no. 23.
Wife's Portrait, The. Seki, *Folktales of Japan,* no. 48.

## 465A-D QUESTS FOR THE IMPOSSIBLE.

In order to protect his wife from the desires of a monarch or to gain a wife for himself, the hero must fulfill a series of seemingly impossible tasks.

### 465A THE QUEST FOR THE UNKNOWN.

Animal Wife, The (Greece). Thompson, *100 Folktales,* no. 33.
Danilo the Luckless. Afanasyev, *Russian Fairy Tales,* p. 255.
Go I Know Not Wither, Bring Back I Know Not What. Afanasyev, *Russian Fairy Tales,* p. 504.
Queen That Got Her Just Deserts, A. Campbell, *Cloudwalking Country,* p. 221.
Turtle and the Chickpea, The. Megas, *Folktales of Greece,* no. 30.
Vaino and the Swan Princess (Finland). Booss, *Scandinavian Tales,* p. 528.
Woman Who Came Down from Heaven, The. Seki, *Folktales of Japan,* no. 23.

### 465B THE QUEST FOR THE LIVING HARP.

Wise Wife, The. Afanasyev, *Russian Fairy Tales,* p. 521.

### 465C A JOURNEY TO THE OTHER WORLD.

Bhrgu's Journey in the Other World. O'Flaherty, *Tales of Sex and Violence,* p. 32.

## 468 THE PRINCESS IN THE TREE THAT REACHED THE SKY.

A king had a tree that reached the sky. He promised a great reward to anyone who could climb to the top and bring him back some of its fruit. A poor swineherd climbed the tree and discovered a different realm. Following many adventures (types 554, 314, 552A), he married a princess from that realm, then returned to earth. The fruit he brought back made the king young again. —Note: For other tales with plants reaching to heaven see types 328, 804A, 1960G.

Tree That Reached Up to the Sky, The. Dégh, *Folktales of Hungary,* no. 6.
Tree That Reached Up to the Sky, The. Dégh, *Studies,* p. 263f.

## 470 FRIENDS IN LIFE AND DEATH.

. Two friends swore that they would never part, not even in death, but one of them soon died. The other was to be married, and—in keeping with the promise—he fetched his friend from the graveyard to serve as his best man. After the wedding ceremony the groom walked his friend back to his grave, but he slipped and broke his neck, and that was the end of him. (Thompson)

Friends in Life and Death (Norway). Thompson, *100 Folktales,* no. 34.

Invited Guest, The. Musick, *Green Hills of Magic,* no. 47.
Isaac Haw and George Villiers. Briggs, *DBF,* pt. B, v. 1, p. 501.
It Serves Me Right! El-Shamy, *Folktales of Egypt,* no. 12.
Lord Middleton and Bocconi. Briggs, *DBF,* pt. B, v. 1, p. 524.
One Night in Paradise. Calvino, *Italian Folktales,* no. 40.

**470\*   RETURNING FROM THE LAND OF THE IMMORTALS.**
Usheen, pursuing a deer, fell into an underground realm where one
could spend a thousand years without aging a day. After a year, or so
it seemed, he requested permission to visit his homeland, and they gave
him a horse, warning him not to dismount. Back in his own country,
he discovered that his friends were long dead and that his house had
crumbled to the earth. Forgetting the warning, he climbed from the
horse, but in an instant the years came upon him, and he fell to the
ground, a helpless old man. Cf. type 766.

Usheen's Return to Ireland. Glassie, *Irish Folktales,* no. 111.

**470A   A SKELETON IS INVITED TO A WEDDING.**   A man
digging in a churchyard found a giant thigh-bone and said, as a joke:
"It would be great fun to have this fellow as a wedding guest." Later
the man married, and a huge fellow appeared at the celebration,
warning the bridegroom not to sneer at dead men's bones. Thanks to
the clever bride, the ghost was locked in at outbuilding before he could
harm her husband. (Simpson)

Bridegroom and the Dead Man, The. Simpson, *Icelandic Folktales,* p. 115.
True Thomas. Briggs, *DBF,* pt. B, v. 1, p. 393.

**471   THE BRIDGE TO THE OTHER WORLD.**   A king promised his
daughter to anyone who could tend his seven foals for a day. Two
brothers tried and failed, but the youngest succeeded, following the
horses across a bridge to another realm. He learned that the horses
were enchanted princes, brothers of the princess he was to marry.
Upon his return he broke the enchantment by cutting off the horses'
heads. (Christiansen)

Seven Foals, The. Christiansen, *Folktales of Norway,* p. 169.
Sheep and the Ram, The (Canada). Dorson, *Folktales around the World,* p.
  450.
Woman with the Three Children, The. Delarue, *French Folktales,* p. 257.

**471A   A BIRD TURNS CENTURIES INTO MINUTES.**   An old
stonemason working on a church paused to listen to the marvelous
song of a bird. He turned to resume his work, but discovered that the
church was finished, with people praying inside. A shaft of light
appeared, and he heard a voice: "That's your ladder to paradise; it's
been waiting for you for three hundred years." (Briggs, "The
Stonemason of the Chartons")

Noontide Ghost, The. Briggs, *DBF*, pt. A, v. 1, p. 426.
Priest Who Had One Small Glimpse of Glory. Paredes, *Folktales of Mexico*,
   no. 38.
Stonemason of the Chartons, The. Briggs, *DBF*, pt. A, v. 1, p. 498.

**471A\*   A VISIT IN HELL.** A wealthy peasant died and went to hell,
leaving two pots of money buried. One day a fiddler accidentally fell
into hell, and the peasant told him about the treasure, instructing him
that it should be given to the poor. The devils forced the fiddler to
play for three years (it seemed to him like three days). When his
strings broke, he escaped, claiming that he would go home and return
with new strings. He told the peasants' sons about the buried treasure,
and they used it for good purposes, thus saving their father. Cf. type
953.

Fiddler in Hell, The. Afanasyev, *Russian Fairy Tales*, p. 180.

**475   HEATING HELL'S KITCHEN.** In return for a promise of
wealth, a discharged soldier agreed to tend the fires in hell's kitchen
for seven years. In one pot he found his former corporal, in another
his former ensign, and in a third his former general, so he threw extra
wood onto the fires. When his time was up the devil rewarded him
with a sack full of sweepings. Back on earth the sweepings turned into
gold. (Grimm) Cf. types 360, 361.

Devil's Sooty Brother, The. Grimm, *Tales*, no. 100.
Legend of Twardowski, The. Musick, *Green Hills of Magic*, no. 1.
Magic Shirt, The. Afanasyev, *Russian Fairy Tales*, p. 110.

**476\*   A MIDWIFE (OR GODMOTHER) FOR THE ELVES.** Elves
invited a girl to hold a child for them at its christening. She stayed at
the celebration for three days, or so she thought. Upon returning
home, she discovered that she had been away for seven years.
(Grimm) Cf. types 503, 503\*, 504, and Christiansen, *Migratory
Legends*, type 5070.

Elves, The. Grimm, *Tales*, no. 39/II.
Fairy Frog, The. O'Sullivan, *Folktales of Ireland*, no. 26.
Fairy Midwife, The. Briggs and Tongue, *Folktales of England*, no. 11.
Fairy Midwife, The (I, II). Briggs, *DBF*, pt. B, v.1, p. 235.
Fairy Ointment. Briggs, *DBF*, pt. B, v.1, p. 238.
How Joan Lost the Sight of One Eye. Briggs, *DBF*, pt. B, v.1, p. 272.
Marie Kirstan the Midwife. Briggs, *DBF*, pt. B, v.1, p. 310.
Midwife, The. Briggs, *DBF*, pt. B, v.1, p. 324.
Midwife and the Frog, The. Dégh, *Folktales of Hungary*, no. 71.
Midwife, the Cat, and the Demons, The. Sabar, *Kurdistani Jews*, p. 190.
Nursing a Fairy. Briggs, *DBF*, pt. B, v.1, p. 330.
Reward of a Midwife, The. Noy, *Folktales of Israel*, no. 12.
Woman Who Suckled a Fairy, The. Briggs, *DBF*, pt. B, v.1, p. 407.

**480** **THE KIND AND THE UNKIND GIRLS.** A girl fell into a well and found herself in the underground realm of Frau Holle. She was kind and industrious, and when it was time for her to return home, Frau Holle rewarded her with gold. Her envious sister, wanting the same reward, jumped down the well. But she was selfish and lazy, and when it was time for her to leave, she received a coat of pitch that never came off. (Grimm)  —See Roberts, *The Tale of the Kind and the Unkind Girls*.

Ash Cakes and Water. Campbell, *Cloudwalking Country*, p. 83.
Baba Yaga, The (Russia). Cole, *Best-Loved Folktales*, no. 92.
Baba Yaga. Afanasyev, *Russian Fairy Tales*, p. 194.
Bottle of Water from the World's End Well, The. Briggs, *DBF*, pt. A, v. 1, p. 167.
Bucket, The. Crane, *Italian Popular Tales*, no. 26.
Cats under the Sea, The. Mathias and Raspa, *Italian Folktales in America*, no. 2.
Cats, The. Calvino, *Italian Folktales*, no. 129.
Corpse Watchers, The. Glassie, *Irish Folktales*, no. 113.
Daughter and Stepdaughter. Afanasyev, *Russian Fairy Tales*, p. 278.
Enchanted Wreath, The (Thorpe). Lang, *Orange Fairy Book*, p. 110.
Fairies, The. Perrault, *Fairy Tales* (trans. Carter), p. 73.
Fairy, The (Perrault). Opie, *Classic Fairy Tales*, p. 129.
Frau Holle. Grimm, *Tales*, no. 24.
Gallymanders! Gallymanders!. Chase, *Grandfather Tales*, no. 2.
Girl Is Carried Away by the River, A. Arewa, *Northern East Africa*, p. 155.
Glass Ball, The. Briggs, *DBF*, pt. A, v. 1, p. 269.
Glass House, The. Briggs, *DBF*, pt. A, v. 1, p. 270.
Gold in the Chimley, The (USA). Clarkson and Cross, *World Folktales*, no. 2.
Gold in the Chimley, The. Dorson, *Buying the Wind*, p. 206.
Gold in the Chimley, The. Roberts, *South from Hell*, no. 16C.
Golden Rain, The. Campbell, *Cloudwalking Country*, p. 32.
Good Girl and the Ornery Girl, The. Randolph, *The Devil's Pretty Daughter*, p. 94.
Green Lady, The (I, II). Briggs, *DBF*, pt. A, v. 1, p. 286.
Green Lady, The. Briggs and Tongue, *Folktales of England*, no. 2.
Hans Frank. Grimm, *Other Tales*, p. 23.
King Frost (Russia). Cole, *Best-Loved Folktales*, no. 94.
King of Colchester's Daughters, The (England). Opie, *Classic Fairy Tales*, p. 207.
Little Crop-Tailed Hen, The. Sampson, *Gypsy Folk Tales*, p. 27.
Little Girl's Sieve, The. Delarue, *French Folktales*, p. 167.
Little Watercress Girl, The. Briggs, *DBF*, pt. A, v. 1, p. 394.
Maiden Bright-Eye (Denmark). Lang, *Pink Fairy Book*, p. 289.
Man with a Long Nose, The. Briggs, *DBF*, pt. A, v. 1, p. 408.
Marion and Jeanne (France). Bødker, *European Folk Tales*, p. 160.
Old Man Who Cut Bamboo, The. Seki, *Folktales of Japan*, no. 34.
Old Man Who Made Flowers Bloom, The. Seki, *Folktales of Japan*, no. 35.
Old Witch, The. Briggs, *DBF*, pt. A, v. 1, p. 432.
Old Witch, The. Jacobs, *More English Fairy Tales*, p. 101.
Old Woman in the Well, The. Delarue, *French Folktales*, p. 164.
Saint Joseph in the Forest. Grimm, *Tales*, no. 201.
Shining, Beautiful Lady, The. Campbell, *Cloudwalking Country*, p. 249.

**500  GUESSING THE HELPER'S NAME.** A miller boasted that his daughter could spin straw into gold. The king put her to the test. Locking her in a room full of straw, he told her that if she turned the straw into gold he would marry her, otherwise she would die. A little man offered to spin the straw into gold in return for her first child. The desperate girl agreed. A year later she brought a baby into the world, and shortly thereafter the dwarf came to claim it. The mother cried so, that he offered to let her keep the baby, if she could guess his name within three days. She tried every name, but none was right. On the third day a messenger reported to her a strange little man he had seen in the forest singing a song about his name "Rumpelstiltskin." When the dwarf discovered that she knew his name, he went into a rage and pulled himself in two. (Grimm) Cf. type 501.

Tom Tit Tot. Briggs and Tongue, *Folktales of England,* no. 3.
Tom Tit Tot. Briggs, *DBF,* pt. A, v. 1, p. 535.
Tom Tit Tot. Jacobs, *English Fairy Tales,* p. 1.
Whuppity Stoorie: I. Briggs, *DBF,* pt. A, v. 1, p. 567.

**501 THE THREE OLD SPINNING WOMEN.** The queen happened by at the moment a woman was beating her daughter for refusing to spin. The mother, ashamed of her daughter's laziness, claimed that the girl was being punished for her insistence on spinning without a pause. The queen liked this, and took the girl to the palace. She gave her three rooms filled with flax and told her that if she could spin it all, she should marry the prince. Soon three old women appeared; one had a flat foot, the other a distorted lip, and the third a misshapen thumb. They offered to complete her task, if she would invite them to the wedding, and she agreed. The three ugly women appeared at the marriage celebration, and when introduced to the prince, they told him that their deformities had come from treading the spinning wheel, licking the thread, and twisting the thread. The alarmed bridegroom proclaimed that his bride should never again touch a spinning wheel. (Grimm) Cf. type 500.

And Seven. Calvino, *Italian Folktales,* no. 5.
Buzz-Buzz Aunty. Villa, *100 Armenian Tales,* no. 38.
Girl That Weren't Ashamed to Own Her Kin, The. Campbell, *Cloudwalking Country,* p. 241.
Gypsy Woman, The (sequel to Tom Tit Tot). Briggs, *DBF,* pt. A, v. 1, p. 539.
Habetrot and Scantlie Mab. Jacobs, *More English Fairy Tales,* p. 195.
Habetrot. Briggs, *DBF,* pt. A, v. 1, p. 303.
Seven Bits of Bacon-Rind, The. Basile, *Pentamerone,* Day 4, Tale 4.
Three Aunts, The (Norway). Thompson, *100 Folktales,* no. 37.
Three Aunts, The. Asbjørnsen and Moe, *East o' the Sun,* p. 193.
Three Spinners, The. Grimm, *Tales,* no. 14.
Three Spinners, The. Ranke, *Folktales of Germany,* no. 39.
Whuppity Stoorie (II). Briggs, *DBF,* pt. A, v. 1, p. 568.

**502 THE WILD MAN AS A HELPER.** A king kept a wild man in a cage. One day the prince's ball fell into the cage, and he unlocked the door, allowing the wild man to escape. Fearing punishment, the boy ran away also, but the wild man promised to come to his aid, whenever he would call out "Iron Hans." The boy became a servant for another king. He went to battle for his new master, but received only a three-legged horse. The wild man came to his aid, bringing him a strong steed. The boy was victorious, winning not only the battle, but also the hand of the princess. (Grimm) Cf. types 314, 530, 531.

Country of the Beautiful Gardens, The. Villa, *100 Armenian Tales,* no. 18.
Georgic and Merlin. Delarue, *French Folktales,* p. 237.
Gold-Bearded Man, The (Hungary). Lang, *Crimson Fairy Book,* p. 198.
Guerrino Sets Free from his Father's Prison a Certain Savage Man. Straparola, *Facetious Nights,* Night 5, Tale 1.

Hairy Man, The. Lang, *Crimson Fairy Book,* p. 22.
Iron Hans. Grimm, *Tales,* no. 136.
Monster's Hairs, The. Villa, *100 Armenian Tales,* no. 22.
Prince Ivan and Princess Martha. Afanasyev, *Russian Fairy Tales,* p. 79.
Seven-Headed Beast, The. Thomas, *It's Good to Tell You,* no. 2.
Three For a Pot. Briggs, *DBF,* pt. A, v. 1, p. 516.

**503   THE HUNCHBACKS AND THE ELVES.** A hunchback heard the elves singing and added his own voice. Delighted by his music, the elves rewarded him by taking the hump from his back. Another hunchback heard of the miracle, went to the same place, and also joined the elves' singing. But he sang badly, so they cursed him by adding a second hump to his back. (Thompson)

Food and Fire and Company. Briggs, *DBF,* pt. A, v. 1, p. 240.
Four Little Dwarfs, The. Pino-Saavedra, *Folktales of Chile,* no. 18.
Gifts from the Pixies. Palmer, *Folklore of Somerset,* p. 21.
Goblin Combe. Briggs and Tongue, *Folktales of England,* no. 8.
Goblin Combe. Briggs, *DBF,* pt. A, v. 1, p. 279.
Hunchback and the Fairies, The. Clouston, *Popular Tales,* v. 1, p. 352.
Hunchback's Gift, The (Ireland). Thompson, *100 Folktales,* no. 38.
Little Folks' Presents, The. Grimm, *Tales,* no. 182.
Miser and the Fairies of the Gump, The. Briggs, *DBF,* pt. A, v. 1, p. 415.
Monkeys' Jizo-Sama, The. Seki, *Folktales of Japan,* no. 37.
Old Men Who Had Wens, The. Seki, *Folktales of Japan,* no. 36.
Playing Blind Beggar. Simpson, *Icelandic Folktales and Legends,* p. 22.
That's Enough to Go on With. Briggs, *DBF,* pt. A, v. 1, p. 505.
Tom Beg and Bill Beg. Killip, *Folklore of the Isle of Man,* p. 29.
Tonino and the Fairies (Spain). Cole, *Best-Loved Folktales,* no. 35.
Two Humpbacks, The. Crane, *Italian Popular Tales,* no. 27.
Two Humps, The. Briggs, *DBF,* pt. A, v. 1, p. 542.
Two Hunchbacks and the Wednesday Witches, The. Walker and Uysal, *Tales in Turkey,* p. 188.
Two Hunchbacks, The. Calvino, *Italian Folktales,* no. 90.

**503\*   HELPFUL ELVES.** During the night elves made shoes for a poor cobbler. To show their thanks, the cobbler and his wife made clothes for the little people. The elves, delighted with their new clothes, never returned, but the shoemaker and his wife prospered. (Grimm, 39/I) —Note: Countless legends describe the pranks—sometimes helpful, often mischievous—of elves and fairies. Cf. types 476\*, 503, 504, and Christiansen, *Migratory Legends,* types 5050-6070.

Elves, The. Grimm, *Tales,* no. 39/I.
Finger Lock. Briggs, *DBF,* pt. A, v. 1, p. 233.
Hand with the Knife, The. Grimm, *Other Tales,* p. 142.

**504   THE CHANGELING** (new classification). This true story took place in 1580 near Breslau. While working in the field, a mother left her newly born child on a stack of hay. When she returned, she knew that the baby lying there was not hers, for it greedily sucked her milk and made inhuman noises. The landowner told her to beat the child with a switch, and she would witness a miracle. She did this, and the devil took his child back, returning the stolen baby. (Grimm, "Beating the Changeling with Switches") Cf. type 476* and Christiansen, *Migratory Legends,* type 5085. —See Hartland, *The Science of Fairy Tales,* pp. 93-134.

Beating the Changeling with Switches. Grimm, *German Legends,* no. 88.
Brewery of Egg-Shells (Croker). McGarry, *Great Folktales of Old Ireland,* p. 39.
Brewery of Egg-Shells (Croker). Yeats, *Fairy and Folk Tales of Ireland,* p. 49.
Caerlaverock Changeling, The. Briggs, *DBF,* pt. B, v. 1, p. 194.
Brewery of Eggshells. Jacobs, *Celtic Fairy Tales,* p. 223.
Changeling, The (I, II). Briggs, *DBF,* pt. B, v. 1, p. 196.
Changeling, The. Grimm, *German Legends,* no. 82.
Changelings (2 tales). Porter, *Folklore of East Anglia,* p. 77.
Changelings, The (Sweden). Booss, *Scandinavian Tales,* p. 306.
Changelings. Yeats, *Fairy and Folk Tales of Ireland,* p. 48.
Changelings in the Water, The. Grimm, *German Legends,* no. 83.
Changelings (numerous accounts). Evans-Wentz, *The Fairy-Faith.*
Changeling, The. El-Shamy, *Folktales of Egypt,* no. 43.
Devonshire Fairies. Campbell, *West Highlands,* v. 2, p. 82.
Elves, The (tale 3). Grimm, no. 39/III.
Fairy Changeling, A (I, II). Briggs, *DBF,* pt. B, v. 1, p. 221.
Fairy Hill Alowe, The. Briggs, *DBF,* pt. B, v. 1, p. 233.
Fairy Nurse, The (Poem by Walsh). Yeats, *Fairy and Folk Tales of Ireland,* p. 51.
Fairy of Corrie Osben and the Tailor. MacDougall, *Highland Fairy Legends,* p. 11.
Fairy Theft. Briggs, *DBF,* pt. B, v. 1, p. 240.
Fairy Theft Prevented. Briggs, *DBF,* pt. B, v. 1, p. 240.
Glengarry Fairy, The. MacDougall, *Highland Fairy Legends,* p. 3.
Inishkeen's on Fire. Glassie, *Irish Folktales,* no. 62.
Johnnie in the Cradle. Briggs, *DBF,* pt. B, v. 1, p. 290.
Kintalen Changeling, The. MacDougall, *Highland Fairy Legends,* p. 8.
Man That Dug Up Arrowheads. Randolph, *Sticks in the Knapsack,* p. 74.
Nursemaid-in-the-Rye, The. Grimm, *German Legends,* no. 90.
Pixie Child and the Human Child, The. Whitlock, *Folklore of Devon,* p. 31.
Red-Haired Tailor of Rannoch and the Fairy, The. MacDougall, *Highland Fairy Legends,* p. 5.
Riddling in the Reek. Aitken, *A Forgotten Heritage,* p. 12.
Smith and the Fairies, The. Campbell, *West Highlands,* v. 2, p. 5.
Stolen Child, The (Yeats). Yeats, *Fairy and Folk Tales of Ireland,* p. 57.
Sutherland Fairies. Campbell, *West Highlands,* v. 2, p. 71.
Tailor and the Changeling, The. Killip, *Folklore of the Isle of Man,* p. 103.
Tailor and the Baby, The. Briggs, *DBF,* pt. B, v. 1, p. 362.
Tailor and the Baby, The. Campbell, *West Highlands,* v. 2, p. 68.
Tailor of Kintalen, The. Briggs, *DBF,* pt. B, v. 1, p. 364.
Tibbie's Bairn. Aitken, *A Forgotten Heritage,* p. 9.
Torr-a-Bhuilg. MacDougall, *Highland Fairy Legends,* p. 1.
True Stories about Fairies (I, II). Briggs, *DBF,* pt. B, v. 1, p. 386.
Two Women from the Underworld. Grimm, *German Legends,* no. 91.
Watching Out for Children. Grimm, *German Legends,* no. 89.
Woman Gives Birth to Water-Kelpie. Briggs, *DBF,* pt. B, v. 1, p. 388.

Woman Had a Baby That Never Grew. Simpson, *Folklore of the Welsh Border*, p. 75.

**505 THE GRATEFUL DEAD MAN.** A wandering tailor came to a poor sinner hanging on the gallows. He paid the judge his last three silver pieces for the body, and gave it a decent burial. Later he was joined by a stranger, who helped him come to a great fortune. The stranger was the man the tailor had taken from the gallows. (Grimm) —Note: Types 505-507C typically begin in a similar manner. The differences lie primarily in the nature of the assistance rendered to the hero by his dead companion. See Gerould, *The Grateful Dead*.

Dead Man's Thanks. Grimm, *Other Tales*, p. 126.
Grateful Fish, The. El-Shamy, *Folktales of Egypt*, no. 5.
Jack and the Ghosts. Briggs, *DBF*, pt. A, v. 1, p. 323.
Kadar and Cannibals. Thundy, *South Indian Folktales*, no. 49.
Man and His Three Sons, The. Saucier, *French Louisiana*, no. 10.
Naked Man, The. Dawkins, *Modern Greek Folktales*, no. 36.
Old Shake-Your-Head. Campbell, *Cloudwalking Country*, p. 98.

**506 THE GRATEFUL DEAD MAN HELPS SAVE THE PRINCESS.**

Bald Man at the Funeral, The. Bushnaq, *Arab Folktales*, p. 125.
Barra Widow's Son, The. Campbell, *West Highlands*, v. 2, p. 121.
Box with Bones, The. Noy, *Folktales of Israel*, no. 50.
Fair Brow. Calvino, *Italian Folktales*, no. 45.
Fair Brow. Crane, *Italian Popular Tales*, no. 35.
Four Eggs a Penny. Briggs, *DBF*, pt. A, v. 1, p. 249.
Golden Duck, The. Musick, *Green Hills of Magic*, no. 45.
John of Calais. Massignon, *Folktales of France*, no. 10.
Joseph Ciufolo, Tiller-Flutist. Calvino, *Italian Folktales*, no. 108.
Shaking-Head. Curtin, *Myths and Folktales of Ireland*, p. 121.

**506A THE GRATEFUL DEAD MAN HELPS FREE THE PRINCESS FROM SLAVERY.**

Dead Man and the Princess Freed from Slavery, The. Grimm, *Other Tales*, p. 123.
Princess Who Was Rescued from Slavery, The (Sweden). Thompson, *100 Folktales*, no. 39.

**507A THE GRATEFUL DEAD MAN HELPS RESCUE THE OGRE'S BRIDE.**

Companion, The. Asbjørnsen and Moe, *Norwegian Folktales*, p. 84.
Hild, Queen of the Elves. Simpson, *Icelandic Folktales and Legends*, p. 43.
Jack and the Giants. Briggs, *DBF*, pt. A, v. 1, p. 326.
John and the Wicked Princess. Roberts, *South from Hell*, no. 17.
Little Cinder Girl, The. Briggs, *DBF*, pt. A, v. 1, p. 383.
Red Etin, The. Briggs, *DBF*, pt. A, v. 1, p. 463.
Traveling Companion, The. Andersen, *Complete Fairy Tales*, no. 7.

## 507B  THE GRATEFUL DEAD MAN HELPS FREE THE GIRL OF A SERPENT.

> Girl Out of Whose Mouth Came a Snake, The (Turkey). Bødker, *European Folk Tales*, p. 205.

## 507C  THE GRATEFUL DEAD MAN AND THE SERPENT GIRL.

> Box with Bones, The. Noy, *Folktales of Israel*, no. 50.
> Helpful Spirit, The. Villa, *100 Armenian Tales*, no. 36.

## 510  THE PERSECUTED HEROINE.  A king asked his three daughters how much they loved him. The youngest claimed he was as dear as salt to her. This answer enraged him, and he ordered her put to death. She escaped to a neighboring kingdom, and a prince fell in love with her. Her father was invited to the wedding, without knowing it was his banished daughter. His meal was served without salt. Suddenly he realized what his daughter had meant. Then she appeared, and everyone rejoiced. (Calvino, "Dear as Salt") Cf. type 923. —See Cox, *Cinderella;* Dundes, *Cinderella: A Casebook;* and Rooth, *The Cinderella Cycle*. Note: Convention varies in distinguishing between types 510 and 510A.

> Barbarina and the Black Snake. Mathias and Raspa, *Italian Folktales in America*, no. 1.
> Dear as Salt. Calvino, *Italian Folktales*, no. 54.
> Dirty Shepherdess, The (Sebillot). Lang, *Green Fairy Book*, p. 180.
> Girl Who Went Through Fire, Water and the Golden Gate, The. Briggs, *DBF*, pt. A, v. 1, p. 268.
> Green Knight, The (Denmark). Lang, *Olive Fairy Book*, p. 152.
> Like Meat Loves Salt. Chase, *Grandfather Tales*, no. 13.
> Magic Orange Tree, The (Haiti). Cole, *Best-Loved Folktales*, no. 187.
> Old Woman's Hide, The. Calvino, *Italian Folktales*, no. 70.
> Princess Mouse-Skin. Grimm, *Other Tales*, p. 44.
> Punchkin. Jacobs, *Indian Fairy Tales*, p. 21.
> Teja and Teji (India). Dorson, *Folktales around the World*, p. 177.
> Three Girls with Journey Cakes, The. Campbell, *Cloudwalking Country*, p. 140.
> True Bride, The. Grimm, *Tales*, no. 186.

## 510A  CINDERELLA.  Cinderella's stepmother and two stepsisters forced her do the hardest work and made her sleep on the cinders by the hearth. When the king announced a great festival, Cinderella went to her mother's grave, and a bird threw a beautiful dress over her. She was the most beautiful girl at the ball, and the prince fell in love with her. At the evening's end she left so quickly that she lost one of her slippers. The next day the prince discovered that Cinderella was the beautiful girl from the ball, because only her foot would fit the lost slipper, and he married her forthwith. (Grimm)

Ashpet. Chase, *Grandfather Tales,* no. 12.
Ashpitel. Briggs, *DBF,* pt. A, v. 1, p. 138.
Benizara and Kakezara. Seki, *Folktales of Japan,* no. 38.
Broken Pitcher, The. Briggs, *DBF,* pt. A, v. 1, p. 171.
Cat Cinderella, The. Basile, *Pentamerone,* Day 1, Tale 6.
Cinder-Maid. Jacobs, *European Folk and Fairy Tales,* no. 1.
Cinderella (France). Dorson, *Folktales around the World,* p. 57.
Cinderella (Perrault). Cole, *Best-Loved Folktales,* no. 1.
Cinderella. Crane, *Italian Popular Tales,* no. 9.
Cinderella. Dawkins, *Modern Greek Folktales,* no. 21.
Cinderella. Eberhard, *Folktales of China,* no. 66.
Cinderella. Falassi, *Folklore by the Fireside,* p. 55.
Cinderella. Grimm, *Tales,* no. 21.
Cinderella. Massignon, *Folktales of France,* no. 43.
Cinderella. Saucier, *French Louisiana,* no. 2.
Cinderella. Villa, *100 Armenian Tales,* no. 30.
Cinderella; or, The Little Glass Slipper. Perrault, *Fairy Tales* (trans. Carter), p. 81.
Cinderilla; or, The Little Glass Slipper (Perrault). Opie, *Classic Fairy Tales,* p. 161.
Essy Pattle and da Blue Yowe. Marwick, *Folklore of Orkney and Shetland,* p. 164.
Fair, Brown, and Trembling. Curtin, *Myths and Folktales of Ireland,* p. 37.
Fair, Brown, and Trembling. Glassie, *Irish Folktales,* no. 112.
Gold Star. Espinosa, *Folklore of Spain in the American Southwest,* p. 184.
Golden Slipper, The. Afanasyev, *Russian Fairy Tales,* p. 44.
Gràttula-Beddàttula. Calvino, *Italian Folktales,* no. 148.
Hearth-Cat, The (Portugal). Thompson, *100 Folktales,* no. 40.
Indian Cinderella, The (Canada). Clarkson and Cross, *World Folktales,* no. 4.
Indian Cinderella, The (Canada). Cole, *Best-Loved Folktales,* no. 179.
Katie Woodencloak. Asbjørnsen and Moe, *East o' the Sun,* p. 357.
Liisa and the Prince (Finland). Booss, *Scandinavian Tales,* p. 573.
Little Cinder-Girl, The. Briggs, *DBF,* pt. A, v. 1, p. 383.
Little Cinder-Girl, The. Sampson, *Gypsy Folk Tales,* p. 77.
Little Red Fish and the Clog of Gold, The. Bushnaq, *Arab Folktales,* p. 181.
Maria Cinderella. Pino-Saavedra, *Folktales of Chile,* no. 19.
Marion and Jeanne (France). Bødker, *European Folk Tales,* p. 160.
Rosina in the Oven. Calvino, *Italian Folktales,* no. 64.
Rushen Coatie. Jacobs, *More English Fairy Tales,* p. 163.
Sharp Grey Sheep, The. Campbell, *West Highlands,* v. 2, p. 300.
Vasilisa the Beautiful. Afanasyev, *Russian Fairy Tales,* p. 439.
Wonderful Birch, The. Lang, *Red Fairy Book,* p. 123.

## 510B  A KING TRIES TO MARRY HIS DAUGHTER.  A dying queen made her husband promise that he would marry only a woman as beautiful as she. When the time came for his remarriage, the only fitting woman he could find was his own daughter, and he told her his intentions to marry her. To gain time, she asked for dresses patterned after the moon, the stars, and the sun, and also for a coat made of every kind of fur, but the king found these and continued to press for marriage. She finally escaped by smearing her face with soot, wrapping herself in the fur coat, and running into the woods. Another king found her there, and she became his kitchen servant, suffering many indignities. With time, however, he discovered her true beauty,

and they married. (Grimm) —Note: Some variants listed below suppress the incest motif.

All-Kinds-of-Fur. Grimm, *Tales,* no. 65.
Allerleirauh (Grimm, altered). Lang, *Green Fairy Book,* p. 276.
Ashey Pelt. Briggs, *DBF,* pt. A, v. 1, p. 140.
Barbarina and the Black Snake. Mathias and Raspa, *Italian Folktales in America,* no. 1.
Bear, The. Lang, *Grey Fairy Book,* p. 269.
Black Yow, The. Briggs, *DBF,* pt. A, v. 1, p. 164.
Cap o' Rushes. Briggs, *DBF,* pt. A, v. 2, p. 387.
Cap o' Rushes. Jacobs, *English Fairy Tales,* p. 51.
Catskins. Chase, *Grandfather Tales,* no. 11.
Catskin. Jacobs, *More English Fairy Tales,* p. 204.
Catskin: The Princess and the Golden Cow. Briggs, *DBF,* pt. A, v. 1, p. 179.
Donkey Skin (France, *Le Cabinet des Fées*). Lang, *Grey Fairy Book,* p. 1.
Donkey Skin. Falassi, *Folklore by the Fireside,* p. 42.
Donkey-Skin. Perrault, *Fairy Tales* (trans. Carter), p. 139.
Fair Maria Wood. Crane, *Italian Popular Tales,* no. 10.
Florinda. Pino-Saavedra, *Folktales of Chile,* no. 21.
Flying Princess, The. Dawkins, *Modern Greek Folktales,* no. 40.
Golden Box, The. Villa, *100 Armenian Tales,* no. 24.
Golden Filly Chest, The. Campbell, *Cloudwalking Country,* p. 196.
Grey Castle, The. Briggs, *DBF,* pt. A, v. 1, p. 298.
Katie Woodencloak (Norway). Thompson, *100 Folktales,* no. 41.
King Who Wished to Marry His Daughter. Campbell, *West Highlands,* v. 1, p. 226.
Like Meat Loves Salt. Chase, *Grandfather Tales,* no. 13.
Little Blue Bonnet, The. Gmelch and Kroup, *To Shorten the Road,* p. 177.
Little Cat Skin. Campbell, *Cloudwalking Country,* p. 82.
Little Stick Figure, The. Pino-Saavedra, *Folktales of Chile,* no. 20.
Margery White Coats. Campbell, *West Highlands,* v. 1, p. 232.
Mossycoat. Briggs and Tongue, *Folktales of England,* no. 4.
Mossycoat. Briggs, *DBF,* pt. A, v. 1, p. 416.
Princess in the Donkey Skin, The. Roberts, *South from Hell,* no. 18.
Princess in the Suit of Leather, The. Bushnaq, *Arab Folktales,* p. 193.
Princess That Wore a Rabbit-Skin Dress. Campbell, *Cloudwalking Country,* p. 161.
Queen with the Golden Hair, The. Campbell, *Cloudwalking Country,* p. 30.
Rashie Coat. Briggs, *DBF,* pt. A, v. 1, p. 455.
Rashiecoat. Aitken, *A Forgotten Heritage,* p. 73.
Rashin Coatie. Briggs, *DBF,* pt. A, v. 1, p. 456.
Red Calf, The. Briggs, *DBF,* pt. A, v. 1, p. 460.
She Donkey's Skin, The. Massignon, *Folktales of France,* no. 44.
She-Bear, The. Basile, *Pentamerone,* Day 2, Tale 6.
Tattercoats. Briggs, *DBF,* pt. A, v. 1, p. 502.
Tattercoats. Jacobs, *More English Fairy Tales,* p. 67.
Tebaldo Wishes to Have His Only Daughter Doralice to Wife. Straparola, *Facetious Nights,* Night 1, Tale 4.
Wooden Maria. Calvino, *Italian Folktales,* no. 103.

**511  ONE-EYE, TWO-EYES, THREE-EYES.** A woman had three daughters. The oldest had only one eye, the second had two eyes, and the third three eyes. The mother, One-Eye, and Three-Eyes hated Two-Eyes; they were cruel to her in every way, and they gave her nothing to eat. One day a wise woman told Two-Eyes what she could say to her goat to cause it to give her a fine meal. The others found out about the goat and killed it. Two-Eyes buried its entrails in front of the house, and the next morning a tree with golden fruit stood there. A handsome knight stopped and asked about the tree. Discovering that only Two-Eyes could pluck its fruit, he married her. (Grimm)

Burenushka, the Little Red Cow. Afanasyev, *Russian Fairy Tales*, p. 146.
Enchanted Prince. Espinosa, *Folklore of Spain in the American Southwest*, p. 191.
One-Eye, Two-Eyes, and Three-Eyes (Germany). Thompson, *100 Folktales*, no. 42.
One-Eye, Two-Eyes, and Three-Eyes. Grimm, *Tales*, no. 130.
One-Eye, Two-Eyes, Three-Eyes. Falassi, *Folklore by the Fireside*, p. 34.
Silver Tree with Golden Apples, A. Campbell, *Cloudwalking Country*, p. 43.
Three Sisters, The. Roberts, *South from Hell*, no. 19B.

**511A   THE LITTLE OX.** A little boy's father gave him a bull calf. Afterward the father died, and the boy's stepfather treated him cruelly, threatening also to kill the bull calf. So the boy ran away with his bull calf. A dragon killed the bull calf. The boy took the bull calf's gut, and when he hit the dragon with it, it killed the dragon, and the boy cut out its tongue. —Continues as type 300. (Jacobs)

Jack and the Bull. Chase, *The Jack Tales*, no. 2.
Jack and the Bull Stripe. Roberts, *South from Hell*, no. 20D.
Jack and the Bull's Horns. Roberts, *South from Hell*, no. 20B.
Little Black Bull, The. Briggs, *DBF*, pt. A, v. 1, p. 380.
Little Bull-Calf, de Three Giants, and de Fiery Dragon, De. Briggs, *DBF*, pt. A, v. 1, p. 382.
Little Bull-Calf, The. Jacobs, *More English Fairy Tales*, p. 186.
Out in the World. Calvino, *Italian Folktales*, no. 172.

**513   THE EXTRAORDINARY COMPANIONS.** A king announced that he would marry his daughter to the man who could build a self-propelled carriage. The youngest of three brothers set out to attempt the task. He was joined by five extraordinary companions: one could eat huge quantities of bread, another had a great thirst, the third could throw stones across the sea, the fourth could hear wool being spun in the center of the earth, and the last could make thirty-six windmills turn with the air from his behind. An old woman helped the boy make the self-propelled carriage, but then the king tried to back away from his bargain, adding one task after the other. The extraordinary companions helped the boy overcome every difficulty. —Note: The plots of types 513, 513A, and 513B differ only in minor details.

Eleven Brothers and Eleven Sisters. Musick, *Green Hills of Magic*, no. 43.
Honey Gatherer's Three Sons (Africa). Clarkson and Cross, *World Folktales*, no. 50.
Leppä Pölkky and the Blue Cross (Finland). Booss, *Scandinavian Tales*, p. 564.

Long, Broad, and Quickeye (Bohemia). Lang, *Grey Fairy Book,* p. 366.
Millionare, His Daughter, and Her Three Suitors. Saucier, *French Louisiana,*
  no. 9.
Self-Propelled Carriage, The (France). Thompson, *100 Folktales,* no. 43.
Self-Propelled Carriage, The. Delarue, *French Folktales,* p. 157.
Simpleton, The (Italy). Lang, *Grey Fairy Book,* p. 309.
Son of the Fisherman, The. Walker and Uysal, *Tales in Turkey,* p. 55.

## 513A  SIX GO THROUGH THE WORLD.

Ash Lad and the Good Helpers. Asbjørnsen and Moe, *Norwegian Folktales,* p.
  170.
Dirt Boy, The. Seki, *Folktales of Japan,* no. 18.
Dreamer and His Dream, The. Villa, *100 Armenian Tales,* no. 16.
Five Scapegraces, The. Calvino, *Italian Folktales,* no. 126.
Flea, The. Basile, *Pentamerone,* Day 1, Tale 5.
Head-Falconer, The (Turkey). Bødker, *European Folk Tales,* p. 209.
How Six Men Got On in the World. Grimm, *Tales,* no. 71.
King of Ireland's Son, The. Glassie, *Irish Folktales,* p. 39.
Sea King and Vasilisa the Wise, The. Afanasyev, *Russian Fairy Tales,* p. 427.
Seven Semyons, The. Afanasyev, *Russian Fairy Tales,* p. 410.
Six Servants, The. Grimm, *Tales,* no. 134.

## 513B  THE LAND AND WATER SHIP.  Cf. type 1889.

Ash Lad and the Good Helpers. Asbjørnsen and Moe, *Norwegian Folktales,* p.
  170.
Boat for Land and Water, A. Calvino, *Italian Folktales,* no. 99.
Boat That Sailed on Land, The. Pourrat, *Treasury of French Tales,* p. 175.
Flying Ship, The (Russia). Lang, *Yellow Fairy Book,* p. 198.
Fool of the World and the Flying Ship (Russia). Cole, *Best-Loved Folktales,*
  no. 91.
Hardy Hardhead. Chase, *The Jack Tales,* no. 11.
How the Hermit Helped to Win the King's Daughter (Sicily). Lang, *Pink Fairy
  Book,* p. 174.
Little Boat That Could Sail on Land and on Sea. Thomas, *It's Good to Tell
  You,* no. 8.
Seven Simons, The (Hungary). Lang, *Crimson Fairy Book,* p. 37.
Three Boys with Journey Cakes, The. Campbell, *Cloudwalking Country,* p.
  140.

## 513C  THE HUNTER'S SON.  The king and his vizier commanded the
son of a hunter to build an ivory palace. The boy used forty barrels of
wine to make a herd of elephants drunk, and thus got enough ivory for
the task. Next they sent the boy to a distant mountain to capture the
sister of seven brothers. On the way the boy was joined by a man who
was always thirsty, one who was always cold, one who was always
hungry, one who could hear everything in the earth, one who could
throw stones great distances, and one who could shake the earth. The
unusual companions performed various tasks, enabling the boy to win
the girl's hand. When she learned what the king and the vizier had
done, she turned them into a cat and a mouse, and the hunter's son
became king. (Dawkins, "The Son of the Hunter")

Hunter and the King's Fair Daughter, The. Noy, *Folktales of Israel,* no. 54.
Huntsman, The. Villa, *100 Armenian Tales,* no. 15.
Johnnie, the Son of the Widow. Dawkins, *Modern Greek Folktales,* no. 42A.
Son of the Hunter, The. Dawkins, *Modern Greek Folktales,* no. 42B.

**514  A GIRL TURNS INTO A MAN.** A man was summoned to war, but his youngest daughter, dressed as a man, volunteered in his place. She fought so bravely that the king chose her as his daughter's husband. At night she placed a sword between herself and her bride. Unhappy with their supposed son-in-law, the king and queen sent her to steal fire from the one-eyed giants. Contrary to their expectation, she succeeded. The defeated giant cursed the victor: "If you are a boy you shall become a girl; if you are a girl you shall become a boy." The curse worked, and the marriage between the princess and the heroine, now a man, became a happy one. (Dawkins) —Cf. types 884-884B*.

Florinda. Pino-Saavedra, *Folktales of Chile,* no. 21.
Indian Princess Borrows a Jinni's Sex, A. Mathers, *1001 Nights,* v. 4, p. 411.
Youngest Child, The. Dawkins, *Modern Greek Folktales,* no. 46.

**514*  THE GIRL WHO MADE THE FATE LAUGH.** A girl picked poppies and sewed them to her dress, which caused a Fate to laugh. To reward her, the Fate caused the king to marry her. Some time later she laughed at her husband's beard, saying it looked like the palace brush. He would have had her killed for this insult, but the Fates came to her rescue. They gave her a handsome brush covered with diamonds and told her to show it to the king as the brush that his beard resembled. This pleased the king, and he forgave his wife for the misunderstanding.

Poppies. Megas, *Folktales of Greece,* no. 32.

**516  FAITHFUL JOHN.** A young king entered a room that had been forbidden him, and fell in love with a girl whose portrait he saw there. His servant, Faithful John, helped him gain the princess's hand. During the wedding celebration the bride fell to the floor, apparently dead. Faithful John had learned from three ravens that this would happen and that the young queen could be saved only by sucking three drops of blood from her breast. This he did, reviving her. The king, outraged at this behavior, sentenced Faithful John to death, but upon hearing about the ravens, he pardoned him. However, as he spoke the pardon, Faithful John turned into stone. Later the queen gave birth to twin boys. One day the stone figure spoke to the king: "You can restore me to life by cutting off your sons' heads and sprinkling me with their blood." Because of the servant's great loyalty, the king did just that, and Faithful John came back to life. Faithful John set the children's heads back in place, and they too were restored to life. (Grimm)

> Dragon and the Snake, The. Thundy, *South Indian Folktales*, no. 44.
> Faithful John (Germany). Thompson, *100 Folktales*, no. 44.
> Faithful John. Grimm, *Tales*, no. 6.
> Father Roquelaure. Delarue, *French Folktales*, p. 86.
> Gold-Rich King, The. Ranke, *Folktales of Germany*, no. 34.
> Golden Princess, The. Campbell, *Cloudwalking Country*, p. 38.
> In Love with a Statue. Crane, *Italian Popular Tales*, no. 17.
> John the True. Jacobs, *European Folk and Fairy Tales*, no. 21.
> Koshchey the Deathless. Afanasyev, *Russian Fairy Tales*, p. 485.
> Ludwig and Iskander. Villa, *100 Armenian Tales*, no. 37
> Moorish Prince and the Christian Prince. Pino-Saavedra, *Folktales of Chile*, no. 22.
> Old Fench. Massignon, *Folktales of France*, no. 2.
> Orphan and the Governor, The. Lindell, *Folk Tales from Kammu*, II, no. 13.
> Pome and Peel. Calvino, *Italian Folktales*, no. 33.
> Raven, The. Basile, *Pentamerone*, Day 4, Tale 9.
> Romance of Mongol Girl and Arab Boy, The (Afghanistan). Dorson, *Folktales around the World*, p. 209.
> Slave, The. Dawkins, *Modern Greek Folktales*, no. 37.

**516C  SAINT JAMES OF GALICIA.** To keep a promise made by his mother, a prince embarked on a pilgrimage to the shrine of Saint James of Galicia. En route he was joined by a faithful companion. They stopped for a rest in another kingdom, and the king decided he wanted the prince to marry his daughter. To keep the pilgrim in his kingdom, he poisoned the companion, but the prince still continued his pilgrimage, carrying his dead friend with him. At the shrine, Saint James accepted the prince's devotions and revived the companion. The prince returned to marry the princess, and then set forth for his own home. His father-in-law still hated the companion, whom he had once poisoned, and caused him to miss the prince's departure. The companion ran after them, but the great exertion caused him to contract leprosy. The prince cared for him, but he became weaker and weaker. Saint James came to him as a physician and told him that only the blood of his daughter would cure the sick man. The prince then opened his daughter's veins, and her blood cleansed the companion of his leprosy. He feared he had killed his daughter, but the next morning she too was alive and well. (Crane)

> Old Man and the Three Brothers, The. Megas, *Folktales of Greece*, no. 42.
> Saint James of Galicia. Crane, *Italian Popular Tales*, no. 61.

**517  THE BOY WHO UNDERSTOOD BIRDS.** A boy, hated by his stepmother, overheard two blackbirds say how he would become king and be served by his parents. The stepmother had the boy set afloat in a river. A princess rescued him. Later he married her and became king. Cf. types 671, 707, 725, 930.

Two Blackbirds, The. Villa, *100 Armenian Tales,* p. 517.

**518  QUARRELING GIANTS LOSE THEIR MAGIC OBJECTS.**
A king whose wife had betrayed him sought revenge. He came to three
giants who were quarreling about the division of their inheritance: a
magic sword, a cloak that made its wearer invisible, and boots that
would transport one anyplace in the world. The man offered to settle
the dispute and took the items, claiming he wanted to see that they were
in good condition. In an instant he wished himself, with the power of
the boots, to the castle where his wife was about to marry another man.
The giants thus lost their magic objects, and with the help of the cloak
and the sword, the betrayed king found his revenge. (Grimm, no. 92)
—Note: The acquisition of magic items in such a manner is found in
diverse tales, for example, types 302, 569, 581.

> Crystal Ball, The. Grimm, *Tales,* no. 197.
> Drummer, The. Grimm, *Tales,* no. 193.
> King of the Golden Mountain, The. Grimm, *Tales,* no. 92.
> Magic Bird-Heart. Villa, *100 Armenian Tales,* no. 12.
> Neapolitan Soldier, The. Calvino, *Italian Folktales,* no. 100.
> Raven, The. Grimm, *Tales,* no. 93.
> Tale within a Tale, A. Bushnaq, *Arab Folktales,* p. 94.

**519  BRUNHILDE, THE STRONG BRIDE.**  Siegfried, in order to
gain the hand of King Gunther's sister, offered to help Gunther woo
Brunhilde, who had announced that she would marry no one who
could not better her in weight casting, javelin throwing, and jumping.
Standing next to Gunther while wearing a cloak that made him
invisible, Siegfried won each contest, and thus Brunhilde had to marry
Gunther. *(Nibelungenlied)*

> Footless Champion and the Handless Champion, The. Afanasyev, *Russian
>    Fairy Tales,* p. 269.
> Giantess Leader, The. Villa, *100 Armenian Tales,* no. 9.
> Hedgy. Musick, *Green Hills of Magic,* no. 23.
> How Gunther won Brunhild. *Nibelungenlied* (trans. Hatto), p. 60.
> Milk of Wild Beasts, The. Afanasyev, *Russian Fairy Tales,* p. 304.

**530  THE PRINCESS ON THE GLASS MOUNTAIN.**  A king gave
his daughter three golden apples and placed her atop a glass hill; he
then promised her to anyone who could ride a horse to the top. Boots,
the youngest of three brothers, tamed a mysterious horse that had been
ravaging his father's field. He rode the horse to the top of the glass
hill, collected the apples, and claimed the princess as his bride.
(Asbjørnsen and Moe, "The Princess on the Glass Hill") Cf. types 314,
502, 531.

> Dapplegrim. Asbjørnsen and Moe, *East o' the Sun,* p. 272.
> Dove Girl, The. Calvino, *Italian Folktales,* no. 164.

Glass Mountain, The (Poland). Lang, *Yellow Fairy Book*, p. 114.
Golden-Bristled Pig, the Golden-Feathered Duck, and the Golden-Maned Mare. Afanasyev, *Russian Fairy Tales*, p. 533.
Jack and the Bull. Chase, *The Jack Tales*, no. 2.
Jack and the Little Bull. Randolph, *Who Blowed Up the Church House?*, p. 133.
Princess and the Peasant, The (Finland). Bødker, *European Folk Tales*, p. 17.
Princess on the Glass Hill, The (Norway). Thompson, *100 Folktales*, no. 45.
Princess on the Glass Hill. Asbjørnsen and Moe, *East o' the Sun*, p. 92.
Princess on the Glass Mountain, The. Grimm, *Other Tales*, p. 26.
Silver, Golden, and Diamond Prince, The. Ranke, *Folktales of Germany*, no. 35.
Three Brothers, The. Musick, *Green Hills of Magic*, no. 31.
Three Castles, The. Calvino, *Italian Folktales*, no. 13.
Wooing of Seppo Ilmarinen, The (Finland). Booss, *Scandinavian Tales*, p. 536.

**531 FERDINAND THE FAITHFUL AND FERDINAND THE UNFAITHFUL.** Ferdinand the Faithful received a key from his godfather, with the instructions that he should open a certain door when he turned fourteen. He thus found a marvelous horse, which became his faithful companion. Ferdinand gained another companion as well, a man named Ferdinand the Unfaithful, but this companion always tried to harm him. The two Ferdinands became servants to the king. At the instigation of Ferdinand the Unfaithful, the king sent Ferdinand the Faithful on a dangerous quest for a princess. With the help of his horse, Ferdinand the Faithful brought back a bride for the king, but the new queen did not love the king, for he had no nose. The queen, in order to demonstrate her magic powers, cut off Ferdinand the Faithful's head and then restored it immediately. The king let her try the same trick on him, but she did not replace his head. After her husband was buried, she married Ferdinand the Faithful. (Grimm) Cf. types 314, 502, 530.

Black King, The; or, Fair Ferentine. Thomas, *It's Good to Tell You*, no. 9.
Blessing Incarnate, The. Dawkins, *More Greek Folktales*, no. 10.
Buideach, the Tinker, and the Black Donkey, The. Glassie, *Irish Folktales*, no. 121.
Corvetto. Basile, *Pentamerone*, Day 3, Tale 7.
Ferdinand the Faithful and Ferdinand the Unfaithful. Grimm, *Tales*, no. 126.
Fioravante and Beautiful Isolina. Calvino, *Italian Folktales*, no. 79.
Firebird and Princess Vasilisa, The. Afanasyev, *Russian Fairy Tales*, p. 494.
Firebird, the Horse of Power, and the Princess Vasilissa, The (Russia). Cole, *Best-Loved Folktales*, no. 93.
Gallant Szérus, The. Dégh, *Folktales of Hungary*, no. 8.
Giant with the Seven Heads, The. Briggs, *DBF*, pt. A, v. 1, p. 265.
Gold Feather. Massignon, *Folktales of France*, no. 11.
Golden Castle That Hung in the Air, The. Asbjørnsen and Moe, *Norwegian Folktales*, p. 139.
Horse of Seven Colors, The. Paredes, *Folktales of Mexico*, no. 35.
Huntsman, The. Villa, *100 Armenian Tales*, no. 15.
King Fortunatus's Golden Wig. Delarue, *French Folktales*, p. 70.
King's Godson and the Baldchin, The. Megas, *Folktales of Greece*, no. 33.

Lovely Florandine, The. Grimm, *Other Tales,* p. 37.
Magic Horse, The. Villa, *100 Armenian Tales,* no. 14.
Mermaid and the Boy, The (Lapland). Lang, *Brown Fairy Book,* p. 165.
Mule, The. Glassie, *Irish Folktales,* no. 116.
Prince, a King, and a Horse, A. Dégh, *Folktales of Hungary,* no. 5.
Servant Who Took the Place of His Master, The (Greece). Thompson, *100
    Folktales,* no. 46.
Servant Who Took the Place of His Master, The. Dawkins, *Modern Greek
    Folktales,* no. 34.
Seven Magic Hairs. Bushnaq, *Arab Folktales,* p. 115.
Ship with Three Decks. Calvino, *Italian Folktales,* no. 3.
Turkey Raiser, The. Saucier, *French Louisiana,* no. 6.

**532\*  GOD'S GODSON.** A poor couple with twelve children could find
no one to be their expected baby's godfather, until Jesus himself
offered his service. At the christening he gave the baby, who was
named Péterke, a calf. When Péterke became twenty, he sought the
hand of the princess. The king agreed, but only if Péterke could plow
a thousand-acre field in a single day. With the help of the calf, now a
bull, he completed the task and married the princess. Cf. type 332.

Péterke. Dégh, *Folktales of Hungary,* no. 7.

**533  THE GOOSEGIRL.** A princess was betrothed to a prince in a
distant kingdom and set forth, accompanied by her maid, to marry
him. En route, the maid forced the princess to exchange places with
her. The false bride married the prince, and the true princess was
forced to tend the geese. Now the false bride was afraid that the
princess's horse, who had the gift of speech, might reveal her secret, so
she had him killed and his head mounted in a gateway. But the horse
still talked to his former mistress about her plight. These miraculous
conversations came to the attention of the king, who then restored the
true bride to her rightful position and had the false bride put to death.
Cf. types 403, 450.

Fair Margaret. Thomas, *It's Good to Tell You,* no. 14.
Fairy Child, The. Villa, *100 Armenian Tales,* no. 3.
Golden Bracelet, The. Campbell, *Cloudwalking Country,* p. 45.
Goose-Girl, The (Germany). Thompson, *100 Folktales,* no. 47.
Goose-Girl, The. Grimm, *Tales,* no. 89.
Jubeinah and the Slave. Bushnaq, *Arab Folktales,* p. 206.
Roswal and Lilian. Briggs, *DBF,* pt. A, v. 2, p. 475.
Treacherous Slave Girl, The. Arewa, *Northern East Africa,* p. 202.
Two Cakes, The. Basile, *Pentamerone,* Day 4, Tale 7.

**533\*  THE SNAKE HELPER.** A girl, carrying lunch to her father,
came upon a snake, who promised her good fortune, if she would take
it home with her. She did as it asked, and from then on her tears
turned to pearls and her laughter produced golden seeds. Later she
became engaged to marry the king, but her jealous sisters cut off her
hands, gouged out her eyes, and left her for dead in the bushes. One of

them then married the king in her place. The snake helped her recover her hands and her eyes. When the false bride gave birth to a child it was a scorpion, but the king gave a party nonetheless. The true bride came, and when the king saw that she laughed golden seeds, he knew what had happened, so he had the two wicked sisters and the scorpion put to death, and he then married his true bride. (Calvino)  Cf. type 433.

Biancabella and the Serpent. Straparola, *Facetious Nights,* Night 1, Tale 3.
Snake, The. Calvino, *Italian Folktales,* no. 12.

## 545B  PUSS-IN-BOOTS.

When Peter's poor parents died, he inherited only a cat. Through various tricks, the cat convinced the king that Peter was a wealthy nobleman. The king, Peter, and the cat went together to a troll's castle, and the cat tricked the troll into looking at the sun, thus killing him. She then asked Peter to cut off her head, which he reluctantly did. In that moment, the cat became a beautiful princess, and she married Peter. (Asbjørnsen and Moe)

Bukhtan Bukhtanovich. Afanasyev, *Russian Fairy Tales,* p. 168.
Dame Cat; or, The Wedding Patron (Greece). Bødker, *European Folk Tales,* p. 197.
Don Joseph Pear. Crane, *Italian Popular Tales,* no. 33.
Earl of Cattenborough, The. Jacobs, *European Folk and Fairy Tales,* no. 11.
Gagliuso. Basile, *Pentamerone,* Day 2, Tale 4.
Gaselle, A. Lang, *Violet Fairy Book,* p. 127.
Gilded Fox, The. Delarue, *French Folktales,* p. 119.
Giovanuzza the Fox. Calvino, *Italian Folktales,* no. 185.
How the Beggar Boy Turned into Count Piro (Sicily). Lang, *Crimson Fairy Book,* p. 243.
Lord Peter. Asbjørnsen and Moe, *East o' the Sun,* p. 295.
Lord Peter (Norway). Thompson, *100 Folktales,* no. 48.
Master Cat, The; or, Puss in Boots (Perrault). Opie, *Classic Fairy Tales,* p. 147.
Mighty Mikko (Finland). Clarkson and Cross, *World Folktales,* no. 3.
Miller and the Fox, The. Villa, *100 Armenian Tales,* no. 10.
Puss in Boots (France). Cole, *Best-Loved Folktales,* no. 3.
Puss in Boots. Crane, *Italian Popular Tales,* no. 34.
Puss in Boots. Massignon, *Folktales of France,* no. 25.
Puss in Boots. Perrault, *Fairy Tales* (trans. Carter), p. 43.
Puss-in-Boots. Grimm, *Other Tales,* p. 29.
Squire Per. Asbjørnsen and Moe, *Norwegian Folktales,* p. 122.

## 545D*  THE BEAN KING.

One day a poor man found a bean. "What luck!" he said to himself, and made plans in his mind how he would plant it and make it multiply until, after a few harvests, he would have storehouses full of beans. With these visions, he borrowed some fine clothes, put the bean in his pocket, and went to a wealthy property owner to lease some warehouses. His clothes made such a good impression, that the rich man offered him his daughter's hand as well. The bean dealer used other tricks as well to make people think he was wealthy, until one day he came to an enormous palace, filled with treasures. A young lady in green appeared and presented it all to him. She was, he now learned, the bean that he had picked up from the ground and carried about in his pocket. (Calvino)

Dealer in Peas and Beans. Calvino, *Italian Folktales,* no. 154.
Man Who Found the Pea (commentary). Dawkins, *Modern Greek Folktales,* no. 63.

**546   A PARROT HELPS THE HERO WIN A PRINCESS.**

Girl with the Golden Hair, The. Thundy, *South Indian Folktales,* no. 54.

**550   THE QUEST FOR THE GOLDEN BIRD.** A king had a tree with golden apples, but every night a golden bird would steal one of the apples. The king's two oldest sons attempted without success to find the golden bird, but the youngest, with the help of a fox that he befriended, succeeded not only in finding the golden bird but also in gaining the hand of a princess. In return, the fox asked the boy to cut off his head. This done, the fox was freed from a magic curse, and he turned into the princess's brother. (Grimm)

Bird Grip, The (Sweden). Lang, *Pink Fairy Book,* p. 132.
Bird of the Golden Feather, The. Bushnaq, *Arab Folktales,* p. 80.
Bird of the Golden Land, The. Campbell, *Cloudwalking Country,* p. 78.
Gold Bird, The (Germany). Thompson, *100 Favorite Folktales,* no. 49.
Golden Bird, The. Grimm, *Tales,* no. 57.
Golden Duck, The. Musick, *Green Hills of Magic,* no. 45.
Golden Nightingale, The. Dawkins, *Modern Greek Folktales,* no. 35A.
Greek Princess and the Young Gardener, The. Jacobs, *More Celtic Fairy Tales,* p. 110.
Horse of Seven Colors, The. Paredes, *Folktales of Mexico,* no. 35.
Jeweled Cage and the Evil Sister, The. Walker and Uysal, *Tales in Turkey,* p. 90.
King of Ireland's Son, The. Glassie, *Irish Folktales,* no. 117.
King of the Herrings, The (I, II). Briggs, *DBF,* pt. A, v. 1, p. 365.
King's Golden Apple Tree, The. Campbell, *Cloudwalking Country,* p. 70.
Lamp Which Never Went Out, The. Dawkins, *Modern Greek Folktales,* no. 35B.
Mac Iain Direach. Campbell, *West Highlands,* v. 2, p. 344.
Monk, The. Megas, *Folktales of Greece,* no. 20.
Mule, The. Glassie, *Irish Folktales,* no. 116.
Nunda, Eater of People, The (Swahili). Lang, *Violet Fairy Book,* p. 249.
Prince Ivan, the Firebird, and the Gray Wolf. Afanasyev, *Russian Fairy Tales,* p. 612.
Prince, A, a King, and a Horse. Dégh, *Folktales of Hungary,* no. 5.
Three Brothers, The. Noy, *Folktales of Israel,* no. 56.
Three Girls with Journey Cakes, The. Campbell, *Cloudwalking Country,* p. 140.
Water of Life, The. Campbell, *Cloudwalking Country,* p. 183.
Witch and Her Servants, The (Russia). Lang, *Yellow Fairy Book,* p. 161.
World Below, The. Villa, *100 Armenian Tales,* no. 34.

**550A  THE ONE GRATEFUL BROTHER.** Three poor brothers set forth to seek better luck. An old man gave one of them a herd of sheep, the second an olive orchard, and the third a bride; he counseled each one to always give to the poor. Disguised as a leper, the old man returned to each of the brothers. The first two rejected him, and they lost their fortunes. The third treated him with kindness, and he received even greater wealth. (Dawkins)

> Only One Brother Was Grateful. Dawkins, *Modern Greek Folktales,* no. 70.
> Three Robbers and El-Khidr. El-Shamy, *Folktales of Egypt,* no. 21.

**551  THE QUEST FOR THE WATER OF LIFE.** A king was very ill, and could be cured only by the water of life. Following unsuccessful attempts by his two older brothers, the youngest son set forth to obtain the magic remedy. A dwarf, whom he befriended, helped him not only to find the water of life for his father but also to protect himself from his envious brothers and to gain the hand of an enchanted princess. (Grimm)

> Bold Knight, The, the Apples of Youth, and the Water of Life. Afanasyev, *Russian Fairy Tales,* p. 314.
> Brown Bear of the Green Glen, The. Campbell, *West Highlands,* v. 1, p. 168.
> Fairy of the Dawn, The (Romania). Lang, *Violet Fairy Book,* p. 165.
> Girl with Golden Hair, The. Thomas, *It's Good to Tell You,* no. 10.
> Golden Bird, The. Asbjørnsen and Moe, *Norwegian Folktales,* p. 49.
> Golden-Headed Fish, The (Armenia). Lang, *Olive Fairy Book,* p. 178.
> Griffin, The. Crane, *Italian Popular Tales,* no. 8.
> King of England and His Three Sons, The. Briggs, *DBF,* pt. A, v. 1, p. 355.
> King of England and His Three Sons, The. Jacobs, *More English Fairy Tales,* p. 142.
> Magic Horse, The. Villa, *100 Armenian Tales,* no. 14.
> Monk, The. Megas, *Folktales of Greece,* no. 20.
> Omadhaun Laois, The. Gmelch and Kroup, *To Shorten the Road,* p. 79.
> Search for the Magic Lake, The (Ecuador). Cole, *Best-Loved Folktales,* no. 198.
> Sleeping Queen, The. Calvino, *Italian Folktales,* no. 61.
> Stolen Crown, The. Calvino, *Italian Folktales,* no. 46.
> Three Orphans, The. Calvino, *Italian Folktales,* no. 138.
> Water of Life, The. Briggs, *DBF,* pt. A, v. 1, p. 560.
> Water of Life, The. Campbell, *Cloudwalking Country,* p. 183.
> Water of Life, The. Grimm, *Tales,* no. 97.
> Well at the World's End, The (Ireland). Thompson, *100 Favorite Folktales,* no. 50.
> Well of the World's End, The. Jacobs, *English Fairy Tales,* p. 215.

**552  THE  GIRLS  WHO  MARRIED  ANIMALS.**  A witch transformed three princes into animals: one a falcon, the second a stag, and the third a dolphin. They married three sisters. The girls' brother, with the help of his animal brothers-in-law rescued another princess from a dragon. The brother married this princess, and the three animals regained their human forms. (Basile) —Note: Tales from this group emphasizing the help given to the hero by his animal brothers-in-law are classified as type 552A. Tales of type 552B focus on the relationship between the brides' father and his animal sons-in-law. Both subcategories are included in the following list.

Animal Sons-in-Law, The (Norway). Bødker, *European Folk Tales,* p. 41.
Crystal Ball, The. Grimm, *Tales,* no. 197.
Fair Fiorita, The. Crane, *Italian Popular Tales,* no. 13.
Maria Morevna. Afanasyev, *Russian Fairy Tales,* p. 553.
Navel of the Earth, The. Megas, *Folktales of Greece,* no. 34.
Ogre's Soul, The. Villa, *100 Armenian Tales,* no. 1.
Princesses Wed to the First Passers-By, The. Calvino, *Italian Folktales,* no. 133.
Sun, the Moon, and the Raven, The. Afanasyev, *Russian Fairy Tales,* p. 588.
Three Animal Kings, The. Basile, *Pentamerone,* Day 4, Tale 3.
Three Princes, The. Dawkins, *Modern Greek Folktales,* no. 23.
Three Sisters, The. Grimm, *Other Tales,* no. 53.
Tree That Reached Up to the Sky, The. Dégh, *Folktales of Hungary,* no. 6.
Weaver's Boy, The. Campbell, *Cloudwalking Country,* p. 85.
What Came of Picking Flowers (Portugal). Lang, *Grey Fairy Book,* p. 93.

**553  THE BIRD HELPER.** A prince came to the aid of a bird fighting with a snake. To show his gratitude, the bird helped the prince find a beautiful princess and obtain a magnificent castle.

Jay Bird That Had a Fight with a Rattle Snake, The. Campbell, *Cloudwalking Country,* p. 132.

**554  THE GRATEFUL ANIMALS.** Three brothers came to an ant hill. The two older ones wanted to destroy it, but the youngest one—whom they called Simpleton—would not allow it. Later the two older ones wanted to catch some ducks and roast them, but Simpleton came to their rescue as well. Further, he also stopped them when they wanted to set fire to a honey tree. Later these animals came to the youngest brother's aid, helping him win the hand of a princess by gathering a thousand scattered pearls, recovering a key from the bottom of a lake, and revealing which of three princesses had eaten honey. (Grimm, no. 62)

Charmed Ring, The. Jacobs, *Indian Fairy Tales,* p. 90.
Child from the Sea, The. Dawkins, *Modern Greek Folktales,* no. 7.
Cinderello. Dawkins, *Modern Greek Folktales,* no. 9.
Cinderello. Megas, *Folktales of Greece,* no. 35.
Fortunio Finds Three Animals and Wins the King's Daughter. Straparola, *Facetious Nights,* Night 3, Tale 4.
Girl with the Golden Hair, The. Thundy, *South Indian Folktales,* no. 54.
Golden-Haired Beauty, The. Pino-Saavedra, *Folktales of Chile,* no. 23.
King of the Herrings, The (I, II). Briggs, *DBF,* pt. A, v. 1, p. 365.
King's Godson and the Baldchin, The. Megas, *Folktales of Greece,* no. 33.
Magic Fruit, The. Arewa, *Northern East Africa,* p. 238.
Master Ever Ready. Grimm, *Other Tales,* p. 41.
Queen Bee, The. Grimm, *Tales,* no. 62.

Red Lion of the Forest, The. Briggs, *DBF*, pt. A, v. 1, p. 470.
Sea-Hare, The. Grimm, *Tales*, no. 191.
Soothsayer's Son, The. Jacobs, *Indian Fairy Tales*, p. 70.
Sultan's Forty Sons, The. Walker and Uysal, *Tales in Turkey*, p. 77.
Thankful Beasts, The. Clouston, *Popular Tales*, v. 1, p. 236.
Three Girls with Journey Cakes, The. Campbell, *Cloudwalking Country*, p. 140.
Tree That Reached Up to the Sky, The. Dégh, *Folktales of Hungary*, no. 6.
White Snake, The. Grimm, *Tales*, no. 17.

## 554B*   THE CHILD WHO WAS RAISED BY AN EAGLE.

Little Wildrose (Romania). Lang, *Crimson Fairy Book*, p. 93.

## 555   THE FISHERMAN AND HIS WIFE.
A fisherman lived with his wife in a miserable hut. One day he caught a fish who claimed to be an enchanted prince, so the fisherman set him free. However, upon hearing this story, the wife insisted that her husband ask the fish to give them a cottage. The husband called upon the fish, and their miserable hut did indeed turn into a pleasant cottage. But the wife was not satisfied for long; next she wanted a stone castle; then to be king, then emperor, and then pope. The husband, each time more reluctantly, asked the fish for these gifts, and each was granted. But the woman was still not satisfied, and finally she asked to be even as God is. This request was met with a great storm, and when the fisherman returned home he found his wife, as in the beginning, sitting in their miserable hut. (Grimm, no. 19)

Fisherman and His Wife, The. Grimm, *Tales*, no. 19.
Gold-Children, The. Grimm, *Tales*, no. 85.
Goldfish, The (Russia). Thompson, *100 Favorite Folktales*, no. 51.
Goldfish, The. Afanasyev, *Russian Fairy Tales*, p. 528.
Little Sardine, The. Delarue, *French Folktales*, p. 226.
My Old Woman Must Be Paid. Simpson, *Icelandic Folktales and Legends*, p. 60.
Old Woman Who Lived in a Vinegar Bottle, The. Briggs, *DBF*, pt. A, v. 1, p. 436.
Pea, The. Massignon, *Folktales of France*, no. 26.
Stone-Cutter, The (Japan). Lang, *Crimson Fairy Book*, p. 192.
Stonecutter, The (Japan). Cole, *Best-Loved Folktales*, no. 118.
Wanto and the Shapeless Thing (Cameroun). Dorson, *Folktales around the World*, p. 360.

## 559   MAKING THE PRINCESS LAUGH.
Jack traded three cows for a magic stick, a singing bee, and a fiddle that played itself. Now the king's daughter would never smile, so the king declared that anyone who could make her laugh could marry her. Jack appeared at court with his magic objects. The princess heard the singing bee, and she smiled; the fiddle playing itself made her smile again; and when Jack turned his stick loose, and it began batting the people about, the

princess laughed out loud. Thus Jack won the hand of the princess. (Briggs) —Cf. types 571, 1642.

> Cockchafer, the Mouse, and the Grasshopper. Basile, *Pentamerone,* Day 3, Tale 5.
> Jack and His Bargains. Briggs, *DBF,* pt. A, v. 1, p. 314.
> Jack from Tubberclare. Gmelch and Kroup, *To Shorten the Road,* p. 62.
> King's Daughter Laughed. Randolph, *The Devil's Pretty Daughter,* p. 83.
> La Ramée. Massignon, *Folktales of France,* no. 14.
> Louse Skin, The. Paredes, *Folktales of Mexico,* no. 37.
> Sultan Offers His Daughter as a Prize. The. Arewa, *Northern East Africa,* p. 236.

**560  THE MAGIC RING.** A boy saved the life of a dog, a cat, and a snake. The snake's father—in gratitude—gave the boy a magic ring, and with its power he won the hand of the princess. However, his bride helped a servant steal the ring, and he used its power to transport her and the castle to the bottom of the sea. The dog and cat whose lives the hero had saved recovered the ring for him. He thus got back his castle and his wife, and the wicked servant was put to death. (Megas)

> Adventures of Mehmet the Mad, The. Walker and Uysal, *Tales in Turkey,* p. 24.
> Cinderello. Dawkins, *Modern Greek Folktales,* no. 9.
> Cinderello. Megas, *Folktales of Greece,* no. 35.
> Cock's Stone, The. Basile, *Pentamerone,* Day 4, Tale 1.
> Enchanted Ring, The (Sebillot). Lang, *Green Fairy Book,* p. 137.
> Enchanted Watch, The (Deulin). Lang, *Green Fairy Book,* p. 43.
> Farmer and the Money-Lender, The. Jacobs, *Indian Fairy Tales,* p. 152.
> Girl with the Golden Hair, The. Thundy, *South Indian Folktales,* no. 54.
> Grateful Animals and the Talisman, The (Greece). Thompson, *100 Folktales,* no. 52.
> Helpful Animals, The. Eberhard, *Folktales of China,* no. 62.
> Jack and His Golden Snuff-Box. Briggs, *DBF,* pt. A, v. 1, p. 334.
> Jack and His Golden Snuff-Box. Jacobs, *English Fairy Tales,* p. 81.
> King of the Golden Mountain, The. Grimm, *Tales,* no. 92.
> Magic Coconut, The. Pino-Saavedra, *Folktales of Chile,* no. 24.
> Magic Ring, The. Calvino, *Italian Folktales,* no. 42.
> Magic Ring, The. Lang, *Yellow Fairy Book,* p. 178.
> Magic Ring, The. Villa, *100 Armenian Tales,* no. 20.
> Poor Woodcutter, The. Paredes, *Folktales of Mexico,* no. 36.
> Prince Green Serpent and La Valeur. Thomas, *It's Good to Tell You,* no. 11.
> Ring of the King of the Djinn, The. Bushnaq, *Arab Folktales,* p. 142.
> Ring, The. Musick, *Green Hills of Magic,* no. 30.
> Snuff-Box, The (Sebillot). Lang, *Green Fairy Book,* p. 145.
> Soria Moria Castle. Asbjørnsen and Moe, *East o' the Sun,* p. 396.
> Soria Moria Castle. Asbjørnsen and Moe, *Norwegian Folktales,* p. 67.
> Wooden Horse, The. Grimm, *Other Tales,* p. 50.

**561  ALADDIN AND HIS MAGIC LAMP.** Aladdin came into the possession of a lamp that, when rubbed, produced a genie who would obey every command. With this power Aladdin gained great wealth and the hand of the princess. But an evil magician stole the lamp and had Aladdin's palace, the princess included, carried away. With the help of a magic ring Aladdin recovered the magic lamp and regained his palace and his wife. *(1001 Nights)*

Ala al-Din and the Wonderful Lamp. Mathers, *1001 Nights,* v. 3, p. 369.

Aladdin and the Enchanted Lamp. Dawood, *Tales from the 1001 Nights,* p. 165.

Aladdin and the Wonderful Lamp (1001 Nights). Cole, *Best-Loved Folktales,* no. 107.

Aladdin and the Wonderful Lamp (1001 Nights). Lang, *Blue Fairy Book,* p. 72.

Cock and the Hand Mill, The. Afanasyev, *Russian Fairy Tales,* p. 387.

Enchanted Ring, The. Afanasyev, *Russian Fairy Tales,* p. 31.

Fisherman's Son and the Magic Ring (Turkey). Clouston, *Popular Tales,* v. 1, p. 330.

Hans and the Wishing Box (Denmark). Clouston, *Popular Tales,* v. 1, p. 327.

How Cajusse Was Married (Italy). Clouston, *Popular Tales,* v. 1, p. 314.

Jenik and His Magic Watch (Bohemia). Clouston, *Popular Tales,* v. 1, p. 321.

Magic Box, The. Afanasyev, *Russian Fairy Tales,* p. 164.

Magic Lamp, The. Ranke, *Folktales of Germany,* no. 40.

Magic Ring, The (Burma). Clouston, *Popular Tales,* v. 1, p. 476.

Magic Ring, The (Greece). Clouston, *Popular Tales,* v. 1, p. 325.

Magic Ring, The (India). Clouston, *Popular Tales,* v. 1, p. 337.

Magic Shirt, The. Afanasyev, *Russian Fairy Tales,* p. 110.

Magic Stone, The (Albania). Clouston, *Popular Tales,* v. 1, p. 324.

Maruf's Magic Ring (Arabic). Clouston, *Popular Tales,* v. 1, p. 470.

Ring and the Lamp, The. Grimm, *Other Tales,* p. 73.

Tushcoon Eigna. Villa, *100 Armenian Tales,* no. 40.

Wishing-Stone, The (Mongolia). Clouston, *Popular Tales,* v. 1, p. 335.

**562  THE SPIRIT IN THE BLUE LIGHT.** A soldier, unfairly dismissed from service, came into the possession of a magic blue lantern. To gain revenge, the soldier had the magic man of the lantern bring the king's daughter to his room every night, but he got caught in this act, and was sentenced to die. At the last moment the magic man came to his rescue, knocking everyone to the ground. The terrified king surrendered not only his daughter, but also his entire kingdom to the soldier. (Grimm)

Blue Light, The. Grimm, *Tales,* no. 116.

Hagop's Wish. Villa, *100 Armenian Tales,* no. 21.

Lars, My Lad! (Sweden). Booss, *Scandinavian Tales,* p. 169.

Soldier of the Blue Light. Roberts, *South from Hell,* no. 22.

Tinder Box, The (Andersen). Opie, *Classic Fairy Tales,* p. 272.

Tinderbox, The. Andersen, *Complete Fairy Tales,* no. 1.

**563  THE TABLE, THE ASS, AND THE STICK.** Three brothers learned different trades. The first became a joiner, and his master presented him with a table that would magically spread itself with fine food, but an innkeeper stole the table. The second became a miller, and his master gave him a donkey that would drop gold pieces, but the innkeeper stole it also. The youngest brother became a turner, and his master gave him a cudgel that would beat anyone its master told it to. Learning about his brothers' losses, the youngest boy set his cudgel to the innkeeper, not calling it off until he returned the stolen donkey and table. (Grimm)

Ari-Ari, Donkey, Donkey, Money, Money! Calvino, *Italian Folktales*, no. 127.

Ass That Lays Money, The (Italy). Thompson, *100 Favorite Folktales*, no. 53.

Ass That Lays Money, The. Crane, *Italian Popular Tales*, no. 32.

Ass, the Table and the Stick, The. Briggs, *DBF*, pt. A, v. 1, p. 141.

Ass, the Table, and the Stick, The. Jacobs, *English Fairy Tales*, p. 206.

Beggar and His Ass, The. Noy, *Folktales of Israel*, no. 20.

Boy and His Wages, The. Briggs, *DBF*, pt. A, v. 1, p. 169.

Boy and the Box, The. Dawkins, *Modern Greek Folktales*, no. 8.

Coffeemill, the Tray, and the Stick, The. Noy, *Folktales of Israel*, no. 21.

Father Grumbler. Lang, *Brown Fairy Book*, p. 77.

Father Louison and the Mother of the Wind. Delarue, *French Folktales*, p. 204.

Frost and His Neighbors. Ranke, *Folktales of Germany*, no. 41.

Invisible Caps and Cloaks. Clouston, *Popular Tales*, v. 1, p. 72, 461.

Jack and the North West Wind. Chase, *The Jack Tales*, no. 5.

Koshalki-Opalki (Poland). Clarkson and Cross, *World Folktales*, no. 1.

Lad Who Went to the North Wind, The. Asbjørnsen and Moe, *East o' the Sun*, p. 228.

Magic Bag, The. Roberts, *South from Hell*, no. 23A.

Magic Gifts, The. Fowke, *Folklore of Canada*, p. 129.

Magic Napkin, The. Massignon, *Folktales of France*, no. 51.

North Wind's Gift, The. Calvino, *Italian Folktales*, no. 83.

Ogre, The (Italy). Lang, *Grey Fairy Book*, p. 344.

Ogre, The. Basile, *Pentamerone*, Day 1, Tale 1.

Old Man La Feve. Thomas, *It's Good to Tell You*, no. 12.

Salt-Grinding Millstones, The. Seki, *Folktales of Japan*, no. 39.

Seven Mysteries of the Luck, The. Briggs, *DBF*, pt. A, v. 1, p. 478.

Smart Brother and the Crazy Brother, The (Turkey). Dorson, *Folktales around the World*, p. 138.

Switch, the Tablecloth, and the Harmonica. Musick, *Green Hills of Magic*, no. 34.

Table-Be-Set, Gold-Donkey, and Cudgel-out-of-the-Sack. Grimm, *Tales*, no. 36.

**564  THE MAGIC PURSE AND "OUT OF THE SACK!"** An old woman constantly abused her husband. One day a crane gave him a magic sack that, at his calling, produced two men who prepared a fine meal. On his way home he stopped at his godmother's house, and she stole the magic sack. Then the crane gave him another sack, one that held two men with clubs. The old man visited his godmother again, and the men with clubs beat her until she returned the stolen sack. The man took both sacks home. He gave his wife a good meal from the one and hung the other nearby. The wife wanted more to eat and went to the nearest sack; out jumped the men with the clubs and beat her without mercy, while her husband walked around laughing. Finally he called them off, and from that time the man and his wife lived in harmony. (Afanasyev)

> Two Out of the Sack (Russia). Thompson, *100 Favorite Folktales*, no. 54.
> Two Out of the Sack. Afanasyev, *Russian Fairy Tales*, p. 321.

**565  THE MAGIC MILL.** A poor man came into the possession of a magic mill that would produce anything he requested. A seaman, tired of long voyages for salt, bought the mill for a high price and set it to work producing salt. To his dismay he couldn't make it stop. His ship filled with salt and sunk. The mill is still at the bottom of the sea grinding away, and that is why the sea is salty. (Asbjørnsen and Moe)

> Master and His Pupil, The. Briggs, *DBF*, pt. A, v. 1, p. 411.
> Mill That Grinds at the Bottom of the Sea, The. Asbjørnsen and Moe, *Norwegian Folktales*, p. 108.
> Mill, The. Megas, *Folktales of Greece*, no. 36.
> Old Handmill, The. Briggs, *DBF*, pt. A, v. 1, p. 427.
> Salt-Grinding Millstones, The. Seki, *Folktales of Japan*, no. 39.
> Sweet Porridge. Grimm, *Tales*, no. 103.
> Water Mother, The. Eberhard, *Folktales of China*, no. 49.
> Why the Sea Is Salt (Norway). Clarkson and Cross, *World Folktales*, no. 58.
> Why the Sea Is Salt. Asbjørnsen and Moe, *East o' the Sun*, p. 8.

**566  FRUIT THAT GROWS HORNS (FORTUNATUS).** A laborer married a princess whom he had rescued from a dragon. But she grew tired of living with him, stole his magic tablecloth, and escaped on his flying carpet. He then discovered two magic trees. Fruit from the first caused horns to grow on one's head; fruit from the other removed them. He found his runaway wife and tricked her into eating the horn-producing apples. When she implored him to make her beautiful again, he beat her severely with an iron rod. When she finally repented and returned the magic items she had stolen, he gave her the fruit that removed the horns. Then they lived happily together. (Afanasyev)

> Adventures of Mehmet the Mad, The. Walker and Uysal, *Tales in Turkey*, p. 24.
> Cabbage-Donkey, The. Grimm, *Tales*, no. 122.
> Fortunatus and His Purse. Lang, *Grey Fairy Book*, p. 74.
> Fortunatus. Briggs, *DBF*, pt. A, v. 1, p. 245.
> Horns (Russia). Thompson, *100 Favorite Folktales*, no. 55.
> Horns. Afanasyev, *Russian Fairy Tales*, p. 292.
> Invisible Caps and Cloaks. Clouston, *Popular Tales*, v. 1, p. 72.
> Johnnie and Tommie. Gmelch and Kroup, *To Shorten the Road*, p. 41.
> Kenneth the Yellow. Campbell, *West Highlands*, v. 1, p. 194.
> Little Soldier, The (Deulin). Lang, *Green Fairy Book*, p. 157.
> Magic Figs, The. Villa, *100 Armenian Tales*, no. 13.
> Magic Flute of Asmodeus, The. Schwartz, *Elijah's Violin*, p. 94.
> Man and His Three Sons, The. Saucier, *French Louisiana*, no. 10.
> Princess with the Horns, The. Calvino, *Italian Folktales*, no. 189.

Shepherd Who Made the King's Daughter Laugh. Crane, *Italian Popular Tales,*
   no. 31.
Three Deserters, The. Massignon, *Folktales of France,* no. 65.
Three Soldiers, The. Campbell, *West Highlands,* v. 1, p. 181.
Three Soldiers, The (another version). Campbell, *West Highlands,* v. 1, p.
   195.
Three Soldiers, The. Jacobs, *European Folk and Fairy Tales,* no. 9.
Tiidu the Piper (Estonia). Lang, *Crimson Fairy Book,* p. 108.
Two Brothers in Fortune. Grimm, *Other Tales,* p. 79.

**567   THE MAGIC BIRD HEART.**   A hunter befriended an old woman
in the forest.   In gratitude, she told him where he could find a cloak
that made its wearer invisible and a bird whose heart, if swallowed,
would give him a gold piece every morning.   He found the magic
cloak, swallowed the bird heart, and set forth.   An old witch who lived
with a beautiful girl took him in; they gave him a drink that brought up
the magic heart, and stole his cloak, leaving him with nothing.
—Continues as type 566. (Grimm)

Bird Liver, The. Campbell, *Cloudwalking Country,* p. 195.
Cabbage Heads That Worked Magic, The. Campbell, *Cloudwalking Country,*
   p. 156.
Cabbage-Donkey, The. Grimm, *Tales,* no. 122.
Crab with the Golden Eggs. Calvino, *Italian Folktales,* no. 146.
Magic Bird-Heart. Villa, *100 Armenian Tales,* no. 12.
Magic Bird, The (Greece). Thompson, *100 Favorite Folktales,* no. 56.
Magic Bird, The. Dawkins, *Modern Greek Folktales,* no. 22.

**567A   THE MAGIC BIRD HEART AND THE TWIN BROTHERS.**
An evil-hearted goldsmith came into the possession of a golden bird,
and knowing that whoever ate its heart and liver would find a piece of
gold beneath his pillow every morning, he ordered the bird cooked.
His nephews, the twin sons of a poor broommaker, were in the kitchen,
and when two little morsels fell out of the bird, they ate them. These
were the heart and liver, and the next morning they found gold pieces
in their beds.   To avenge his loss, the goldsmith tricked the
broommaker into abandoning the twins in the forest.   —Continues as
type 303. (Grimm, no. 60)

Duck with Golden Eggs, The. Afanasyev, *Russian Fairy Tales,* p. 541.
Johnnie and Tommie. Gmelch and Kroup, *To Shorten the Road,* p. 41.
Magic Bird-Heart. Villa, *100 Armenian Tales,* no. 12.
Two Brothers in Fortune. Grimm, *Other Tales,* p. 79.
Two Brothers, The. Grimm, *Tales,* no. 60.

**569   THE KNAPSACK, THE HAT, AND THE HORN.**   A boy found
a magic table cloth in the woods.   Not seeing its owner, he took it with
him.   He came to a man who owned a knapsack that would, on
command, yield seven warriors.   The boy traded the magic cloth for
the knapsack, but he then called up the seven warriors, who stole back
the cloth for him.   Next he came to a man who had a magic hat with the

power of twelve cannons. He gave this man the magic cloth in return for the hat, but once again he recovered the cloth with the help of the warriors from the knapsack. A third man had a magic horn that would cause any fortification to crumble. As before, he traded the cloth for the horn, having his warriors take back the cloth. He then went to war, making peace only after the king agreed to give him his daughter in marriage. His bride discovered the secret of the knapsack, and she turned its warriors against their former master. But he still had the horn, and he blew on it until the castle fell in, crushing the king and his daughter to death. Then he was king, and no one dared to oppose him. (Grimm)  Cf. types 518, 581.

Ciccu (Sicily). Lang, *Pink Fairy Book,* p. 339.
Go I Know Not Wither, Bring Back I Know Not What. Afanasyev, *Russian Fairy Tales,* p. 504.
Habie's Whistle. Briggs, *DBF,* pt. A, v. 1, p. 306.
How the Raja's Son Won the Princess Labam (India).  Cole, *Best-Loved Folktales,* no. 144.
How the Raja's Son Won the Princess Labam. Jacobs, *Indian Fairy Tales,* p. 3.
King of the Cats, The. Briggs, *DBF,* pt. A, v. 1, p. 350.
Knapsack, the Hat, and the Horn, The. Grimm, *Tales,* no. 54.
Magic Knapsack, The. Briggs, *DBF,* pt. A, v. 1, p. 396.
Sticks in the Knapsack. Randolph, *Sticks in the Knapsack,* p. 3E.
Three Treasures of the Giants, The. Lang, *Orange Fairy Book,* p. 177.

**570   THE RABBIT HERD.**  A king announced that the man who could cure his sick daughter could have her hand in marriage.  A simpleton set out to try his luck and en route was kind to an old man.  The man blessed the simpleton's medicine and gave him a magic flute as well. The medicine worked, but the king, not wanting his daughter to marry a simpleton, gave him an additional task; he was to tend 300 rabbits without losing one.  To make him fail, the princess asked him for a rabbit, but he would not give her one until she went behind the bushes with him.  Afterward he played his magic flute, and the rabbit jumped from the princess's basket and returned to the herd.  Next the queen asked for a rabbit.  She too had to go behind the bushes with the simpleton, and she too lost the rabbit when he played the magic flute. Finally the king tried.  The simpleton made him lick a dead donkey's behind for a rabbit, but it too returned to the herd when the simpleton played his flute.  The king then gave the simpleton another task; he was to talk three bags full.  In the presence of the court, the simpleton began to tell about going behind the bushes with the princess, but she shut him up, saying: "That bag's full!"  The queen stopped him in the same way, when he started to tell about her, as did the king when he started talking about the dead donkey.  Thus the princess had to marry him after all.  (Ranke)

Eighteen Rabbits, The. Sampson, *Gypsy Folk Tales,* p. 66.

Fill, Bowl! Fill! Chase, *The Jack Tales,* no. 10.
Fill, Bowl, Fill! Randolph, *Who Blowed Up the Church House?,* p. 17.
Fill, Bowl, Fill. Randolph, *Pissing in the Snow,* no. 29.
Hare Herd, The. Ranke, *Folktales of Germany,* no. 42.
Ignez Was a Burro. Dorson, *Buying the Wind,* p. 423.
Jesper Who Herded the Hares (Scandinavia). Lang, *Violet Fairy Book,* p. 205.
Jock and His Lulls. Briggs, *DBF,* pt. A, v. 1, p. 336.
Kings's Daughter Who Could Never Get Enough Figs, The. Calvino, *Italian Folktales,* no. 47.
King's Hares, The (Norway). Thompson, *100 Favorite Folktales,* no. 57.
Magic Fife, The. Afanasyev, *Erotic Tales,* p. 41.
Riddle, The. Espinosa, *Folklore of Spain in the American Southwest,* p. 178.
Temptations (Denmark). Booss, *Scandinavian Tales,* p. 488.
Three May Peaches, The. Delarue, *French Folktales,* p. 3.
Wonderful Whistle, The. Afanasyev, *Russian Secret Tales,* p. 169.

**571  ALL STICK TOGETHER.** A simpleton shared his lunch with an old man, and in return the man gave him a golden goose. Everyone who touched the goose stuck fast to it, and soon it had attracted many people, all hopelessly attached. The simpleton pulled his unusual following to the palace of a princess who never laughed. The king had decreed that whoever could make her laugh would become her husband. When the princess saw the strange spectacle, she laughed aloud. Hence, the simpleton married her, and when the king died, he inherited the kingdom as well. (Grimm)

Dove and the Fox, The (Italy). Dorson, *Folktales around the World,* p. 74.
Gilly and His Goat Skin Clothes. Campbell, *Cloudwalking Country,* p. 100.
Golden Goose, The. Grimm, *Tales,* no. 64.
Jack and the King's Girl. Chase, *The Jack Tales,* no. 9.
Kid, The. Delarue, *French Folktales,* p. 263.
King's Daughter Laughed. Randolph, *The Devil's Pretty Daughter,* p. 83.
Lamb with the Golden Fleece, The (Hungary). Thompson, *100 Folktales,* no. 58.
Lazy Jack. Briggs, *DBF,* pt. A, v. 2, p. 150.
Lazy Jack. Jacobs, *English Fairy Tales,* p. 152.
Magic Swan, The (Kletke). Lang, *Green Fairy Book,* p. 175.
Royal Candlestick, The. El-Shamy, *Folktales of Egypt,* no. 7.
Quack Quack! Stick to My Back! Calvino, *Italian Folktales,* no. 38.
Taper-Tom Who Made the Princess Laugh. Asbjørnsen and Moe, *Norwegian Folktales,* p. 20.

**571B  THE HIMPHAMP.** A merchant's wife asked him to bring her a wondrous wonder, a marvelous marvel, but in all his travels he could not find one. Finally an old man sold him a goose, claiming it was what he was seeking. The merchant gave his wife the goose, and during his next absence, she invited her lover to a goose dinner with her. However, they both became attached to the goose, and it pulled them into the street. Everyone who came to their aid became stuck as well. Then the merchant appeared, and he gave his wife a thorough beating, repeating with each blow: "Here is your wondrous wonder, your marvelous marvel!" —Note: The more traditional form of this tale (not available in a current English translation) casts the lover as a king and his mistress as a blacksmith's wife, while the magic object—called a "himphamp" or other nonsense term—is an iron chamber pot that traps the lovers in a compromising situation.

> Wondrous Wonder, Marvelous Marvel. Afanasyev, *Russian Fairy Tales,* p. 13.

**576  THE MAGIC KNIFE.** A king told a suitor that he could marry the princess only if he tamed three wild horses and brought him as much gold as they could carry. The princess gave the boy a magic knife that helped him fulfill these tasks, and the two were married.

> Enchanted Knife, The (Serbia). Lang, *Violet Fairy Book,* p. 199.

**577  THE KING'S TASKS.** A king promised his daughter's hand to the man who could cut down a giant oak that was blocking his light and also dig him a well that would hold water for a year. No one could accomplish these tasks, because for every chip that was cut from the tree, two grew back in its place, and further, the castle was located high on a hill of solid rock. Boots, the youngest of three brothers, happened to find an ax that chopped by itself and a spade that dug by itself. Taking these to the castle, he commanded them to cut and dig. In a short time the tree had been felled and the well was full of water, and Boots married the princess. (Asbjørnsen and Moe) Cf. type 313.

> Ax, the Spade, and the Walnut, The. Musick, *Green Hills of Magic,* no. 44.
> Boots and His Brothers (Norway). Clarkson and Cross, *World Folktales,* no. 45.
> Boots and His Brothers. Asbjørnsen and Moe, *East o' the Sun,* p. 330.
> Jack and the Miller's Daughter. Roberts, *South from Hell,* no. 24.
> Madschun (Turkey). Lang, *Olive Fairy Book,* p. 1.
> Three Brothers and the Three Tasks, The. Briggs, *DBF,* pt. A, v. 1, p. 507.

**580  BELOVED OF WOMEN.** Each of three brothers was granted a wish. The two older ones requested endless wealth, but the youngest one, whom they called Boots, asked that every woman who saw him should fall in love with him. Then they set forth into the world. At their first three stops the innkeepers' wives fell so in love with Boots that they gave him magic gifts: scissors that made fine clothes, a table cloth that created marvelous meals, and a tap that produced the best ale and wine. When the princess heard of these marvelous things she asked to see them, and in the course of events she fell in love with Boots. Thus he married the princess and inherited the kingdom. (Asbjørnsen and Moe)

> Best Wish, The. Asbjørnsen and Moe, *East o' the Sun,* p. 252.
> One Who is Loved By Womankind Will Never Find Himself in Need. Christiansen, *Folktales of Norway,* p. 234.

**580\*   MONEY WITHOUT END.**   A stranger gave a man a florin, telling him to buy himself a glass of whiskey, which he did, putting the change in his pocket. Later he found the same florin in his pocket. So it went for a long time: he spent the florin often, but it always returned to his pocket. Finally, overcome with fear, he threw the coin away, saying: "May the devil go with you!" This time it vanished for good. (O'Sullivan)

> Buideach, the Tinker, and the Black Donkey, The. Glassie, *Irish Folktales,* no. 121.
> Fairy Money. O'Sullivan, *Folktales of Ireland,* no. 28.
> Fairy Shilling, The. Glassie, *Irish Folktales,* no. 74.
> King Neptune's Diamonds. Musick, *Green Hills of Magic,* no. 51.
> Man Who Sold His Shadow, The. Musick, *Green Hills of Magic,* no. 2.
> Rich Beggar and His Wonderful Purse, The. Noy, *Folktales of Israel,* no. 19.

**581   THE TWIN BROTHERS AND THEIR MAGIC OBJECTS.**   A poor couple had many children. The woman gave birth once again, this time to twins. Not wanting to be a burden, the two boys immediately set forth into the world. They christened each other in a brook, and then parted. The younger came to an old hag with only one eye, which he stole, giving it back only after she gave him a magic sword. In a similar manner he acquired other magic gifts from two other one-eyed women. —Continues as type 303.

> Shortshanks. Asbjørnsen and Moe, *East o' the Sun,* p. 131.

**585   SPINDLE, SHUTTLE, AND NEEDLE.**   An orphan girl's only inheritance was a little house, a spindle, a shuttle, and a needle. One day her spindle danced away, leaving a trail of golden thread, until it came to the king, who was passing through the village while on a quest for a bride. Next the shuttle escaped, weaving a carpet as it ran; and the needle flew about her room, covering everything with beautiful cloth and curtains. Drawn by the thread from the spindle, the king appeared at her door, and he asked the little seamstress to be his bride. (Grimm)

> Jack and the Ghosts. Briggs, *DBF,* pt. A, v. 1, p. 323.
> Spindle, Shuttle, and Needle. Grimm, *Tales,* no. 188.
> Spindle, the Shuttle, and the Needle—All Golden, The. Campbell, *Cloudwalking Country,* p. 27.

**590   THE MAGIC BELT.**   A boy, walking with his mother, found a little blue belt, and when he put it on, it made him strong enough to pick up a hill. They found shelter in a house where a giant troll lived. In the night, the boy heard the giant say to his mother: "We two could live happily together, if we could get rid of your son." In the following days they gave the boy dangerous tasks, hoping he would be killed, but with the help of his magic belt, he always completed them safely. Finally the mother succeeded in taking the belt away from him, then she and the troll burned out his eyes and set him adrift. However, lions he had earlier befriended rescued him and restored his sight. He sneaked back to the troll's castle and put on the magic belt. He struck his mother dead, then burned out the troll's eyes and set him adrift to die. More adventures followed, and he rescued a princess, winning her hand in marriage. (Asbjørnsen and Moe)

Black Crow and the White Cheese, The. El-Shamy, *Folktales of Egypt*, no. 2.
Blue Band, The. Christiansen, *Folktales of Norway*, p. 193.
Blue Belt, The (Norway). Thompson, *100 Favorite Folktales*, no. 59.
Blue Belt, The. Asbjørnsen and Moe, *East o' the Sun*, p. 155.
Child Is Promised to a Lion, A. Arewa, *Northern East Africa*, p. 156.
Foolish Boy, The. Pino-Saavedra, *Folktales of Chile*, no. 25.
Gallant Szérus, The. Dégh, *Folktales of Hungary*, no. 8.
King's Son Who Is Afraid of Nothing, The. Grimm, *Tales*, no. 121.
Strigla, The (The Gelló). Dawkins, *Modern Greek Folktales*, no. 27.
Strong Prince, The (Hungary). Lang, *Crimson Fairy Book*, p. 145.
Wonderful Sword, The. Gmelch and Kroup, *To Shorten the Road*, p. 156.

**592 DANCING IN THORNS.** A traveler befriended a dwarf, and in return received three things: a gun that would always hit its mark, a fiddle that would cause everyone to dance who heard it, and the gift that no one could refuse to grant any favor he might ask. Soon afterward he met a Jew listening to a bird perched high in a tree. The traveler shot the bird, and it fell into a thorn bush. "Fetch the bird," he said, and the Jew had to obey. With the Jew in the thorn bush, the man began to play the fiddle, forcing the Jew to dance until he was scratched and cut all over. He would not stop playing until the Jew gave him his purse of gold. The Jew reported the incident, and the fiddler was brought to court and sentenced to be hanged. The judge granted him one last request: to play his fiddle. The music caused the hangman, the judge, and everyone else to dance until they fell to the ground. The fiddler threatened to play more if the Jew did not confess to his past crimes. He did so, and was hanged as a thief. (Grimm) —Note: In many older versions of this tale, a monk—not a Jew—is the cruel fiddler's victim.

Friar and the Boy, The. Briggs, *DBF*, pt. A, v. 1, p. 250.
Gifts of the Magician, The (Finland). Lang, *Crimson Fairy Book*, p. 134.
Jew in the Thorns, The. Grimm, *Tales*, no. 110.
Jew That Danced among the Thorns, The. Campbell, *Cloudwalking Country*, p. 224.
Little Freddie and His Fiddle. Asbjørnsen and Moe, *Norwegian Folktales*, p. 61.
Poor Man's Son, The. Saucier, *French Louisiana*, no. 20.

**593 BLOWING UP THE FIRE.** Kiot-Jean loved Jacqueline, but her father would not approve their marriage. To help Kiot-Jean, an old

shepherd gave him some red powder, which, at his next visit to
Jacqueline, he sprinkled on the fire. One after the other, everyone in
the household came to blow up the fire, but then they could not stop
blowing. They all puffed and puffed until the father gave Kiot-Jean
permission to marry Jacqueline, thus lifting the curse. (Delarue)

Aunt Kate's Goomer-Dust. Randolph, *The Devil's Pretty Daughter,* p. 15.
How Kiot-Jean Married Jacqueline. Delarue, *French Folktales,* p. 267.

**610  FRUIT TO CURE THE PRINCESS.** A king proclaimed that
anyone who cured his sick daughter could have her hand in marriage.
The oldest of three brothers set forth with a basket of apples, hoping
that this would be the right medicine. On the way he met a little man
who asked what he had in the basket. "Frog legs," he answered. When
the princess opened the basket, it was indeed filled with frog legs, and
the boy was driven away. The second brother had a similar
experience, ending up with a basket of hog bristles. The youngest
brother tried his luck as well, but he told the little man that his basket
contained apples to cure the princess, and that is indeed what happened.
(Grimm) —Continues as type 461.

Griffin, The. Grimm, *Tales,* no. 165.
Kings's Daughter Who Could Never Get Enough Figs, The. Calvino, *Italian
    Folktales,* no. 47.

**612  THE THREE SNAKE-LEAVES.** A man married a princess, who
made him promise, that he would be buried with her, should she die
first. Shortly thereafter she fell sick and died, and he had himself
locked in her tomb. Inside he saw a snake, which he cut into pieces.
To his amazement another snake appeared carrying three green leaves,
with which it brought the dead snake back to life. The man placed the
leaves on his dead wife's eyes and mouth, and she too came back to life.
But a change had come over her. She soon fell in love with a sea
captain, and, while on a voyage with her husband, she and the captain
threw the husband overboard, and he drowned. However, the man's
faithful servant saw what had happened, and he fished his dead master
from the sea and revived him with the snake-leaves. When his wife
and her lover landed, they were caught in their lies. Her father, the
king, sent them both back to sea in a ship that had been pierced with
holes, and they soon sank and drowned. (Grimm) Cf. Christiansen,
*Migratory Legends,* type 3030.

Captain and the General, The. Calvino, *Italian Folktales,* no. 179.
Governor's Son, The. Lindell, *Folk Tales from Kammu,* II, no. 14.
Lion's Grass, The. Calvino, *Italian Folktales,* no. 194.
Snake-Doctor, The. Campbell, *Cloudwalking Country,* p. 188.
Three Snake-Leaves, The. Grimm, *Tales,* no. 16.
Tobey the King Snake. Randolph, *The Talking Turtle,* p. 68.

**613 THE TWO TRAVELERS: TRUTH AND FALSEHOOD.** A good-natured tailor and an evil-spirited shoemaker met on their travels. The tailor ran out of food, and the shoemaker would share his bread only in return for his companion's eyes. Thus, having to choose between starvation and blindness, the tailor gave up his eyes. Later he learned from two crows that the dew would restore a blind person's sight. He accordingly washed his eye sockets with dew, and his vision returned. —Continues as type 554. (Grimm, "The Two Travelers")

Good Apprentice and the Bad, The. Bushnaq, *Arab Folktales*, p. 129.
Good Man and the Bad Man, The. Clouston, *Popular Tales*, v. 1, p. 249, 464.
Gossiping Animals, The. Eberhard, *Folktales of China*, no. 55.
Grateful Beasts, The (Hungary). Lang, *Yellow Fairy Book*, p. 64.
Lion, the Leper and the Tod, The. Briggs, *DBF*, pt. A, v. 1, p. 121.
Miser and a Generous Man, A. Noy, *Folktales of Israel*, no. 22.
Mountain of the Sun, The. Noy, *Folktales of Israel*, no. 23.
Noble and the Vile, The. El-Shamy, *Folktales of Egypt*, no. 14.
Rich Boy and the Poor Boy, The. Villa, *100 Armenian Tales*, no. 41.
Right and Wrong. Afanasyev, *Russian Fairy Tales*, p. 202.
Shoemaker and the Tailor, The. Grimm, *Other Tales*, p. 64.
Three Pedlars, The (Netherlands). Bødker, *European Folk Tales*, p. 104.
True and Untrue (Norway). Thompson, *100 Favorite Folktales*, no. 60.
Truth and Falsehood. Megas, *Folktales of Greece*, no. 41.
True and Untrue. Asbjørnsen and Moe, *East o' the Sun*, p. 1.
Truth or Lies? Which Pays Best? Dawkins, *Modern Greek Folktales*, no. 73.
Two Brothers, The. Basile, *Pentamerone*, Day 4, Tale 2.
Two Brothers, The. Massignon, *Folktales of France*, no. 45.
Two Muleteers, The. Calvino, *Italian Folktales*, no. 184.
Two Neighbors, The. Megas, *Folktales of Greece*, no. 40.
Two Travelers, The. Grimm, *Tales*, no. 107.
Worker and the Drone, The. Grimm, *Other Tales*, p. 78.

**621 THE LOUSE SKIN.** A king came into the possession of a louse so large that he was able to have a coat made for his daughter from its skin. He then announced that anyone who could guess what kind of skin it was could have the princess's hand in marriage. A boy named Jesper set out to try his luck. On the way he shared his bread with an ant, and the ant became his companion. At the palace the ant crept into the princess's bedroom and overheard her talking about her louse-skin coat. He reported this to Jesper, who was thus able to guess the secret and marry the princess. (Thompson)

Comte de Mes Comtes, The. Massignon, *Folktales of France*, no. 30.
Flea, The. Basile, *Pentamerone*, Day 1, Tale 5.
Louse Hide. Calvino, *Italian Folktales*, no. 104.
Louse Skin, The (Denmark). Thompson, *100 Favorite Folktales*, no. 61.
Louse Skin, The. Paredes, *Folktales of Mexico*, no. 37.
Rather Unusual Frog, The. Roberts, *South from Hell*, no. 25.
Serpent Son, The (Italy). Bødker, *European Folk Tales*, p. 182.
Silent Princess, The. Dawkins, *Modern Greek Folktales*, no. 48.
Sixth Captain's Tale, The. Mathers, *1001 Nights*, v. 4, p. 373.

**650 A  THE YOUNG GIANT.**  A small boy was carried away by a giant, who nurtured him for four years.  The boy became so strong that he could uproot the largest oak.  He then returned home, but his parents did not want this giant for a son, so he became a smith's apprentice.  For wages he asked only to be allowed to give his master two blows.  The smith, a miser, agreed, but when payday came, the young giant kicked him over four loads of hay.  Next he found work on a farm, where the bailiff similarly agreed to accept blows instead of paying the young giant.  On payday he received such a blow that he was never seen again.  Then the young giant took up his walking stick, a great iron bar, and went on his way.  (Grimm, no. 90)

Aay Cet Reey.  Lindell, *Folk Tales from Kammu*, II, no. 8.
Aliosha Popovich.  Afanasyev, *Russian Fairy Tales*, p. 67.
Big Sixteen and the Devil.  Botkin, *Treasury of American Folklore*, p. 721.
Boy That Had a Bear for a Daddy, The.  Campbell, *Cloudwalking Country*, p. 190.
Devil's Tale, The.  Sampson, *Gypsy Folk Tales*, p. 13.
Fourteen.  Calvino, *Italian Folktales*, no. 96.
Hedgy.  Musick, *Green Hills of Magic*, no. 23.
Ilya Muromets and the Dragon.  Afanasyev, *Russian Fairy Tales*, p. 569.
Ivanko the Bear's Son.  Afanasyev, *Russian Fairy Tales*, p. 221.
Jack the Bear.  Gmelch and Kroup, *To Shorten the Road*, p. 112.
Jack the Cobbler—the Widow's Son from Ireland.  Gmelch and Kroup, *To Shorten the Road*, p. 131.
Kondoy (Mexico).  Dorson, *Folktales around the World*, p. 499.
Little Fourteen; or, As Strong as Fourteen.  Massignon, *Folktales of France*, no. 46.
Nodey, the Priest's Grandson.  Afanasyev, *Russian Fairy Tales*, p. 173.
Strong Hans.  Grimm, *Tales*, no. 166.
Strong Jack.  Briggs, *DBF*, pt. A, v. 1, p. 499.
Three Blue Stones, The.  Delarue, *French Folktales*, p. 276.
Tom and the Giant Blunderbuss.  Briggs, *DBF*, pt. A, v. 1, p. 524.
Tom Hickathrift.  Briggs, *DBF*, pt. A, v. 1, p. 529.
Tom Hickathrift.  Jacobs, *More English Fairy Tales*, p. 46.
Twenty-One-Year Old Giant, The.  Briggs, *DBF*, pt. A, v. 1, p. 541.
Widow and the Brigand, The.  Calvino, *Italian Folktales*, no. 145.
Young Giant, The (Germany).  Thompson, *100 Favorite Folktales*, no. 62.
Young Giant, The.  Grimm, *Tales*, no. 90.

**650 C  SIEGFRIED SLAYS THE DRAGON.**  Siegfried killed a dragon and bathed in its blood, which made him invulnerable to any weapon, except for one spot between his shoulder blades where a leaf had fallen, keeping the blood from his skin.  His treacherous companion Hagen learned of this one vulnerable spot, and stabbed Siegfried in the back.  *(Nibelungenlied)*

Hedgy.  Musick, *Green Hills of Magic*, no. 23.
Siegfried Slays the Dragon.  Hatto, *Nibelungenlied*, pp. 28, 121.

**652  THE BOY WHOSE WISHES ALWAYS COME TRUE.**  An angel promised a childless queen that she would give birth to a son whose every wish would come true. Shortly after the birth of the child, the palace cook stole him away. The prince, in his place of exile, wished a pretty girl for a companion, and she immediately stood before him. The cook, afraid of the boy's power, asked the girl to kill the boy, but the boy discovered the plot and turned the cook into a black dog and the girl into a carnation. He then returned to his own country and was reunited with his mother and father. He transformed the carnation back into a beautiful girl, and the two were married. (Grimm, no. 76)

Carnation, The. Grimm, *Tales,* no. 76.
Duck-Dog, The (Canada). Dorson, *Folktales around the World,* p. 429.
Girl That Changed into a Flower Bloom. Campbell, *Cloudwalking Country,* p. 247.
Myrtle, The. Basile, *Pentamerone,* Day 1, Tale 2.
Pink, The. Grimm, *Other Tales,* p. 143.
Wonder Child, The (Netherlands). Bødker, *European Folk Tales,* p. 108.

**652A  THE MYRTLE.** See type 407A.

**653  THE SKILLFUL BROTHERS.** Four brothers learned trades. The first became a thief, the second an astronomer, the third a hunter, and the fourth a tailor. To demonstrate their skills to their father, the astronomer spotted five eggs in a distant tree, the thief stole them without disturbing the mother bird, the hunter hit all five with a single shot, the tailor sewed them back together, and finally the thief replaced them, unharmed, in the nest. Next the brothers set forth and, using their unusual skills, freed a princess from a dragon. Because each had contributed equally to her rescue, the king gave her to none of them, instead rewarding each with half a kingdom. (Grimm)

Five Brothers, The (Chile). Cole, *Best-Loved Folktales,* no. 200.
Five Brothers, The. Pino-Saavedra, *Folktales of Chile,* no. 26.
Five Sons, The. Basile, *Pentamerone,* Day 5, Tale 7.
Four Brothers, The (2 variants). Arewa, *Northern East Africa,* p. 251.
Four Clever Brothers, The. Clouston, *Popular Tales,* v. 1, p. 277.
Four Skillful Brothers, The. Grimm, *Tales,* no. 129.
Miller's Four Sons, The (France). Thompson, *100 Favorite Folktales,* no. 63.
Three Sons, The. Briggs, *DBF,* pt. A, v. 1, p. 521.
Wake-Well and His Brothers (Iceland). Bødker, *European Folk Tales,* p. 53.

**653A  THE RAREST GIFT.** A king offered his daughter's hand to the suitor who could bring her the rarest gift. Three brothers set out to find such a present. One acquired a magic carpet that could take its owner anywhere in the world, the second found a telescope that could see hundreds of miles, even through walls, and the third came into the possession of grapes that could cure any illness. With the telescope the brothers discovered that the princess had taken ill and was dying. The second brother's carpet carried them to her in an instant, and the youngest brother cured her with his grapes.  Because the boys all contributed to the princess's cure, each had an equal claim for her hand.  The king settled the dispute by marrying her to a fourth suitor, who had brought her nothing.  (Calvino)

Many Dilemmas of the Padishah's Three Sons, The.  Walker and Uysal, *Tales in Turkey,* p. 123.
Princess Nur al-Nihar and the Lovely Jinniyah.  Mathers, *1001 Nights,* v. 3, p. 550.
Royal Candlestick, The.  El-Shamy, *Folktales of Egypt,* no. 7.
Salamanna Grapes.  Calvino, *Italian Folktales,* no. 65.
Who Cured the Princess?  Noy, *Folktales of Israel,* no. 53.

**654  WHICH BROTHER HAS THE BEST SKILL?**    A father announced that he would leave his house to the one of his three sons who best learned his trade.  The oldest son learned blacksmithing, and demonstrated his skill by shoeing a horse at full gallop.  The middle son became a barber, and for his masterpiece, he shaved a rabbit running at full speed.  The youngest son became a fencing master, and he showed his skill by fighting off a rain storm with his sword.  The father judged this last feat to be the greatest and gave the house to the youngest son, who in turn invited his two brothers to live with him. (Grimm)

Skillful Brothers, The.  Roberts, *South from Hell,* no. 26.
Three Brothers, The.  Grimm, *Tales,* no. 124.
Three Skilful Son, The.  Pourrat, *Treasury of French Tales,* p. 1.
Trita and His Brothers.  O'Flaherty, *Tales of Sex and Violence,* p. 53.

**655  THE THREE CLEVER BROTHERS.**    Three clever brothers approached a judge to settle a dispute about their inheritance.  On the way they stopped at a grassy spot, and from faint traces of evidence deduced that a camel without a tail, blind in one eye, and loaded with fat on one side and sweets on the other had rested there before breaking away from its master.  When they met the man who owned the camel, he accused them of stealing it, because they knew so much.  However, they explained to the judge how they had made their clever deductions, and he was so impressed that he offered them lodging in his house.  The boys continued their deductions as they ate, the oldest determining that the roast was actually dog meat, the second adding that the cook was in her days of uncleanliness, and the third concluding that their host was a bastard.  With this the judge stepped from his hiding place and declared the youngest boy disinherited, adding his own deduction: "It takes a bastard to know a bastard."  (Bushnaq) —Note: The episode of the strayed camel is classified type 655A.

Guessing Children, The.  Walker and Uysal, *Tales in Turkey,* p. 114.
Judge of Horses, Diamonds, and Men, A.  Noy, *Folktales of Israel,* no. 36.
Three Mohammads, The.  Bushnaq, *Arab Folktales,* p. 345.

**660 THE THREE DOCTORS.** Three army surgeons possessed a magic healing salve. One evening in a tavern, to show off their abilities, one cut off his own hand, the other tore out his own heart, and the third gouged out his own eyes, intending to restore them in the morning. However, during the night a cat ran off with the hand, heart, and eyes. The maid, who had left the cupboard door open, replaced the missing items with a thief's hand from the gallows, a cat's eyes, and a pig's heart from the slaughter room. In the morning the three surgeons fastened these organs to themselves with their salve. The thief's hand continued to steal, the cat's eyes pursued mice in the dark, and the doctor with the pig's heart rooted about in the dirt with his nose. (Grimm)

> Doctors Ain't Smart as They Think They Be. Campbell, *Cloudwalking Country,* p. 187.
> Medical Expert from Lisnaskea, A. Glassie, *Irish Folktales,* no. 41.
> Three Army Surgeons, The. Grimm, *Tales,* no. 118.

**665 THE MAN WHO COULD FLY LIKE A BIRD, SWIM LIKE A FISH, AND RUN LIKE A RABBIT.** A stranger offered three brothers gold, silver, or the ability to learn an art. The older two chose gold and silver, but the youngest boy, a simpleton, preferred to learn an art, so the gentleman taught him to fly like a bird, swim like a fish, and run like a rabbit. Later the simpleton went to war with the king. As they approached the enemy the king despaired, for he had left important papers at home. He offered his daughter's hand to anyone who could bring them within one day. The simpleton ran over the fields like a rabbit, flew over a forest like a bird, and swam across a great water like a fish. The king got his papers in time and won the war, and the simpleton won the hand of the princess, becoming the king's successor. (Ranke)

> Peasant and His Three Sons, The. Ranke, *Folktales of Germany,* no. 43.
> Speedy Messenger, The. Afanasyev, *Russian Fairy Tales,* p. 124.
> Speedy Messenger, The (Russia). Thompson, *100 Favorite Folktales,* no. 64.

**670 ANIMALS TEACH A MAN HOW TO HANDLE HIS WIFE.** A man had the ability to understand the language of animals. One day he laughed aloud at a conversation he had overheard between a bull and a donkey. His wife wanted to know why he was laughing. He responded that it would cost him his life if he told her. Still, she would not relent, insisting that he reveal his secret. Now the man had a rooster which could satisfy fifty hens, and the merchant overheard the rooster talking with the dog. "Our master could solve his problem easily," he said. "He need only beat her until she either dies or repents." The man took the rooster's advice, delivering blows until his wife passed out. When she could speak again, she said: "I repent," and from that time they had a happy marriage. *(1001 Nights)* Cf. types 900, 901, 903A\*, 910A, 1376A\*.

Animal Languages, The. Ranke, *Folktales of Germany,* no. 44.
Animal Talk and the Nosy Wife. Calvino, *Italian Folktales,* no. 177.
Billy Goat and the King, The (India). Lang, *Olive Fairy Book,* p. 211.
Bold Cock, The. Pourrat, *Treasury of French Tales,* p. 92.
Donkey Who Gave Advice, the Ox Who became Sick, and the Rooster Who
    Was Clever, The. Sabar, *Folk Literature of the Kurdistani Jews,* p. 181.
Fable of the Ass, the Bull and the Husbandman, The. Mathers, *1001 Nights,*
    v. 1, p. 6.
He Heard Animals Talking. Randolph, *Sticks in the Knapsack,* p. 108.
Language of Animals, The (Bulgaria). Thompson, *100 Folktales,* no. 65.
Language of Beasts, The. Lang, *Crimson Fairy Book,* p. 55.
Man Could Understand His Animals' Talk, A (3 variants). Arewa, *Northern
    East Africa,* p. 167.
Ox and Ass. Megas, *Folktales of Greece,* no. 14.
Rooster's Advice, The. Villa, *100 Armenian Tales,* no. 78.
Rooster, The. Musick, *Green Hills of Magic,* no. 63.
Shepherd and the Snake, The. Massignon, *Folktales of France,* no. 69.
Suleyman and the Little Owl. Bushnaq, *Arab Folktales,* p. 244.
Then the Merman Laughed. Simpson, *Icelandic Folktales and Legends,* p. 92.
Three Laughs of the Leipreachán, The. O'Sullivan, *Folktales of Ireland,* no.
    30.
Tom and Jerry. Randolph, *The Talking Turtle,* p. 102.

**671  THE BOY WHO LEARNED THE LANGUAGES OF ANIMALS.** A count had a son who was a simpleton. After three years of study, the boy claimed only to have learned the languages of the dogs, the birds, and the frogs. The count, in dismay, drove him away. On his travels the simpleton learned of a great treasure from barking dogs, and from croaking frogs he learned that he himself would be the next pope. Thus, he entered the church where the cardinals had met, and two white doves flew to his shoulders. The cardinals took this to be a sign from heaven, and they consecrated him as the new pope. (Grimm) Cf. types 517, 707, 725, 930.

Animal Speech. Calvino, *Italian Folktales,* no. 23.
Bobino. Lang, *Grey Fairy Book,* p. 197.
Language of Animals, The. Crane, *Italian Popular Tales,* no. 43.
Language of Animals, The. Jacobs, *European Folk and Fairy Tales,* no. 8.
Little Lad Who Became a Bishop, The. Massignon, *Folktales of France,* no.
    18.
Magic Ear, The. Seki, *Folktales of Japan,* no. 40.
Three Languages, The (Italy). Thompson, *100 Folktales,* no. 66.
Three Languages, The. Grimm, *Tales,* no. 33.

**672  THE GIFT OF THE KING OF SNAKES.** A boy befriended a snake, who in return told him to go to his father, the king of snakes, and ask that they touch their tongues together. The king of snakes only reluctantly fulfilled this wish, and from that time forth the boy had great knowledge and power as a healer.

Lochman Hehkeem. Villa, *100 Armenian Tales*, no. 98.

**672B   THE TOAD'S CROWN.** A little girl saw a toad and spread out a blue handkerchief for it. The toad returned with a small gold crown, laid it on the blue cloth, and went away again. The girl picked up the crown. When the toad returned and couldn't find its crown, it struck its head against a rock until it died.

Tales of the Toad (II). Grimm, *Tales*, no. 105.

**673   THE WHITE SNAKE'S MEAT.** There was a king who seemed to know every secret. After every meal he always ate from a mysterious covered dish. One day his trusted servant was overcome with curiosity and looked in the dish. There he saw the meat of a white snake, and he ate a little piece. Soon he discovered that the snake's meat had given him the power to understand the language of birds and animals. —Continues as type 554. (Grimm)

Sir James Ramsay of Bamff. Briggs, *DBF,* pt. B, v. 2, p. 578.
White Snake, The. Grimm, *Tales,* no. 17.

**675   THE SIMPLETON WHOSE WISHES ALWAYS CAME TRUE.** Simple Hans had the power to make wishes come true. He wished the princess pregnant, and she did indeed have a child. The king set the princess, the child, and Simple Hans adrift at sea in a barrel. Simple Hans wished them safely ashore, and then he created a splendid castle, where they lived happily together. One day the king chanced upon the castle. His daughter, unrecognized, entertained him, but before he left, she hid a golden cup in his pocket. She then sent her horsemen after him, who accused him of stealing the cup. He insisted that he did not know how it came to be in his pocket. "One must not judge by appearances," said his daughter, making herself known to him. Then they all lived happily together. (Grimm)

A Simple Fellow Gets Back His Wits by the Help of a Tunny Fish. Straparola, *Facetious Nights,* Night 3, Tale 1.
Bertoldino (Italy). Dorson, *Folktales around the World,* p. 68.
Cloven Youth, The. Calvino, *Italian Folktales,* no. 34.
Emelya the Simpleton. Afanasyev, *Russian Fairy Tales,* p. 46.
Half-Man. Delarue, *French Folktales,* p. 272.
Lazy Boy, The (Denmark). Thompson, *100 Favorite Folktales,* no. 67.
Little Man with the Scabby Head, The. Dawkins, *Modern Greek Folktales,* no. 4.
Miss Laa, the Governor's Daughter. Lindell, *Folk Tales from Kammu,* II, no. 16.
Moustafat. Saucier, *French Louisiana,* no. 12.
Peruonto. Basile, *Pentamerone,* Day 1, Tale 3.
Simple Hans. Grimm, *Other Tales,* p. 35.
Ugly Yann. Massignon, *Folktales of France,* no. 3.

**676 OPEN, SESAME!** Ali Baba, a poor woodcutter, observed a troop of thieves approach a cliff. Upon their command "Open, Sesame!" a doorway opened in the rocks, and the thieves disappeared inside. Later Ali Baba tried the command himself. Discovering a treasure trove inside, he took what he needed for his family. With time, his wealthy, but envious brother also learned the secret and let himself into the cave. But overcome with greed, he forgot the magic word; the thieves caught him inside, and killed him. —Continues as type 954. *(1001 Nights)*

> Ali Baba and the Forty Thieves *(1001 Nights)*. Cole, *Best-Loved Folktales,* no. 108.
> Ali Baba and the Forty Thieves. Mathers, *1001 Nights,* v. 4, p. 100.
> Forty Thieves, The *(1001 Nights)*. Lang, *Blue Fairy Book,* p. 242.
> Forty Thieves, The (commentary). Dawkins, *Modern Greek Folktales,* no. 52.
> Forty-One Robbers, The. Mathias and Raspa, *Italian Folktales in America,* no. 6.
> How Black Snake Caught the Wolf. Harris, *Daddy Jake,* no. 4.
> Jewel Stone, The. Pino-Saavedra, *Folktales of Chile,* no. 27.
> Man Who Robbed the Robbers, The. Calvino, *Italian Folktales,* no. 193.
> Rabbit and Bear inside the Elephant. Dorson, *Negro Tales,* p. 18.
> Simeli Mountain. Grimm, *Tales,* no. 142.
> Thirteen Bandits, The. Calvino, *Italian Folktales,* no. 137.
> Wise Maiden and the Seven Robbers, The. Afanasyev, *Russian Fairy Tales,* p. 134.

**681 THE SULTAN'S BATH SHOWS HIM A NEW LIFE.** A sultan climbed into his bathtub and suddenly found himself changed into a woman and standing by a river. A Bedouin forced her (the transformed woman) to join his three other wives and many children. Everyone abused the newcomer. The next day they sent her to the river to wash dirty clothes. She jumped into the water and immediately found herself in the royal bathtub, transformed back into a man as though nothing had happened.

> Grateful Fish, The. El-Shamy, *Folktales of Egypt,* no. 5.
> It Happened in a Bath. Villa, *100 Armenian Tales,* no. 70.

**700 TOM THUMB.** A peasant and his wife had no children. One day she said: "I wish we had a child, even if it were only as big as a thumb." Seven months later she gave birth to a boy, who was only the size of a thumb. One day a cow swallowed the little boy, who had been asleep in the hay. He escaped when the cow was slaughtered, only to be eaten alive by a wolf. From inside its belly he told the wolf the way to his father's kitchen, instructing it to eat its fill. When the wolf had eaten so much it could no longer squeeze through the entrance, the boy began to shout. Attracted by the noise, his father killed the wolf and rescued him. (Grimm, no. 37) Cf. type 327B.

Dathera Dad. Briggs, *DBF,* pt. B, v. 1, p. 205.
Grain-of-Millet. Delarue, *French Folktales,* p. 217.
Hazel-Nut Child (Bukovina). Lang, *Yellow Fairy Book,* p. 222.
Inchelina. Andersen, *Complete Fairy Tales,* no. 5.
Little Chick-Pea. Crane, *Italian Popular Tales,* no. 77.
Little Lasse (Topelius). Lang, *Lilac Fairy Book,* p. 132.
Little One Inch. Seki, *Folktales of Japan,* no. 28.
Mundig. Villa, *100 Armenian Tales,* no. 29.
Pepper-Corn. Crane, *Italian Popular Tales,* p. 375.
Pete and the Ox. Calvino, *Italian Folktales,* no. 91.
Strange Adventures of Little Maia, The. Lang, *Olive Fairy Book,* p. 130.
Thomas of the Thumb. Campbell, *West Highlands,* v. 3, p. 127.
Thumbelina (Inchelina). Andersen, *Complete Fairy Tales,* no. 5.
Thumbikin. Asbjørnsen and Moe, *East o' the Sun,* p. 372.
Thumbkin. Jacobs, *European Folk and Fairy Tales,* no. 24.
Thumbling's Travels. Grimm, *Tales,* no. 45.
Thumbthick. Grimm, *Tales,* no. 37.
Tom Thumb (Germany). Thompson, *100 Favorite Folktales,* no. 68.
Tom Thumb. Briggs, *DBF,* pt. A, v. 1, p. 531.
Tom Thumb. Jacobs, *English Fairy Tales,* p. 140.
Tom Thumb. Massignon, *Folktales of France,* no. 19.
Tom Thumbe (England). Opie, *Classic Fairy Tales,* p. 41.
Tommelise (Andersen). Opie, *Classic Fairy Tales,* p. 290.
Young Giant, The. Grimm, *Tales,* no. 90.

**701** **THE GIANT'S TOY.** A giant picked up a man and took him home in his pocket, but the giant's mother made him put the little worm back where he had found him, and thus the man escaped. (Ranke) Cf. Christiansen, *Migratory Legends,* type 5015.

Giant of Grabbist and the Dorcas Jane, The. Briggs and Tongue, *Folktales of England,* no. 29.
Giant's Toy, The. Ranke, *Folktales of Germany,* no. 20.
Toy for the Giant, A. Lindow, *Swedish Legends and Folktales,* no. 17.

**704** **THE PRINCESS AND THE PEA.** To determine whether or not a certain girl was a true princess, and thus worthy of her son, the old queen gave her a bed with twenty mattresses, and beneath them all she hid a pea. The next morning, the girl complained that a terrible bump in her bed had bruised her black and blue. Now everyone knew that she was a genuine princess, and the prince married her forthwith.

Princess on the Pea, The (Andersen). Opie, *Classic Fairy Tales,* p. 286.
Princess and the Pea, The. Andersen, *Complete Fairy Tales,* no. 3.

**705** **A MIRACULOUS BIRTH.** A childless wife bought a pomegranate from a vendor who claimed the fruit would bring pregnancy. But the woman's husband ate the pomegranate, and he bore a baby girl. Then a falcon stole the child and reared it in a nest high in a tree. One day the sultan's son saw the girl in the nest, and he fell in love with her. The boy's grandmother helped bring the girl down from the tree, and soon the two were married. —Continues as type 706. (Dorson)

Child from the Sea, The. Dawkins, *Modern Greek Folktales,* no. 7.
Falcon's Daughter, The (Egypt). Dorson, *Folktales around the World,* p. 159.

**706   THE GIRL WITHOUT HANDS.** An old man approached a poor
miller, offering to make him wealthy in return for what was standing
behind his mill. Thinking that the stranger meant his apple tree, the
miller agreed, but at that moment his daughter was standing behind the
mill. However, because of her piety, the devil could not take her, so he
threatened to take the miller instead, unless the miller would cut off his
daughter's hands. The girl let her father do this, and then she went
forth into the world. A king, attracted by her great beauty, had silver
hands made for her and married her. After a year, the king had to go
on a journey, and in his absence the young queen gave birth to a son.
The devil intercepted the letter telling the king the good news,
changing it to read that his wife had delivered a monster. The king
responded, saying that the queen should be given good care. The devil
changed this letter to read that the queen and the child should be put to
death. The threatened mother and child escaped into the forest, where
they lived many years. An angel restored her hands, and with time the
king found his wife and son. (Grimm)

Armless Maiden, The (Russia). Thompson, *100 Folktales,* no. 69.
Armless Maiden, The. Afanasyev, *Russian Fairy Tales,* p. 294.
Biancabella Is Sent Away in Order That She May Be Put to Death. Straparola,
   *Facetious Nights,* Night 3, Tale 3.
Boy Cuts Off His Sister's Hand, A. Arewa, *Northern East Africa,* p. 175.
Cruel Stepmother, The. Briggs, *DBF,* pt. A, v. 1, p. 197.
Daughter Doris. Briggs, *DBF,* pt. A, v. 1, p. 201.
Doña Bernarda. Espinosa, *Folklore of Spain in the American Southwest,* p.
   179.
Falcon's Daughter, The (Egypt). Dorson, *Folktales around the World,* p. 159.
Girl with No Hands, The. Musick, *Green Hills of Magic,* no. 33.
Girl without Any Hands, The. Campbell, *Cloudwalking Country,* p. 163.
Girl without Arms, The. Seki, *Folktales of Japan,* no. 30.
Girl without Hands, The. Grimm, *Tales,* no. 31.
Girl without Hands, The. Ranke, *Folktales of Germany,* no. 36.
John and Mary; or, The Girl with the Chopped-Off Hands. Thomas, *It's Good
   to Tell You,* no. 13.
Maiden without Hands in Romanian Folklore, The. Dégh, *Studies,* p. 319.
Mariam. Villa, *100 Armenian Tales,* no. 32.
Olive. Calvino, *Italian Folktales,* no. 71.
One-Handed Girl, The (Africa). Lang, *Lilac Fairy Book,* p. 185.
Rising Water, Talking Bird and Weeping Tree. Saucier, *French Louisiana,* no.
   7.
Turkey Hen, The. Calvino, *Italian Folktales,* no. 141.
Woman with Her Hands Cut Off, The. Massignon, *Folktales of France,* no.
   31.

**706B   THE GIRL WHO GAVE HER HANDS TO HER BROTHER.**
A widowed king proposed marriage to his own sister, a woman named
Penta, expressing his love for her with great vigor. Above all, he

proclaimed, it was her hand that enchanted him. Beside herself, Penta had a slave cut off her hands and had them delivered to her brother in a porcelain bowl. He flew into a rage and had Penta set adrift at sea, but another king rescued her, and in due course they were married. —Continues in the manner of the type 706 tale abstracted above.

Girl with the Maimed Hands, The. Basile, *Pentamerone,* Day 3, Tale 2.

**707  DANCING WATER, SINGING APPLE, AND SPEAKING BIRD.** A king overheard three sisters talking. One boasted that if she were married to the king, she would bear him two sons with apples in their hands and a daughter with a star on her forehead. This so impressed the king that he married the girl, and the three children were born, just as she had promised. However, the envious sisters bribed the nurse to put puppies in the place of the newborns and to leave the babies outside for the dogs to eat. A fairy rescued them, and when they had grown, they moved into a house near the palace. Their aunts recognized them and conspired to destroy them. They sent the boys on dangerous quests for the dancing water and the singing apple, thinking they would be killed, but they returned safely. However, on the last quest, the search for the speaking bird, the boys relaxed their guard, and were turned to stone. Their sister followed their tracks and broke the spell, and they returned with the speaking bird, who revealed to them the truth about their mother, now in exile, and their wicked aunts. The king restored their mother to her rightful place and had the evildoers put to death. (Thompson) Cf. types 517, 671, 725, 930.

Ancilotto, King of Provino, Takes to Wife the Daughter of a Baker. Straparola, *Facetious Nights,* Night 4, Tale 3.
Bird of Truth, The. Lang, *Orange Fairy Book,* p. 292.
Boy Who Had a Moon on His Forehead and a Star on His Chin, The. Jacobs, *Indian Fairy Tales,* p. 156.
Boys with the Golden Stars, The (Romania). Lang, *Violet Fairy Book,* p. 299.
Dancing Water, Singing Apple, Speaking Bird. Jacobs, *European Folk Tales,* no. 7.
Dancing Water, the Singing Apple, and the Speaking Bird, The (Italy). Thompson, *100 Folktales,* no. 70.
Dancing Water, Singing Apple, and Speaking Bird. Crane, *Italian Popular Tales,* no. 4.
Farizad of the Rose's Smile. Mathers, *1001 Nights,* v. 3, p. 439.
Fine Greenbird, The. Calvino, *Italian Folktales,* no. 87.
Golden Eggplant, The. Seki, *Folktales of Japan,* no. 49.
Golden-Haired Twins, The. Villa, *100 Armenian Tales,* no. 31.
Little Cinder-Girl, The. Sampson, *Gypsy Folk Tales,* p. 77.
Nightingale That Shrieked, The. Bushnaq, *Arab Folktales,* p. 89.
Promises of the Three Sisters, The. El-Shamy, *Folktales of Egypt,* no. 9.
Singing Branch, the Bird of Truth, and the Water of Youth, The. Pourrat, *Treasury of French Tales,* p. 138.
Singing Tree and the Talking Bird, The. Afanasyev, *Russian Fairy Tales,* p. 184.

Speckled Bull, The. O'Sullivan, *Folktales of Ireland*, no. 19.
Three Blind Queens. Calvino, *Italian Folktales*, no. 113.
Three Little Birds, The. Grimm, *Tales*, no. 96.
Three Sisters and Their Wishes for a Husband. Dawkins, *Modern Greek Folktales*, no. 31.
Two Wives, The. Arewa, *Northern East Africa*, p. 197.
Vile Mother-in-Law, The (Greece). Bødker, *European Folk Tales*, p. 189.
Water of Life, The (Spain). Lang, *Pink Fairy Book*, p. 184.

**708  THE WONDER-CHILD.**  A wicked washerwoman gave the princess food that made her pregnant. The girl, accused of unchastity, was set adrift on a lake, where she gave birth to a squirrel. The squirrel rescued her and made the truth known about the conception. (Briggs)

Birth of Saint Kentigern, The. Rowling, *Folklore of the Lake District*, p. 62.
Little Fox, De. Briggs, *DBF*, pt. A, v. 1, p. 388.
Little Squirrel, The. Briggs, *DBF*, pt. A, v. 1, p. 394.

**709  SNOW-WHITE.**  A queen asked her magic mirror who was the fairest in the land, and it always responded that she herself was, until Snow-White, her stepdaughter [her real daughter in the Grimms' earliest versions], became seven years old and more beautiful than the queen. The envious queen ordered a hunter to kill Snow-White, but instead he abandoned her in the woods, and she found her way to the house of the seven dwarfs. The wicked queen followed her there and, after two unsuccessful attempts to kill her, poisoned her with an apple. The dwarfs built a glass coffin for her. One day a prince saw the coffin and fell in love with the body inside. The dwarfs took pity on him and gave him the coffin. As his servants began to move it, one of them stumbled, and the shock dislodged the piece of poisoned apple from Snow-White's throat. She came back to life, and she and the prince  married soon afterward. (Grimm)

Bella Venezia. Calvino, *Italian Folktales*, no. 109.
Blanca Rosa and the Forty Thieves. Pino-Saavedra, *Folktales of Chile*, no. 28.
Crystal Casket, The. Crane, *Italian Popular Tales*, no. 21.
Giricoccola. Calvino, *Italian Folktales*, no. 50.
Gold-Tree and Silver-Tree. Jacobs, *Celtic Fairy Tales*, p. 88.
Little Snow-White. Grimm, *Tales*, no. 53.
Myrsina; or, Myrtle. Megas, *Folktales of Greece*, no. 37.
Nourie Hadig. Villa, *100 Armenian Tales*, no. 2.
Our Lady of the Rosary. Espinosa, *Folklore of Spain in the American Southwest*, p. 180.
Snow White. Dawkins, *Modern Greek Folktales*, no. 20.
Snow-White (Germany). Thompson, *100 Favorite Folktales*, no. 71.
Snow-White. Briggs, *DBF*, pt. A, v. 1, p. 494.
Snowdrop (Grimm, Altered). Opie, *Classic Fairy Tales*, p. 230.
Snowwhite. Jacobs, *European Folk and Fairy Tales*, no. 25.
Stepchild That Was Treated Mighty Bad, A. Campbell, *Cloudwalking Country*, p. 53.
Wildwood King, The. Calvino, *Italian Folktales*, no. 111.

Young Slave, The. Basile, *Pentamerone,* Day 2, Tale 8.

**710  OUR LADY'S CHILD.** A poor woodcutter and his wife had a three-year old girl, but no way to support her. The Virgin Mary took the child to live with her in heaven. When she was fourteen years old, the Virgin Mary gave her the keys to the thirteen doors of heaven, with the instructions that she was not to open the thirteenth door. The girl opened the twelve doors and rejoiced in the magnificence behind each, and finally unlocked the thirteenth as well. Inside was the Trinity, sitting in fire and splendor. When the Virgin Mary returned, she knew the girl had opened the forbidden door, but the girl would not admit her transgression, so she was thrown out of heaven. A king found her on earth and married her, although she had lost the power of speech, because of her unwillingness to confess. A further punishment, the Virgin Mary took each of her newborn children away from her. After the loss of three children, the people insisted that she be judged. Unable to defend herself, she was sentenced to die at the stake. Finally, the executioner's fire melted her pride, and she cried out: "Yes, Mary, I did it." In that instant, rain fell from heaven to extinguish the flames, and Mary returned her three missing children. Now forgiven, she had happiness the rest of her life. (Grimm)

> Girl with the Golden Finger, The. Campbell, *Cloudwalking Country,* p. 47.
> Goat Face, The. Basile, *Pentamerone,* Day 1, Tale 8.
> Juanita. Pino-Saavedra, *Folktales of Chile,* no. 29.
> Lassie and Her Godmother, The. Asbjørnsen and Moe, *East o' the Sun,* p. 188.
> Our Lady's Child. Grimm, *Tales,* no. 3.
> Wild Sow of the Forest, The. Gmelch and Kroup, *To Shorten the Road,* p. 103.

**711  THE BEAUTIFUL AND THE UGLY TWIN.** An old woman told a childless queen how to cause two flowers to grow from beneath her bed, and that by eating one of them the queen would conceive. However, the queen ate both flowers, and she gave birth to twin girls. The older twin, who was very ugly, was born riding a goat and carrying a wooden spoon, but the younger one was lovely. Once, after the girls were grown, witches replaced the beautiful twin's head with that of a calf. Tatterhood, so they called the ugly twin, set forth with her sister to regain her human head. Mounted on her goat and armed with her wooden spoon, Tatterhood attacked the witches, forcing them to return her sister's head. Then Tatterhood sailed with her twin to a kingdom where a widowed king was looking for a bride. He fell in love with the beautiful twin, but Tatterhood would agree to the marriage only if the king's son would marry her, and the king forced him to do so. On their way to the wedding, the prince was very sullen. "Why don't you ask me why I ride this goat?" said Tatterhood. So the prince asked, and instantly the goat turned into a horse. "Why don't you ask why I carry this wooden spoon?" she continued. No sooner had he asked, than the spoon became a silver wand. "Now ask why I am so ugly," she said. He so asked, and in an instant she became the most beautiful girl in the world. (Asbjørnsen and Moe)

Dullness and Wit Borrowed from Each Other. Pourrat, *Treasury of French Tales*, p. 69.
Kate Crackernuts. Briggs, *DBF,* pt. A, v. 1, p. 344.
Kate Crackernuts. Jacobs, *English Fairy Tales*, p. 198.
Mop Head. Christiansen, *Folktales of Norway*, p. 252.
Ricky with the Tuft. Perrault, *Fairy Tales* (trans. Carter), p. 97.
Tatterhood. Asbjørnsen and Moe, *East o' the Sun*, p. 345.

**712 THE SLANDERED WIFE.** A merchant left his beautiful and virtuous wife in the care of a friend. The friend wanted to take her as a mistress, but she refused. To gain revenge, the friend wrote to the merchant that his wife was leading a life of sin. The husband replied that she should be buried alive, and the friend did just that. Shepherds rescued her from her grave, and after many hardships, she put on a monk's robe and heard confessions. Her husband, now blind, and the friend, with paralyzed hands, came to the monk and confessed their sins. Finally she revealed her true identity to her husband. In that instant his sight was restored, and they lived happily together. Cf. type 881.

Mersina, Myrtle. Dawkins, *Modern Greek Folktales,* no. 58.

**715 HALF-CHICK.** Two women had a rooster. They split it in two; one ate her half, the other kept hers. While scratching about, Half-Chick uncovered a bushel of money, but a miller, who happened to pass by, took the money, leaving only three heads of wheat in exchange. To right the wrong, Half-Chick, followed by a fox, a wolf, a colony of ants, and a river, went to the miller's house. They brought so much destruction that the miller had to return the money. Half-Chick carried it back to the good woman, and they lived happily together. (Delarue)

Cock Who Went Traveling, The. Ranke, *Folktales of Germany,* no. 11.
Drakestail (France). Cole, *Best-Loved Folktales,* no. 6.
Drakestail. Lang, *Red Fairy Book,* p. 202.
Half Chicken. Massignon, *Folktales of France,* no. 53.
Half-Chick, The (Spain). Cole, *Best-Loved Folktales,* no. 37.
Half-Chick, The (Spain). Lang, *Green Fairy Book,* p. 27.
Half-Chick. Delarue, *French Folktales,* p. 312.
Half-Rooster. Thomas, *It's Good to Tell You,* no. 15.
Sparrow and the King, The (Tunisia). Dorson, *Folktales around the World,* p. 164.
Teenchy-Tiny Duck, The. Harris, *Uncle Remus and the Little Boy,* no. 5.

**720  MY MOTHER KILLED ME; MY FATHER ATE ME.** A woman offered her stepson an apple from a chest, but when he stooped over to take it, she slammed the lid, cutting off his head. Then she cut up the body and served it to his father as black pudding. Later a bird lighted on a mill and sang: "My mother killed me; my father ate me." At his request, the miller gave him a millstone, placing it around his neck as if it were a collar. Then he flew to his father's house and sang the same song. When the stepmother looked out the window, the bird dropped the millstone, crushing her to death. Then the little boy was standing there, alive once again, and he went inside with his father and his sister. (Grimm)

Applie and Orangie (Scotland). Dorson, *Folktales around the World*, p. 37.
Fair Ellen of Radcliffe. Briggs, *DBF*, pt. B, v. 2, p. 47.
Green Bird, The. Bushnaq, *Arab Folktales*, p. 150.
June Apple Tree, The. Campbell, *Cloudwalking Country*, p. 212.
Juniper Tree, The. Grimm, *Tales*, no. 47.
Juniper, The (Germany). Thompson, *100 Favorite Folktales*, no. 72.
Little Bird, The. Briggs, *DBF*, pt. A, v. 1, p. 378.
Little Rosy. Briggs and Tongue, *Folktales of England*, no. 5.
Milk-White Doo, The. Briggs, *DBF*, pt. A, v. 1, p. 414.
My Mother Killed Me, My Father Ate Me. Abrahams, *Afro-American Folktales*, no. 33.
Orange and Lemon. Briggs, *DBF*, pt. A, v. 1, p. 441.
Pennywinkle! Pennywinkle! Randolph, *Who Blowed Up the Church House?*, p. 53.
Rose-Tree, The. Briggs, *DBF*, pt. A, v. 1, p. 472.
Rose-Tree, The. Jacobs, *English Fairy Tales*, p. 15.
Rosy. Briggs, *DBF*, pt. A, v. 1, p. 473.
Satin Frock, The. Briggs, *DBF*, pt. A, v. 1, p. 476.
Silver Tree, The. Roberts, *South from Hell*, no. 27A.

**725  THE BOY WHO WOULDN'T TELL HIS DREAMS.** A boy stayed in bed longer than usual in order to finish a dream. But when he wouldn't tell the dream, his father drove him away. He went to the home of a rich man, but he wouldn't tell the dream here either, so the rich man had him put in a pit. He escaped, and the rich man's daughter hid him. Later a king threatened to make war on the rich man, but the boy saved him by solving riddles and accomplishing difficult tasks. In the end he married both the rich man's daughter and the daughter of the king who had threatened to make war. (Musick) Cf. types 517, 671, 707, 930.

Auspicious Dream, The. Walker and Uysal, *Tales in Turkey*, p. 132.
Boy Who Could Keep a Secret, The (Hungary). Lang, *Crimson Fairy Book*, p. 62.
Boy Who Wouldn't Tell His Dreams, The. Musick, *Green Hills of Magic*, no. 46.
Dreamer and His Dream, The. Villa, *100 Armenian Tales*, no. 16.
Weaver's Dream, The. Bushnaq, *Arab Folktales*, p. 326.
Wild Man and His Daughter. Dawkins, *More Greek Folktales*, no. 7.

Young Son of the Ploughman, The. Dawkins, *Modern Greek Folktales*, no. 53.

**726  THE OLDEST MAN.**  A stranger asked an old man why he was crying. "Because my father whipped me," was the answer. "Your father? What age are you?" "Seventy-three." The stranger then found the old man's father and asked why he had punished his son. "Because," came the answer, "the nasty little fellow was making faces at his grandfather." (Briggs, "The Oldest on the Farm")

> Key of Craigiehow, The. Briggs, *DBF*, pt. A, v. 1, p. 346.
> Old Man Crying, The. Dorson, *Buying the Wind*, p. 86.
> Old Parr. Briggs, *DBF*, pt. B, v. 2, p. 102.
> Old Troll and the Handshake, The. Christiansen, *Folktales of Norway*, p. 82.
> Oldest in the Farm, The. Briggs, *Folklore of the Cotswolds*, p. 79.
> Oldest Inhabitant, The. Randolph, *Sticks in the Knapsack*, p. 8.
> Oldest on the Farm, The. Briggs, *DBF*, pt. A, v. 2, p. 212.
> Oldest Person, The. Clouston, *Popular Tales*, v. 2, p. 96.
> Painswick Ancients, The. Briggs, *DBF*, pt. A, v. 2, p. 215.
> Three Old Men of Painswick, The. *Briggs,* DBF, pt. A, v. 2, p. 216.

**726\* THE OLD MEN AND THE BURIED TREASURE.**  A poor Irish farmer left his wife and children to seek better luck elsewhere. On his travels he met two shriveled old men who told him about a treasure buried on his farm. In return, they asked him to bring them the razor he would find with the gold. He did this, gaining wealth for himself and his family. The razor rejuvenated the two old men.

> Seán Na Bánóige. O'Sullivan, *Folktales of Ireland*, no. 36.

**729  THE AX, LOST IN THE RIVER.**  A woodcutter lost his ax in the river, and Hermes, feeling pity, brought up a gold ax from the river bottom and gave it to him, although the man admitted that this was not the one he had lost. Hoping for the same reward, the man's friend threw his ax into the river. Hermes again delivered a gold ax, which the man claimed as his own. Knowing this to be a lie, Hermes took away the gold ax. Thus the man lost his ax and gained nothing in its place.

> Honesty Is the Best Policy. Handford, *Aesop*, no. 156.

**735A  BAD LUCK, IMPRISONED AND RELEASED.**  A poor man captured Bad Luck in a chest and buried it in the earth. From that day forth he prospered. His wealthy and spiteful brother decided to release Bad Luck and thus return his brother to misfortune. However, when the spiteful brother opened the chest, Bad Luck attached himself to him, and in a short time he became a penniless beggar. (Afanasyev)

> Two Kinds of Luck. Afanasyev, *Russian Fairy Tales*, p. 501.
> Woe (Russia). Cole, *Best-Loved Folktales*, no. 98.

**736A THE RING IN THE FISH.** A queen gave a ring — a gift from her husband — to her lover. The king took it from the man's finger while he slept and threw it into the river, then asked his wife to return the gift. Unable to produce the ring, she was imprisoned. In despair, she asked for Saint Kentigern's help. He told her servant to fish in a certain place. Upon so doing, the servant caught a salmon with the ring in its mouth, and the queen was freed. (Rowling) Cf. type 2204; Christiansen, *Migratory Legends,* type 7050.

> Cinderello. Megas, *Folktales of Greece,* no. 35.
> John of Horsill (II). Briggs, *DBF,* pt. B, v. 2, p. 240.
> Kentigern Returns an Adulteress's Ring. Rowling, *Folklore of the Lake District,* p. 66.
> Ring and the Fish, The. Clouston, *Popular Tales,* v. 1, p. 398.
> Saint Egwin. Briggs, *DBF,* pt. B, v. 2, p. 440.
> Salomo's Ring Is Stolen. Arewa, *Northern East Africa,* p. 19.
> Too Lucky Man, The. Dawkins, *More Greek Folktales,* no. 20.

**737 CONJURING UP ONE'S FUTURE HUSBAND.** A girl, wishing to see her future husband, performed the necessary rituals. A hunter appeared, but left his knife behind when he departed. Later he married the girl. Happening onto the lost knife in her chest, he went into a rage and killed her with it. (Grimm)

> Dumb Supper, The. Roberts, *South from Hell,* no. 28A.
> Saint Andreas' Eve. Grimm, *German Legends,* no. 115.

**745A WEALTH FINDS ITS PREDESTINED OWNER.** A saddlemaker saved a hundred gold coins, and for safekeeping sewed them into a saddle. Without thinking, he sold the saddle to a stranger. A year later the stranger returned the saddle for repairs, so the saddlemaker recovered his lost wealth. (Bushnaq)

> Miser of Winchelsea, The. Briggs, *DBF,* pt. B, v. 2, p. 268.
> Sultan's Camp Followers, The. Bushnaq, *Arab Folktales,* p. 339.

# Religious Tales

**750A GOOD WISHES AND FOOLISH WISHES.** A poor widow
gave lodging to Saint Peter, and he rewarded her with the promise that
she would continue to do all day what she first did. Not knowing what
he meant, she turned to her weaving, as planned. Seemingly driven by
magic, the loom produced cloth the entire day. Learning of this
miracle, a wealthy, but mean-spirited woman asked Peter for the same
gift, and he agreed. However, this woman's first activity of the
morning was to relieve herself, and that is how she spent the entire
day. (Calvino) —Note: A common variant relates how a foolish
person, granted three wishes, uses the first two to his or her detriment,
and then must use the third to undo the unwanted consequences. For
example, in "The Three Wishes" from *1001 Nights* a man, dissatisfied
with his virility, wishes himself a giant "zabb." But then, discovering
himself so monstrously endowed that he can hardly move, he wishes
himself a smaller one, and it disappears altogether. He must use his
third and final wish to restore himself to his original condition.

Avaricious and Envious. Jacobs, *Aesop,* no. 54.
Bomere Pool. Briggs, *DBF,* pt. B, v. 2, p. 167.
Foolish Wishes, The. Perrault, *Fairy Tales* (trans. Carter), p. 131.
Hospitality. Calvino, *Italian Folktales,* no. 41.3.
Lord, Saint Peter, and the Blacksmith, The. Crane, *Italian Popular Tales,* no.
    51.
Old Couple's Three Wishes. Dorson, *Buying the Wind,* p. 83.
Poor and the Rich, The (Germany). Thompson, *100 Folktales,* no. 73.
Poor and the Rich, The. Ranke, *Folktales of Germany,* no. 56.
Poor Man and the Rich Man, The. Grimm, *Tales,* no. 87.
Ridiculous Wishes (France). Clarkson and Cross, *World Folktales,* no. 51.
Saint Peter and Two Women (Sweden). Booss, *Scandinavian Tales,* p. 190.
Sausage, The (Sweden). Booss, *Scandinavian Tales,* p. 179.
Simmer Water. Briggs, *DBF,* pt. B, v. 2, p. 349.
Three Wishes, The (de Beaumont). Opie, *Classic Fairy Tales,* p. 199.
Three Wishes, The. Briggs, *DBF,* pt. A, v. 1, p. 522.
Three Wishes, The. Briggs, *DBF,* pt. A, v. 2, p. 309.
Three Wishes, The. Jacobs, *More English Fairy Tales,* p. 107.
Three Wishes, The. Mathers, *1001 Nights,* v. 3, p. 27.

Three Wishes, The. Musick, *Green Hills of Magic,* no. 37.
Three Wishes, The. Randolph, *Who Blowed Up the Church House?,* p. 139.
Traveller's Cornsack, The. Briggs, *DBF,* pt. B, v. 2, p. 377.
Two Neighbours, The. Pourrat, *Treasury of French Tales,* p. 171.

## 750B  HOSPITALITY REWARDED.

A poor woman was boiling stones to make her children think they were peas. She received Christ at the door, and the stones turned into peas. (Briggs, "Christ and the Peas") Cf. type 751D*.

Christ and the Peas. Briggs, *DBF,* pt. A, v. 1, p. 107.
Choja Who Became a Monkey, The. Seki, *Folktales of Japan,* no. 41.
Golden Frogs of Bovey Tracey, The. Briggs, *DBF,* pt. B, v. 2, p. 419.
Kind Old Woman and the Hob, The. Raven, *Folklore of Staffordshire,* p. 104.
Lake of Langui, The (Peru). Dorson, *Folktales around the World,* p. 545.
Poor Widow and Her Son, The. Briggs, *DBF,* pt. A, v. 1, p. 448.
Telltale Pepper Bush, The. Abrahams, *Afro-American Folktales,* no. 26.

## 750D  THREE BROTHERS AND THEIR GIFTS FROM HEAVEN.

An old man granted wishes to three brothers, on the condition that they would always share with the poor. The first received a herd of sheep, the second a great olive orchard, and the third a spring that ran honey. Only the youngest kept his promise, and the first two brothers lost their wealth. (Megas)

Old Man and the Three Brothers, The. Megas, *Folktales of Greece,* no. 42.
Only One Brother Was Grateful. Dawkins, *Modern Greek Folktales,* no. 70.
Three Robbers and El-Khidr. El-Shamy, *Folktales of Egypt,* no. 21.

## 750F*  THE BLESSING FROM THE TWELVE MEN.

After baking bread for a rich woman, a poor woman would wash the dough from her hands, and make gruel for her children. But then the rich woman made her wash her hands before leaving, so her children had nothing. While searching for food, the poor woman came upon twelve men, who asked her what she thought of the various seasons. She said only good things, and they rewarded her with a jar full of gold. Learning about this event, the rich woman sought out the twelve men, but she said only bad things about the seasons. The men sent her home with a jar full of snake. (Megas)

Twelve Months, The (Greece). Cole, *Best-Loved Folktales,* no. 44.
Twelve Months, The. Megas, *Folktales of Greece,* no. 39.

## 750H*  A CARDPLAYER ENTERS PARADISE.

A cardplayer hosted Christ and his twelve disciples, and Christ offered the man entrance into heaven. When his time came, the cardplayer reported at the gate to Paradise, bringing twelve unworthy companions as well. Christ had to let them all enter, because he too had taken twelve guests to the cardplayer's house.

Cardplayer in Paradise, The. Megas, *Folktales of Greece,* no. 43.

**750\*\*\*\* THE VIRGIN MARY AND THE ANIMALS.** The Virgin Mary attempted to hide among some goats, but they bleated. From that day forth their shameful parts have been exposed for all to see.

Virgin Mary and the Goats, The. Bushnaq, *Arab Folktales,* p. 298.

**751A THE GREEDY WOMAN IS TURNED INTO A BIRD.** A miserly woman offered to make a roll for the Lord and Saint Peter from a tiny piece of dough. It grew to a large size, so she pulled off a tiny piece for her guests, but this one grew as well. Unwilling to give them a large piece, she sent them away hungry. To punish her greed, the Lord turned her into a woodpecker. (Asbjørnsen and Moe)

Black Woodpecker, The. Ranke, *Folktales of Germany,* no. 57.
First Cornish Mole, The. Briggs, *DBF,* pt. A, v. 1, p. 107.
Gertrude's Bird. Asbjørnsen and Moe, *East o' the Sun,* p. 213.
Greedy Peasant-Woman, The. Briggs, *DBF,* pt. A, v. 1, p. 112.
Owl Was a Baker's Daughter, The. Briggs, *DBF,* pt. A, v. 1, p. 124, 443.

**751C\* WEALTH LEADS TO PRIDE.** A poor beggar came into the possession of a donkey that dropped gold and silver coins. His wealth led to hardheartedness. Then his donkey was stolen, and he was soon reduced to his former state.

Beggar and his Ass, The. Noy, *Folktales of Israel,* no. 20.

**751D\* THE HOSPITABLE THIEVES.** The Lord and his apostles were turned away by a landowner, but a band of thieves shared their meal with them, and the apostles blessed them.

Tale the Robbers Tell, A. Calvino, *Italian Folktales,* no. 165.3.

**752 MARY AND THE PLOWMEN** (new classification). On their flight to Egypt, the Virgin Mary and Jesus passed farmers sowing their seed. Miraculously, the plants were ready to harvest the same day. When soldiers asked the farmers if they had seen the woman and child, they answered: "Yes, on the day we planted this crop." And the soldiers gave up their pursuit.

Virgin Mary and the Plowmen, The. Bushnaq, *Arab Folktales,* p. 299.

**752A THRESHING WITH FIRE.** The Lord set fire to a large stack of sheaves, and the flames threshed them clean, leaving the grain, chaff, and straw all neatly stacked in separate piles. A greedy woman tried the same trick with a new load of sheaves, but succeeded only in burning down her barn. (Calvino)

Buckwheat. Calvino, *Italian Folktales,* no. 41.4.

Christ and Peter (Netherlands). Bødker, *European Folk Tales,* p. 112.
Story about Our Lord Jesus Christ, A. Ranke, *Folktales of Germany,* no. 59.

**753  CHRIST AND THE SMITH.** Our Lord demonstrated his power to a smith. First he took off a horse's legs, remade the shoes in the furnace, then replaced the legs. Next put the smith's old mother in the flames, and she came at a lovely young woman. The smith tried to do the same miracles with a gentleman's horse and an old beggar woman. He burned the horse's legs to ashes, and it did not go any better for the old woman. (Asbjørnsen and Moe)

Blacksmith from Ireland, The. Briggs, *DBF,* pt. A, v. 1, p. 165.
Blacksmith That Tried Doctoring. Campbell, *Cloudwalking Country,* p. 191.
Christ and the Blacksmith. Musick, *Green Hills of Magic,* no. 56.
Christ Is the Better Smith. Paredes, *Folktales of Mexico,* no. 39.
Little Old Man Made Young by Fire, The. Grimm, *Tales,* no. 147.
Lord, Saint Peter, and the Apostles, The. Crane, *Italian Popular Tales,* no. 50.
Lord, Saint Peter, and the Blacksmith. Crane, *Italian Popular Tales,* no. 51.
Master-Smith, The. Asbjørnsen and Moe, *East o' the Sun,* p. 105.
Old Smith, The. Briggs, *DBF,* pt. A, v. 1, p. 428.
Put the Old Woman in the Furnace. Calvino, *Italian Folktales,* no. 165.2.
Saint Aloys and the Lame Nag. Briggs and Tongue, *Folktales of England,* no. 36.
Saint Aloys and the Lame Nag. Briggs, *DBF,* pt. B, v. 2, p. 433.
Smith and His Dame, The. Briggs, *DBF,* pt. A, v. 1, p. 490.
Will the Smith. Briggs, *DBF,* pt. A, v. 1, p. 574.

**753A  UNSUCCESSFUL RESUSCITATION.** Brother Merry saw Saint Peter bring a dead princess back to life. He tried unsuccessfully to achieve the same cure on another dead princess. In the end, Saint Peter appeared and corrected his errors, bringing the second girl back to life. (Grimm)

Brother Merry. Grimm, *Tales,* no. 81.
Lochman Hehkeem. Villa, *100 Armenian Tales,* no. 98.

**754  MONEY BRINGS MISFORTUNE.** A wealthy man gave a poor porter some money, which brought the porter many concerns. He asked the rich man for more money, which brought more unhappiness, so he asked for still more. The rich man, angry at the porter's greed and lack of gratitude, pushed him down the stairs. The porter struck his head and became blind, and then had to live as a beggar.

Porter Who Lost His Appetite, The. Noy, *Folktales of Israel,* no. 15.

**756  GREEN LEAVES ON A DRY STICK.** Tannhäuser visited the women in the Mountain of Venus, but then confessed his sins to Pope Urban. He responded by stating that Tannhäuser would not be forgiven until a dry stick would sprout green leaves. Three days later, the Pope's stick did indeed begin to sprout green leaves. (Grimm)

Boy Who Made a Trip to Hell, The. Musick, *Green Hills of Magic,* no. 57.
Legend of Twardowski, The. Musick, *Green Hills of Magic,* no. 1.
Lot and the Devil. Bushnaq, *Arab Folktales,* p. 292.
Mountain of Venus, The. Baring-Gould, *Curious Myths of the Middle Ages,*
    no. 10.
Tannhäuser. Grimm, German *Legends,* no. 171.

**756A THE SELF-RIGHTEOUS HERMIT.** A hermit made a cruel remark about a sinner being led to the gallows. His penance was to carry about a dry branch until three green twigs would sprout from it, which did indeed happen during the night that he died.

Three Green Branches, The. Grimm, *Tales,* no. 206.

**756B RECOVERING THE DEVIL'S CONTRACT.** The devil tricked a poor man into signing over his unborn son. When the boy was grown he found his way to hell and recovered the paper his father had signed in blood. (Ranke)

Boy Who Made a Trip to Hell, The. Musick, *Green Hills of Magic,* no. 57.
Friar on Errigal, The. O'Sullivan, *Folktales of Ireland,* no. 22.
Legend of Twardowski, The. Musick, *Green Hills of Magic,* no. 1.
Road to Hell, The. Ranke, *Folktales of Germany,* no. 58.

**756C THE GREATER SINNER.** A man who had killed ninety-nine people was given the penance to stand in a cemetery until his staff sprouted green leaves. While there, he saw a man trying to violate a woman's corpse. To protect the dead woman's honor, he killed the man with his staff. The following day his staff had sprouted green leaves. (El-Shamy)

Greater Sinner, The (2 tales). Dawkins, *Modern Greek Folktales,* no. 82A,B.
Greater Sinner, The (Greece). Thompson, *100 Folktales,* no. 74.
Killer of Ninety-Nine, The. El-Shamy, *Folktales of Egypt,* no. 22.

**758 EVE'S UNEQUAL CHILDREN.** God blessed Eve's children. To one he said: "You shall be a peasant," to another "You, a fisherman," and so forth. Eve complained that the children received different blessings, but God explained that not everyone can be a prince. Laborers and servants are also necessary. (Grimm)

Eve's Unequal Children. Grimm, *Tales,* no. 180.
In This World One Weeps and Another Laughs. Crane, *Italian Popular Tales,*
    no. 52.
Origin of Elves, The. Simpson, *Icelandic Folktales and Legends,* p. 14.

**759 DIVINE ACTS ARE VINDICATED.** A man was angry with Saint Joseph, for two of his sons had died on his day. Then the saint appeared to him and explained that had the boys lived longer they would have been hanged as criminals and condemned to hell. (Dorson)

How God's Wheel Turns. O'Sullivan, *Folktales of Ireland,* no. 23.
Mass of Saint Joseph (Spain). Dorson, *Folktales around the World,* p. 66.
Righteous Man, Black Man, and Moses. Sabar, *Kurdistani Jews,* p. 179.
Shall Not the Judge of All the Earth Do Right? Dawkins, *Modern Greek Folktales,* no. 84.

## 759B   A SIMPLE SAINT ATTENDS MASS. A priest invited a shepherd, who never went to church, to attend mass. The simple man came to the service and hung his coat on a sunbeam. Seeing the coat hanging in mid air, the priest knew that the shepherd was a saint.

An Actual Saint. Glassie, *Irish Folktales,* no. 14.

## 760*   THE CONDEMNED SOUL. —Miscellaneous tales.

Condemned Lover, The (Peru). Dorson, *Folktales around the World,* p. 533.
Saint Augustine in Long Compton. Briggs, *Folklore of the Cotswolds,* p. 71.

## 760A*   THE DEATH OF A MISER. A miser, fearing death, swallowed his gold coins. The devil shook the dead man until the coins fell out, then said to the sexton who was keeping watch: "The money is yours, but the bag is mine."

Death of a Miser. Afanasyev, *Russian Fairy Tales,* p. 268.

## 762   THE WOMAN WITH 365 CHILDREN. A countess accused a woman who had just given birth to twins of having had two lovers. As punishment for her rash judgment, the countess shortly thereafter became pregnant and subsequently gave birth to 365 children.

As Many Children as There Are Days. Grimm, *German Legends,* no. 584.

## 763   TREASURE FINDERS MURDER ONE ANOTHER. Six men found a pot of gold. Three went to town for food while the others guarded the treasure. To make their shares larger, the three who stayed behind decided to kill those who had gone for food. For the same reason, the three who went to town put poison in their companions' food. Thus three were struck dead, and three died of poisoned food. (Villa)

Chaucer's Pardoner's Tale. Clouston, *Popular Tales,* v. 2, p. 379.
It Served the Bastards Right. Randolph, *Sticks in the Knapsack,* p. 77.
Pardoner's Tale, The. Chaucer, *The Canterbury Tales,* p. 262.
Poor Man's Trust in God, The. Sabar, *Kurdistani Jews,* p. 145.
Soul-Taker, The. Villa, *100 Armenian Tales,* no. 51.

## 764   THE GHOST'S SON. A rejected suitor died, but came back from the grave and made his beloved pregnant. The child became a priest. It was prophesied that on the occasion of his first mass, the church with its congregation would be swallowed by the earth. A brave man, after

after hearing the prophecy, stabbed the priest to death, and thus saved the church.

Ghost's Son, The. Simpson, *Icelandic Folktales and Legends,* p. 136.

**766   THE MAGIC SLEEP.**   Holger the Dane sleeps in the castle Kronborg, and if Denmark should ever be in danger, he will awaken and come to her aid. (Andersen)  Cf. type 470*.

Arthur and His Knights Asleep in Alderley Edge. Simpson, *Folklore of the Welsh Border,* p. 34.
Canobie Dick and Thomas of Ercildoun. Briggs, *DBF,* pt. B, v. 2, p. 176.
Emperor Charles in Wonder Mountain. Grimm, *German Legends,* no. 28.
Fairies of Merlin's Craig, The. Briggs, *DBF,* pt. B, v. 1, p. 215.
Frederick Barbarossa at Kyffhausen. Grimm, *German Legends,* no. 23.
Giant's Cave of South Barrule, The. Killip, *Folklore of the Isle of Man,* p. 152.
Hunter and His Hounds: A Legend of Brinkburn. Briggs, *DBF,* pt. B, v. 2, p. 238.
Holger the Dane. Andersen, *Complete Fairy Tales,* no. 38.
Key of Craigachow, The. Briggs, *DBF,* pt. A, v. 1, p. 346.
King Arthur at Sewingshields. Briggs, *DBF,* pt. B, v. 2, p. 243.
King Herla. Briggs, *DBF,* pt. A, v. 1, p. 363.
Noontide Ghost, The. Briggs, *DBF,* pt. A, v. 1, p. 426.
Piper of Glendovon, The. Briggs, *DBF,* pt. B, v. 1, p. 336.
Potter Thompson. Briggs, *DBF,* pt. B, v. 2, p. 319.
Seven Men Sleeping in a Cave, The. Grimm, *German Legends,* no. 392.
Seven Sleepers of Ephesus. Baring-Gould, *Curious Myths of the Middle Ages,* no. 4.
Silver Horseshoe, The. Briggs, *DBF,* pt. B, v. 2, p. 348.
Sir Guy the Seeker. Briggs, *DBF,* pt. B, v. 2, p. 353.
Sleeping Giant of Castle Rushen, The. Killip, *Folklore of the Isle of Man,* p. 18.
Stonemason of the Charltons, The. Briggs, *DBF,* pt. A, v. 1, p. 498.
Three Tells, The. Grimm, *German Legends,* no. 298.
Wizard of Alderley Edge, The. Briggs, *DBF,* pt. B, v. 2, p. 398.

**766\*   REFUSING TO HELP A STRANGER.**   An old man asked a little girl to wash his tired feet, but she ran away from him. The man disappeared, and a few days later the little girl died. (Musick)

Agkon, the Greedy Son (Philippines). Dorson, *Folktales around the World,* p. 257.
He Walked on Earth. Musick, *Green Hills of Magic,* no. 58.

**767   FOOD FOR THE CRUCIFIX.**   A child shared his lunch with the crucifix in a cathedral, then crossed his arms and died. The pastor declared that the child was a saint. (Calvino)

Child That Fed the Crucifix, The. Calvino, *Italian Folktales,* no. 186.
Food for the Crucifix. Pino-Saavedra, *Folktales of Chile,* no. 30.
Heavenly Wedding, The. Grimm, *Tales,* no. 209.

**768 SAINT CHRISTOPHER CARRIES THE CHRIST CHILD.** A giant carried travelers across a great river, an easy task due to his great strength. One night he answered a small child's call and lifted him to his shoulders. As he made his way across the stream the child became heavier and heavier, and he reached the opposite shore only with great difficulty. "You seemed as heavy as the whole world," said the giant, setting down his rider. "Yes," answered the child. "I carry the world's sins. Tonight you have borne them." (Briggs)

> Kristaps. Carpenter, *A Latvian Storyteller*, p. 223.
> Saint Christopher Carries the Christ Child. Briggs, *Folklore of the Cotswolds*, p. 154.

**769 A CHILD RETURNS FROM THE DEAD.** A child, who had stolen a few coins and hidden them beneath the floor, died, but could not rest in its grave, until the parents found the stolen money and gave it to the poor.

> Stolen Farthing, The. Grimm, *Tales*, no. 154.

**774 JESUS AND SAINT PETER.** The Lord, traveling with his apostles, asked each of them to carry a stone. Peter chose the smallest one he could find. Later, the Lord turned the stones into bread, so Peter received only a small roll. They set out again, and the Lord repeated the commandment. This time Peter picked the largest stone he could find, but they soon came to a town where bread was plentiful, so Peter ended up carrying the heavy stone for nothing. (Calvino, "Stones to Bread")

> How Saint Peter Happened to Join Up with the Lord. Calvino, *Italian Folktales*, no. 41.1.
> Jesus and Saint Peter in Friuli. Calvino, *Italian Folktales*, no. 41.
> Jesus and Saint Peter in Sicily. Calvino, *Italian Folktales*, no. 165.
> Lord, Saint Peter, and the Apostles, The. Crane, *Italian Popular Tales*, no. 50.
> Saint Peter and the Horseshoe. Dégh, *Folktales of Hungary*, no. 22.
> Stones to Bread. Calvino, *Italian Folktales*, no. 165.1.

**776 KILLING THE GOOSE THAT LAID THE GOLDEN EGGS** (new classification). A man had a goose that laid a golden egg every day. As he grew rich from the sale of these eggs, he also became greedy, so he killed the goose and cut it open, hoping to find a great treasure. But there was no gold inside, and that was the end of his golden eggs. (Aesop)

> Gold-Producing Animals. Clouston, *Popular Tales*, v. 1, p. 123.
> Goose with the Golden Eggs (Aesop). Cole, *Best-Loved Folktales*, no. 41.
> Goose with the Golden Eggs, The. Jacobs, *Aesop*, no. 57.
> Grasp All, Lose All (India). Lang, *Olive Fairy Book*, p. 234.
> Much Wants More. Handford, *Aesop*, no. 178.

**777  THE WANDERING JEW.**  A Jewish shoemaker refused to allow Jesus to rest for a moment on his doorstep as he carried his cross to the place of crucifixion.  He was therefore cursed to wander about the earth for ever, not even finding rest in death.  (Baring-Gould) —See Anderson, *The Legend of the Wandering Jew.*

> Buttadeu. Crane, *Italian Popular Tales,* no. 59.
> Curse of the Shoemaker. Briggs, *DBF,* pt. B., v. 2, p. 597.
> Desperate Malchus. Crane, *Italian Popular Tales,* no. 57.
> Judas. Crane, *Italian Popular Tales,* no. 56.
> Malchus at the Column. Crane, *Italian Popular Tales,* no. 58.
> Pilate. Crane, *Italian Popular Tales,* no. 55.
> Roving Jew, The. Dorson, *Buying the Wind,* p. 507.
> Wandering Jew in England. Briggs, *DBF,* pt. B., v. 2, p. 595.
> Wandering Jew in Staffordshire, The. Raven, *Folklore of Staffordshire,* p. 30.
> Wandering Jew, The. Baring-Gould, *Curious Myths of the Middle Ages,* no. 1.
> Wandering Jew. Briggs, *DBF,* pt. B., v. 2, p. 597.

**779  DIVINE REWARDS AND PUNISHMENTS.**  —Miscellaneous tales.

> Bones of Father Adam, The. Bushnaq, *Arab Folktales,* p. 303.
> Count Robert. Pourrat, *Treasury of French Tales,* p. 155.
> Devil Who Was a Potter, The. Afanasyev, *Russian Fairy Tales,* p. 576.
> Ear of Grain, The. Grimm, *Tales,* no. 194.
> Fra Ignazio. Calvino, *Italian Folktales,* no. 191.
> Gentleman Who Kicked a Skull, The. Crane, *Italian Popular Tales,* no. 71.
> Gossips of Saint John. Crane, *Italian Popular Tales,* no. 72.
> Groomsman, The. Crane, *Italian Popular Tales,* no. 69.
> Letter to God, The. Sabar, *Kurdistani Jews,* p. 184.
> Mercy of God, The (2 tales). Dawkins, *Modern Greek Folktales,* no. 83A,B.
> Musicians on the Gallows, The. Grimm, *Other Tales,* p. 90.
> Parish Priest of San Marcuola, The. Crane, *Italian Popular Tales,* no. 70.
> Poor Wretch, The. Afanasyev, *Russian Fairy Tales,* p. 177.
> Sainte Madeleine. Pourrat, *Treasury of French Tales,* p. 34.
> Star Talers, The. Grimm, *Tales,* no. 153.
> Steel Cane, The (Armenia). Lang, *Olive Fairy Book,* p. 301.
> Stone Statue, The (Sweden). Booss, *Scandinavian Tales,* p. 206.
> Willful Child, The. Grimm, *Tales,* no. 117.

**779B\*  NAUGHTY CHILDREN LOSE THEIR MOTHER.**  Two girls were very naughty to their mother, so she left them, and instead a woman with glass eyes and a wooden tail came to be their mother.

> Pear-Drum, The. Briggs, *DBF,* pt. A, v. 2, p. 554.

**779C\*  HARDHEARTED CHILDREN ARE PUNISHED.**  An old couple asked their married son to give them some corn. Although his corn bins were full, he told them that he had not yet harvested his crop, and he sent them away with only a few handfuls. Later he discovered that all his corn had been eaten by weevils.

Hard-Hearted Son, The. Paredes, *Folktales of Mexico,* no. 40.

**780   THE SINGING BONE.** A king promised his daughter's hand to whoever could kill the wild boar that was ravaging his land. A simple, kind-hearted boy killed the boar, but his older brother struck him dead, buried his body, and claimed the princess for himself. Years afterward a shepherd made a flute from a bone that he had found in the sand, and it sang a song that told the story of the murder. The shepherd took the miraculous flute to the king, who had the the older brother put to death. (Grimm)

> Binnorie. Briggs, *DBF,* pt. A, v. 1, p. 152.
> Binnorie. Jacobs, *English Fairy Tales,* p. 44.
> Bul-Bul Bird, The (Latvia). Cole, *Best-Loved Folktales,* no. 90.
> Flower of Lily-Lo, The. Paredes, *Folktales of Mexico,* no. 41.
> Griffin, The. Crane, *Italian Popular Tales,* no. 8.
> Jealous Sister, The. Arewa, *Northern East Africa,* p. 143.
> Kumba Kills His Wife's Sister. Arewa, *Northern East Africa,* p. 144.
> Laurel Flower, The. Massignon, *Folktales of France,* no. 66.
> Little Bird, The; or, The Singing Bones. Saucier, *French Louisiana,* no. 16.
> Little Ripen Pear, The. Roberts, *South from Hell,* no. 30A.
> Magic Fiddle, The. Jacobs, *Indian Fairy Tales,* no. 40.
> Magic Flute, The. Fowke, *Folklore of Canada,* p. 280.
> Miraculous Pipe, The. Afanasyev, *Russian Fairy Tales,* p. 425.
> Murder of Saint Kenelm, The. Raven, *Folklore of Staffordshire,* p. 29.
> Peacock Feather, The. Calvino, *Italian Folktales,* no. 180.
> Quendreda Has King Kenelm Killed. Briggs, *Folklore of the Cotswolds,* p. 69.
> Rose of Peppermette, The. Thomas, *It's Good to Tell You,* no. 16.
> Saint Kenelm. Briggs, *DBF,* pt. B, v. 2, p. 448.
> Singing Bone, The (Italy). Thompson, *100 Folktales,* no. 75.
> Singing Bone, The. Grimm, *Tales,* no. 28.
> Singing Bones, The. Abrahams, *Afro-American Folktales,* no. 30.
> Singing Bones, The. Botkin, *Treasury of American Folklore,* p. 678.
> Skeleton's Song, The. Seki, *Folktales of Japan,* no. 42.
> Wicked Stepmother, The. Randolph, *The Talking Turtle,* p. 16.

**780C   THE TELL-TALE HEAD.** A merchant murdered his companion in a deserted area. A year later, passing through the same area, he saw a watermelon growing out of season, picked it, and put it in his bag. He showed it to the sheriff. They cut it open, and inside was the head of the murdered man. The merchant confessed to the crime.

> Sidi 'Aabdul-Rahman. El-Shamy, *Folktales of Egypt,* no. 37.

**781   A BIRD REPORTS THE MURDER OF A CHILD.** A gentleman passed the house where a small boy lived with his mother. "Mother's going to put me in the oven," said the boy to him, but the man paid no heed and left. A little later a magpie flew repeatedly across his path, so he returned to the house. The woman had gone, and he found the little boy roasting in the oven. Cf. type 960A.

Good Magpie, The.  Briggs, *DBF*, pt. B, v. 2, p. 768.

**782  THE EMPEROR WHO HAD GOAT'S EARS.**  Czar Trojan had ears like a goat.  Every day a barber was brought to the palace to shave him, after which the czar would ask what he had seen.  If the barber answered truthfully, the czar had his head cut off.  Finally a barber came who claimed to have seen nothing unusual, so the czar paid him well, and had him return regularly.  But the barber told his secret to a hole in the ground, and a tree grew out of the hole, and shepherds made a flute from one of the tree's branches, and the flute sang about the czar's ears, so soon everyone knew the czar's secret, and there was nothing he could do about it.  (Cole)

> Czar Trojan's Ears (Yugoslavia).  Cole, *Best-Loved Folktales,* no. 101.
> Goat's Ears of the Emperor Trojan, The (Serbia).  Lang, *Violet Fairy Book,* p. 52.

**785  WHO ATE THE LAMB'S HEART?**  Peter and his companion were cooking a lamb.  While Peter was not looking, the companion ate the heart, but denied this when Peter asked him about it.  Later they received a bag of gold for having cured a princess.  Peter divided the gold into three parts: one for himself, one for the companion, and one for the one who ate the lamb's heart.  Now the companion readily admitted that he was the one who had eaten the lamb's heart.  (Grimm)

> Brother Merry.  Grimm, *Tales,* no. 81.
> Hare Liver, The.  Calvino, *Italian Folktales,* no. 41.2.
> Saint Peter's Chicken.  Pourrat, *Treasury of French Tales,* p. 134.

**785A  THE FOWL WITH ONE LEG.**  A cook, preparing a crane for his master, gave one of the legs to his lover.  Questioned about the missing leg, he claimed that cranes have but one leg.  The next day, to prove his point, he showed his master some cranes standing on one leg.  But the master shouted, and the cranes, both legs clearly visible, flew away.  To this, the cook replied that had he so shouted at the dinner table, the roasted bird would also  have produced a second leg.

> Currado's Cook Converts His Master's Anger into Laughter.  Boccaccio, *Decameron,* Day 6, Tale 4.

**791  SAINT PETER AND JESUS TRADE PLACES IN BED.**  Jesus and Saint Peter found shelter in a hayloft during harvest time.  At dawn the mistress of the house gave Peter a whack to rouse him out of bed to help with the threshing.  He traded places with Jesus, and went back to sleep.  The woman returned to give the other man a blow, and hit Peter again.  (Calvino)

> Buckwheat.  Calvino, *Italian Folktales,* no. 41.4.
> Christ and Peter (Netherlands).  Bødker, *European Folk Tales,* p. 112.

Saint Peter and the Horseshoe. Dégh, *Folktales of Hungary*, no. 22.
Story about Our Lord Jesus Christ, A. Ranke, *Folktales of Germany*, no. 59.

**800   THE TAILOR IN HEAVEN.**   A dishonest tailor died, but he talked his way past Saint Peter, thus gaining entrance into heaven. One day he observed an old washerwoman stealing an item of clothing from her laundry work. Angered, the self-righteous tailor threw the Lord's golden footstool at her. Discovering the tailor's quickness to judge others, the Lord cast him out of heaven. (Grimm)

> Tailor in Heaven, The. Grimm, *Tales*, no. 35.
> Tailor in Heaven, The. Ranke, *Folktales of Germany*, no. 60.

**801   THE FAULT-FINDER IN HEAVEN.**   Master Pfriem, a shoemaker, found fault with everyone. One night he dreamed he had died and gone to heaven. There he saw a cart stuck in a deep hole and watched as angels hitched horses both to the front and rear of the cart. "How stupid!" he cried, and wanted to show the angels the right way to hitch horses to a cart, but even as he spoke, the horses, which had wings that he had not seen, flew into the air, pulling the cart straight up out of the hole. Master Pfriem awoke from his dream, but still he continued to find fault with everyone and everything. (Grimm) Cf. type 1248.

> It Serves Me Right! El-Shamy, *Folktales of Egypt*, no. 12.
> Master Pfriem. Grimm, *Tales*, no. 178.

**802   THE PEASANT AND THE RICH MAN IN HEAVEN.**   A peasant and a rich man arrived in heaven at the same time. The rich man was met with great jubilation, while the peasant was ignored. He asked Saint Peter why this was so, and received the answer that a rich man's arrival in heaven was cause for a great celebration, because it happened only once in a hundred years, whereas poor people entered every day. (Grimm) Cf. type 1738.

> Crowdy of Hightworth. Briggs, *DBF*, pt. A, v. 2, p. 50.
> Peasant in Heaven, The. Grimm, *Tales*, no. 167.
> Pitman's Dream, A. Briggs, *DBF*, pt. A, v. 2, p. 236.
> Saint Anthony's. Briggs, *DBF*, pt. A, v. 2, p. 255.

**804   SAINT PETER'S MOTHER.**   Saint Peter received permission to pull his mother from purgatory. Many other souls took hold of her skirt, wanting to be pulled into heaven with her, but she pushed them aside. Noting the hardness of her heart, Saint Peter let go of her, and she fell back into purgatory. (Grimm)

> Poor Compadre, The. Pino-Saavedra, *Folktales of Chile*, no. 31.
> Saint Peter's Mamma. Calvino, *Italian Folktales*, no. 165.5.
> Saint Peter's Mother. Crane, *Italian Popular Tales*, p. 192.
> Saint Peter's Mother. Grimm, *Other Tales*, p. 134.

Santa Catalina (Spain). Dorson, *Folktales around the World*, p. 64.

**804A  THE PLANT THAT REACHED HEAVEN.** An old man planted a head of cabbage that grew until it reached heaven. He wanted to carry his wife to the top, so she climbed into a bag, which he held between his teeth as he climbed. Impatiently, she asked "Is it far?" and when he opened his mouth to answer, the bag fell to the ground, and she was killed. —Note: For other tales with plants reaching to heaven see types 328, 468, 1960G.

Fox Physician, The. Afanasyev, *Russian Fairy Tales*, p. 15.

**804B  BUILDING A CHURCH IN HELL.** A man promised his new-born son to the devil. The boy reported to hell at the appointed time, and immediately began to build a church. The devil could not have this, so he threw the boy out.

Legend of Twardowski, The. Musick, *Green Hills of Magic*, no. 1.

**805  SAINT JOSEPH THREATENS TO LEAVE HEAVEN.** Saint Peter barred a man, who in life had addressed all his prayers to Saint Joseph, from entering heaven. He had, claimed Peter, neglected the other saints. Hearing this, Saint Joseph threatened to take his wife and son and leave heaven, so Peter let him in after all.

Devotee of Saint Joseph. Calvino, *Italian Folktales*, no. 28.

**809*  A SINGLE GOOD DEED.** God granted one hour in paradise but the rest of eternity in hell to a sinner who had performed but a single good deed in life. Similarly, a righteous man who had committed a single sin was given one hour in hell and the rest of eternity in paradise. The sinner offered to give his hour in paradise to the righteous man, and God was so touched that he forgave him his sins. .Thus both men were saved. (Sabar)

By Virtue of a Single Good Deed. Sabar, *Kurdistani Jews*, p. 142.
Man Who Didn't Perform His Prayers, The. El-Shamy, *Folktales of Egypt*, no. 19.

**810  THE DEVIL LOSES A SOUL THAT WAS PROMISED HIM.** A poor man in despair signed a pact with the devil, agreeing, in return for wealth, to renounce God. Later he repented and entered a church, where he prayed for many days. The Virgin Mary brought him the pact he had signed. He burned it and returned to his family. (Bødker)

Blacksmith Who Sold Himself to the Devil, The. Briggs, *DBF*, pt. A, v. 1, p. 167.
Child Promised to the Devil, The. Massignon, *Folktales of France*, no. 70.
Child, the Snake, and Our Lady, The. Pourrat, *Treasury of French Tales*, p. 105.

Faustus. Briggs, *DBF,* pt. B, v. 1, p. 96.
King of the Golden Mountain, The. Grimm, *Tales,* no. 92.
Legend of Twardowski, The. Musick, *Green Hills of Magic,* no. 1.
Licentiate of Saint Andrews, The. Briggs, *DBF,* pt. B, v. 1, p. 111.
Liombruno. Calvino, *Italian Folktales,* no. 134.
Lionbruno. Crane, *Italian Popular Tales,* no. 36.
Man Who Wouldn't Go Out at Night, The. Briggs, *DBF,* pt. A, v. 1, p. 407.
Mangy One, The. Calvino, *Italian Folktales,* no. 110.
Mother's Dream, The. Briggs, *DBF,* pt. B, v. 2, p. 555.
Nix Naught Nothing. Jacobs, *English Fairy Tales,* p. 33.
Poor Man Who Sold His Soul to the Devil, The (Greece). Bødker, *European
    Folk Tales,* p. 203.
Poor Man Who Wanted to Become Rich. Dawkins, *Modern Greek Folktales,*
    no. 59.
Round Square, The. Briggs, *DBF,* pt. B, v. 1, p. 132.
Svein Unafraid. Christiansen, *Folktales of Norway,* p. 159.
Three Princesses of Whiteland, The. Asbjørnsen and Moe, *East o' the Sun,* p.
    181.
Vicar and the Devil, The. Briggs, *DBF,* pt. B, v. 1, p. 149.

## 810A* THE DEVIL BUILDS A CHURCH IN ONE NIGHT. A
certain town entered an agreement with the devil. He would build
them church in one night, if they would give him a certain number of
unbaptized babies. However, if he could not finish the task before the
cock crowed, the town would owe him nothing. Only the outside
plastering remained undone as dawn approached. Then an old woman
from the town entered the chicken coop and lit a candle, causing the
cock to crow before sunrise. Thus the devil lost his wager.

> How the Devil Constructed a Church (Honduras). Cole, *Best-Loved Folktales,*
> no. 194.

## 812 THE DEVIL'S RIDDLE. Three deserters from the army entered
an agreement with the devil. He was to serve them for seven years, but
then they would become his property, unless they could solve a riddle
he would give them. As the seven years approached their end, the
three came upon an old woman, who happened to be the devil's
grandmother. She helped them discover the answer to the riddle, and
thus they were saved. (Grimm, no. 125)

> Bhrgu's Journey in the Other World. O'Flaherty, *Tales of Sex and Violence,*
> p. 32.
> Devil and His Grandmother, The. Campbell, *Cloudwalking Country,* p. 246.
> Devil and His Grandmother, The. Grimm, *Tales,* no. 125.
> Devil and the Three Soldiers, The. Grimm, *Other Tales,* p. 88.
> Devil's Riddles, The. Briggs, *DBF,* pt. A, v. 1, p. 123.
> Man in the Wilderness, The. Briggs, *DBF,* pt. A, v. 1, p. 403.
> Man Who Found the Pea (commentary). Dawkins, *Modern Greek Folktales,*
> no. 63.
> Three Traveling Artisans, The. Ranke, *Folktales of Germany,* no. 28.
> Wife of the Gandharva in the Waters. O'Flaherty, *Tales of Sex and Violence,*
> p. 87.

**813 A CARELESS WORD SUMMONS THE DEVIL.** A man asked his wife for five shillings to go drinking, but she would not give it to him. "Then I'll sell myself to the devil for it!" he responded. The next night a stranger gave him five shillings. Some time later this same stranger appeared to him at midnight and took him away. (Briggs, "The Man That Sold His Soul to the Devil")

> El Caballo con Alas (The Horse with Wings). Musick, *Green Hills of Magic,* no. 4.
> Man That Sold His Soul to the Devil, The. Briggs, *DBF,* pt. B, v. 1, p. 115.
> Squeeze-Penny and the Devil. Pourrat, *Treasury of French Tales,* p. 111.
> White Mare of Whitestonecliffe, The. Briggs, *DBF,* pt. B, v. 2, p. 391.

**815 KEEPING WATCH AT A RICH MAN'S GRAVE.** A dying rich man offered a poor man eight measures of grain if he would keep watch at his grave for three nights. The poor man agreed, and—in the company of an old soldier—took up his position in the churchyard. The devil approached and offered them as much gold as would fit in a boot, if they would vacate their post. —Continues as type 1130.

> Grave Mound, The. Grimm, *Tales,* no. 195.

**815\* A CRAFTSMAN REFUSES THE DEVIL'S MONEY.** A tailor, while measuring a man for a suit of clothes, noticed that he had hooves for feet. He made and delivered the suit, but would not take the man's payment. If he had, it would have cost him his soul. (Briggs, "The Devil and the Tailor")

> Cresswell Tailor, The. Briggs, *DBF,* pt. B, v. 1, p. 56.
> Devil and the Blacksmith, The. Briggs, *DBF,* pt. B, v. 1, p. 72.
> Devil and the Tailor, The. Briggs, *DBF,* pt. A, v. 1, p. 210.

**817\* THE DEVIL LEAVES UPON HEARING GOD'S NAME.** The devil kept stealing firewood from a certain house, until a tinker volunteered to stand guard. The devil approached and asked who was there, upon which the tinker said: "It's me and God." The devil fled and never returned. (Briggs, "The Timber and the Devil")

> Devil's Bolts. Briggs, *DBF,* pt. B, v. 1, p. 85.
> Diabolic Invitation. Briggs, *DBF,* pt. B, v. 1, p. 93.
> El Caballo con Alas. Musick, *Green Hills of Magic,* no. 4.
> Shrove Tuesday Visitor, The (Canada). Clarkson and Cross, *World Folktales,* no. 34.
> Timber and the Devil, The. Briggs, *DBF,* pt. B, v. 1, p. 144.

**819\* THE DEVIL'S PORTRAIT.** A boy carved a figure of the devil. The devil came to him and told him to change the eye. A priest told the boy to cut the eye out, or the devil would get him. The devil returned, and when he saw the carving with the missing eye, he vanished in flames.

Little Boy and the Devil, The. Briggs, *DBF,* pt. B, v. 1, p. 113.

**820   THE DEVIL AS A LABORER.**   Davies tricked the devil into spreading his field with manure. (Briggs)

> Devil Who Was a Potter, The. Afanasyev, *Russian Fairy Tales,* p. 576.
> How Davies Had the Muck Spread. Briggs, *DBF,* pt. B, v. 1, p. 66.
> Jack and the Devil. Simpson, *Folklore of the Welsh Border,* p. 58.

**821   THE DEVIL AS ADVOCATE.**   A treacherous innkeeper, himself guilty of many crimes, accused an innocent traveler of robbery. A stranger in a red cap defended the traveler in court, proving his innocence and exposing the innkeeper's crimes as well. Cf. type 360.

> Treacherous Innkeeper, The. Briggs, *DBF,* pt. B, v. 1, p. 145.

**821A   THE DEVIL RESCUES AN ACCUSED MAN.**   A poor boy innocently acquired a sum of money, but the mayor stole it from him. The boy accused him of the theft, but was then sentenced to die for slandering a person of rank. At the execution, a strange gentleman appeared, and, after hearing the boy's story, asked the mayor to swear: "May the devil take me if I am a thief!" The mayor did so, and in that instant, the gentleman took him by the collar and flew off through the air with him.

> How the Devil Fetched the Mayor. Ranke, *Folktales of Germany,* no. 64.

**821B   CHICKENS FROM BOILED EGGS.**   A sailor ordered cooked eggs at a tavern, but had to leave before he could pay. Years later he returned, and the innkeeper gave him a huge bill, based on the cost of all the chickens the eggs might have produced had they hatched. The sailor, unable to pay, was brought to trial. His lawyer arrived late at court, and explained to the judge that he had been planting cooked beans. The innkeeper interrupted: "How can a man plant cooked beans?" The lawyer answered: "How can chicks hatch from cooked eggs?" Thus the sailor won his case. (Megas)  —Note: In some versions, the lawyer is identified as the devil.

> Eggs. Megas, *Folktales of Greece,* no. 53.
> George Buchanan and the Eggs. Briggs, *DBF,* pt. A, v. 1, p. 100.
> Nasreddin Khoja as Witness. Walker and Uysal, *Tales in Turkey,* p. 236.

**821C   THE DEVIL PROMISES HELP, BUT RENEGES** (new classification).   A thief and the devil entered into an agreement to work together. Finally the man was caught and sentenced to die. The devil stood beneath the gallows to catch him as he fell, but at the last moment he stepped aside, and the thief hanged.

Devil Who Wore Out Forty Pairs of Tsarouchia. Megas, *Folktales of Greece*, no. 44.

**822  THE LAZY BOY AND THE INDUSTRIOUS GIRL.**  The Lord and Saint Peter met a lazy boy and an industrious girl. "Those two should get married," remarked the Lord. "The one makes up for what the other lacks."

Christ and Peter (Netherlands). Bødker, *European Folk Tales*, p. 112.

**822\*  THE DEVIL AS CREDITOR.**  A poor farmer borrowed a barrel of money from a stranger in the woods. He agreed to bring the money back after a certain time and call "Koop!" three times. This he did, and a voice answered: "Koop is dead; keep what you have."

Dead Creditor, The. Ranke, *Folktales of Germany*, no. 65.

**826  THE DEVIL WRITES A LIST IN CHURCH.**  A pious man observed the devil, seated beneath the pulpit, writing a list of all those who whispered, slept, or otherwise misbehaved in church. "You won't trick me!" thought the man, but when the devil stretched his parchment to make room for more names, the man laughed out loud, and the devil wrote down his name as well. (Lindow)

Devil in the Church, The. Lindow, *Swedish Legends and Folktales*, no. 77.
Goblin on the Church-Beam, The. Simpson, *Icelandic Folktales and Legends*, p. 192.

**830C  IF GOD WILLS.**  A certain man had no time for religion. In spite of his wife's pleas, he would not say "If God wills," as he made plans for the day. Then one day a soldier forced him to leave his work and accompany him to town; from then on he ended every statement with "If God wills." (Bushnaq)

If God Wills. Bushnaq, *Arab Folktales*, p. 284.
Those Stubborn Souls, The Biellese. Calvino, *Italian Folktales*, no. 20.

**831  THE PRIEST IN THE GOATSKIN.**  A poor peasant found a buried treasure. A greedy priest, hoping to frighten the peasant into giving him the treasure, sewed himself into a goatskin and went to the peasant's house, disguised as the devil. The peasant would not open his door. When the priest returned home, he discovered that the goatskin had grown to his body, and it could not be removed. (Afanasyev)

Treasure-Trove. Afanasyev, *Russian Fairy Tales*, p. 550.
Treasure, The (Russia). Cole, *Best-Loved Folktales*, no. 97.

**832  A FISH FOR EACH CHILD.**  A poor fisherman always caught the same number of fish as he had children. When one of the children died, he caught one less fish.

Victory in the Time of Famine. Glassie, *Irish Folktales,* no. 107.

**834  THE POOR BROTHER'S TREASURE.** Some one knocked at a poor man's window and asked him to fetch a treasure; he was afraid to go, but he did tell his rich brother about the incident. The following night the knocking sounded again, and the rich brother followed the stranger, but he found only a dead horse. In anger, he cut off one of the horse's legs and threw it through his brother's window. In the morning a great pile of gold coins lay on the brother's floor. (Ranke)

> Dream, The. Musick, *Green Hills of Magic,* no. 55.
> Jar Full of Ants, A. Eberhard, *Folktales of China,* no. 12.
> Poor Brother's Treasure, The. Ranke, *Folktales of Germany,* no. 37.
> Three Godfathers, The. Musick, *Green Hills of Magic,* no. 52.
> Two Brothers, The (USA). Dorson, *Folktales around the World,* p. 493.

**834A  A POT OF GOLD AND A POT OF SNAKES.** An honest man found a pot of gold and told his dishonest neighbor about it. The neighbor dug up the pot, but found it filled with snakes. For revenge, he poured the snakes down the honest man's chimney, but instead of snakes, gold coins fell into the room. (Seki)

> Blind Wolf. Musick, *Green Hills of Magic,* no. 53.
> Luck from Heaven and Luck from Earth. Seki, *Folktales of Japan,* no. 44.
> Three Godfathers, The. Musick, *Green Hills of Magic,* no. 52.

**835A\*  THE DRUNK MAN IN THE CELLAR.** Attempting to cure a heavy drinker, a minister carried him, unconscious, into a cellar. When the drinker awoke, the minister said: "We are both dead." "How long have you been here?" asked the drinker. "A fortnight," answered the minister. "Then you must know your way around," said the drinker. "Can you find me something to drink?" The minister then saw that he had tackled a hopeless case. (Briggs, "Not So Easy Cured")

> Clerk of Bartholmy, The. Briggs, *DBF,* pt. A, v. 2, p. 37.
> Not So Easy Cured. Briggs, *DBF,* pt. A, v. 2, p. 202.

**836F\*  THE MISER AND THE EYE OINTMENT.** A man came into the possession of a magic ointment that, when applied to one eye, would show him the location of buried treasure. He was warned that if he applied it to both eyes, he would go blind, but he failed to heed the warning, and lost his sight.

> Patient Suitor, The. Villa, *100 Armenian Tales,* no. 17.

**837  A WICKED LANDLORD POISONS HIS OWN SON.** A landlord, tired of seeing an old beggar woman, gave her a poisoned cake. She, in turn, gave the cake to the landlord's son, who stopped at her hut while hunting in the woods. He fell dead after the first bite. (Noy)

Beggar's Bread, The. Musick, *Green Hills of Magic,* no. 59.
Ditch-Digger Falls into His Own Ditch. Villa, *100 Armenian Tales,* no. 43.
Do Good, Do Good. Dance, *Folklore from Contemporary Jamaicans,* no. 101.
Landlord and His Son, The. Noy, *Folktales of Israel,* no. 17.

**838    A THIEF REPROACHES HIS MOTHER.** A thief, being led to the gallows, stopped as though to whisper to his mother. Instead, he nearly bit off her ear. Then he said aloud: "If you had punished me when I was young, I would not be here today."

Spare the Rod and Spoil the Child. Handford, *Aesop,* no. 168.
Young Thief and His Mother, The. Jacobs, *Aesop,* no. 44.

**839    THE GREATEST SIN.** The devil showed a hermit that drunkenness is the greatest of all sins, because all other sins can follow it.

Hermit and the Devil, The. Ranke, *Folktales of Germany,* no. 61.

**841    ONE BEGGAR PRAISES GOD; ONE PRAISES THE KING.** A king observed two beggars, one praising God and the other the king. The king had two loaves of bread baked, one filled with gold, which he gave to the beggar who praised him, and a plain loaf, which went to the beggar who praised God. However, the beggar who praised the king thought that his loaf was too heavy, so he traded it to the other beggar for the lighter loaf, and thus he lost his treasure. (Noy, "He Who Gives Thanks")

He Who Gives Thanks to the King and He Who Gives Thanks to the Almighty. Noy, *Folktales of Israel,* no. 34.
Kitchen Deity, The. Eberhard, *Folktales of China,* no. 79.
Tailor with His Luck Locked Up, The. Noy, *Folktales of Israel,* no. 67.

**844    A HAPPY MAN'S SHIRT.** A king was told that he could cure his son of melancholy by finding a man who was thoroughly happy and then exchanging shirts with him. The king finally found such a person, but the happy man wore no shirt. (Calvino)

Happy Man's Shirt, The. Calvino, *Italian Folktales,* no. 39.
King's Unhappy Son, The. Musick, *Green Hills of Magic,* no. 60.
Shoes for the King. Randolph, *Who Blowed Up the Church House?,* p. 130.

**845    THE OLD MAN AND DEATH.** An old woodcutter, too weary to pick up his bundle of sticks, cried out: "I wish that death would take me!" As he spoke, death appeared, but then the old man changed his mind. "Would you help me lift this load to my shoulders?" he now asked.

Old Man and Death, The. Jacobs, *Aesop,* no. 69.

**846 THE DEVIL IS BLAMED; GOD IS PRAISED.** The devil complained to God that, whatever the actual cause, he was always blamed for mankind's bad luck, whereas God always received credit for good fortune. (Ranke)

> Devil and Our Lord, The. Ranke, *Folktales of Germany,* no. 62.
> Devil Gets Blamed, The. Carpenter, *A Latvian Storyteller,* p. 179.
> No Justice on Earth. Abrahams, *Afro-American Folktales,* no. 21.

**848\* SAINT NICHOLAS AND THE THIEF.** A thief, about to be captured, prayed to Saint Nicholas, offering a huge candle in return for escape. The saint provided a piece of carrion for the man to hide in, but he would not accept the gift of the candle from a thief.

> Father Nicholas and the Thief. Afanasyev, *Russian Fairy Tales,* p. 145.

**849\* THE CROSS AS SECURITY.** A bankrupt merchant borrowed 50,000 rubles from a Tartar, pledging only the church cross as security. His voyage was profitable, but on his return trip, fearing a shipwreck, he sealed the Tartar's money in a barrel and threw it overboard; miraculously, the barrel drifted down the Danube to the Tartar's house, and he recovered it himself. Impressed with the power of the cross, the Tartar had himself and his family baptized.

> Cross is Pledged as Security, The. Afanasyev, *Russian Fairy Tales,* p. 159.

# Romantic Tales

**850  THE PRINCESS'S BIRTHMARKS.**  A king announced that any suitor who could identify the princess's birthmarks could marry her. A swineherd knew how to make his pigs dance by playing a flute. One day the princess saw his dancing pigs and asked to have one, but he consented only after she lifted her skirt to her navel for him. Thus he learned that she had three golden hairs on her belly, and with this information he won her hand in marriage. (Ranke)

> Clever Little Tailor, The. Grimm, *Tales,* no. 114.
> Golden Breasts, Diamond Navel, Chain of Gold. Abrahams, *Afro-American Folktales,* no. 75.
> Self-Playing Gusla, The. Afanasyev, *Russian Fairy Tales,* p. 211.
> Simple Lad and Three Little Pigs. Pino-Saavedra, *Folktales of Chile,* no. 32.
> Swineherd, The. Andersen, *Complete Fairy Tales,* no. 22.
> Swineherd Who Married a Princess, The (Germany). Dorson, *Folktales around the World,* p. 87.
> Swineherd Who Married a Princess. Ranke, *Folktales of Germany,* no. 46.
> Tamacasti. Parades, *Folktales of Mexico,* no. 4.

**851  WINNING THE PRINCESS WITH A RIDDLE.**  A princess said that she would marry whoever could give her a riddle that she could not answer. A prince told her this riddle: "One slew none and yet slew twelve." The princess could not guess the answer (a raven that had eaten the meat of a poisoned horse and was in turn eaten by twelve men), so she had to marry the prince. (Grimm, "The Riddle")

> Bierde. Crane, *Italian Popular Tales,* no. 14.
> Ignes Was a Burro. Dorson, *Buying the Wind,* p. 423.
> Man Who Put His Mother Over His Shoulder and Rode His Father, The. El-Shamy, *Folktales of Egypt,* no. 11.
> Princess Who Wanted to Solve Riddles, The (Russia). Thompson, *100 Folktales,* no. 76.
> Princess Who Wanted to Solve Riddles, The. Afanasyev, *Russian Fairy Tales,* p. 115.
> Riddle, The. Espinosa, *Folklore of Spain in the American Southwest,* p. 178.
> Riddle, The. Grimm, *Tales,* no. 22.
> Riddle, The. Megas, *Folktales of Greece,* no. 49.

Riddles, The. Villa, *100 Armenian Tales,* no. 19.
Ridere (Knight) of Riddles, The. Campbell, *West Highlands,* v. 2, p. 36.
Sea-Hare, The. Grimm, *Tales,* no. 191.
Son of the Merchant from Milan. Calvino, *Italian Folktales,* no. 62.
Three Killed Florrie, Florrie Killed Ten. Abrahams, *Afro-American Folktales,*
   no. 86.
Three Shining Stones, The. Parades, *Folktales of Mexico,* no. 42.
Young Prince, The. Briggs, *DBF,* pt. A, v. 2, p. 505.

**852 FORCING THE PRINCESS TO SAY "THAT'S A LIE!"** A
princess was such a storyteller that her father promised her hand to
anyone who could make her say "That's a lie!" A simple boy tried his
luck by telling one tall tale after the other, but the princess responded
to each with a casual "I dare say." Finally the boy claimed to have seen
his mother boxing the ears of her father, to which the princess angrily
remarked: "That's a lie!" Thus the simple boy won the princess.
(Asbjørnsen and Moe) Cf. type 1920H.

   Ash Lad Who Made the Princess Say, "You're a Liar!" Asbjørnsen and Moe,
      *Norwegian Folktales,* p. 17.
   Boots Who Made the Princess Say, "That's a Story." Asbjørnsen and Moe,
      *East o' the Sun,* p. 48.
   Great Liar, The. O'Sullivan, *Folktales of Ireland,* no. 53.
   Great Lie, The. Noy, *Folktales of Israel,* no. 44.
   Jack and the King. Briggs, *DBF,* pt. A, v. 2, p. 411.
   King of the Liars, The. Briggs, *DBF,* pt. A, v. 2, p. 424.
   Lies, The. Megas, *Folktales of Greece,* no. 69.
   Master and the Tenant Farmer, The. Massignon, *Folktales of France,* no. 47.
   Shepherd Who Got the King's Daughter. Delarue, *French Folktales,* p. 343.
   Third Captain's Tale, The. Mathers, *1001 Nights,* v. 4, p. 354.

**853 CATCHING THE PRINCESS WITH HER OWN WORDS.**
There was a princess with such a fast tongue that the king promised to
marry her to anyone who could outwit her with words. Boots, the
youngest of three brothers, decided to try his luck, and on the way to
the palace he picked up a number of items from the side of the road: a
broken plate, a dead magpie, and an old shoe sole. Boots and the
princess began their battle of words. "Can I cook my magpie here?" he
asked. "The fat will run out of it," she answered. "We'll catch it in
this," he replied, holding up the broken plate. "Are you trying to wear
out my tongue with your nonsense?" she asked. "No," he replied,
"here is one that's already worn out," and pulled out the shoe sole. The
princess had nothing else to say, and Boots thus won her hand in
marriage. (Asbjørnsen and Moe, "Taming the Shrew")

   Blockhead-Hans. Lang, *Yellow Fairy Book,* p. 313.
   Clod Hans. Andersen, *Complete Fairy Tales,* no. 76.
   Daft Jack and the Heiress. Briggs, *DBF,* pt. A, v. 2, p. 397.
   Dirty Jack. Roberts, *South from Hell,* no. 31.
   Foolish Brother, The. Briggs, *DBF,* pt. A, v. 2, p. 405.
   Little John ('Tit Jean) I. Saucier, *French Louisiana,* no. 17.

Prick Teaser, The. Randolph, *Pissing in the Snow,* no. 94.
Princess of Canterbury, The. Briggs, *DBF,* pt. A, v. 2, p. 452.
Princess of Canterbury. Jacobs, *More English Fairy Tales,* p. 229.
Princess Who Always Had to Have the Last Word, The. Asbjørnsen and Moe, *Norwegian Folktales,* p. 77.
Quare Jack. Dorson, *Buying the Wind,* p. 172.
Rich Man's Daughter, The. Randolph, *Pissing in the Snow,* no. 11.
She Always Answered No. Randolph, *Who Blowed Up the Church House?,* p. 6.
Taming the Shrew. Asbjørnsen and Moe, *East o' the Sun,* p. 129.
Three Questions, The. Briggs, *DBF,* pt. A, v. 2, p. 495.
Twigmuntus, Cowbelliantus, Perchnosius (Sweden). Booss, *Scandinavian Tales,* p. 199.

**853A  THE PRINCESS ALWAYS ANSWERS "NO!"** A king told his daughter to say "no" to every request of a certain suitor. The suitor asked: "Do you think the guards should stay here in our presence?" and "Do you think we should keep the lamps lit?" The princess said "no" each time, which satisfied the suitor completely. (Calvino)

No! Afanasyev, *Russian Secret Tales,* p. 42
Prick Teaser, The. Randolph, *Pissing in the Snow,* no. 94.
Shepherd at Court, The. Calvino, *Italian Folktales,* no. 60.
Three Shining Stones, The. Parades, *Folktales of Mexico,* no. 42.

**854  MONEY DOES EVERYTHING.** A wealthy man boasted that money could do anything. The king bet him that, in spite of his great wealth, he could not seduce the princess, who was kept locked under seven keys. The man had a giant golden turkey made, and he got inside it, then had an old woman pull the turkey past the palace, shouting "See the turkey for fifty pesos." The king paid the woman to take the turkey to his daughter, who wanted to keep it in her room. Thus the wealthy man won his bet, and after the child was born, he married the princess. (Pino-Saavedra) Cf. type 860A*.

He Who Has Money Does What He Likes. Pino-Saavedra, *Folktales of Chile,* no. 33.
Money Can Do Everything. Calvino, *Italian Folktales,* no. 7.

**858  TO YOUR GOOD HEALTH!** A king insisted that whenever he sneezed everyone had to say "To your good health!" A certain shepherd refused to do this, and was brought to court. The king threatened him with many torments, but the shepherd always answered: "I will not say it until the princess is my wife." Finally, in desperation, the king gave him the hand of his daughter. At the wedding celebration, the king sneezed, and the shepherd cried out: "To your good health!"

To Your Good Health! (Russia) Lang, *Crimson Fairy Book,* p. 29.

**859  THE PENNILESS SUITOR.** Hans's uncle wanted to find him a wife, so he told him to put on a pair of patched pants and to hold a farthing in his hand until he returned. The uncle then went to a rich peasant's daughter in the next village and said: "Won't you marry my Hans. He has a piece of money in his hand and a lot of patches." The girl's father understood patches of land, so he agreed to the marriage. —Note: The story of the patches is classified 859A; the episode with the coin in hand is type 859B.

> Hans Gets Married. Grimm, *Tales,* no. 84.

**860A\*  THE HIDDEN PRINCESS.** A king hid his daughter in a secure place and then announced that any man who could find her within eight days should have her to wife. A young man had the figure of a lion made from gold and hid himself inside. An old woman took the lion to the king, who immediately wanted it for his daughter. Thinking himself alone, he took the lion to the princess in her secret room, and thus the suitor discovered the hiding place and married her. Cf. type 854.

> Golden Lion, The (Sicily). Lang, *Pink Fairy Book,* p. 223.

**870  THE ENTOMBED PRINCESS.** A princess wanted to marry a certain prince, but her father preferred another suitor. To break her will, the king locked her in a dark tower. After seven years, she dug herself free. Her father's kingdom, in the meantime, had been laid waste by invaders. After much travail, she found her beloved prince, and they married. (Grimm)

> Finn King's Daughter, The. Christiansen, *Folktales of Norway,* p. 147.
> Genevieve de Brabant. Saucier, *French Louisiana,* no. 1.
> Girl Clad in Mouseskin (Denmark). Booss, *Scandinavian Tales,* p. 493.
> Maid Maleen. Grimm, *Tales,* no. 198.
> Princess in the Earth Cave, The (Sweden). Thompson, *100 Folktales,* no. 77.
> Princess Who Was Hidden Underground (Germany). Lang, *Violet Fairy Book,* p. 316.
> Salento and Sølento (Norway). Bødker, *European Folk Tales,* p. 37.

**870A  THE GOOSEGIRL.** A goosegirl told a passing prince that he would marry her, but he chose a princess instead. The prince had a magic stone that could tell whether or not a girl had had a previous lover. Fearing the stone, the prince's fiancée asked the goosegirl to take her place in the marriage bed. She did this, and the stone told the prince that his mate was a virtuous maiden. But when the princess replaced the goosegirl in bed, the stone revealed that she already had three children. And so it came to be that the prince rejected the princess and took the goosegirl for his bride. (Asbjørnsen and Moe)

> Destined Girl Wins Her Place as the Prince's Bride, The. Dawkins, *Modern Greek Folktales,* no. 44.
> Duncombe. Briggs, *DBF,* pt. B, v. 2, p. 196.
> Little Annie the Goose-Girl. Asbjørnsen and Moe, *East o' the Sun,* p. 414.
> Little Lucy Goosey Girl. Christiansen, *Folktales of Norway,* p. 183.

**870B\*   THE TRUE BRIDE SEWS A WEDDING DRESS.** A prince sought the hand of Princess Signy, but he was deceived by a witch who took on a beautiful shape. He brought her a piece of beautiful brocade for her wedding dress, but the false bride did not know how to sew and had to enlist the help of Signy. The prince discovered the fraud, had the witch put to death, and married Signy.

> Asmund and Signy (Iceland). Lang, *Brown Fairy Book,* p. 275.

**870D\*   THE MAGIC MIRROR.** A prince required a girl of fifteen who was both beautiful and a virgin. He found her with the help of a magic mirror that could reveal the state of a woman's virtue. *(1001 Nights)*

> Juan, Pedro, and Diego. Pino-Saavedra, *Folktales of Chile,* no. 34.
> Mirror of Virgins, The. Mathers, *1001 Nights,* v. 3, p. 358.

**871   THE PRINCE'S PORTRAIT.** A merchant's daughter saw a portrait of the Prince of Persia and fell in love with him. Her father carried her messages of love to the prince, but he haughtily rejected them. So she herself set out for Persia and, with the help of magic gifts, won the prince's love.

> Haughty Prince. Calvino, *Italian Folktales,* no. 102.

**871A   THE WIFE WITH AN UNDERGROUND LOVER.** A man saw his wife arise from bed in the middle of the night. He followed her to a cave where she met a black lover. The deceived husband cut off the lover's head and turned his wife into a black dog, which he kept and punished daily with a whip. (Bushnaq) Cf. type 449.

> Queen Who Was a Witch, The. Noy, *Folktales of Israel,* no. 51.
> Tale within a Tale, A. Bushnaq, *Arab Folktales,* p. 94.
> Underground Marriage, The. Dawkins, *Modern Greek Folktales,* no. 41.
> Underground Marriage, The. Dawkins, *Modern Greek Folktales,* no. 41.

**873   THE KING DISCOVERS HIS UNKNOWN SON.** A prince fell in love with a woman from a portrait, and set forth to find her. He found her in a distant city and spent several days and nights with her before they had to part. Years later, after he had become king, he discovered the son that had been born of that union, and he married his erstwhile beloved.

> King Clarion of Talagante. Pino-Saavedra, *Folktales of Chile,* no. 35.

**873\*   LOVE ADVENTURE TOLD SYMBOLICALLY.** A countess visited a prince at night in his room, without revealing her identity. Later, after hearing her recite a symbol-filled poem, he recognized his lover and married her. (Calvino)

Count's Sister, The. Calvino, *Italian Folktales,* no. 167.
Rose in the Chest, The. Bushnaq, *Arab Folktales,* p. 355.

**875   THE CLEVER PEASANT GIRL.** A peasant's daughter helped her father win a dispute by solving riddles. Impressed with her cleverness, the king gave her additional tasks: to present herself neither naked nor clothed and neither walking nor riding. She succeeded at these tasks by placing herself in a net and letting a horse pull her to the palace. The king was so pleased with her cleverness that he married her, and he called upon her often for advice. (Jacobs) —Note: The tales listed below typically contain several episodes of types 875A-E or other similar events. Cf. types 921, 1533, 1663.

Basil Plant, The. Pino-Saavedra, *Folktales of Chile,* no. 36.
Catherine, Sly Country Lass. Calvino, *Italian Folktales,* no. 72.
Chick-Pea Seller's Daughter, The. Mathers, *1001 Nights,* v. 4, p. 210.
Clever Daughter, The. Fowke, *Folklore of Canada,* p. 280.
Clever Girl, The. Crane, *Italian Popular Tales,* no. 108.
Clever Girl, The. Crane, *Italian Popular Tales,* p. 311.
Clever Lass, The. Jacobs, *European Folk and Fairy Tales,* no. 23.
Clever Manka (Czechoslovakia). Clarkson and Cross, *World Folktales,* no. 13.
Clever Manka (Czechoslovakia). Cole, *Best-Loved Folktales,* no. 99.
Clever Minister's Daughter, The. Bushnaq, *Arab Folktales,* p. 354.
Clever Peasant Girl, The (Italy). Thompson, *100 Favorite Folktales,* no. 78.
Clever Peasant Girl, The. Dawkins, *Modern Greek Folktales,* no. 65.
Daughters of the Broom Thief, The. Walker and Uysal, *Tales in Turkey,* p. 135.
Farmer's Clever Daughter, The. Ranke, *Folktales of Germany,* no. 47.
Gobborn Seer, The. Briggs, *DBF,* pt. A, v. 1, p. 277.
Governor Tries to Cheat the Orphan, The. Lindell, *Folk Tales from Kammu,* II, no. 15.
Intended Divorce, The. Clouston, *Popular Tales,* v. 2, p. 327.
King's Son and the Poor Man's Daughter, The. Musick, *Green Hills of Magic,* no. 68.
Not Driving and Not Riding. Asbjørnsen and Moe, *Norwegian Folktales,* p. 137.
Peasant's Clever Daughter, The. Grimm, *Tales,* no. 94.
Pottle o' Brains, A. Briggs, *DBF,* pt. A, v. 2, p. 238.
Stone of Gold, The. Mathias and Raspa, *Italian Folktales in America,* no. 10.
What Is the Fastest Thing in the World? Megas, *Folktales of Greece,* no. 50.
What Melody Is the Sweetest. Noy, *Folktales of Israel,* no. 61.
Wise Little Girl, The. Afanasyev, *Russian Fairy Tales,* p. 252.
Women's Wiles. Bushnaq, *Arab Folktales,* p. 318.

**875A   REVEALING A THEFT WITH RIDDLES.** A king asked his servant to deliver a round cake and thirty biscuits to a peasant's daughter, who was reputed to be the cleverest girl in the world. The girl sent back the message that it was the fifteenth day of the month and half moon. Through this riddle, the king discovered that his servant had eaten half the cake and fifteen of the biscuits. (Jacobs)

Clever Girl, The. Crane, *Italian Popular Tales,* no. 108.
Clever Lass, The. Jacobs, *European Folk and Fairy Tales,* no. 23.
Daughters of the Broom Thief. Walker and Uysal, *Tales in Turkey,* p. 135.
Riddle, The. Dawkins, *Modern Greek Folktales,* no. 67.

**875B TASK AND COUNTERTASK.** The tsar set a task for a peasant's daughter, renowned for her cleverness. She was to weave a towel
from one silken thread. She responded by giving the tsar a twig and
telling him she would weave the towel on the loom that he had made
from the twig. Other tasks and countertasks followed, and in the end
the tsar, impressed with the girl's quick wit, married her. (Afanasyev)

Sultan's Camp Followers, The. Bushnaq, *Arab Folktales,* p. 339.
Wise Little Girl, The. Afanasyev, *Russian Fairy Tales,* p. 252.

**875D IS THE FISH MALE OR FEMALE?** A queen asked whether
the fish she had just been served was male or female, at which the fish
laughed aloud. Seeking an explanation, the king called in a boy known
for his wisdom. The boy required the queen's forty maids to undress.
They were all young men in disguise. The fish had laughed, explained
the clever boy, because the queen had asked a senseless question about
the fish's sex, while she had surrounded herself with men dressed as
women. The king had his wife and the forty men put to death. (Villa)

Clever Boy, The. Villa, *100 Armenian Tales,* no. 67.
Gobborn Seer. Jacobs, *More English Fairy Tales,* p. 60.
Male or Female? Mathers, *1001 Nights,* v. 2, p. 387.
Why the Fish Laughed. Jacobs, *Indian Fairy Tales,* p. 186.

**875E A JUDGMENT CONCERNING THE BIRTH OF A CALF.**
A man stole a calf, claiming that it was the offspring of his mare. The
judge, after hearing the claim, ordered that a sack of flour be loaded
on the back of a mouse. "That would crush the mouse," exclaimed the
defendant. "Your claim is just as absurd," said the judge, and awarded
the plaintiff not only the calf, but the horse as well.

Hashish-Eater in Judgment, The. Mathers, *1001 Nights,* v. 3, p. 548.

**877 THE OLD WOMAN WHO WAS SKINNED.** A king saw a
woman's delicate hand through a shutter, and asked her to marry him,
not knowing that she was eighty years old. When he saw her without
her veil, he threw her out the window. Passing fairies felt compassion,
and they turned her into a beautiful young woman. The king took her
back. When the queen's ninety-year old sister saw the transformation,
she too wanted youth and beauty, and asked repeatedly for the secret.
The now young queen told her sister that she had removed her old
skin. The old woman tried this, but it killed her. (Crane)

Jealous Sisters, The. Dawkins, *More Greek Folktales,* no. 17.

King Who Wanted a Beautiful Wife, The (Italy). Thompson, *100 Folktales*, no. 79.
King Who Wanted a Beautiful Wife, The. Crane, *Italian Popular Tales*, no. 25.
King Who Would Have a Beautiful Wife, The (Sicily). Lang, *Pink Fairy Book*, p. 162.
Old Woman Who Was Skinned, The. Basile, *Pentamerone*, Day 1, Tale 10.
One-Tooth and Two-Teeth. Bushnaq, *Arab Folktales*, p. 169.
Three Crones, The. Calvino, *Italian Folktales*, no. 29.

**879   THE SUGAR PUPPET.** A prince engaged in a war of wits with the woman he loved, but she always bettered him, once even making him kiss her donkey's tail. Fearing retribution, she placed a life-sized doll made of sweets in her bed.  He did indeed stab the doll, but immediately repented of his brash act. She emerged from her hiding place, and they had a happy life together from then on. (Calvino)

Basil Plant, The. Pino-Saavedra, *Folktales of Chile*, no. 36.
Clever Maria (Portugal). Lang, *Crimson Fairy Book*, p. 359.
Convent of Nuns and Monastery of Monks. Calvino, *Italian Folktales*, no. 195.
Fanfinette and the King's Son. Massignon, *Folktales of France*, no. 48.
Pot of Marjoram, The. Calvino, *Italian Folktales*, no. 21.
Sapia Liccarda. Basile, *Pentamerone*, Day 3, Tale 4.
Viola. Basile, *Pentamerone*, Day 2, Tale 3.

**881   A SLANDERED WIFE PROVES HER INNOCENCE.** Upon hearing his young wife falsely accused of infidelity, a prince ordered her killed, but she escaped. Disguised as a man, she returned to the court, exposed the man who had slandered her, and then revealed herself to her now repentant husband. (Calvino) Cf. type 712.

King of Spain and the English Milord. Calvino, *Italian Folktales*, no. 158.
Flight of Birds, The (resembles type 1431). Briggs, *DBF*, pt. A, v. 1, p. 238.

**882   THE WAGER ON THE WIFE'S FIDELITY.** To win a wager, a man hid himself in a chest and had himself smuggled into a merchant's wife's bedroom. From this hiding place he learned the location of a birthmark on the woman, and thus convinced the merchant that his wife had been unfaithful. The angered husband ordered his wife killed, but she escaped, dressed as a man. Keeping the male disguise, she eventually became a counselor to the sultan. With time she had her husband and his slanderous friend brought to court, and the entire story came to light. The friend was put to death, and the husband and wife were reunited. (Boccaccio) Cf. type 892.

Bernabò Orders His Wife Killed. Boccaccio, *Decameron*, Day 2, Tale 9.
Chest, The. Campbell, *West Highlands*, v. 2, p. 9.
Great Narbone, The. Calvino, *Italian Folktales*, no. 176.
Imogen and Posthumus. Shakespeare, *Cymbeline*.
Innkeeper of Moscow, The. Ranke, *Folktales of Germany*, no. 38.
'Piniated Englishman and Hellfire Jack, De. Briggs, *DBF*, pt. A, v. 2, p. 451.

Wager on the Wife's Chastity, The. Pino-Saavedra, *Folktales of Chile*, no. 37.
Wormwood. Calvino, *Italian Folktales*, no. 157.

**882A\*  ENTRAPPED SUITORS ARE FORCED TO WORK.**  A
wright's beautiful wife was plagued with offers from various
gentlemen, so she finally agreed to let them visit her.  However, she
trapped them in an underground chamber, and forced them to spin flax
for her as penance for their folly.  Cf. types 1359C, 1730.

Wright's Chaste Wife, The. Briggs, *DBF*, pt. A, v. 2, p. 503.

**883A  THE SLANDERED MAIDEN.**  A man and woman left their
daughter with a priest while they made a pilgrimage.  The priest
attempted to seduce the girl, but she refused him.  Angered, he wrote
to the father, accusing the girl of grievous acts.  The father hence
commanded that she be put to death, but she escaped into the forest,
where a prince found her and married her.  With time the entire story
came to light, and the priest was put to death. (Villa)

Girl Outwits Three Men, The. Bushnaq, *Arab Folktales*, p. 361.
Girl Who Was Left at Home, The (commentary). Dawkins, *Modern Greek
   Folktales*, no. 57.
Herb of Love, The. Dawkins, *More Greek Folktales*, no. 23.
Honor. Villa, *100 Armenian Tales*, no. 48.
Immoral Khoja and the Daughter of the Aga, The. Walker and Uysal, *Tales in
   Turkey*, p. 215.
Lady and the Hind, The. Pourrat, *French Tales*, p. 197.

**883B  PUNISHING THE SEDUCER.**  A prince seduced two sisters,
leaving each with a child.  The third sister, Fanfinette, disguised
herself as a doctor and convinced the prince that he himself had given
birth to the two babies.  With time he proposed marriage to Fanfinette.
—Continues as type 879. (Massignon)

Amorous Prince Outwitted. Thundy. *South Indian Folktales*, no. 55.
Fanfinette and the King's Son. Massignon, *Folktales of France*, no. 48.

**884  THE FORSAKEN FIANCEE.**  A prince and a princess were engaged to marry.  He returned to his own country to see his dying
father, who made him promise to marry another woman instead.  The
forsaken fiancée, dressed like a man, pursued her beloved, ultimately
causing him to recall his love for her.  He explained his situation to his
second fiancée with the parable of the lost key: A man lost a key and
had a replacement made.  Later, he found the original key, so he no
longer needed the replacement. (Grimm, no. 67)

Beausoleil. Thomas, *It's Good to Tell You*, no. 18.
Belluccia. Basile, *Pentamerone*, Day 3, Tale 6.
King of Portugal's Son. Calvino, *Italian Folktales*, no. 68.
Princess Plumpkins (Pachoulenia). Megas, *Folktales of Greece*, no. 51.

Swallow, The. Megas, *Folktales of Greece,* no. 71.
True Bride, The. Grimm, *Tales,* no. 186.
Twelve Huntsmen, The. Grimm, *Tales,* no. 67.

### 884A  A WOMAN DISGUISED AS A MAN IS WOOED. A

woman, separated from her husband, disguised herself as a man and
became the king's servant. The queen tried to seduce the servant, but
met only resistance. She then claimed "he" had tried to rape her, and
the servant was sentenced to die. At the gallows, the missing husband
suddenly appeared and exposed the accused's breasts, thus revealing
the queen's wickedness. (Dawkins) Cf. type 318.

Lord of the World Below, The. Dawkins, *Modern Greek Folktales,* no. 17.
Work of the Genii, The. Villa, *100 Armenian Tales,* no. 11.

### 884B  THE GIRL AS A SOLDIER. Theodora, to save her father from

military service, dressed herself as a man and joined the army. After
three years of service she married a companion, who had long
suspected that she was not a man. (Dawkins)

Fanta-Ghirò the Beautiful. Calvino, *Italian Folktales,* no. 69.
Girl Who Pretended to Be a Boy, The. Lang, *Violet Fairy Book,* p. 320.
Theodora in the Army. Dawkins, *Modern Greek Folktales,* no. 47A.

### 884B*  A GIRL DISGUISED AS A MAN DECEIVES THE KING.

Vasilisa rode a horse, shot a gun, and did other things quite like a man.
Dressed in men's clothes, she visited the king. He sensed that the youth
was a girl and tried to trick her into revealing her sex, but she
outwitted him at every turn. (Afanasyev)

First Sword and Last Broom. Calvino, *Italian Folktales,* no. 124.
Foppish King, The. Calvino, *Italian Folktales,* no. 188.
Sir Northwind. Dawkins, *Modern Greek Folktales,* no. 47B.
Vasilisa, the Priest's Daughter. Afanasyev, *Russian Fairy Tales,* p. 131.

### 885A  A LADY REVIVES AT HER LOVER'S VOICE. An English

lady was denied the right to marry her lover in Scotland, but her
parents did promise that should could be buried in Scotland, should she
die. She then took a powerful sleeping potion, and seemed to die.
However, at the churchyard in Scotland, her lover's voice brought her
back to life, and they were married.

Gay Goshawk, The. Briggs, *DBF,* pt. A, v. 1, p. 261.

### 887  GRISELDA. A nobleman married a woman from the lower class,

and then tested her patience and loyalty by taking her children from
her and pretending to marry another woman. She proves herself by
enduring his abuse without complaint, so in the end her children are
returned to her, and she is given the full status of nobility. (Boccaccio)

Clerk's Tale, The (Griselda). Chaucer, *Canterbury Tales*, p. 340.
Griselda. Boccaccio, *Decameron*, Day 10, Tale 10.
Nut-Brown Maid, The. Briggs, *DBF*, pt. A, v. 2, p. 450.

**888   A WIFE RESCUES HER HUSBAND FROM SLAVERY.** A count fell into slavery in Turkey. His shirt, which his wife had made for him, never soiled, a sign of her continued fidelity. She disguised herself as a pilgrim and, through her great skill as a harpist, accomplished his release. (Grimm)

Faithful Wife, The. Grimm, *Other Tales*, p. 128.
Lute Player, The (Russia). Lang, *Violet Fairy Book*, p. 70.
Tests of Chastity. Clouston, *Popular Tales*, v. 1, p. 168.

**888A   A CLEVER WIFE SAVES HER HUSBAND'S FORTUNE.** A man gambled away all of his belongings. Humiliated, he reported the bad news to his wife. She responded by confessing that the gamesters had been hired by her to teach him a lesson. In truth, he had lost nothing. (Briggs, "Hedges the Gamester")

Hedges the Gamester. Briggs, *DBF*, pt. B, v. 2, p. 223.
Right Nought. Briggs, *DBF*, pt. A, v. 2, p. 252.

**889   THE TRUTHFUL SERVANT.** A landowner's kinsman bet that he could make Kyriakos the trusted goatherd tell a lie. The kinsman sent his wife to Kyriakos, and she seduced him into killing a prize goat for her. When the landowner asked about the goat, Kyriakos was tempted to say that it had died or fallen into the sea, but in the end he could only tell the truth, and thus his master won the wager. (Bødker)

Isotta and the Cowherd. Straparola, *Facetious Nights*, Night 3, Tale 5.
Master Truthful (Greece). Bødker, *European Folk Tales*, p. 201.
Steward Truth. Calvino, *Italian Folktales*, no. 187.
Truthful Joseph. Crane, *Italian Popular Tales*, no. 48.

**890   A POUND OF FLESH.** A recently married merchant failed to return his godfather's ship within the agreed upon time. His penalty was to have a pound of flesh cut from his rump or to go to jail, so he went to jail. His bride disguised herself as a viceroy and confronted the godfather. She maintained that he could cut out a chunk of flesh, but if it weighed any more or any less than a pound, then he, the godfather, would have to pay. Not wishing to gamble, he gave up his claim and released the debtor to the viceroy, who then revealed herself as the youth's wife. (Pino-Saavedra)

Bassanio, Portia, and Shylock. Shakespeare, *The Merchant of Venice*.
One Gram More, One Gram Less. Sabar, *Kurdistani Jews*, p. 155.
White Onion. Pino-Saavedra, *Folktales of Chile*, no. 38.

**891   A WIFE, IN DISGUISE, SEDUCES HER OWN HUSBAND.**
A sultan married a saddlemaker's daughter, but then refused to
consummate the marriage. She, dressed as a man, followed him to his
camp and engaged him in chess, letting him win. As a prize, she
offered to let him sleep with her slave; then she presented herself, now
disguised as a harem girl, to the Sultan. This happened three times,
over a period of three years, and she conceived three children.
Finally, the Sultan learned the truth and accepted his wife and children.
(Bushnaq) Cf. type 1379.

> Catherine the Wise. Calvino, *Italian Folktales,* no. 151.
> Sapia. Basile, *Pentamerone,* Day 6, Tale 6.
> Gilette and Bertrand. Boccaccio, *Decameron,* Day 3, Tale 9.
> Helena and Bertram. Shakespeare, *All's Well That Ends Well.*
> Sultan's Camp Followers, The. Bushnaq, *Arab Folktales,* p. 339.
> Three Measures of Salt, The. Dawkins, *Modern Greek Folktales,* no. 45.

**891A   THE GIRL IN THE TOWER.** A king loved his daughter so
much that he kept her in a glass tower. One day she found a bone in
her food and threw it against a window, breaking it. Below she
observed a crier shouting praises to Sir Nerak. She decided she must
marry Sir Nerak, or die; but Sir Nerak refused her proposals. She
threatened to kill herself, unless her father set her adrift in a chest, so
he did as she requested. The tide carried her to Sir Nerak's palace, and
when he saw the beautiful princess, he asked her to marry him.
(Dawkins) Cf. types 310, 898.

> Face, The. Basile, *Pentamerone,* Day 3, Tale 3.
> Girl Shut Up in a Tower, The. Dawkins, *Modern Greek Folktales,* no. 30.

**891B\*   THE KING'S GLOVE.** A king desired his squire's beautiful
wife and entered the chamber where she was asleep. Removing his
glove, he reached to caress her, but then checked himself and left. The
squire found the king's glove on his wife's bed and said nothing, but
from that time forth, much to his wife's puzzlement and dismay, he
would not touch her. Finally the king discovered the grief he had
caused, and he told the couple what had happened. (Calvino)

> Firuz and His Wife. Mathers, *1001 Nights,* v. 4, p. 227.
> Left-Handed Squire, The. Calvino, *Italian Folktales,* no. 160.
> Lion Who Walked in the Garden, The. Noy, *Folktales of Israel,* no. 59.
> Vineyard I Was and Vineyard I Am. Crane, *Italian Popular Tales,* no. 42.

**892   THE SLANDERED FIANCEE.** A king was to marry a merchant's daughter, but his spiteful general claimed that she was a fallen
woman. To prove his charge, he paid an old woman to steal the girl's
ring and to discover the location of her secret birthmark, but with time
his wickedness became known. The slanderer was hanged, and the
king married his fiancée. (Afanasyev) Cf. type 882.

Bejeweled Boot, The. Calvino, *Italian Folktales*, no. 159.
Imogen and Posthumus. Shakespeare, *Cymbeline*.
Merchant's Daughter and Slanderer. Afanasyev, *Russian Fairy Tales*, p. 415.

**893  A TEST OF FRIENDSHIP.** To test their loyalty, a man carried a bloody sack containing a freshly slaughtered calf to first one friend and then another, claiming to have killed a man and asking for help in burying the body. Only one person offered aid. (Briggs) Cf. type 1381C.

Tests of Friendship. Bushnaq, *Arab Folktales*, p. 300.
True Friendship. Briggs, *DBF*, pt. A, v. 2, p. 497.

**894  THE GHOULISH SCHOOLMASTER.** A girl saw her schoolmaster tear raw meat from a horse with his teeth. The ghoul tormented her for many years, asking her repeatedly what she had seen. She endured in silence, and finally he left her in peace. (Bushnaq)

Deceived Girl and the Stone of Suffering. Noy, *Folktales of Israel*, no. 48.
Lost Shoe of Gold, A. Bushnaq, *Arab Folktales*, p. 132.
Nourie Hadig. Villa, *100 Armenian Tales*, no. 2.
Ogre Schoolmaster, The. Dawkins, *Modern Greek Folktales*, no. 33.
Prince in a Swoon, The. Dawkins, *Modern Greek Folktales*, no. 32.
Sleeping Prince, The. Megas, *Folktales of Greece*, no. 29.

**897  THE CRUEL SISTERS-IN-LAW.** A giantess lived with her seven giant brothers and their wives. Her sisters in law were jealous, so they put a snake in her food, and she swallowed it. Later it came out to drink at a brook, and a plowman killed it. Learning of their wives' wickedness, the brothers threw them over a cliff.

Seven Giant Brothers, The. Villa, *100 Armenian Tales*, no. 7.

**898  THE DAUGHTER OF THE SUN.** Astrologers predicted that a princess would conceive a baby from the sun. To prevent this, the king placed her in a tower, but when the girl was almost twenty, she climbed to one of the high windows, was touched by the sun, and became pregnant. After the baby was born she was abandoned in a bean patch by the princess's maid. She was discovered by a king, and when she grew up she married a prince. (Calvino) Cf. type 891A.

Daughter of the Sun, The. Calvino, *Italian Folktales*, no. 74.
Fairy Orlanda, The. Crane, *Italian Popular Tales*, no. 30.
First Story of the Parrot. Crane, *Italian Popular Tales*, no. 47.1
Silent Princess, The (Turkey). Lang, *Olive Fairy Book*, p. 318.
Silent Princess, The. Dawkins, *Modern Greek Folktales*, no. 48.
Terrible Head, The. Lang, *Blue Fairy Book*, p. 182.
White Doe, The (d'Aulnoy). Lang, *Orange Fairy Book*, p. 201.

**898\*** **THE DAUGHTER GIVEN TO THE SUN.** A childless woman asked the sun for a daughter, promising to give her back at the age of twelve. This happened, but the sun, seeing the girl's longing for her mother, helped her to return home.

> Maroula. Megas, *Folktales of Greece,* no. 38.

**899** **A WIFE SACRIFICES HERSELF FOR HER HUSBAND.** Death came to take a man, but agreed to give him more time, if he could find a friend who would lend him some years. All of his friends turned him down, but his wife, not wanting to live without him, offered half of her remaining years, and death left without a victim. (Musick)

> Angel of Death and the Rabbi's Son, The. Sabar, *Kurdistani Jews,* p. 136.
> Look in Your Own Backyard. Musick, *Green Hills of Magic,* no. 9.

**900** **KING THRUSHBEARD.** A haughty princess turned down every suitor arranged by her father. She especially ridiculed a man with a crooked chin, calling him King Thrushbeard. To punish her, her father gave her to a beggar. Now she had to work at the hardest tasks, and she rued her former pride. Finally the beggar revealed his true identity. He was King Thrushbeard in disguise. (Grimm) Cf. types 670, 901, 903A\*, 910A, 986.

> Baron's Haughty Daughter, The. Ranke, *Folktales of Germany,* no. 48.
> Cannetella (Italy). Lang, *Grey Fairy Book,* p. 332.
> Comte de Mes Comtes, The. Massignon, *Folktales of France,* no. 30.
> Crumb in the Beard, The (Italy). Thompson, *100 Favorite Folktales,* no. 80.
> Crumb in the Beard, The. Crane, *Italian Popular Tales,* no. 29.
> Haaken Grizzlebeard. Christiansen, *Folktales of Norway,* p. 186.
> Hacon Grizzlebeard. Asbjørnsen and Moe, *East o' the Sun,* p. 39.
> Ina the King. Briggs, *DBF,* pt. B, v. 2, p. 77.
> Jealous Sister, The. Arewa, *Northern East Africa,* p. 143.
> King Thrushbeard. Grimm, *Tales,* no. 52.
> Mincing Princess, The. Calvino, *Italian Folktales,* no. 175.
> Old Bushy Beard. Campbell, *Cloudwalking Country,* p. 244.
> Pride Punished. Basile, *Pentamerone,* Day 4, Tale 10.
> Swineherd, The (Andersen). Opie, *Classic Fairy Tales,* p. 303.
> Swineherd, The. Andersen, *Complete Fairy Tales,* no. 22.

**900A** **THE GIRL WITH A GOAT FACE.** With the help of a fairy, a peasant girl became the wife of a king, but she showed no gratitude, so the fairy cursed her with the face of a goat. Only after she humbled herself did she regain her human face. (Basile)

> Buffalo Head. Calvino, *Italian Folktales,* no. 67.
> Goat Face, The. Basile, *Pentamerone,* Day 1, Tale 8
> Goat-Faced Girl, The (Italy). Lang, *Grey Fairy Book,* p. 84.
> Invisible Grandfather. Calvino, *Italian Folktales,* no. 35.

**901   TAMING THE SHREW.** A man married a beautiful, but obstinate woman. After the ceremony, he warned his horse to take care in crossing a stream, but still it splashed water on the bride's dress. The man responded by shooting it to death. "I never say a thing twice," he explained. The bride took this lesson to heart and became the most obedient wife, and they lived happily together for many years. (Clarkson and Cross) Cf. types 670, 900, 903A*, 910A.

> Girl That Wouldn't Do a Hand's Turn, The. Campbell, *Cloudwalking Country,* p. 220.
> He Counted Up to Three. Randolph, *Sticks in the Knapsack,* p. 71.
> Most Obedient Wife, The (Denmark). Clarkson and Cross, *World Folktales,* no. 12.
> Reason to Beat Your Wife. El-Shamy, *Folktales of Egypt,* no. 56.
> Taming of the Shrew, The. Afanasyev, *Russian Fairy Tales,* p. 161.
> Taming of the Shrew, The (examples and commentary). Brunvand, *American Folklore,* p. 360.
> Petruchio and Katharina. Shakespeare, *The Taming of the Shrew.*
> You Haven't Packed the Saddle. Dorson, *Buying the Wind,* p. 351.

**902*   CURING THE LAZY WOMAN.** A man married a girl who was so lazy that she would throw dirty clothes into the fire instead of washing them. Angered, her husband wrapped her in a bundle of straw and took her back to her parents, where he left her. (Dégh)

> Lazybones (Hungary). Dorson, *Folktales around the World,* p. 114.
> Lazybones. Dégh, *Folktales of Hungary,* no. 12.

**903A*   TAMING A QUICK-TEMPERED WIFE.** A man walked home with his new bride, who had a reputation for her quick temper. A barking dog approached them, but the groom refused to hit the dog with his stick. "This is not intended for dogs," he explained. The bride soon learned what the stick was intended for, and in a short time she became a good and loving wife. Cf. types 670, 900, 901, 910A.903A*, 1376A*.

> Watchers at the Well, The. Briggs, *DBF,* pt. A, v. 1, p. 554.

**910A   ENIGMATIC ADVICE PROVES TO BE VALUABLE.** Solomon said to a man who had asked how to handle an obstinate wife: "Go to Goosebridge." At Goosebridge the man saw a man beating a mule that would not cross the bridge. Understanding Solomon's wisdom, the man took a stick to his wife, and from that time forth she was an obedient and loving woman. (Boccaccio) Cf. types 670, 900, 901, 903A*.910A, 1376A*.

> Go to Goosebridge. Boccaccio, *Decameron,* Day 9, Tale 9.
> Master Vavasour and Turpin His Man. Briggs, *DBF,* pt. A, v. 2, p. 180.

**910B ADVICE WELL TAKEN.** A man was away from home for twenty years. He met a man who advised him: "Keep cool; don't cut off a head." Upon arriving home he saw his wife in bed with two young men. Drawing his sword, he approached them to kill the presumed lovers, but suddenly remembered the advice and lay down his sword. His wife awoke and said: "Children, your father has come back!" Then he learned that during his absence his wife had borne him twins. (Afanasyev, "Good Advice")

> Cheater Cheated, The. Afanasyev, *Russian Fairy Tales*, p. 228.
> Do Neither Kindness nor Yet Unkindness. Dawkins, *More Greek Folktales*, no. 16.
> Five Counsels, The. Paredes, *Folktales of Mexico*, no. 43.
> Five Wise Words of the Guru, The (India). Lang, *Olive Fairy Book*, p. 167.
> Gobborn Seer, The. Briggs, *DBF*, pt. A, v. 1, p. 277.
> Good Advice. Afanasyev, *Russian Fairy Tales*, p. 289.
> He Wins Who Waits (Armenia). Lang, *Olive Fairy Book*, p. 289.
> Ivan. Briggs, *DBF*, pt. A, v. 2, p. 488.
> Ivan. Jacobs, *Celtic Fairy Tales*, p. 195.
> Ivan (Wales). Clarkson and Cross, *World Folktales*, no. 53.
> Long Wait, A. Musick, *Green Hills of Magic*, no. 64.
> Patient Suitor, The. Villa, *100 Armenian Tales*, no. 17.
> Pottle o' Brains, A. Briggs, *DBF*, pt. A, v. 2, p. 238.
> Rich Tom of Ireland. Roberts, *South from Hell*, no. 32A.
> Solomon's Advice. Calvino, *Italian Folktales*, no. 192.
> Tale within a Tale, A. Bushnaq, *Arab Folktales*, p. 94.
> Three Admonitions, The. Crane, *Italian Popular Tales*, no. 41.
> Three Counsels, The. Espinosa, *Folklore of Spain in the American Southwest*, p. 185.
> Three Good Advices, The. Briggs, *DBF*, pt. A, v. 2, p. 491.
> Three Questions, The. Tolstoy, *Fables and Fairy Tales*, p. 82.
> Three Words of Advice, The (Greece). Thompson, *100 Favorite Folktales*, no. 81.
> Three Words of Advice, The. Dawkins, *Modern Greek Folktales*, no. 75A.
> Tinner of Chyannor, The. Briggs, *DBF*, pt. A, v. 2, p. 495.
> Wisely Spent. Villa, *100 Armenian Tales*, no. 6.
> Yalla Britches. Briggs, *DBF*, pt. A, v. 2, p. 504.
> Years Are as Days. Noy, *Folktales of Israel*, no. 46.

**910C CONSIDER THE CONSEQUENCES.** A king's enemy bribed his barber to cut his throat. About to commit the murder, he saw a maxim on the shaving mug: "Do nothing without considering the consequences." Shaken, he confessed everything to his intended victim. (Clouston)

> Do Not Do Anything without Considering Its End. Walker and Uysal, *Tales in Turkey*, p. 179.
> How a King's Life Was Saved by a Maxim. Clouston, *Popular Tales*, v. 2, p. 317, 491.

**910D A MAN HANGS HIMSELF AND FINDS A TREASURE.** A wealthy man told his spendthrift son that he should hang himself from a certain pillar if he ever became destitute. The son lost everything, and followed his father's advice. When he tried to hang himself, the pillar crumbled, revealing the treasure that his father had hidden inside. (Noy)

Heir of Linne, The. Briggs, *DBF,* pt. A, v. 2, p. 406.
Heir of Linne, The. Clouston, *Popular Tales,* v. 2, p. 53.
Spendthrift Son, The. Musick, *Green Hills of Magic,* no. 62.
Spendthrift Son, The. Noy, *Folktales of Israel,* no. 14.
Timon Discovers a Treasure. Shakespeare, *Timon of Athens.*
Two Brothers, The. Basile, *Pentamerone,* Day 4, Tale 2.

**910E   TREASURE IN THE VINEYARD.** A dying farmer told his sons to dig in the vineyard for a treasure. They dug everywhere but found nothing. However, from the good cultivation, the vines yielded a bumper crop.

Treasure Trove. Handford, *Aesop,* no. 172.

**910F   THE STRENGTH OF A BUNDLE OF STICKS.** A man whose sons were always quarreling asked them to break a tied bundle of sticks, but they could not. He then untied the bundle and asked them to break the sticks one at a time, which they did with ease. From this they learned the strength of unity. (Aesop)

Bundle of Sticks, The. Jacobs, *Aesop,* no. 72.
Quarreling Sons and the Bundle of Sticks, The. Arewa, *Northern East Africa,* p. 242.
Unity Is Strength. Handford, *Aesop,* no. 173.
Vinegrower, the Priest, the Frankish Priest, and the Chotzas, The. Megas, *Folktales of Greece,* no. 52.

**910G   BUYING ADVICE.** A man bought advice from a dervish. Although at first he did not understand the sayings, with time they brought him wealth and happiness. (Villa)

Advice That Cost a Thousand Ryo, The. Seki, *Folktales of Japan,* no. 46.
Lac of Rupees for Bit of Advice. Jacobs, *Indian Fairy Tales,* p. 103.
Pottle o' Brains, A. Briggs, *DBF,* pt. A, v. 2, p. 238.
Pottle o' Brains. Jacobs, *More English Fairy Tales,* p. 134.
Wisely Spent. Villa, *100 Armenian Tales,* no. 6.

**911\*   A FATHER'S ADVICE.** A dying father gave his son three pieces of advice: "Tell no secret to your wife. Do not make a friend of a soldier. Never rear up a castaway bastard." Time proved the wisdom of the old man's words. (Dawkins)

Father's Advice, A. Bushnaq, *Arab Folktales,* p. 289.
Three Words of Advice, The. Dawkins, *Modern Greek Folktales,* no. 75B.
We Two against Fortune. Bushnaq, *Arab Folktales,* p. 295.

**915B  THE CLEAN SISTER AND THE DIRTY SISTER** (new classification). A mother favored one of her two daughters, and never made her work. The other had to do all the household chores. The two girls married, and the favored one, not knowing how to work, kept house so poorly that her husband soon abandoned her. The daughter who had learned to work as a child organized her household well, and had a good marriage.

Souillon. Massignon, *Folktales of France*, no. 32.

**920B  WHAT KIND OF BIRD?** To determine which of three princes should become king, each was asked what kind of bird he would prefer to be. The first answered: "A hawk, because it resembles a knight." The second said: "An eagle, because all other birds fear it." The third replied: "A starling, because it gains its living without injury to anyone." The third prince was chosen to succeed his father as king.

Sons of the Conqueror, The. Briggs, *DBF*, pt. B, v. 2, p. 129.

**920C  SHOOTING AT THE FATHER'S CORPSE.** To settle an inheritance dispute between three brothers, Friar Bacon had the dead father removed from his grave, then said that the brother who could strike the body closest to the heart would receive the estate. The youngest brother refused to shoot, and Friar Bacon awarded him the estate, for he had thus proven his love to his father.

Friar Bacon (V). Briggs, *DBF*, pt. B, v. 2, p. 657.

**921  THE PEASANT'S CLEVER SON.** A landlord came to collect the rent, and the farmer's son engaged him in conversation, speaking in riddles. The landlord was so impressed with the boy's wit that he gave him free rent until Christmas. (Briggs, "The Clever Boy") Cf. type 875.

Clever Boy, The. Briggs, *DBF*, pt. A, v. 2, p. 391.
Discreet Answers. Briggs, *DBF*, pt. A, v. 2, p. 58.
Farmer Gag's Clever Son. Briggs, *DBF*, pt. A, v. 2, p. 79.
Jack and the Vicar. Briggs, *DBF*, pt. A, v. 2, p. 135.
Jack Hornby. Briggs, *DBF*, pt. A, v. 2, p. 133.
King and Old George Buchanan, The. Dorson, *Buying the Wind*, p. 181.
King and the Hermit, The. Briggs, *DBF*, pt. A, v. 2, p. 418.
King and the Northern Man, The. Briggs, *DBF*, pt. A, v. 2, p. 433.
King and the Tanner, The. Briggs, *DBF*, pt. A, v. 2, p. 437.
King Mátyás and His Scholars. Dégh, *Folktales of Hungary*, no. 17.
Kutsa Seduces Indra's Wife. O'Flaherty, *Tales of Sex and Violence*, p. 75.
Lord Craven. Briggs, *DBF*, pt. A, v. 2, p. 157.
Pedro de Urdemalas and the Priest. Paredes, *Folktales of Mexico*, no. 55.
Right Answer to the Right Question, The. Noy, *Folktales of Israel*, no. 37.
Under the Earth I Go. Briggs, *DBF*, pt. A, v. 2, p. 501.

**921A  THE FOUR PAYMENTS.** The tsar asked a peasant how he spent his money. The man answered: "One fourth goes to taxes, one fourth pays a debt, one fourth I lend, and one fourth I throw away." Then the peasant explained his riddle: "I pay a debt by supporting my aged father, I make a loan by feeding my son, and I throw money away by feeding my daughter." (Afanasyev)

> King and the Basket Weaver, The. Megas, *Folktales of Greece*, no. 54.
> Peter the First and the Peasant. Tolstoy, *Fables & Fairy Tales*, p. 22.
> Peter the Great and the Stone Mason (Russia). Dorson, *Folktales around the World*, p. 127.
> Riddles. Afanasyev, *Russian Fairy Tales*, p. 29.

**921B\*  BEGGAR, THIEF, AND MURDERER.** A friar predicted the future for three children. One would become a beggar, the second a thief, and the third a murderer. Then he advised the children's mother: "Let the one destined to become a beggar be a friar; the one that is to become a thief, an attorney; and the murderer, make him a physician."

> Friar Who Told Three Children's Fortunes. Briggs, *DBF*, pt. A, v. 2, p. 93.

**921C\*  ASTRONOMER, WATCHMAKER, AND DOCTOR.** A simple miller's ordinary wisdom exceeded that of the learned people who were his guests.

> Otto's Astronomer, Watchmaker, and Doctor. Megas, *Folktales of Greece*, no. 55.

**921D\*  WITTY RESPONSES.** —Miscellaneous tales.

> Abu Nuwas and the Hundred Eggs. Bushnaq, *Arab Folktales*, p. 276.
> Blind Man and the Virgin, The. Storer, *Facetiae of Poggio*, no. 97.
> Dhuha in His Old Age. Bushnaq, *Arab Folktales*, p. 259.
> Djuha and the Donkey. Bushnaq, *Arab Folktales*, p. 254.
> Djuha and the Hunter's Gift. Bushnaq, *Arab Folktales*, p. 257.
> Djuha and the Tough Chicken. Bushnaq, *Arab Folktales*, p. 256.
> Djuha Fries Quails. Bushnaq, *Arab Folktales*, p. 256.
> Englishman, An. Storer, *Facetiae of Poggio*, no. 19.
> Learned Man and the Boatman, The. Pourrat, *French Tales*, p. 57.
> Lorenzo de' Medici. Storer, *Facetiae of Poggio*, no. 22.
> Messer Nicholas. Storer, *Facetiae of Poggio*, no. 14.
> Old Wine. Storer, *Facetiae of Poggio*, no. 1.
> Saint or Horse (Yiddish). Cole, *Best-Loved Folktales*, no. 105.
> Tosetto of Padua. Storer, *Facetiae of Poggio*, no. 39.
> Truth, The. Bushnaq, *Arab Folktales*, p. 288.

**921E\*  THE POTTER AND THE TSAR.** Impressed with a potter's wisdom, the tsar decreed that everyone use only earthenware at receptions, and the potter became wealthy.

> Potter, The. Afanasyev, *Russian Fairy Tales*, p. 208.

**921F  A  WIFE  SOLVES  RIDDLES  BY  DECEPTION** (new classification).

> Liver of the Wise and Liver of the Foolish. El-Shamy, *Folktales of Egypt,* no. 10.

**921F\*  PLUCKING THE GEESE.** A soldier impressed the tsar with his ability to solve riddles. As a reward, the tsar promised to send him thirty geese to pluck. The geese were noblemen, and using the same riddles he had learned from the tsar, the soldier made himself wealthy.

> Clever Answers. Afanasyev, *Russian Fairy Tales,* p. 578.

**922  THE KING, THE ABBOT, AND THE SHEPHERD.** A jealous king threatened to take an abbot's life if he could not answer three questions. A shepherd offered to take the abbot's place at the trial. Dressed in a monk's robe, he heard the first two questions and gave witty answers. The king's final question was: "What am I thinking?" The shepherd replied: "You think I am the abbot, but in truth I am a shepherd." The king was so pleased with the clever answers that he pardoned the abbot and gave the shepherd a pension. (Jacobs)

> Cook, The. Crane, *Italian Popular Tales,* no. 91.
> Dispute in Sign Language, A (Israel). Dorson, *Folktales around the World,* p. 169.
> Dispute in Sign Language, A. Noy, *Folktales of Israel,* no. 38.
> Farmer's Answers, The. Glassie, *Irish Folktales,* no. 23.
> Independent Bishop, The. Briggs, *DBF,* pt. A, v. 2, p. 408.
> King and the Bishop, The (Denmark). Thompson, *100 Favorite Folktales,* no. 82.
> King John and the Abbot of Canterbury. Briggs, *DBF,* pt. A, v. 2, p. 423.
> King John and the Abbot of Canterbury. Jacobs, *More English Fairy Tales,* p. 159.
> King John and the Abbot. Child, *English and Scottish Ballads,* no. 45.
> King Matt and the Wise Old Farmer. Musick, *Green Hills of Magic,* no. 69.
> Kunz and His Shepherd (Jewish). Clarkson and Cross, *World Folktales,* no. 11.
> Little Shepherd Boy, The. Grimm, *Tales,* no. 152.
> Miller, The. Briggs, *DBF,* pt. A, v. 2, p. 485.
> Parson and Sexton. Asbjørnsen and Moe, *Norwegian Folktales,* p. 15.
> Riddle Test, The. Fowke, *Folklore of Canada,* p. 164.
> Thoughtless Abbot, The (Italy). Cole, *Best-Loved Folktales,* no. 33.
> Thoughtless Abbot, The. Crane, *Italian Popular Tales,* no. 92.
> Three Questions, The. Campbell, *West Highlands,* v. 2, p. 406.
> Three Questions, The. Glassie, *Irish Folktales,* no. 22.
> Three Questions, The. Paredes, *Folktales of Mexico,* no. 44.
> Three Questions. Briggs, *DBF,* pt. A, v. 2, p. 495.
> Three Riddles, The. *Folklore of Spain in the American Southwest,* p. 179.
> Two Little Scotch Boys. Briggs and Tongue, *Folktales of England,* no. 63.
> Two Little Scotch Boys. Briggs, *DBF,* pt. A, v. 2, p. 336.
> What Melody is the Sweetest. Noy, *Folktales of Israel,* no. 61.
> Wise Man's Questions, The. Randolph, *The Talking Turtle,* p. 25.

Without Worry (Netherlands). Bødker, *European Folk Tales*, p. 103.

**922A  A MINISTER PROVES HIS INNOCENCE.**  A clever shepherd became minister to the king, only to be unjustly accused of theft. The investigators found something hidden in his room: not the jewels he was accused of stealing, but his shepherd's clothing. He explained that he had kept them as a reminder of his former happy, carefree days. Hearing this, the king declared him innocent. (Villa)

> Servant When He Reigns, A. Now, *Folktales of Israel*, no. 60.
> Under Suspicion. Villa, *100 Armenian Tales*, no. 90.

**922B  THE KING'S FACE ON THE COIN.**  A king commanded a basket weaver to not reveal a certain secret unless he should see the king's face; in the king's absence the man revealed the secret. When asked by the king why he had disobeyed, the man said: "But sir, I could see your face on the coin in my hand." Impressed with the basket weaver's wit, the king made him Grand Vizier. (Megas)

> Clever Peasant, The. Crane, *Italian Popular Tales*, no. 107.
> King and the Basket Weaver, The. Megas, *Folktales of Greece*, no. 54.
> King Mátyás and His Scholars. Dégh, *Folktales of Hungary*, no. 17.

**923  LOVE LIKE SALT.**  A princess told her father that she loved him like salt. Insulted, he ordered her killed, but she escaped and married a neighboring prince. Her father was invited to the wedding banquet, not knowing his daughter was the bride. His food was served without salt, which showed him what she had meant. She revealed herself to him, and everyone celebrated. (Calvino). Cf. type 510.

> Cap o' Rushes. Briggs, *DBF*, pt. A, v. 2, p. 387.
> Dear as Salt. Calvino, *Italian Folktales*, no. 54.
> Goose-Girl at the Well, The. Grimm, *Tales*, no. 179.
> King Lear and Cordelia. Shakespeare, *King Lear*.
> Old Woman's Hide, The. Calvino, *Italian Folktales*, no. 70.
> Princess Mouse-Skin. Grimm, *Other Tales*, p. 44.
> Princess Who Loved Her Father Like Salt. Dawkins, *Modern Greek Folktales*, no. 77.
> Salt and Bread (Sweden). Cole, *Best-Loved Folktales*, no. 85.
> Sugar and Salt. Briggs, *DBF*, pt. A, v. 2, p. 487.
> Three Killed Florrie, Florrie Killed Ten. Abrahams, *Afro-American Folktales*, no. 86.
> Water and Salt. Crane, *Italian Popular Tales*, no. 23.
> Who is Blessed with the Realm, Riches, and Honor? Noy, *Folktales of Israel*, no. 57.

**923B  A WOMAN MAKES HER OWN FORTUNE.**  A king overheard his daughter say: "It is the woman who is important and not her husband." This so angered him that he married her to a man who had nothing. However, through her determination and with good luck she and her husband soon were able to build a palace across from that of the king. (Villa) —Continues as type 412.

Fairy Child, The. Villa, *100 Armenian Tales*, no. 3.
Lazy Ahmet and the Padishah's Daughter. Walker and Uysal, *Tales in Turkey*, p. 172.
Who is Blessed with the Realm, Riches, and Honor? Noy, *Folktales of Israel*, no. 57.
Wisely Spent. Villa, *100 Armenian Tales*, no. 6.

**924  FIGHTING WITH SYMBOLS.** A stranger came to a padishah's court, drew a circle, and sat in it. A weaver, known for his wisdom, also drew a circle and sat down. The stranger responded by scattering grain upon the ground, whereupon the weaver released a rooster that ate the grain, setting two walnuts in the circle as well. Then the stranger departed, and did not return. The weaver explained: The stranger in his circle was claiming dominion. The grain represented his soldiers. The weaver's rooster symbolized his nation's resistance, and the two walnuts showed that he was willing to wager his testicles on the outcome.

Wise Old Weaver, The. Walker and Uysal, *Tales in Turkey*, p. 183.

**924A  DEBATING WITH SYMBOLS.** A priest and a rabbi debated, using sign language. The priest pointed a finger at the rabbi, who answered by pointing two fingers. Then the priest scattered grain on the floor, whereupon the rabbi released a hen that ate up the seeds. Later the rabbi explained: The priest had threatened, by pointing, to put out one of the rabbi's eyes. The answer was a threat to put out both of the priest's eyes. The priest's grain symbolized the Jews, scattered throughout the world. The rabbi's hen represented the Messiah that would gather them together.

Dispute in Sign Language, A (Israel). Dorson, *Folktales around the World*, p. 169.
Dispute in Sign Language, A. Noy, *Folktales of Israel*, no. 38.

**924B  SIGN LANGUAGE MISUNDERSTOOD.** A scholar lifted his forefinger to say "there is but one God" in sign language. The village idiot thought he was threatening to poke out his eye and responded with two outstretched fingers, signifying: "I can poke out both of your eyes!" But the scholar understood the two fingers to mean "Allah has no equal!" and he congratulated the simpleton for his great understanding of symbols. (Bushnaq)

Professor of Signs, The (I, II). Briggs, *DBF*, pt. A, v. 2, p. 455.
Stuck to Some Great Door. Walker and Uysal, *Tales in Turkey*, p. 119.
Wise Man and Bahlul, The. Bushnaq, *Arab Folktales*, p. 277.

**926  TWO WOMEN CLAIM ONE CHILD.**  Two women, each claiming motherhood of a child, came before Solomon. He stated that the child should be cut in two parts, with each woman receiving half. Upon hearing this judgment, one woman relinquished her claim, in order to save the child. The judge then gave her the whole child, stating that she had proven her true maternal love. (Bible)

> Recalling Solomon. Storer, *Facetiae of Poggio*, no. 144.
> Solomon and the Two Women. Bible: 1 Kings 3: 16-28.
> Solomon and the Two Women. Rhys-Davids, *Jataka*, p. xiv.

**926C  WISE JUDGES.**  A rich merchant lost a purse containing two thousand rubles, half of which he offered to whoever returned it. A poor man brought him the purse, but to avoid paying the reward, the merchant claimed there had been a precious stone in the purse as well, and accused the finder of having stolen it. The case came before a judge, who gave the purse with all its contents to the poor man, explaining: "If the merchant's purse contained a precious stone, then this must not be it." (Tolstoy, "The Merchant and the Purse.")

> Clever Judge, A (China). Cole, *Best-Loved Folktales*, no. 130.
> Famous Judge, A. Fisher, *Idaho Lore*, p. 51.
> It Could Always Be Worse (Yiddish). Cole, *Best-Loved Folktales*, no. 103.
> Just Judge, A. Tolstoy, *Fables and Fairy Tales*, p. 59.
> Justice. Bushnaq, *Arab Folktales*, p. 293.
> King Who Changed His Ways, The. Bushnaq, *Arab Folktales*, p. 297.
> Lost Purse, The. Clouston, *Popular Tales*, v. 2, p. 367.
> Merchant and the Purse, The. Tolstoy, *Fables and Fairy Tales*, p. 50.
> One Gram More, One Gram Less. Sabar, *Kurdistani Jews*, p. 155.
> Precocious Children. Clouston, *Popular Tales*, v. 2, p. 12.

**927  OUT-RIDDLING THE JUDGE.**  A man sentenced to death stated a riddle that the judge could not solve, and thus gained his freedom. (Briggs, "The Life-Saving Riddle")

> Life-Saving Riddle, The (I-III). Briggs, *DBF*, pt. A, v. 2, p. 440.
> Out-Riddling the Judge. Glimm, *Flatlanders and Ridgerunners*, p. 15.
> Under the Earth I Go. Briggs, *DBF*, pt. A, v. 2, p. 501.

**929  CLEVER DEFENSES.**  —Miscellaneous tales.

> Madonna Filippa Is Discovered by Her Husband with a Lover. Boccaccio, *Decameron*, Day 6, Tale 7.
> Man Who Put Up Such a Good Defense, The. Pourrat, *French Tales*, p. 9.
> Merchant and the Folk of Falsetown, The. Clouston, *Popular Tales*, v. 2, p. 99.
> Si'Djeha and the Qadi's Coat. Bushnaq, *Arab Folktales*, p. 266.

**930  A POOR BOY TO MARRY A RICH GIRL.**  After hearing a prophecy that a poor farmer's infant son would someday become his heir, a wealthy merchant bought the boy and abandoned him in the forest. A hunter found the baby and raised him. Years later the merchant, while buying furs from the hunter, met the boy and heard the story of how he had been found. Alarmed, he sent the boy to his house carrying a sealed letter. The letter instructed his wife to have the boy hanged. En route, while the boy was resting, two rogues opened the letter, thinking there was money inside. After reading the message, they replaced it with a note commanding the merchant's daughter to marry the messenger. Thus the prophecy was fulfilled. —Continues as type 461. (Booss) Cf. types 517, 671, 707, 725.

Abraham Our Father and the Dogs. Noy, *Folktales of Israel*, no. 25.
Antti and the Wizard's Prophecy (Finland). Booss, *Scandinavian Tales*, p. 547.
Bride Who Had Never Been Kissed, The. Briggs, *DBF*, pt. A, v. 2, p. 380.
Chance and the Poor Man. Megas, *Folktales of Greece*, no. 46.
Child Whose Shirt Stuck to His Skin, The. Sabar, *Kurdistani Jews*, p. 172.
Devil with the Three Golden Hairs, The. Grimm, *Tales*, no. 29.
Dragon and the Enchanted Filly, The. Calvino, *Italian Folktales*, no. 75.
Emperor's Lesson, The. Villa, *100 Armenian Tales*, no. 47.
Fairest of All Others. Briggs, *DBF*, pt. A, v. 1, p. 225.
Fish and the Ring, The. Briggs, *DBF*, pt. A, v. 1, p. 236.
Fish and the Ring, The. Jacobs, *English Fairy Tales*, p. 190.
Ismailian Merchant, The. Calvino, *Italian Folktales*, no. 152.
King Who Would Be Stronger than Fate (India). Lang, *Brown Fairy Book*, p. 300.
Man Born to Be King, The. Dawkins, *Modern Greek Folktales*, no. 50.
Mandorlinfiore. Calvino, *Italian Folktales*, no. 112.
Miller's Son, The. Clouston, *Popular Tales*, v. 2, p. 458.
Rich Peter the Pedlar. Asbjørnsen and Moe, *East o' the Sun*, p. 199.
Stepney Lady, The. Briggs, *DBF*, pt. A, v. 1, p. 497.
Tanzara and Dyeer. Villa, *100 Armenian Tales*, no. 27.
What God Wrote Cannot Be Unwritten. Bushnaq, *Arab Folktales*, p. 147.
What Is Inscribed on the Brow the Eye Will See. Bushnaq, *Arab Folktales*, p. 172.
With God's Will All Is Possible. Noy, *Folktales of Israel*, no. 49.

**930A A POOR GIRL TO MARRY A RICH BOY.** —Note: This tale is similar to type 930, except that the genders are reversed.

Soused in the Cistern. Dawkins, *Modern Greek Folktales*, no. 51.

**931 OEDIPUS.** It was prophesied that Rosa would have a son by her father and then later marry this son. To prevent this, she had her father killed. An apple tree grew from his grave; Rosa ate one of its apples, and thus conceived. Further attempting to thwart the prophecy, Rosa slashed the newborn baby about the chest and set it adrift at sea. A sailor rescued the infant and raised it. Years later the youth married Rosa. When she saw the scars on his chest and heard the story of his rescue from the sea she knew that the prophecy had been fulfilled. She then jumped to her death from the roof of a house. (Dawkins)

Crivoliu. Crane, *Italian Popular Tales,* p. 201.
Rich Man and His Three Daughters, The. Dawkins, *Modern Greek Folktales,* no. 62.

**934  PROPHECY OF DEATH.** A Gypsy prophesied that a boy would drown. To prevent this, the mother built a house high on a hill, but a spring emerged from the ground, drowning both mother and child. (Briggs, "Osmotherly")

Death of King Ella, The. Briggs, *DBF,* pt. B, v. 2, p. 30.
Foretelling the Future. Villa, *100 Armenian Tales,* no. 44.
Lailoken's Triple Death. Rowling, *Folklore of the Lake District,* p. 52.
Maiden Castle. Rowling, *Folklore of the Lake District,* p. 31.
Mother's Dream, The, or, Benjie Spedlands. Briggs, *DBF,* pt. B, v. 2, p. 555.
No Escape from Fate. Noy, *Folktales of Israel,* no. 13.
Osmotherly. Briggs, *DBF,* pt. B, v. 2, p. 294.

**934E\*  A DAUGHTER IS CURSED AT BIRTH.** It was prophesied that an infant girl would burn her father's castle, have a baby before marrying, and kill a man. Each prediction came true, but the girl's good stepmother helped her to escape from any evil consequences.

Hild the Good Stepmother (Iceland). Bødker, *European Folk Tales,* p. 56.

**935  A PRODIGAL SON'S RETURN.** Jan, a blacksmith's son, left home. Good fortune came his way, and he married a princess. En route to visit his parents and brother he lost his horse and fine clothes in a card game. Arriving in rags, he took his old place at the forge. Later the princess arrived. Without knowing she was their son's wife, the family gave her shelter. To their surprise, she chose to sleep next to Jan, and thus they learned that he had married a princess. (Bødker)

How a Smith Made His Fortune (Germany). Bødker, *European Folk Tales,* p. 87.
Man and His Three Sons. Roberts, *South from Hell,* no. 33.

**938  FIRST MISFORTUNE, THEN GOOD LUCK.** A shepherd had a dream in which a man told him that both misfortune and good luck would befall him, and then asked him which he would prefer first. The shepherd asked for the bad luck first. Shortly thereafter his wife was abducted, one son was carried away by a wolf, and another was lost in a river. Later the shepherd found himself in a place where a new ruler was to be chosen by freeing a bird and seeing where he lit. The bird chose the shepherd. With time he was reunited with his wife and his two sons, whose lives had been miraculously spared. (Villa)
—Note: Aarne and Thompson add two subtypes: 938A, where a girl choses good fortune in old age rather than in youth, and 938B where a

newly married couple makes this choice. I have combined these very similar subtypes under number 938.

Catherine and Her Destiny (Sicily). Lang, *Pink Fairy Book*, p. 167.
Catherine and Her Fate. Crane, *Italian Popular Tales*, no. 28.
Ill-Fated Princess, The. Megas, *Folktales of Greece*, no. 47.
Shepherd's Dream, The. Villa, *100 Armenian Tales*, no. 50.
Slave Mother, The. Calvino, *Italian Folktales*, no. 131.
Sultan Hasan. El-Shamy, *Folktales of Egypt*, no. 15.
Troubles in Youth Rather Than in Old Age. Walker and Uysal, *Tales in Turkey*, p. 84.

## 939A  A RETURNING SON IS KILLED BY HIS PARENTS.  A couple granted lodging to a stranger, but during the night they murdered him for the money he was carrying. The next day they discovered that the stranger was their own son, who had been abroad for many years. (Briggs, "The Penryn Tragedy")

Jack White's Gibbet. Briggs and Tongue, *Folktales of England*, no. 46.
Lay Ghost-Layer, A. Briggs, *DBF*, pt. B, v. 1, p. 516.
Penryn Tragedy, The. Briggs, *DBF*, pt. B, v. 2, p. 304.
Son Murdered by His Parents, The. Briggs and Tongue, *Folktales of England*, no. 26.

## 945  INTELLIGENCE OR LUCK?  Intelligence, seeking to settle an argument with Luck, entered a simple plowboy, who immediately left his field to seek a better life. He soon became a contender for the princess's hand, but in so doing he offended the king and was sentenced to die. Then Luck made her entry, causing the executioner to break his sword, and the king to issue a last-minute pardon. Thus Luck proved her superiority over Intelligence. (Thompson)

Carpenter, the Tailor, and the Rabbi, The. Sabar, *Kurdistani Jews*, p. 185.
Four Men and One Miracle. Bushnaq, *Arab Folktales*, p. 306.
Girl Out of Whose Mouth Came a Snake, The (Turkey). Bødker, *European Folk Tales*, p. 205.
Intelligence and Luck (Czechoslovakia). Cole, *Best-Loved Folktales*, no. 100.
Intelligence and Luck (Czechoslovakia). Thompson, *100 Favorite Folktales*, no. 83.
Luck and Good Sense. Dawkins, *More Greek Folktales*, no. 19.
Many Dilemmas of the Padishah's Three Sons, The. Walker and Uysal, *Tales in Turkey*, p. 123.
Royal Candlestick, The. El-Shamy, *Folktales of Egypt*,Silent Princess, The. Dawkins, *Modern Greek Folktales*, no. 48.

## 946A*  BALDAK BORISIEVICH.  A seven-year-old Russian hero traveled to Turkey where he caused the sultan to suffer many indignities before hanging him with a silken noose.

Baldak Borisievich. Afanasyev, *Russian Fairy Tales*, p. 90.

**947  PURSUED BY BAD LUCK.**  A poor woodcutter was attacked by wolves.  He ran across a bridge to escape, but it collapsed under his weight.  Some fishermen rescued him and placed him against a wall to warm him in the sun.  Just as he came to his senses, the wall collapsed and killed him.  (Grimm)

> Ill Luck.  Grimm, *Other Tales,* p. 122.
> I've Seen (It) with My Own Eyes; Nobody Told Me!  El-Shamy, *Folktales of Egypt,* no. 13.

**947A  PREDESTINED BAD LUCK.**  A poor weaver learned that a certain waterspout represented his predestined fortune.  To make it yield more water, he drove an awl into its head, but succeeded only in stopping the flow completely.  He sat at his loom chanting: "I saw it and I stopped it."  The princess, thinking he had spied her doing something in secret, stuffed a goose with thirty dinars and gave it to him, but he sold the goose for two dinars.  Ultimately, this story came to the king's attention, and he rewarded the weaver with a sack of gold, but as he left the palace, he stumbled and fell, hitting his head on a stone and killing himself.  (Bushnaq)

> God Disposes.  Bushnaq, *Arab Folktales,* p. 286.
> Sackmaker, The.  Megas, *Folktales of Greece,* no. 48.
> Tailor with His Luck Locked Up, The.  Noy, *Folktales of Israel,* no. 67.
> Unfortunate Shoemaker, The.  Sabar, *Kurdistani Jews,* p. 148.
> When the Wheel of Fortune Turns.  Noy, *Folktales of Israel,* no. 10.

**947B\*  THE GODDESS OF FATE ALLOTS GOOD AND BAD LUCK.**  A traveler found shelter at a woman's house.  During the night he saw her climb into a pot of boiling water, hang herself, cut her throat, count money into a bag, put on a silken dress, and sit and read.  The next morning she explained.  She was the Queen of the Planets, and each activity from the previous night would determine the fate of children born at that particular time.

> Queen of the Planets, The.  O'Sullivan, *Folktales of Ireland,* no. 37.

**949\*  A RICH MAN LEARNS TO BEG.**  A rich merchant fell in love with a beggar's beautiful daughter, but before the girl's father would consent to the marriage, the merchant had to put on rags and beg for one day.  At the day's end, the father explained: "Now I know that even if your business should fail, you could support my daughter."

> Test, The.  Villa, *100 Armenian Tales,* no. 53.

**950  THE THIEF'S CORPSE.**  Two brothers found a way into the king's treasury and stole a bag of gold.  Discovering his loss, the king set a trap by covering the treasury floor with pitch.  The thieves returned, and one became helplessly trapped.  To protect his brother, the trapped man asked him to cut off his head so his body could not be identified. The unfettered thief complied. Later the king displayed the headless corpse in public, hoping to capture the other thief by noting who mourned the dead man, but the brother eluded this trap. (Noy)

> Ali Baba and the Forty Thieves. Mathers, *1001 Nights*, v. 4, p. 100.
> Brother's Love, A. Noy, *Folktales of Israel*, no. 33.
> Hagop's Wish. Villa, *100 Armenian Tales*, no. 21.
> Mason and His Son, The. Crane, *Italian Popular Tales*, no. 44.
> Prince Ferdinand. Ranke, *Folktales of Germany*, no. 49.
> Quico and Caco. Pino-Saavedra, *Folktales of Chile*, no. 39.
> Robbers, The. Villa, *100 Armenian Tales*, no. 73.
> Robbery of the King's Treasury. Clouston, *Popular Tales*, v. 2, p. 115, 480.
> Thief in the King's Treasury, The. Dawkins, *Modern Greek Folktales*, no. 56.
> Treasure Chamber of Rhampsinitus, The. (Herodotus) Thompson, *100 Folktales*, no. 84.

**951  A DISGUISED KING JOINS A BAND OF THIEVES.** A king disguised himself to see how poor people lived and made friends with three fellows who were plotting to rob the royal treasury. The three were captured, but when they recognized the king as a former friend, he pardoned them. (Noy) —Note: I have combined Aarne-Thompson subtypes 951A-C into one number.

> When I Lift the Left Moustache. Noy, *Folktales of Israel*, no. 32.
> King Mátyás and the Hussars. Dégh, *Folktales of Hungary*, no. 15.

**952  THE KING AND THE SOLDIER.** A new recruit entered the regiment where his older brother was general. The general, unwilling to recognize his own kin, ordered his brother whipped, so the latter deserted and fled into the forest. There he met a stranger who had become lost while hunting, and the two joined company. During the night they were attacked by robbers, and the soldier killed them all. Then the stranger revealed that he was the king; he made the deserter a general and demoted the older brother to private. (Afanasyev)

> Boot of Buffalo Leather, The. Grimm, *Tales*, no. 199.
> Hussar Stroke, A. Dégh, *Folktales of Hungary*, no. 14.
> Soldier and the King, The. Afanasyev, *Russian Fairy Tales*, p. 563.
> Why the Executioner Is Called Assessor (Sweden). Booss, *Scandinavian Tales*, p. 229.

**953  THREE FRIGHTFUL TALES.** A beautiful woman offered to marry the man who related the most frightful adventure. The first told of his capture by a giant, and how he had escaped by offering to fix his captor's guitar (cf. type 471A*). The second told how his ship had lost its provisions, forcing the crew to cannibalize one another in order that a few might live. The third told of trading places with a corpse he had found under his bed at an inn. Later the murderous innkeeper stabbed the corpse, enabling the intended victim to escape (cf. type 956A). It is not known which story won.

Three Tales by Three Sons . Calvino, *Italian Folktales,* no. 163.

**954  KILLING THE THIEVES HIDDEN IN CASKS.**  To gain revenge against Ali Baba (cf. type 676), the robber chief hid his men in casks and, claiming to be an oil merchant, gained lodging in his enemy's house. But a watchful servant discovered the plot and poured boiling oil into the casks, killing the villains before they could mount their attack. *(1001 Nights)*

Ali Baba and the Forty Thieves. Mathers, *1001 Nights,* v. 4, p. 100.
Jewel Stone, The. Pino-Saavedra, *Folktales of Chile,* no. 27.
Wise Maiden and the Seven Robbers, The. Afanasyev, *Russian Fairy Tales,* p. 134.

**955  THE ROBBER BRIDEGROOM.**  A woman went unannounced to her fiancé's home, where she saw him murder and dismember another young woman. Taking a severed finger as evidence, she reported what she had seen, and the villain was brought to justice. (Grimm) Cf. types 311, 312.

Bobby Rag. Briggs, *DBF,* pt. A, v. 2, p. 375.
Cellar of Blood, The. Briggs, *DBF,* pt. A, v. 2, p. 390.
Doctor Forster. Briggs, *DBF,* pt. A, v. 1, p. 214.
Girl Who Got Up a Tree, The. Briggs, *DBF,* pt. A, v. 2, p. 405.
Jack and His Master. Roberts, *South from Hell,* no. 34.
Lass 'At Seed Her Awn Graave Dug, The. Briggs, *DBF,* pt. B, v. 2, p. 87.
Lonton Lass, The. Briggs, *DBF,* pt. B, v. 2, p. 256.
Marriage of a Queen and a Bandit, The. Calvino, *Italian Folktales,* no. 169.
Mary, the Maid of the Inn. Briggs, *DBF,* pt. B, v. 2, p. 263.
Mister Fox's Courtship. Briggs and Tongue, *Folktales of England,* no. 43.
Mister Fox's Courtship. Briggs, *DBF,* pt. A, v. 2, p. 448.
Mister Fox. Briggs, *DBF,* pt. A, v. 2, p. 446.
Mister Fox. Jacobs, *English Fairy Tales,* p. 148.
Mister Fox. Randolph, *The Devil's Pretty Daughter,* p. 95.
Old Foster. Dorson, *Buying the Wind,* p. 192.
Oxford Student, The. Briggs, *DBF,* pt. B, v. 2, p. 103.
Riddle Me, Riddle Me Right. Fowke, *Folklore of Canada,* p. 141.
Robber Bridegroom, The. Grimm, *Tales,* no. 40.
Sir Richard Baker. Briggs, *DBF,* pt. B, v. 2, p. 353.

**956A  AT THE MURDERER'S HOUSE.**  A gentleman and his servant took lodging at an inn. While stabling the horses, the servant discovered bags filled with human legs. Thus forewarned, the two travelers waited in their room with loaded pistols, and they shot the murderers as they entered. (Briggs, "The Black and His Master")

Black and His Master, The. Briggs, *DBF,* pt. A, v. 2, p. 375.
Burker Tale, A (I-III). Briggs, *DBF,* pt. B, v. 2, p. 14.
Murder Hole, The. Briggs, *DBF,* pt. B, v. 2, p. 274.

Thomas of Reading. Briggs, *DBF,* pt. B, v. 2, p. 370.

**956B   A GIRL KILLS A BAND OF ROBBERS.**  Six brothers planned to rob a mill. They climbed through a small window, but as each one entered, the miller's daughter cut off his head with her father's sword. However, she only wounded the last man, and he escaped. To gain revenge, he disguised himself and returned as a suitor. He lured the girl to his house, where he tried to kill her, but she escaped. In the end, he was captured and killed. (Sampson) Cf. Christiansen, *Migratory Legends,* type 8025.

> Brave Maid-Servant, The. Briggs, *DBF,* pt. B, v. 2, p. 171.
> Girl and the Thief, The. Massignon, *Folktales of France,* no. 57.
> Girl That Wouldn't Do a Hand's Turn, The. Campbell, *Cloudwalking Country,* p. 220.
> Hand, The. Briggs, *DBF,* pt. A, v. 1, p. 307.
> Legend of the Sword, The. Briggs, *DBF,* pt. B, v. 2, p. 89.
> Maid of the Mill, The. Sampson, *Gypsy Folk Tales,* p. 102.
> One-Handed Murderer. Calvino, *Italian Folktales,* no. 89.
> Robber and the Housekeeper, The. Briggs, *DBF,* pt. A, v. 2, p. 457.
> Robber Captain, The. Dawkins, *More Greek Folktales,* no. 22.
> Robber Who Was Hurt (examples and commentary). Brunvand, *The Choking Doberman,* p. 37.
> Robbers, The. Afanasyev, *Russian Fairy Tales,* p. 419.

**958C\*   THE ROBBER DISGUISED AS A CORPSE.**  A woman disguised herself as a corpse. Her traveling companion claimed to be taking her to her burial; then they robbed the people who gave them lodging. They tried this with Candy Ashcraft, but she saw the supposed corpse move, and waited up with a hatchet. When the woman sat up in her coffin, gun in hand, Candy struck her dead, and then killed the accomplice as he came through the door.

> What Candy Ashcraft Done. Randolph, *The Devil's Pretty Daughter,* p. 6.

**958D\*   THE ROBBER DISGUISED AS A WOMAN.**  A robber entered a house disguised as a beggar woman. The cook noticed the boots and spurs beneath his dress and killed him with the kitchen poker. (Briggs, "The Cook at Combwell")

> Cook at Combwell, The. Briggs, *DBF,* pt. B, v. 2, p. 183.
> Long Pack, The. Briggs, *DBF,* pt. B, v. 2, p. 254.

**958E\*   THE HAND OF GLORY.**  A maid at an inn pretended to be asleep and watched a traveler afix a candle to a dead man's hand, while saying: "Let those who are asleep be asleep." When he went outside to summon his robber accomplices, the maid locked the door. She could not awaken anyone in the house until she broke the hand's spell by throwing skimmed milk over it. (Briggs, "The Hand of Glory" [I])

Hand of Glory, The (I-III). Briggs, *DBF*, pt. B, v. 2, p. 534.
Hand of Glory, The. Rowling, *Folklore of the Lake District*, p. 26.
Mummified Arm, The. Raven, *Folklore of Staffordshire*, p. 18.

**960  THE SUN BRINGS ALL TO LIGHT.** A tailor beat and robbed a
Jew, who said as he died: "The sun will bring it to light." Years later
the tailor sat looking at the sun's reflections and said: "It wants to bring
it to light, but it cannot." His wife overheard him and asked what he
meant. He told her the secret, and she, in turn, confided in her best
friend. Soon the whole town knew. The tailor was brought to trial and
condemned. (Grimm) Cf. type 1381C.

Blind Eye of Gibbie Laa. Marwick, *Folklore of Orkney and Shetland*, p. 181.
Bright Sun Will Bring It to Light, The. Grimm, *Tales*, no. 115.
Burgess the Miner. Briggs, *DBF*, pt. B, v. 2, p. 497.
There Is Righteousness. Villa, *100 Armenian Tales*, no. 52.

**960A  BIRDS WITNESS A CRIME.** Two men killed a shepherd. Not
long afterward crows began to fly about their heads, bringing them
into suspicion. With time the truth was discovered, and the murderers
were hanged. (Briggs, "The Shepherd and the Crows") Cf. type 781.

Shepherd and the Crows, The. Briggs, *DBF*, pt. B, v. 2, p. 577.
Shepherd of Black Mountain and the Crows. Simpson, *Folklore of the Welsh
    Border*, p. 53.
Thomas Elks and the Raven. Simpson, *Folklore of the Welsh Border*, p. 52.

**964  A THIEF BETRAYS HIMSELF.** A curate, in order to determine
who had stolen a goose, asked everyone in church to sit. Then he said:
"The person who stole the goose is not yet seated." "Yes I am," replied
the thief, and thus revealed his guilt. (Briggs)

Thief Detected, The. Briggs, *DBF*, pt. A, v. 2, p. 292.
Thief's Hat, The. Carpenter, *A Latvian Storyteller*, p. 210.

**967  SAVED BY A SPIDER WEB.** A holy man, pursued by enemies,
took refuge in a cave. A spider spun a web across the opening, leading
the pursuers to think that no one had entered, and they went away.

Old Woman and the Spider, The. Briggs, *DBF*, pt. B, v. 2, p. 558.

**968  ROBBERS AND MURDERERS.** —Miscellaneous Tales.

Farmer and the Footpads, The. Briggs, *DBF*, pt. B, v. 2, p. 200.
Pride Goeth before a Fall. Jacobs, *Indian Fairy Tales*, p. 132.

**973  THROWING A MAN OVERBOARD TO STOP A STORM.**

Brown Robyn's Confession. Briggs, *DBF*, pt. A, v. 1, p. 173.
Jonah and the Whale. Bible: Jonah, 1-2.

## 974 A RETURNING MAN'S WIFE IS ABOUT TO REMARRY.

Drake and His Lady. Briggs, *DBF*, pt. B, v. 2, p. 39.
Drake's Cannon-Ball. Briggs, *DBF*, pt. B, v. 2, p. 39.
Hind Horn. Briggs, *DBF*, pt. A, v. 2, p. 407.
Mab's Cross. Briggs, *DBF*, pt. B, v. 2, p. 257.
Old Roe and His Dog. Simpson, *Folklore of the Welsh Border*, p. 45.
Sir Francis Drake Returns. Whitlock, *Folklore of Devon*, p. 73.
Sir Francis Drake's Postponed Wedding. Palmer, *Folklore of Somerset*, p. 70.
Sir Thomas Bonham Returns to His Wife. Whitlock, *Folklore of Wiltshire*, p. 100.
Two Irish Lads in Canada. Briggs, *DBF*, pt. A, v. 2, p. 499.

## 976 WHICH WAS THE NOBLEST ACT? A man agreed to let his bride keep a previously arranged rendezvous with her former lover. En route, the woman was captured by a robber, but after hearing her story, he conducted her to the lover, who, in turn, took her safely back to her husband. (Chaucer)

Franklin's Tale, The. Chaucer, *Canterbury Tales*, p. 427.
Guessing Children, The. Walker and Uysal, *Tales in Turkey*, p. 114.

## 980 CHILDREN NEGLECT THEIR OLD PARENTS.

Mercer's Son of Midhurst, The. Briggs, *DBF*, pt. B, v. 2, p. 266.
Ungrateful Son, The. Clouston, *Popular Tales*, v. 2, p. 372.

## 980A HALF A BLANKET. A man wanted to send his old father away with half a blanket, but his wife thought they should give the him it all. Then their child, who had never spoken before, said: "Give him half a blanket and leave the other half with me, for I'll need it when it's my turn to send you away." The couple quickly decided to allow the old father to stay.

Half a Blanket. Glassie, *Irish Folktales*, no. 24.

## 980B THE WOODEN BOWL. An old man spilled his soup and let food dribble from his mouth, so his son made him sit behind the stove and eat from a wooden bowl. One day the man saw his own son, a boy of four, carving a piece of wood. "This is a bowl for you to eat from when you are old," he explained. He immediately restored the old grandfather to his former place at the table.

Old Grandfather and His Grandson, The. Grimm, *Tales*, no. 78.

## 980C DRAGGING THE OLD FATHER ONLY TO THE GATE. A man in the prime of life abused his aging father; he would strike him and even drag him out of the house by his hair. When he too became old his son treated him the same way. One day the son dragged him out

the door and onto the street. "You go too far!" cried the old man. "I never dragged my old father beyond the gate."

> Turn About Is Fair Play. Pourrat, *Treasury of French Tales,* p. 163.

**980D A TOAD IN THE FACE OF AN UNGRATEFUL SON.** A man, about to eat a roasted chicken, saw his aged father coming, and hid the bird so he would not have to share it. After the old man left, the son resumed eating, but the chicken became a toad and jumped into his face, and it stayed there for the rest of his life.

> Ungrateful Son, The. Grimm, *Tales,* no. 145.

**981 SAVED BY AN OLD MAN'S WISDOM.** Long ago people too old to work were thrown into a canyon, but instead of doing this, one family hid their old grandfather. At this time, the ruler commanded the villagers to make a rope from ashes, but no one could do this until the old man suggested burning an ordinary rope and leaving the ashes intact. When the ruler learned about the old man's wisdom, he decreed that henceforth old people should not be abandoned. (Seki)

> Mountain Where Old People Were Abandoned, The (Japan). Dorson, *Folktales around the World,* p. 243.
> Mountain Where Old People Were Abandoned, The. Seki, *Folktales of Japan,* no. 53.
> Old Man's Wisdom Saves the Kingdom, An. Arewa, *Northern East Africa,* p. 180.

**982 THE OLD FATHER'S TREASURE.** An old man, thinking himself near death, divided his property among his sons. But he did not die, and his sons treated their now impoverished father cruelly. To correct this, he obtained four bags full of gravel, and pretended they contained money he had received in payment of an old debt. Hoping for an added inheritance, the sons immediately became attentive to his every need. (Jacobs)

> How the Wicked Sons Were Duped. Jacobs, *Indian Fairy Tales,* p. 221.
> Ungrateful Sons, The. Briggs, *DBF,* pt. A, v. 2, p. 502.

**986 A LAZY MAN FINDS A TREASURE.** To punish his proud daughter, a king married her to a lazy pauper. She, in turn, threatened to beat her husband if he did not go to the mountains for wood, and there he found a buried treasure. —Continues as type 412. (Villa) Cf. type 900.

> Fairy Child, The. Villa, *100 Armenian Tales,* no. 3.
> Lazy Ahmet and the Padishah's Daughter. Walker and Uysal, *Tales in Turkey,* p. 172.

**990 A DEAD WOMAN REVIVED BY A GRAVE ROBBER.** A woman died and was placed in a tomb. The sexton opened the vault to steal her jewels. Unable to remove a ring, he began to cut off her finger, but this brought her back to life. In terror, the sexton ran over a cliff. The woman returned to her home, and she lived many more years. (Briggs and Tongue)

> Buried Alive. Dorson, *Buying the Wind,* p. 310.
> Buried Alive. Dorson, *Negro Tales,* p. 219.
> Dangerous Post, The. Pourrat, *Treasury of French Tales,* p. 14.
> Florence Wyndham Comes Back to Life. Palmer, *Folklore of Somerset,* p. 90.
> Lady Mount Edgcumbe and the Sexton. Whitlock, *Folklore of Devon,* p. 98.
> Lady Restored to Life (I-VII). Briggs, *DBF,* pt. B, v. 2, p. 83.
> Thievish Sexton, The. Briggs and Tongue, *Folktales of England,* no. 42.

**992 AN ADULTERESS EATS HER LOVER'S HEART.** Discovering that his wife had a lover, Guillaume murdered him and had his heart served to her. Upon learning the truth of her meal, she jumped from a window and killed herself. (Boccaccio)

> Eaten Heart, The (commentary and examples). Legman, *Rationale of the Dirty Joke,* v. 1, p. 650.
> Guillaume Causes His Wife to Eat the Heart of Her Lover. Boccaccio, *Decameron,* Day 4, Tale 9.
> Lover's Heart, The. Clouston, *Popular Tales,* v. 2, p. 187.
> Tancredi Kills His Daughter's Lover. Boccaccio, *Decameron,* Day 4, Tale 1.

**992A A WOMAN DRINKS FROM HER LOVER'S SKULL.** A prince killed his stepmother's black lover. She found the corpse and made a cup from the skull, a chair from the leg bones, and a mirror frame from the arm bones. She then gave the prince the riddle: "I drink Moor; I sit Moor; I see Moor." He solved it in the presence of a judge, who then condemned the queen to death. (Calvino)

> Moor's Bones, The. Calvino, *Italian Folktales,* no. 121.
> Riddle, The. Dawkins, *Modern Greek Folktales,* no. 67.

# Anecdotes

**1000  THE BARGAIN NOT TO BECOME ANGRY.** Jack went to work for a neighboring farmer. "I cannot stand angry talk," said the farmer. "If either of us loses his temper, the other can cut a strip of skin out of his back, from neck to waist." The master then tried to make Jack angry by giving him only a crust of bread for a whole day's food, so Jack sold one of his master's sheep for food. Later the master told Jack to clean the horses, so he killed them and cleaned out their insides. The master barely managed to hold his temper. The next day he asked his wife to spy on Jack from behind a bush, but Jack saw her and shot her in the leg. Finally the master went into a rage, and thus lost the bet. (Jacobs) —Note: Types 1000-1029 depict contracts in which clever workers better their masters in ways suggested above. The various episodes are found in numerous combinations.

Anger Bargain, The (Denmark). Thompson, *100 Folktales*, no. 85.
Big Jack and Little Jack. Chase, *Jack Tales*, no. 7.
Black Dog, The. Pino-Saavedra, *Folktales of Chile*, no. 40.
Boy Who Heard the Dew When It Fell, The. Bushnaq, *Arab Folktales*, p. 367.
Farmer and Hired Help (Afghanistan). Cole, *Best-Loved Folktales*, no. 111.
Hunchback, The. Saucier, *French Louisiana*, no. 21.
In the Hillman's Service (Denmark). Bødker, *European Folk Tales*, p. 78.
It Just Suits Me. Randolph, *The Talking Turtle*, p. 20.
Keep Cool. Jacobs, *European Folk and Fairy Tales*, no. 15.
Keloghlan and the Köse, The. Walker and Uysal, *Tales in Turkey*, p. 71.
Lose Your Temper, and You Lose Your Bet. Calvino, *Italian Folktales*, no.
Mac-a-Rusgaich. Campbell, *West Highlands*, v. 2, p. 318.
March and April. Massignon, *Folktales of France*, no. 13.
Ogre Outwitted, The (commentary). Dawkins, *Modern Greek Folktales*, no. 5.
Peter the Rogue. Espinosa, *Folklore of Spain in the American Southwest*, p.
Pope, His Wife, His Daughter, and His Man. Afanasyev, *Russian Secret*
Quick-Witted. Villa, *100 Armenian Tales*, no. 71.

**1002  GIVING AWAY THE MASTER'S PROPERTY.**

In the Hillman's Service (Denmark). Bødker, *European Folk Tales*, p. 78.

**1003  COMING HOME WHEN THE DOG DOES.** The master sent Esben to plow, telling him to come home when the dog did. At midday Esben gave the dog a whack. The poor beast ran home howling, and Esben followed. (Thompson)

Anger Bargain, The (Denmark). Thompson, *100 Folktales,* no. 85.
Black Dog, The. Pino-Saavedra, *Folktales of Chile,* no. 40.
In the Hillman's Service (Denmark). Bødker, *European Folk Tales,* p. 78.
Keloghlan and the Köse, The. Walker and Uysal, *Tales in Turkey,* p. 71.
Quick-Witted. Villa, *100 Armenian Tales,* no. 71.

**1004  HOGS IN THE MUD; SHEEP IN THE AIR.** Esben stole his master's pigs, then cut off their tails, which he poked into a mudhole. "The pigs have fallen into the mud," he reported, "and only their tails are left above ground." The master tried to pull the pigs out, but he only got the tails. (Thompson)

Anger Bargain, The (Denmark). Thompson, *100 Folktales,* no. 85.
Aunt Tempy's Story. Harris, *Nights with Uncle Remus,* no. 41.
Boy Receives Payment for an Ox Tail. Arewa, *Northern East Africa,* p. 171.
Brother Rabbit Gets the Provisions. Harris, *Nights with Uncle Remus,* no. 39.
Giufà's Exploits. Crane, *Italian Popular Tales,* no. 103.
Hare and the Hyena, The. Arewa, *Northern East Africa,* p. 33.
How Mister Rabbit Saved His Meat. Harris, *Uncle Remus,* no. 20.
Hunchback, The. Saucier, *French Louisiana,* no. 21.
In the Hillman's Service (Denmark). Bødker, *European Folk Tales,* p. 78.
Lose Your Temper, and You Lose Your Bet. Calvino, *Italian Folktales,* no.
Pedro Animales Fools His Boss. Pino-Saavedra, *Folktales of Chile,* no. 41.
Pedro de Urdemalas (Chile). Clarkson and Cross, *World Folktales,* no. 49.
Rogue and the Herdsman, The (Iceland). Lang, *Crimson Fairy Book,* p. 253.

**1005  BUILDING A BRIDGE WITH SLAIN CATTLE.** Esben built a bridge by killing four of his master's cows and placing them in the brook. (Thompson)

Anger Bargain, The (Denmark). Thompson, *100 Folktales,* no. 85.
In the Hillman's Service (Denmark). Bødker, *European Folk Tales,* p. 78.
Mac-a-Rusgaich. Campbell, *West Highlands,* v. 2, p. 318.

**1006  CASTING EYES.** The master allowed Esben to attend a party, but asked him to cast an eye in his direction from time to time. So Esben killed four of the master's sheep and put their eyes in his picket. As the party progressed, he cast these eyes at his master. (Thompson) Cf. type 1685.

Anger Bargain, The (Denmark). Thompson, *100 Folktales,* no. 85.
Casting Sheep's Eyes. Roberts, *South from Hell,* no. 64.
Fool, The. Crane, *Italian Popular Tales,* no. 104.
In the Hillman's Service (Denmark). Bødker, *European Folk Tales,* p. 78.
Mac-a-Rusgaich. Campbell, *West Highlands,* v. 2, p. 318.
Pat and the Five Pigeons. Briggs, *DBF,* pt. A, v. 1, p. 191.

**1006\*  KILL THE SHEEP THAT IS LOOKING AT YOU.** Ivanko's master asked him to slaughter a sheep. "Which one?" asked Ivanko. "The one that looks at you," was the answer. So Ivanko killed the entire flock, because they all looked at him.

Ivanko the Bear's Son. Afanasyev, *Russian Fairy Tales*, p. 221.

**1007  KILLING THE MASTER'S LIVESTOCK.** —Miscellaneous.

Abu Nuwas Travels with the Caliph. Bushnaq, *Arab Folktales*, p. 275.
Big Jack and Little Jack. Chase, *Jack Tales*, no. 7.
Keloghlan and the Köse, The. Walker and Uysal, *Tales in Turkey*, p. 71.
Simpleton Brother, The. Dawkins, *Modern Greek Folktales*, no. 64.

**1008  LIGHTING THE WAY BY SETTING THE BARN AFIRE.**

Anger Bargain, The (Denmark). Thompson, *100 Folktales*, no. 85.
In the Hillman's Service (Denmark). Bødker, *European Folk Tales*, p. 78.

**1009  GUARDING THE DOOR BY CARRYING IT AWAY.** A gentlewoman told her servant to pull the door after him and follow her. Accordingly, he pulled the door from its hinges and carried it with him. (Briggs, "The French Manservant") Cf. type 1653A.

French Manservant, The. Briggs, *DBF*, pt. A, v. 2, p. 92.
Ivanko the Bear's Son. Afanasyev, *Russian Fairy Tales*, p. 221.
Keloghlan and the Köse, The. Walker and Uysal, *Tales in Turkey*, p. 71.
Mister Vinegar. Briggs, *DBF*, pt. A, v. 2, p. 548.
Mister Vinegar. Jacobs, *English Fairy Tales*, p. 28.
Pulling the Door. Briggs, *DBF*, pt. A, v. 2, p. 243.
Stupid Peikko (Finland). Booss, *Scandinavian Tales*, p. 581.

**1010  FIXING THINGS UP.** The master told Esben to fix up the manure pile, so he hauled all the furniture outside and placed it there. (Thompson)

Anger Bargain, The (Denmark). Thompson, *100 Folktales*, no. 85.
In the Hillman's Service (Denmark). Bødker, *European Folk Tales*, p. 78.

**1011  CUTTING DOWN THE ORCHARD.** Jack made the job of picking apples easier for himself by first cutting down the trees. (Chase)

Big Jack and Little Jack. Chase, *Jack Tales*, no. 7.
Black Dog, The. Pino-Saavedra, *Folktales of Chile*, no. 40.
Keloghlan and the Köse, The. Walker and Uysal, *Tales in Turkey*, p. 71.

**1012  CLEANING THE MASTER'S CHILD.** Told to clean the master's child, Esben stripped him naked, scrubbed him a brook, and hung him up to dry. By the time the mistress got to him, the child had frozen to death. (Bødker) Cf. type 1681B.

In the Hillman's Service (Denmark). Bødker, *European Folk Tales*, p. 78.
Keloghlan and the Köse, The. Walker and Uysal, *Tales in Turkey*, p. 71.

## 1013  BATHING THE GRANDMOTHER IN BOILING WATER.
Cf. type 1681B.

Fool's Luck. Villa, *100 Armenian Tales*, no. 62.
Simpleton Brother, The. Dawkins, *Modern Greek Folktales*, no. 64.

## 1029  THE BARGAIN ENDS WHEN THE CUCKOO SINGS.
Pírolo and a priest agreed to not get angry before the cuckoo sang.
After suffering many indignities, the priest dressed his maid in
feathers and sent her to the roof to sing like a cuckoo, hoping thus to
end the wager. Pírolo shot the strange bird, whereupon the priest
lost his temper, and hence the bet.

Lose Your Temper, and You Lose Your Bet. Calvino, *Italian Folktales*, no.

## 1030  MAN AND OGRE SHARE THE HARVEST. The devil agreed
to help a peasant, in return for half the harvest. The devil was to take
everything that grew above ground and the peasant everything that
grew below the earth. The peasant planted turnips, and the devil
received only worthless leaves. The following year the devil asked to
reverse the arrangement. This time the peasant planted wheat, and
the devil harvested only worthless roots. (Grimm)  Cf. type 9B.
—Note: Types 1030-1114 depict partnerships or contests through
which a clever hero outwits or intimidates an ogre (often the devil).
The episodes are found in various combinations.

Bobtail and the Devil. Roberts, *South from Hell*, no. 39.
Bogie's Field, The. Briggs, *DBF*, pt. B, v. 1, p. 26.
Cut Legs and the Devil. Dorson, *Jonathan Draws the Long Bow*, p. 55.
Davies and his Friend in Partnership. Briggs, *DBF*, pt. B, v. 1, p. 65.
Davies and the Man in Black. Briggs, *DBF*, pt. B, v. 1, p. 65.
Devil and the Farmer, The. Carpenter, *A Latvian Storyteller*, p. 177.
Devil and the Good Lord, The. Massignon, *Folktales of France*, no. 33.
Devil and the Peasant, The. Pourrat, *Treasury of French Tales*, p. 118.
Farmer and the Boggart, The. Briggs, *DBF*, pt. B, v. 1, p. 28.
God and the Devil Share the Harvest (Latvia). Cole, *Best-Loved Folktales*, no.
How Bobtail Beat the Devil. Chase, *Grandfather Tales*, no. 9.
Jack and the Devil. Simpson, *Folklore of the Welsh Border*, p. 58.
Little Bull with the Golden Horns, The. Thomas, *It's Good to Tell You*, no. 6.
Living King of Hell Dies of Anger, The. Eberhard, *Folktales of China*, no. 70.
Partnership between Wolf and Mouse. El-Shamy, *Folktales of Egypt*, no. 49.
Peasant and the Devil, The. Grimm, *Tales*, no. 189.
Peasant, the Bear, and the Fox, The. Afanasyev, *Russian Fairy Tales*, p. 288.
Sheer Crops (USA, Black). Clarkson and Cross, *World Folktales*, no. 44.
Swindler, The. Handford, *Aesop*, no. 167.
Tops and the Butts, The. Briggs, *DBF*, pt. B, v. 1, p. 145.

**1036  THE HOGS WITH CURLY TAILS.** Bobtail and the devil raised hogs together. When the time came to divide the animals, Bobtail took those with curly tails, and the devil is still looking for his hogs, the ones with straight tails. (Roberts)

> Bobtail and the Devil. Roberts, *South from Hell*, no. 39.
> Cut Legs and the Devil. Dorson, *Jonathan Draws the Long Bow*, p. 55.
> Dickey Kent, the Devil and the Pigs. Briggs, *DBF*, pt. B, v. 1, p. 94.
> How Bobtail Beat the Devil. Chase, *Grandfather Tales*, no. 9.
> Jack and the Devil. Simpson, *Folklore of the Welsh Border*, p. 58.
> Jack o' Kent and the Pigs. Briggs, *DBF*, pt. B, v. 1, p. 107.

**1045  PULLING DOWN THE FOREST WITH A ROPE.** A boy intimidated the devil by wrapping a rope around the forest and threatening to pull down all the trees at once. (Ranke)

> How El Bizarron Fooled the Devil (Cuba). Cole, *Best-Loved Folktales*, no.
> Inheritance, The (Finland). Bødker, *European Folk Tales*, p. 26.
> Jack in the Giants' Newground (USA). Cole, *Best-Loved Folktales*, no. 176.
> Jack in the Giants' Newground. Chase, *Jack Tales*, no. 1.
> Old Magician Sabino, The. Mathias and Raspa, *Italian Folktales in America*,
> Stupid Peikko (Finland). Booss, *Scandinavian Tales*, p. 582.
> Youngest Brother and the Stupid Devil, The. Ranke, *Folktales of Germany*,

**1049  THE HEAVY AX OR THE GIANT BUCKET.** The hero frightened a giant by threatening to cut down the whole forest with a single blow and by offering to bring the entire well into the house. (Grimm)

> Baldchin and the Drakos, The. Megas, *Folktales of Greece*, no. 57.
> Giant and the Tailor, The. Grimm, *Tales*, no. 183.
> Gypsy and the Bear, The. Musick, *Green Hills of Magic*, no. 66.
> Herr Lazarus and the Draken. Lang, *Grey Fairy Book*, p. 136.
> Jack in the Giants' Newground (USA). Cole, *Best-Loved Folktales*, no. 176.
> Jack in the Giants' Newground. Chase, *Jack Tales*, no. 1.
> Mac-a-Rusgaich. Campbell, *West Highlands*, v. 2, p. 318.
> Old Magician Sabino, The. Mathias and Raspa, *Italian Folktales in America*,
> Stan Bolovan (Romania). Lang, *Violet Fairy Book*, p. 111.

**1050  A CONTEST IN FELLING TREES.** Matti engaged Peikko, the stupid ogre, in a contest to pull up a large tree. After trying in vain, Peikko fell back exhausted. Unseen by his opponent, Matti cut down the tree with his ax.

> Stupid Peikko (Finland). Booss, *Scandinavian Tales*, p. 583.

**1051  SPRINGING WITH A BENT TREE.** A giant bent a tree down for the Brave Little Tailor to pick some fruit. He let go, and the tailor flew into the air. The latter claimed that he had jumped over the tree on purpose, a feat that the giant could not match. (Grimm, no. 20)

Brave Little Tailor, The. Grimm, *Tales*, no. 20.
Giant and the Tailor, The. Grimm, *Tales*, no. 183.

**1052  A CONTEST IN CARRYING A TREE.** The Brave Little Tailor offered to carry the branches—the heaviest part, he claimed—if the giant would carry the trunk. The giant lifted the trunk to his shoulder, and the tailor rode along behind, astride a limb. (Grimm)

Aay Caan Laay. Lindell, Folk *Tales from Kammu,* II, no. 3.
Brave Little Tailor, The. Grimm, *Tales,* no. 20.
Tailor and the Giants, The. Roberts, *South from Hell,* no. 62B.

**1053  SHOOTING WILD BOARS.** The hero intimidated a giant by threatening to shoot a thousand wild boars with a single shot.

Giant and the Tailor, The. Grimm, *Tales,* no. 183.

**1060  SQUEEZING WATER FROM A STONE.** The Brave Little Tailor showed his strength by squeezing a piece of cheese, which the giant supposed to be a stone, until liquid ran from it. (Grimm)

Ash Lad Who Had An Eating Match with the Troll. Asbjørnsen and Moe, *Norwegian Folktales,* p. 81.
Baldchin and the Drakos, The. Megas, *Folktales of Greece,* no. 57.
Boots Who Ate a Match with the Troll. Asbjørnsen and Moe, *East o' the Sun,*
Brave Little Tailor, The. Grimm, *Tales,* no. 20.
How Mister Rabbit Succeeded in Raising a Dust. Harris, *Uncle Remus,* no.
Jack in the Giants' Newground (USA). Cole, *Best-Loved Folktales,* no. 176.
Jack in the Giants' Newground. Chase, *Jack Tales,* no. 1.
Jack Strong, Slayer of Five Hundred. Calvino, *Italian Folktales,* no. 97.
Jack the Giant Killer. Campbell, *West Highlands,* v. 2, p. 342.
Jack the Giant Killer. Dorson, *Buying the Wind,* p. 168.
Old Magician Sabino, The. Mathias and Raspa, *Italian Folktales in America,*
Stan Bolovan (Romania). Lang, *Violet Fairy Book,* p. 111.
Stupid Peikko (Finland). Booss, *Scandinavian Tales,* p. 583.
Tailor and the Giants, The. Roberts, *South from Hell,* no. 62B.

**1061  BITING STONES.** A tailor outwitted a bear by eating nuts while giving the bear stones to eat. (Grimm) Cf. type 1133.

Clever Little Tailor, The. Grimm, *Tales,* no. 114.
Hunter and the Forest-Goblin, The. Afanasyev, *Erotic Tales,* p. 93.
Hunter and the Satyr, The. Afanasyev, *Russian Secret Tales,* p. 47.

**1062  A CONTEST IN THROWING STONES.** The Brave Little Tailor threw a bird into the air, pretending it was a stone, and thus won a throwing contest with a giant. (Grimm)

Brave Little Tailor, The. Grimm, *Tales,* no. 20.
John and the Giants. Musick, *Green Hills of Magic,* no. 26.
Mac-a-Rusgaich. Campbell, *West Highlands,* v. 2, p. 318.
Old Magician Sabino, The. Mathias and Raspa, *Italian Folktales in America,*

Stupid Peikko (Finland). Booss, *Scandinavian Tales,* p. 583.
Tailor and the Giants, The. Roberts, *South from Hell,* no. 62B.

**1063  A CONTEST IN THROWING THE GIANT'S CLUB.** A boy entered a throwing contest with a giant. "I hope you don't mind losing your club," the boy said, "because I intend to throw it out of sight into the sea." Not wanting to lose his club, the giant resigned. (Campbell)

Ivanko the Bear's Son. Afanasyev, *Russian Fairy Tales,* p. 221.
Jack in the Giants' Newground (USA). Cole, *Best-Loved Folktales,* no. 176.
Jack in the Giants' Newground. Chase, *Jack Tales,* no. 1.
Jack the Giant Killer. Campbell, *West Highlands,* v. 2, p. 342.
Stan Bolovan (Romania). Lang, *Violet Fairy Book,* p. 111.

**1063A  SHOUTING A WARNING.** Jack engaged in a throwing contest with a giant, but when Jack shouted a warning to the people across the sea, the giant resigned without making Jack throw the weight. (Calvino)

How El Bizarron Fooled the Devil (Cuba). Cole, *Best-Loved Folktales,* no.
Jack Strong, Slayer of Five Hundred. Calvino, *Italian Folktales,* no. 97.
John and the Giants. Musick, *Green Hills of Magic,* no. 26.
Samson and Satan. Botkin, *Treasury of American Folklore,* p. 724.

**1063B  THROWING A CLUB TO CONSTANTINOPLE.** A shepherd, engaged in a show of strength with a family of ogres, threatened to throw a club to Constantinople. They stopped him, for their sisters lived in Constantinople, and they feared for their safety. (Megas)

Baldchin and the Drakos, The. Megas, *Folktales of Greece,* no. 57.
Jack the Giant Killer. Dorson, *Buying the Wind,* p. 168.

**1066  THE HANGING GAME.** Two men came to a gallows and decided to see what it was like to be hanged. The one agreed to let the other down when he whistled that he had had enough. But the hanging man never whistled, so his companion emptied his pockets and left. (Campbell)

Fly Which Raised the Fish, The. Campbell, *West Highlands,* v. 2, p. 272.
Three-Legged Hare, The. Briggs, *DBF,* pt. B, v. 1, p. 143.

**1070  A WRESTLING CONTEST WITH AN OGRE.** John Trevail accepted a wrestling match with the devil. With the help of a parson, who provided mystical charms, John won the match.

Prize Wrestler and the Demon, The. Briggs, *DBF,* pt. B, v. 1, p. 124.

**1071  A WRESTLING CONTEST WITH A BEAR.** A boy agreed to wrestle with an ogre, only if the latter would first challenge the boy's old grandfather, and the boy pointed him in the direction of a bear, who mauled the ogre terribly. (Ranke)

Inheritance, The (Finland). Bødker, *European Folk Tales,* p. 26.
Youngest Brother and the Stupid Devil, The. Ranke, *Folktales of Germany,*

**1072  A RACE WITH THE TRICKSTER'S SON (A RABBIT).** A trickster convinced an ogre to enter a race with his three-year old son, who he said was asleep under certain bush. But under the bush was a rabbit, and it ran away so fast that the ogre had no chance. (Ranke)

Inheritance, The (Finland). Bødker, *European Folk Tales,* p. 26.
Ivanko the Bear's Son. Afanàsyev, *Russian Fairy Tales,* p. 221.
Youngest Brother and the Stupid Devil, The. Ranke, *Folktales of Germany,*

**1073  A CLIMBING CONTEST WITH A SQUIRREL.** An ogre entered a climbing contest with the hero's daughter, but the hero matched him against a squirrel, and the ogre lost. (Ranke) Cf. types 1227, 2028.

Inheritance, The (Finland). Bødker, *European Folk Tales,* p. 26.
Youngest Brother and the Stupid Devil, The. Ranke, *Folktales of Germany,*

**1074  A RACE IS WON BY A LOOK-ALIKE HELPER.** A girl challenged Old Nick to a race. Her twin sister situated herself at the end of the course, making Old Nick think he had lost. He tried three times, but finally had to acknowledge himself beaten. (Booss) —Note: Tales with this plot using animal actors (usually a hare and two hedgehogs) are classified as type 275A*.

Davies Sets the Devil to Race with a Hedgehog. Briggs, *DBF,* pt. B, v. 1, p.
Devil and Rabbit. Carpenter, *A Latvian Storyteller,* p. 179.
Gypsy and the Bear, The. Musick, *Green Hills of Magic,* no. 66.
How the Hedgehog Ran the Devil to Death. Briggs, *DBF,* pt. A, v. 1, p. 116.
Old Nick and the Girl (Sweden). Booss, *Scandinavian Tales,* p. 203.

**1082  CARRYING A HORSE BETWEEN ONE'S LEGS.** Ivanko engaged the devil in a carrying contest. The devil started by lifting a horse to his back and carrying it until he was exhausted. Ivanko bettered his opponent by claiming to carry the horse effortlessly between his legs. Actually he mounted it and let the horse carry him. (Afanasyev)

Ivanko the Bear's Son. Afanasyev, *Russian Fairy Tales,* p. 221.
Youngest Brother and the Stupid Devil, The. Ranke, *Folktales of Germany,*

**1085  SPLITTING A LOG BARE-HANDED.** Cenco split a log completely through with an ax and wedges, then placed the two halves back together. He partially split a second log and propped the

pieces apart with wooden spikes. Then he demonstrated his strength
to a magician by pretending to split the first log with his bare hands.
When the magician tried the same feat on the second log, Cenco
knocked out the spikes. The half-split log sprang shut, trapping the
magician by his fingers. Cf. types 151, 157A, 1160.

Old Magician Sabino, The. Mathias and Raspa, *Italian Folktales in America,*

**1088   A CONTEST IN EATING.** A boy engaged in an eating match
with a troll, tricking him by putting the food into a bag under his
shirt. To show the troll how one could eat still more, he pretended to
cut open his belly by slitting the bag. The troll followed his example,
and killed himself. (Asbjørnsen and Moe)

Ash Lad Who Had an Eating Match with the Troll. Asbjørnsen and Moe,
  *Norwegian Folktales,* p. 81.
Big Wind, The. Briggs, *DBF,* pt. A, v. 1, p. 147.
Boots Who Ate a Match with the Troll. Asbjørnsen and Moe, *East o' the Sun,*
Brother Rabbit's Barbecue. Harris, *Seven Tales of Uncle Remus,* no. 4.
Child Rowland. Briggs, *DBF,* pt. A, v. 1, p. 180.
Clever Little Tailor, The. Briggs, *DBF,* pt. A, v. 1, p. 190.
Clever Little Tailor, The. Briggs, *DBF,* pt. A, v. 1, p. 190.
Jack and the Giants (England). Opie, *Classic Fairy Tales,* p. 64.
Jack in the Giants' Newground (USA). Cole, *Best-Loved Folktales,* no. 176.
Jack in the Giants' Newground. Chase, *Jack Tales,* no. 1.
Jack the Giant Killer. Campbell, *West Highlands,* v. 2, p. 342.
Jack the Giant Killer. Dorson, *Buying the Wind,* p. 168.
Jack the Giant-Killer. Briggs, *DBF,* pt. A, v. 1, p. 331.
John and the Giants. Musick, *Green Hills of Magic,* no. 26.
Little Thumb and the Giant. Randolph, *The Devil's Pretty Daughter,* p. 53.
Mac-a-Rusgaich. Campbell, *West Highlands,* v. 2, p. 318.
Pot Belly, Big Mouth, and Skinny Legs. Saucier, *French Louisiana,* no. 23.

**1089   A CONTEST IN THRESHING.** Mac-a-Rusgaich won a
threshing contest with a giant because the latter struck the sheaves so
hard that they bounced onto the rafters.

Mac-a-Rusgaich. Campbell, *West Highlands,* v. 2, p. 318.

**1090   A CONTEST IN MOWING.** Mac-a-Rusgaich won a mowing
contest with a giant by taking the shorter inside swath for himself and
giving the giant the longer outside swath. (Campbell)

Devil's Whetstone, The. Briggs, *DBF,* pt. B, v. 1, p. 92.
Farmer and the Bogart, The. Briggs, *DBF,* pt. B, v. 1, p. 28.
Hob Thrust. Briggs, *DBF,* pt. B, v. 1, p. 269.
How Davies and the Devil Had a Mowing Contest. Briggs, *DBF,* pt. B, v. 1,
Jack and the Devil. Simpson, *Folklore of the Welsh Border,* p. 58.
Longstone, The. Briggs, *DBF,* pt. B, v. 1, p. 113.
Mac-a-Rusgaich. Campbell, *West Highlands,* v. 2, p. 318.
Sir Barnabas Bromgrave Mows a Match with the Devil. Porter, *Folklore of
  East Anglia,* p. 105.
Sir Barney Brograve and the Devil. Briggs, *DBF,* pt. B, v. 1, p. 137.

**1091** **AN UNHEARD-OF HORSE.** A peasant won a bet with the devil by riding to him on an animal the devil could not identify. The unfamiliar mount was the peasant's own wife with her hair combed over her face and a carrot emerging from her behind. (Afanasyev)

Devil and the Peasant, The. Pourrat, *Treasury of French Tales,* p. 118.
Peasant and the Devil, The. Afanasyev, *Russian Secret Tales,* p. 49.

**1092** **AN UNHEARD-OF BIRD.** The devil agreed to relinquish his claim on a certain man if the latter could bring him a bird that he, the devil, had never seen before. The man won by sticking many kinds of feathers onto his wife and then presenting her as a bird. (Pino-Saavedra)

Hunter's Joke, The (Finland). Dorson, *Folktales around the World,* p. 97.
Unknown Bird, The. Pino-Saavedra, *Folktales of Chile,* no. 42.

**1093** **CONTESTS IN WIT.** —Miscellaneous anecdotes.

Fause Knight Upon the Road (I-II), The. Briggs, *DBF,* pt. A, v. 1, p. 230.
Harpkin. Briggs, *DBF,* pt. A, v. 1, p. 232.

**1096** **A CONTEST IN SEWING.** A tailor won a sewing match with the devil by threading the latter's needle with a hundred yards of thread. (Briggs)

Devil and the Tailor, The. Briggs, *DBF,* pt. A, v. 1, p. 211.
Tailor Who Sold His Soul to the Devil, The. Paredes, *Folktales of Mexico,* no.

**1097** **A HOUSE OF STONE AND A HOUSE OF ICE.** One winter the Lord built himself a house of ice and the devil built himself a house of stone. The ice house was so beautiful that the devil exchanged his stone house for it, but the sun soon melted the devil's new house. Cf. type 43.

Devil and the Good Lord, The. Massignon, *Folktales of France,* no. 33.

**1115** **ATTEMPTING TO KILL THE HERO IN HIS BED.** Instead of using the bed offered by the giant, the Brave Little Tailor slept in a corner. During the night the giant broke the bed in two with a great iron bar. To his astonishment and fear, the tailor was still alive the following morning. (Grimm) Cf. types 327, 327B, 1153.

Adventures with Giants. Clouston, *Popular Tales,* v. 1, p. 133.
Brave Little Tailor, The. Grimm, *Tales,* no. 20.
Gourd of Blood, The. Mathias and Raspa, *Italian Folktales in America,* no. 7.
Gypsy and the Bear, The. Musick, *Green Hills of Magic,* no. 66.
Herr Lazarus and the Draken. Lang, *Grey Fairy Book,* p. 136.
How El Bizarron Fooled the Devil (Cuba). Cole, *Best-Loved Folktales,* no.
In the Hillman's Service (Denmark). Bødker, *European Folk Tales,* p. 78.

Jack Strong, Slayer of Five Hundred. Calvino, *Italian Folktales*, no. 97.
John and the Giants. Musick, *Green Hills of Magic*, no. 26.
Little Thumb and the Giant. Randolph, *The Devil's Pretty Daughter*, p. 53.
Mister Fox and Miss Goose. Harris, *Nights with Uncle Remus*, no. 1.
Outwitting Giants. Villa, *100 Armenian Tales*, no. 64.
Stan Bolovan (Romania). Lang, *Violet Fairy Book*, p. 111.

**1119  OGRES KILL THEIR OWN CHILDREN.** A witch planned to kill her stepdaughter while she slept, but during the night the intended victim traded places with her stepsister, so the witch ended up killing her own daughter. (Grimm) —Note: This motif is frequently an integral part of types 327 and 327B. Many tales listed above under those numbers are traditionally categorized under type 1119 as well.

Halfman. Lang, *Violet Fairy Book*, p. 345.
How Wiley Wolf Rode in the Bag. Harris, *Told by Uncle Remus*, no. 3.
Next to the River. Randolph, *Sticks in the Knapsack*, p. 116.
Stepmother Kills Her Own Daughter, A. Arewa, *Northern East Africa*, p. 197.
Sweetheart Roland. Grimm, *Tales*, no. 56.

**1120  THE OGRE DROWNS HIS OWN WIFE.** A keloghlan lifted a köse's sleeping wife into his own bed, then, imitating the woman's voice, said: "Husband, let's throw the keloghlan into the river, bed and all." The köse, half asleep, threw the bed into the water, and thus drowned his own wife. (Walker and Uysal)

Keloghlan and the Köse, The. Walker and Uysal, *Tales in Turkey*, p. 71.
Peter the Rogue. Espinosa, *Folklore of Spain in the American Southwest*, p.

**1121  BURNING THE WITCH IN HER OWN OVEN.** Baba Yaga captured a brave youth and intended to bake him alive. He pretended to not know how to lie on the baking pan. Baba Yaga showed him by curling up on the pan, and he quickly pushed her into the stove. Cf. type 327A.

Baba Yaga and the Brave Youth. Afanasyev, *Russian Fairy Tales*, p. 76.
Esben and the Witch (Denmark). Lang, *Pink Fairy Book*, p. 258.
Garden Witch, The. Calvino, *Italian Folktales*, no. 181.
Giant's Treasure, The (Sweden). Bødker, *European Folk Tales*, p. 33.
Hansel and Gretel. Grimm, *Tales*, no. 15.
Jack in the Giants' Newground (USA). Cole, *Best-Loved Folktales*, no. 176.
Jack in the Giants' Newground. Chase, *Jack Tales*, no. 1.
Jack the Giant Killer. Dorson, *Buying the Wind*, p. 168.

**1122  KILLING THE OGRE'S WIFE .** —Miscellaneous tricks.

Halfman. Lang, *Violet Fairy Book*, p. 345.
Rooster-Brother. Villa, *100 Armenian Tales*, no. 76.

**1130  A BOOT FULL OF MONEY.** To fulfill his half of a bargain, the devil agreed to fill a peasant's boot with money. However, the peasant held out a boot without a sole, and with all his wealth the devil was unable to fill it. (Ranke)

Devil Duped, The. Ranke, *Folktales of Germany,* no. 68.
Devil's Boot, The. Massignon, *Folktales of France,* no. 58.
General Moulton and the Devil. Dorson, *Jonathan Draws the Long Bow,* p.
General Staats and the Devil. Musick, *Green Hills of Magic,* no. 5.
Grave Mound, The. Grimm, *Tales,* no. 195.
Stupid Peikko (Finland). Booss, *Scandinavian Tales,* p. 583.

**1133  CASTRATING AN OGRE TO MAKE HIM STRONG.** A hunter gave an ogre a bullet for a nut, and he was, of course, unable to crack it with his teeth. "Let me castrate you, and you'll be able to crack nuts with ease!" the hunter said, biting a real nut himself to prove the point. Thus the ogre lost his manhood. Cf. type 1061.

Hunter and the Forest-Goblin, The. Afanasyev, *Erotic Tales,* p. 93.
Hunter and the Satyr, The. Afanasyev, *Russian Secret Tales,* p. 47.

**1134  AN OGRE INJURES HIMSELF TO BECOME STRONG.** Jack tricked a giant into thinking he could run faster by cutting out his intestines, but the giant succeeded only in killing himself. (Calvino)

How Mister Lion Lost His Wool. Harris, *Uncle Remus and Brer Rabbit,* no.
Jack Strong, Slayer of Five Hundred. Calvino, *Italian Folktales,* no. 97.

**1135  BLINDING AN OGRE WITH AN EYE OINTMENT.** A man offered to cure a giant's squinty eye with a special ointment. The giant lay down, and the man poured boiling oil into his eyes, blinding him.

Florentine, The. Calvino, *Italian Folktales,* no. 76.

**1137  BLINDING AN OGRE WITH A STAKE.** Odysseus drove a heated stake into the one eye of his captor Polyphemus, a Cyclops, and blinded him, thus enabling him and his fellow travelers to escape. (Thompson)

Birth of Finn MacCumhail, The. Glassie, *Irish Folktales,* no. 109.
Blinded Giant, The. Jacobs, *More English Fairy Tales,* p. 92.
Burn Sel,' Blame Sel' for It. Briggs, *DBF,* pt. B, v. 1, p. 194.
Cyclops, The. Dawkins, *More Greek Folktales,* no. 4A.
Donald Cameron and the Brownies. Briggs, *DBF,* pt. B, v. 1, p. 207.
Fairy Dell of Cromarty, The. Briggs, *DBF,* pt. B, v. 1, p. 222.
Jack and the Giant of Dalton Mill. Briggs, *DBF,* pt. A, v. 1, p. 325.
Maggie Moloch. Briggs, *DBF,* pt. B, v. 1, p. 307.
Man Who Blinded the Ogre, The. Dawkins, *More Greek Folktales,* no. 4B.
Masell. Briggs, *DBF,* pt. A, v. 1, p. 410.
Massell. Briggs, *DBF,* pt. B, v. 1, p. 314.
Me A'an Sel'. Briggs, *DBF,* pt. B, v. 1, p. 314.
One-Eye. Calvino, *Italian Folktales,* no. 115.

Polyphemus, the Cyclops (Homer). Thompson, *100 Folktales,* no. 86.
Robber and His Sons, The. Grimm, *Other Tales,* p. 111.

**1138   GILDING THE OGRE'S BEARD.** Matti offered to dye Peikko's beard red. Following the trickster's directions, the ogre held his
beard in a pot of melted tar until it cooled. But the solidified tar held
the beard fast, and Peikko had to cut it off to free himself. (Booss)

Pedro de Urdemalas and the Priest. Paredes, *Folktales of Mexico,* no. 55.
Stupid Peikko (Finland). Booss, *Scandinavian Tales,* p. 587.

**1145   FRIGHTENING THE OGRE BY BURNING TWIGS.** Peikko ate so much at a wedding feast that it appeared there would be
nothing for the other guests. The host thus threw some green twigs
on the fire. When they began to hiss, he said: "There must be a snake
in the house!" and Peikko ran away in fright.

Stupid Peikko (Finland). Booss, *Scandinavian Tales,* p. 586.

**1146   THE OGRE TAKES A MILLSTONE TO BE A PEARL.**
Matti gave Peikko a millstone, claiming it was one of his mother's
pearls. With the millstone tied around his neck, the ogre tried to row
across a lake, but the weight sunk his boat and pulled him to the
bottom.

Stupid Peikko (Finland). Booss, *Scandinavian Tales,* p. 587.

**1149   MAKING THE OGRE FEAR CHILDREN.** Lazarus warned a
draken that his children loved draken meat, but the draken still came
for a visit. Coached by their father, the children called out "draken
meat!" as the ogre approached, and the draken ran away terrified.
(Lang, "Herr Lazarus and the Draken")

Herr Lazarus and the Draken. Lang, *Grey Fairy Book,* p. 136.
Stan Bolovan (Romania). Lang, *Violet Fairy Book,* p. 111.

**1151   FRIGHTENING THE OGRE WITH GIANT SHOES.** To
stop Peikko from stealing his grain, a miller made a pair of huge
birch-bark shoes and left them in front of his shed. When Peikko saw
the shoes he thought they were owned by a giant, and ran away
terrified.

Stupid Peikko (Finland). Booss, *Scandinavian Tales,* p. 587.

**1153   ALL THE MONEY THE TRICKSTER CAN CARRY.** A
hillman agreed to pay Esben all the money he could carry, if his
services were satisfactory. The boy tricked him repeatedly, so the
hillman attempted to end their contract by killing him in his bed.
However, Esben escaped (cf. type 1115). Fearing the boy's apparent

strength, the hillman paid him a cart filled with money to break their contract.

In the Hillman's Service (Denmark). Bødker, *European Folk Tales*, p. 78.

**1157 THE OGRE SMOKES A GUN FOR A PIPE.** A hunter offered a young devil his gun, claiming it was a pipe. The devil put the barrel in his mouth, and the hunter pulled the trigger. "Your tobacco is too sharp for me!" said the devil, and disappeared. (Ranke)

Devil and the Man, The. Ranke, *Folktales of Germany*, no. 69.
Eileschpijjel's Smoke Pipe. Dorson, *Buying the Wind*, p. 131.
How Herman Maki Met the Devil or One of His Little Cousins, Dorson, *Bloodstoppers and Bearwalkers*, p. 143.
Morgan Jones and the Devil. Dorson, *Jonathan Draws the Long Bow*, p. 55.

**1159 CATCHING THE WOULD-BE MUSICIAN IN A CRACK.** A bear, hoping to learn to play the violin, let a tailor place his paws in a vise, but the tailor closed the vise and captured the bear. Later, the bear attacked the tailor and his bride but the tailor spread his legs in the form of a vise. The assailant, afraid of being caught again, ran away. (Grimm, "The Clever Little Tailor") —Note: In less delicate tellings, it is the hero's wife who frightens away the ogre with her spread legs. Cf. types 151, 1160.

Clever Little Tailor, The. Grimm, *Tales*, no. 114.
Strange Musician, The. Grimm, *Tales*, no. 8.

**1160 CATCHING THE DEVIL BY THE NOSE.** A man tricked the devil into sticking his nose through a crack in the door, then he pushed his knife into the crack, pinning the devil. Later the devil nearly caught the man's wife, but she saved herself by taking off her pants; the devil fled, fearing that he would get his nose caught in another crack. Cf. types 151, 157A, 1085, 1159.

Devil Caught, The. Dorson, *Buying the Wind*, p. 78.

**1161 THE BEAR TRAINER AND HIS CAT.** A band of trolls ascended upon a house where a bear trainer with his bear had stopped for the night. Catching only a glimpse of the sleeping animal, the trolls thought it was a cat, but once awakened, it unleashed its full strength upon the intruders. Later the the trolls asked the house owner about his cat. "She had seven kittens," answered the man. The trolls never again approached that house. (Asbjørnsen and Moe) Cf. Christiansen, *Migratory Legends*, type 6015.

Bear Trainer and the Trolls, The. Lindow, *Swedish Legends and Folktales*,
Cat on the Dovrefell, The. Asbjørnsen and Moe, *East o' the Sun*, p. 90.

Christmas Visitors and the Tabby Cat, The.  Christiansen, *Folktales of Elves' Dance on New Year's Eve*.  Simpson, *Icelandic Folktales and Legends,*

**1164  THE WOMAN AND THE OGRE IN THE PIT.**  A man threw his shrewish wife into a deep pit.  After three days of peace he lowered her a rope to see how she was doing, but instead of his wife, he pulled out a devil.  The imp promised to make the man wealthy if he would not force him back into the netherworld with the tormenting woman.  (Afanasyev)

Bad Wife, The.  Afanasyev, *Russian Fairy Tales,* p. 56.
Talkative Wife, The.  Villa, *100 Armenian Tales,* no. 79.

**1164A  THE DEVIL'S MOTHER-IN-LAW.**  The devil married a young woman.  Her mother discovered his identity and trapped him in a bottle which she then buried in a snowbank.  He tricked a man into releasing him, but the man learned about devil's marriage and frightened him away by making him think that his mother-in-law was arriving.  Cf. type 1862B.

Don Demonio's Mother-in-Law (Spain).  Cole, *Best-Loved Folktales,* no. 34.

**1165  THE TROLL AND THE CHRISTENING.**  A farmer invited a troll, known for his generous gifts, to his child's christening feast.  After having presented his gift, the troll was told that the Drumbeater (thunder) would also attend the feast, so the troll, who was afraid of thunder and lightning, did not attend.

Old Man from Haberg, The.  Lindow, *Swedish Legends and Folktales,* no. 23.

**1169  THE TRANSPOSED HEADS.**  Two brothers cut off each other's heads in a fight over the one man's wife.  A dervish joined the heads to the corpses, bringing the men back to life.  However, the heads ended up on the wrong bodies, which raises the question: "To which man did the woman now belong?"

Girl Out of Whose Mouth Came a Snake, The (Turkey).  Bødker, *European Folk Tales,* p. 205.

**1170  THE DEVIL, THE PEDLAR, AND THE OLD WOMAN.**  A pedlar agreed to give himself to the devil in return for help in selling all his goods.  He then saved himself by having a shrewish old woman climb into his bag just before the devil came to get him.  Seeing the old woman, the devil had to admit defeat, for no one would ever buy such an item.

Old Nick and the Pedlar (Sweden).  Booss, *Scandinavian Tales,* p. 224.

**1174   THE MASTER'S MAGIC BOOK.** Cromwell's servant opened his master's giant Bible, hoping to discover its power. A band of tiny men emerged from the book, shouting: "Give me work!" The quick-thinking servant commanded them to make him ropes of sand, which they were unable to do, so they returned to the book from which they came. (Glassie) Cf. type 325* and Christiansen, *Migratory Legends,* type 3020.

> Cromwell's Bible. Glassie, *Irish Folktales,* no. 99.
> Devil and the Schoolmaster, The. Briggs, *DBF,* pt. B, v. 1, p. 81.
> Devil at Vale Royal Abbey, The. Briggs, *DBF,* pt. B, v. 1, p. 83.
> Ghost of Cranmere Pool, The. Whitlock, *Folklore of Devon,* p. 55.
> Inexperienced Use of the Black Book. Christiansen, *Folktales of Norway,* p.
> Ivanko the Bear's Son. Afanasyev, *Russian Fairy Tales,* p. 221.
> Michael Scott and the Devil. Briggs, *DBF,* pt. B, v. 1, p. 116.
> Peasant Tricks the Devil, A. Ranke, *Folktales of Germany,* no. 70.
> Sands of Cocker, The. Briggs, *DBF,* pt. B, v. 1, p. 134.
> Schoolmaster at Bury, The. Briggs, *DBF,* pt. B, v. 1, p. 135.
> Threshing-Flail from Heaven, The. Grimm, *Tales,* no. 112.
> Tregeagle Makes a Rope of Sand. Deane and Shaw, *Folklore of Cornwall,* p.
> William de Tracey's Penance. Palmer, *Folklore of Somerset,* p. 131.

**1175   STRAIGHTENING A CURLY HAIR.** The devil worked for a farmer and completed every task, until asked to hammer a curly hair straight. The more he hammered, the curlier the hair became. He finally gave up and went away.

> Devil and the Farmer, The. Briggs, *DBF,* pt. A, v. 1, p. 208.

**1179   THE DEVIL MANS A PUMP.** The devil signed on as a ship-mate and was to get the captain's soul unless the latter could give him a task he couldn't do. The captain put a pump through a hole in the ship into the water and asked the devil to pump the ship dry. He pumped and pumped and finally had to admit defeat.

> Outwitting the Devil. Lindow, *Swedish Legends and Folktales,* no. 76.

**1179\*   AN OGRE HOLDS THE SHIP BY ITS ANCHOR.** Unable to weigh anchor, a sailor dove to investigate and found that a sea woman was holding it with her foot. She released the anchor only after the sailor promised to return and marry her. Later he was carried away by a wave and never seen again.

> Cluasach and the Sea-Woman (Ireland). Bødker, *European Folk Tales,* p. 135.

**1180   WATER IN A SIEVE.** A girl came under the power of an ogre. She handed him a sieve and asked him to fetch her a drink of water, then made her escape while he was trying to fill it. (Briggs, "Water in a Sieve") —Note: The heroines of type 480 tales often must fulfill this seemingly impossible task.

Bingie Drains the Cranmere Pool. Whitlock, *Folklore of Devon,* p. 55.
Girl Who Fetched Water in a Riddle, The. Briggs, *DBF,* pt. A, v. 1, p. 267.
How Davies Puzzled the Devil. Briggs, *DBF,* pt. B, v. 1, p. 66.
Marion and Jeanne (France). Bødker, *European Folk Tales,* p. 160.
Water in a Sieve. Briggs, *DBF,* pt. A, v. 1, p. 561.

**1185  THE FIRST CROP.** A man purchased land, agreeing to make payment upon harvesting its first crop. He planted acorns. —Note: In German and Scandinavian versions, this contract is made with the devil rather than with a human seller.

First Crop, The. Briggs, *DBF,* pt. B, v. 2, p. 203.

**1187  TO LIVE AS LONG AS A CANDLE LASTS.** One night near twelve o'clock a mysterious stranger appeared in Betty's room, saying she would have to go with him when her candle was gone. She screamed, and her family fetched the parson. He blew out the candle and locked it in the church, thus foiling the devil. (Briggs, "Betty's Candle")

Betty's Candle. Briggs, *DBF,* pt. B, v. 1, p. 45.
Candle, The. Briggs, *DBF,* pt. B, v. 1, p. 53.
Coals on the Devil's Hearth. Glassie, *Irish Folktales,* no. 44.
Demon Lover, The. Whitlock, *Folklore of Devon,* p. 24.
Demon Mason, The. Briggs, *DBF,* pt. B, v. 1, p. 68.
Devil at Little Dunkeld Manse, The. Briggs, *DBF,* pt. B, v. 1, p. 76.
Green Mist, The. Briggs and Tongue, *Folktales of England,* no. 12.
Lawyer and the Devil, The. Glassie, *Irish Folktales,* no. 43.
Mister Pengelly and the Devil. Briggs, DBF, pt. A, v. 2, p. 186.

**1191  THE DEVIL BUILDS A BRIDGE.** The devil helped build the bridge across the Main River between Frankfurt and Sachsenhausen. His payment was to be the first living thing that crossed the bridge. The devil completed his work one night, and at dawn the next morning the master builder drove a rooster across the bridge, thus cheating the devil of a human soul. (Grimm)

Bridge at Kentchurch, The. Briggs, *DBF,* pt. B, v. 1, p. 52.
Bridge at Kirkby Lonsdale, The. Rowling, *Folklore of the Lake District,* p. 23.
Bridge to Sachsenhausen, The. Grimm, *German Legends,* no. 186.
Curious Cat, The. Briggs and Tongue, *Folktales of England,* no. 51.
Curious Cat, The. Briggs, *DBF,* pt. B, v. 1, p. 60.
Devil's Bridge at Kirkby Lonsdale, The. Briggs, *DBF,* pt. B, v. 1, p. 88.
Devil's Bridge, The (I, II). Briggs, *DBF,* pt. B, v. 1, p. 86.
Jack and the Devil. Simpson, *Folklore of the Welsh Border,* p. 58.
Kilgrim Bridge. Briggs, *DBF,* pt. B, v. 2, p. 242.
Satan Outwitted. Dorson, *Jonathan Draws the Long Bow,* p. 55.

**1199  DEATH WAITS FOR THE MAN TO PRAY.** The angel Gabriel came to take a man, but agreed to spare him until he had said a last prayer. The man refused to pray, so the angel had to wait.

Some time later Gabriel disguised himself as a small boy and asked the man to help him read a school lesson. The passage was a prayer, so the man had to surrender to the angel. (Villa)

Soul-Taking Angel, The. Villa, *100 Armenian Tales,* no. 45.
Town That Had Faith in God, The. Noy, *Folktales of Israel,* no. 8.

**1199B   AN ENDLESS SONG.** The devil agreed to carry a traveler as long as the latter could entertain him with a song. At the song's end, the man would have to carry the devil. The traveler climbed on the devil's back and sang, "Yallehr, yallehr," repeating the same word over and over again until he reached his destination. —Cf. types 227, 1376A*, 2013, 2300, 2320.

Devil's Yallehr. Villa, *100 Armenian Tales,* no. 75.
Words without End. Abrahams, *Afro-American Folktales,* p. 1.

**1200   PLANTING SALT.** Simpletons variously sow salt like grain, plant coins, spread manure around their churches to make them grow larger, and perform similar agricultural idiocies.

Growing the Church. Briggs, *DBF,* pt. A, v. 2, p. 112.
Making the Bishops Channings Church Spire Grow. Whitlock, *Folklore of Wiltshire,* p. 179.
Master Southam Mucks the Church Tower. Briggs, *Folklore of the Cotswolds,*
Men of Coombe Make the Church Grow. Briggs, *Folklore of the Cotswolds,*
Nicobore and His Money. Briggs, *DBF,* pt. A, v. 2, p. 200.
People from Schwarzenborn Sow Salt. Ranke, *Folktales of Germany,* no.
Pevensey Follies. Briggs, *DBF,* pt. A, v. 2, p. 233.
Wiltshire Follies. Briggs, *DBF,* pt. A, v. 2, p. 349.

**1201   PROTECTING THE PLANTED FIELD.** A cow got into a planted field, but the men of Schwarzenborn did not want to send anyone to drive it out, for fear of trampling the crop. The mayor solved the problem by having two men carry the man who was to chase away the cow.

People from Schwarzenborn Protect Their Seed. Ranke, *Folktales of Germany,* no. 71C.

**1202   HARVESTING GRAIN WITH A CANNON.** Cf. type 1650.

Three Children of Fortune, The. Grimm, *Tales,* no. 70.

**1210   GRAZING THE COW ON THE ROOF.** Cf. types 1384 and 1408.

Biggest Fool, The. Dorson, *Negro Tales,* p. 260.
Foolish John (2 versions). Saucier, *French Louisiana,* no. 22.
Grazing the Cow on the Roof. Clouston, *Book of Noodles,* p. 196.

Half Booby and the Shower of Milk Porridge. Campbell, *West Highlands,* v.
   2, p. 400.
Lutoniushka. Afanasyev, *Russian Fairy Tales,* p. 336.
Old Bachelor, The. Saucier, *French Louisiana,* no. 27.
Parish Bull Eats the Grass from the Wall, The. Ranke, *Folktales of Germany,*
There's Bigger Fools Than Tildy. Randolph, *The Devil's Pretty Daughter,* p.
Three More Bigger Fools. Dorson, *Negro Tales,* p. 101.
Three Sillies, The (I, II). Briggs, *DBF,* pt. A, v. 2, p. 304.
Three Sillies, The. Jacobs, *English Fairy Tales,* p. 9.
Three Sillies, The. Roberts, *South from Hell,* no. 58.

**1213   THE PENT CUCKOO.** The men of Borrowdale tried to capture
a cuckoo by building a fence around its nesting tree, but however
high they built the fence, it always escaped by flying just over the top.
(Briggs and Tongue)

Borrowdale Cuckoo, The. Briggs and Tongue, *Folktales of England,* no. 72.
Borrowdale Cuckoo. Briggs, *DBF,* pt. A, v. 2, p. 25.
Borrowdale Folk and Their Cuckoo. Rowling, *Folklore of the Lake District,* p.
Cornishmen Attempt to Catch Cuckoos in Flight. Dorson, *Bloodstoppers,* p.
Cuckoo-Penners. Briggs, *DBF,* pt. A, v. 2, p. 51.
Wise Men of Gotham, The: Of Hedging a Cuckoo. Briggs, *DBF,* pt. A, v. 2,
Yabberton Yawnies. Briggs, *DBF,* pt. A, v. 2, p. 362.

**1214   THE PERSUASIVE AUCTIONEER.**   A farmer auctioned his
cow, and upon hearing the animal's description, he bought it himself.

Clark County Farmer Buys His Own Cow, A. Fisher, *Idaho Lore,* p. 96.

**1215   THE MAN, THE BOY, AND THEIR DONKEY.**  A passerby
chided a man and a boy for not riding their donkey, so the boy
mounted the beast. The next passerby criticized him for not letting
his father ride, so they exchanged places. Then someone said that the
boy should not have to walk, so the man pulled him up beside him.
The next person shamed them for overloading the poor animal, so,
having tried every alternative, they tied the donkey's feet together
and carried it between them on a pole. Struggling to get free, the
donkey fell over a bridge and drowned.

Man, the Boy and the Donkey, The (Aesop). Cole, *Best-Loved Folktales,* no.
Man, the Boy, and the Donkey, The. Jacobs, *Aesop,* no. 63.

**1215A   TRYING TO PLEASE TWO WIVES** (new classification). A
man, whose hair was turning gray, had a young wife and an old wife.
The young woman pulled out his gray hairs to make him look
younger, while the older woman, pulled out the black hairs. Soon he
was bald. (Aesop)

Man and His Two Wives, The. Jacobs, *Aesop,* no. 45.
Plucked Clean. Handford, *Aesop,* no. 182.
When One Man Has Two Wives. Bushnaq, *Arab Folktales,* p. 370.

**1218   A PEASANT HATCHES EGGS.** A peasant let a crow carry off the hens, so his wife forced him to sit on the eggs to finish hatching them. (Afanasyev)

> Husband Who Hatched Eggs, The. Afanasyev, *Russian Secret Tales,* p. 45.
> Peasant Hatches Eggs, A. Afanasyev, *Erotic Tales,* p. 83.
> Vardiello. Basile, *Pentamerone,* Day 1, Tale 4.

**1227   JUMPING AFTER A SQUIRREL.** A hunter climbed a tree in pursuit of a squirrel. The squirrel jumped to another tree, and the man tried to follow, but fell to the ground and killed himself. Cf. types 1073, 2028.

> Dick and Dock. Roberts, *South from Hell,* no. 56.
> Irishmen Squirrel Hunting. Roberts, *South from Hell,* no. 40.

**1229   HOLDING A WOLF BY THE TAIL.** A man crawled into a wolf's den to take the cubs. No sooner had he entered, than the mother wolf returned. She was half inside when the man's companion took hold of her tail to prevent her from reaching the man in the den. The struggling wolf created a cloud of dust. "What is the meaning of the dust?" asked the man inside. His friend replied: "If the wolf's tail breaks, you'll know the meaning of the dust." Cf. type 1900.

> If the Wolf's Tail Breaks. Clouston, *Book of Noodles,* p. 91.

**1229\*   SHOVELING NUTS WITH A HAYFORK.**

> Six Sillies, The. Lang, *Red Fairy Book,* p. 186.

**1231   PLANNING AN ATTACK ON A HARE.** Seven men made plans to attack a strange beast, which in truth was only a hare. (Grimm) Cf. types 1281, 1310\*, 1319A\*.

> Assynt Man and the Hare, The. Campbell, *West Highlands,* v. 2, p. 399.
> Seven Swabians, The. Grimm, *Tales,* no. 119.
> Wise Men of Gotham, The (III). Briggs, *DBF,* pt. A, v. 2, p. 355.

**1240   A FOOL CUTS OFF THE BRANCH HE IS SEATED ON.**

> Fool Cuts Off the Branch on Which He Is Seated. Clouston, *Book of Noodles,*
> Grind the Coffee. Randolph, *The Devil's Pretty Daughter,* p. 103.

**1241A   TYING UP A CLIFF.** The men of Austwick were afraid that a nearby cliff might fall down, so they bound it with ropes. Their efforts were not in vain, for the cliff still stands.

> Austwick Carles (III). Briggs, *DBF,* pt. A, v. 2, p. 12.

**1242  LOADING THE WOOD.**  A man loaded a wagon with wood, saying with each piece, "If the horses can pull this piece they can pull the next one too." He overloaded the wagon, and the horses couldn't move it. Hence he began removing wood, saying with each piece, "If they can't pull this piece they can't pull the next one either." He returned home with an empty wagon.

Wagon Load, The. Dorson, *Buying the Wind,* p. 131.

**1242A  CARRYING THE LOAD TO SPARE THE HORSE.**  A man with a heavy sack mounted his horse. In order to spare the beast, he held the sack on his own back. (Clouston)

Fool Carries a Sack of Meal to Spare His Horse, A. Clouston, *Book of Loading the Ass.* Megas, *Folktales of Greece,* no. 59.
Pal Hall's Quiffs. Briggs, *DBF,* pt. A, v. 2, p. 218.
Wise Men of Gotham, The (I). Briggs, *DBF,* pt. A, v. 2, p. 354.

**1244  STRETCHING THE BENCH.**  A certain bench could seat six men, but in cold weather, when they wore heavy coats, there was room for only five. Taking off their coats, they pulled at the bench to stretch it. Now it held all six, until they put their coats back on.

Stretching the Bench. Ranke, *Folktales of Germany,* no. 73.

**1245  CARRYING SUNLIGHT INTO A WINDOWLESS HOUSE.**

Austwick Carles (IV). Briggs, *DBF,* pt. A, v. 2, p. 12.
Biggest Fool, The. Dorson, *Negro Tales,* p. 260.
Coggeshall Jobs (V). Briggs, *DBF,* pt. A, v. 2, p. 43.
Gothamites Carry Light into Their House. Clouston, *Book of Noodles,* p. 57.
Jimmy Smuggles and His Friends. Simpson, *Folklore of Sussex,* p. 156.
Silly Girl, The. Dorson, *Negro Tales,* p. 105.
There's Bigger Fools Than Tildy. Randolph, *The Devil's Pretty Daughter,* p.
Three More Bigger Fools. Dorson, *Negro Tales,* p. 101.

**1248  LOADING A BEAM CROSSWISE ON A WAGON.**  Cf. type 801.

Bolliton Jackdaws. Briggs, *DBF,* pt. A, v. 2, p. 24.
Fool Loads a Beam Crosswise on His Chariot, A *(Gesta Romanorum).*
  Clouston, *Book of Noodles,* p. 117.
Master Pfriem. Grimm, *Tales,* no. 178.

**1250  A HUMAN WELL ROPE.**  To reach the bottom of a well, one man took hold of a bar and lowered his feet into the hole. A second man held onto the first man's feet, and so on, until the load grew too heavy for the man on top. "Let me spit on my hands," he shouted. He released his grip, and they all fell into the well. (Ranke)

Irishmen Looking for Gold. Roberts, *South from Hell,* no. 41A.

Let Me Spit on My Hands. Fowke, *Folklore of Canada,* p. 165.
Moon in the Well, The. Briggs, *DBF,* pt. A, v. 2, p. 193.
People from Schwarzenborn Measure the Depth of the Well. Ranke, *Folktales of Germany,* no. 71E.
Seven Brothers in the Well, The. Pourrat, *Treasury of French Tales,* p. 11.

**1250A  BUILDING A LADDER OF BOXES.** Two fools tried to reach a high place by climbing on boxes stacked atop one another. Running out of boxes, the man on the ground took the one from the bottom, and everything fell down.

Take One from the Bottom. Fowke, *Folklore of Canada,* p. 163.

**1255  DIGGING A HOLE TO BURY A PILE OF EARTH.** The men of Essex dug a well but were unhappy with the great pile of earth that resulted. After careful deliberation they decided to dig a hole and bury it. (Briggs)

Essex Men's Well, The. Briggs, *DBF,* pt. A, v. 2, p. 74.
People from Schwarzenborn Dig a Well. Ranke, *Folktales of Germany,* no.

**1260  MAKING PORRIDGE IN A WHIRLPOOL.** Some men from Gotham decided to make porridge in a river whirlpool. They threw oatmeal into the bubbling water then, one after the other, they jumped in themselves to taste the results.

Gothamites Make Oatmeal in a Whirlpool. Clouston, *Book of Noodles,* p. 43.
Porridge in the Whirlpool, The. Briggs, *DBF,* pt. A, v. 2, p. 360.

**1263  EATING PORRIDGE AND MILK IN TWO ROOMS.** A foolish woman ate her porridge in the kitchen, while repeatedly running to the cellar for a spoonful of milk.

Lutoniushka. Afanasyev, *Russian Fairy Tales,* p. 336.

**1270  DRYING CANDLES IN THE OVEN.**

Yabberton Yawnies. Briggs, *DBF,* pt. A, v. 2, p. 362.

**1271C*  A CLOAK FOR A TREE.** Foolish John went to the store to buy cloth for his mother, but returning home he wrapped it around a tree that he thought must be freezing in the cold. (Dorson)

Foolish John and the Errands. Dorson, *Buying the Wind,* p. 250.
Old Roadman, The. Briggs, *DBF,* pt. A, v. 2, p. 210.

**1272A  TEN CAPS FROM ONE PIECE OF CLOTH** (new classification). A miser asked a tailor to make ten caps from a piece of cloth that was big enough for only one. The tailor agreed, but the miser was not at all happy with the tiny caps that resulted.

Miser of Castro, The. Megas, *Folktales of Greece*, no. 60.

**1276\* PRAYING FOR A CHANGE IN THE WIND.** A woman found going against the wind very difficult, and prayed that its direction would change. After she reached her destination her prayer was answered, and she had to struggle against the wind all the way home.

Answer to Prayer. Briggs, *DBF*, pt. A, v. 2, p. 6.

**1278   MARKING THE BOAT.** During a war some villagers sunk their bell in a lake. To mark the hiding place, they cut a notch in the boat at the spot where they had dropped the bell. (Ranke)

Irishman Loses a Shovel Overboard, An. Clouston, *Book of Noodles*, p. 99.
Marking the Boat (I-III). Briggs, *DBF*, pt. A, v. 2, p. 177.
Notch Marks the Spot, A. Randolph, *Who Blowed Up the Church House?*, p.
People from Schwarzenborn Hide a Bell. Ranke, *Folktales of Germany*, no.
Two Newfoundland Fishermen. Fowke, *Folklore of Canada*, p. 145.

**1278\* HIDING A KNIFE BENEATH A CLOUD.** Some men from Austwick left a knife on a moor at the edge of a cloud's shadow. When they returned the cloud was gone, and they never found the knife. (Briggs)

Gothamites Leave a Knife beneath a Cloud. Clouston, *Book of Noodles*, p.
Whittle to the Tree. Briggs, *DBF*, pt. A, v. 2, p. 348.

**1281   BURNING THE BARN TO DESTROY AN ANIMAL.** To rid themselves of a frightening animal in their hayloft (it was only an owl) some peasants set fire to their barn. (Grimm, no. 174) Cf. types 1231, 1282, 1310\*, 1319A\*, 1650, 1651.

Owl, The. Grimm, *Tales*, no. 174.
Three Children of Fortune, The. Grimm, *Tales*, no. 70.

**1281A   THE MAN-EATING COW.** A piper found a dead man on the road. He wanted the corpse's boots, but because of the frost he could get them only by cutting off the dead man's feet. Later he found lodging at a farm and bedded down with the cows. Freeing the boots from the severed feet, he departed early the next morning. A servant found the feet, and presumed that a cow had eaten the piper. (O'Sullivan)

Cow That Ate the Piper, The. O'Sullivan, *Folktales of Ireland*, no. 51.
Man Who Had a Calf, The. Dorson, *Buying the Wind*, p. 87.

**1282   BURNING DOWN A HOUSE TO RID IT OF INSECTS.** Cf. type 1281.

Wise Men of Gotham, The (II). Briggs, *DBF,* pt. A, v. 2, p. 354.

**1284 A FOOL DOES NOT KNOW HIMSELF.** A bearded Irishman asked to be wakened early. During the night some wags shaved him. As he hurried away the next morning he noticed the missing beard and complained that they had wakened the wrong man. (Briggs, "The Wrong Man") Cf. types 1336A, 1383.

Eli. Megas, *Folktales of Greece,* no. 58.
Highlander with the Blackened Face, The. Clouston, *Book of Noodles,* p. 6.
Puzzled Carter, The. Briggs, *DBF,* pt. A, v. 2, p. 244.
Seán Na Scuab. O'Sullivan, *Folktales of Ireland,* no. 52.
There's Bigger Fools Than Tildy. Randolph, *The Devil's Pretty Daughter,* p.
Two Husbands, The. Noy, *Folktales of Israel,* no. 69.
Where is the Jar? Noy, *Folktales of Israel,* no. 70.
Wrong Man, The. Briggs, *DBF,* pt. A, v. 2, p. 362.

**1286 JUMPING INTO BREECHES.** Fools try to get dressed by standing up their breeches and jumping into them, both feet at once.

Bastianelo (Italy). Clarkson and Cross, *World Folktales,* no. 62.
Clever Elsie and Her Companions (Italy). Thompson, *100 Folktales,* no. 88.
Lutoniushka. Afanasyev, *Russian Fairy Tales,* p. 336.
Silly Girl, The. Dorson, *Negro Tales,* p. 105.
Six Sillies, The. Lang, *Red Fairy Book,* p. 186.
Three More Bigger Fools. Dorson, *Negro Tales,* p. 101.
Three Sillies, The (I, III). Briggs, *DBF,* pt. A, v. 2, p. 301, 305.
Three Sillies, The. Jacobs, *English Fairy Tales,* p. 9.
Three Sillies, The. Roberts, *South from Hell,* no. 58.

**1287 FOOLS CANNOT COUNT THEMSELVES.** Twelve men of Gotham were afraid that one of their group was lost, because each time they counted, the counter forgot himself. (Jacobs)

Counting Noses. Dorson, *Buying the Wind,* p. 133.
Foolish Weaver, The (Pushtu). Lang, *Orange Fairy Book,* p. 124.
Fools Count Themselves (several variants). Clouston, *Book of Noodles,* p.
Irishmen Looking for Gold. Roberts, *South from Hell,* no. 41A.
Seven Brothers in the Well, The. Pourrat, *Treasury of French Tales,* p. 11.
Wise Men of Gotham, The: Of Counting. Briggs, *DBF,* pt. A, v. 2, p. 353.
Wise Men of Gotham, The: Of Counting. Jacobs, *More English Fairy Tales,* p.

**1288 FOOLS CANNOT FIND THEIR OWN LEGS.** Seven brothers sat in a circle and could not get up, because they could not tell which set of legs belonged to which man. (Jacobs)

Drovers Who Lost Their Feet, The. Paredes, *Folktales of Mexico,* no. 47.
Half Booby and the Shower of Milk Porridge. Campbell, *West Highlands,* v. 2, p. 400.
Macandrew Family, The. Jacobs, *More Celtic Fairy Tales,* p. 97.

**1290 A FOOL MISTAKES A FLAX FIELD FOR A LAKE.**

Fog Fishing'. Glimm, *Flatlanders and Ridgerunners,* p. 31.
Rooster's Beam, The. Grimm, *Tales,* no. 149.

**1291   SENDING ONE CHEESE AFTER ANOTHER.**   A fool
dropped a cheese, and it rolled away, so he threw another one after it,
hoping it would bring the first one back.

Assynt Woman and the Cheeses, The. Campbell, *West Highlands,* v. 2, p.
Freddy and Katy Lizzy. Grimm, *Tales,* no. 59.
Gothamite Sends One Cheese after Another, A. Clouston, *Book of Noodles,*
Iverness Wife and the Balls of Worsted, The. Campbell, *West Highlands,* v.
Wise Men of Gotham: Of Sending Cheeses. Briggs, *DBF,* pt. A, v. 2, p. 351.
Wise Men of Gotham: Of Sending Cheeses. Jacobs, *More English Fairy Tales,*

**1291B   A FOOL GREASES CRACKED EARTH WITH BUTTER.**

Foolish John and the Errands. Dorson, *Buying the Wind,* p. 250.
Freddy and Katy Lizzy. Grimm, *Tales,* no. 59.

**1291C   EXPECTING A TABLE TO WALK ON ITS OWN LEGS.**

Assynt Man's Mistakes, The. Campbell, *West Highlands,* v. 2, p. 397.
Ivanushko the Little Fool. Afanasyev, *Russian Fairy Tales,* p. 62.

**1294   BEHEADING A STUCK CALF.**

Calf's Head Gets Stuck in a Pot, The. Clouston, *Book of Noodles,* p. 89.
Calf's Head Gets Stuck in the Gate, The. Briggs, *DBF,* pt. A, v. 2, p. 31.

**1296   THE FOOL'S ERRAND.**   A fool is sent for an imaginary item,
such as a left-handed wrench.

Art of the Tongue, The. Legman, *Rationale of the Dirty Joke,* vol. 1, p. 510.
Fish Warden. Glimm, *Flatlanders and Ridgerunners,* p. 174.
Snipe Hunting. Glimm, *Flatlanders and Ridgerunners,* p. 12.

**1297\*   FOOLS WALK INTO A RIVER AND DROWN.**

Austwick Carles (I). Briggs, *DBF,* pt. A, v. 2, p. 10.
Seven Swabians, The. Grimm, *Tales,* no. 119.

**1305A   THE TAILOR AND THE MISER'S GOLD.**   A tailor talked a
miser into giving him some of his gold, for, as he said, the miser
could gain only so much satisfaction from looking at it.

Damer's Gold. O'Sullivan, *Folktales of Ireland,* no. 49.

**1305B   THE MISER AND HIS STOLEN GOLD.**   A thief stole a
miser's buried gold.   Discovering the empty hole, the miser
bemoaned his loss.  A neighbor commented: "You only looked at
your gold.  Now look at the hole; it will do you just as much good."
(Aesop)

Miser and His Gold, The. Jacobs, *Aesop,* no. 62.
Miser Who Was Robbed, The. Pourrat, *Treasury of French Tales,* p. 31.
Miser, The. Daly, *Aesop Without Morals,* no. 225.
Where Your Treasure Is, There Will Your Heart Be Also. Handford, *Aesop,*

**1310 DROWNING AN EEL.** Discovering that an eel had eaten the other fish from their pond, the men of Gotham punished it by throwing it into the water to drown. (Jacobs)

Gothamites Drown an Eel. Clouston, *Book of Noodles,* pp. 21, 33.
Mole of Jarnages, The. Delarue, *French Folktales,* p. 338.
Wise Men of Gotham: Of Drowning Eels. Briggs, *DBF,* pt. A, v. 2, p. 352.
Wise Men of Gotham: Of Drowning Eels. Jacobs, *More English Fairy Tales,*

**1310A THROWING A RABBIT INTO A BRIAR PATCH.** Cf. type 175.

How Mister Rabbit Was Too Sharp for Mister Fox. Harris, *Uncle Remus,* no.

**1310C THROWING A BIRD OVER A CLIFF.**

Six Hungry Beasts (Finland). Lang, *Crimson Fairy Book,* p. 233.

**1310\* MISTAKING A CRAB FOR A MONSTER.** Some villagers found a crab that had fallen from a fisherman's basket and took it to be a horrible monster. (Briggs, "The Shapwick Monster") Cf. types 1231, 1281, 1319A\*.

Dabchick, The. Briggs, *DBF,* pt. A, v. 2, p. 53.
Folkestone Fiery Serpent, The. Briggs, *DBF,* pt. A, v. 2, p. 88.
Irishmen Deer Hunting. Roberts, *South from Hell,* no. 43.
Lincolnshire Yellowbreasts. Briggs, *DBF,* pt. A, v. 2, p. 153.
Shapwick Monster, The. Briggs, *DBF,* pt. A, v. 2, p. 262.

**1313 THE MAN WHO THOUGHT HE WAS DEAD.** An abused boy, tired of life, drank what he thought was poison, but in truth was only wine. He then laid himself in a freshly dug grave. Hearing music from a nearby wedding, he fancied that he was already in paradise. (Grimm)

Now I Should Laugh, If I Were Not Dead (Iceland). Clarkson and Cross, *World Folktales,* no. 65.
Poor Boy in the Grave, The. Grimm, *Tales,* no. 185.
Vardiello. Basile, *Pentamerone,* Day 1, Tale 4.

**1313A A PREDICTION OF DEATH IS TAKEN SERIOUSLY.** A man heard a prediction that he would die when his donkey brayed three times. Shortly thereafter the donkey brayed three times, so the man lay down and thought himself dead.

How to Behave in Heaven. Walker and Uysal, *Tales in Turkey,* p. 228.

**1315   A TRAIN IS TAKEN FOR AN ANIMAL.** Dinah, seeing her first train, threw it some fodder. From the way it puffed, she knew that it must be hungry.

Po' Thing. Dorson, *Negro Tales,* p. 237.

**1316   MISTAKING A RABBIT FOR A SHEEP.** A worker took longer than expected to bring in the sheep, because, as he explained, of the little brown one. It was a hare. (Briggs, "The Hunted Hare")

Difficulty for the Baby-Sitter. Briggs, *DBF,* pt. A, v. 2, p. 220.
Hunted Hare, The. Briggs, *DBF,* pt. A, v. 2, pp. 64, 126.

**1318   MISTAKING AN ORDINARY OBJECT FOR A GHOST.** Cf. type 326B*.

Ghost, The. Fowke, *Folklore of Canada,* p. 170.
Old Marster and the Hant. Dorson, *Negro Tales,* p. 176.

**1319   A FOOL THINKS A PUMPKIN IS A HORSE'S EGG.**

Beni-Jennad Buys a Melon instead of a Mule (Algeria and India). Clouston, *Book of Noodles,* p. 37.
Horse's Egg. Briggs, *DBF,* pt. A, v. 2, p. 120.
Irishman and Punkin. Dorson, *Negro Tales,* p. 252.
Irishmen and the Pumpkin, The. Roberts, *South from Hell,* no. 46.
Macandrew Family, The. Jacobs, *More Celtic Fairy Tales,* p. 97.
Mare's Egg, The. Simpson, *Folklore of Sussex,* p. 157.
Mare's Egg. Briggs, *DBF,* pt. A, v. 2, p. 175.
Mare's Nest, The. Randolph, *Who Blowed Up the Church House?,* p. 144.
Pedro Urdimale, the Little Fox, and the Mare's Egg. Pino-Saavedra, *Folktales of Chile,* no. 43.
Racehorse Eggs. Fisher, *Idaho Lore,* p. 131.

**1319A*   FOOLS MISTAKE A WATCH FOR A GHOST.** Some men from Austwick found a watch. Alarmed at its ticking, they beat it to pieces with their sticks. (Briggs, "The Austwick Carles and the Watch") Cf. types 1231, 1281, 1310*.

Austwick Carles and the Watch, The. Briggs, *DBF,* pt. A, v. 2, p. 13.
Irishman and the Watch (2 tales). Roberts, *South from Hell,* no. 47.
Red Hot Shilling in Darlaston, The. Raven, *Folklore of Staffordshire,* p. 147.
The Cannings Men and the Watch. Whitlock, *Folklore of Wiltshire,* p. 180.
Three Irish Tramps. Briggs, *DBF,* pt. A, v. 2, p. 297.
We Killed Him. Briggs, *DBF,* pt. A, v. 2, p. 345.

**1319J*   FOOLS EAT BEETLES FOR BERRIES.**

Has Plummocks Legs? Briggs, *DBF,* pt. A, v. 2, p. 114.
Irishmen Eating Dungbeetles. Roberts, *South from Hell,* no. 44.

**1319*   MISTAKEN IDENTITIES.** —Miscellaneous tales.

Dick and Dock. Roberts, *South from Hell,* no. 56.
Irishman and the Fiddler. Roberts, *South from Hell,* no. 52.
Irishman and the Turtle. Roberts, *South from Hell,* no. 49.
Irishman Hunting for an American Man. Roberts, *South from Hell,* no. 50B.

## 1321  FOOLS ARE FRIGHTENED.  —Miscellaneous tales.

Battle of the Boards, The. Roberts, *South from Hell,* no. 48A.
Henry S. of Trenit Heron. Briggs, *DBF,* pt. A, v. 2, p. 116.
Seven Swabians, The. Grimm, *Tales,* no. 119.

## 1321C  A FOOL IS FRIGHTENED BY HUMMING BEES.

Foolish German, The. Afanasyev, *Russian Fairy Tales,* p. 600.

## 1322A*  A FOOL IS FRIGHTENED BY AN OWL.

Farmer Tickle and the Owl. Briggs, *DBF,* pt. A, v. 2, p. 83.
Hangman's Stone, The. Briggs, *DBF,* pt. B, v. 2, p. 220.
Henpecked Husband. Briggs, *DBF,* pt. A, v. 2, p. 115.
How Mister Lenine Gave Up Courting. Briggs, *DBF,* pt. A, v. 2, p. 122.
Jacob Stone and the Owl. Briggs, *DBF,* pt. A, v. 2, p. 136.
Jacob Stone Is Frightened by an Owl. Palmer, *Folklore of Somerset,* p. 143.
Man Who Answered the Owl, The. Briggs, *Folklore of the Cotswolds,* p. 78.
Sheep-Stealers of the Blackdown Hills, The.  Briggs, *DBF,* pt. B, v. 2, p.
Take Two wi't. Briggs, *DBF,* pt. A, v. 2, p. 291.

## 1325A  MOVING THE FIREPLACE.  A fool, seated next to the fire, became too hot and sent for a mason to move the fireplace.  The mason asked the fool to go for a walk while he completed the task, which he did by moving the man's chair, but he charged a handsome price for the job.

Macandrew Family, The. Jacobs, *More Celtic Fairy Tales,* p. 97.

## 1326  MOVING THE CHURCH.  The people of Schwarzenborn wanted their church moved back a little, so they all pushed at it.  One man grew too hot and took off his coat, placing it behind the church. Someone stole the coat.  The people thought they had pushed the church over it, and they congratulated one another on their success. (Ranke)

Coggeshall Jobs: Moving the Church. Briggs, *DBF,* pt. A, v. 2, p. 43.
Men of Belmont Move Their Church, The. Clouston, *Book of Noodles,* p. 55.
Moving the Church. Ranke, *Folktales of Germany,* no. 74.
There's Bigger Fools Than Tildy. Randolph, *The Devil's Pretty Daughter,* p.

## 1327  EMPTYING A BAG OF MEAL.  A fool overheard two men debating, and to demonstrate the emptiness of their arguments, he emptied the bag of meal he was carrying into the river.

Wise Men of Gotham: Of Buying Sheep. Briggs, *DBF,* pt. A, v. 2, p. 350.
Wise Men of Gotham: Of Buying Sheep. Jacobs, *More English Fairy Tales,* p.

**1328A\*    THE OVERSALTED SOUP.** "Don't forget to salt the soup,"
said a woman; then everyone in the household put salt in the soup.

Well-Salted Soup, The. Pourrat, *Treasury of French Tales,* p. 16.

**1333    THE SHEPHERD WHO CRIED "WOLF!" TOO OFTEN.** A
shepherd shouted that a wolf was in his flock, and the townspeople
ran to his aid, only to discover that it was a joke. Later a wolf did
attack his sheep; the shepherd again cried for help, but this time no
one believed him.

Crying Wolf Too Often. Handford, *Aesop,* no. 196.
Shepherd's Boy, The. Jacobs, *Aesop,* no. 43.

**1334    THE LOCAL MOON.** A fool away from home greeted the moon
in surprise, for he thought it was from his home town. (Briggs, "The
Slibburn Müne")

Cannings Vawk and the Comet. Briggs, *DBF,* pt. A, v. 2, p. 31.
Slibburn Müne, The. Briggs, *DBF,* pt. A, v. 2, p. 278.
Sun and the Moon, The. Pourrat, *Treasury of French Tales,* p. 6.

**1335    THE EATEN MOON.** A man watched the moon's reflection in
the pond where his horse was drinking. The moon disappeared
behind a cloud, and the man thought his horse had eaten it, so he cut
the beast open to recover the moon. (Briggs, "The Eaten Moon")

Eaten Moon, The. Briggs, *DBF,* pt. A, v. 2, p. 67.
Old Moon Broken Up into Stars, The. Briggs, *DBF,* pt. A, v. 2, p. 210.
Three Sillies, The. Roberts, *South from Hell,* no. 58.

**1335A    RESCUING THE MOON.** Fools try to pull the moon from a
pond.

Coggeshall Jobs (II). Briggs, *DBF,* pt. A, v. 2, p. 43.
Darlaston Geese. Briggs, *DBF,* pt. A, v. 2, p. 55.
Gorran Men Attempt to Trap the Moon in a Bucket, The. Deane and Shaw,
    *Folklore of Cornwall,* p. 139.
Khoja Pulls the Moon from the Well, The. Clouston, *Book of Noodles,* p. 92.
Moon in the Mill-Pond, The. Harris, *Nights with Uncle Remus,* no. 19.
Three Sillies, The. Jacobs, *English Fairy Tales,* p. 9.
Wise Men of Gotham (III). Briggs, *DBF,* pt. A, v. 2, p. 360.

**1335\*    FOOLS MISTAKE THE SETTING SUN FOR A CAMP-
FIRE.**

Brother Rabbit Gets the Provisions. Harris, *Nights with Uncle Remus,* no. 39.
Why Brother Fox's Legs Are Black. Harris, *Uncle Remus and His Friends,*

## 1336  FOOLS MISTAKE THE MOON FOR A CHEESE.

Buried Moon, The. Jacobs, *More English Fairy Tales*, p. 110.
Elbington Man Fishes for Cheese, An. Briggs, *Folklore of the Cotswolds*, p.
Moon in the Horsepond, The. Briggs, *DBF*, pt. A, v. 2, p. 192.
Moon in the Well, The. Briggs, *DBF*, pt. A, v. 2, p. 193.
People of Piddinghoe Fish for the Moon, The. Simpson, *Folklore of Sussex*,
Wiltshire Moonraker, The. Whitlock, *Folklore of Wiltshire*, p. 178.

## 1336A  A WOMAN DOES NOT RECOGNIZE HER OWN REFLECTION. A woman found a mirror among her husband's things and thought it was a photograph of his lover. She took some satisfaction in the fact that she was a "bloomin' old geyser." (Briggs, "The Farmer and His Wife and the Mirror") CF. type 1284.

Farmer and His Wife and the Mirror, The. Briggs, *DBF*, pt. A, v. 2, p. 84.
First Mirror, The. Glassie, *Irish Folktales*, no. 27.
Looking Glass, The. Dorson, *Buying the Wind*, p. 81.
Mirror, The (China). Clarkson and Cross, *World Folktales*, no. 63.
Mister Fox and the Deceitful Frogs. Harris, *Uncle Remus*, no. 14.

## 1339  FOOLS EATING UNFAMILIAR FOOD.

Bahlul and the Sweetmeats. Bushnaq, *Arab Folktales*, p. 276.
First Banana, The. Briggs, *DBF*, pt. A, v. 2, p. 87.

## 1339D  FOOLS EAT A WHOLE PORTION OF PEPPER.

Irishmen and the Red Pepper. Roberts, *South from Hell*, no. 42.

## 1342  HOT AND COLD WITH THE SAME BREATH. A satyr watched a man warm his hands with his breath. When the same man later cooled his steaming porridge by blowing on it, the satyr grew afraid, not wanting to be around a person who could blow hot and cold with the same breath.

Man and the Satyr, The. Jacobs, *Aesop*, no. 56.

## 1345*  STORIES DEPENDING ON PUNS. Example: Silk is a good name for a soldier, because silk can never be worsted. (Briggs, "Captain Silk")

Captain Silk. Briggs, *DBF*, pt. A, v. 2, p. 32.
Messer Paolo Marchese. Storer, *Facetiae of Poggio*, no. 25.

## 1347  FOOLS CHOOSE A LIVING CRUCIFIX. A sculptor taking an order for a crucifix from some simple peasants jokingly asked if they wanted a dead one or a living one. They decided upon a living one, reasoning that if their fellow villagers preferred a dead statue, they could easily kill it.

Some Peasants Who Bought a Crucifix. Storer, *Facetiae of Poggio,* no. 24.

**1347\* THE STATUE'S FATHER.** A man prayed before a statue in church. Later the priest replaced the statue with a smaller image, and when the man returned, he thought the new statue was the larger one's son. Cf. type 1476A.

Big Christ and the Little Christ, The. Paredes, *Folktales of Mexico,* no. 69.

**1349\* FOOLS.** —Miscellaneous tales.

Coat o' Clay. Jacobs, *More English Fairy Tales,* p. 82.
Irishman Who Bought a Mule. Roberts, *South from Hell,* no. 53.
Irishmen and the Hornet's Nest. Roberts, *South from Hell,* no. 45.
Ivanushko the Little Fool. Afanasyev, *Russian Fairy Tales,* p. 62.
Lancashire Follies. Briggs, *DBF,* pt. A, v. 2, p. 147.
Lazy Irishman, The. Roberts, *South from Hell,* no. 54.
Man Who Put Up Such a Good Defence, The. Pourrat, *French Tales,* p. 9.

**1349D\* TRICKING SOMEONE INTO HITTING A ROCK.** A Yankee held his hand above a rock. He asked an Irishman to hit it, then moved his hand, and the Irishman hit the rock. The Irishman tried the same trick, but he held his hand in front of his face, instead of over a rock, and his intended victim knocked him down.

Irishman Shows Pat a Yankee Trick. Dorson, *Buying the Wind,* p. 93.

**1350 A MAN FEIGNS DEATH TO TEST HIS WIFE.** A man pretended to be dead, and just as he suspected, within a short time his wife invited a young man into her bedroom. The "corpse" jumped from his resting place and attacked the couple with a stick. (Glassie) Cf. types 65, 1510.

Loving Wife, The. Briggs, *DBF,* pt. A, v. 2, p. 168.
Shadow of the Glen, The. Glassie, *Irish Folktales,* no. 25.

**1351 THE SILENCE WAGER.** A husband and wife argued as to which one should return a borrowed kettle. They settled the matter with a silence wager; the first one to speak would return the kettle. Days later the king came to their door and requested a light for his lantern. When the couple answered with silent gestures, the king thought they were mad and ordered them taken away. Then the man broke the silence, saying: "I'll return the kettle!" (Massignon)

Barring the Door (numerous variants). Clouston, *Book of Noodles,* pp. 107, He Who Speaks First. Massignon, *Folktales of France,* no. 59.
Jamming Pan, The. Briggs, *DBF,* pt. A, v. 2, p. 137.
Silence Wager, The. Briggs and Tongue, *Folktales of England,* no. 74.
Silent Couple, The. Clouston, *Popular Tales,* v. 2, p. 15.
Wager, The. Crane, *Italian Popular Tales,* no. 95.

**1352A  A PARROT'S TALES PREVENT AN ADULTERY.** A merchant gave his wife a parrot, and its tales so captured the woman's interest that they kept her from entertaining would-be lovers during her husband's absences. Cf. types 237, 243, 1422.

> Merchant, His Wife, and His Parrot, The. Clouston, *Popular Tales,* v. 2, p.
> Parrot, The (3 versions). Crane, *Italian Popular Tales,* nos. 45-47.
> Parrot, The. Calvino, *Italian Folktales,* no. 15.

**1353  THE OLD WOMAN AS THE DEVIL'S HELPER.** An old woman, promised a pair of shoes by the devil if she could bring discord to a happily married couple, told the wife that she could increase her husband's love by cutting a few hairs from his chin. She then told the husband that his wife was plotting to cut his throat while he slept. The man pretended to sleep. Seeing his wife silently approaching with a razor, he struck her dead with a stick. (Ranke) Cf. type 1378.

> Old Woman Sows Discord, An. Ranke, *Folktales of Germany,* no. 66.
> With Her Godmother to Josefsdal. Lindow, *Swedish Legends and Folktales,*

**1354  THE ANGEL OF DEATH AND THE MARRIED COUPLE.** A man near death asked his wife to put on her most beautiful dress and sit near him. She protested that this would be inappropriate, upon which he confessed his hope that the angel of death would take the beautiful woman instead of him.

> Stories from Nasreddin Hodja (Turkey). Bødker, *European Folk Tales,* p.

**1355A  THE LORD ABOVE AND THE LORD BELOW.** A woman hid one lover in the canopy of her bed and another one beneath her bed. Her husband came to her and proclaimed his wish for another child, saying: "The Lord above will provide." The man in the canopy responded: "Why not the lord below?"

> The Lord Above Will Provide. Legman, *Rationale of the Dirty Joke,* vol. 1, p.

**1355B  A FARMER SEEKS HIS LOST CALF AMONG LOVERS.** Two lovers were sporting beneath a tree that a farmer had climbed hoping to spot a lost calf. The man admired his partner's body, exclaiming: "What I can see!" "Do you see my calf?" interrupted the farmer. "I think I see its tail." (Legman)

> Calf, The. Legman, *Rationale of the Dirty Joke,* v. 1, p. 381.
> Speckle-Ass Bull, The. Randolph, *Pissing in the Snow,* no. 72.

**1355C  THE ONE ABOVE US WILL PROVIDE.** A deserter hid himself in a hayloft. Two lovers came into the barn and began to cuddle. "If we have a baby, who will take care of it?" asked the girl.

Her companion replied: "There is one above us who will provide for it." "No I won't!" shouted the soldier from his hiding place. The terrified lovers fled, abandoning their clothes.

Deserter, The. Afanasyev, *Russian Secret Tales,* p. 183.

## 1358A  A DEVIL JUMPS FROM A LOVER'S HIDING PLACE.
Lorenzo Dow observed how a woman, hearing her husband, had hid her lover under some flax remnants. Dow claimed to be able to conjure up the devil, and proved his point by setting fire to the flax. The lover, covered with flames, bolted from his hiding place and ran out the door. The husband maintained to his dying day that he had seen Satan himself. (Briggs) Cf. types 1535, 1725.

Hussar Stroke, A. Dégh, *Folktales of Hungary,* no. 14.
Lorenzo Dow and the Devil. Briggs, *DBF,* pt. A, v. 2, p. 157.

## 1358C  EXPOSING A FAITHLESS WIFE.
A farmhand observed his mistress with the man next door, and told the neighbor that the husband knew everything. He then told his master that the neighbor wanted to borrow an ax. Seeing the husband approaching with an ax, the frightened neighbor fled. Thus the man learned of his wife's faithlessness, and she gave her word never to stray again. (Asbjørnsen and Moe)

Clever Son and the Confused Lovers, The. Walker and Uysal, *Tales in Turkey, p. 153.*
Tom Totherhouse. Asbjørnsen and Moe, *East o' the Sun,* p. 411.

## 1359  OUTWITTING A FAITHLESS WIFE.
—Miscellaneous tales. Cf. types 1360C, 1380.

Cut Their Knockers Off! Randolph, *Pissing in the Snow,* no. 22.
Dimitrio Surprises His Wife Polissena with a Priest. Straparola, *Facetious Nights,* Night 1, Tale 5.
Lion the Color of Yellow Silk, A. Bushnaq, *Arab Folktales,* p. 338.
Simplicio Is Enamoured of Giliola, the Wife of a Peasant. Straparola, *Facetious Nights,* Night 2, Tale 5.
Thomas of Reading. Briggs, *DBF,* pt. B, v. 2, p. 370.

## 1359C  WOULD-BE LOVERS POSE AS NAKED STATUES.
A priest, a cantor, and a blacksmith, one after the other, came to a sculptor's wife hoping to seduce her. Upon undressing, each man heard a noise and hid in a cupboard. Her husband then returned with a woman who had ordered statues of three saints. He opened the cupboard; the customer was pleased with what she saw, except—she said—the statues were too realistic. The sculptor offered to remove the offending parts, and approached the cupboard with a knife. The "statues" suddenly came to life and fled. Cf. types 882A*, 1730.

Live Statues, The. Fowke, *Folklore of Canada,* p. 284.

**1360C  OLD HILDEBRAND.**  A peasant learned that his wife and a priest had conspired to be together during his absence. Hence he had a friend carry him, hidden in a basket, into his own house. From his hiding place he heard his wife and the priest celebrating their trickery with a merry song. He added his own verse before driving the priest out with blows. (Grimm)

> Husband and Wife. Afanasyev, *Russian Fairy Tales,* p. 369.
> Little Dickey Milburn. Briggs, *DBF,* pt. A, v. 2, p. 154.
> Little Dicky Whigburn. Legman, *Rationale of the Dirty Joke,* vol. 1, p. 770.
> Neighbour, The. Basile, *Pentamerone,* Day 2, Tale 10.
> Old Hildebrand. Grimm, *Tales,* no. 95.
> Piety in Excess. Walker and Uysal, *Tales in Turkey,* p. 212.
> Song of the Thief (Poland). Dorson, *Folktales around the World,* p. 107.
> Untrue Wife's Song, The (2 variants). Dorson, *Buying the Wind,* p. 209.

**1361  THREE LOVERS AND A HOT KISS.**  A woman hid one lover in a trunk in order to take a second one into her bed. Meanwhile, a third lover, a blacksmith, clamored at her window for a kiss, and as a joke she presented him with her bare bottom. Recognizing her trick and seeking revenge, the blacksmith returned with a heated iron and called out for another kiss.  This time the man from the bed presented his behind, and the blacksmith applied the hot iron. The burned man shouted "fire!" and the man in the trunk, afraid that the house was ablaze, called for help. The noise soon roused the entire neighborhood. (Randolph)

> Miller's Tale, The. Chaucer, *Canterbury Tales,* p. 105.
> Pope and His Man, The (2 versions). Afanasyev, *Russian Secret Tales,* p.
> Priest and His Hired Hand, The. Afanasyev, *Erotic Tales,* p. 49.
> Three Lovers, The. Dorson, *Buying the Wind,* p. 427.
> Tote Out the Big Trunk. Randolph, *Sticks in the Knapsack,* p. 99.

**1362  THE SNOW CHILD.**  A soldier returned home after an absence of seven years and learned that his wife now had a two-year-old son. She explained that she had conceived from snow that had fallen on her. The man accepted her story, but one day he took the boy away and returned without him. As he explained to his wife, the two had gone for a walk in the hot sun, and the boy had simply melted away. (Musick)

> Snow Boy, The. Musick, *Green Hills of Magic,* no. 61.
> Twelve-Months' Child, A. Storer, *Facetiae of Poggio,* no. 55.
> Woman Whose Husband Went to Mecca, The. Bushnaq, *Arab Folktales,* p.

**1363  LODGERS SLEEP WITH THE HOST'S WIFE AND DAUGHTER.**  In part by design and in part by accident, a man, his wife, their daughter, and two lodgers repeatedly exchange bed partners as the night progresses. Cf. type 1544.

Father, Daughter, and Boyfriend. Legman, *Rationale of the Dirty Joke,* vol. 1, Jenkins Boys, The. Randolph, *Who Blowed Up the Church House?,* p. 29.
Miller of Abingdon, The. Briggs, *DBF,* pt. A, v. 2, p. 442.
Mush for Supper. Roberts, *South from Hell,* p. 255.
Reeve's Tale, The. Chaucer, *Canterbury Tales,* p. 125.
Two Guests Sleep with the Host's Wife and Daughter. Boccaccio, *Decameron,* Day 9, Tale 6.

### 1365  THE OBSTINATE WIFE. —Miscellaneous tales.

When Twice as Many Is Half the Trouble. Bushnaq, *Arab Folktales,* p. 332.
Woman's Way. Afanasyev, *Russian Fairy Tales,* p. 599.

### 1365A  SEEKING A CONTRARY WIFE UPSTREAM. A man's wife fell into a river, and he sought her upstream, explaining to the incredulous onlookers that she was too contrary to drift with the current. *(1001 Nights)*

Contrary Wife, The. Briggs and Tongue, *Folktales of England,* no. 75.
Contrary Wife, The. Briggs, *DBF,* pt. A, v. 2, p. 47.
Goha Seeks His Wife Upstream. Mathers, *1001 Nights,* v. 4, p. 305.
How Madde Coomes, When His Wife Was Drowned, Sought Her against the Streame. Briggs, *DBF,* pt. A, v. 2, p. 122.
Man Who Sought for His Wife Drowned in a Stream, A. Storer, *Facetiae of Poggio,* no. 62.
Old Woman against the Stream, The. Asbjørnsen and Moe, *Norwegian Folktales,* p. 112.
Parcel, The. Porter, *Folklore of East Anglia,* p. 165.
Pig-Headed Wife, The (Finland). Booss, *Scandinavian Tales,* p. 579.
Pig-Headed Wife, The (Finland). Clarkson and Cross, *World Folktales,* no.
Pig-Headed Wife, The (Finland). Cole, *Best-Loved Folktales,* no. 87.
Scissors. Jacobs, *European Folk and Fairy Tales,* no. 4.
She Floated Upstream. Randolph, *Hot Springs and Hell,* no. 62.

### 1365B  KNIFE OR SCISSORS? A man and his wife had an argument about how something had been cut. He insisted it had been done with a knife, while she maintained it had been cut with scissors. Their argument intensified, and he finally pushed her into a pond, shouting "knife!" as she sunk. He thought this would be the last word, but as the woman disappeared, she reached two fingers above the water and made the sign of a pair of scissors. (Briggs)

Knife or Scissors. Briggs, *DBF,* pt. A, v. 2, p. 144.
Knife or Scissors. Briggs and Tongue, *Folktales of England,* no. 76.
Old Woman Who Was Always Saying "Scissors." Dorson, *Buying the Wind,* Obstinate Wife. Fowke, *Folklore of Canada,* p. 188.
Scissors They Were. Crane, *Italian Popular Tales,* no. 96.
Scissors! El-Shamy, *Folktales of Egypt,* no. 57.
Scissors. Jacobs, *European Folk and Fairy Tales,* no. 4.
Stubborn Wife, The. *Afanasyev, Russian Fairy Tales,* p. 280.

Stubborn Wife, The. Legman, *Rationale of the Dirty Joke,* vol. 1, p. 186.
Wasn't She Spunky?. Dorson, *Jonathan Draws the Long Bow,* p. 230.

**1365C   THE WOMAN WHO CALLED HER HUSBAND LOUSY.** A woman called her husband a lousy rascal, and he responded with blows. He beat her until she could not talk, but she still got the last word by pretending to crack a louse between her thumbnails. (Dorson)

Quarrelsome Couple. Dorson, *Negro Tales,* p. 275.
Woman Who Insisted on Calling Her Husband Lousy, A. Storer, *Facetiae of Poggio,* no. 61.

**1365J\*   ASKING BY OPPOSITES.** A man learned to deal with his obstinate wife by asking her to do the opposite of what he actually wanted. Thus while wanting to oppose him, she did his will.

Bad Wife, The. Afanasyev, *Russian Fairy Tales,* p. 56.

**1366A\*   A HORSE FOR A HUSBAND WHO RULES HIS HOUSE.** A man set forth to find a husband who was in command, taking with him two horses, one black and one white, and twenty-five hens. The horses were to be gifts for husbands in charge; the hens were for wives who ruled. Soon all but one of the hens had been given away, but the horses were still unclaimed. Finally he found a husband who seemed to be in command, and he offered him a horse. He selected the white one. As the giver turned to leave, the man's wife said: "Take the black one instead!" Accordingly, the husband asked for an exchange, but in return for the white horse he received only a hen. (Dorson) Cf. type 1375.

Grey Mare Is the Better Horse, The (I, II). Briggs, *DBF,* pt. A, v. 2, p. 110.
Looking for a Man Boss. Dorson, *Buying the Wind,* p. 82.

**1370   THE LAZY WIFE.** —Miscellaneous tales. Example: A farmer attempted to rouse his lazy wife one morning by shouting "Fire!" "Where?" responded the woman, startled from her sleep. "In everyone's house but ours," answered the husband. (Briggs and Tongue)

Lazy Wife, The (I, II). Briggs, *DBF,* pt. A, v. 2, p. 152.
Lazy Wife, The. Briggs and Tongue, *Folktales of England,* no. 79.

**1372   PRESCRIBING BLOWS.** A man attempted to describe his wife's illness to the druggist. The latter lost his patience and slapped the man twice, saying "Give her two of these." The customer later returned and delivered a blow to the druggist. "One was enough," he explained. Cf. type 1557.

Lapatossu and the Druggist. Dorson, *Bloodstoppers and Bearwalkers*, p. 149.

**1372\* PRESCRIBING GOOD FOOD.** Anancy pretended to have a sickness that could be cured only by eating an entire goat. Thus he was able to have a feast without sharing with his wife.

Bone Sweet, The. Dance, *Folklore from Contemporary Jamaicans*, no. 14A.

**1373 WEIGHING THE CAT.** Goha bought a large piece of mutton for dinner, but his wife ate it, blaming the cat. Goha put the cat on the scales, and finding that it weighed less than the missing meat, caught his wife in her lie. *(1001 Nights)*

Djuha's Meat Disappears. Bushnaq, *Arab Folktales*, p. 255.
Goha Weighs the Cat. Mathers, *1001 Nights*, v. 4, p. 298.

**1375 THE SEARCH FOR A HUSBAND WHO CAN RULE.** A gentleman offered a pair of new boots to any husband who was not afraid of his wife. A peasant claimed the prize, but refused the gentleman's offer of boot grease to go with them. It might, he explained, stain his shirt, and that would irk his wife. Upon hearing this, the gentleman took back the boots. (Storer) Cf. type 1366A\*.

Abu Nuwas and the Caliph's Queen. Bushnaq, *Arab Folktales*, p. 274.
Henpecked Husband, The. Briggs, *DBF*, pt. A, v. 2, p. 115.
Husbands and Wives. Storer, *Facetiae of Poggio*, no. 141.

**1376A\* A HUSBAND WEANS HIS WIFE FROM STORIES.** An innkeeper's wife would accept only those guests who could tell stories, and he sought to break her of this practice. One night they took in an old man who agreed to tell stories the whole night, but only on the condition that he not be interrupted. The woman agreed, and the old man began: "An owl flew into a garden, sat on a tree trunk, and drank some water." He repeated this one sentence over and over again, until finally the woman interrupted. She had broken her promise, and her husband beat her so hard that from that time on she never wanted to hear another story. (Afanasyev) —Note: For additional accounts of endlessly repeating stories see types 227, 1199B, 2013, 2300, 2320. For additional stories of women "corrected" by beating see types 564, 670, 903A\*, 910A.

Cúchulainn and the Smith's Wife. O'Sullivan, *Folktales of Ireland*, no. 16.
How a Husband Weaned His Wife from Fairy Tales. Afanasyev, *Russian Fairy Tales*, p. 308.

**1377 AN ADULTERESS LOCKS HER HUSBAND OUT.** A woman, thinking her husband was too drunk to miss her, visited her lover. But her husband did notice her absence, and he locked her out. When her pleas to open the door went unanswered, she threatened to jump into the well. Her husband came to rescue her, and she slipped inside and locked him out. He raised a din, and the neighbors demanded an explanation. The woman, with a great show of piety, claimed that she had locked him out to cure him of his drunkenness.

Tofano Locks His Wife Out . Boccaccio, *Decameron,* Day 7, Tale 4.

**1378  A PRESENT FOR A MISTRESS.** An old woman entered a wager with the devil that she was his equal in causing discord. To prove her wiliness she purchased a piece of distinctive cloth from a merchant, claiming that it was her son's gift for his mistress. She then went to the merchant's house and asked his wife if she might enter and say her prayers. Before leaving she hid the cloth in the clothes basket, where the husband found it. Concluding that his wife was the mistress mentioned by the old woman, he beat her and sent her back to her parents. The devil had to concede that the old woman was his equal. Cf. type 1353.

Old Woman and the Devil, The. Bushnaq, *Arab Folktales,* p. 359.

**1378B\*  A WIFE'S TEMPORARY REIGN.** An ambitious woman asked the village council to elect her mayor, which they did. She ruled, drank with the peasants, and took bribes. However, she had not yet collected the poll tax when a Cossack came for it, so he gave her a good thrashing. Now she no longer wanted to be mayor, and resigned herself to being an obedient wife.

Mayoress, The. Afanasyev, *Russian Fairy Tales,* p. 141.

**1379  A WIFE TAKES THE PLACE OF HER HUSBAND'S LOVER.** A man asked a maid in his household for certain favors, and she finally agreed. Before the rendezvous she reported the matter to her mistress. At the appointed time the wife herself went to the dark meeting place, and thus the husband had an affair with his own wife. Cf. type 891.

English Dyer Who Had an Adventure with His Wife, An. Storer, *Facetiae of Poggio,* no. 116.

**1379\*  FALSE PARTS.** A newly married woman got ready for bed by taking off a wig, a glass eye, and a wooden leg. The startled husband responded by asking her to throw him the part he was most interested in. (Randolph)

Better End, The. Randolph, *Pissing in the Snow,* no. 38.
Man Who Came Apart, The. Fisher, *Idaho Lore,* p. 121.

**1380  A FAITHLESS WIFE WISHES HER HUSBAND BLIND.** An old peasant discovered that his young wife was receiving secret visits from a young man. To avenge himself, he disguised himself as a hermit and told his wife he would grant her a wish. She wished that her husband would go blind, and he accordingly feigned blindness. The lover soon came to visit, and the old man killed him, making it look like he had choked on his food. Cf. types 1359, 1405, 1462, 1575.

False Old Mawkin, The. Briggs, *DBF*, pt. A, v. 2, p. 78.
Nicholas the Hermit (2 versions). Afanasyev, *Russian Secret Tales*, p. 218.

**1381  A MAN DISCREDITS HIS TALKATIVE WIFE.**  A poor peasant found a buried treasure while plowing. Before telling his wife, he bought a hare, which he threw into a tree, and a fish, which he hung on a bush. At the time he showed his wife the treasure, he also "discovered" the fish in the bush and the hare in the tree. She told the neighbors about the treasure and soon thereafter was summoned to court. The talkative woman explained that she and her husband had found the treasure the same day they had caught a fish in a bush and a hare in a tree. The magistrate concluded that she had lost her wits and dismissed the case. (Dégh)

Chatterbox, The. Megas, *Folktales of Greece*, no. 62.
How a Fish Swam in the Air and a Hare in the Water. Lang, *Violet Fairy*
Indiscreet Wife, The. Afanasyev, *Russian Fairy Tales*, p. 226.
Stroke of Luck, A (Hungary). Cole, *Best-Loved Folktales*, no. 102.
Stroke of Luck, A. Dégh, *Folktales of Hungary*, no. 13.

**1381B  A MOTHER PROTECTS HER HALF-WITTED SON.**  A half-witted boy stole some planks from a wrecked ship. His mother knew that if questioned he would admit to the crime, so while he slept she sprinkled porridge in the doorway. When he awoke, she told him that during the night it had rained porridge. When the officials asked him about the wood, he admitted the theft, on the night that it rained porridge. Upon hearing this, the officials dismissed him. Cf. type 1600.

Bahlul and the Owl. Bushnaq, *Arab Folktales*, p. 278.
Cook, the Policeman, and the Parrot, The. Briggs, *DBF*, pt. A, v. 2, p. 229.
Half Booby and the Shower of Milk Porridge. Campbell, *West Highlands*, v. 2, p. 400.
Silly Jack and the Factor. Briggs, *DBF*, pt. A, v. 2, p. 265.

**1381C  A WIFE TALKS ABOUT HER HUSBAND'S CRIME.**  To test his wife's ability to keep a secret, a man killed a goat and buried its body, then told his wife he had murdered a man. The woman told a friend, who in turn told someone else, and soon the whole town knew. The police came to investigate, but found only a goat in the grave. (Espinosa) Cf. type 893.

Murdered Packman, The. Pourrat, *Treasury of French Tales,* p. 77.
Story of the Goat, The. Espinosa, *Folklore of Spain in the American Southwest,* p. 179.

## 1381D  A WIFE EMBELLISHES HER HUSBAND'S SECRET.
Ivan, to test his wife's ability to keep a secret, told her that in the privy a crow had flown from his behind. The woman immediately told a neighbor the secret, but said it had been two crows. This neighbor told another woman, raising the number of crows to three. And so it went, until one day a man asked Ivan: "Is it true that twelve crows flew from your behind?"

Talkative Wife, The. Afanasyev, *Russian Secret Tales,* p. 188.

## 1381E  A MAN FINDS A PURSE AND STARTS SCHOOL.
An old man found found a purse filled with money. No longer poor, he decided he should learn to read, and he started school. Some time later a gentleman came by and asked if anyone had found a purse. The old man replied that he had found a purse, but it had been before he started school. The gentleman answered: "That was before I was born," and rode off cursing the old man's impudence. (Briggs, "The Portmantle")

John and Sally. Briggs, *DBF,* pt. A, v. 2, p. 140.
Old Roadman, The. Briggs, *DBF,* pt. A, v. 2, p. 210.
Portmantle, The. Briggs, *DBF,* pt. A, v. 2, p. 238.

## 1383  A WOMAN DOES NOT KNOW HERSELF.
Elsie went to cut grain, but instead of working, she lay down to nap. When she did not return home, her husband found her in the field still asleep. To teach her a lesson, he covered her with a net sewn with bells. When she finally awoke, the bells confused her, and she wondered who she was. Arriving at home, she knocked at a window and asked if Elsie were inside. "Yes, she is here," answered the husband. "Oh, God!," she replied, "then I'm not me!" With that she ran out of the village, never to return. (Grimm, "Clever Elsie") Cf. type 1284.

Clever Elsie. Grimm, *Tales,* no. 34.
Freddy and Katy Lizzy. Grimm, *Tales,* no. 59.
Giske. Christiansen, *Folktales of Norway,* p. 164.
Goosey Grizzel. Asbjørnsen and Moe, *East o' the Sun,* p. 221.
Lawkamercyme. Briggs, *DBF,* pt. A, v. 2, p. 539.
Lawkamercyme. Jacobs, *More English Fairy Tales,* p. 65.
Not a Pin to Choose between Them. Asbjørnsen and Moe, *East o' the Sun,* p.
Sam and Sooky. Chase, *Grandfather Tales,* no. 17.
Sean na Scuab. O'Sullivan, *Folktales of Ireland,* no. 52.

## 1384  A MAN SEEKS SOMEONE AS STUPID AS HIS WIFE.
A man left his wife in charge of selling three cows to a cattle dealer, with the warning that he would color her black and blue if she

behaved stupidly. In spite of his warning, she lost the cows to a swindler (cf. type 1385). The husband returned, but instead of delivering the promised beating at once, he told her he would spare her if in three days he could find someone as stupid as she. —Continues as type 1540. (Grimm, no. 104) Note: Type 1384 tales typically include several episodes about fools, especially types 1245, 1286, 1326, 1385, 1387, 1450, 1540, 1653.

Amari Seeks a Bigger Fool Than His Wife. Arewa, *Northern East Africa*, p.
Bastianelo (Italy). Clarkson and Cross, *World Folktales*, no. 62.
Bastianelo. Crane, *Italian Popular Tales*, no. 93.
Believing Husbands, The (Scotland). Lang, *Lilac Fairy Book*, p. 332.
Cicco Petrillo. Calvino, *Italian Folktales*, no. 105.
Clever Elsie and Her Companions (Italy). Thompson, *100 Folktales*, no. 88.
Clever People, The. Grimm, *Tales*, no. 104.
Great Need, The. Dorson, *Buying the Wind*, p. 132.
Half Booby and the Shower of Milk Porridge. Campbell, *West Highlands*, v. 2, p. 400.
Hamdullah, Nisan, and Iyyar. Sabar, *Folk Literature of the Kurdistani Jews*,
Lad 'At Went Oot to Look for Fools, Th'. Briggs, *DBF*, pt. A, v. 2, p. 144.
Lutoniushka. Afanasyev, *Russian Fairy Tales*, p. 336.
Not a Pin to Choose between Them. Asbjørnsen and Moe, *East o' the Sun*, p.
Old Bachelor, The. Saucier, *French Louisiana*, no. 27.
Simple-Minded Jeanne. Delarue, *French Folktales*, p. 347.
Six Sillies, The. Lang, *Red Fairy Book*, p. 186.
Some Wives Are That Way. Christiansen, *Folktales of Norway*, p. 208.
There's Bigger Fools Than Tildy. Randolph, *The Devil's Pretty Daughter*, p.
Three More Bigger Fools. Dorson, *Negro Tales*, p. 101.
Three Noodles, or: The Heavens Might Have Fallen. Briggs, *DBF*, pt. A, v.
Three Sillies, The. Jacobs, *English Fairy Tales*, p. 9.
Three Sillies, The. Roberts, *South from Hell*, no. 58.
Three Sillies. Briggs, *DBF*, pt. A, v. 2, p. 301.
Three Wise Men, The. Campbell, *West Highlands*, v. 2, p. 28.
Woman Called Rice Pudding, The. Bushnaq, *Arab Folktales*, p. 374.

**1385 A WOMAN ACCEPTS HER OWN COW AS SECURITY.** A woman sold three cows to a stranger. He claimed to have left his money at home, so he took only two of the cows, leaving the third one behind as a security deposit. He never returned. —Continues as type 1384. (Grimm) Cf. type 1541.

Clever People, The. Grimm, *Tales*, no. 104.
Ninety-Nine Hens and a Rooster. Megas, *Folktales of Greece*, no. 63.

**1385* A WOMAN LOSES HER HUSBAND'S MONEY.** A man had saved up a good number of gold coins. He told his wife that they were counters for games and hid them. Later some pedlars came by with clay pots for sale. She gave them the yellow counters for their pots. (Grimm) Cf. type 1541.

Freddy and Katy Lizzy. Grimm, *Tales*, no. 59.
Shining Fish. Calvino, *Italian Folktales*, no. 118.

**1386 FEEDING THE CABBAGE.** To make her cabbage grow, a woman placed pieces of fat on the plants in the garden, but a dog ate all the fat. —Continues as type 1387.

> Fattening Up the Cabbage. Carpenter, *A Latvian Storyteller,* p. 189.
> Presentneed, Bymeby, and Hereafter. Chase, *Grandfather Tales,* no. 16.

**1387 A WOMAN DRAWS BEER IN THE CELLAR.** Katy Lizzy was in the cellar drawing beer when she remembered that upstairs she had left sausages within reach of the dog. Leaving the tap open, she ran upstairs, but the dog had already made off with the sausages. Returning to the cellar she discovered that the beer had run out over everything. To prevent her husband from noticing the spilled beer, she emptied a sack of flour onto the floor. —Continues as types 1653A, 1383, 1791. (Grimm) Cf. type 1408.

> Fattening Up the Cabbage. Carpenter, *A Latvian Storyteller,* p. 189.
> Freddy and Katy Lizzy. Grimm, *Tales,* no. 59.

**1387A A FOOLISH WIFE THROWS THINGS AWAY.** A woman became angry with the dishes in her cupboard for rattling when she walked across the floor, so she threw them out the window. Later, she told the fish she was cleaning to stop looking at her. When they refused to close their eyes, she threw them down the well.

> Foolish Woman, The. Harris, *Daddy Jake,* no. 11.

**1405 THE LAZY SPINNING WOMAN.** A lazy woman claimed that she could not spin, for she had no reel for the yarn. Her husband agreed to make a reel and went into the forest to cut a piece of wood. She ran ahead and hid herself in a thicket. When he approached, she called out: "He who cuts wood for reels shall die." Alarmed, the husband returned home with no wood, and the woman continued her evil ways. (Grimm) Cf. types 1380, 1462, 1575.

> Lazy Spinning Woman, The. Grimm, *Tales,* no. 128.
> Lazy Woman, The. Ranke, *Folktales of Germany,* no. 50.
> Sam and Sooky. Chase, *Grandfather Tales,* no. 17.

**1406 THE MERRY WIVES' WAGER.** Two women argued as to which one's husband was the greater fool. The first, to prove her point, pretended to spin thread that was too fine to be seen. Her husband believed her story and put on the clothes she thus made. The second woman convinced her husband that he had died. He lay quietly in his coffin until his naked friend came by, at which he cried out: "I should laugh, if I were not dead." Thus it came out how the women had tricked their husbands, and for their part they received a public whipping. (Clarkson and Cross) Cf. type 1620.

Believing Husbands, The (Scotland). Lang, *Lilac Fairy Book*, p. 332.
Gown in the Bathhouse, The. Bushnaq, *Arab Folktales*, p. 334.
Merry Wives, The (Denmark). Lang, *Pink Fairy Book*, p. 297.
Now I Should Laugh, If I Were Not Dead (Iceland). Clarkson and Cross, *World Folktales*, no. 65.
Sgire Mo Chealag. Campbell, *West Highlands*, v. 2, p. 388.
Stupid Men and Shrewish Wives. Christiansen, *Folktales of Norway*, p. 206.
Two Husbands, The. Noy, *Folktales of Israel*, no. 69.
Two Old Women's Bet, The (USA). Cole, *Best-Loved Folktales*, no. 175.
Two Old Women's Bet. Chase, *Grandfather Tales*, no. 18.
Which Was the Foolishest? (Iceland). Lang, *Brown Fairy Book*, p. 270.

**1407    A MISER SUSPECTS HIS WIFE OF EATING TOO MUCH.**
A miser suspected his wife of eating too much and spied on her from the chimney, but she built a fire and nearly suffocated him. Later he hid himself in a feather bed to see what she ate, and she beat the bed with a stick. Last he hid himself in an empty barrel, and she poured boiling lye in the barrel, scalding him terribly. —Continues as type 1407A. (Booss)

All I Possess! (Sweden). Booss, *Scandinavian Tales*, p. 221.
Father of Farts, The. Mathers, *1001 Nights*, v. 3, p. 523.

**1407A    A MISER GIVES HIS WIFE EVERYTHING HE OWNS.**
A miser, near death, watched his wife preparing a lavish meal for herself and her guests. "All I possess!" he cried, bemoaning the loss of the food. His words were interpreted as his last will, and thus his wife inherited all his possessions. (Booss)

All I Possess! (Sweden). Booss, *Scandinavian Tales*, p. 221.
Seven Lamb Heads, The. Calvino, *Italian Folktales*, no. 170.
Wife Who Lived on Wind, The. Calvino, *Italian Folktales*, no. 156.

**1408    THE MAN WHO DID HIS WIFE'S WORK.** A man traded jobs with his wife for a day. He began with the churning, but soon went to the cellar for ale. He had just inserted the tap when he remember the unguarded churn; he ran upstairs, but the pig had already spilled the cream. Meanwhile, the ale ran onto the cellar floor. He refilled the churn. This time he strapped it to his back, intending to churn as he walked, but he bent over and spilled it. Then he led the cow across a plank to the cottage roof, where she could graze on the sod. To keep her from falling off, he lowered her rope down the chimney, tying the end to his own leg. But the cow fell from the roof, drawing the man up the chimney. His wife, returning from the field, saw the cow dangling from the roof and cut the rope. Inside, she found her husband stuck head-first in the porridge pot. (Asbjørnsen and Moe) Cf. type 1387.

Cow on the Roof, The (Wales). Clarkson and Cross, *World Folktales*, no. 8.

Cow on the Roof, The. Cole, *Best-Loved Folktales*, no. 68.
Husband Who Hatched Eggs, The. Afanasyev, *Russian Secret Tales*, p. 45.
Husband Who Was to Mind the House. Asbjørnsen and Moe, *East o' the Sun*,
Man Does a Woman's Work, A. Afanasyev, *Erotic Tales*, p. 79.
Old Man in a Wood, The. Briggs, *DBF*, pt. A, v. 2, p. 208.
Old Man Who Lived in a Wood, The. Briggs, *DBF*, pt. A, v. 2, p. 209.
Peasant Hatches Eggs, A. Afanasyev, *Erotic Tales*, p. 83.
Peasant Who Did His Wife's Work, The. Afanasyev, *Russian Secret Tales*, p.
Simple John and His Twelve Misfortunes. Briggs, *DBF*, pt. A, v. 2, p. 269.
Simple Simon's Misfortunes. Briggs, *DBF*, pt. A, v. 2, p. 270.
Too-Submissive Husband, The. Pourrat, *Treasury of French Tales*, p. 148.

**1408B   A WOMAN FILLS HER HUSBAND'S REQUESTS.** A man was looking for a reason to beat his wife, to show her who was the master of the house, but she always met his every request. One day he asked for fish, and she prepared it three ways. Just before dinner, the baby made a mess on the floor, and the mother covered it with a dish. At dinner time the husband asked for fried fish, and she brought him fried fish. He changed his mind, asking for baked fish, and she brought that. Then he demanded a casserole, and she had a casserole as well. Finally he said, in desperation: "I'd rather eat shit." At this the wife turned over the dish on the floor, saying: "Here it is!"

Reason to Beat Your Wife. El-Shamy, *Folktales of Egypt*, no. 56.

**1410   A HUSBAND AS HIS WIFE'S CONFESSOR.** A man suspected that his wife had a lover, so he disguised himself as a priest and heard her confession. She, recognizing her husband, confessed to being in love with a priest. The husband, determined to catch the culprit, stood watch at the front door, thus allowing his wife to admit her lover through another entrance. Later she told her husband that she had seen through his disguise, and that he himself was the priest whom she had named. The relieved husband now let down his guard, making it easier for the woman to receive her lover. (Boccaccio)

Jealous Husband Disguises Himself as a Priest. Boccaccio, *Decameron,* Day
Wife's Confession, The. Storer, *Facetiae of Poggio*, no. 45.

**1415   LUCKY HANS.** For seven years' work Hans received a piece of gold as big as his head. He traded the gold for a cow, the cow for a pig, the pig for a goose, and the goose for a stone. He accidentally dropped the stone down a well, but praised his luck, for he had grown weary from carrying it. (Grimm) Cf. types 170A, 1642, 1655

Barter. Afanasyev, *Russian Fairy Tales*, p. 338.
Gudbrand of the Hillside. Asbjørnsen and Moe, *Norwegian Folktales*, p. 178.
Gudbrand on the Hill-Side (Norway). Clarkson and Cross, *World Folktales*,
Gudbrand on the Hill-Side. Asbjørnsen and Moe, *East o' the Sun*, p. 149.

Gudbrand on the Hillside (Norway). Thompson, *100 Folktales,* no. 87.
Hans in Luck. Grimm, *Tales,* no. 83.
Hedley Kow, The. Jacobs, *More English Fairy Tales,* p. 55.
Jack's Wonderful Bargains. Briggs, *DBF,* pt. A, v. 2, p. 135.
Jean-Baptiste's Swaps. Delarue, *French Folktales,* p. 352.
Mister Vinegar. Briggs, *DBF,* pt. A, v. 2, p. 548.
Mister Vinegar. Jacobs, *English Fairy Tales,* p. 28.
Setting Down the Budget. Randolph, *The Devil's Pretty Daughter,* p. 20.
What Father Does Is Always Right. Andersen, *Complete Fairy Tales,* no. 106.

**1416    THE MOUSE IN THE SILVER DISH.** A master, in order to
test his servant's obedience, invited him to dinner. He told him to eat
everything he wanted, but warned him not to take the cover from one
particular silver dish. He then left the servant alone. Unable to control his curiosity, the guest peeked inside the forbidden dish. Out ran
a mouse, revealing his disobedience. (Jacobs)

Bob Appleford's Pig. Briggs, *DBF,* pt. A, v. 2, p. 24.
Clock, The. Briggs, *DBF,* pt. A, v. 2, p. 40.
Lost Paradise, A (France). Lang, *Lilac Fairy Book,* p. 62.
Poor People Who Wanted to Be Rich, The. Ranke, *Folktales of Germany,* no.
Son of Adam, A. Briggs, *DBF,* pt. A, v. 2, p. 279.
Son of Adam, A. Jacobs, *More English Fairy Tales,* p. 118.
That's None of Your Business. Briggs, *DBF,* pt. A, v. 2, p. 292.

**1417    THE WIFE WHO PUT ANOTHER WOMAN IN HER BED.**
A man discovered that his wife's lover was about to enter the house
and gave pursuit. During his absence, the wife had her maid take her
place in bed. When the husband returned from his unsuccessful
chase, he released his anger against the woman in his bed, beating her
and cutting off her hair. The next morning, the wife—with no sign
of bruises and with a full head of hair—accused her husband of
drunkenness. The maid received a handsome reward from her
mistress for the abuse that she had borne. (Boccaccio)

Monna Deceives Her Husband by Putting Another Woman in Her Bed.
Boccaccio, *Decameron,* Day 7, Tale 8.
Wise Men of Gotham, The (V). Briggs, *DBF,* pt. A, v. 2, p. 355.

**1418    THE OATH OF CHASTITY.** A woman had a lover who visited
her often. Her husband grew suspicious, and insisted that she swear
an oath of chastity at a certain holy place where anyone who swore
falsely would be struck by lightning. Her lover owned a stable, and
the woman and her husband rented a donkey from him for the
pilgrimage. The woman slipped from the donkey, and she fell to the
ground, with her skirts about her waist, revealing her nakedness to
the donkey driver. At the holy place she swore that no man had ever
seen her nakedness, save her own husband and the stable owner.
God, in his wisdom, accepted the oath. (Bushnaq)

Chain of Truth, The. Bushnaq, *Arab Folktales,* p. 348.
Erminione Accuses His Wife Filenia before a Tribunal. Straparola, *Facetious Nights,* Night 4, Tale 2.
The Ordeal. Gottfried von Strassburg, *Tristan,* ch. 23.
Tests of Chastity. Clouston, *Popular Tales,* v. 1, p. 168.

**1418\*** **A MAN OVERHEARS HIS WIFE'S CONFESSION.** A man hid under his daughter's bed on her wedding night and heard her confess to her husband that she had had other lovers. The groom angrily jumped out of bed, saying: "I'm heading for Texas!" The girl began to cry, and her mother came to comfort her. "You shouldn't have told him," the mother said. "I've never told your pappy about the men I used to run around with." With that the old man jumped from his hiding place under the bed and yelled: "I'm heading for Texas too!"

Heading for Texas. Randolph, *The Devil's Pretty Daughter,* p. 61.

**1419** **A WOMAN AND HER LOVER TRICK HER HUSBAND.** Thia, hearing her husband return, quickly hid her lover behind a door. Welcoming her husband, she told him of a charm she had learned during his absence that would keep the hawks from their chickens. He had only to cover his head while she recited a certain chant. The husband eagerly followed her directions, enabling the lover to escape unseen. (Straparola)

Little Ab and the Scalding Barrel. Randolph, *Who Blowed Up the Church House?,* p. 52.
Man Who Understood Women, The. Mathers, *1001 Nights,* v. 3, p. 543.
Marsilio Takes to Flight While Thia Works a Spell for Her Husband. Straparola, *Facetious Nights,* Night 5, Tale 4.
Shoemaker's Lesson, The. Porter, *Folklore of East Anglia,* p. 166.

**1419B** **A WOMAN SUBSTITUTES AN ANIMAL FOR HER CAPTURED LOVER.** A man locked his wife's lover in a chest. While the husband was making preparations to take the chest to the governor as proof of his wife's infidelity, she secretly released the prisoner and put a baby donkey in his place. Upon seeing the animal, the governor had the husband arrested, but his wife interceded on his behalf, claiming that his behavior had been the result of a seizure. (Bushnaq)

Gown in the Bathhouse, The. Bushnaq, *Arab Folktales,* p. 334.
Women's Mischief. Afanasyev, *Russian Secret Tales,* p. 239.

**1419C** **THE HUSBAND WITH ONE EYE.** A woman was

saying: "I dreamed that you can now see from this eye as well."
Meanwhile, her lover slipped out the door unseen. (Clouston)

Husband with One Eye, The. Clouston, *Popular Tales and Fictions,* v. 1, p.
Returning Husband, The. Briggs, *DBF,* pt. A, v. 2, p. 250.

### 1419D   TWO LOVERS PRETEND TO BE A MURDERER AND HIS FUGITIVE.
A woman had two lovers in her house when her husband returned unexpectedly. She instructed the one to rush from the house waving his dagger and shouting: "I'll kill him." She then told her husband that the other lover was a stranger whom she had hidden from a would-be murderer, and the husband congratulated her for her selfless and courageous act.

Isabella's Husband Returns Unexpectedly. Boccaccio, *Decameron,* Day 7,

### 1419G   THE PRIEST'S BREECHES.
A friar visited a certain woman to hear her confession. Her suspicious husband entered their room, only to discover that the friar had hurriedly departed, leaving his breeches behind. Enraged, the husband confronted the churchman. The latter explained that they were the breeches of Saint Francis, and that he had taken this relic to the woman's house to cure her. With great ceremony the breeches were brought back to the monastery and placed with other sacred relics. (Storer)

Abbess and the Priest's Breeches, The. Boccaccio, *Decameron,* Day 9, Tale 2.
How a Friar's Breeches Became Sacred Relics. Storer, *Facetiae of Poggio,* no.

### 1419H   A WOMAN WARNS HER LOVER WITH A SONG.
A woman's lover approached her window, thinking her husband was away. To warn him that her husband was with her, she sang her baby a lullaby that included the lines: "Begone, my love and my dear, thou canst not have a lodging here." (Briggs, "The Untrue Wife's Song")

Exorcism, The. Briggs, *DBF,* pt. A, v. 2, p. 74.
Gianni Hears Tapping at His Door in the Night. Boccaccio, *Decameron,* Day
No Use to Rattle the Blind. Randolph, *Pissing in the Snow,* no. 44.
Untrue Wife's Song, The. Briggs, *DBF,* pt. A, v. 2, p. 339.

### 1420C   BORROWING MONEY FROM A LOVER'S HUSBAND.
A man borrowed money from a friend, then used this money to buy love from the friend's wife. He told the friend he had repaid the loan to his wife, who—of course—could not reveal the circumstances under which she had received the funds. (Boccaccio)

Gulfardo Borrows Money to Pay for His Friend's Wife's Love. Boccaccio,
*Decameron,* Day 8, Tale 1.
Shipman's Tale, The. Chaucer, *Canterbury Tales,* p. 174.

**1420E BUYING LOVE WITH A FUR COAT.** Abu Nuwas gave a minister's wife his handsome fur coat in return for her favors. Upon leaving her house he dropped a cup onto the steps. Then he began to cry and moan that his coat had been confiscated because he had broken a cup. The minister's wife, unwilling to reveal the actual circumstances, quickly returned the coat.

Abu Nuwas and the Fur Cloak. Bushnaq, *Arab Folktales,* p. 273.

**1422 THE PARROT AND THE ADULTEROUS WOMAN.** A parrot revealed his mistress's adulterous behavior. The husband thought it was lying and killed it, but later he learned the truth of the parrot's story. Cf. types 237, 243, 1352A.

The Husband and the Parrot. Lang, *1001 Nights,* p. 30.

**1423 THE ENCHANTED TREE.** Lydia conspired with her husband's servant Pyrrhus, devising a plan through which they might make love in the master's presence. Accordingly, one day when the three were walking in the garden, Lydia requested a pear from a certain tree. Pyrrhus climbed after the fruit, but once in the tree, he called to his master: "Have you no shame, making love like that in broad daylight?" The master demanded an explanation for the strange remark, and Pyrrhus concluded that the pear tree was enchanted, giving the impression of unreal happenings below. To test the theory, the master climbed the tree, and he too saw a strange occurrence: his wife and his servant making love. Convinced that the tree was bedeviled, he had it cut down immediately. (Boccaccio)

Apple Tree, The. Dorson, *Buying the Wind,* p. 449.
Bewitched Tree, The. Briggs, *DBF,* pt. A, v. 2, p. 20.
Blind Man and His Wife, The. Briggs, *DBF,* pt. A, v. 2, p. 22.
Lydia and Pyrrhus Make Love beneath a Tree. Boccaccio, *Decameron,* Day 7,
Merchant's Tale, The. Chaucer, *Canterbury Tales,* p. 375.

**1424 CURING AN UNBORN CHILD.** A priest convinced a peasant's wife that she was pregnant with a child lacking arms and legs. She let the priest finish the job that her husband ostensibly had left undone. (Afanasyev) Cf. type 1547*.

Curing the Unborn Child (anecdotes with commentary). Legman, *Rationale of
the Dirty Joke,* vol. 1, p. 130.
Friar Rinaldo Goes to Bed with His Godchild's Mother. Boccaccio,
*Decameron,* Day 7, Tale 3.
Pope and the Peasant, The (3 versions). Afanasyev, *Russian Secret Tales,* p.

**1424\* A WOMAN ASSUMES A VULGAR NAME.** A peasant found a buried treasure, but a soldier stole it from him. The peasant's wife overtook the soldier, who agreed to be her companion. Feigning embarrassment, she told him her name was "Shit." During the night she took the treasure and returned to her husband. Discovering his loss, the soldier called out the woman's name repeatedly, but succeeded only in getting himself evicted from the inn.

> Curious Names. Afanasyev, *Russian Secret Tales,* p. 245.

**1425 PUTTING THE DEVIL INTO HELL.** Rustico, a monk, instructed Alibech, a beautiful young woman, concerning the differences between their anatomy. He possessed a devil, and she a hell; and they took great pleasure in putting the devil into hell where he belonged. (Boccaccio)

> Alibech Puts the Devil Back in Hell. Boccaccio, *Decameron,* Day 3, Tale 10.
> Glory-Pole, The. Randolph, *Pissing in the Snow,* no. 76.
> Judgement Regarding Some Cows, A. Afanasyev, *Erotic Tales,* p. 75.
> Putting the Pope in Rome. Afanasyev, *Russian Secret Tales* (notes), p. 285.
> Sentence Concerning the Cows, The. Afanasyev, *Russian Secret Tales,* p.
> We Call It Lapland. Randolph, *The Talking Turtle,* p. 36.

**1425B\* YOU'RE NOT RELATED TO YOUR FATHER.** A man told his son to be careful about choosing a girlfriend, because he had sown wild oats in his youth, and many of the girls in town were in truth the boy's sisters. Upon hearing this, the boy's mother told him that she too had sown wild oats, and that he wasn't related to his father. (Dorson)

> Father and Mother Both "Fast." Dorson, *Buying the Wind,* p. 79.
> You Ain't No Kin to Pa! Legman, *Rationale of the Dirty Joke,* vol. 1, p. 444.

**1430 AIR CASTLES.** A girl, carrying a pail of milk on her head, made plans for the money she would get from the milk. A new dress and a hat would make her look elegant. Lost in thought, she tossed her head to show off her dream clothes, and in so doing spilled all of the milk. (Aesop)

> Barber's Fifth Brother, The. Mathers, *1001 Nights,* v. 1, p. 250.
> Beggar's Plan, The. Afanasyev, *Russian Fairy Tales,* p. 599.
> Broken Pot, The. Jacobs, *Indian Fairy Tales,* p. 38.
> Buttermilk Jack. Briggs, *DBF,* pt. A, v. 1, p. 105.
> Day Dreaming. Jacobs, *European Folk and Fairy Tales,* no. 14.
> Daydreamer, The. Afanasyev, *Russian Fairy Tales,* p. 161.
> Don't Count Your Chickens. Bushnaq, *Arab Folktales,* p. 285.
> Don't Count Your Chickens Until They Are Hatched! Clouston, *Popular Tales,*
>     v. 2, p. 432.
> Lad and the Fox, The (Sweden). Booss, *Scandinavian Tales,* p. 203.
> Lazy Heinz. Grimm, *Tales,* no. 164.
> Lean Lisa. Grimm, *Tales,* no. 168.
> Milkmaid and Her Pail, The. Jacobs, *Aesop,* no. 77.

**1430A FOOLISH CONCERNS FOR AN UNBORN CHILD.** A woman accidentally dropped a log on the hearth, then broke into tears. Her husband rushed to her aid, and she explained her plight: "If our Lutoniushka were married, and if he had a son, and if this son had been sitting here, I would have hit him with the log." (Afanasyev) Cf. type 1450.

> Lutoniushka. Afanasyev, *Russian Fairy Tales*, p. 336.
> Sievemaker and the Ass, The. Megas, *Folktales of Greece*, no. 64.

**1440 A HORSE INSTEAD OF A BRIDE.** An old landowner repeatedly asked a girl to marry him. Finally the girl's father tricked the unwanted suitor by promising him his filly, although the landowner thought he was to receive the daughter. As promised, the horse, dressed like a bride, was delivered to the landowner's chamber.

> Squire's Bride, The. Asbjørnsen and Moe, *Norwegian Folktales*, p. 56.

**1443\* THE MAN WHO COULD NOT JUMP OVER A PILLOW.** A man and a woman shared a bed one night, separated by a pillow. The next day the woman ridiculed her partner's athletic abilities with the taunt: "You couldn't even jump over a pillow."

> You Couldn't Even Jump Over a Pillow. Legman, *Rationale of the Dirty Joke*, vol. 1, p. 123.

**1445\* KNEADING DOUGH.** A woman was told that the secret of making good bread was to knead the dough until her backside was wet with sweat. And she followed this advice, checking her bare behind every few minutes with her doughy hand to see if it was wet yet. The bread was good, but no one would have eaten it, if they had known how it had been made.

> Intelligent House-Wife, The. Afanasyev, *Russian Secret Tales*, p. 41.
> Wash the Bottom. Afanasyev, *Russian Secret Tales*, p. 13.

**1447\* BATHING A DIRTY PERSON.** A man from southern Egypt went to a public bath in Cairo, and it took hours of scrubbing just to reach his undershirt.

> Body Scrub, The. El-Shamy, *Folktales of Egypt*, no. 69.

**1450 CLEVER ELSIE.** Elsie went to the cellar to draw beer and noticed an ax hanging on the wall. She began to cry, because—as she explained—if she were married, and if she had a son, and if the son went to the cellar to draw beer, the ax might fall and kill him. A suitor, impressed with her cleverness, married her. —Continues as type 1383. (Grimm) Cf. type 1430A. Note: Type 1450 tales typically include numerous episodes describing foolish behavior, for example, types 1384 and 1387.

Bastianelo (Italy). Clarkson and Cross, *World Folktales*, no. 62.
Bastianelo (Italy). Cole, *Best-Loved Folktales*, no. 31.
Bastianelo. Crane, *Italian Popular Tales*, no. 93.
Clever Elsie and Her Companions (Italy). Thompson, *100 Folktales*, no. 88.
Clever Elsie, The. Ranke, *Folktales of Germany*, no. 76.
Clever Elsie. Grimm, *Tales*, no. 34.
Foolish Women, The (commentary). Dawkins, *Modern Greek Folktales*, no.
Hamdullah, Nisan, and Iyyar. Sabar, *Kurdistani Jews*, p. 157.
If He Had Been There, He Would Have Been Killed (several variants). Clouston, *Book of Noodles*, p. 191.
Simple-Minded Jeanne. Delarue, *French Folktales*, p. 347.
Six Sillies, The. Lang, *Red Fairy Book*, p. 186.
There's Bigger Fools Than Tildy. Randolph, *The Devil's Pretty Daughter*, p.
Three Innocents, The. Massignon, *Folktales of France*, no. 38.
Three More Bigger Fools. Dorson, *Negro Tales*, p. 101.
Three Sillies, The. Jacobs, *English Fairy Tales*, p. 9.
Three Sillies, The. Roberts, *South from Hell*, no. 58.
Three Wise Men, The. Campbell, *West Highlands*, v. 2, p. 28.
What Shall Baby's Name Be? (Sweden). Booss, *Scandinavian Tales*, p. 186.

**1451 A SUITOR CHOOSES THE THRIFTY GIRL.** A lazy and wasteful girl was engaged to be married. Her fiancé discovered that her servant had made a dress from the remnants of flax she had wasted while spinning, and he decided to marry the thrifty girl instead. (Grimm)

Half-Cup of Tea, The. Briggs and Tongue, *Folktales of England*, no. 49.
Hurds, The. Grimm, *Tales*, no. 156.

**1452 CHOOSING A BRIDE BY HOW SHE CUTS CHEESE.** Three potential brides sliced cheese for a suitor. One cut the rind too thick, wasting good cheese. One cut the rind too thin. One cut off the right amount, and the suitor chose her. (Grimm)

Best of Three, The (2 variants). Dorson, *Buying the Wind*, p. 146.
Choice of a Servant, The. Briggs, *DBF*, pt. A, v. 1, p. 106.
Choosing a Bride. Grimm, *Tales*, no. 155.

**1453 THE KEY IN THE FLAX.** A suitor, visiting a potential bride, secretly hid a key in the flax on her spinning wheel. He came back a few days later, and she had not yet found the key, so he knew that she had not been attending to her spinning. He did not return.

Key in the Distaff, The. Asbjørnsen and Moe, *Norwegian Folktales*, p. 128.

**1456 THE BLIND FIANCEE.** A young woman was almost blind. To hide this from her suitor, she and her mother stuck a pin in the gatepost. Later the girl, sitting on the porch with her suitor, asked: "Isn't that a pin sticking in the gatepost?" The young man investigated, and came back marvelling at the girl's sharp eyesight. Later that evening, the girl thought she saw the cat on the table, and chased it away with her hand. It was a pitcher of milk, and she knocked it onto her guest. He did not return. (Randolph)

Nearsighted Old Lady. Dorson, *Negro Tales,* p. 98.
Old Lady with Poor Eyesight, The. Dorson, *Buying the Wind,* p. 90.
Pin in the Gatepost, The. Randolph, *Who Blowed Up the Church House?,* p.

## 1459** A GIRL'S FAMILY PUTS ON A SHOW OF WEALTH.

How One Went Out to Woo. Asbjørnsen and Moe, *East o' the Sun,* p. 104.

## 1462 A SUITOR PRETENDS TO BE AN ANGEL.
A lazy boy from a poor family disguised himself as a priest and hid behind a shrine in his wealthy neighbor's house. When the rich family assembled for dinner, he stepped from behind the shrine and instructed the man to marry one of his daughters to the neighbor's son. The very next morning the rich man presented a marriage proposal. Thus the poor boy married a rich girl. (Seki) Cf. types 1380, 1405, 1575.

MacCulloch's Courtship. Briggs, *DBF,* pt. B, v. 2, p. 92.
Old Black-Oak Knows Best. Randolph, *The Devil's Pretty Daughter,* p. 92.
Three Year Sleeping Boy, The. Seki, *Folktales of Japan,* no. 54.

## 1476 PRAYING FOR A HUSBAND.

Saint Agnes's Well. Briggs, *DBF,* pt. B, v. 2, p. 341.

## 1476A PRAYING TO A STATUE'S MOTHER.
A girl, thinking herself alone in Saint Anne's Chapel, prayed for a husband. The sexton, out of sight behind a statue of Saint Anne, surprised her with a sarcastic response. The girl, thinking the answer had come from the child Mary, answered: "Hold your tongue, and let your mother speak!" (Grimm) Cf. type 1347*.

Girl from Brakel, The. Grimm, *Tales,* no. 139.
Maid Who Wanted to Marry, The. Briggs, *DBF,* pt. A, v. 2, p. 169.
Nowt But a Tailor. Briggs, *DBF,* pt. A, v. 2, p. 204.

## 1476B THE GIRL WHO MARRIED THE DEVIL.
A girl declared that she would marry only a man dressed in gold. Her father gave a party, and a man dressed in gold appeared and danced with her. It was the devil, and he took her away with him. (Botkin) Cf. type 363.

Devil Marriage, The. Botkin, *American Folklore,* p. 725.
Man with the Fiery Rose, The. Pourrat, *French Tales,* p. 189.

**1479\* AN OLD WOMAN STAYS OUT ALL NIGHT.** An old woman was promised that if she would take off her clothes and stay on the roof all night, she would get a young man for a husband. She spent the whole night naked on the roof, even though it was very cold. Cf. type 1500.

Young Man in the Morning. Dorson, *Negro Tales,* p. 261.

**1500 THE OLD WOMAN'S CURE** (new classification). A ninety-year old woman complained of imaginary sicknesses, and her son sent for a doctor. The doctor prescribed marriage for the old woman, explaining that every time the wind lifted her skirts, the thought of a bridegroom entered her mind. (Bushnaq) Cf. type 1479\*.

Cure, The. Bushnaq, *Arab Folktales,* p. 331.
Mad Woman, A. Störer, *Facetiae of Poggio,* no. 70.
Man Who Asked Pardon of His Sick Wife, A. Storer, *Facetiae of Poggio,* no.
Widow Who Desired a Husband, A. Storer, *Facetiae of Poggio,* no. 87.

**1510 THE WIDOW OF EPHESUS.** A widow had a wooden likeness made of her deceased husband. She kept the statue under her bed by day and took it into her bed each night. A young man was attracted to the widow, if not for love then because of her wealth. He secretly took the place of the wooden statue one night. The next day the widow used the statue for firewood. (Briggs) Cf. types 65, 1350, 1352\*.

Old John and Young John. Briggs, *DBF,* pt. A, v. 2, p. 207.
Widow of Ephesus, The. Legman, *Rationale of the Dirty Joke,* vol. 1, p. 650.

**1511\* THE MESSAGE OF THE BELLS.** A widow, contemplating remarriage, heard the church bells say: "You shall be wed; take him to your board and bed." She married, but her new husband turned out to be a wife beater. She heard the bells again, but now they said: "You were wrong to be wed; now he rules your board and bed." (Pourrat)

Take Him or Leave Him. Pourrat, *French Tales,* p. 123.
Talking Cat, The (French Canada). Cole, *Best-Loved Folktales,* no. 178.

**1516B\* MARRIAGE AS A SUBSTITUTE FOR PURGATORY.** A man who had suffered from a bad marriage was excused from purgatory and admitted directly into paradise. A second man, who had married one shrewish woman, then a second, and even a third, expected similar treatment, but Saint Peter blocked his way. "Paradise," he explained, "is for the unfortunate, not the imbeciles."

Two Ill-Married Men, The. Pourrat, *French Tales,* p. 153.

**1525  THE MASTER THIEF.** —Miscellaneous anecdotes. Tales listed under this number usually include one or more episodes described under the subdivisions 1525A-1525R and other related types.

> Boy Who Outwitted the Robber, The. Briggs, *DBF*, pt. A, v. 2, p. 377.
> Canny Jack. Briggs, *DBF*, pt. A, v. 2, p. 386.
> Clever Jack. Briggs, *DBF*, pt. A, v. 2, p. 392.
> Corvetto. Basile, *Pentamerone*, Day 3, Tale 7.
> Crack and Crook. Calvino, *Italian Folktales*, no. 17.
> Crafty Miller, The. Briggs, *DBF*, pt. A, v. 2, p. 275.
> Facetia of Some Thieves. Storer, *Facetiae of Poggio*, no. 143.
> Fox Eats the Arab's Chickens, The. Arewa, *Northern East Africa*, p. 139.
> How Jack Became a Master Thief. Briggs, *DBF*, pt. A, v. 2, p. 408.
> Ixte'que (The Thief). Paredes, *Folktales of Mexico*, no. 45.
> Jack and His Master. Briggs, *DBF*, pt. A, v. 2, p. 412.
> Jack the Cunning Thief. Jacobs, *More Celtic Fairy Tales*, p. 11.
> Jack the Highway Robber. Gmelch and Kroup, *To Shorten the Road*, p. 53.
> Jack the Robber. Briggs, *DBF*, pt. A, v. 2, p. 413.
> Lothian Tom. Briggs, *DBF*, pt. A, v. 2, p. 158.
> Maltman and the Poller, The. Briggs, *DBF*, pt. A, v. 2, p. 170.
> Master Thief, The (Scotland). Thompson, *100 Folktales*, no. 89.
> Miser, The. Afanasyev, *Russian Fairy Tales*, p. 58.
> One-Sided Boy, The (Korea). Dorson, *Folktales around the World*, p. 296.
> Quare Jack. Dorson, *Buying the Wind*, p. 172.
> Rabbit and Fox Go Fishing. Dorson, *Negro Tales*, p. 28.
> Roclore (I, II). Saucier, *French Louisiana*, nos. 14, 15.
> Roclore. Dorson, *Buying the Wind*, p. 253.
> When Ben Sikran Owed Money. Bushnaq, *Arab Folktales*, p. 271.

**1525A  STEALING A HORSE, SHEET, AND PARSON.** A count challenged a thief to steal his horse, the sheet upon which he and his wife slept, and the parson. The thief met the first test by giving drugged wine to the stable guards. He approached the second task by cutting a corpse from the gallows. Carrying the body on his shoulders, he climbed to the count's bedroom window. The count shot the supposed intruder, and the thief dropped the dead man. The count left his wife to investigate, and the thief entered the bedroom. Disguising his voice, he said to the countess: "The poor sinner is dead. Give me the sheet to cover his body." The woman complied, and the thief won the second test. Next the thief disguised himself as Saint Peter and approached the church, calling out that judgment day was here, and that anyone wishing to go to heaven should enter his sack. The parson crept inside, giving the master thief his victory. (Grimm) —Note: When it appears alone, the episode of the dupe hoping to enter heaven in a sack is classified as type 1737.

> Cassandrino Steals the Praetor's Bed and Horse. Straparola, *Facetious Nights*, Night 1, Tale 2.
> Dickey of Kingswood. Briggs, *DBF*, pt. B, v. 2, p. 36.
> Frankie-Boy's Trade. Calvino, *Italian Folktales*, no. 117.
> Jack and the Doctor's Girl. Chase, *Kurdistani Jews* no. 13.

Jack Tale. Chase, *Jack Tales,* p. 195.
Master Thief, The. Asbjørnsen and Moe, *East o' the Sun,* p. 232.
Master Thief, The. Grimm, *Tales,* no. 192.
Master Thief, The. Jacobs, *European Folk Tales,* no. 16.
Master Thief. Thomas, *It's Good to Tell You,* no. 19.
Paying the Scot-Ale. Briggs, *DBF,* pt. B, v. 2, p. 297.
Robbers, The. Villa, *100 Armenian Tales,* no. 73.
Smith's Servant, The. Campbell, *West Highlands,* v. 2, p. 273.
Son of the Scottish Yeoman, The. Campbell, *West Highlands,* v. 2, p. 253.
Thief, The. Afanasyev, *Russian Fairy Tales,* p. 590.
Three Brothers, The. Espinosa, *Folklore of Spain in the American Southwest,*
    p. 188.

**1525D  THE THIEF'S BAIT.** A thief placed two boots some distance
apart on a narrow trail. A man on a horse carrying a lamb saw the
first boot, bemoaned the fact that it did not have a mate, and tossed it
aside. When he came to the second boot, he tied the horse and lamb
to a tree, and ran back to recover the one he had discarded. The thief
mounted the horse, picked up the lamb, and rode away. (Espinosa)

Boy That Was Trained to Be a Thief, The. Campbell, *Cloudwalking Country,*
    p. 170.
Cobbler and the Calf, The. Clouston, *Popular Tales,* v. 2, p. 43.
Man and His Boots, The. Harris, *Uncle Remus and His Friends,* no. 22.
Master Thief, The. Jacobs, *European Folk Tales,* no. 16.
Master Thief. Thomas, *It's Good to Tell You,* no. 19.
Mister Fox Goes a-Hunting, but Mister Rabbit Bags the Game. Harris, *Uncle
    Remus,* no. 15.
Shifty Lad, The (Scotland). Lang, *Lilac Fairy Book,* p. 1.
Soldier's Riddle, A. Afanasyev, *Russian Fairy Tales,* p. 117.
Tall Fellow's Turkey, A. Randolph, *The Devil's Pretty Daughter,* p. 70.
Three Brothers, The. Espinosa, *Folklore of Spain in the American Southwest,*
    p. 188.

**1525G  A THIEF ASSUMES DISGUISES.**

Quico and Caco. Pino-Saavedra, *Folktales of Chile,* no. 39.
Smith's Servant, The. Campbell, *West Highlands,* v. 2, p. 273.
Son of the Scottish Yeoman, The. Campbell, *West Highlands,* v. 2, p. 253.

**1525H  THIEVES ROB EACH OTHER.** Cf. types 1525R, 1525N.

Cheater Cheated, The. Afanasyev, *Russian Fairy Tales,* p. 228.
Crack, Crook, and Hook. Calvino, *Italian Folktales,* no. 123.
Pre Scarpafico Dupes Three Robbers. Straparola, *Facetious Nights,* Night 1,
    Tale 3.
Quico and Caco. Pino-Saavedra, *Folktales of Chile,* no. 39.
Robber's Cunning against Another Robber, A. Briggs, *DBF,* pt. A, v. 2, p.
    253.
Two Pickpockets. Briggs, *DBF,* pt. A, v. 2, p. 337.

**1525J*  A THIEF LEAVES FOOD HE THINKS IS POISONED.**

Brother Rabbit Pretends to Be Poisoned. Harris, *Nights with Uncle Remus,* no. 50.

Mrs. Partridge Has a Fit. Harris, *Uncle Remus and His Friends,* no. 7.

## 1525M HIDING A STOLEN SHEEP IN A CRADLE.

Baby in the Cradle. Randolph, *The Devil's Pretty Daughter,* p. 19.
Baby in the Crib (USA, Black). Clarkson and Cross, *World Folktales,* no. 47.
Isaac Lowndes Steals a Buck. Simpson, *Folklore of the Welsh Border,* p. 50.

## 1525N TWO THIEVES TRICK EACH OTHER. Cf. types 1525H, 1525R.

King of Cheats, The (India). Dorson, *Folktales around the World,* p. 187.

## 1525Q TWO THIEVES WITH THE SAME WIFE. A night thief and a day thief discovered that they were both married to the same woman. She decided to live with the one who best proved his skill, so they entered into a thievery contest. (Dorson)

Matching Wits. Villa, *100 Armenian Tales,* no. 72.
Two Thieves with the Same Wife, The (Afghanistan). Dorson, *Folktales around the World,* p. 223.

## 1525Q* THE THIEF'S SONG. A thief, while dancing with the tavernkeeper's wife, noticed where their money was hidden. He sang a song that told his accomplice where to look, and thus the tavernkeeper lost his money.

Song of the Thief, The (Poland). Dorson, *Folktales around the World,* p. 107.

## 1525R A YOUNG ROBBER TRICKS HIS OLDER BROTHERS. Cf. types 1525H, 1525N.

Quare Jack. Dorson, *Buying the Wind,* p. 172.

## 1526A WINNING SUPPER BY A TRICK.

Achichinque, El. Paredes, *Folktales of Mexico,* no. 48.
Tom Tram's Merry Tales. Briggs, *DBF,* pt. A, v. 2, p. 318.

## 1527A TRICKING A ROBBER INTO WASTING HIS BULLETS. A highwayman forced a pedlar to hand over his valuables. To prove he had been robbed, the pedlar asked the highwayman to shoot a hole through one side of his coat, then through the other side, and then through his hat. The robber complied, using up all of his ammunition. Then the pedlar produced a hidden pistol and forced the highwayman to surrender all of his loot. (Glassie)

Enchanted Steed, The. Briggs, *DBF,* pt. B, v. 2, p. 46.

Farmer Dean's Wager with the Highwaymen. Whitlock, *Folklore of Wiltshire*, p. 104.
Willie Brennan. Glassie, *Irish Folktales*, no. 104.

**1528   THE BIRD UNDER THE TRICKSTER'S HAT.** Pedro, seeing two gentlemen on horseback approaching him, placed his hat over the pile of dung he had just made. He told the gentleman he was watching a golden partridge under his hat, and that he would take it out if he could get some help. One of the men lent him his horse to go for help, and Pedro rode away, never to return. The man decided to uncover the golden bird by himself; he was not happy with what he found. Cf. type 1542A.

Pedro Urdemales Cheats Two Horsemen (Chile). Dorson, *Folktales around the World*, p. 558.
Pedro Urdemales Cheats Two Horsemen. Pino-Saavedra, *Folktales of Chile*, no. 44.

**1529   A THIEF CLAIMS TO HAVE BEEN A DONKEY.** A poor man stole a rich man's donkey, then placed himself in the harness. When the rich man discovered him, the thief claimed that demons had turned him into a donkey, but that at last he was redeemed. The rich man, not wanting to get involved with demons, let the man go. (Noy)

Donkey Driver and the Thief, The (Arabia). Cole, *Best-Loved Folktales*, no. 110.
John Brodison and the Policeman. Glassie, *Irish Folktales*, no. 35.
Magical Transformations. Clouston, *Popular Tales*, v. 1, p. 447.
Metamorphosis, The. Briggs, *DBF*, pt. A, v. 2, p. 183.
Monks and the Donkey, The. Musick, *Green Hills of Magic*, no. 74.
Passover Miracle, The. Noy, *Folktales of Israel*, no. 65.
Pedlar's Ass, The. Briggs, *DBF*, pt. A, v. 2, p. 233.

**1529A\*   WINNING A BET BY EATING DISGUSTING FOOD.** Rob entered a bet with a gentleman as to which could eat the most disgusting food. While alone, Rob mixed some gingerbread and beer together in a chamber pot, then ate it in the gentleman's presence. Thinking he knew what was in the pot, the gentleman refused to try it, and Rob won the bet.

Rob Hall and the Gentleman. Briggs, *DBF*, pt. A, v. 2, p. 253.

**1530   HOLDING UP A ROCK.** Seeing the coyote approaching, the rabbit positioned himself beneath a large rock and then pretended to hold it up. "I'm holding up this rock," he explained. "They're going to bring my dinner to me here." Hoping to get the promised dinner for himself, the coyote took the rabbit's place, thus allowing the rabbit to escape. (Paredes)

Hare Tricks a Hyena into Holding Up a Stone, A (4 variants). Arewa, *Northern East Africa*, p. 99.
How Brer Rabbit Saved Brer B'ar's Life. Harris, *Uncle Remus and the Little Boy*, no. 4
Mouse and the Fox, The (Peru). Dorson, *Folktales around the World*, p. 527.
Old Granny Grinny Granny. Abrahams, *Afro-American Folktales*, no. 50.
Old Grinny Granny Wolf. Harris, *Nights with Uncle Remus*, no. 54.
Rabbit and the Coyote, The. Paredes, *Folktales of Mexico*, no. 26.
Tricky Yankee, The. Dorson, *Buying the Wind*, p. 187.

**1533 DIVIDING THE FOWL.** A peasant gave the king a chicken. The king asked how it should be divided. The peasant gave him the head, for he was the head of state; the wings and legs went to the members of the court, for they followed the king's orders; and he kept the rest (actually the largest part), for he was just a lowly peasant. The king was so pleased with the clever explanations, that he gave the peasant a handsome reward. (Villa) Cf. types 875, 1663.

Clever Girl, The. Crane, *Italian Popular Tales*, no. 108.
Capon Carver, The (Albania). Clouston, *Popular Tales*, v. 2, p. 493.
Capon Carver, The (Talmud). Clouston, *Popular Tales*, v. 2, p. 329.
Clever Girl, The. Crane, *Italian Popular Tales*, p. 311.
Dividing the Goose. Afanasyev, *Russian Fairy Tales*, p. 579.
How the Peasant Divided the Geese. Tolstoy, *Fables and Fairy Tales*, p. 52.
Just Deserts. Bushnaq, *Arab Folktales*, p. 371.
King's Son and the Poor Man's Daughter, The. Musick, *Green Hills of Magic*, no. 68.
Master John Scot. Briggs, *DBF*, pt. B, v. 2, p. 94.
Prince Who Became a Pauper, The. Sabar, *Kurdistani Jews*, p. 183.
Riddle, The. Dawkins, *Modern Greek Folktales*, no. 67.
Test of the Chicken, The. Villa, *100 Armenian Tales*, no. 74.

**1534 JUSTICE RESTORED WITH UNJUST DECISIONS.** A poor man borrowed a horse from his rich brother, and while in his possession, the horse accidentally lost its tail. The rich man set out to bring a complaint before the judge; his brother had no choice but to follow. They found lodging with a peasant. The poor brother accidentally fell on the peasant's child, crushing it to death, so the peasant too decided to file a complaint with the judge. Arriving in town, the poor man concluded that his case was hopeless, and he jumped from a bridge. He fell upon an old man, killing him, and the old man's son brought charges to the judge. The judge ordered the poor man to keep his brother's horse until it grew another tail. Further, he decided that the poor man should take the peasant's wife and produce a new son by her. Last, he ordered the man whose father had been killed to jump from the bridge and land on the defendant. To avoid these settlements, the plaintiffs had to give the poor man a great sum of money. (Afanasyev)

Judge and the Baker, The. El-Shamy, *Folktales of Egypt*, no. 54.
Judgment of the Qadi, The. Bushnaq, *Arab Folktales*, p. 322.

Man with Many Court Cases, A. Noy, *Folktales of Israel,* no. 16.
Rich Brother and the Poor Brother, The (Portugal). Lang, *Lilac Fairy Book,* p. 173.
Shemiaka the Judge. Afanasyev, *Russian Fairy Tales,* p. 625.
Shemiaka the Judge. Thompson, *100 Favorite Folktales,* no. 90.

## 1534A* SUBSTITUTING THE MAN TO BE HANGED. A cobbler murdered one of his customers and was sentenced to die. Upon being reminded that the town had only one cobbler, the judge reconsidered his sentence. There were two roofers, so he sentenced one of them to be hanged instead.

Chelm Justice (Yiddish). Cole, *Best-Loved Folktales,* no. 104.

## 1535 THE RICH PEASANT AND THE POOR PEASANT. A rich peasant killed his poor neighbor's only horse. Hoping to recover part of his loss, the poor peasant started off for market with the horse's skin. He stopped at the house of a man whose wife had just received the sexton as a guest. The peasant watched as the husband returned unexpectedly and the sexton hid himself in a chest. Taking advantage of the situation, the poor peasant claimed to have a magic horsehide, one that could conjure up the devil. To demonstrate, he produced a devil from the chest, a devil who looked just like the sexton. The impressed farmer offered an entire bushel of money for the magic hide. When the poor peasant's neighbor learned how much the horsehide had brought, he killed all of his horses and took the skins to market, but when he told the shoemakers and tanners his expected price, he received only abuse. —Continues as type 1737. (Andersen) Note: Tales of this type typically contain numerous episodes of trickery. Cf. types 1358, 1539, 1725

Artful Lad, The (Sweden). Booss, *Scandinavian Tales,* p. 208.
Big Peter and Little Peter. Asbjørnsen and Moe, *East o' the Sun,* p. 336.
Buddy. Gmelch and Kroup, *To Shorten the Road,* p. 126.
Carambot. Thomas, *It's Good to Tell You,* no. 20.
Dirty Jack. Roberts, *South from Hell,* no. 31.
Eobhan Eurrach. Campbell, *West Highlands,* v. 2, p. 249.
Goldsmith's Fortune, The (Pathan). Lang, *Orange Fairy Book,* p. 106.
Gourd of Blood, The. Mathias and Raspa, *Italian Folktales in America,* no. 7.
Heifer Hide, The. Chase, *Jack Tales,* no. 17.
Huddon and Duddon and Donald O'Leary. Glassie, *Irish Folktales,* no. 118.
Ivanushko the Little Fool. Afanasyev, *Russian Fairy Tales,* p. 62.
Jack and the Giants. Briggs, *DBF,* pt. A, v. 1, p. 326.
Jack and the Sack. Randolph, *The Devil's Pretty Daughter,* p. 67.
John Outwits Mister Berkeley. Abrahams, *Afro-American Folktales,* no. 97.
Köse and the Sultan, The. Walker and Uysal, *Tales in Turkey,* p. 150.
Liar Mvkang and the Rich Villagers (Burma). Dorson, *Folktales around the World,* p. 279.
Liar Mvkang Sells Ashes (Burma). Dorson, *Folktales around the World,* p. 281.

Little Claus and Big Claus (Andersen). Thompson, *100 Favorite Folktales,* no. 91.
Little Claus and Big Claus. Andersen, *Complete Fairy Tales,* no. 2.
Little Fairly. Clouston, *Popular Tales,* v. 2, p. 229, 489.
Little Peasant, The. Grimm, *Tales,* no. 61.
Magic Cowhide, The. Randolph, *The Devil's Pretty Daughter,* p. 105.
Magic Horn, The. Randolph, *The Devil's Pretty Daughter,* p. 87.
Man with No Beard, The. Dawkins, *Modern Greek Folktales,* no. 69.
Master Sly (Luxembourg). Bødker, *European Folk Tales,* p. 99.
Misery. Afanasyev, *Russian Fairy Tales,* p. 20.
Ogre and His Farmer, The. Pourrat, *French Tales,* p. 207.
Peasant Pewit, The. Ranke, *Folktales of Germany,* no. 51.
Pedro Urdemales Cheats Two Horsemen (Chile). Dorson, *Folktales around the World,* p. 558.
Pedro Urdemales Cheats Two Horsemen. Pino-Saavedra, *Folktales of Chile,* no. 44.
Poor Brother and the Rich, The. Campbell, *West Highlands,* v. 1, p. 237.
Precious Hide, The. Afanasyev, *Russian Fairy Tales,* p. 156.
Ribin, Robin, and Levi the Dun. Campbell, *West Highlands,* v. 2, p. 243.
Sheep for the Asking. Briggs, *DBF,* pt. A, v. 2, p. 262.
Si' Djeha's Miracles. Bushnaq, *Arab Folktales,* p. 266.
Two Woodcutters, The. Roberts, *South from Hell,* no. 59.

**1536 DISPOSING OF A CORPSE.** A family was vacationing abroad, when father's old stepmother died. To avoid unnecessary bureaucracy, they tied her body in a bundle on the roof of their car, hoping to carry her home in this manner. While they were in a cafe, someone stole their car, bundle and all. (Briggs and Tongue) Cf. type 1537.

Dead Body, The. Afanasyev, *Russian Fairy Tales,* p. 118.
Dead Cat in the Package, The (A,B). Brunvand, *The Choking Doberman,* p. 216.
Köse Who Became Muhtar, The. Walker and Uysal, *Tales in Turkey,* p. 156.
Nicholas the Hermit. Afanasyev, *Russian Secret Tales,* p. 218.
Plenty Clooked! Fisher, *Idaho Lore,* p. 75.
Purloined Corpses (examples and commentary). Brunvand, *The Vanishing Hitchhiker,* ch. 5.
Runaway Grandmother, The. Brunvand, *The Choking Doberman,* p. 219.
Stolen Corpse, The. Briggs and Tongue, *Folktales of England,* no. 48.
Stolen Corpse, The (I, II). Briggs, *DBF,* pt. B, v. 2, p. 769.
Swede and His Corpse, The. Fisher, *Idaho Lore,* p. 73.
Three Knights and the Lady, The. Clouston, *Popular Tales,* v. 2, p. 332.

**1536A THE WOMAN IN THE CHEST.** A priest, wanted to spy on the schoolmaster, whom he suspected of thievery. He put his mother in a chest, then took it to the teacher for safekeeping. The teacher discovered the spy and killed her, making it look like she had choked on a piece of bread. When the priest found his dead mother, he was afraid he would be accused of killing her, and he paid the teacher to help him prop her body at the top of a stairway in a tavern. A waitress accidentally knocked her down the stairs. Fearing prosecution, she paid the teacher to help her put the body in a field.

A farmer, thinking it was a thief, struck the body with a stick. He too paid the teacher to remove the corpse. The teacher placed it in a sack and carried it into the woods, where he discovered some robbers. He took one of their sacks, leaving the sack containing the body with them. (Ranke) Cf. type 1537.

> Miserly Rich Man, The, and the Unlucky Poor Man. Pino-Saavedra, *Folktales of Chile,* no. 45.
> Whiteshirt. Dégh, *Folktales of Hungary,* no. 9.
> Woman in the Chest, The. Ranke, *Folktales of Germany,* no. 52.

**1536B   THREE HUNCHBACKS PLUS ONE.** A woman was married to a very jealous man who was a hunchback. One day she invited three organ grinders into her house. They were identical triplets, and like her husband hunchbacks. Hearing her husband approaching and fearing his jealousy, she hid the three strangers in a chest. After her husband left, she opened the chest, but the three men were dead. She hired a servant to throw, as she stated, a dead hunchback into the river. When the servant came back, she showed him the body of the second hunchback, and the confused servant thought that the body had returned. He carried, as he presumed, the body to the river a second time, and a third time as well. After his third trip he saw the hunchbacked husband returning home and concluded that it was the corpse coming back a fourth time. Undaunted, he threw the husband in the river. The woman thus ridded herself not only of the three dead guests, but of her tyrannical husband as well. (Pourrat)

> Baker and Jack the Fool, The. Briggs, *DBF,* pt. A, v. 2, p. 17.
> Crazy Mehmet and the Three Priests. Walker and Uysal, *Tales in Turkey,* p. 218.
> Pedro Urdimale and the Dead Priests. Pino-Saavedra, *Folktales of Chile,* no. 46.
> Three Hunchbacks, The. Pourrat, *French Tales,* p. 60.

**1537   KILLING A CORPSE.** An old man choked on a bone and died. Afraid that he would be accused of murder, the host took the body to the road and propped it up. Some travelers thought the corpse was a highwayman and threw rocks at it. Seeing that the man was dead, they thought that they would be hanged for murder, so they leaned the body against a farmer's shed. The farmer thought it was a prowler and shot him. So it continued, until two rogues, also thinking they had killed the man, tied the body to a wild horse and sent him on his way. (Chase) Cf. type 1536.

> Clever Lord, The. Seki, *Folktales of Japan,* no. 56.
> Köse Who Became Muhtar, The. Walker and Uysal, *Tales in Turkey,* p. 156.
> Monk of Leicester, Who Was Four Times Slain and Once. Briggs, *DBF,* pt. A, v. 2, p. 190.
> Old Dry Frye. Chase, *Grandfather Tales,* no. 10.

**1538  THE BOY AND THE COW THIEVES.** A band of thieves stole a cow from a cowherd. Disguised as a girl, a doctor, and a priest, the boy visited the thieves and carried away all their wealth.

John the Cowherd. *Folklore of Spain in the American Southwest*, p. 182.

**1539  TRICKSTERS AND THEIR VICTIMS.** Campriano pushed a few coins into his mule's rear end and then demonstrated to some strangers how the animal made droppings of gold. They bought the mule for a good price. When they came back to complain that the mule dropped only ordinary dung for them, Campriano pretended to pick a fight with his wife. He stabbed her (so it seemed—actually he struck an ox bladder filled with animal blood that they previously had placed under her clothing), then brought her back to life with a "magic" straw. The yokels bought the straw and stabbed their own wives to death, to teach them a lesson. This time the straw did not work, and they were imprisoned for life. (Calvino) Cf. types 1535, 1542, 1737.

Biter Bit, The (Kletke). Lang, *Green Fairy Book*, p. 194.
Bragging Brian. Campbell, *West Highlands*, v. 2, p. 247.
Campriano. Calvino, *Italian Folktales*, no. 82.
Cap That Paid, The. Briggs, *DBF*, pt. A, v. 2, p. 33.
Coyote Tricks the White Man (American Indian). Clarkson and Cross, *World Folktales*, no. 46.
Cunning Shoemaker, The (Sicily). Lang, *Pink Fairy Book*, p. 154.
Hamdullah, Nisan, and Iyyar. Sabar, *Kurdistani Jews*, p. 157.
Irishman's Hat, The. Briggs and Tongue, *Folktales of England*, no. 69.
Irishman's Hat, The. Briggs, *DBF*, pt. A, v. 2, p. 129.
Jester, The. Afanasyev, *Russian Fairy Tales*, p. 151.
King of Cheats, The (India). Dorson, *Folktales around the World*, p. 187.
Köse and the Sultan, The. Walker and Uysal, *Tales in Turkey*, p. 150.
Little Peasant, The. Grimm, *Tales*, no. 61.
Magic Horn, The. Randolph, *The Devil's Pretty Daughter*, p. 87.
Mangoose and Mangoes. Thundy, *South Indian Folktales*, no. 34.
Oxford Student Steals the Landlord's Horse. Briggs, *Folklore of the Cotswolds*, p. 79.
Peasant Sells a Cow as a Goat, A. Ranke, *Folktales of Germany*, no. 53.
Pedro de Urdemalas and the Gringo (I, II). Paredes, *Folktales of Mexico*, nos. 53A, B.
Pedro de Urdemalas (Chile). Clarkson and Cross, *World Folktales*, no. 49.
Pedro Urdemales Cheats Two Horsemen (Chile). Dorson, *Folktales around the World*, p. 558.
Pedro Urdemales Cheats Two Horsemen. Pino-Saavedra, *Folktales of Chile*, no. 44.
Peter the Rogue. Espinosa, *Folklore of Spain in the American Southwest*, p. 182.
Scarpafico Dupes Three Robbers. Straparola, *Facetious Nights*, Night 1, Tale 3.
Schemer and the Flute, The. Musick, *Green Hills of Magic*, no. 67.
Si' Djeha Cheats the Robbers. Bushnaq, *Arab Folktales*, p. 260.
Uncle Capriano. Crane, *Italian Popular Tales*, no. 105.

Very Bad Boy, A (France). Lang, *Lilac Fairy Book,* p. 110.
Wise Men of Gotham: Of Sending Rent. Jacobs, *More English Fairy Tales,* p. 226.

**1540   THE MAN FROM PARADISE.** A beggar knocked at the door of a widow who had remarried, saying he was from Paris. The woman understood "Paradise" and gave the man a bundle of clothes for her deceased husband. When her new husband heard this news, he mounted his horse to overtake the trickster. The thief saw him coming and hid the bundle. When asked if he had seen a man carrying a package, the trickster said that the man had run into a field. The husband asked him to hold his horse while he ran after the villain. The trickster retrieved the package, mounted the horse, and quickly rode away. (Thompson)

> Amari Seeks a Bigger Fool Than His Wife. Arewa, *Northern East Africa,* p. 166.
> Clever People, The. Grimm, *Tales,* no. 104.
> Good Wife and the Bad Husband, The (India). Clouston, *Book of Noodles,* p. 213.
> Great Need, The. Dorson, *Buying the Wind,* p. 132.
> Hamdullah, Nisan, and Iyyar. Sabar, *Kurdistani Jews,* p. 157.
> Jack Hannaford. Briggs, *DBF,* pt. A, v. 2, p. 131.
> Jack Hannaford. Jacobs, *English Fairy Tales,* p. 40.
> Man from Paradise, The (France). Thompson, *100 Favorite Folktales,* no. 92.
> Ninety-Nine Hens and a Rooster. Megas, *Folktales of Greece,* no. 63.
> Not a Pin to Choose between Them. Asbjørnsen and Moe, *East o' the Sun,* p. 173.
> Visitor from Paradise, A. Jacobs, *European Folk and Fairy Tales,* no. 19.
> Woman Called Rice Pudding, The. Bushnaq, *Arab Folktales,* p. 374.

**1541   FOR THE LONG WINTER.** In preparation for the month of Ramadan, a man stored up great quantities of food, always telling his wife: "Save this is for Ramadan." One day the wife overheard two camel drivers, one whose name was Ramadan. Hearing the name, she opened the door and gave him all that her husband had saved. (Bushnaq) Cf. types 1385, 1385*.

> Christmas. Crane, *Italian Popular Tales,* no. 94.
> Fattening Up the Cabbage. Carpenter, *A Latvian Storyteller,* p. 189.
> Good Fortune; or, The Miser and His Wife. Briggs, *DBF,* pt. A, v. 2, p. 104.
> Great Need, The. Dorson, *Buying the Wind,* p. 132.
> Hamdullah, Nisan, and Iyyar. Sabar, *Kurdistani Jews,* p. 157.
> Hereafterthis. Briggs, *DBF,* pt. A, v. 2, p. 116.
> Hereafterthis. Jacobs, *More English Fairy Tales,* p. 7.
> Hoyik and Boyik. Briggs, *DBF,* pt. A, v. 2, p. 125.
> Long Day, The. Carpenter, *A Latvian Storyteller,* p. 192.
> Miser and His Wife, The. Briggs, *DBF,* pt. A, v. 2, p. 104.
> Presentneed, Bymeby, and Hereafter. Chase, *Grandfather Tales,* no. 16.
> Silly Girl, The. Dorson, *Negro Tales,* p. 105.
> Simple Wife, The. Bushnaq, *Arab Folktales,* p. 373.
> Thriftless Wife, The. Briggs, *DBF,* pt. A, v. 2, p. 310.

**1542A A TRICKSTER BORROWS A HORSE.** A man wanted to see some of Peter's famous tricks. Peter told him he had left them at home, but if he could borrow the man's horse, he would fetch them. The man agreed, and Peter rode off, shouting: "This is one of my tricks." (Espinosa) —Note: this episode is frequently built into other tales. Cf. types 1528, 1535, 1539, 1737.

> Coyote Tricks the White Man (American Indian). Clarkson and Cross, *World Folktales*, no. 46.
> Peter the Rogue. Espinosa, *Folklore of Spain in the American Southwest*, p. 182.

**1542\*\* RESTORED VIRGINITY.** A woman repeatedly visited a doctor to have her virginity restored. His normal fee was fifteen pounds, but the last time he charged a hundred. "This time I installed a zipper," he explained. (El-Shamy)

> Instant Virginity. El-Shamy, *Folktales of Egypt*, no. 68.
> Shepherd, The. Afanasyev, *Russian Secret Tales*, p. 173.
> Tacking on Her Maidenhead. Randolph, *Pissing in the Snow*, no. 41.
> Two Little Balls of Yarn. Legman, *Rationale of the Dirty Joke*, vol. 1, p. 141, 333.

**1543\* A WIFE GIVES HER HUSBAND MONEY TO BUY A BETTER PENIS.** Cf. type 1543A\*.

> Enchanted Ring, The. Afanasyev, *Russian Secret Tales*, p. 65.
> Fearful Bride, The. Afanasyev, *Erotic Tales*, p. 67.
> Miller's Prick, The. Randolph, *Pissing in the Snow*, p. 66.
> Timorous Young Girl, A. Afanasyev, *Russian Secret Tales*, p. 29.

**1543A\* THE COMB.** A man seduced a priest's daughter by offering to lend her his "comb." (Afanasyev)

> Comb, The. Afanasyev, *Erotic Tales*, p. 19.
> Comb, The. Afanasyev, *Russian Secret Tales*, p. 127.
> Loss of Jenkin-Horn, The. Randolph, *Pissing in the Snow*, no. 15.
> Magic Ring, The. Afanasyev, *Erotic Tales*, p. 23.

**1543C\* THE PATIENT WITH NO SENSE OF TASTE.** A man complained to a doctor that he could taste nothing. The doctor went to the outhouse and filled a large capsule with fresh hockey, then asked the patient to chew it. "That tastes like shit!" responded the man. "You can taste as well as anyone," replied the doctor, and charged him his regular fee.

> Dutch Doctor, The. Randolph, *Pissing in the Snow*, no. 32.

**1544 GAINING LODGING AND FOOD BY TRICKERY.** Cf. types 1363, 1526.

Ben Sikran Improves the Couscous. Bushnaq, *Arab Folktales,* p. 270.
Parson and the Clerk, The (Sweden). Booss, *Scandinavian Tales,* p. 232.

**1544A\* A SOLDIER'S RIDDLE.** An old woman teased two soldiers with a riddle. They answered with another riddle and stole a chicken from her oven, leaving an old shoe in its place.

Soldier's Riddle, A. Afanasyev, *Russian Fairy Tales,* p. 117.

**1545 THE BOY WITH FANCIFUL NAMES.** A new farmhand told the farmer his name was "Fuckemboth," but he told the farmer's wife and daughter that he was called "Beans." During the night the farmer heard a strange noise coming from his wife's bed. "It's just Beans on my stomach," explained the wife. A little later similar noises came from his daughter's bed, and she called out the same explanation. Suddenly the farmer thought of his hired hand and he hollered out his name, but no one answered. (Randolph) Cf. type 1563.

Johnnie Fuckerfast. Legman, *Rationale of the Dirty Joke,* vol. 1, p. 106.
King of Cheats, The (India). Dorson, *Folktales around the World,* p. 187.
New Hired Man, The. Randolph, *Pissing in the Snow,* no. 23.
Pedro de Urdemalas and the House with Strange Names (I). Paredes, *Folktales of Mexico,* no. 54A.
Pedro de Urdemalas and the Priest. Paredes, *Folktales of Mexico,* no. 55.
Quevedo Works as a Cook (Peru). Dorson, *Folktales around the World,* p. 541.

**1545B THE BOY WHO KNEW NOTHING OF SEX.** A priest, wanting to protect his wife and daughter, hired a servant who claimed to know nothing of sex. But the boy's ignorance was merely a guise, and he soon seduced both the priest's wife and his daughter. (Afanasyev)

New Hired Man, The. Randolph, *Pissing in the Snow,* no. 23.
Pope, His Wife, His Daughter, and His Man, The. Afanasyev, *Russian Secret Tales,* p. 94.

**1547\* SEDUCING A WOMAN WITH THE PROMISE OF A GIFTED BABY.** Cf. type 1424.

Making the Baby into a Violinist (anecdotes with commentary). Legman, *Rationale of the Dirty Joke,* vol. 1, p. 130.
This Will Be a Pope! Legman, *Rationale of the Dirty Joke,* vol. 1, p. 469.

**1548 NAIL SOUP.** A tramp talked a housewife into making nail soup for him. He provided the nail, while she contributed flour, meat, potatoes, and vegetables. (Booss)

Friar and the Whetstone, The. Briggs, *DBF,* pt. A, v. 2, p. 94.
Old Woman and the Tramp (Sweden). Booss, *Scandinavian Tales,* p. 182.

Old Woman and the Tramp (Sweden). Clarkson and Cross, *World Folktales,*
no. 64.
Old Woman and the Tramp (Sweden). Cole, *Best-Loved Folktales,* no. 84.
Soup from a Stone. Dorson, *Jonathan Draws the Long Bow,* p. 226.

**1551 BUYING A COW AS A GOAT.** One at a time, three tricksters
asked a peasant with a cow what he wanted for his goat. Thoroughly
confused, he finally sold it as a goat. (Ranke)

Irishman Bets with Bartender. Dorson, *Buying the Wind,* p. 92.
Peasant Sells a Cow as a Goat, A. Ranke, *Folktales of Germany,* no. 53.
Scarpafico Is Duped by Three Robbers. Straparola, *Facetious Nights,* Night 1,
Tale 3.
Sharpers and the Simpleton, The. Clouston, *Popular Tales,* v. 2, p. 27, 473.

**1555A PAYING FOR ONE ITEM WITH ANOTHER.** A man
ordered a bag of peanuts, but before paying, he exchanged them for a
bottle of bear. When the storekeeper asked to be paid for the beer,
the man said: "I paid with peanuts." "But you didn't pay for the
peanuts," replied the storekeeper. The man answered: "I don't have
them; you do."

Paying for Beer with Peanuts. Dorson, *Buying the Wind,* p. 88.

**1555B TRADING WATER FOR RUM.** A sot had a tavernkeeper fill
his bottle with rum. The customer could produce no money, so the
tavernkeeper demanded the rum back. The sot dutifully handed him
a full bottle from beneath his coat. However, it was a bottle of water
that he had prepared in advance.

Trading Water for Rum. Dorson, *Jonathan Draws the Long Bow,* p. 226.

**1556 DOUBLE FUNERAL MONEY.** Abu Nowas told the sultan that
his wife had died, and the sultan gave him money for the funeral.
Then the wife of Abu Nowas went to the sultan and begged money
for her husband's burial, and the ruler again complied.

Death of Abu Nowas and of His Wife, The (Tunisia). Lang, *Crimson Fairy
Book,* p. 273.

**1557 THE CIRCULATING SLAP.** The son of Walter Raleigh made
an improper remark at the dinner table, and his father punished him
with a slap. The son, wanting revenge but not daring to strike his
father, hit the gentleman seated next to him, saying: "Box about,
'twill come to my father anon." Cf. type 1372.

Box About. Briggs, *DBF,* pt. A, v. 2, p. 28.

**1558 A MAN IS INVITED BECAUSE OF HIS CLOTHES.** Giufà
was never invited anywhere until his mother bought him a

gentleman's suit of clothes. Now he was invited to a fine dinner. He filled his pockets with food, saying: "Eat, my clothes, for they invited you, not me!" (Calvino)

Djuha's Sleeve. Bushnaq, *Arab Folktales*, p. 257.
Eat Your Fill, My Fine Clothes! Calvino, *Italian Folktales*, no. 190.5.
Eat, My Clothes! Crane, *Italian Popular Tales*, no. 102.

**1559B\*   THE UGLIER FOOT.** A woman noticed a tailor's foot, and commented how ugly it was. "I bet there is an even uglier one here in the house," he responded. The woman accepted the bet, whereupon the tailor revealed his other foot, which was indeed uglier than the first one.

Uglier Foot, The. O'Sullivan, *Folktales of Ireland*, no. 54.

**1561   EATING THREE MEALS ONE AFTER THE OTHER.** A servant proposed that he eat his lunch immediately following breakfast, in order to save time walking back and forth from the field. The master agreed. Next, using a similar argument, he received the master's approval to eat dinner. Following dinner, according to time-honored custom, he retired to bed. (Afanasyev)

Boy That Was Foolish Wise, The. Campbell, *Cloudwalking Country*, p. 165.
Breakfast, Lunch, and Dinner. Carpenter, *A Latvian Storyteller*, p. 188.
Good Pope, The. Afanasyev, *Russian Secret Tales*, p. 250.
Lad Who Was Never Hungry, The. Briggs and Tongue, *Folktales of England*, no. 80.
Lad Who Was Never Hungry, The. Briggs, *DBF*, pt. A, v. 2, p. 147.
Mac-a-Rusgaich. Campbell, *West Highlands*, v. 2, p. 318.
Mean Rich Man, The. Dorson, *Buying the Wind*, p. 447.
Useful Appetite, A. Briggs, *DBF*, pt. A, v. 2, p. 341.

**1562   THINK THREE TIMES BEFORE YOU SPEAK.** A man told his boy to always think three times before he spoke. The next day the boy came to his father, who was was standing with his back to the fire, and slowly started a sentence three times: "Father, I think—." Finally he finished: "that your coat is on fire!" (Briggs, "Father, I Think—")

Father, I Think—. Briggs, *DBF*, pt. A, v. 2, p. 85.
Father, I Think. Briggs and Tongue, *Folktales of England*, no. 64.
King Edward and the Salad. Briggs and Tongue, *Folktales of England*, no. 65.
King Edward VII and the Salad. Briggs, *DBF*, pt. A, v. 2, p. 143.
Minstrel and His Pupil, The (Turkey). Clouston, *Book of Noodles*, p. 166.
They Took His Word! Briggs, *DBF*, pt. A, v. 2, p. 292.
Think Thrice Before You Speak. Dorson, *Buying the Wind*, p. 146.

**1562A   THE HOUSE WITH THE STRANGE NAMES.** A master taught his maid new names for all the things in the house. She was to say barnacle for bed, squibs and crackers for trousers, white-faced simminy for cat, and so forth. During the night the house caught fire, and by the time the maid reported it with the new language, it was too late. Cf. type 1940.

Barn Is Burning, The. Abrahams, *Afro-American Folktales,* no. 100.
Clever Apprentice, The. Briggs, *DBF,* pt. A, v. 2, p. 37.
Don Nippery Septo. Briggs, *DBF,* pt. A, v. 2, p. 61.
Easy Decree. Briggs, *DBF,* pt. A, v. 2, p. 66.
Master and Servant. Briggs, *DBF,* pt. A, v. 2, p. 180.
Master of All Masters. Briggs, *DBF,* pt. A, v. 2, p. 178.
Master of All Masters. Jacobs, *English Fairy Tales,* p. 220.
Pedro de Urdemalas and the House with Strange Names (II). Paredes, *Folktales of Mexico,* no. 54B.
Tom Ten per Cent. Briggs, *DBF,* pt. A, v. 2, p. 317.

**1562B\* THE WHOLE LOAF OF BREAD.** A priest gave his laborer a loaf of bread with the instructions to eat his fill, let the dog eat his fill, and bring back the loaf whole. The laborer fed himself and dog from the inside of the loaf, leaving the outer crust intact. The priest, pleased with his cleverness, added to his wages.

Priest's Laborer, The. Afanasyev, *Russian Fairy Tales,* p. 332.

**1563 A SERVANT TAKES ADVANTAGE OF HIS MASTER'S WIFE AND DAUGHTERS.** Pedro Animales' boss sent him to the house for three tools: a shovel, a pike, and a crowbar. At the house, Pedro told his master's wife and two daughters that the boss had ordered them to give themselves to him. They didn't believe him, so he shouted to the waiting man: "All three?" "Yes, all three!" was the impatient reply. Thus Pedro Animales had his will of the three women, but then he had to flee. (Pino-Saavedra) Cf. type 1545.

Big Jack and Little Jack. Chase, *Jack Tales,* no. 7.
Brother Rabbit and Miss Nancy. Harris, *Told by Uncle Remus,* no. 16.
It Didn't Cost Him Nothing. Randolph, *Pissing in the Snow,* no. 16.
Lose Your Temper, and You Lose Your Bet. Calvino, *Italian Folktales,* no. 56.
New Hired Man, The. Randolph, *Pissing in the Snow,* no. 23.
New or the Old, The. El-Shamy, *Folktales of Egypt,* no. 58.
Pedro Animales Fools His Boss. Pino-Saavedra, *Folktales of Chile,* no. 41.
Pope and His Man, The (2 versions). Afanasyev, *Russian Secret Tales,* p. 112.
Pope and the Peasant, The. Afanasyev, *Russian Secret Tales,* p. 106.
Priest and His Hired Hand, The. Afanasyev, *Erotic Tales,* p. 49.

**1565 A WAGER NOT TO SCRATCH.** The padishah offered a reward to three peasants if they could refrain from scratching for one hour. Toward the end of the hour their itching became unbearable, so they pointed to various things, sneaking a scratch as they moved their hands. The padishah saw what they were doing, but rewarded them for their cleverness. (Walker and Uysal)

> Brother Rabbit and the Mosquitoes. Harris, *Nights with Uncle Remus,* no. 37.
> How the Three Itching Peasants Won Their Rewards. Walker and Uysal, *Tales in Turkey,* p. 142.

**1566A\* KILLING THE ROOSTER THAT WAKES YOU.** The maids in a certain household grew angry with the rooster for waking them, and they killed it. Then their mistress required them to arise even earlier.

> Out of the Frying-Pan into the Fire. Handford, *Aesop,* no. 184.

**1567 THE HUNGRY SERVANT.** —Miscellaneous tales.

> Take a Pinch of Salt with It. Briggs, *DBF,* pt. A, v. 2, p. 290.

**1567F ONE COW WITH TWO CALVES.** A New Mexican was in a house in California, but no one invited him to eat. "In New Mexico the cows all have two calves," he told the men at the table. They wanted to know how one cow could feed two calves. "Just like here," he said. "One calf sucks and one watches." Then the men invited him to eat with them.

> New Mexican and the Californians, The. Dorson, *Buying the Wind,* p. 445.

**1567G GOOD FOOD CHANGES THE SONG.** A farmer heard his workers singing: "Curds and whey, ivvery day." He told his wife to improve their fare, and the next day he heard them singing, while mowing like steam engines: "'Am an' eggs, mind thi legs." (Briggs, "The Hungry Mowers")

> Farmer and His Man, The. Briggs, *DBF,* pt. A, v. 2, p. 81.
> Grace before Meat (6 examples). Fowke, *Folklore of Canada,* p. 161.
> Hungry Mowers, The. Briggs, *DBF,* pt. A, v. 2, p. 125.
> Rate for a Job, The. Briggs, *DBF,* pt. A, v. 2, p. 245.

**1571\* FINDING AN EXCUSE TO BEAT ONE'S MASTER.**

> Tailor, the King and His Servants, The. Briggs, *DBF,* pt. A, v. 2, p. 288.

**1572D\* ACCEPTING A GIFT NOT OFFERED SERIOUSLY.**

> Quarrelsome Demyan. Afanasyev, *Russian Fairy Tales,* p. 163.

**1574 THE TAILOR'S DREAM.** A tailor dreamed he had died and gone to hell, where Satan confronted him with a great patchwork web consisting of the pieces of cloth he had stolen while on earth. Awakening, he told the dream to his foreman. Later the foreman caught him stealing a piece of scarlet cloth and reminded him of the dream. "It's all right," responded the tailor. "There was nothing this color in the web."

Tailor's Dream, The. Clouston, *Popular Tales*, v. 2, p. 79.

**1575  A SERVANT PRETENDS TO BE AN ANGEL.** A tailor kept his apprentices working until eleven every night. One evening the tailor was returning from town through the forest, and two apprentices hid themselves near the path. As the master approached, one of them said: "If thou keepest thy lads at work till eleven, thou shalt not enter the kingdom of heaven." The master never again required his apprentices to work so late. (Briggs, "The Tailor and His Apprentices") Cf. types 1380, 1405, 1462.

John Drew the Shoemaker. Briggs, *DBF*, pt. A, v. 2, p. 140.
Tailor and His Apprentices, The. Briggs, *DBF*, pt. A, v. 2, p. 288.

**1577*  A BLIND BEGGAR IS ROBBED.** A shopkeeper discovered where four blind beggars hid their money, and stole it. But he felt pity when they came begging, and gave them a coin. One of the beggars could eat no food purchased with his own money. The bread bought with the shopkeeper's coin stuck in his throat, so they knew that he was the thief. They raised a great hue, forcing him to return their money. (Noy, "The Shopkeeper and the Four Blind Beggars.")

Porter Who Lost His Appetite, The. Noy, *Folktales of Israel*, no. 15.
Shopkeeper and Four Blind Beggars, The. Noy, *Folktales of Israel*, no. 18.

**1579  FERRYING A GOAT, A WOLF, AND A CABBAGE.** How can one carry a goat, a wolf, and a cabbage across a river in a boat that will hold only one baggage item per trip? The goat cannot be left alone with the cabbage, nor the wolf with the goat. One solution: Take the goat first, leaving the wolf with the cabbage. Then get the cabbage and bring back the goat. Then take the wolf and leave it again with the cabbage. Return for the goat. (Carpenter)

Goat, Wolf, and Cabbage. Carpenter, *A Latvian Storyteller*, p. 231.
Three Men and Three Women Cross a River (2 variants). Arewa, *Northern East Africa*, p. 255.

**1585  THE LAWYER'S CRAZY CLIENT.** A man sold a calf three times and was hence charged with fraud. His lawyer advised him to answer every question: "Oink, oink." The defendant followed this advice; the judge declared him crazy and set him free. Having won the case, the lawyer asked for his fee, but all he received was the client's answer: "Oink, oink." (Fowke) Cf. type 1589.

Calf Sold Three Times, The. Fowke, *Folklore of Canada*, p. 57.

Pierre Patelin; or, Of Him That Paid His Debt with Crying "Bea." Briggs, *DBF*, pt. A, v. 2, p. 235.
Rick Tyler and the Lawyer. Randolph, *Who Blowed Up the Church House?*, p. 152.

**1586 THE FLY ON THE JUDGE'S NOSE.** A fool complained to a judge about being annoyed by flies. The judge responded that he was at liberty to strike a fly wherever he might see one. Shortly thereafter, a fly lit on the judge's nose, and the fool pursued it with his fist, smashing the judge's nose. (Clouston)

Fly on the Judge's Nose, The (examples with commentary). Clouston, *Popular Tales and Fictions*, v. 1, p. 55.
Giufà and the Judge. Crane, *Italian Popular Tales*, no. 100.
Little Omelet, The. Crane, *Italian Popular Tales*, no. 101.

**1588\*\* A CHEATER IS CAUGHT WITH HIS OWN WORDS.** A suitor entered a marriage agreement that promised him board for ten years. Ten days after the marriage, the father-in-law informed him that the contract was now over, for according to the Torah, years are as days. The bridegroom responded by threatening to leave his wife, because she was still childless. Under Jewish law a wife who did not give birth within ten years could be divorced. The father-in-law agreed to uphold the original contract.

Years Are as Days. Noy, *Folktales of Israel*, no. 46.

**1589 THE CASE OF THE LAWYER'S DOG.** A dog stole meat from a butcher, and the butcher asked a lawyer if the dog's owner could be sued. "Yes," answered the lawyer. "The dog is yours," replied the butcher. "You owe me 4s. 6d. for the meat." The lawyer responded: "My consultation fee is 6s. 8d. You owe me the difference." (Briggs, "The Lawyer's Dog Steals Meat") Cf. type 1585.

Case Is Altered, The. Briggs, *DBF*, pt. a, v. 2, p. 34.
Lawyer's Dog Steals Meat, The. Briggs, *DBF*, pt. A, v. 2, p. 150.

**1590 DIRT IN THE TRESPASSER'S SHOES.** The king warned George Buchanan to never set foot on Scotland's soil again. George went to England and filled the bottoms of his shoes with dirt. Then he returned to Scotland, standing on English soil. (Dorson, "The King and Old George Buchanan")

King and Old George Buchanan, The. Dorson, *Buying the Wind*, p. 181.
Roclore (I, II). Saucier, *French Louisiana*, nos. 14, 15.
Roclore. Dorson, *Buying the Wind*, p. 253.

**1591 THE THREE JOINT DEPOSITORS.** Three men deposited money with a woman, under the condition that she repay it when the three returned together. One of the three, however, convinced her to pay him the entire sum, and he absconded. The remaining two brought suit against her, but the judgment went against them. The court concluded that the defendant had not refused payment to all three depositors, appearing at the same time, as specified by the original agreement. Thus, she would not be accountable until such time that all three jointly asked for repayment. (Briggs, "The Three Joint Depositors")

George Buchanan as Advocate. Briggs, *DBF,* pt. A, v. 2, p. 95.
Three Friends and the Innkeeper of Kayseri. Walker and Uysal, *Tales in Turkey,* p. 149.
Three Graziers and the Alewife, The. Clouston, *Popular Tales,* v. 2, p. 1.
Three Joint Depositors, The. Briggs, *DBF,* pt. A, v. 2, p. 298.

**1592   THE IRON-EATING MICE.** A peasant promised his master a gift of cheese, but the mice ate it. Hearing this, the master grew angry, claiming the peasant's story was impossible. Later the master claimed that he had rubbed his plow with oil to prevent rust, but that the mice had eaten off the iron points. The peasant asked why it was that mice could not eat his cheese, but that they could eat the master's iron. All who heard the story sided with the master.

Peasant and the Master, The. Crane, *Italian Popular Tales,* no. 37.

**1592B   THE POT THAT HAD A CHILD AND DIED.** A man borrowed a large pot from his neighbor. He returned it with a small pot inside. "Your pot had a child," explained the borrower. The neighbor laughed, and took both pots. Later the man borrowed the large pot again, but this time he did not return it. "Your pot died," he claimed. "A pot cannot die," objected the neighbor. "If a pot can give birth, then it can die," replied the borrower. (Bushnaq)

Djuha Borrows a Pot. Bushnaq, *Arab Folktales,* p. 254.
Goha Borrows a Stewpot. Mathers, *1001 Nights,* v. 4, p. 299.
Stories from Nasreddin Hodja (Turkey). Bødker, *European Folk Tales,* p. 213.

**1600   SUBSTITUTING AN ANIMAL FOR A CORPSE.** A simpleton inadvertently killed the rent collector. His mother helped him hide the corpse, but then secretly replaced it with a dead goat. When questioned by the police about the missing man, the simpleton admitted his deed and showed where he had buried the body. Finding only a goat, the police dropped the case.

Silly Jack and the Factor. Briggs, *DBF,* pt. A, v. 2, p. 265.

**1610   SHARING STROKES WITH THE KING'S GUARD.** A soldier found the king's lost ring and returned it. Before the guard would let him enter, the soldier had to sign a note promising him half of whatever reward he might receive. The king offered the soldier two thousand rubles, but the soldier asked for two hundred lashes instead. The puzzled king made preparation for the whipping, and discovered the note. The king gave the guard not half but all the promised lashes, and then rewarded the soldier with three thousand rubles and discharged him from further duty. (Afanasyev) Cf. type 1689A.

Firrazzanu and the Letter to the Commandant. Crane, *Italian Popular Tales,* p. 291.
Just Reward, The (Russia). Thompson, *100 Favorite Folktales,* no. 93.
Just Reward, The. Afanasyev, *Russian Fairy Tales,* p. 39.
Poor Man and the Gateman Share Strokes, The. Arewa, *Northern East Africa,* p. 202.

**1611   A SAILOR FALLS FROM THE MAST.** A sailor was showing off high on the mast when he lost his balance. The rigging broke his fall, and he landed feet-first, unhurt on the deck. "Do that if you can!" he shouted to another sailor.

Do That If You Can. Briggs, *DBF,* pt. A, v. 2, p. 58.

**1612   A CONTEST IN SWIMMING.** A non swimmer entered a swimming contest with an expert. The novice began loading himself with provisions, including a sword to fend off sea monsters. This frightened the expert, and he withdrew.

George Buchanan and the Drover. Briggs, *DBF,* pt. A, v. 2, p. 99.

**1613   PLAYING CARDS AS A PRAYER BOOK.** A constable criticized a man for amusing himself with cards while in church. The man explained: "The deuce stands for the two testaments, the three for the Holy Trinity, the four for the four evangelists." Reaching the Jack, he concluded: "The Jack represents a knave like the constable." (Fowke) Cf. types 1827A, 1839.

Perpetual Almanack, The. Briggs, *DBF,* pt. B, v. 2, p. 107.
Richard's Cards. Fowke, *Folklore of Canada,* p. 56.

**1617   AN UNJUST BANKER IS TRICKED INTO REPAYING A DEPOSIT.** A poor man deposited his savings with the mayor, but when he later asked for repayment, the mayor refused. A rich lady came to the poor man's aid. She brought the mayor a bag of gems, asking if he would keep them for her. At that moment—as planned—the poor man appeared and asked for his money. The mayor, wanting to impress the lady with his honesty, repaid the entire sum. Then the lady made an excuse and left with her jewels. (Villa)

Ashman's Money, The. Villa, *100 Armenian Tales,* no. 66.
Sicilian Lady Relieves a Merchant of His Goods, A. Boccaccio, *Decameron,*
    Day 8, Tale 10.

**1620    THE EMPEROR'S NEW CLOTHES.** Two tricksters pretended
to sew clothes for the emperor from cloth that was invisible to those
unfit for office. No one admitted to not being able to see the clothes
until a child, seeing the emperor parade down the street, exclaimed:
"He has nothing on!" Cf. type 1406.

Emperor's New Clothes, The. Andersen, *Complete Fairy Tales,* no. 9.

**1626    DREAM BREAD.** Three men had but one loaf of bread. They
agreed that the person who had the most wonderful dream should
receive the entire loaf. The next morning the first two told their
dreams. Then the third one said: "I dreamed that in the night I got
hungry and got up and ate the loaf." (Dorson)

Bakalawa Story, The. Noy, *Folktales of Israel,* no. 45.
Dream Bread. Briggs, *DBF,* pt. A, v. 2, p. 64.
Faith of Three Fellows, The. Briggs, *DBF,* pt. A, v. 2, p. 76.
I Ate the Loaf (Spain). Cole, *Best-Loved Folktales,* no. 36.
Man with the Pie, The. Megas, *Folktales of Greece,* no. 70.
Three Dreams. Fowke, *Folklore of Canada,* p. 165.
Three Dreams, The. Randolph, *The Devil's Pretty Daughter,* p. 145.
Three Irish Tramps. Briggs, *DBF,* pt. A, v. 2, p. 297.
Three Irishmen Have a Dream Contest. Dorson, *Buying the Wind,* p. 91.
Three Travellers and the Loaf, The. Clouston, *Popular Tales,* v. 2, p. 86.
Two Millers and the Charcoal-Burner. Pourrat, *French Tales,* p. 115.
Two Psychiatrists, The. Paredes, *Folktales of Mexico,* no. 59.

**1628*  PRETENDING TO SPEAK A FOREIGN LANGUAGE.** Cf.
type 1641C.

Rich Man's Two Sons, The. Briggs, *DBF,* pt. A, v. 2, p. 251.
Rich Man's Two Sons, The. Briggs and Tongue, *Folktales of England,* no.
    66.

**1640    THE BRAVE LITTLE TAILOR.** A tailor killed seven flies
with one stroke. He embroidered "Seven with one blow" on a sash,
and proudly set forth. A giant saw the emblem and interpreted it to
mean that the tailor had downed seven men with one blow.
—Continues as types 1060, 1062, 1052, 1051, 1115. (Grimm) Note:
Type 1640 tales usually contain several episodes from types 1000-
1199.

Bear Killer, The. Lindell, *Folk Tales from Kammu,* II, no. 6.
Brave Kong (Cambodia). Clarkson and Cross, *World Folktales,* no. 61.
Brave Little Tailor, The (Germany). Thompson, *100 Favorite Folktales,* no.
    94.
Brave Little Tailor, The. Grimm, *Tales,* no. 20.

Cobbler, The. Crane, *Italian Popular Tales,* no. 19.
Dozen at One Blow, A. Jacobs, *European Folk and Fairy Tales,* no. 10.
Foma Berennikov. Afanasyev, *Russian Fairy Tales,* p. 284.
Herr Lazarus and the Draken. Lang, *Grey Fairy Book,* p. 136.
Ivan the Simpleton. Afanasyev, *Russian Fairy Tales,* p. 142.
Jack and the Varmints (USA). Clarkson and Cross, *World Folktales,* no. 43.
Jack and the Varmints. Chase, *Jack Tales,* no. 6.
Jack in the Giants' Newground (USA). Cole, *Best-Loved Folktales,* no. 176.
Jack in the Giants' Newground. Chase, *Jack Tales,* no. 1.
Jack Strong, Slayer of Five Hundred. Calvino, *Italian Folktales,* no. 97.
Jack the Giant-Killer (I, II). Briggs, *DBF,* pt. A, v. 1, pp. 329, 331.
John and the Giants. Musick, *Green Hills of Magic,* no. 26.
John Balento. Calvino, *Italian Folktales,* no. 199.
John Glaick, the Brave Tailor. Briggs, *DBF,* pt. A, v. 1, p. 341.
Johnny Gloke. Jacobs, *More English Fairy Tales,* p. 78.
Old Cobbler, The (Belgium). Bødker, *European Folk Tales,* p. 156.
Old Magician Sabino, The. Mathias and Raspa, *Italian Folktales in America,* no. 9.
Outwitting Giants. Villa, *100 Armenian Tales,* no. 64.
Stupid John Nightgown Who Killed Seven at One Push. Espinosa, *Folklore of Spain in the American Southwest,* p. 184.
Tailor and the Giants, The. Roberts, *South from Hell,* no. 62B.
Tailor, The. Massignon, *Folktales of France,* no. 4.
Valiant John. Thomas, *It's Good to Tell You,* no. 21.
Widow's Son, A. Glassie, *Irish Folktales,* no. 114.

**1641 DOCTOR KNOW-ALL.** A peasant named Crab claimed to be Dr. Know-All. A nobleman who had lost some money invited Crab to dinner. When the first course was served, Crab said to his wife: "That is the first one." The servant, who had helped to steal the money, thought he meant: "That is the first thief." In a like manner, Crab accidentally identified the second and third thieves, and they all confessed. (Grimm) —Continues with similar fortunate accidents.

Almondseed and Almondella. Megas, *Folktales of Greece,* no. 68.
Brother Rabbit Has Fun at the Ferry. Harris, *Uncle Remus and His Friends,* no. 3.
Charcoal Burner, The. Asbjørnsen and Moe, *Norwegian Folktales,* p. 25.
Clever Gypsy, The. Briggs, *DBF,* pt. A, v. 2, p. 39.
Clever Irishman, The. Briggs, *DBF,* pt. A, v. 2, p. 39.
Conjuror, The; or, The Turkey and the Ring. Briggs, *DBF,* pt. A, v. 2, p. 46.
Crab (Italy). Clarkson and Cross, *World Folktales,* no. 9.
Crab (Italy). Cole, *Best-Loved Folktales,* no. 30.
Crab (Italy). Thompson, *100 Favorite Folktales,* no. 95.
Crab. Crane, *Italian Popular Tales,* no. 109.
Cricket. Delarue, French Folktales, p. 66.
Cricket Is Caught. Saucier, *French Louisiana,* no. 24B.
Cunning Old Wizard; or, Jean Malin. Saucier, *French Louisiana,* no. 24A.
Doctor Know-All. Ranke, *Folktales of Germany,* no. 54.
Dr. Know-All. Grimm, *Tales,* no. 98.
Fortuneteller, The. Musick, *Green Hills of Magic,* no. 54.
Gaping Woman, The. Roberts, *South from Hell,* no. 63.
Goldhair Becomes Minister. Eberhard, *Folktales of China,* no. 11.
Harisarman. Jacobs, *Indian Fairy Tales,* p. 85.
Idle Ahmad. Bushnaq, *Arab Folktales,* p. 350.

King's Jewel, The. Saucier, *French Louisiana,* no. 24.
Lucky Imposter, The. Clouston, *Popular Tales,* v. 2, p. 413.
Old Coon, The. Dorson, *Negro Tales,* p. 172.
Peasant Astrologer, The. Calvino, *Italian Folktales,* no. 25.
Robin's Escape. Glassie, *Irish Folktales,* no. 28.
Roclore. Dorson, *Buying the Wind,* p. 253.
Second Sight. Randolph, *The Devil's Pretty Daughter,* p. 133.
Sham Wise Man, The. Paredes, *Folktales of Mexico,* no. 57.
Society of Khrap, The. Legman, *Rationale of the Dirty Joke,* vol. 1, p. 153.

**1641C  THE PEASANT WHO SPOKE LATIN.**  A peasant accidentally spoke some words that sounded like Latin. His learning so impressed the king, that he gave him his daughter and half the kingdom. Cf. type 1628*.

> Twigmuntus, Cowbelliantus, Perchnosius (Sweden). Booss, *Scandinavian Folk Tales,* p. 199.

**1642  THE GOOD BARGAIN.**  A peasant sold his cow for seven talers. Returning home he passed a pond filled with croaking frogs. He understood them to say: "Eight, eight." "No, seven," he called back. When the frogs replied: "Eight, eight," he threw the seven talers at them, shouting: "Count it for yourself!"  —Continues with similar blunders. (Grimm) Cf. type 1415.

> Bahlul and the Owl. Bushnaq, *Arab Folktales,* p. 278.
> Foolish John and the Errands. Dorson, *Buying the Wind,* p. 250.
> Good Bargain, The. Grimm, *Tales,* no. 7.
> Irishmen and the Frogs. Dorson, *Negro Tales,* p. 250.
> Keloghlan Who Would Not Tell, The. Walker and Uysal, *Tales in Turkey,* p. 161.
> Vardiello. Basile, *Pentamerone,* Day 1, Tale 4.

**1643  SELLING GOODS TO A STATUE.**  Giufà attempted to sell a piece of cloth to a statue. When it did not pay him, he struck it with a hoe, uncovering a treasure that had been hidden inside. (Calvino)

> Giufà and the Plaster Statue. Calvino, *Italian Folktales,* no. 190.1.
> Giufà and the Plaster Statue. Crane, *Italian Popular Tales,* no. 99.

**1645  TREASURE AT HOME.**  A pedlar who lived in Swaffham dreamed that good fortune would befall him at London Bridge. Hence he traveled to the bridge, and there told his dream to a shopkeeper. The Londoner replied: "You are a fool to take such a journey." He then told the pedlar of a dream he had had describing a treasure trove in Swaffham. From the description, the pedlar recognized his own orchard. He rushed home and found the treasure. (Jacobs)

> Dream, The. Dawood, *1001 Nights,* p. 328.
> Dreams of Gold. Glassie, *Irish Folktales,* no. 76.

How Dundonald Castle Was Built. Briggs, *DBF,* pt. B, v. 2, p. 234.
John Chapman Goes to London Bridge. Porter, *Folklore of East Anglia,* p. 126.
Pedlar of Swaffham, The (I-III). Briggs, *DBF,* pt. B, v. 2, p. 298.
Pedlar of Swaffham, The. Jacobs, *More English Fairy Tales,* p. 98.
Swaffham Tinker, The. Briggs, *DBF,* pt. B, v. 1, p. 364.
Upsall Castle. Briggs, *DBF,* pt. B, v. 2, p. 385.

**1645A THE DREAM OF BURIED TREASURE.** A traveler dreamed that he found a barrel of money in a burial mound. Later he came to such a mound and dug up a hidden treasure. (Simpson)

Dreamer and the Treasure, The. Simpson, *Icelandic Folktales and Legends,* p. 186.
Man Who Bought a Dream, The (Japan). Dorson, *Folktales around the World,* p. 245.
Man Who Bought a Dream, The. Seki, *Folktales of Japan,* no. 45.
Sleeping King, The. Grimm, *German Legends,* no. 433.

**1645B\* GOD WILL PROVIDE.** A poor man who trusted in God hired his donkey to strangers, who loaded it with a treasure. Then they fell to fighting among themselves, and soon all three were dead from their wounds. The donkey, still laden with gold, returned to its master. (Bushnaq)

Fortune and the Wood-Cutter (Asia Minor). Lang, *Brown Fairy Book,* p. 202.
God Will Provide. Bushnaq, *Arab Folktales,* p. 307.
Laziness Rewarded. Paredes, *Folktales of Mexico,* no. 58.
Poor Man's Trust in God, The. Sabar, *Kurdistani Jews,* p. 145.

**1650 THREE BROTHERS INHERIT A ROOSTER, A SCYTHE, AND A CAT.** A man left his oldest son a rooster, the next a scythe, and the youngest a cat, telling them to seek their fortunes where such things were unknown. The first boy found a land without roosters. The people there were so pleased with its ability to crow at fixed hours that they gave a donkey laden with gold for it. The second son found a country where the peasants harvested their grain with cannons, and they gave him a great fortune for his scythe. The third found an island overrun with mice, and he sold his cat for the greatest fortune of all. —Continues as type 1281. (Grimm) Cf. types 1202, 1651.

Gilded Fox, The. Delarue, *French Folktales,* p. 119.
Inheritance, The (Finland). Bødker, *European Folk Tales,* p. 26.
Three Children of Fortune, The. Grimm, *Tales,* no. 70.

**1651 DICK WHITTINGTON AND HIS CAT.** —Essentially the same as the cat episode in type 1650.

Cottager and His Cat, The (Iceland). Lang, *Crimson Fairy Book,* p. 174.
Dick Whittington and His Cat. Briggs, *Folklore of the Cotswolds,* p. 60.

King of the Canaries, The. Storer, *Facetiae of Poggio,* no. 113.
Three Children of Fortune, The. Grimm, *Tales,* no. 70.
Three Pennies, The. Afanasyev, *Russian Fairy Tales,* p. 113.
Whittington and His Cat. Briggs, *DBF,* pt. B, v. 2, p. 139.
Whittington and His Cat. Clouston, *Popular Tales,* v. 2, p. 65.
Whittington and His Cat. Jacobs, *English Fairy Tales,* p. 167.
Whittington. Lang, *Blue Fairy Book,* p. 206.

**1651A  SALT IN A SALTLESS LAND.** A sailor with a ship loaded with salt landed in a land that knew no salt. He traded his entire cargo, measure for measure, for silver and gold. (Afanasyev)

Boat Loaded with. . ., A. Calvino, *Italian Folktales,* no. 173.
Salt (Russia). Cole, *Best-Loved Folktales,* no. 96.
Salt (Russia). Thompson, *100 Favorite Folktales,* no. 96.
Salt. Afanasyev, *Russian Fairy Tales,* p. 40.

**1652  THE FIDDLER AND THE WOLVES.** A boy sat in the rafters of a kiln playing the fiddle. A pack of wolves heard him and entered the building, and the boy locked them inside. A traveler heard the wolves howling and the boy fiddling, and he stopped to see what was happening. When he opened the kiln door, the wolves all escaped. The boy claimed that these were the emperor's wolves, and that he was teaching them to play the fiddle. The frightened traveler gave the boy thousands of marks.

Inheritance, The (Finland). Bødker, *European Folk Tales,* p. 26.

**1653  THE ROBBERS UNDER THE TREE.** Mr. and Mrs. Vinegar lived in a vinegar bottle. One day she broke the house with her broom. There was nothing left but the door, so they picked it up and set forth to seek their fortune. At nightfall they found themselves in a forest. They climbed a tree, pulling up the door behind them. A band of robbers met under the tree to divide their booty. Mr. Vinegar was so frightened that he let the door fall. The terrified robbers ran away, leaving their money behind. (Jacobs).

Hereafterthis. Briggs, *DBF,* pt. A, v. 2, p. 116.
Inheritance, The (Finland). Bødker, *European Folk Tales,* p. 26.
Lucky Table, The (Costa Rica). Cole, *Best-Loved Folktales,* no. 196.
Michel Michelkleiner's Good Luck (Luxembourg). Bødker, *European Folk Tales,* p. 98.
Mister Vinegar. Jacobs, *English Fairy Tales,* p. 28.
Quare Jack. Dorson, *Buying the Wind,* p. 172.
Thriftless Wife, The. Briggs, *DBF,* pt. A, v. 2, p. 310.
Tinker's Wife, The. Briggs, *DBF,* pt. A, v. 2, p. 314.
Wedding Gift. Musick, *Green Hills of Magic,* no. 65.

**1653A  SECURING THE DOOR.** Freddy and Lizzy set forth to overtake a swindler. Freddy asked Lizzy to secure the house door and then to follow him. She secured the door by taking it off its hinges and carrying it with her. —Continues as type 1653. (Grimm) Cf. type 1009.

> Freddy and Katy Lizzy. Grimm, *Tales*, no. 59.
> Giufà, Pull the Door after You! Calvino, *Italian Folktales*, no. 190.6.
> Hereafterthis. Jacobs, *More English Fairy Tales*, p. 7.
> Silly Girl, The. Dorson, *Negro Tales*, p. 105.
> Visitor from Paradise, A. Jacobs, *European Folk and Fairy Tales*, no. 19.

### 1653B TWO BROTHERS IN A TREE. Cf. types 1653, 1653A.

> Fool and His Brother, The. Paredes, *Folktales of Mexico*, no. 62.
> Fool's Luck. Villa, *100 Armenian Tales*, no. 62.
> Simpleton Brother, The. Dawkins, *Modern Greek Folktales*, no. 64.

### 1653F A FOOL FRIGHTENS ROBBERS BY TALKING TO HIMSELF.

> Brave Laborer, The. Afanasyev, *Russian Fairy Tales*, p. 276.
> Giufà, the Moon, the Robbers, and the Cops. Calvino, *Italian Folktales*, no. 190.2.
> Old One-Eye. Chase, *Grandfather Tales*, no. 23.

### 1654 ROBBERS FLEE FROM A SUPPOSED CORPSE. To escape from his creditors, Giufà pretended to die, and his body was carried into the church. That night some robbers came into the church to divide a sack of stolen money. Giufà sat up in his coffin, and the terrified robbers ran away, leaving their money behind. (Calvino)

> Giufà and the Red Beret. Calvino, *Italian Folktales*, no. 190.3.
> Giufà's Exploits. Crane, *Italian Popular Tales*, no. 103.
> Miser, The. Afanasyev, *Russian Fairy Tales*, p. 58.
> Partnership of the Thief and the Liar. Lang, *Grey Fairy Book*, p. 67.
> Persistent Creditor and Dishonest Debtor. Walker and Uysal, *Tales in Turkey*, p. 145.
> Stingy and Naggy. El-Shamy, *Folktales of Egypt*, no. 55.
> Two Thieves (Russia). Dorson, *Folktales around the World*, p. 129.

### 1655 PROFITABLE EXCHANGES. A traveler left a pea at an inn. The landlady's chicken ate the pea, so the man took the chicken in exchange. At his next stop, a pig ate his chicken, so the man took the pig. Then a horse killed his pig, so he took the horse. At the next inn, the landlord's daughter took the horse to the river to drink; it fell in and was carried away. The man demanded the girl in exchange for the lost horse. Afraid that she would escape, he put her in a sack. The landlady at the next inn released the girl, placing a big dog in her place. When the man opened the sack, the dog flew out at him, and no one knows what happened next. (Jacobs) Cf. types 170A, 545B*, 1415.

> All Change. Jacobs, *European Folk and Fairy Tales*, no. 2.

Exchanges (5 variants). Arewa, *Northern East Africa*, p. 244.
Grain of Wheat, The. Pourrat, *French Tales*, p. 165.
How the King Recruited His Army. Harris, *Uncle Remus and His Friends*, no. 24.
It Started with a Thorn. Villa, *100 Armenian Tales*, no. 96.
Pedro Urdimale Makes Exchanges. Pino-Saavedra, *Folktales of Chile*, no. 47.
Sexton's Nose, The. Crane, *Italian Popular Tales*, no. 79.
Sparrow, The. El-Shamy, *Folktales of Egypt*, no. 50.
Stubborn Keloghlan, The. Walker and Uysal, *Tales in Turkey*, p. 163.
Travels of a Fox, The (USA). Clarkson and Cross, *World Folktales*, no. 41.
Turlendu. Delarue, *French Folktales*, p. 319.

**1656 LURING UNWANTED SOULS OUT OF HEAVEN.** There were too many Welshmen in heaven, so Saint Peter stepped outside and called: "Roasted Cheese!" All the Welshmen ran out to get some, and Peter barred the gate behind them. —Note: In Eastern Europe the story is told how Jews were drawn from heaven with the promise of a used clothing sale in hell.

Cause Bob. Briggs, *DBF,* pt. A, v. 2, p. 35.

**1661 THE MULTIPLE TAX.** A padishah granted a weaver the right to extract a tax from anyone who was also a weaver, anyone whose name was Hasan, anyone who was bald, and anyone who had two wives. The first man he confronted met all the requirements, and had to pay a fourfold tax. With time the weaver's tax charter caused an uproar among the people, and the padishah withdrew it. Impressed with the weaver's cleverness, he made him an advisor.

Wise Old Weaver, The. Walker and Uysal, *Tales in Turkey*, p. 183.

**1663 DIVIDING EGGS AMONG MEN AND WOMAN.** A man, asked to divide five eggs justly among two men and one woman, gave each man one and the woman three. He reasoned that nature had already provided the men with two eggs apiece. (Bushnaq) Cf. types 875, 1533.

Just Deserts. Bushnaq, *Arab Folktales*, p. 371.
Nasreddin Khoja Dividing Five Eggs. Walker and Uysal, *Tales in Turkey*, p. 233.

**1675 THE OX THAT LEARNED TO TALK.** A childless couple "adopted" an ox. The sexton, in return for money and provisions, offered to teach it to speak. To cover his fraud, he slaughtered the ox and reported that it had run away. Later the couple learned of a merchant named Peter Ox who lived in a neighboring town. They saw in him their lost son and named him their heir. The merchant, who had no living parents, was also pleased with newly discovered kin. (Thompson)

One-Eyed Cadi, The. Noy, *Folktales of Israel,* no. 66.
Ox as Mayor, The (Germany). Dorson, *Folktales around the World,* p. 90.
Ox as Mayor, The. Ranke, *Folktales of Germany,* no. 77.
Peter Bull (Denmark). Cole, *Best-Loved Folktales,* no. 82.
Peter Bull (Denmark). Lang, *Pink Fairy Book,* p. 126.
Peter Ox (Denmark). Thompson, *100 Favorite Folktales,* no. 97.

**1676  A SHAM GHOST IS FRIGHTENED BY HIS VICTIM.** A sexton, annoyed by a half-witted girl who sang hymns in the churchyard, dressed in a sheet to frighten her. When she saw him she cried out: "Run, white soul, or the black soul will catch you!" The terrified sexton ran for his life. Never again did he interfere with the girl who sang hymns. (Briggs, "Netherbury Churchyard Legend")

Croydon Devil Claims His Own, The. Briggs, *DBF,* pt. B, v. 1, p. 59.
Idiot, The. Briggs, *DBF,* pt. B, v. 2, p. 239.
Netherbury Churchyard Legend, The. Briggs, *DBF,* pt. B, v. 2, p. 276.

**1676A  A SHAM GHOST IS FRIGHTENED BY A MONKEY.** A man dressed himself in a sheet to frighten a little boy. The man's pet monkey, unbeknown to him, pulled a cloth over his head and followed. When the boy saw them he shouted: "Run, big fraid, or little fraid will catch you!" The terrified man ran home, and never tried to scare the boy again. (Roberts)

Big Fraid and Little Fraid. Roberts, *South from Hell,* no. 60A.
Black Devil and White Devil. Briggs, *DBF,* pt. B, v. 1, p. 23.
Lantern Lads, The. Briggs, *DBF,* pt. B, v. 1, p. 299.
Mock Ghost and Real Ghost. Briggs, *DBF,* pt. B, v. 1, p. 541.
Two Ghosts, The. Briggs, *DBF,* pt. B, v. 1, p. 594.
White Bucca and the Black, The. Briggs, *DBF,* pt. B, v. 1, p. 38.

**1676B  THE GIRL WHO DIED OF FRIGHT.** To prove her courage, a girl went to a graveyard after dark. She caught her clothing on a stick, and—thinking a spirit had her—she died of fright. (Dorson)

Girl Who Died of Fright, The. Dorson, *Buying the Wind,* p. 310.
Rider in the Brambles, The. Paredes, *Folktales of Mexico,* no. 61A.
Stake in the Graveyard, The. Paredes, *Folktales of Mexico,* no. 61B.

**1678  THE BOY WHO HAD NEVER SEEN A WOMAN.** A man lived alone in the mountains with his boy. When the boy was fourteen years old they went to town together, and the boy saw—for his first time—a pretty girl. "That's a devil red-hot from hell," explained the father. Before leaving town the father offered to buy the boy a new shotgun or a pony. The boy answered: "No, just get me one of those devils red-hot from hell." (Randolph)

Boy Who Had Never Seen a Woman. Boccaccio, *Decameron,* Day 4, Introduction.
King Neptune's Diamonds. Musick, *Green Hills of Magic,* no. 51.

Woman-Hater's Son, The. Randolph, *The Devil's Pretty Daughter,* p. 120.

**1681B   THE FOOL AS A HOUSEKEEPER.**   A fool reported to his brother that their old mother was ill. "Heat some water for a bath, while I go for a doctor," said the bright one.   The fool filled the tub with boiling water, then put his grandmother in it.   She died. (Paredes) Cf. types 1012, 1013.

> Clever Servant, The. *Grimm, Tales,* no. 162.
> Fool and His Brother, The. Paredes, *Folktales of Mexico,* no. 62.

**1682   THE HORSE THAT ATE STRAW.**   A man trained a horse to eat nothing but straw, but it died. (Clouston)

> Jew and His Horse, The. Carpenter, *A Latvian Storyteller,* p. 204.
> Training a Horse to Live on Straw. Clouston, *Book of Noodles,* p. 2.

**1682*   MAKING A STUBBORN MULE GO.**   A man put a dime's worth of stinging salve on his mule's tail to make it go.   Then he had to get twenty cents' worth for himself, in order to catch his runaway mule. (Randolph)

> High-Life on the Mule. Randolph, *Hot Springs and Hell,* no. 323.
> Quick Ass, The. El-Shamy, *Folktales of Egypt,* no. 61.

**1684A*   THE LONG NIGHT.**   As a joke, an innkeeper locked two travelers in their windowless room.   Throughout the next day, whenever they would knock on their door to be let out, he would shout back: "Be quiet. It's night and people are trying to sleep."

> Land of the Long Nights, The. Pourrat, *French Tales,* p. 42.

**1685   A FOOL'S COURTSHIP AND MARRIAGE.**   —A numskull makes foolish mistakes while courting and on his wedding night.

> Casting Sheep's Eyes. Roberts, *South from Hell,* no. 64.
> Foolish Bridegroom. Legman, *Rationale of the Dirty Joke,* vol. 1, p. 152.
> Gothamite Casts Sheep-Eyes at a Fair Maid, A. Clouston, *Book of Noodles,*
> Numskull Groom on His Wedding Night, The. Legman, *Rationale of the Dirty Joke,* vol. 1, p. 126.
> Pike's Head, The. Afanasyev, *Erotic Tales,* p. 45.
> Pike's Head, The. Afanasyev, *Russian Secret Tales,* p. 16.
> Silly Boy, The (Sweden). Bødker, *European Folk Tales,* p. 28.

**1687   THE FORGOTTEN WORD.**   A woman sent her son to buy soap. As he walked, he kept saying "soap, soap," to remind himself of what he was to fetch. A passerby thought the boy was making fun of him and scolded him. The boy responded: "I'm sorry I done it," but then forgot the soap, now repeating "I'm sorry I done it" as he walked. He came to a woman who had just dropped a basket of eggs. Thinking he was ridiculing her, she pushed him into a ditch. Covered with mud,

he continued on his way. The next person he met told him to go
home and wash with soap. At last he remembered what he had been
sent for, and he went to the store and bought some soap. (Chase)
—Cf. type 1696.

Soap Boy, The. Roberts, *South from Hell,* no. 65.
Soap, Soap, Soap! Chase, *Grandfather Tales,* no. 14.
Stupid's Cries. Jacobs, *More English Fairy Tales,* p. 211.
Stupid's Mistaken Cries. Briggs, *DBF,* pt. A, v. 2, p. 284.

**1689    THE GIFT THAT WAS THROWN AT THE GIVER.** A
peasant selected a basket of large turnips as a gift for the emir, but
then decided that figs would be more appropriate. The emir was in a
sour mood and had his servants pelt the peasant with the figs. "Thank
God they weren't turnips!" cried the peasant. The emir, upon
hearing the peasant's explanation for the unusual remark, changed
his mood and gave the man a purse of gold. (Bushnaq)

Djuha and the Basket of Figs. Bushnaq, *Arab Folktales,* p. 258.
Luckily, They Are Not Peaches. Clouston, *Popular Tales,* v. 2, p. 467.
Nasreddin Khoja and Tamerlane. Walker and Uysal, *Tales in Turkey,* p. 229.
Thank God It Wasn't a Peso. Paredes, *Folktales of Mexico,* no. 63.

**1689A    TWO PRESENTS FOR THE KING.** A poor man harvested a
giant turnip and gave it to the king. The amused monarch responded
with a generous reward. The poor man's wealthy brother, hoping
for an even greater reward, presented the king with horses and gold.
The king gave him the giant turnip in return. (Grimm) —Note: This
tale often includes an episode of type 1610. For additional tales of
giant vegetables see types 1920A, 1960D, 2044.

Deal That Went to the Dogs, A. Dégh, *Folktales of Hungary,* no. 16.
Test of the Chicken, The. Villa, *100 Armenian Tales,* no. 74.
Turnip, The. Grimm, *Tales,* no. 146.

**1692    THE STUPID THIEF.** Goosey Grizzel joined a band of thieves.
They sent her into a well-stocked kitchen to steal food.
Overwhelmed with the choices, she called out, asking which items
she should steal. This woke the household, and Goosey had to flee
empty handed. (Asbjørnsen and Moe)

Goosey Grizzel. Asbjørnsen and Moe, *East o' the Sun,* p. 221.
Letter to the Almighty, A. Noy, *Folktales of Israel,* no. 35.

**1693    A FOOL TAKES INSTRUCTIONS LITERALLY.** Example:
A farmer instructed his new shepherd about repelling wild animals.
"Throw rocks at them like these," he said. Later a leopard
approached the flock, and the shepherd ran home to pick up the rocks
that the farmer had pointed out. When he returned to the flock, the

leopard had already done his damage. (Lang, "The Foolish Weaver")

Foolish Weaver, The (Pushtu). Lang, *Orange Fairy Book*, p. 124.
Fool, The. Crane, *Italian Popular Tales*, no. 104.
I Know What I Have Learned (Denmark). Lang, *Pink Fairy Book*, p. 148.
Letter to the Almighty, A. Noy, *Folktales of Israel*, no. 35.
Naar. Lindell, *Folk Tales from Kammu*, II, no. 1.

**1696  WHAT SHOULD I HAVE SAID?** A fool says and does the right things, but always on the wrong occasions, for example mourning at a wedding or rejoicing at a funeral. Cf. type 1687.

Arrant Fool, The. Afanasyev, *Russian Fairy Tales*, p. 334.
Clever Hans. Grimm, *Tales*, no. 32.
Fool, The (Venice). Clouston, *Book of Noodles*, p. 127.
Giufà and the Wineskin. Calvino, *Italian Folktales*, no. 190.4.
Going Traveling. Grimm, *Tales*, no. 143.
Heart, Liver, and Lights. Campbell, *Cloudwalking Country*, p. 94.
Jack and the King's Girl. Chase, *Jack Tales*, no. 9.
Jack's Rewards and What He Did With Them. Briggs, *DBF*, pt. A, v. 2, p. 134.
Jock and His Mother. Briggs, *DBF*, pt. A, v. 1, p. 340.
Johnny Raggie Comes Ta Grace. Marwick, *Folklore of Orkney and Shetland*, p. 172.
Lazy Jack (England). Clarkson and Cross, *World Folktales*, no. 60.
Lazy Jack. Briggs, *DBF*, pt. A, v. 2, p. 150.
Lazy Jack. Jacobs, *English Fairy Tales*, p. 152.
Silly Boy, The (Sweden). Bødker, *European Folk Tales*, p. 28.
Silly Matt (Norway). Clouston, *Book of Noodles*, p. 123.
Simpleton, The. Grimm, *Other Tales*, p. 95.
Some Other Small Gut. Randolph, *The Devil's Pretty Daughter*, p. 72.
Stupid Drover, The. Paredes, *Folktales of Mexico*, no. 64.
Stupid's Mistaken Cries. Briggs, *DBF*, pt. A, v. 2, p. 285.
Village Fool, The. Dorson, *Buying the Wind*, p. 343.
What Am I to Say? Megas, *Folktales of Greece*, no. 67.
What Should I Have Said? (Russia). Thompson, *100 Folktales*, no. 98.
You Shouldn't Say That, Karagöz! Walker and Uysal, *Tales in Turkey*, p. 159.

**1697  WE THREE; FOR MONEY.** Three innocent foreigners unwittingly confess to a murder because of their limited vocabulary. Cf. type 360.

Three Dunces, The. Espinosa, *Folklore of Spain in the American Southwest*, p. 185.
Three Foreigners, The. Briggs and Tongue, *Folktales of England*, no. 70.
Three Foreigners, The. Briggs, *DBF*, pt. A, v. 2, p. 294.
Three Journeymen, The. Grimm, *Tales*, no. 120.
We Killed Him. Briggs, *DBF*, pt. A, v. 2, p. 345.
We Ourselves. Pino-Saavedra, *Folktales of Chile*, no. 48.
We Three Hielanmen. Briggs, *DBF*, pt. A, v. 2, p. 345.

**1698  A DEAF MAN'S COMICAL ANSWERS.**

Deaf Man's Answers, The. Randolph, *Who Blowed Up the Church House?*, p. 80.
Hard of Hearing: A Love Story. Dorson, *Jonathan Draws the Long Bow*, p. 98.
She Wanted a Whisk Broom. Randolph, *Sticks in the Knapsack*, p. 109.
She Who Understood Best. Bushnaq, *Arab Folktales*, p. 376.
She's Got One Spoiled Tit. Randolph, *The Talking Turtle*, p. 39.
Son of a Bishop, The. Randolph, *The Talking Turtle*, p. 118.

### 1698C  A SHOUTING MATCH BETWEEN TWO WHO THINK EACH OTHER DEAF.

Firrazzanu's Wife and the Queen. Crane, *Italian Popular Tales*, no. 98.

### 1698J  A DEAF MAN'S MEMORIZED ANSWERS.  A deaf man, carving an ax handle, noticed a visitor approaching, so he quickly thought out answers to the questions he thought would be asked. "First he will ask what I am making," thought the man. But actually the visitor said: "Good day," to which the deaf man said: "An ax handle." "Next," thought the deaf man, "he will ask about my mare." Instead, the man asked about his daughter, and received the answer "She's in the barn, heavy with foal." —Similar absurdities follow. (Asbjørnsen and Moe)

Deaf Man and the Pig Trough, The. Briggs and Tongue, *Folktales of England*, no. 71.
Good Day, Fellow! Axe Handle! Asbjørnsen and Moe, *Norwegian Folktales*, p. 158.

### 1698K  THE FOREIGN SALESMAN.  —Similar to type 1698J, except that the misunderstandings stem from language problems instead of from deafness. Cf. type 1699.

Buyer and the Seller, The. Briggs, *DBF*, pt. A, v. 2, p. 30.

### 1699  A FOREIGNER'S COMICAL ANSWERS.

Charity Will Save from Death. Noy, *Folktales of Israel*, no. 39.
Englishman and Highlandman. Briggs, *DBF*, pt. A, v. 2, p. 69.
Fool, The. Dorson, *Buying the Wind*, p. 450.
Paut Ar Ir? Carpenter, *A Latvian Storyteller*, p. 194.
Rosary of Amozoc, The. Paredes, *Folktales of Mexico*, no. 65.
Two Farmers, The. Dorson, *Buying the Wind*, p. 451.

### 1700  I DON'T KNOW.  Comical situations result when the expression "I don't know," spoken in a foreign language, is misunderstood.

Colored Man and the Mexicans, The. Dorson, *Negro Tales*, p. 79.
I Don't Know. Carpenter, *A Latvian Storyteller*, p. 158.
No Estiendo. Dorson, *Buying the Wind*, p. 452.
Old Gram Shaw. Dorson, *Buying the Wind*, p. 90.

**1705   AN ANIMAL TALKS BACK.** A farmer scolded his ox: "Stupid fool, who taught you to be so awkward?" The ox replied: "You did!" (Briggs)

> Farmer and His Ox, The. Briggs and Tongue, *Folktales of England,* no. 84.
> Farmer and His Ox, The. Briggs, *DBF,* pt. A, v. 2, p. 82.
> Talk (Africa). Clarkson and Cross, *World Folktales,* no. 36.
> Things That Talked, The. Abrahams, *Afro-American Folktales,* no. 106.

**1725   AN AMOROUS PARSON IS TRAPPED IN A CHEST.** A parson visiting a married woman was surprised by her returning husband and had to hide in a chest half filled with soot. The husband, who knew of the parson's presence, took the chest to town and amused himself by displaying the black devil he had captured. (Afanasyev) Cf. types 1358A, 1535.

> Hussar Stroke, A. Dégh, *Folktales of Hungary,* no. 14.
> Pope Who Neighed Like a Stallion, The. Afanasyev, *Russian Secret Tales,* p. 190.

**1726*  A SEDUCTION WITH LOST EARRINGS.** A man whose wife had been seduced by the priest planned his revenge. He visited the priest's wife and secretly pocketed her earrings. When she missed them, he surmised that she had sat on them and had thus lost them in a certain place. Fortunately, he possessed the right tool for probing. Only after numerous tries did he find the lost earrings.

> Pope and the Peasant, The. Afanasyev, *Russian Secret Tales,* p. 102.

**1730   LOVERS IN A CHEST.** A woman, for her own reasons, invited five lovers to visit her, scheduling them at short intervals. The first had just gotten undressed when he heard the second one coming; thinking it was her husband, he hid in a large chest. And so it continued until all five men were trapped in the same chest. (*1001 Nights,* "A Woman's Trick") Cf. types 882A*, 1359C.

> Cunning Woman, The (3 versions). Afanasyev, *Russian Secret Tales,* p. 200.
> Honest Wife, The. Megas, *Folktales of Greece,* no. 66.
> Lady and Her Suitors, The. Clouston, *Popular Tales,* v. 2, p. 289.
> Live Statues, The. Fowke, *Folklore of Canada,* p. 284.
> Painted Priests, The. Musick, *Green Hills of Magic,* no. 72.
> Perfidy of Wives , The. Mathers, (Frame Story) *1001 Nights,* v. 4, p. 89.
> Woman's Trick, A. Mathers, *1001 Nights,* v. 3, 225.

**1735   A SERMON ON GIVING AND RECEIVING.** A priest promised that whatever a person would give to the church would come back a hundredfold. A poor man, at the priest's insistence, gave a calf. The calf broke away from its new pasture, leading the priest's cows back to the poor man. The priest, because of his promise, had to give up his runaway cattle. (Paredes)

God Gives a Hundred for One. Paredes, *Folktales of Mexico,* no. 66.
Sentence Concerning the Cows, The. Afanasyev, *Russian Secret Tales,* p. 141.

**1735A  A BOY SINGS THE WRONG SONG IN CHURCH.** A parson, whose meat had been stolen, heard a boy singing: "We have seven geese and an old one, too. The meat of the priest is hanging in the chimney, too." He asked the boy to sing this song in church. The boy told his parents, and they taught him new words. When Sunday came, the boy sang: "We have seven young geese and an old one, too. The priest sleeps with the cook and with the maiden, too." (Ranke)

Man That Stole the Parson's Sheep. Briggs and Tongue, *Folktales of England,* no. 62.
Man That Stole the Parson's Sheep, The. Briggs, *DBF,* pt. A, v. 2, p. 173.
Parson and the Shepherd Lad, The. Briggs, *DBF,* pt. A, v. 2, p. 232.
Priest's Pig, The. Massignon, *Folktales of France,* no. 5.
Wee Boy and Minister Gray, The. Briggs, *DBF,* pt. A, v. 2, p. 344.
Wrong Song, The. Ranke, *Folktales of Germany,* no. 55.

**1736A  THE SWORD THAT TURNED TO WOOD.** A soldier lost his sword and carved a replacement from wood. Later he was commanded to execute a comrade. He said: "If God grants this condemned man his life, let Him turn my sword to wood." He drew his sword, and sure enough, it had "miraculously" turned to wood. (Dégh)

Blessed Be God Day by Day. Noy, *Folktales of Israel,* no. 30.
King Mátyás and the Hussars. Dégh, *Folktales of Hungary,* no. 15.

**1737  TRADING PLACES WITH THE TRICKSTER IN A SACK.** Jack was sentenced to die for something bad he had done. The posse tied him up in a sack, and two soldiers carried him toward the river, where they were to drown him. They stopped for a drink at a tavern, leaving Jack outside. Jack started to yell that he was being forced to marry Polly Brown. A simple country boy, who thought that to marry Polly Brown would not be a bad thing, untied the sack and traded places with Jack. Thus they threw the country boy in the river, and Jack went free. (Randolph) —Note: Similar episodes are often included in types 1525A, 1535, and 1539.

Aay Caan Laay. Lindell, *Folk Tales from Kammu,* II, no. 3.
Brother Rabbit's Cradle. Harris, *Told by Uncle Remus,* no. 12.
Brother 'Possum Gets in Trouble. Harris, *Nights with Uncle Remus,* no. 32.
Canny Jack. Briggs, *DBF,* pt. A, v. 2, p. 386.
Creeturs Go to the Barbecue. Harris, *Uncle Remus and Brer Rabbit,* no. 1
In Some Lady's Garden. Harris, *Nights with Uncle Remus,* no. 31.

Incorrigible Youth, The. Briggs, *DBF*, pt. A, v. 2, p. 314.
Jack and the Sack. Randolph, The Devil's Pretty Daughter, p. 67.
Little Peasant, The. Grimm, *Tales,* no. 61.
Mister Fox Gets into Serious Business. Harris, *Uncle Remus,* no. 29.
Mister Rabbit and Mister Bear. Harris, *Uncle Remus,* no. 23.
Roclore. Dorson, *Buying the Wind,* p. 253.
Turnip, The. Grimm, *Tales,* no. 146.

**1738  NO PRIESTS IN HEAVEN.** A priest scolded a farmer for not attending church. Later the farmer told the priest he had dreamed he had died and reported to heaven. Saint Peter would not admit him, for he had not taken the Lord's Supper. "Is there no priest here who can offer it to me?" asked the farmer. "No, there are no priests in heaven," was the answer. —Note: Similar tales, told about lawyers, are classified type 1860A. Cf. type 802.

All Priests Go to Hell. Paredes, *Folktales of Mexico,* no. 67.
Black John's Dream. Briggs, *DBF,* pt. A, v. 2, p. 22.
Crowdy of Highworth. Briggs, *DBF,* pt. A, v. 2, p. 50.
Dream, The. Ranke, *Folktales of Germany,* no. 79.
Of the Beggar's Answer to Mister Skelton the Poet. Briggs, *DBF,* pt. A, v. 2, p. 276.
Old Charley Creed. Briggs and Tongue, *Folktales of England,* no. 82.
Old Charley Creed. Briggs, *DBF,* pt. A, v. 2, p. 206.
Parson's Meeting, The. Briggs and Tongue, *Folktales of England,* no. 59.
Parson's Meeting, The. Briggs, *DBF,* pt. A, v. 2, p. 231.
Preachers around the Fire. Randolph, *Hot Springs and Hell,* no. 157.

**1738C\*  MARKING SINS WITH CHALK.** Two chaps died and were on their way to heaven. Each was to mark the sins of the other with chalk on the ladder as they ascended. The one went ahead, but soon returned. "I came back for more chalk," he explained. (Briggs and Tongue, "The Two Chaps Who Went to Heaven")

Three Premiers Who Went to Heaven. Briggs and Tongue, *Folktales of England,* no. 58.
Two Chaps Who Went to Heaven. Briggs and Tongue, *Folktales of England,* no. 57.

**1739  THE MAN WHO THOUGHT HE WAS PREGNANT.** —Tricksters convince a man that he is pregnant.

Gown in the Bathhouse, The. Bushnaq, *Arab Folktales,* p. 334.
Man That Had a Baby, The. Randolph, *Pissing in the Snow,* no. 13.
Man Who Had a Calf, The. Dorson, *Buying the Wind,* p. 87.
Pope Who Begot a Calf, The. Afanasyev, *Russian Secret Tales,* p. 89.
Rectal Motherhood (anecdotes with commentary). Legman, *Rationale of the Dirty Joke,* v. 1, p. 596.
Simone Persuades Calandrino That He Is Pregnant. Boccaccio, *Decameron,* Day 9, Tale 3.

**1739A\*  PREGNANT WITH GAS.** A woman convinced her miserly husband that his gas pains from overeating were symptoms of pregnancy, and that a giant fart was the delivery of a child. In shame, the man left town. He returned years later, only to learn that his wife had disappeared with his wealth. *(1001 Nights)*

Viola Tricks the Prince into Thinking He Has Given Birth. Basile, *Pentamerone,* Day 2, Tale 3.
Father of Farts, The. Mathers, *1001 Nights,* v. 3, p. 523.

**1741   THE GUEST FLEES TO SAVE HIS EARS.** A servant girl sampled the chicken dinner she was cooking for her master and his guest, and before she knew it, she had eaten both chickens. To save herself, she told the guest that her master intended to cut off his ears, so he—understandably—fled when he saw the host approaching with a carving knife. The cook then told the master that the guest had stolen both chickens and run away. (Grimm)

Butcher's Tale, The. Mathers, *1001 Nights,* v. 4, p. 98.
Clever Gretel. Grimm, *Tales,* no. 77.
Give Me Even One. Dance, *Folklore from Contemporary Jamaicans,* no. 79.
Guest Who Ran Away, The. Bushnaq, *Arab Folktales,* p. 33.

**1750   THE TURKEYS WHO TALKED TOO MUCH.** A clever woman, in return for lavish provisions, took the queen's turkeys away, promising to train them to talk. She reported to the queen that the turkeys had learned their lessons well, but that they would say only one thing: "The princess had a lover." The queen insisted that the turkeys be killed, so the woman did not have to return them.

Talking Turkeys, The. Bushnaq, *Arab Folktales,* p. 325.

**1777A\*   SEXTON AND PRIEST TRADE PLACES.** A priest asked a confessing sexton about the money stolen from the poor box. The sexton claimed to not be able to hear the questions, so the puzzled priest traded places with him. Now the sexton asked about the seduction of his wife, and the priest could hear nothing. (Paredes)

I Can't Hear a Thing. Paredes, *Folktales of Mexico,* no. 68.
Who's Been Stealing My Cigars? Legman, *Rationale of the Dirty Joke,* vol. 1, p. 715.

**1781   PARSONS BOAST ABOUT THEIR PURSUITS.** At a camp meeting, each of two parsons would say "Amen!" whenever a woman passed whom he had seduced. The one priest said "Amen, amen!" as the other's wife and daughter walked by. No one knew the cause of the fight that ensued. (Randolph)

Hermit Who Had Many Women, A. Storer, *Facetiae of Poggio,* no. 13.
Lawyer and a Doctor, A. Legman, *Rationale of the Dirty Joke,* v. 1, p. 757.
Two Preachers, The. Randolph, *Pissing in the Snow,* no. 17.

**1785B THE PARSON HITS A NEEDLE.** Mischievous boys hid some needles in pulpit's covering. During his sermon, the pastor asked "Who created the world?" slamming his hand onto the pulpit. In pain, he cried: "It was those damned boys!"

Damned Boys, The. Ranke, *Folktales of Germany,* no. 78.

**1791 DIVIDING UP THE DEAD.** Two men, a fat one and a thin one, overheard boys in a graveyard dividing nuts: "One for you and one for me." They thought it was devils dividing souls. Then one of the boys said: "I'll take the fat one and you get the thin one." The two terrified men ran for their lives. (Randolph) —Note: The frightened dupes in this tale are most often a parson and a sexton.

Bag of Nuts, The (I, II). Briggs, *DBF,* pt. A, v. 2, p. 14.
Black and His Master, The. Briggs, *DBF,* pt. A, v. 2, p. 375.
Churchyard, The. Briggs and Tongue, *Folktales of England,* no. 60.
Churchyard, The. Briggs, *DBF,* pt. A, v. 2, p. 36.
Devil and the Angel, The. Roberts, *South from Hell,* no. 67A.
Devil in the Graveyard, The. Randolph, *Who Blowed Up the Church House?,* p. 25.
Dividing Souls. Dorson, *Negro Tales,* p. 48.
Dividing Up the Dead. Randolph, *Who Blowed Up the Church House?,* p. 83.
Freddy and Katy Lizzy. Grimm, *Tales,* no. 59.
Is He Fat? (England). Thompson, *100 Favorite Folktales,* no. 99.
Mother Elston's Nuts. Briggs, *DBF,* pt. A, v. 2, p. 193.
Old Woman Who Cracked Nuts, The. Briggs, *DBF,* pt. A, v. 2, p. 211.
One for You. Fowke, *Folklore of Canada,* p. 189.
Three in One. Briggs, *DBF,* pt. A, v. 2, p. 295.
Two Tailors, The. Briggs, *DBF,* pt. A, v. 2, p. 338.

**1792 STEALING STOLEN GOODS.** A man had a barrel of whiskey that he did not want to share with his family. A friend suggested that he hide the barrel and report that it had been stolen. This he did, but when he went to recover it, he discovered that his friend had already helped himself to the "stolen" drink. —Note: This tale is often told of a parson seeking a way to avoid sharing recently slaughtered meat.

Three Barrels of Whiskey. Randolph, *The Devil's Pretty Daughter,* p. 151.

**1804 IMAGINED PENANCE FOR AN IMAGINED SIN.** A priest charged a man fifteen dollars as penance for an intended sin. "The intention is as bad as the act," explained the priest. The man responded by going through the motion of payment with an empty hand. "My intention to pay is as good as the actual money," he explained.

Confession. Dorson, *Buying the Wind,* p. 448.

**1807 A PRIEST ABSOLVES THE MAN WHO STOLE HIS CAP.** A greedy priest charged a fee for hearing confessions. A poor man stole the priest's fur cap to get the money for the fee. The priest, without knowing whose cap the man had stolen, absolved him.

Greedy Pope, The. Afanasyev, *Russian Secret Tales,* p. 148.

**1824  PARODY SERMONS.**

Friar Cipolla's Sermon. Boccaccio, *Decameron,* Day 6, Tale 10.
Reverend John Dod's Sermon upon Malt. Briggs, *Folklore of the Cotswolds,* p. 77.
Sermon upon Malt, A. Briggs, *DBF,* pt. B, v. 2, p. 125.
Tom's Conversion. Briggs, *DBF,* pt. A, v. 2, p. 315.

**1826  A PASTOR FINDS AN EXCUSE TO NOT PREACH.** Nasr-ed-Din Hodja asked his followers if they knew what he was going to preach. When they answered "no," he left the mosque, saying: "I cannot preach an unknown subject." The following Friday he asked the same question, but this time the congregation said "yes." Again he left without preaching, saying this time: "If you already know the sermon, I have no need to preach." (Clarkson and Cross)

Nasr-ed-Din Hodja (Turkey). Clarkson and Cross, *World Folktales,* no. 48.
Secret Wisdom. Randolph, *Sticks in the Knapsack,* p. 129.

**1827A  A PARSON DROPS HIS CARDS.** A parson lifted his arms while preaching, and a deck of cards flew into the congregation. Pretending he had intentionally thrown the cards, he scolded the youth for not knowing their catechism as well as they knew cards. Cf. types 1613, 1839.

Parson and the Cards, The. Briggs, *DBF,* pt. A, v. 2, p. 230.

**1829  A LIVE PERSON TAKES THE PLACE OF A SAINT.** In celebration of holy week, some worshippers hired a man to dress in the clothing of Jesus Christ and lie in a coffin. They had just begun to walk around the coffin praying and singing, when the man lying there broke wind. (Paredes)

Live Statues, The. Fowke, *Folklore of Canada,* p. 284.
On Holy Week (Mexico). Dorson, *Folktales around the World,* p. 502.
On Holy Week. Paredes, *Folktales of Mexico,* no. 70.

**1830  THE CANDIDATE WHO PROMISED TO CONTROL THE WEATHER.** A candidate for public office promised to deliver the kind of weather everyone wanted. However, after he was installed, the townspeople could not agree upon what to request, so the weather continued as before.

Promising Candidate. Briggs, *DBF,* pt. A, v. 2, p. 241.

**1831A  INAPPROPRIATE ACTS IN CHURCH.** —Miscellaneous.

> Angry Choir-Leader, The. Briggs, *DBF*, pt. A, v. 2, p. 6.

**1832\*  A BOY ANSWERS A PARSON.**  A parson asked who was the worst sinner. A boy replied: "Moses, for he broke all the commandments." (Briggs, "Breaking the Commandments")

> Boy and the Parson, The. Briggs, *DBF*, pt. A, v. 2, p. 28.
> Breaking the Commandments. Briggs, *DBF*, pt. A, v. 2, p. 29.

**1832E\*  A PRIEST TEACHES A BOY GOOD MANNERS.**  A man sent his son with a string of trout for the priest. The boy, unhappy with the task, dropped the fish on the priest's chair and started to leave. The priest, wanting to teach the boy good manners, suggested that they exchange roles. He politely handed the fish to the boy, whereupon the boy gave him twenty-five cents, thus showing that he expected to be paid for his services. —Continues as type 1832J\*.

> String of Trout, The (Canada). Dorson, *Folktales around the World,* p. 448.

**1832J\*  A PRIEST TEACHES A BOY HOW TO CHOOSE.**  A priest laid twenty-five cents on one corner of a table, fifty cents on another, and a dollar on the third. "If you take the twenty-five cents you'll go to heaven," he explained. "Take the fifty cents and you'll go to purgatory; take the dollar and you'll go to hell. Now choose." The boy scooped up all the money, saying: "I'll take it all, then I'll be able to go where I want to."

> String of Trout, The (Canada). Dorson, *Folktales around the World,* p. 448.

**1832M\*  REPEATING THE PRIEST'S WORDS.**  A woman was told to repeat everything the priest said. And she dutifully mimicked his every statement: "Who are you?," "What do you want?," and finally: "Are you mad?"

> Performing the Five Precepts (Ceylon). Clouston, *Book of Noodles,* p. 69.

**1833  APPLYING A SERMON.** —Humorous interpretations of sermons.

> Curate and the Fool, The. Briggs, *DBF*, pt. A, v. 2, p. 52.
> Long-Winded Preacher, A. Briggs, *DBF*, pt. A, v. 2, p. 156.
> Parson Spry's Sermon. Briggs, *DBF*, pt. B, v. 2, p. 297.
> Sermon on the Arrest of Jesus, The. Paredes, *Folktales of Mexico,* no. 72.
> Skelton (III). Briggs, *DBF*, pt. A, v. 2, p. 273.

**1833A  INTERRUPTING A SERMON.**  A preacher liked to get half drunk before giving his sermon, so he sent his son to a moonshiner named Paul for a bottle of whisky. The boy did not return until after the sermon had started. The preacher told of Paul's coming down from Gotha and called out: "And what did Paul say?" The boy answered: "Paul say you pay him for that first quart of whiskey you had and he'll let you have another'n." (Dorson)

Famous Sermon, The. Paredes, *Folktales of Mexico,* no. 73.
Parson and the Parrot, The. Briggs, *DBF,* pt. A, v. 2, p. 227.
Parson and the Parrot, The. Briggs and Tongue, *Folktales of England,* no. 61.
Philip Spencer. Briggs, *DBF,* pt. A, v. 2, p. 234.
What Did Paul Say? Dorson, *Negro Tales,* p. 255.

**1833E   UNEXPECTED ANSWERS TO PRIEST'S QUESTIONS.** Example: A priest says to a simple person, "God died for you," and receives the response, "I didn't know he was sick." (Dance)

Me Never Even Know Him Sick. Dance, *Folklore from Jamaicans,* no. 141.
Minister and the Woman in the Woods, The. Dorson, *Buying the Wind,* p. 89.
Wanted a Pup. Briggs, *DBF,* pt. A, v. 2, p. 343.

**1835D\*   DON'T LET YOUR MIND WANDER.** A parson offered to give a horse to a man if the latter could say one *Pater noster* to the end without thinking of something else. The man began to pray, but after a few words he asked: "Will you include a saddle and bridle?" Thus he lost the bargain.

Ploughman That Said His Paternoster, The. Briggs, *DBF,* pt. A, v. 2, p. 237.

**1838   THE PARSON RIDES A PIG.** A pig ran between a parson's legs, thus forcing him to ride it. He shouted to his congregation: "Stick to God; I have to leave with the devil!"

Pig in the Church, The. Ranke, *Folktales of Germany,* no. 80.

**1839   CARD-PLAYING PARSONS.** —Miscellaneous anecdotes. Cf. types 1613, 1827A.

Cock-Fighting Parson, The. Briggs, *DBF,* pt. A, v. 2, p. 42.
Parson and His Boon-Companions, The. Briggs, *DBF,* pt. A, v. 2, p. 229.
Wold Forred. Briggs, *DBF,* pt. A, v. 2, p. 361.

**1840A   A BULL FOR A SAINT.** A man promised a saint a bull in return for a certain blessing. When the man delivered the bull, he asked the saint's image where he wanted it. Receiving no answer, he tied the bull to the statue and left. The bull pulled the statue over and dragged it out of the church.

Miracle of San Pedro Piedra Gorda. Paredes, *Folktales of Mexico,* no. 71.

**1840B   A THIEVING PARSON BLESSES HIMSELF.** A churchman stole eels from a miller's pond. The miller reported his loss to the thief himself, who assured him that he would place a curse on the culprit in his next sermon. The next Sunday, the churchman, in Latin, blessed the thief and cursed the victim. (Briggs, "The Miller's Eels")

> Miller's Eels, The. Briggs, *DBF,* pt. A, v. 2, p. 185.
> Poetic Truth. Briggs, *DBF,* pt. A, v. 2, p. 237.

**1842  AN ANIMAL'S BURIAL.** A goat, rooting in the earth, uncovered a treasure. When it later died, his thankful owners asked the priest to give it a Christian burial. The priest was outraged at the request, until offered fifty rubles for the service. He quickly determined that the goat was a Christian, and deserved a proper burial. (Afanasyev)

> Burial of the Dog (and the Goat), The. Afanasyev, *Russian Secret Tales,* p. 135.
> Curate Who Buried a Little Dog, A. Storer, *Facetiae of Poggio,* no. 10.
> Wayfarer and His Ass, The. Noy, *Folktales of Israel,* no. 1.

**1843  A PARSON VISITS THE DYING.** —Miscellaneous anecdotes.

> Dilemma, The. Villa, *100 Armenian Tales,* no. 69.
> Honest MacGregor, An. Briggs, *DBF,* pt. A, v. 2, p. 118.

**1847*  AN EXCHANGE OF HOLY WORDS.** A man put a sign on his apple tree: "These apples are for the festival." When he went on Saturday to pick the fruit, he found the tree bare. Someone had written on the back of his sign: "All is safely gathered in."

> Thieves and the Apples, The. Briggs, *DBF,* pt. A, v. 2, p. 293.

**1848*  A STONE FOR EACH MASS** (new classification). A man dropped a stone through a slot into a box for each mass that he attended. Although he went every day for many years, the box never became full. One day he opened the box and found only five stones. The priest explained that had he heard the mass only five times in such a way that it had counted.

> Pious Man, The. Glassie, *Irish Folktales,* no. 13.

**1848A  THE PASTOR'S CALENDAR.** —Ignorant churchmen confuse the holidays. Cf. type 2012.

> Priest Who Did Not Know When Palm Sunday Fell, A. Storer, *Facetiae of Poggio,* no. 23.
> Priest Who Made Baskets, The. Briggs, *DBF,* pt. A, v. 2, p. 240.
> Resurrexi. Briggs, *DBF,* pt. A, v. 2, p. 249.

**1861   JOKES ON JUDGES.** A farmer needed a judge's signature on a contract, but the latter refused to sign without a bribe. The farmer filled a jar nearly to the top with dung, upon which he placed a thin layer of cheese. Presenting this to the judge, he asked: "Is it right for you to demand such presents?" "Let us not go too deeply into that," answered the judge, adding: "This is fine cheese." "Let us not go too deeply into that," responded the farmer. Cf. type 1586.

> Let Us Not Go Too Deeply into That. Walker and Uysal, *Tales in Turkey,* p. 249.

**1862B   THE DEVIL AND THE DOCTOR IN PARTNERSHIP.** A devil tried marriage, but his wife made life miserable for him, so he left her. Then he became a partner with a sham doctor. The devil agreed to enter a princess's body, causing her to become ill. The doctor would propose à cure, the devil would leave, and the doctor would collect a reward. However, once inside the princess, the devil refused to leave. The doctor got the better of him by announcing that the devil's wife was arriving. Hearing this, the devil immediately left the princess, and in an instant she recovered. (Calvino) Cf. type 1164A.

> Devil Makes Trial of Matrimony, The. Straparola, *Facetious Nights,* Night 2, Tale 4.
> Lame Devil. Calvino, *Italian Folktales,* no. 162.

**1862C   AN APPRENTICE DIAGNOSES BY INFERENCE.** A doctor, in the presence of his apprentice, told a sick man that he had eaten too many cockles. Afterward he explained to the apprentice that his diagnosis had been based on the large pile of cockle shells he had seen outside the door. Using the same method, the apprentice, having seen fox tails hanging in a sick man's entryway, accused the patient of eating too many foxes. (Briggs)

> Doctor's Apprentice, The. Briggs, *DBF,* pt. A, v. 2, p. 59.
> Doctor's Apprentice, The. Crane, *Italian Popular Tales,* no. 97.
> I Infer You Have Eaten a Horse (Turkey). Clouston, *Book of Noodles,* p. 168.

**1875   ESCAPING FROM A BARREL BY SEIZING A TAIL.** Michel set forth to seek his fortune. A band of robbers attacked him in the woods, taking his bundle and nailing him inside a cask to perish. A dog came sniffing around the cask, and Michel managed to grab its tail through the bung hole. The terrified dog ran off, pulling the cask behind him. It finally shattered, freeing its prisoner. —Continues in a manner similar to type 130. (Bødker) Cf. type 1900.

Fantastic Adventures of Cadiou the Tailor, The. Delarue, *French Folktales,* p. 322.
Marshal in the Barrel, The. Randolph, *The Devil's Pretty Daughter,* p. 58.
Michel Michelkleiner's Good Luck (Luxembourg). Bødker, *European Folk Tales,* p. 98.
Scalded Wolf, The (France). Dorson, *Folktales around the World,* p. 59.
Scalded Wolf, The. Massignon, *Folktales of France,* no. 61.
Tin Can on the Cow's Tail, The. Briggs, *DBF,* pt. A, v. 2, p. 314.

**1876   CHICKENS ON A STRING.** A man who had exchanged jobs for the day with his wife (type 1408) tied their chickens together to make tending them easier. A hawk seized one of them and carried away the entire flock in one swoop. (Afanasyev)

Man Does a Woman's Work, A. Afanasyev, *Erotic Tales,* p. 79.
Peasant Who Did His Wife's Work, The. Afanasyev, *Russian Secret Tales,* p. 50.
Poor Boy in the Grave, The. Grimm, *Tales,* no. 185.

**1880   A MAN IS SHOT FROM A CANNON.** Baron Münchhausen crawled into a cannon to escape the heat of the sun, and fell asleep. They discharged the cannon, sending the baron across the Thames River. He landed in a haystack without disturbing his sleep.

*Baron Munchausen* (ed. Darton), ch. 19.

**1881   CARRIED THROUGH THE AIR BY GAME BIRDS.** A hunter swam underwater in a pond filled with wild ducks, and tied their feet to a long line. The ducks flew away, carrying him with them dangling from the line. (Chase)

Boy and the Turkeys, The. Randolph, *The Devil's Pretty Daughter,* p. 101.
Catching Wild Geese. Dorson, *Jonathan Draws the Long Bow,* p. 229 (footnote).
Dalbec Flies through the Air. Fowke, *Folklore of Canada,* p. 83.
Dick and Dock. *Roberts, South from Hell,* no. 56.
King of Liars, The. Briggs, *DBF,* pt. A, v. 2, p. 424.
Lost Lake. Fisher, *Idaho Lore,* p. 132.
Only a Fair Day's Huntin'. Chase, *Grandfather Tales,* no. 20.

**1881\*   BIRDS FLY AWAY WITH A TREE.** To capture the crows that were stealing from his pear trees, a farmer coated the branches with bird lime. The crows, unable to free themselves, flew away with all five trees.

Crows Fly Away with the Pear-Trees, The. Briggs, *DBF,* pt. A, v. 2, p. 50.

**1882   A BURIED MAN DIGS HIMSELF FREE.** A man was digging a well when the earth collapsed, burying him alive. He ran to a neighbor and borrowed a shovel so he could dig himself free. (Randolph)

Dick and Dock. Roberts, *South from Hell,* no. 56.
Irishman Saves Himself First. Dorson, *Buying the Wind,* p. 91.
Long High Jump, A. Fisher, *Idaho Lore,* p. 116.
Long-Handled Shovel, A. Randolph, *The Devil's Pretty Daughter,* p. 128.

**1889 MUNCHAUSEN TALES.** —Note: Types 513, 1880, 1881, 1889A-1889P, 1890, 1894, 1896, 1910, and 1930 form a canon of tall tales made famous by the German "Liar Baron" Karl Friedrich Hieronymus Freiherr von Münchhausen (1720-1797). Stories of his adventures, obviously based on folklore, first appeared in print in the *Vade Mecum für lustige Leute,* nos. 8, 10 (Berlin, 1781, 1783). Rudolf Erich Raspe, a German exile in England, incorporated the stories into a continuous account, publishing them anonymously under the title *Baron Munchausen's Narrative of His Marvellous Travels and Campaigns in Russia* (Oxford, 1786 [actually 1785]). The tales returned to Germany via the popular translations (1786, 1788) of Gottfried August Bürger. Apart from their literary heritage, the individual stories have flourished in folk tellings.

**1889A SHOOTING OFF THE LEADER'S TAIL.** A hunter saw a buck deer holding onto a doe's tail with his teeth. He shot off the doe's tail and took it home. The buck followed, still holding the tail in his mouth. (Dorson)

*Baron Munchausen* (ed. Darton), ch. 3.
Curt Goes Deer Hunting. Dorson, *Buying the Wind,* p. 75.

**1889B TURNING AN ANIMAL INSIDE OUT.** Captain Benson's dog swallowed his favorite knife. To retrieve it, the captain put his hand down the dog's throat until he reached the tail, and then turned the animal inside out. (Dorson)

*Baron Munchausen* (ed. Darton), ch. 4.
Captain Benson's Dog. Dorson, *Jonathan Draws the Long Bow,* p. 107.
Don Bartolo. Paredes, *Folktales of Mexico,* no. 20.

**1889C THE DEER WITH A FRUIT TREE AS ANTLERS.** A hunter, out of normal shot, loaded his gun with cherry stones. He hit a stag in the head, but the blow only stunned him. A year or two later he saw the same stag, who now had a cherry tree growing from his head. *(Baron Munchausen)*

*Baron Munchausen* (ed. Darton), ch. 4.
Robert and the Peachtree. Roberts, *South from Hell,* no. 69A.

**1889D A TREE GROWS OUT OF A HORSE.**

*Baron Munchausen* (ed. Darton), ch. 5.

**1889F FROZEN SOUNDS.** One cold morning, the hired man went to the barn, whistling as usual. The notes froze, hanging in front of him. He snapped them off and brought them inside. When they thawed, they made the sweetest music you ever heard. (Glimm)

> *Baron Munchausen* (ed. Darton), ch. 6.
> Coldest Morning Ever, The. Glimm, *Flatlanders and Ridgerunners*, p. 39.
> Sounds Freezing (3 variants). Fowke, *Folklore of Canada*, p. 183.

**1889G ANOTHER WORLD INSIDE A GIANT FISH.**

> *Baron Munchausen* (ed. Darton), ch. 8, 20.

**1889H ANOTHER WORLD BENEATH THE SEA.**

> *Baron Munchausen* (ed. Darton), ch. 11, 15.
> Cluasach and the Sea-Woman (Ireland). Bødker, *European Folk Tales*, p. 135.

**1889K DESCENDING ON A ROPE MADE OF CHAFF.**

> *Baron Munchausen* (ed. Darton), ch. 6.
> Threshing-Flail from Heaven, The. Grimm, *Tales*, no. 112.

**1889L THE SPLIT DOG.** A hunting dog ran into an ax left in a stump and cut itself in two. Dr. Bates put it back together with his sticking salve. However, by mistake he put two of the legs up and two down. But this didn't stop the dog from chasing rabbits. It would run on two legs until they got tired, then turn over and run on the other two. (Glimm)

> Amasa Abbey's Dog. Dorson, *Jonathan Draws the Long Bow*, p. 102.
> Appy Boz'll. Briggs, *DBF,* pt. A, v. 2, p. 10.
> Dog and the Hares, The. Briggs and Tongue, *Folktales of England*, no. 89.
> Dog and the Hares, The. Briggs, *DBF,* pt. A, v. 2, p. 60.
> Dr. Bates's Sticking Salve. Glimm, *Flatlanders and Ridgerunners*, p. 31.
> Split Dog: Great Bird. Fowke, *Folklore of Canada*, p. 184.
> Split Dog, The. Roberts, *South from Hell*, no. 69C.

**1889M SNAKEBITE CAUSES AN OBJECT TO SWELL.**

> Snakes. Fisher, *Idaho Lore*, p. 130.
> Swollen Hoe Handle, The. Roberts, *South from Hell*, no. 74A.
> Swollen Tree, The. Roberts, *South from Hell*, no. 74B.

**1889N AN EXTRAORDINARY HUNTING DOG.** Cf. type 1920F*.

> *Baron Munchausen* (ed. Darton), ch. 5, 17.

**1889P A HORSE IS CUT IN TWO, THEN SEWN TOGETHER.** Cf. type 1911A.

> *Baron Munchausen* (ed. Darton), ch. 5.

**1890  THE LUCKY SHOT.** Just as a hunter fired at a rabbit the rabbit ran into a covey of partridges, and with one shot the hunter killed one rabbit and eleven birds. The sound of the shot flushed a turkey, and the man shot it with the other barrel. The dead turkey fell into a tree, and while getting it down, the man discovered a great cache of honey. Later he flushed another rabbit. Not having reloaded, he threw his gun at it. When he went to recover his gun, he fell through a rotten plank covering an underground treasure trove. (Harris)

Fool for Luck, A. Harris, *Uncle Remus and His Friends,* no. 21.
Jack's Hunting Trips. Chase, *Jack Tales,* no. 16.
John of Horsill (I). Briggs, *DBF,* pt. B, v. 2, p. 240.
Only a Fair Day's Huntin'. Chase, *Grandfather Tales,* no. 20.
Shooting the Foxes with One Bullet. Carpenter, *A Latvian Storyteller,* p. 239.
Sir Gammer Vans. Jacobs, *More English Fairy Tales,* p. 43.
Tall Hunting Tale. Roberts, *South from Hell,* no. 70.

**1890D  THE RAMROD SHOT.** A hunter, about to be attacked by a snake, fired a shot at game birds. The recoil knocked the ramrod loose; it fell down the snake's neck and choked it to death. Cf. type 1894.

Only a Fair Day's Huntin'. Chase, *Grandfather Tales,* no. 20.

**1890E  THE BENT GUN BARREL.** A hunter with a double-barreled gun saw a flock of ducks approaching from one side and a flock of geese from the other. He bent his barrels apart, pulled the triggers, and shot both the ducks and the geese. (Chase)

Amasa Abbey's Circular Gun. Dorson, *Jonathan Draws the Long Bow,* p. 102.
Dalbec's Wonderful Shot. Fowke, *Folklore of Canada,* p. 82.
Ninety-Nine Pigeons. Glimm, *Flatlanders and Ridgerunners,* p. 36.
Only a Fair Day's Huntin'. Chase, *Grandfather Tales,* no. 20.

**1890F  A LUCKY SHOT.** —Miscellaneous anecdotes.

*Baron Munchausen* (ed. Darton), ch. 3, 10.
Dalbec and the Geese. Fowke, *Folklore of Canada,* p. 83.
How Dave McDougall Hunted Wild Geese. Fowke, *Folklore of Canada,* p. 189.

**1891B\*  CATCHING HARES WITH SNUFF.** To catch hares in the wintertime, place snuff beneath a balanced stone. The hare will smell the snuff and hit against the stone, which will fall down and kill him.

Catching Hares in Winter. Ranke, *Folktales of Germany,* no. 81.

### 1893A* TWO HARES RUN INTO EACH OTHER AND ARE CAUGHT.

Two Hares, The (I, II). Briggs, *DBF*, pt. A, v. 2, p. 335.

### 1894 SHOOTING A RAMROD FULL OF BIRDS. A man took aim at the finches settling in his cherry tree. With one shot he skewered twenty-four of them to the tree with his ramrod. (Briggs)

*Baron Munchausen* (ed. Darton), ch. 20.
Shooting Finches. Briggs, *DBF*, pt. A, v. 2, p. 265.
Shooting Robins with a Ramrod. Dorson, *Jonathan Draws the Long Bow*, p. 115.

### 1895 CATCHING FISH IN WADING BOOTS.

Boy and the Fish Warden, The. Glimm, *Flatlanders and Ridgerunners*, p. 180.
Jack's Hunting Trips. Chase, *Jack Tales*, no. 16.
Only a Fair Day's Huntin'. Chase, *Grandfather Tales*, no. 20.
Sixty Pounds of Salmon in His Boots. Dorson, *Jonathan Draws the Long Bow*, p. 6.
Tall Hunting Tale. Roberts, *South from Hell*, no. 70.
Thomas Moore Catches Shad in His Trousers. Dorson, *Jonathan Draws the Long Bow*, p. 111.

### 1896 MAKING AN ANIMAL JUMP OUT OF ITS SKIN. A hunter, not wanting to kill the silver fox, nor to damage its pelt, loaded his gun with a nail. He fired, nailing the animal to a tree by its tail. Then he whipped it until it ran of out its skin. (Dorson, "How We Caught the Silver Fox in Finland")

*Baron Munchausen* (ed. Darton), ch. 3.
Cold Snap of '83 in Thebes, The. Dorson, *Buying the Wind*, p. 346.
How We Caught the Silver Fox in Finland, Dorson, *Bloodstoppers and Bearwalkers*, p. 144.

### 1900 ESCAPING FROM A HOLLOW TREE ON A BEAR'S TAIL. A hunter climbed down a hollow tree to capture the bear cubs inside. Just then the mother bear returned, climbing down the inside of the tree backwards. The man saved himself by taking hold of the bear's tail and poking her with his knife. She pulled him to the top. He then slid down the outside of the tree and shot the bear. (Roberts, no. 71B) Cf. types 1229, 1875.

Bears in a Holler Tree. Roberts, *South from Hell*, no. 71B.
Dalbec and the Bear. Fowke, *Folklore of Canada*, p. 82.
Jack on a Hunting Trip. Roberts, *South from Hell*, no. 71A.
Jack's Hunting Trips. Chase, *Jack Tales*, no. 16.
What Darkens the Hole? Dorson, *Negro Tales*, p. 253.

### 1910 A WOLF HARNESSES ITSELF BY EATING A HORSE.

*Baron Munchausen* (ed. Darton), ch. 2.
Parson and the Poor Man, The. Dégh, *Folktales of Hungary,* no. 10.

## 1911A  THE HORSE WITH A BROKEN BACK AND A SHEEP'S
SKIN.  A man placed such a load on his mare that it broke her back.
He skinned the animal, wrapped the load in her hide, and carried it
home himself.  But the horse followed him home.  Feeling sorry for
the animal, shivering in the cold, the man threw a sheep skin over
her.  The skin took root and became her new hide, producing more
wool than forty sheep. (Chase) Cf. type 1889P.

Amasa Abbey's Horse. Dorson, *Jonathan Draws the Long Bow,* p. 102.
Basket-Maker's Donkey, The. Briggs, *DBF,* pt. A, v. 2, p. 17.
Corpus Delicti. Fisher, *Idaho Lore,* p. 139.
Great Liar, The. O'Sullivan, *Folktales of Ireland,* no. 53.
Horse's Last Drunk, The. Glassie, *Irish Folktales,* no. 38.
Old Roaney. Chase, *Grandfather Tales,* no. 22.
Wool and Withies. Briggs, *DBF,* pt. A, v. 2, p. 362.

## 1912  A CAT KILLS MICE WITH ITS WOODEN PAW.

Cat with the Wooden Paw, The. Dorson, *Buying the Wind,* p. 348.

## 1916  THE BREATHING TREE.  A hunter noticed a tree with a crack
that opened and closed.  Puzzled, he cut the tree down.  It was
completely filled with coons.  Their breathing made the crack open
and close.

Major Brown's Coon Story. Dorson, *Jonathan Draws the Long Bow,* p. 227.

## 1920  A CONTEST IN LYING.  The person who tells the biggest lie
wins a prize.

Beardless Man and the Cake, The. Dawkins, *Modern Greek Folktales,* no. 68.
Bishop Wins the Lying Contest, The. Raven, *Folklore of Staffordshire,* p.
    145.
Bragging Englishman. Roberts, *South from Hell,* no. 72.
Cole-Wort, The. Briggs, *DBF,* pt. A, v. 2, p. 44.
Finest Liar in the World, The (Serbia). Lang, *Violet Fairy Book,* p. 17.
Four Fellows and Their Three Dogs, The. Briggs, *DBF,* pt. A, v. 2, p. 91.
Great Lie, The. Noy, *Folktales of Israel,* no. 44.
Long-Bow Story, A. Lang, *Olive Fairy Book,* p. 64.
Man Who Bounced, The. Briggs and Tongue, *Folktales of England,* no. 90.
Man Who Bounced, The. Briggs, *DBF,* pt. A, v. 2, p. 174.
Mark Twain in the Fens. Briggs, *DBF,* pt. A, v. 2, p. 176.
Mister Sharp and the Old Soldier. Randolph, *The Devil's Pretty Daughter,* p.
    154.
My Return from the War of Independence. Walker and Uysal, *Tales in Turkey,*
    p. 165.
Prize for Lying, The. Briggs, *DBF,* pt. A, v. 2, p. 241.
Seminole Medicine. Randolph, *Pissing in the Snow,* no. 31.
Tall Tale of the Merchant's Son, The. Noy, *Folktales of Israel,* no. 24.
Three Turnips, The. Briggs, *DBF,* pt. A, v. 2, p. 309.

Village of Lies, The. Megas, *Folktales of Greece,* no. 69.

**1920A  ONE LIE BEGETS ANOTHER.**  A man boasted about a giant cabbage he had seen.  His companion  responded with a story of a giant kettle.  "What was it for?" asked the first.  "To cook your cabbage in," was the answer. (Storer) Cf. types 1960D, 1960F.

> Big Cabbage. Dorson, *Negro Tales,* p. 245.
> Cabbage and the Cauldron, The. Storer, *Facetiae of Poggio,* no. 96.
> Chilean Swindlers, The. Pino-Saavedra, *Folktales of Chile,* no. 49.
> Mark Twain in the Fens. Briggs and Tongue, *Folktales of England,* no. 91.

**1920B  NO TIME TO LIE.**  They asked the town liar to tell one of his stories, but he said he had no time, for—as he said—he had to fetch a doctor for an injured man.  They soon discovered, that the story of the injured man was a lie. (Dorson, "Art Church Tells a Lie")

> Champion, The. Randolph, *Who Blowed Up the Church House?,* p. 13.
> Too Busy to Lie. Dorson, *Buying the Wind,* p. 357.
> Art Church Tells a Lie. Dorson, *Buying the Wind,* p. 67.

**1920D  REDUCING THE SIZE OF THE LIE.**  A noblemen was telling lies.  "I shot three hares with one shot," he claimed.  No one believed him, so he called his servant in as a witness.  "It was a pregnant hare with two young ones inside her," said the servant, and no one could challenge that.

> Helping to Lie. Ranke, *Folktales of Germany,* no. 82.

**1920E  A CONSPIRACY OF LIARS.**  Two liars became partners. The first bet the king a large sum that he had seen a cauliflower that filled twelve tubs.  The partner, pretending to be a stranger, corroborated the story, and the liar won the bet. (Lang)

> Chilean Swindlers, The. Pino-Saavedra, *Folktales of Chile,* no. 49.
> Partnership of the Thief and the Liar. Lang, *Grey Fairy Book,* p. 67.

**1920E\*  SEEING OR HEARING AN ENORMOUS DISTANCE.**

> Captain Benson Hears the Mouse on the Weather-Cock. Dorson, *Jonathan Draws the Long Bow,* p. 108.

**1920F\* THE INTELLIGENT DOG.**  Dr. Fell claimed that his dog would round up the cows and sheep, bring them home through a hole in the fence, then go back and fix the hole in the fence.  Cf. type 1889N.

> Doctor Fell's Dog. Briggs, *DBF,* pt. A, v. 2, p. 59.
> Smart Dog. Glimm, *Flatlanders and Ridgerunners,* p. 49.

**1920H   EXCHANGING A STORY FOR FIRE.**   A boy offered to tell an old beekeeper a story in exchange for fire. They agreed that if the man interrupted him, the boy could cut three strips of flesh from his back. The boy told many lies without interruption, but when he said, "my grandfather was riding on your grandfather," the old man broke in. The boy thus got his fire and three strips of flesh. —Cf. type 852

If You Don't Like It, Don't Listen. Afanasyev, *Russian Fairy Tales*, p. 345.

**1920H\*   THE LANTERN AND THE FISH.**   A man claimed to have caught a yard-long fish. His friend responded by saying he had found a lantern, still lit, on the bottom of a creek. The first man could not believe this story, so the second one said: "I'll blow out my lantern if you'll take two feet from your fish."

Trout Too Big. Glimm, *Flatlanders and Ridgerunners*, p. 48.

**1927   THE COLD MAY NIGHT.**   Birds and fish recollect their marvelous experiences on the coldest night ever.

Cold May Night, The (Ireland). Dorson, *Folktales around the World*, p. 6.
Cold May Night, The. O'Sullivan, *Folktales of Ireland*, no. 11.

**1930   SCHLARAFFENLAND (THE LAND OF COCKAIGNE).**   A fantasy land is described in which plows pull themselves without horses, doves attack wolves, frogs thresh corn, and so forth. (Grimm, "Cockaigne")

*Baron Munchausen* (ed. Darton), ch. 18, 20.
Chilean Swindlers, The. Pino-Saavedra, *Folktales of Chile*, no. 49.
Cockaigne. Grimm, *Tales*, no. 158.
Doun on Yon Bank. Briggs, *DBF*, pt. A, v. 2, p. 518.
Down Underground. Briggs, *DBF*, pt. A, v. 2, p. 63.
I Saddled My Sow. Briggs, *DBF*, pt. A, v. 2, p. 537.
Jack the Giant-Killer (II). Briggs, *DBF*, pt. A, v. 1, p. 331.
Land in Which Impossible Things Happened, A. Arewa, *Northern East Africa*, p. 151.
Mother Shipton's House. Briggs, *DBF*, pt. A, v. 2, p. 549.
Nomansland in Cornucopia. Boccaccio, *Decameron*, Day 8, Tale 3.
One Sesame Seed, The. El-Shamy, *Folktales of Egypt*, no. 3.
Pynots in the Crabtree, The. Briggs, *DBF*, pt. A, v. 2, p. 245.
Rabbits Baste Themselves. Briggs, *DBF*, pt. A, v. 2, p. 245.
Singing Geese, The. Botkin, *American Folklore*, p. 680.
Sir Gammer Vans. Briggs, *DBF*, pt. A, v. 2, p. 558.
Tall Tale from Ditmarsh, The. Grimm, *Tales*, no. 159.
Thrawn Sang, A. Briggs, *DBF*, pt. A, v. 2, p. 563.
Vision of MacConglinney, The. Jacobs, *More Celtic Fairy Tales*, p. 67.
Wee Yowe, The. Briggs, *DBF*, pt. A, v. 2, p. 576.

**1940   EXTRAORDINARY NAMES.**   A girl lived in Walpe with her husband Cham and their child Wild who slept in a cradle named Hippodadle. Cf. type 1562A.

Household Servants. Grimm, *Tales,* no. 140.

**1950** **A CONTEST IN LAZINESS.** A king offered to bequeath his kingdom to the one of his three sons who proved himself the laziest. The first claimed he was too lazy to close his eyes, even if rain drops were falling in them. The second said he was too lazy to pull his feet back from a fire. The third said that if he were being hanged and someone place a knife in his hand, he would be too lazy to cut the rope. The king declared this last son his successor. (Grimm, no. 151)

> Fimber Village Tales. Briggs, *DBF,* pt. A, v. 2, p. 86.
> Laziest Trick, The. Randolph, *Hot Springs and Hell,* no. 345.
> Lazy Yankees (several examples). Dorson, *Jonathan Draws the Long Bow,* p. 253.
> Science of Laziness, The. Calvino, *Italian Folktales,* no. 44.
> Three Lazy Ones, The. Grimm, *Tales,* no. 151.
> Three Lazy Ones. Briggs, *DBF,* pt. A, v. 2, p. 299.
> Twelve Lazy Servants, The. Grimm, *Tales,* no. 151*.
> Who Is the Laziest? El-Shamy, *Folktales of Egypt,* no. 62.

**1951** **A LAZY MAN REFUSES A GIFT.** A yankee refused the gift of a bushel of corn, because it was not shelled.

> Is It Shelled? Dorson, *Jonathan Draws the Long Bow,* p. 253.

**1960** **GIANT ANIMALS OR GIANT OBJECTS.**

**1960A** **THE GIANT ANIMAL.**

> Big Possum, The. Roberts, *South from Hell,* no. 73.
> Bunyan's Blue Ox. Fowke, *Folklore of Canada,* p. 168.
> Paul Bunyan's Cornstalk (USA). Cole, *Best-Loved Folktales,* no. 174.
> Threshing-Flail from Heaven, The. Grimm, *Tales,* no. 112.

**1960B** **THE GIANT FISH.**

> Apply Boswell Stories. Briggs, *DBF,* pt. A, v. 2, p. 8.
> Fish Story, A. Musick, *Green Hills of Magic,* no. 75.
> Fruit Peddler, The. Saucier, *French Louisiana,* no. 28.
> My Pet Charlie. Roberts, *South from Hell,* no. 75.
> Pike with the Long Teeth, The. Afanasyev, *Russian Fairy Tales,* p. 54.
> Riding Rainbows. Fisher, *Idaho Lore,* p. 127.

**1960D** **THE GIANT VEGETABLE.** Cf. types 1920A, 1689A, 2044.

> Big Connecticut Pumpkins. Dorson, *Jonathan Draws the Long Bow,* p. 129.
> Big Potato, A. Glassie, *Irish Folktales,* no. 36.
> Giant Parsnips. Briggs, *DBF,* pt. A, v. 2, p. 104.
> Great Liar, The. O'Sullivan, *Folktales of Ireland,* no. 53.
> Great Turnips, The. Briggs, *DBF,* pt. A, v. 2, p. 109.
> Great Turnip, The. Simpson, *Folklore of Sussex,* p. 157.

Idaho Potatoes. Fisher, *Idaho Lore,* p. 139.
Mark Twain in the Fens. Briggs and Tongue, *Folktales of England,* no. 91.
My Return from the War of Independence. Walker and Uysal, *Tales in Turkey,*
    p. 165.
Partnership of the Thief and the Liar. Lang, *Grey Fairy Book,* p. 67.
Three Turnips, The. Briggs, *DBF,* pt. A, v. 2, p. 309.
Turnip, The. Grimm, *Tales,* no. 146.
Village of Lies, The. Megas, *Folktales of Greece,* no. 69.

### 1960F   THE GIANT KETTLE.   Cf. type. 1920A.

My Return from the War of Independence. Walker and Uysal, *Tales in Turkey,*
    p. 165.

### 1960G   THE GIANT PLANT.   Cf. types 328, 468, 804A.

Paul Bunyan's Cornstalk (USA). Cole, *Best-Loved Folktales,* no. 174.
Tall Cornstalk, The. Chase, *Grandfather Tales,* no. 21.
Tall Story, A. Grimm, *Other Tales,* p. 145.
Tall Tale of the Merchant's Son, The. Noy, *Folktales of Israel,* no. 24.
Threshing-Flail from Heaven, The. Grimm, *Tales,* no. 112.
Village of Lies, The. Megas, *Folktales of Greece,* no. 69.

### 1960H   THE GIANT SHIP.

Two Ships, The. Saucier, *French Louisiana,* no. 26.

### 1960J   THE GIANT BIRD.

Little Bird Grows, The. Abrahams, *Afro-American Folktales,* no. 42.
Sun, Earth, and Creation, The. Thundy, *South Indian Folktales,* no. 4.

### 1960M   GIANT  INSECTS.

Kittle and the Mosquitoes, The. Glimm, *Flatlanders and Ridgerunners,* p. 40.
Mosquitoes and Pot. Fowke, *Folklore of Canada,* p. 186.
New Jersey Terror. Fisher, *Idaho Lore,* p. 138.

### 1960Z   GIANT OBJECTS.   —Miscellaneous tales.

Big as an Idaho Potato. Fisher, *Idaho Lore,* p. 126.
Big Snow, A. Fisher, *Idaho Lore,* p. 123.
Finn and the Dragon. Briggs, *DBF,* pt. A, v. 1, p. 234.
Great Bed of War, The. Jones-Baker, *Folklore of Hertfordshire,* p. 192.
Great Wind, The. Briggs, *DBF,* pt. A, v. 2, p. 110.
Mester Ship, The. Marwick, *Folklore of Orkney and Shetland,* p. 128.
Munchausen Tethers His Horse to a Church Steeple [nearly buried in snow].
    *Baron Munchausen* (ed. Darton), ch. 2.

### 1962   AT MY FATHER'S BAPTISM.   —A pastiche of tall tales.

When I Was a Kid of Ten. Dégh, *Folktales of Hungary,* no. 32.
When I Was a Miller. Dégh, *Folktales of Hungary,* no. 31.

**1962A INTIMIDATING AN OPPONENT.** A bully challenged Barney Beal to a fight. Before the contest began, Barney lifted a large barrel of water and drank from the bunghole. Seeing Barney's strength, the bully withdrew from the fight.

How Barney Beal Awed the Bully of Peak's Island. Dorson, *Buying the Wind,* p. 49.

**1965 KNOIST AND HIS THREE SONS.** One of Knoist's sons was blind, one lame, and one naked. The blind one shot a hare, the lame one caught it, and the naked one put it in his pocket. (Grimm) Cf. type 2335.

Five Men. Briggs, *DBF,* pt. A, v. 2, p. 520.
Knoist and His Three Sons. Grimm, *Tales,* no. 138.
Lying Tale, A. Briggs, *DBF,* pt. A, v. 2, p. 542.
Sevenfold Liar, The. Briggs, *DBF,* pt. A, v. 2, p. 261.
Three Brothers, The. Crane, *Italian Popular Tales,* no. 84.

# Formula Tales

**2010** **TALES BUILT ON THE NUMBER TWELVE.** —Note: Aarne and Thompson distinguish subtypes 2010A, "Twelve Days of Christmas" (e.g., Chase) and 2010B, "Twelve Kinds of Food" (e.g., Fowke).

> First Night of Christmas, The. Fowke, *Folklore of Canada*, p. 289.
> Twelve Days of Christmas, The. Chase, *Grandfather Tales*, p. 176.
> Twelve Truths of the World, The. Espinosa, *Folklore of Spain in the American Southwest*, p. 195.

**2012** **A FORGETFUL MAN COUNTS THE DAYS OF THE WEEK.** An absent-minded priest made one basket each day of the week. When he counted six completed baskets, he knew it was Sunday. Cf. type 1848A.

> Priest Who Made Baskets, The. Briggs, *DBF*, pt. A, v. 2, p. 240.

**2013** **SHALL I TELL IT AGAIN?** Once there was a cat, with its paws made of cloth, and its eyes turned back. Do you want me to tell it again? Cf. types 227, 1199B, 1376A*, 2300, 2320.

> Round. Paredes, *Folktales of Mexico,* no. 80.

**2014** **CONTRADICTIONS OR EXTREMES** —Chain tales.

> Bad, Not Bad. Afanasyev, *Russian Secret Tales,* p. 15.
> It Weren't Neither of Us! Briggs, *Folklore of the Cotswolds,* p. 80.
> Tall Tale, A. Bushnaq, *Arab Folktales,* p. 314.
> Twernt Neither of Us! Whitlock, *Folklore of Wiltshire,* p. 181.

**2014A** **GOOD NEWS AND BAD NEWS ABOUT A WEDDING.** A man reported his wedding to a friend. "Good news!" responded the latter. "She was a shrew," continued the first. "Bad news!" said the friend. "With her dowry I bought a house," continued the first. "Good news!" congratulated the friend. "The house burned down," replied the first. "Bad news!" said the other. "Not all bad," said the first, "for she burned up with it!" (Briggs) Cf. type 96*.

Comme Ça. Pourrat, *Treasury of French Tales,* p. 233.
Gabe Says It Ain't So Bad. Randolph, *The Talking Turtle,* p. 72.
Good and Bad News. Briggs, *DBF,* pt. A, v. 2, p. 104.
Some Bad News. Pourrat, *Treasury of French Tales,* p. 235.

**2015  THE STUBBORN GOAT.** A goat that was shedding on one side locked himself in a peasant's house. A hare, a wolf, and a cock tried to make him open the door, but he refused, threatening to break their ribs. Then a bee flew in and stung him on his shedding side. The goat ran away and never returned. (Afanasyev)  Cf. types 212, 2030.

Coué or Couette. Massignon, *Folktales of France,* no. 39.
Goat Shedding on One Side, The. Afanasyev, *Russian Fairy Tales,* p. 312.
Making Hairlock Come Home (Norway). Clouston, *Popular Tales,* v. 1, p. 299.
Petuzzo. Falassi, *Folklore by the Fireside,* p. 75.
Ram in the Chile Patch, The. Paredes, *Folktales of Mexico,* no. 76.
Skinned Goat, The. Ranke, *Folktales of Germany,* no. 9.

**2016  THE COW THAT WOULDN'T STAND STILL.** —A chain tale involving a stick, a butcher, a silver penny, a weary lady with golden hair, and a fine laddie with a sharp sword, each of whom plays a role in making the wee, wee cow stand still so the wee, wee mannie can milk her. Cf. type 2030.

Wee, Wee Mannie, The (Scotland). Cole, *Best-Loved Folktales,* no. 67.
Wee, Wee Mannie, The. Briggs, *DBF,* pt. A, v. 2, p. 576.
Wee, Wee Mannie, The. Jacobs, *More English Fairy Tales,* p. 192.

**2019  PIF PAF POLTRIE.** —A nonsense tale about courting.

Fair Katrinelje and Pif Paf Poltrie. Grimm, *Tales,* no. 131.

**2021  THE DEATH OF THE LITTLE HEN.** The little hen choked on a nut. The cock ran to seek help, but when he returned, the hen had already died. Six mice pulled her funeral carriage, but they slipped into a stream and drowned. The little cock dug her a grave; then he sat down and mourned until he died. (Grimm) —Note: Aarne and Thompson categorize the episode (told as a chain tale) describing the futile search for help as type 2021A.

Cock and Hen a-Nutting. Asbjørnsen and Moe, *East o' the Sun,* p. 378.
Cock and Hen a-Nutting (Norway). Clouston, *Popular Tales,* v. 1, p. 300.
Death and Burial of Poor Hen-Sparrow (India). Clouston, *Popular Tales,* v. 1, p. 304.
Death of Chanticleer, The (Norway). Clouston, *Popular Tales,* v. 1, p. 302.
Death of the Cock, The. Afanasyev, *Russian Fairy Tales,* p. 17.

Death of the Little Hen, The. Grimm, *Tales,* no. 80.

**2021B   THE COCK KNOCKS OUT THE HEN'S EYE.** The cock put out the hen's eye, because the hazel tree tore his trousers. The hazel tree tore his trousers, because the goats ate its bark. —The chain continues, ending with a wolf carrying off a pig, because God told him to.

Cock and the Hen, The. Afanasyev, *Russian Fairy Tales,* p. 309.

**2022   AN ANIMAL MOURNS THE DEATH OF A SPOUSE.** A flea and a louse were brewing beer. The louse fell in and was killed. A door, a broom, a cart, an ash pile, a tree, and a girl all joined the flee in mourning the louse's death. Then a spring broke loose and drowned all the mourners. (Grimm)

Flea and the Louse, The. Briggs, *DBF,* pt. A. v. 2, p. 522.
Flech an' da Loose Shackin' Dir Sheets, Da. Briggs, *DBF,* pt. A, v. 2, p. 521.
Little Louse and Little Flea. Grimm, *Tales,* no. 30.
Little Sausage and Little Mouse. Ranke, *Folktales of Germany,* no. 6.
Rat and the She Rat, The. Massignon, *Folktales of France,* no. 34.
Titty Mouse and Tatty Mouse. Briggs, *DBF,* pt. A, v. 2, p. 574.
Titty Mouse and Tatty Mouse. Jacobs, *English Fairy Tales,* p. 77.

**2022B   THE HEN LAYS AN EGG; THE MOUSE BREAKS IT.** A hen laid an egg, and it rolled into a corner, where a mouse broke it. The gatepost shrieked and the swilltub leaked. A girl carrying water dropped her buckets, and her mother spilled her dough. Her father, a priest, tore the pages from his book and scattered them on the floor.

Hen, The. Afanasyev, *Russian Fairy Tales,* p. 27.

**2023   THE ANT WHO MARRIED A MOUSE.** An ant found a penny and bought herself a ribbon. She put it on and sat in the window, watching the passersby. Many animals asked for her hand, and she chose the mouse, because she liked the way he sang. But the mouse fell into the stewpot and was killed. (Crane, no. 90)

Ant and the Mouse, The. Crane, *Italian Popular Tales,* no. 90.
Cat and the Mouse, The. Crane, *Italian Popular Tales,* no. 82.
Little Cockroach Martina (Cuba). Dorson, *Folktales around the World,* p. 508.
Pérez the Mouse. Paredes, *Folktales of Mexico,* no. 77.
Sister Cat (Italy). Dorson, *Folktales around the World,* p. 72.

**2025   THE FLEEING PANCAKE.** A pancake rolled out the door and down the road. Many animals tried to stop it, but it rolled past them all. A pig offered to carry it across a brook. The pancake agreed, and the pig swallowed it in one gulp. (Thompson)

Bear Ate Them Up, The. Randolph, *Sticks in the Knapsack,* p. 59.
Bun, The. Afanasyev, *Russian Fairy Tales,* p. 447.

Gingerbread Boy, The (USA). Clarkson and Cross, *World Folktales,* no. 39.
Johnny-Cake. Jacobs, *English Fairy Tales,* p. 155.
Little Cake, The. Briggs, *DBF,* pt. A, v. 2, p. 540.
Pancake, The (Norway). Thompson, *100 Favorite Folktales,* no. 100.
Wee Bannock, The. Briggs, *DBF,* pt. A, v. 2, p. 575.
Wee Bannock, The. Jacobs, *More English Fairy Tales,* p. 73.

**2027 THE CAT THAT WAS A GLUTTON.** A cat ate a bowl of porridge, a trough of drippings, a man, a woman, a cow, and many other
things. She tried to eat a goat on a bridge as well, but he butted her
off. She split open, and everyone she had eaten escaped. (Asbjørnsen
and Moe) Cf. types, 122E, 2028.

Cat and the Parrot, The (India). Clarkson and Cross, *World Folktales,* no. 35.
Tabby Who Was Such a Glutton. Asbjørnsen and Moe, *Norwegian Folktales,*
   p. 161.

**2028 THE TROLL (OR BEAR) THAT ATE PEOPLE.** A bear ate
a boy, a girl, a man, and a woman. He tried to eat a squirrel, but it
escaped up a tree. The bear followed it, and the squirrel jumped to
the next tree. The bear tried to jump also, but he fell to the ground
and split open, freeing all the people he had eaten. (Chase) Cf. types
123, 122E, 333, 1227, 2027.

Bad Bear, The. Roberts, *South from Hell,* no. 77B.
Bear Ate Them Up, The. Randolph, *Sticks in the Knapsack,* p. 59.
Cat and the Parrot, The (India). Clarkson and Cross, *World Folktales,* no. 35.
Greedy Fat Man. Roberts, *South from Hell,* no. 77C.
Sody Sallyraytus. Chase, *Grandfather Tales,* no. 7.
Whale That Followed the Ship, The. Briggs, *DBF,* pt. A, v. 2, p. 347.

**2029 CHAINS OF EVENTS.** —Miscellaneous tales.

Bird and the Mason, The (Ceylon). Clouston, *Popular Tales,* v. 1, p. 311.
Castle of the Fly, The. Afanasyev, *Russian Fairy Tales,* p. 25.
Crystal Rooster. Calvino, *Italian Folktales,* no. 98.
Darning-Needle, A. Lang, *Yellow Fairy Book,* p. 319.
Feast Day, A. Crane, *Italian Popular Tales,* no. 83.
Godmother Fox. Crane, *Italian Popular Tales,* no. 81.
Green Gourd, The. Chase, *Grandfather Tales,* no. 24.
Kid, a Kid, My Father Bought, A (Talmud). Clouston, *Popular Tales,* v. 1, p.
   291.
Making Pitidda Sweep the House (Sicily). Clouston, *Popular Tales,* v. 1, p.
   298.
Moorachug and Menachaig (Scotland). Clouston, *Popular Tales,* v. 1, p. 297.
Munachar and Manachar (Ireland). Cole, *Best-Loved Folktales,* no. 58.
Nightingale That Shrieked, The. Bushnaq, *Arab Folktales,* p. 89.
Stars in the Sky, The. Jacobs, *More English Fairy Tales,* p. 177.

**2030 THE PIG THAT WOULDN'T GO OVER THE STILE.** —A
chain tale involving a dog, a stick, fire, water, an ox, a butcher, a
rope, a rat, a cat, a cow, and a haystack, each of which plays a role in

helping a little old woman force her pig to jump over a stile. (Briggs, I) Cf. types 2015, 2016.

A Chain of Won'ts. Abrahams, *Afro-American Folktales,* no. 102.
Cat and Mouse, The. Briggs, *DBF,* pt. A, v. 2, p. 512.
Cat and the Mouse, The. Jacobs, *English Fairy Tales,* p. 188.
Contrarious Pig, The. Campbell, *Cloudwalking Country,* p. 202.
God Damn the Wind. Randolph, *The Talking Turtle,* p. 61.
I Went to Market. Briggs, *DBF,* pt. A, v. 2, p. 538.
Minette and Her Rollers. Saucier, *French Louisiana,* no. 29.
Old Woman and Her Pig, The (I-III). Briggs, *DBF,* pt. A, v. 2, p. 551.
Old Woman and Her Pig, The. Jacobs, *English Fairy Tales,* p. 20.
Old Woman and the Crooked Sixpence, The. Clouston, *Popular Tales,* v. 1, p. 294.
Petuzzo. Falassi, *Folklore by the Fireside,* p. 75.
Wife and Her Bush of Berries, The. Briggs, *DBF,* pt. A, v. 2, p. 579.

## 2030J  A DISOBEDIENT CHILD IS PUNISHED.

Moorachug and Meenachug. Campbell, *West Highlands,* v. 1, p. 161.
Pitidda. Crane, *Italian Popular Tales,* no. 78.

## 2031  STRONG, STRONGER, AND STRONGEST.

An ant broke its leg in the snow and brought suit. The judge condemned the snow for considering itself so mighty. The snow answered that the sun was mightier still, for it could melt snow. The sun replied that the cloud was mightier still, for it could cover the sun. —The chain continues with the wind blowing the cloud, a wall stopping the wind, a mouse gnawing the wall, a cat chasing the mouse, etc., until it reaches God, the mightiest of all. (Paredes)

Ibotity Breaks His Leg (Madagascar). Clouston, *Popular Tales,* v. 1, p. 309.
Little Ant, The. Paredes, *Folktales of Mexico,* no. 78.
Thrush, The. Pino-Saavedra, *Folktales of Chile,* no. 50.

## 2031C  A MIGHTY BRIDEGROOM FOR A MOUSE.

A mouse asked the mighty sun to marry his daughter. The sun said a cloud would be better, for a cloud could cover the sun. The cloud admitted that the wind was stronger than he. The wind sent the mouse to a tower who could withstand his strongest gusts. The tower complained that mice were eating him up, so the father chose a mouse to marry his daughter. (Megas)

Mole's Bridegroom, The. Seki, *Folktales of Japan,* no. 13.
Mouse and His Daughter, The. Megas, *Folktales of Greece,* no. 16.

## 2032  THE WOUNDED COCK.

A mouse in a tree threw a nut to his friend the cock, hitting him on the head. The cock went to a woman for a bandage. —The chain continues, involving a dog, a baker, a forest, and a fountain. The cock finally gets his bandage. (Crane) Cf. type 2034.

Cock and the Mouse, The (Italy). Cole, *Best-Loved Folktales,* no. 32.
Cock and the Mouse, The. Crane, *Italian Popular Tales,* no. 80.
Little Hen, The. Massignon, *Folktales of France,* no. 35.
Sexton's Nose, The. Crane, *Italian Popular Tales,* no. 79.

**2033 HENNY-PENNY THINKS THE SKY IS FALLING.** Something hit Henny-Penny on the head, so she set off to report to the king that the sky was falling. She was joined by Cocky-Locky, Ducky-Daddles, Goosey-Poosey, and Turkey-Lurkey. On the way they were attacked by Foxy-Woxy. Henny-Penny barely escaped. She ran back home, and never told the king that the sky was falling. (Jacobs) Cf. type 20C.

Brother Rabbit Takes Some Exercise. Harris, *Nights with Uncle Remus,* no. 20.
Chicken-Licken. Briggs, *DBF,* pt. A, v. 2, p. 515.
Chickie Birdie. Briggs, *DBF,* pt. A, v. 2, p. 516.
Cock and Hen That Went to the Dovrefell, The. Asbjørnsen and Moe, *East o' the Sun,* p. 353.
End of the World, The (Finland). Booss, *Scandinavian Tales,* p. 589.
Hen and Her Fellow Travellers, The. Briggs, *DBF,* pt. A, v. 2, p. 531.
Henny-Penny. Briggs, *DBF,* pt. A, v. 2, p. 532.
Henny-Penny. Jacobs, *English Fairy Tales,* p. 113.
Little Chicken Kluk (Denmark). Booss, *Scandinavian Tales,* p. 500.
Plop! (Tibet). Clarkson and Cross, *World Folktales,* no. 37.

**2034 THE MOUSE REGAINS ITS TAIL.** A cat bit off a mouse's tail, and would not return it until the mouse brought her some milk. The cow would not give milk, until she got some hay. —The chain continues with a farmer, a butcher, and a baker. (Briggs) Cf. type 2032.

Bird Who Lost His Nose, The. Fowke, *Folklore of Canada,* p. 287.
Cat and the Mouse, The. Briggs, *DBF,* pt. A, v. 2, p. 512.
Cat and the Mouse, The (England). Clarkson and Cross, *World Folktales,* no. 38.
Exchanges (2 variants). Arewa, *Northern East Africa,* p. 247.
How Society Can Get Back Its Medicine (Liberia). Dorson, *Folktales around the World,* p. 344.
How the Fox Got Back His Tail. Bushnaq, *Arab Folktales,* p. 220.

**2035 THE HOUSE THAT JACK BUILT.** —A chain tale in verse about people, animals, and things (including a priest all shaven and shorn, a man all tattered and torn, a maiden all forlorn, and a cow with a crumpled horn) associated with the house that Jack built.

House That Jack Built, The. Briggs, *DBF,* pt. A, v. 2, p. 535.
House That Jack Built, The. Clouston, *Popular Tales,* v. 1, p. 289.

**2039 THE LOST HORSESHOE NAIL.** A merchant failed to replace the missing nail from the shoe of his horse. The shoe came off, and the horse fell down, breaking its leg. The merchant was forced to carry his goods home on his own back, all for the want of a nail. (Grimm)

> Nail, The. Grimm, *Tales,* no. 184.
> Nail, The. Pourrat, *Treasury of French Tales,* p. 126.

**2040**  **FROM BAD TO WORSE.**  A messenger reported bad news in installments: The magpie is dead. From eating too much horseflesh. Your father's horses. They died from overwork. From carrying water. Water needed to fight the fire when your father's house burned down. The fire was set by torches at your mother's funeral. She collapsed at the death of your father. He died from the news that you had lost everything in a bank failure. (Jacobs)

> From Bad to Worse. Villa, *100 Armenian Tales,* no. 95.
> Goat Comes Back, The. Afanasyev, *Russian Fairy Tales,* p. 61.
> How Si' Djeha Staved Off Hunger. Bushnaq, *Arab Folktales,* p. 264.
> Loss of Old Bugler, The. Randolph, *Sticks in the Knapsack,* p. 54.
> Munuck. Villa, *100 Armenian Tales,* no. 97.
> News! Briggs, *DBF,* pt. A, v. 2, p. 199.
> News! Jacobs, *More English Fairy Tales,* p. 182.

**2044**  **PULLING UP THE TURNIP.**  Grandfather could not pull up the turnip he had planted, so he called grandmother. Grandpa pulled on the turnip, grandma pulled grandpa, granddaughter pulled grandma, puppy pulled granddaughter, five beetles pulled puppy, and they pulled up the turnip. Cf. type 1960D.

> Turnip, The. Afanasyev, *Russian Fairy Tales,* p. 26.

**2075**  **TALES IMITATING ANIMAL SOUNDS.**  Cf. type 236*.

> Bittern and Hoopoe, The. Grimm, *Tales,* no. 173.
> Tales of the Toad (III). Grimm, *Tales,* no. 105.
> Talking Animals. Paredes, *Folktales of Mexico,* no. 79.
> The Crumbs on the Table. Grimm, *Tales,* no. 190.

**2202**  **THE STORYTELLER IS KILLED IN HIS OWN STORY.**

> Boy and the Buffalo, The (Cameroun). Dorson, *Folktales around the World,* p. 377.
> Killed by a Bear. Fowke, *Folklore of Canada,* p. 180.

**2204**  **FALSE EXPECTATIONS.**  A man threw two rings, gifts from two girls, into the sea, saying he would marry the girl who could regain her ring. Years later one of the girls was cleaning a fish. She cut into it and what did she find? Guts. Cf. type 736A.

> Two Rings, The. Briggs, *DBF,* pt. A, v. 2, p. 338.

**2251  THIS TALE WOULD HAVE BEEN LONGER.**  A sheep became mired in a peat bog. The shepherd took hold of its tail and pulled, and he pulled! He pulled until the tail broke, and if it had not been for that, this tale would have been longer.

> Tail, The. Campbell, *West Highlands,* v. 2, p. 494.

**2260  THE GOLDEN KEY.**  A boy found a golden key in the snow. Nearby was an iron chest. He turned the key in the lock, and when he has opened the lid, we will learn what wonderful things were inside.

> Golden Key, The. Grimm, *Tales,* no. 200.

**2271  MOCK STORIES.**  Example: I'll tell you a story about Jack O'Nory, and now my story's begun; I'll tell you another about Jack and his brother, and now my story is done. (Personal recollection, Idaho, 1940's)

> Barber, The. Crane, *Italian Popular Tales,* no. 75.
> Mister Attentive. Crane, *Italian Popular Tales,* no. 74.

**2300  ENDLESS TALES.**  Example: A man had a huge barn filled with corn. There was a hole in the roof just large enough for one locust. A locust crawled through the hole and took a grain of corn, then another locust came and took another grain of corn, then.... —Repeats endlessly. (Briggs, I)  Cf. types 227, 1199B, 1376A*, 2013, 2320.

> Black One, White One, and Plucked One. Massignon, *Folktales of France,* no. 56.
> Endless Story, An (Japan). Clarkson and Cross, *World Folktales,* no. 40A.
> Endless Story, An. Seki, *Folktales of Japan,* no. 14.
> Endless Tale, The (I-III). Briggs, *DBF,* pt. A, v. 2, p. 519.
> Hunting the Old Iron. Randolph, *Who Blowed Up the Church House?,* p. 79.
> Locusts Got the Corn. Randolph, *The Devil's Pretty Daughter,* p. 75.
> Round the Campfire. Randolph, *The Devil's Pretty Daughter,* p. 25.
> Shepherd, The. Crane, *Italian Popular Tales,* no. 40.
> Treasure, The. Crane, *Italian Popular Tales,* no. 39.

**2320  ROUNDS.**  —Tales that repeatedly begin over again.  Cf. types 227, 1199B, 1376A*, 2013, 2300.

> Dark and Stormy Night, A (USA). Clarkson and Cross, *World Folktales,* no. 40B.
> Endless Tale, The. Briggs and Tongue, *Folktales of England,* no. 92.
> It Was a Dark and Stormy Night. Briggs, *DBF,* pt. A, v. 2, p. 520.
> Jean Baribeau. Fowke, *Folklore of Canada,* p. 58.
> Round. Paredes, *Folktales of Mexico,* no. 80.

**2335  CONTRADICTIONS.**  Example: One dark night in the middle of the day, two dead boys came out to play. Back to back they faced each other, drew their swords and shot each other. A deaf policeman heard the noise, came inside and shot the two dead boys. (Personal recollection, Idaho, 1940's) Cf. type 1965.

Droll Man, The.  Saucier, *French Louisiana*, no. 25.
Five Men.  Briggs, *DBF*, pt. A, v. 2, p. 520.
Nonsense Rhymes.  Palmer, *Folklore of Somerset*, p. 147.
Once There Were Three.  El-Shamy, *Folktales of Egypt*, no. 53.
Skoonkin Huntin', The.  Chase, *Grandfather Tales*, no. 15.

# The Grimms' Tales

---

[†] Type titles not given resemble the tales' titles.

19. The Fisherman and His Wife (Von dem Fischer un syner Fru). Type 555.

20. The Brave Little Tailor (Das tapfere Schneiderlein). Type 1640. Includes episodes of type 1060, *Squeezing Water from a Stone;* type 1062, *A Contest in Throwing Stones;* type 1052, *A Contest in Carrying a Tree;* type 1051 *Springing with a Bent Tree;* type 1115, *Attempting to Kill the Hero in His Bed.*

21. Cinderella (Aschenputtel). Type 510A.

22. The Riddle (Das Rätsel). Type 85, *Winning the Princess with a Riddle.*

23. The Mouse, the Bird, and the Sausage (Von dem Mäuschen, Vögelchen und der Bratwurst). Type 85.

24. Frau Holle (Frau Holle). Type 480, *The Kind and the Unkind Girls.*

25. The Seven Ravens (Die sieben Raben). Type 451, *The Brothers Who Were Turned into Birds.*

26. Little Red-Cap (Rotkäppchen). Type 333, *Red Riding Hood.*

27. The Bremen Town Musicians (Die Bremer Stadtmusikanten). Type 130, *Outcast Animals Find a New Home.*

28. The Singing Bone (Der singende Knochen). Type 780.

29. The Devil with the Three Golden Hairs (Der Teufel mit den drei goldenen Haaren). Type 461, *Three Hairs from the Devil;* type 930, *The Prophecy That a Poor Boy Will Marry a Rich Girl.*

30. Little Louse and Little Flea (Läuschen und Flöhchen). Type 2022, *An Animal Mourns the Death of a Spouse.*

31. The Girl without Hands (Das Mädchen ohne Hände). Type 706.

32. Clever Hans (Der gescheite Hans). Type 1696, *What Should I Have Said?*

33. The Three Languages (Die drei Sprachen). Type 671.

34. Clever Elsie (Die kluge Else). Type 1450. Ends with an episode of type 1383, *A Woman Does Not Know Herself.*

35. The Tailor in Heaven (Der Schneider im Himmel). Type 800.

36. Table-Be-Set, Gold-Donkey, and Cudgel-out-of-the-Sack (Tischchendeckdich, Goldesel und Knüppel aus dem Sack). Type 563, introduced by type 212, *The Goat That Lied.*

37. Thumbthick (Daumesdick). Type 700, *Tom Thumb.* Includes an episode of type 41, *Overeating in the Pantry.*

38. Mrs. Fox's Wedding (Die Hochzeit der Frau Füchsin). Two tales. Type 65, *Mrs. Fox's Suitors.*

39. The Elves (Die Wichtelmänner). Three tales. Tale one: type 503*, *Helpful Elves.* Tale two: type 476*, *A Midwife (or Godmother) for the Elves.* Tale three: type 504 (new classification), *The Changeling;* also classified as a migratory legend, type 5085.

40. The Robber Bridegroom (Der Räuberbräutigam). Type 955.

41. Herr Korbes (Herr Korbes). Type 210, *The Traveling Animals and the Wicked Man.*

42. The Godfather (Der Herr Gevatter). Type 332, *Godfather Death.*

43. Frau Trude (Frau Trude). Type 334, *At the Witch's House.*

44. Godfather Death  (Der Gevatter Tod).  Type 332.

45. Thumbling's Travels  (Daumerlings Wanderschaft).  Type 700, *Tom Thumb*.

46. Fitcher's Bird  (Fitchers Vogel).  Type 311, *The Heroine Rescues Herself and Her Sisters*.  Similar to type 312, *Bluebeard*.

47. The Juniper Tree  (Von dem Machandelboom).  Type 720, *My Mother Killed Me; My Father Ate Me*.

48. Old Sultan  (Der alte Sultan).  Type 101, *The Old Dog Rescues the Child*.  Concludes with an episode of type 104, *War between the Village Animals and the Forest Animals*.

49. The Six Swans  (Die sechs Schwäne).  Type 451, *The Brothers Who Were Turned into Birds*.

50. Little Briar-Rose  (Dornröschen).  Type 410, *Sleeping Beauty*.

51. Foundling-Bird  (Fundevogel).  Type 313A, *The Girl Helps the Hero Flee*.

52. King Thrushbeard  (König Drosselbart).  Type 900.

53. Little Snow-White  (Sneewittchen).  Type 709.

54. The Knapsack, the Hat, and the Horn  (Der Ranzen, das Hütlein und das Hörnlein).  Type 569.

55. Rumpelstiltskin  (Rumpelstilzchen).  Type 500, *Guessing the Helper's Name*.

56. Sweetheart Roland  (Der Liebste Roland).  Type 1119, *Ogres Kill Their Own Children,* followed by type 313C, *The Girl Helps the Hero Flee; the Forgotten Fiancée*.

57. The Golden Bird  (Der goldene Vogel).  Type 550.

58. The Dog and the Sparrow  (Der Hund und der Sperling).  Type 248, *The Man, the Dog, and the Bird*

59. Freddy and Katy Lizzy  (Der Frieder und das Catherlieschen).  Types 1387, *A Woman Draws Beer in the Cellar;* 1385*, *A Woman Loses Her Husband's Money;* 1291B, *A Fool Greeses the Cracked Earth with Butter;* 1291, *Sending One Cheese After Another;* 1653A, *Securing the Door;* 1653, *The Robbers under the Tree;* 1383, *A Woman Does Not Know Herself;* 1791, *Dividing Up the Dead*.

60. The Two Brothers  (Die zwei Brüder).  Type 567A, *The Magic Bird Heart;* followed by type 303, *The Blood Brothers*.  Includes an episode of type 300, *The Dragon Slayer*.

61. The Little Peasant  (Das Bürle).  Type 1535, *The Rich Peasant and the Poor Peasant (Unibos)*.  Includes an episode of type 1737, *Trading Places with the Trickster in a Sack*.  Similar to type 1539, *Tricksters and Their Victims*.

62. The Queen Bee  (Die Bienenkönigin).  Type 554, *The Grateful Animals*.

63. The Three Feathers  (Die drei Federn).  Type 402, *The Animal Bride*.

64. The Golden Goose  (Die goldene Gans).  Type 571, *All Stick Together,* plus an episode of type 513B, *The Land and Water Ship*.

65. All-Kinds-Of-Fur  (Allerleirauh).  Type 510B, *A King Tries to Marry His Daughter*.

66. The Hare's Bride  (Häsichenbraut).  Type 311, *The Heroine Rescues Herself and Her Sisters*.

67. The Twelve Huntsmen  (Die zwölf Jäger).  Type 884, *The Forsaken Fiancée*.

68. The Thief and His Master (De Gaudeif un sien Meester). Type 325, *The Magician and His Pupil.*

69. Jorinde and Joringel (Jorinde und Joringel). Type 405.

70. The Three Children of Fortune (Die drei Glückskinder). Type 1650, *Three Brothers Inherit a Rooster, a Scythe, and a Cat.* Includes episodes of types 1202, *Harvesting Grain with a Cannon;* 1651, *Dick Whittington and His Cat;* and 1281, *Burning the Barn to Destroy an Unknown Animal.*

71. How Six Men Got On in the World (Sechse kommen durch die ganze Welt). Type 513A.

72. The Wolf and the Man (Der Wolf und der Mensch). Type 157, *Learning to Fear Man.*

73. The Wolf and the Fox (Der Wolf und der Fuchs). Type 41, *Overeating in the Pantry.*

74. The Fox and His Cousin (Der Fuchs und die Frau Gevatterin). Type 152A*, *The Scalded Wolf,* followed by type 4, *Getting a Ride by Pretending to Be Injured.*

75. The Fox and the Cat (Der Fuchs und die Katze). Type 105, *The Cat's Only Trick.*

76. The Carnation (Die Nelke). Type 652, *The Boy Whose Wishes Always Come True.*

77. Clever Gretel (Das kluge Gretel). Type 1741, *The Guest Flees to Save His Ears.*

78. The Old Grandfather and His Grandson (Der alte Großvater und der Enkel). Type 980B, *The Wooden Bowl.*

79. The Nixie (Die Wassernixe). Type 313A, *The Girl Helps the Hero Flee.*

80. The Death of the Little Hen (Von dem Tode des Hühnchens). Type 2021. Includes an episode of type 2021A *The Cock Seeks Help for the Choking Hen.*

81. Brother Merry (Bruder Lustig). Includes episodes of type 785, *Who Ate the Lamb's Heart?;* type 753A, *The Unsuccessful Resuscitation;* type 330B, *The Devil in the Sack;* type 330*, *Entering Heaven by a Trick;*

82. Gambling Hansel (De Spielhansl). Type 330A, *The Smith's Three Wishes.*

83. Hans in Luck (Hans im Glück). Type 1415.

84. Hans Gets Married (Hans heiratet). Types 859B, *The Penniless Wooer: Money in Hand,* and 859A, *The Penniless Wooer: Patch of Land.*

85. The Gold-Children (Die Goldkinder). Type 555, *The Fisherman and His Wife,* followed by type 303, *Blood Brothers.*

86. The Fox and the Geese (Der Fuchs und die Gänse). Type 227, *The Geese's Eternal Prayer.*

87. The Poor Man and the Rich Man (Der Arme und der Reiche). Type 750A, *Good Wishes and Foolish Wishes.*

88. The Singing, Springing Lark (Das singende springende Löweneckerchen). Type 425C, *Beauty and the Beast.*

89. The Goose-Girl (Die Gänsemagd). Type 533.

90. The Young Giant (Der junge Riese). Type 650A. Introduced with an episode of type 700, *Tom Thumb.*

91. The Gnome (Dat Erdmänneken). Type 301A, *The Quest for the Vanished Princesses.*

92. The King of the Golden Mountain (Der König vom goldenen Berge). Type 401A, *The Enchanted Princess in Her Castle*. Introduced with an episode of type 810, *The Devil Loses a Soul That Was Promised Him*. Includes episodes of type 560, *The Magic Ring*, and type 518, *Quarreling Giants Lose Their Magic Objects*.

93. The Raven (Die Rabe). Type 401. *The Girl Transformed into an Animal*. Includes an episode of type 518, *Quarreling Giants Lose Their Magic Objects*.

94. The Peasant's Clever Daughter (Die kluge Bauerntochter). Type 875.

95. Old Hildebrand (Der alte Hildebrand). Type 1360C.

96. The Three Little Birds (De drei Vügelkens). Type 707, *The Dancing Water, the Singing Apple, and the Speaking Bird*.

97. The Water of Life (Das Wasser des Lebens). Type 551.

98. Dr. Know-All (Doktor Allwissend). Type 1641.

99. The Spirit in the Bottle (Der Geist im Glas). Type 331.

100. The Devil's Sooty Brother (Des Teufels rußiger Bruder). Type 475, *Heating Hell's Kitchen*.

101. Bearskin (Der Bärenhäuter). Type 361.

102. The Wren and the Bear (Der Zaunkönig und der Bär). Type 222, *The War between the Birds and the Beasts*.

103. Sweet Porridge (Der süße Brei). Type 565, *The Magic Mill*.

104. The Clever People (Die klugen Leute). Type 1384, *A Man Seeks Someone as Stupid as His Wife*. Includes episodes of type 1385, *A Woman Accepts Her Own Cow as Security*, and type 1540, *The Man from Paradise*.

105. Tales of the Toad (Märchen von der Unke). Three tales. Tale 1: type 285, *The Child and the Snake*. Tale 2: type 672B, *The Toad's Crown*. Tale 3: type 2075 *Imitating Animal Sounds*.

106. The Poor Miller's Boy and the Cat (Der arme Müllerbursch und das Kätzchen). Type 402, *The Animal Bride*.

107. The Two Travelers (Die beiden Wanderer). Type 613, followed by type 554, *The Grateful Animals*.

108. Hans-My-Hedgehog (Hans mein Igel). Type 441.

109. The Little Shroud (Das Totenhemdchen). Unclassified.

110. The Jew in the Thorns (Der Jude im Dorn). Type 592, *Dancing in Thorns*.

111. The Trained Huntsman (Der gelernte Jäger). Type 304.

112. The Threshing-Flail from Heaven (Der Dreschflegel vom Himmel). A combination of types 1960A, *The Giant Animal;* 1960G, *The Giant Plant;* and 1889K, *A Rope Made of Chaff*.

113. The Two Kings' Children (De beiden Künigeskinner). Type 313C, *The Girl Helps the Hero Flee; the Forgotten Fiancée*.

114. The Clever Little Tailor (Vom klugen Schneiderlein). An expurgated version of type 850, *The Princess's Birthmarks*. Includes episodes of type 1061, *Biting Stones* and 1159, *Catching the Would-Be Musician in a Crack* (expurgated).

115. The Bright Sun Will Bring It to Light (Die klare Sonne bringt's an den Tag). Type 960, *The Sun Brings All to Light*.

116. The Blue Light  (Das blaue Licht).  Type 562, *The Spirit in the Blue Light.*

117. The Willful Child  (Das eigensinnige Kind).  Type 779, *Divine Rewards and Punishments.*

118. The Three Army Surgeons  (Die drei Feldscherer).  Type 660, *The Three Doctors.*

119. The Seven Swabians  (Die sieben Schwaben).  Several episodes, mostly of type 1321, *Fools Are Frightened.*  One episode is type 1231, *Planning the Attack on a Hare.*  Conclusion belongs to type 1297*, *Fools Walk into a River and Drown.*

120. The Three Journeymen  (Die drei Handwerksburschen).  Type 360, *The Three Apprentices and the Devil.*  Similar to type 1697, *We Three, for Money.*

121. The King's Son Who Is Afraid of Nothing  (Der Königssohn, der sich vor nichts fürchtet).  Type 590, *The Magic Belt;* and type 401A, *The Enchanted Princess in Her Castle.*

122. The Cabbage-Donkey  (Der Krautesel).  Type 567, *The Magic Bird Heart.*  Similar to type 566, *Fruit That Grows Horns (Fortunatus).*

123. The Old Woman in the Forest  (Die Alte im Wald).  Type 442.

124. The Three Brothers  (Die drei Brüder).  Type 654, *Which Brother Has the Best Skill?*

125. The Devil and His Grandmother  (Der Teufel und seine Großmutter).  Type 812, *The Devil's Riddle.*

126. Ferdinand the Faithful and Ferdinand the Unfaithful  (Ferenand getrü un Ferenand ungetrü).  Type 531.

127. The Iron Stove  (Der Eisenofen).  Type 425A, *The Animal Bridegroom.*

128. The Lazy Spinning Woman  (Die faule Spinnerin).  Type 1405.

129. The Four Skillful Brothers  (Die vier kunstreichen Brüder).  Type 653.

130. One-Eye, Two-Eyes, and Three-Eyes  (Einäuglein, Zweiäuglein und Dreiäuglein).  Type 511.

131. Fair Katrinelje and Pif Paf Poltrie  (Die schöne Katrinelje und Pif Paf Poltrie).  Type 2019.

132. The Fox and the Horse  (Der Fuchs und das Pferd).  Type 47A, *Catching a Horse by the Tail.*

133. The Shoes That Were Danced to Pieces  (Die zertanzten Schuhe).  Type 306, *The Danced-Out Shoes.*

134. The Six Servants  (Die sechs Diener).  Type 513A, *Six Go through the Whole World.*

135. The White Bride and the Black Bride  (Die weiße und die schwarze Braut).  Type 403A, *The Black and the White Bride: The Wishes.*

136. Iron Hans  (Der Eisenhans).  Type 502, *The Wild Man as a Helper.*

137. The Three Black Princesses  (De drei schwatten Prinzessinnen).  Similar to type 401A, *The Enchanted Princess in Her Castle.*

138. Knoist and His Three Sons  (Knoist un sine dre Sühne).  Type 1965.

139. The Girl from Brakel  (Dat Mäken von Brakel).  Type 1476A, *Praying to the Statue's Mother.*

140. Household Servants  (Das Hausgesinde).  Type 1940, *Extraordinary Names.*

141. The Little Lamb and the Little Fish (Das Lämmchen und Fischchen). Type 450, *Little Brother, Little Sister.*

142. Simeli Mountain (Simeliberg). Type 676, *Open Sesame.*

143. Going Traveling (Up Reisen gohn). Type 1696, *What Should I Have Said?*

144. The Little Donkey (Das Eselein). Type 430, *The Donkey Bridegroom.*

145. The Ungrateful Son (Der undankbare Sohn). Type 980D, *A Toad in the Face of an Ungrateful Son.*

146. The Turnip (Die Rübe). Types 1960D, *The Giant Vegetable;* and 1689A, *Two Presents for the King.* Includes an episode of type 1737, *Trading Places with the Trickster in a Sack.*

147. The Little Old Man Made Young by Fire (Das junggeglühte Männlein). Type 753, *Christ and the Smith.*

148. The Lord's Animals and the Devil's (Des Herrn und des Teufels Getier). Unclassified.

149. The Rooster's Beam (Der Hahnenbalken). Unclassified. Contains an episode similar to type 1290, *A Fool Mistakes a Flax Field for a Lake.*

150. The Old Beggar-Woman (Die alte Bettelfrau). Unclassified.

151. The Three Lazy Ones (Die drei Faulen). Type 1950, *A Contest in Laziness.*

151* The Twelve Lazy Servants (Die zwölf faulen Knechte). Type 1950, *A Contest in Laziness.*

152. The Little Shepherd Boy (Das Hirtenbüblein). Type 922, *The King, the Abbot, and the Shepherd.*

153. The Star Talers (Die Sterntaler). Type 779, *Divine Rewards and Punishments.*

154. The Stolen Farthing (Der gestohlene Heller). Type 769, *A Child Returns from the Dead.*

155. Choosing a Bride (Die Brautschau). Type 1452, *Choosing a Bride by How She Cuts Cheese.*

156. The Hurds (Die Schlickerlinge). Type 1451, *A Suitor Chooses the Thrifty Girl.*

157. The Sparrow and His Four Children *(Der Sperling und seine vier Kinder).* Similar to type 157, *Learning to Fear Man.*

158. The Tale of Cockaigne (Das Märchen vom Schlauraffenland). Type 1930.

159. The Tall Tale from Ditmarsh (Das Diethmarsische Lügenmärchen). Type 1930, *Schlaraffenland.*

160. A Riddling Tale (Rätselmärchen). Type 407, *The Girl as a Flower.*

161. Snow-White and Rose-Red (Schneeweißchen und Rosenrot). Type 426, *The Two Girls, the Bear, and the Dwarf.*

162. The Clever Servant (Der kluge Knecht). Similar to type 1681B, *The Fool as a Housekeeper.*

163. The Glass Coffin (Der gläserne Sarg). Type 410, *Sleeping Beauty.*

164. Lazy Heinz (Der faule Heinz). Type 1430, *Air Castles.*

165. The Griffin (Der Vogel Greif). Type 610, *Fruit to Cure the Princess;* and type 461, *Three Hairs from the Devil.*

166. Strong Hans (Der starke Hans). Type 650A, *The Young Giant;* and type 301A, *The Quest for the Vanished Princesses.*

167. The Peasant in Heaven (Das Bürle im Himmel). Type 802.

168. Lean Lisa (Die hagere Liese). Type 1430, *Air Castles.*

169. The Hut in the Forest (Das Waldhaus). Type 431.

170. Sharing Joy and Sorrow (Lieb und Leid teilen). Unclassified.

171. The Wren (Der Zaunkönig). Type 221, *The Wren Becomes King of the Birds.*

172. The Flounder (Die Scholle). Type 250A, *The Flounder's Crooked Mouth.*

173. The Bittern and Hoopoe (Rohrdommel und Wiedehopf). Type 236*, *Imitating Bird Sounds.* Compare type 2075, *Imitating Animal Sounds.*

174. The Owl (Die Eule). Type 1281, *Burning the Barn to Destroy an Unknown Animal.*

175. The Moon (Der Mond). Unclassified.

176. The Duration of Life (Die Lebenszeit). Types 173 and 828, *Men, Animals, and the Span of Life.* (Categorized under two different numbers by Aarne-Thompson.)

177. Death's Messengers (Die Boten des Todes). Type 335.

178. Master Pfriem (Meister Pfriem). Type 801. Includes an episode of type 1248, *Loading a Beam Crosswise on a Wagon.*

179. The Goose-Girl at the Well (Die Gänsehirtin am Brunnen). Type 923, *Love Like Salt.*

180. Eve's Unequal Children (Die ungleichen Kinder Evas). Type 758.

181. The Nixie in the Pond (Die Nixe im Teich). Type 316.

182. The Little Folks' Presents (Die Geschenke des kleinen Volkes). Type 503, *The Hunchbacks and the Elves.*

183. The Giant and the Tailor (Der Riese und der Schneider). Type 1049, *The Heavy Ax;* 1053, *Shooting Wild Boars;* and 1051, *Springing with a Bent Tree.*

184. The Nail (Der Nagel). Type 2039, *The Lost Horseshoe Nail.*

185. The Poor Boy in the Grave (Der arme Junge im Grab). Episodes include type 1876, *Chickens on a String,* and type 1313, *The Man Who Thought He Was Dead.*

186. The True Bride (Die wahre Braut). Type 510, *The Persecuted Heroine;* followed by type 884, *The Forsaken Fiancée.*

187. The Hare and the Hedgehog (Der Hase und der Igel). Type 275A*, *The Race between the Hedgehog and the Hare.* Compare type 1074, *A Race Is Won by a Look-Alike Helper.*

188. Spindle, Shuttle, and Needle (Spindel, Weberschiffchen und Nadel). Type 585.

189. The Peasant and the Devil (Der Bauer und der Teufel). Type 1030, *Man and Ogre Share the Harvest.*

190. The Crumbs on the Table (Die Brosamen auf dem Tisch). Type 236*, *Imitating Bird Sounds.* Compare type 2075, *Imitating Animal Sounds.*

191. The Sea-Hare (Das Meerhäschen). Type 554, *The Grateful Animals.* Similar to 851, *Winning the Princess with a Riddle.*

192. The Master Thief (Der Meisterdieb). Type 1525A, *Stealing the Count's Horse, Sheet, and Parson.*

193. The Drummer (Der Trommler). Type 400, *The Quest for a Lost Bride;* and type 313C, *The Girl Helps the Hero Flee; the Forgotten Fiancée.* Includes an episode of type 518, *Quarreling Giants Lose Their Magic Objects.*

194. The Ear of Grain (Die Kornähre). Type 779, *Divine Rewards and Punishments.*

195. The Grave Mound (Der Grabhügel). Similar to type 815, *Keeping Watch at a Rich Man's Grave.* Contains an episode of type 1130, *A Boot Full of Money.*

196. Old Rinkrank (Oll Rinkrank). Similar to type 311, *The Heroine Rescues Herself and Her Sisters.*

197. The Crystal Ball (Die Kristallkugel). Type 552A, *The Girls Who Married Animals.* Includes episodes of type 302, *The Giant Whose Heart Was in an Egg,* and type 518, *Quarreling Giants Lose Their Magic Objects.*

198. Maid Maleen (Jungfrau Maleen). Type 870, *The Entombed Princess.*

199. The Boot of Buffalo Leather (Der Stiefel von Büffelleder). Type 952, *The King and the Soldier.*

200. The Golden Key (Der goldene Schlüssel). Type 2260.

201. St. Joseph in the Forest (Der heilige Joseph im Walde). Type 480, *The Kind and the Unkind Girls.*

202. The Twelve Apostels (Die zwölf Apostel). Unclassified.

203. The Rose (Die Rose). Unclassified.

204. Poverty and Humility Lead to Heaven (Armut und Demut führen zum Himmel). Unclassified.

205. God's Food (Gottes Speise). Unclassified.

206. The Three Green Branches (Die drei grünen Zweige). Type 756A, *Green Leaves on a Dry Stick.*

207. Our Lady's Little Glass (Muttergottesgläschen). Unclassified.

208. The Aged Mother (Die alte Mütterchen). Unclassified.

209. The Heavenly Wedding (Die himmlische Hochzeit). Type 767, *Food for the Crucifix.*

210. The Hazel Switch (Die Haselrute). Unclassified.

# Secondary Literature

Aarne, Antti and Thompson, Stith. *The Types of the Folktale: A Classification and Bibliography.* FF Communications, no. 184. Helsinki: Suomalainen Tiedeakatemia, 1961.

Abrahams, Roger D. *The Man-of-Words in the West Indies: Performance and the Emergence of Creole Culture.* Baltimore: Johns Hopkins University Press, 1983.

Anderson, George, K. *The Legend of the Wandering Jew.* Providence: Brown University Press, 1965.

Arewa, Erastus Ojo. *A Classification of the Folktales of the Northern East African Cattle Area by Types.* Folklore of the World. New York: Arno Press, 1980.

Azzolina, David S. *Tale Type and Motif Indexes: An Annotated Bibliography.* Folklore Series. New York: Garland Publishing, 1985.

Bächtold-Stäubli, Hanns, ed. *Handwörterbuch des deutschen Aberglaubens.* 10 vols. Berlin: Walter de Gruyter, 1927-1942. Reprint. Berlin, Walter de Gruyter, 1987.

Baer, Florence C. *Sources and Analogues of the Uncle Remus Tales.* FF Communications, no. 228. Helsinki: Suomalainen Tiedeakatemia, 1981.

Bagdanavicius, Vytautas. *Cultural Wellsprings of Folktales,* translated from the Lithuanian by Jeronimas Zemkalnis. New York: Manyland Books, 1970.

Baughman, Ernest W. *Type and Motif Index of the Folktales of England and North America.* Indiana University Folklore Series, no. 20. The Hague: Mouton, 1966.

Bausinger, Hermann. *Formen der "Volkspoesi,"* 2nd ed. Berlin: Erich Schmidt Verlag, 1980.

Beitl, Richard, and Beitl, Klaus. *Wörterbuch der deutschen Volkskunde,* 3rd ed. Kröners Taschenausgabe, vol. 127. Stuttgart: Alfred Kröner Verlag, 1974.

Beit, Hedwig von (Hedwig Roques-von Beit). *Das Märchen: Sein Ort in der geistigen Entwicklung.* Bern and Munich: Francke, 1965.

Beit, Hedwig von (Hedwig Roques-von Beit). *Symbolik des Märchens: Versuch einer Deutung,* 2nd ed. Bern: Francke, 1960.

Bettelheim, Bruno. *The Uses of Enchantment: The Meaning and Importance of Fairy Tales.* New York: Alfred A. Knopf, 1976.

Blackham, H. J. *The Fable as Literature.* London: Athlone Press, 1985.

Bolte, Johannes, and Polívka, Georg. *Anmerkungen zu den Kinder- und Hausmärchen der Brüder Grimm.* 5 vols. Leipzig, 1913-1932. Reprint. Hildesheim: Georg Olms Verlagsbuchhandlung, 1963.

Bødker, Laurits. *Folk Literature (Germanic). International Dictionary of Regional European Ethnology and Folklore,* vol. 2. Copenhagen: Rosenkilde and Bagger, 1965.

Brackert, Helmut, ed. *Und wenn sie nicht gestorben sind: Perspektiven auf das Märchen.* Edition Suhrkamp, no. 973. Frankfurt am Main: Suhrkamp Verlag, 1980.

Briggs, Katharine M. *Abbey Lubbers, Banshees, and Boggarts: An Illustrated Encyclopedia of Fairies.* New York: Pantheon Books, 1979. An abridged and simplified version of the author's Encyclopedia of Fairies, which was originally published under the title *A Dictionary of Fairies.*

Briggs, Katherine M. *An Encyclopedia of Fairies, Hobgoblins, Brownies, Bogies, and other Supernatural Creatures.* New York: Pantheon, 1976. First edition published under the title: *A Dictionary of Fairies.*

Brunvand, Jan Harold. *The Choking Doberman and Other "New" Urban Legends.* New York: W. W. Norton, 1984.

Brunvand, Jan Harold. *The Study of American Folklore: An Introduction,* 2nd edition. New York: W. W. Norton, 1978.

Brunvand, Jan Harold. *The Vanishing Itchhiker: American Urban Legends and Their Meanings.* New York: W. W. Norton, 1981.

Campbell, Joseph. *The Flight of the Wild Gander: Explorations in the Mythological Dimension.* Chicago: Regnery Gateway, 1969.

Christiansen, Reidar Th. *Studies in Irish and Scandinavian Folktales..* Folklore of the World. Copenhagen: Rosenkilde and Bagger, 1959. Reprint. New York: Arno Press, 1980

Christiansen, Reidar Th. *The Migratory Legends.* FF Communications, no. 175. Helsinki: Suomalainen Tiedeakatemia, 1958. Reprint. New York: Arno Press, 1977.

Clouston, W. A. *The Book of Noodles: Stories of Simpletons; or, Fools and Their Follies.* London: Elliot Stock, 1888. Reprint. Detroit: Gale Research Company, 1969.

Clouston, W. A. *Popular Tales and Fictions: Their Migrations and Transformations.* 2 vols. Edinburgh: William Blackwood and Sons, 1887. Reprint. Detroit: Singing Tree Press, 1968.

Cox, Marian Roalfe. *Cinderella: Three Hundred and Forty-five Variants of Cinderella, Catskin, and Cap O' Rushes, Abstracted and Tabulated, with a Discussion of Mediaeval Analogues, and Notes.* London: Published for the Folk-Lore Society by David Nutt, 1893. Introduction by Andrew Lang.

Crowley, Daniel J., ed. *African Folklore in the New World.* Austin: University of Texas Press, 1977.

Dégh, Linda. *Märchen, Erzähler und Erzählgemeinschaft dargestellt an der ungarischen Volksüberlieferung,* Berlin: Akademie Verlag, 1962. Translated by Emily M. Schossberger as *Folktales and Society: Story-Telling in a Hungarian Peasant Community.* Bloomington: Indiana University Press, 1969.

Dégh, Linda, ed. *Studies in East European Folk Narrative.* [Bloomington]: American Folklore Society and the Indiana University Folklore Monographs Series, 1978.

Delarue, Paul. *Le conte populaire français: Catalogue raisonné des versions de France et des pays de langue française d'outre-mer,* vol. 1. Paris: Éditions Érasme, 1957. Volumes 3 and 4, co-edited by Marie-Louise Tenèze, were published 1964 and 1976 by Maisonneuvre et Larose.

Denecke, Ludwig. *Jacob Grimm und sein Bruder Wilhelm.* Realienbücher für Germanisten, no. M100. Stuttgart: J. B. Metzlersche Verlagsbuchhandlung, 1971.

*Deutsches Jahrbuch für Volkskunde.* Institut für Deutsche Volkskunde an der Deutschen Akademie der Wissenschaften zu Berlin. Berlin: Akademie Verlag, 1955-.

Dorson, Richard M. *American Folklore.* The Chicago History of American Civilization. Chicago: University of Chicago Press, 1959.

Dorson, Richard M. *Folklore and Fakelore: Essays toward a Discipline of Folk Studies.* Cambridge: Harvard University Press, 1976.

Dorson, Richard M., ed. *Folklore and Folklife: An Introduction.* Chicago: University of Chicago Press, 1972.

Dorson, Richard M., ed. *Peasant Customs and Savage Myths: Selections from the British Folklorists.* 2 vols. Chicago: University of Chicago Press, 1968.

Dundes, Alan, ed. *Cinderella: A Case Book.* New York: Wildman Press, 1983.

Dundes, Alan. *Interpretting Folklore.* Bloomington: Indiana University Press, 1980.

Dundes, Alan. *Life is Like a Chicken Coop Ladder: A Portrait of German Culture Through Folklore.* New York: Columbia University Press, 1984.

Dundes, Alan, ed. *Oedipus: A Folklore Casebook.* See Edmunds, Lowell.

Dundes, Alan. *The Study of Folklore.* Englewood Cliffs, N. J.: Prentice-Hall, 1965.

Dundes, Alan, and Carl R. Pagter. *Urban Folklore from the Paperwork Empire.* Memoir Series, vol. 62. Austin, Texas: American Folklore Society, 1975.

Edmunds, Lowell, and Dundes, Alan, eds. *Oedipus: A Folklore Casebook.* New York: Garland Publishing, 1983.

Ellis, John M. *One Fairy Story Too Many: The Brothers Grimm and Their Tales.* Chicago: University of Chicago Press, 1983.

*Enzyklopädie des Märchens.* See Ranke, Kurt, ed.

Europäische Märchengesellschaft, *Veröffentlichungen.* Many publications, various authors.

Evans-Wentz, W. Y. *The Fairy-Faith in Celtic Countries.* N.P.: University Books, 1966. First published 1911.

*Fabula: Zeitschrift für Erzählforschung/ Journal of Folktale Studies/ Revue d'Etudes sur le Conte Populaire.* Berlin: Walter de Gruyter, 1958-.

Falassi, Alessandro. *Folklore by the Fireside: Text and Coantext of the Tuscan Veglia.* Austin: University of Texas Press, 1980. Foreword by Roger D. Abrahams.

Flowers, Helen H. *A Classification of Folktales of the West Indies by Types and Motifs.* Ph.D. dissertation, Indiana University, 1952. Reprint. Folklore of the World. New York: Arno Press, 1980.

*Folk-Lore: A Quarterly Review of Myth, Tradition, Institution and Customs.* Folk-Lore Society. London: David Nutt, 1890-.

*Folklore Fellows Communications.* Helsinki: Suomalainen Tiedeakatemia, 1910-.

Franz, Marie-Louise von. *An Introduction to the Psychology of Fairy Tales.* Irving, Texas: Spring Publications and University of Dallas, 1978.

Franz, Marie-Louise von. *Problems of the Feminine in Fairy Tales.* Irving, Texas: Spring Publications and University of Dallas, 1972.

Franz, Marie Louise von. *Shadow and Evil in Fairy Tales.* New York: Spring Publications, 1974.

Fromm, Erich. *The Forgotten Language: An Introduction to the Understanding of Dreams, Fairy Tales and Myths.* New York: Grove Press, 1951.

Gerould, Goldon Hall. *The Grateful Dead: The History of a Folk Story.* Publications of the Folk-Lore Society, no. 60. London: David Nutt, 1908. Reprint. Folcroft, Pennsylvania: Folcroft Library Editions, 1973.

Gose, Elliott B., Jr. *The World of the Irish Wonder Tale: An Introduction to the Study of Fairy Tales.* Toronto: University of Toronto Press, 1985.

Hartland, Edwin Sidney. *The Science of Fairy Tales: An Inquiry into Fairy Mythology.* London: Walter Scott, 1891. Reprint. Detroit: Singing Tree Press, 1968.

Hennig, Dieter, and Bernhard Lauer, eds. *Die Brüder Grimm: Dokumente ihres Lebens und Wirkens.* Kassel: Verlag Weber and Weidemeyer, 1985. 200 Jahre Brüder Grimm, vol. 1.

Heuscher, Julius E. *A Psychiatric Study of Myths and Fairy Tales,* 2nd ed. Springfield, Illinois: Charles C. Thomas, [1974].

Hultkrantz, Åke. *General Ethnological Concepts. International Dictionary of Regionql European Ethnology and Folklore,* vol. 1. Copenhagen: Rosenkilde and Bagger, 1960.

Hurreiz, Sayyid H. *Ja'aliyyin Folktales.* Indiana University African Series, vol. 8. Bloomington: Indiana University, 1977.

Jobes, Gertrude. *Dictionary of Mythology, Folklore, and Symbols.* 2 vols. New York: The Scarecrow Press, 1961.

Jolles, André. *Einfache Formen: Legende, Sage, Mythe, Rätsel, Spruch, Kasus, Memorabile, Märchen, Witz.* Konzepte der Sprach- und Literaturwissenschaft, no. 15. Tübingen: Max Niemeyer Verlag, 1974. First published 1930.

Jordan, Rosan A., and Susan J. Kalcik, eds. *Women's Folklore. Women's Culture.* Publications of the American Folklore Society, New Series, vol. 8. Philadelphia: University of Pennsylvania Press, 1985.

*Journal of American Folklore.* American Folklore Society, 1888-.

Karlinger, Felix. *Grundzüge einer Geschichte des Märchens im deutschen Sprachraum.* Grundzüge, vol. 51. Darmstadt: Wissenschaftliche Buchgesellschaft, 1983.

Karlinger, Felix. *Legendenforschung: Aufgaben und Ergebnisse.* Darmstadt: Wissenschaftliche Buchgesellschaft, 1986.

Karlinger, Felix, ed. *Wege der Märchenforschung.* Wege der Forschung, vol. 255. Darmstadt: Wissenschaftliche Buchgesellschaft, 1973.

Keightley, Thomas. *The Fairy Mythology, Illustrative of the Romance and Superstition of Various Countries,* 1850. Reprint. New York: Haskell House, 1968.

Kiefer, Emma Emily. *Albert Wesselski and Recent Folktale Theories.* Indiana University Publications, Folklore Series, no. 3. Bloomington: Indiana University, 1947.

Laiblin, Wilhelm, ed. *Märchenforschung und Tiefenpsychologie.* Wege der Forschung, vol. 102. Darmstadt: Wissenschaftliche Buchgesellschaft, 1975.

Leach, Maria, ed., and Fried, Jerome, assoc. ed. *Funk and Wagnalls Standard Dictionary of Folklore, Mythology, and Legend.* San Francisco: Harper and Row, 1984.

Legman, G. *The Horn Book: Studies in Erotic Folklore and Bibliography.* New Hyde Park, N.Y.: University Books, 1964.

Legman, G. *Rationale of the Dirty Joke: An Analysis of Sexual Humor.* First Series. New York: Grove Press, 1968. Second series: New York: Breaking Point, 1975.

Lindfors, Bernth, ed. *Forms of Folklore in Africa: Narrative, Poetic, Gnomic, Dramatic.* Austin: University of Texas Press, 1977.

Lüthi, Max. *Das europaische Volksmärchen: Form und Wesen,* 4th ed. Uni Taschenbucher, no. 312. Munich: Francke Verlag, 1974. Translated by John D. Niles as *The European Folktale: Form and Nature.* Folklore Studies in Translation. Bloomington: Indiana University Press, 1986.

Lüthi, Max. *Das Volksmärchen als Dichtung: Asthetik und Anthropologie.* Düsseldorf: Diederichs, 1975. Translated by Jon Erickson as *The Fairytale as Art Form and Portrait of Man.* Folklore Studies in Translation. Bloomington: Indiana University Press, 1987.

Lüthi, Max. *Es war einmal: Vom Wesen des Volksmärchens,* 4th ed. Gottingen: Vandenhoeck and Ruprecht, 1973.

Lüthi, Max. *Märchen,* 3rd ed. Realienbücher für Germanisten, no. M16. Stuttgart: J. B. Metzlersche Verlagsbuchhandlung, 1968.

Lüthi, Max. *So leben sie noch heute: Betrachtungen zum Volksmärchen.* Kleine Vandenhoeck-Reihe, nos. 294-296. Göttingen: Vandenhoeck and Ruprecht, 1969.

*Märchen der Weltliteratur.* Köln: Eugen Diederichs Verlag. Many collections, various editors. Most volumes include scholarly appendices.

Mallet, Carl-Heinz. *Kennen Sie Kinder? Wie Kinder denken, handeln und fühlen, aufgezeigt an vier Grimmschen Märchen.* Munich: Deutscher Taschenbuch Verlag, 1985. Afterord by Bruno Bettelheim. Translated by Joachim Neugroschel as *Fairy Tales and Children: The Psychology of Children Revealed through Four of Grimm's Fairy Tales.* New York: Schocken Books, 1984.

Meacham, Mary. *Information Sources in Children's Literature: A Practical Reference Guide for Children's Librarians, Elementary School Teachers, and Students of Children's Literature.* Contributions in Librarianship and Information Science, No. 24. Westport, Connecticut: Greenwood Press, 1978.

Mieder, Wolfgang, ed. *Grimms Märchen—modern: Prosa, Gedichte, Karikaturen.* Arbeitshefte für den Unterricht. Reclams Universal- Bibliothek, no. 9554. Stuttgart: Phillipp Reclam, 1979.

Michaelis-Jena, Ruth. *The Brothers Grimm.* London: Routledge and Kegan Paul, 1970.

Moser-Rath, Elfriede. *"Lustige Gesellschaft": Schwank und Witz des 17. und 18. Jahrhunderts in kultur- und sozialgeschichtlichem Kontext.* Stuttgart: J. B. Metzlersche Verlagsbuchhandlung, 1984.

Nissen, Walter. *Die Brüder Grimm und ihre Märchen.* Göttingen; Vandenhoeck und Ruprecht, 1984. Foreword by Rolf Wilhelm Brednich.

Nitschke, August. *Soziale Ordnungen im Spiegel der Märchen.* 2 vols. Problemata vols. 53, 54. Stuttgart-Bad Cannstatt: Friedrich Frommann Verlag, 1976/1977.

Oinas, Felix J., and Stephen Soudakoff, trans. and eds. *The Study of Russian Folklore.* Indiana University Folklore Institute, Monograph Series, vol. 25. The Hague: Mouton, 1975.

Pelton, Robert D. *The Trickster in West Africa: A Study of Mythic Irony and Sacred Delight.* Hermeneutics: Studies in the History of Religion. Berkeley: University of California Press, 1980.

Peppard, Murray B. *Paths Through the Forest: A Biography of the Brothers Grimm.* New York: Holt, Rinehart and Winston, 1971.

Perry, B. E. *The Origin of the Book of Sindbad.* Supplement-Serie zu Fabula, series B: Untersuchungen, vol. 3. Berlin: Walter de Gruyter and Company, 1960.

Petzoldt, Leander, ed. *Vergleichende Sagenforschung.* Wege der Forschung, vol. 152. Darmstadt: Wissenschaftliche Buchgesellschaft, 1969.

Pflieger, Pat. *Reference Guide to Modern Fantasy for Children.* Westport, Connecticut: Greenwood Press, 1984.

Propp, Vladimir. *Morphology of the Folktale,* translated by Laurence Scott. Austin: University of Texas Press, 1968.

Propp, Vladimir. *Theory and History of Folklore,* translated by Ariadna Y. Martin et al., edited by Anatoly Liberman. Theory and History of Literature, vol. 5. Minneapolis: University of Minnesota Press, 1984.

Ranke, Kurt. *Die Welt der Einfachen Formen: Studien zur Motiv-, Wort- und Quellenkunde.* Berlin: Walter de Gruyter, 1978.

Ranke, Kurt, ed. *Enzyklopädie des Märchens: Handwörterbuch zur historischen und vergleichenden Erzählforschung,* edited by Kurt Ranke, in collaboration with Hermann Bausinger, Wolfgang Brückner, Max Lüthi, Lutz Röhrich und Rudolf Schenda. To encompass 12 volumes. Published thus far: vols. 1-4 (A-Förster).

Ritz, Hans. *Die Geschichte vom Rotkäppchen: Ursprünge, Analysen, Parodien eines Märchens.* Emstal: Muriverlag, 1981.

Ritz, Hans. *Steit um Rotkäppchen: Eine Geschichte aus der Kulturindustrie.* Göttingen: Muriverlag, 1984.

Roberts, Warren E. *The Tale of the Kind and the Unkind Girls: Aa-Th 480 and Related Tales.* Supplement-Serie zu Fabula, series B: Untersuchungen, vol. 1. Berlin: Walter de Gruyter and Company, 1958.

Röhrich, Lutz. *Sage.* Sammlung Metzler, no. M55. Stuttgart: J. B. Metzlersche Verlagsbuchhandlung, 1966.

Röhrich, Lutz, and Mieder, Wolfgang. *Sprichwort.* Sammlung Metzler, no. M154. Stuttgart: J. B. Metzlersche Verlagsbuchhandlung, 1977.

Röhrich, Lutz. *Der Witz: Figuren, Formen, Funktionen.* Stuttgart: J. B. Metzler, 1977.

Röhrich, Lutz. *Märchen und Wirklichkeit.* Wiesbaden: Franz Steiner Verlag, 1974.

Röhrich, Lutz. *Sage und Märchen: Erzählforschung heute.* Freiburg: Herder, 1976.

Rölleke, Heinz. *Die Märchen der Brüder Grimm: Eine Einführung.* Artemis Einführungen, vol. 18. Munich and Zürich: Artemis Verlag, 1985.

Rölleke, Heinz. *"Wo das Wünschen noch geholfen hat": Gesammelte Aufsätze zu den "Kinder- und Hausmärchen" der Brüder Grimm.* Wuppertaler Schriftenreihe Literatur, vol. 23. Bonn: Bouvier Verlag Herbert Grundmann, 1985.

Rooth, Anna Birgitta. *The Cinderella Cycle.* Lund: C. W. K. Gleerup, 1951.

Sale, Roger. *Fairy Tales and After: From Snow White to E. B. White.* Cambridge: Harvard University Press, 1983.

Scherf, Walter. *Lexikon der Zaubermärchen.* Kröners Taschenausgabe, vol. 472. Stuttgart: Alfred Kröner Verlag, 1982.

Schneiderman, Leo. *The Psychology of Myth, Folklore, and Religion.* Chicago: Nelson-Hall, 1981.

Schwarzbaum, Haim. *Studies in Jewish and World Folklore.* Supplement- Serie zu Fabula, series B: Untersuchungen, vol. 3. Berlin: Walter de Gruyter and Company, 1968.

Seitz, Gabriele. *Die Brüder Grimm: Leben, Werk, Zeit.* München: Winkler Verlag, 1984.

Shannon, George W. B., ed. *Folk Literature and Children: An Annotated Bibliography of Secondary Materials.* Westport, Connecticut: Greenwood Press, 1981.

Sparing, Margarethe Wilma. *The Perception of Reality in the Volksmärchen of Schleswig-Holstein: A Study in Interpersonal Relationships and World View.* Lanham, New York: University Press of America, 1984.

Swahn, Jan-Öjvind. *The Tale of Cupid and Psyche.* Lund: Gleerup, 1955.

Thompson, Stith. *Motif-Index of Folk-Literature: A Classification of Narrative Elements in Folktales, Ballads, Myths, Fables, Mediaeval Romances, Exempla, Fabliaux, Jest-Books, and Local Legends.* Revised and enlarged edition. 6 vols. Bloomington: Indiana University Press, 1955-1958.

Thompson, Stith. *The Folktale.* Berkeley: University of California Press, 1977. First published 1946.

Ussher, Arland, and Metzradt, Carl von. *Enter These Enchanted Woods: An Interpretation of Grimm's Fairy Tales.* Chester Springs, Pennsylvania: Dufour Editions, 1966.

Waelti-Walters, Jennifer. *Fairy Tales and the Female Imagination.* Montreal: Eden Press, 1982.

Weber-Kellermann, Ingeborg. *Deutsche Volkskunde: Zwischen Germanistik und Sozialwissenschaften.* Stuttgart: J. B. Metzlersche Verlagsbuchhandlung, 1969.

*Western Folklore.* California Folklore Society. 1942-.

Wittgenstein, Ottokar G. Graf. *Märchen, Träume, Schicksale: Autoritäts-, Partnerschafts-und Sexualprobleme im Spiegel zeitloser Bildersprache.* Geist und Psyche, no. 2114. Munich: Kindler Taschenbücher, 1973.

*Zeitschrift für Volkskunde.* Deutsche Gesellschaft für Volkskunde. Stuttgart: W. Kohlhammer, 1891-.

Zipes, Jack. Breaking the Magic Spell: Radical Theories of Folk and Fairy Tales. Austin: University of Texas Press, 1979.

Zipes, Jack. *Fairy Tales and the Art of Subversion: The Classical Genre for Children and the Process of Civilization.* New York: Wildman Press, 1983.

Zipes, Jack. *Rotkäppchens Lust und Leid: Biographie eines europäischen Märchens.* Cologne: Eugen Diderichs Verlag, 1982.

Zipes, Jack. *The Trials and Tribulations of Little Red Riding Hood: Versions of the Tale in Sociocultural Context.* South Hadley, Massachusetts: Bergin and Garvey, 1983.

# Folktale Collections

Abrahams, Roger D. *African Folktales: Traditional Stories of the Black World.* New York: Pantheon Books, 1983.

Abrahams, Roger D., ed. *Afro-American Folktales: Stories from Black Traditions in the New World.* New York: Pantheon Books, 1985.

Aesop. *Aesop without Morals: The Famous Fables, and a Life of Aesop,* translated and edited by Lloyd W. Daly. New York: Thomas Yoseloff, 1961.

Aesop. *Fables of Aesop,* translated by S. A. Handford. Harmondsworth, Middlesex, England: Penguin Books, 1964.

Aesop. *The Fables of Aesop,* edited and retold by Joseph Jacobs. New York: Schocken Books, 1966. First published 1894.

Aesop. *Fables of Aesop According to Sir Roger L'Estrange.* Paris: Harrison, 1931. Reprint. New York: Dover, 1967.

Afanasyev, Aleksandr. *Erotic Tales of Old Russia,* selected and translated by Yury Perkov. Oakland: Scythian Books, 1980. Bilingual edition.

Afanasyev, Aleksandr. *Russian Fairy Tales,* translated by Norbert Guterman. New York: Pantheon Books, 1945. Folkloristic commentary by Roman Jakobson.

Afanasyev, Aleksandr. *Russian Secret Tales: Bawdy Folktales of Old Russia.* New York: Brussel and Brussel, 1966. Annotations by Giuseppe Pitre. Introduction by G. Legman.

Aitken, Hannah, ed. *A Forgotten Heritage: Original Folk Tales of Lowland Scotland.* Totowa, New Jersey: Rowman and Littlefield, 1973.

Al-Shahi, Ahmed, and Moore, F. C. T., trans. and eds. *Wisdom from the Nile: A Collection of Folk-Stories from Northern and Central Sudan.* Oxford: Clarendon Press, 1978.

Andersen, Hans Christian. *The Complete Fairy Tales and Stories,* translated by Erik Christian Haugaard. Garden City, New York: Anchor Press/Doubleday, 1983. Foreword by Virginia Haviland.

Apuleius, Lucius. *The Golden Ass,* translated by Jack Lindsay. Bloomington: Indiana University Press, 1962.

*Arabian Nights, The. See* Dawood, N. J.; Lang, Andrew; and Mathers, Powys.

Asbjørnsen, Peter Christen and Moe, Jørgen. *Norwegian Folk Tales,* translated by Pat Shaw Iversen and Carl Norman. Oslo: Dreyers Forlag, 1978.

Asbjørnsen, Peter Christen and Moe, Jørgen. *Norwegian Folk Tales,* translated by Pat Shaw and Carl Norman. New York: Pantheon Books, 1960.

Asbjørnsen, Peter Christen, and Moe, Jørgen. *East o' the Sun and West o' the Moon,* translated by George Webbe Dasent. New York: Dover, 1970. Republication of all the stories by Asbjørnsen and Moe in *Popular Tales from the Norse,* 3rd edition. Edinburgh: David Douglass, 1888.

Aswell, James R., Willhoit, Julia, Edwards, Jennette, Miller, E. E., and Lipscomb, Lena. *God Bless the Devil! Liars' Bench Tales.* Chapel Hill: University of North Carolina Press, 1940. Reprint. Knoxville: University of Tennessee Press, 1985. New introduction by Charles K. Wolfe.

Baring-Gould, Sabine. *Curious Myths of the Middle Ages,* edited and with an introduction by Edward Hardy. New York: Oxford University Press, 1978. First published 1866.

Bascom, William R. *African Dilemma Tales.* World Anthropology, edited by Sol Tax. The Hague: Mouton Publishers, 1975.

Basile, Giambattista. *The Pentamerone* , translated from the Italian of Benedetto Croce, edited with notes by N. M. Penzer. Dutton, New York, 1932. Reprint. Westport, Connecticut: Greenwood Press, 1979. First published 1634/1636 as *Lo Cunto de li Cunti.*

Berry, James. *Tales of Old Ireland,* edited by Gertrude M. Horgan. Dolmen Press, 1966. Reprint. Salem, New Hampshire: Salem House, 1984.

Boase, Wendy. *The Folklore of Hampshire and the Isle of Wight.* The Folklore of the British Isles. Totowa, New Jersey: Rowman and Littlefield, 1976.

Boccaccio, Giovanni. *The Decameron,* translated and with an introduction by G. H. McWilliam. New York: Penguin Books, 1972.

Bødker, Laurits; Hole, Christina; and D'Aronco, G., eds. *European Folk Tales.* European Folklore Series, vol. 1. Copenhagen: Rosenkilde and Bagger, 1963.

Boos, Claire, ed. *Scandinavian Folk and Fairy Tales: Tales from Norway, Sweden, Denmark, Finland, Iceland.* New York: Avenel Books, 1984.

Botkin, B. A., ed. *A Treasury of American Folklore: Stories, Ballads, and Traditions of the People.* New York: Crown Publishers, 1944. Foreword by Carl Sandburg

Boucher, Alan, ed. and trans. *Icelandic Folktales,* 3 vols. Reykjavik: Icelandic Review Library, 1977.

Brackert, Helmut, and Volkmar Sander, eds. *Jakob and Wilhelm Grimm and Others: German Fairy Tales.* The German Library, vol. 29. New York: Continuum, 1985. Includes tales by the Grimms (translated by Margaret Hunt), Ludwig Bechstein (translated by Martha Humphreys), and Iring Fetscher (translated by Martha Humphreys). Foreword by Bruno Bettelheim.

Briggs, Katharine M., and Tongue, Ruth L., eds. *Folktales of England.* Folktales of the World. Chicago: University of Chicago Press, 1965. Foreword by Richard M. Dorson.

Briggs, Katherine M., ed. *British Folktales.* New York: Pantheon Books, 1977.

Briggs, Katherine M., ed. *A Dictionary of British Folk-Tales in the English Language,* pt. A, 2 vols., pt. B, 2 vols. London: Routledge and Kegan Paul, 1970, 1971.

Briggs, Katharine M. *The Folklore of the Cotswolds.* The Folklore of the British Isles. Totowa, New Jersey: Rowman and Littlefield, 1974.

Buber, Martin. *Tales of the Hasidim: The Early Masters.* New York: Schocken Books, 1975.

Bushnaq, Inea, ed. and trans. *Arab Folktales.* New York: Pantheon Books, 1986.

Calvino, Italo. *Italian Folktales,* translated by George Martin. New York: Pantheon Books, 1980.

Campbell, J. F. *Popular Tales of the West Highlands: Orally Collected.* 4 vols. London: Alexander Gardner, 1890-1893. Reprint. Detroit: Singing Tree Press, 1969.

Campbell, Marie. *Tales from the Cloud Walking Country.* Bloomington: Indiana University Press, 1958. Reprint. Westport, Connecticut: Greenwood Press, 1976.

Carpenter, Inta Gale. *A Latvian Storyteller.* Folklore of the World. New York: Arno Press, 1980.

Chase, Richard, ed. *Grandfather Tales: American-English Folk Tales.* Boston: Houghton Mifflin Company, 1948.

Chase, Richard, ed. *The Jack Tales: Told by R. M. Ward and his Kindred in the Beech Mountain Section of Western North Carolina and by Other Descendents of Council Harmon (1803-1896) Elsewhere in the Southern Mountains; with Three Tales from Wise County, Virginia.* Cambridge, Mass.: Houghton Mifflin Company, 1943.

Chaucer, Geoffrey. *The Canterbury Tales,* translated by Nevill Coghill. Harmondsworth, Middlesex, England: Penguin Books, 1977.

Christiansen, Reidar, ed. *Folktales of Norway,* translated by Pat Shaw Iversen. Folktales of the World. Chicago: University of Chicago Press, 1964. Foreword by Richard M. Dorson.

Clarkson, Atelia, and Cross, Gilbert B., eds. *World Folktales: A Scribner Resource Collection.* New York: Charles Scribner's Sons, 1980.

Cole, Joanna, ed. *Best-Loved Folktales of the World.* Garden City, New York: Anchor Press/Doubleday, 1982.

Crane, Thomas Frederick. *Italian Popular Tales.* Boston and New York: Houghton, Mifflin and Company, 1885.

Curtin, Jeremiah, ed. *Myths and Folk Tales of Ireland.* New York: Dover, 1975. Originally published as *Myths and Folk-Lore of Ireland,* Boston: Little, Brown and Company, 1890.

Dadié, Bernard Binlin. *The Black Cloth: A Collection of African Folktales,* translated by Karen C. Hatch. Amherst: University of Massachusetts Press, 1987. Foreword by Es'kia Mphahlele.

Dance, Daryl C. *Folklore from Contemporary Jamaicans.* Knoxville: University of Tennessee Press, 1985.

David, Alfred and Meek, Mary Elizabeth, eds. *The Twelve Dancing Princesses and Other Fairy Tales.* Bloomington: Indiana University Press, 1974.

Dawkins, R. M., ed. and trans. *Modern Greek Folktales.* Oxford, England: Clarendon Press, 1953. Reprint. Westport, Connecticut: Greenwood Press, 1974.

Dawkins, R. M., ed. and trans. *More Greek Folktales.* London: Carendon Press, 1955. Reprint. Westport, Connecticut: Greenwood Press, 1974.

Dawood, N. J., trans. *Tales from the Thousand and One Nights.* Harmondsworth, Middlesex, England: Penguin Books, 1983.

Daly, Lloyd W., trans. *See* Aesop.

Deane, Tony, and Tony Shaw. *The Folklore of Cornwall*. The Folklore of the British Isles. Totowa, New Jersey: Rowman and Littlefield, 1975. Introduction by Venetia J. Newall.

Dégh, Linda, ed. *Folktales of Hungary,* translated by Judit Halász. Folktales of the World. Chicago: University of Chicago Press, 1965. Foreword by Richard M. Dorson.

Delarue, Paul, ed. *The Borzoi Book of French Folk Tales,* translated by Austin E. Fife. New York: Alfred A. Knopf, 1956.

Domenichi, Lodovico. *See* Storer, Edward, trans.

Dorson, Richard M. *America in Legend: Folklore from the Colonial Period to the Present.* New York: Pantheon Books, 1973.

Dorson, Richard M. *Bloodstoppers and Bearwalkers: Folk Traditions of the Upper Peninsula.* Cambridge: Harvard University Press, 1952.

Dorson, Richard M. *Buying the Wind: Regional Folklore in the United States.* Chicago: University of Chicago Press, 1964.

Dorson, Richard M., ed. *Folktales Told around the World.* Chicago: University of Chicago Press, 1975.

Dorson, Richard M. *Jonathan Draws the Long Bow.* Cambridge: Harvard University Press, 1946.

Dorson, Richard M. *Negro Folktales in Michigan.* Cambridge: Harvard University Press, 1956. Reprint. Westport, Connecticut: Greenwood Press, 1974.

Dorson, Richard M. *Negro Tales from Pine Bluff, Arkansas, and Calvin, Michigan.* Bloomington: Indiana University Press, 1958. Reprint. New York: Kraus Reprint Corporation, 1968.

Eberhard, Wolfram, ed. *Folktales of China,* translated from the German by Desmond Parsons. Folktales of the World. Chicago: University of Chicago Press, 1965. Foreword by Richard M. Dorson.

El-Shamy, Hasan M., ed. and trans. *Folktales of Egypt.* Folktales of the World. Chicago: University of Chicago Press, 1980. Foreword by Richard M. Dorson.

Erdoes, Richard, and Ortiz, Alfonso, eds. *American Indian Myths and Legends.* New York: Pantheon Books, 1984.

Espinosa, Aurelio M. *The Folklore of Spain in the American Southwest: Traditional Spanish Folk Literature in Northern New Mexico and Southern Colorado.* Edited by J. Manuel Espinosa. Norman: University of Oklahoma Press, 1985.

Feldman, Susan, ed. *African Myths and Tales.* New York: Dell Publishing Co., 1963.

Fisher, Vardis, director. *Idaho Lore.* Prepared by the Federal Writers' Project of the Work Projects Administration, Vardis Fisher, State Director. American Guide Series. Caldwell, Idaho: Caxton Printers, 1939.

Ford, Patrick K, ed. and trans. *The Mabinogi and other Medieval Welsh Tales.* Berkeley: University of California Press, 1977.

Fowke, Edith. *Folklore of Canada.* Toronto: McClelland and Stewart, 1976.

Gantz, Jeffrey, trans. and ed. *Early Irish Myths and Sagas.* Harmondsworth, Middlesex, England: Penguin Books, 1981.

Glassie, Henry, ed. *Irish Folktales.* New York: Pantheon Books, 1985.

Glimm, James York, ed. *Flatlanders and Ridgerunners: Folktales from the Mountains of Northern Pennsylvania.* Pittsburgh: University of Pittsburgh Press, 1983.

Gmelch, George, and Ben Kroup, eds. *To Shorten the Road.* Toronto: Macmillan of Canada, 1978.

Grieg, Francis. *Heads You Lose and Other Apocryphal Tales.* New York: Crown Publishers, 1982. Originally published 1981 in Great Britain under the title *The Bite and Other Apocryphal Tales.*

Grimm, *Jacob and Wilhelm. Grimms' Other Tales,* selected by Wilhelm Hansen, translated by Ruth Michaelis-Jena and Arthur Ratcliff. Edinburgh: Canongate, 1984. First published 1956 in a limited edition by Golden Cockerel Press, London.

Grimm, Jacob and Wilhelm. *Grimms' Tales for Young and Old,* translated by Ralph Manheim. Garden City, New York: Anchor Press/Doubleday, 1977.

Grimm, Jacob and Wilhelm. *The Complete Grimm's Fairy Tales,* translated by Margaret Hunt, revised by James Stern. New York: Pantheon Books, 1972. Introduction by Padraic Colum, folkloristic commentary by Joseph Campbell.

Grimm, Jacob and Wilhelm. *The German Legends of the Brothers Grimm,* 2 vols., edited and translated by Donald Ward. Philadelphia: Institute for the Study of Human Issues, 1981.

Grimm, Jacob and Wilhelm. *The Grimms' German Folk Tales,* translated by Francis P. Magoun, Jr., and Alexander H. Krappe. Carbondale: Southern Illinois University Press, 1960.

Handford, S. A., trans. *See* Aesop.

Harris, Joel Chandler. *The Complete Tales of Uncle Remus,* compiled by Richard Chase. Boston: Houghton Mifflin Company, 1955. Includes:

*Uncle Remus: His Songs and His Sayings,* first published in New York: D. Appleton and Company, 1880.

*Nights with Uncle Remus: Myths and Legends of the Old Plantation,* first published in Boston: James R. Osgood and Company, 1883.

*Daddy Jake, the Runaway: And Short Stories Told after Dark,* first published in New York: Century Company, 1889.

*Uncle Remus and His Friends: Old Plantation Stories, Songs, and Ballads with Sketches of Negro Character,* first published in Boston: Houghton Mifflin and Company, 1892.

*Told by Uncle Remus: New Stories of the Old Plantation,* first published in New York: McClure, Phillips and Company, 1905.

*Uncle Remus and Brer Rabbit,* first published in New York: Frederick A. Stokes Company, 1907.

*Uncle Remus and the Little Boy,* first published in Boston: Small, Maynard and Company, 1910.

*Uncle Remus Returns,* first published in Boston: Houghton Mifflin Company, 1918.

*Seven Tales of Uncle Remus,* edited by Thomas H. English, Atlanta: Emory University, 1948.

Hartland, Edwin Sidney, ed. *English Fairy and Other Folk Tales.* London: Walter Scott Publishing Co., [ca. 1890].

Hazlitt, W. Carew, ed. *Shakespeare Jest-Books: Reprints of the Early and Very Rare Jest-Books Supposed to Have Been Used by Shakespeare.* 3 vols. London: Willis and Sotheran, 1864.

Hoogasian-Villa, Susie. *See* Villa, Susie Hoogasian.

Hunt, Robert. *Popular Romances of the West of England; or, The Drolls, Traditions, and Superstitions of Old Cornwall,* 2nd ed., London: John Camden Hotten, 1871.

Hyde-Chambers, Fredrick and Audrey. *Tibetan Folk Tales.* Boulder and London: Shambhala, 1981.

Jacobs, Joseph, ed. *See also* Aesop.

Jacobs, Joseph, ed. *Celtic Fairy Tales.* New York: Dover, 1968. Originally published 1892.

Jacobs, Joseph, ed. *English Fairy Tales.* New York: Dover, 1967. Reprint of the 3rd edition, as published by G. P. Putnam's Sons and David Nutt in 1898.

Jacobs, Joseph, ed. *Indian Fairy Tales.* New York: Dover, 1969. Originally published 1892.

Jacobs, Joseph, ed. *More Celtic Fairy Tales.* New York: Dover, 1968. Originally published 1894.

Jacobs, Joseph, ed. *More English Fairy Tales.* New York: G. P. Putnam's Sons, n.d.

Jacobs, Joseph, ed. *European Folk and Fairy Tales.* New York: G. P. Putnam's Sons, copyright 1916.

Jones-Baker, Doris. *The Folklore of Hertfordshire.* The Folklore of the British Isles. Totowa, New Jersey: Rowman and Littlefield, 1977.

Killip, Margaret. *The Folklore of the Isle of Man.* The Folklore of the British Isles. Totowa, New Jersey: Rowman and Littlefield, 1976.

Lang, Andrew, ed. *Arabian Nights.* London: Longmans, 1951.

Lang, Andrew, ed. *The Blue Fairy Book.* New York: Dover, 1965. Originally published circa 1889.

Lang, Andrew, ed. *The Brown Fairy Book.* New York: Dover, 1965. Originally published 1904.

Lang, Andrew, ed. *The Crimson Fairy Book.* New York: Dover, 1967. Originally published 1903.

Lang, Andrew, ed. *The Green Fairy Book.* New York: Dover, 1965. Originally published circa 1892.

Lang, Andrew, ed. *The Grey Fairy Book.* New York: Dover, 1967. Originally published 1900.

Lang, Andrew, ed. *The Lilac Fairy Book.* New York: Dover, 1968. Originally published 1910.

Lang, Andrew, ed. *The Olive Fairy Book.* New York: Dover, 1968. Originally published 1907.

Lang, Andrew, ed. *The Orange Fairy Book.* New York: Dover, 1968. Originally published 1906.

Lang, Andrew, ed. *The Pink Fairy Book.* New York: Dover, 1967. Originally published 1897.

Lang, Andrew, ed. *The Red Fairy Book.* New York: Dover, 1966. Originally published 1890.

Lang, Andrew, ed. *The Violet Fairy Book.* New York: Dover, 1966. Originally published 1901.

Lang, Andrew, ed. *The Yellow Fairy Book.* New York: Dover, 1966. Originally published 1894.

Lindell, Kristina, and Jan-Öjvind Swahn and Damrong Tayanin, eds. *Folk Tales from Kammu II: A Story-Teller's Tales.* Scandinavian Institute of Asian Studies Monograph Series, no. 40. London and Malmö: Curzon Press, 1980.

Lindow, John, ed. *Swedish Legends and Folktales.* Berkeley: University of California Press, 1978.

Lönnrot, Elias, ed. *The Kalevala: or, Poems of the Kaleva District,* translated, and with foreword and appendices by Francis Peabody Magoun, Jr. Cambridge: Harvard University Press, 1963.

MacDougall, James. *Highland Fairy Legends.* Collected from oral tradition by Rev James MacDougall. Edited by Rev George Calder with a new introduction by Dr Alan Bruford. Ipswich and Cambridge, England: D. S. Brewer; Totowa, N. J.: Rowman and Littlefield, 1978. Originally published as *Folk Tales and Fairy Lore in Gaelic and English,* Edinburgh, 1910.

Marwick, Ernest W. *The Folklore of Orkney and Shetland.* The Folklore of the British Isles. Totowa, New Jersey: Rowman and Littlefield, 1975.

Massignon, Geneviève, ed. *Folktales of France,* translated by Jacqueline Hyland. Chicago: University of Chicago Press, 1968. Foreword by Richard M. Dorson.

Mathers, Powys, trans. *The Book of the Thousand Nights and One Night,* rendered into English from the literal and complete French translation of Dr. J. C. Mardrus., 4 vols. London: Routledge and Kegan Paul, Ltd., 1964.

Mathias, Elizabeth, and Richard Raspa. *Italian Folktales in America.* Wayne State University Folklore Archive Study Series. Detroit: Wayne State University Press, 1985. Foreword by Roger D. Abrahams.

McGarry, Mary, ed. *Great Folktales of Old Ireland.* New York: Bell Publishing Company, 1972.

Megas, Georgios A., ed. *Folktales of Greece,* translated by Helen Colaclides. Folktales of the World. Chicago: University of Chicago Press, 1970. Foreword by Richard M. Dorson.

Miller, Elaine K. *Mexican Folk Narrative from the Los Angeles Area.* Publications of the American Folklore Society, Memoir Series, vol. 56. Austin: University of Texas Press, 1973.

Münchhausen, Baron von. *See* Raspe, Rudolf Erich.

Musick, Ruth Ann. *Green Hills of Magic: West Virginia Folktales from Europe.* Lexington: University Press of Kentucky, 1970.

Musick, Ruth Ann. *The Telltale Lilac Bush and Other West Virginia Ghost Tales.* Lexington: University of Kentucky Press, 1965.

Noy, Dov., ed. *Folktales of Israel,* translated by Gene Baharav. Folktales of the World. Chicago: University of Chicago Press, 1963. Foreword by Richard M. Dorson.

O'Flaherty, Wendy Doniger. *Tales of Sex and Violence: Folklore, Sacrifice, and Danger in the Jaiminiya Brahmana.* Chicago: University of Chicago Press, 1985.

O'Sullivan, Sean, ed. and trans. *Folktales of Ireland.* Folktales of the World. Chicago: University of Chicago Press, 1966. Foreword by Richard M. Dorson.

Opie, Iona and Peter, eds. *The Classic Fairy Tales.* New York: Oxford University Press, 1980.

Palmer, Kinglsey. *The Folklore of Somerset.* The Folklore of the British Isles. Totowa, New Jersey: Rowman and Littlefield, 1976.

Palmer, Roy. *The Folklore of Warwickshire.* The Folklore of the British Isles. Totowa, New Jersey: Rowman and Littlefield, 1976.

Paredes, Américo, ed. and trans. *Folktales of Mexico.* Folktales of the World. Chicago: University of Chicago Press, 1970. Foreword by Richard M. Dorson.

Perrault, Charles. *Perrault's Complete Fairy Tales,* translated by A. E. Johnson and others. New York: Dodd, Mead and Company, 1961.

Perrault, Charles. *Perrault's Fairy Tales,* translated by A. E. Johnson. New York: Dover, 1969.

Perrault, Charles. *The Fairy Tales of Charles Perrault,* translated by Angela Carter. New York: Avon Books, 1979. Foreword by Angela Carter.

Pino-Saavedra, Yolando, ed. *Folktales of Chile,* translated by Rockwell Gray. Folktales of the World. Chicago: University of Chicago Press, 1967. Foreword by Richard M. Dorson.

Poggio Bracciolini. *See* Storer, Edward, trans.

Porter, Enid. *The Folklore of East Anglia.* The Folklore of the British Isles. Totowa, New Jersey: Rowman and Littlefield, 1974.

Postma, Minnie. *Tales from the Basotho,* translated from Afrikaans by Susie McDermid. Publications of the American Folklore Society, Memoir Series, vol. 59. Austin: University of Texas Press, 1974.

Pourrat, Henri, ed. *A Treasury of French Tales,* translated by Mary Mian. Boston: Houghton Mifflin, 1954.

Randolph, Vance. *The Devil's Pretty Daughter and Other Ozark Folk Tales.* New York: Columbia University Press, 1955. Notes by Herbert Halpert.

Randolph, Vance. *Hot Springs and Hell and Other Folk Jests and Anecdotes from the Ozarks.* Hatboro, Pennsylvania: Folklore Associates, 1965.

Randolph, Vance. *Pissing in the Snow and Other Ozark Folktales.* New York: Avon Books, 1977. Introduction by Rayna Green. Annotations by Frank A. Hoffmann.

Randolph, Vance. *Sticks in the Knapsack and Other Ozark Folk Tales.* New York: Columbia University Press, 1958. Notes by Ernest W. Baughman.

Randolph, Vance. *The Talking Turtle and Other Ozark Folk Tales.* New York: Columbia University Press, 1957. Notes by Herbert Halpert.

Randolph, Vance. *We Always Lie to Strangers: Tall Tales from the Ozarks.* New York: Columbia University Press, 1951.

Randolph, Vance. *Who Blowed Up the Church House? and Other Ozark Folk Tales.* New York: Columbia University Press, 1952. Notes by Herbert Halpert.

Ranke, Kurt, ed. *Folktales of Germany,* translated by Lotte Baumann. Folktales of the World. Chicago: University of Chicago Press, 1966. Foreword by Richard M. Dorson.

Raspe, Rudolf Erich. *Singular Travels, Campaigns and Adventures of Baron Munchhausen.* New York: Chanticleer Press, 1948. Introduction by John Carswell.

Raspe, Rudolf Erich. *The Surprising Adventures of Baron Munchhausen,* edited by F. J. Harvey Darton. London: Navarre Society, 1930. Based on the earliest complete edition (1786).

Raven, Jon. *The Folklore of Staffordshire.* The Folklore of the British Isles. Totowa, New Jersey: Rowman and Littlefield, 1978.

Ross, Mabel H., and Walker, Barbara K. *On Another Day: Tales Told among the Nkundo of Zaïre.* Hamden, Connecticut: Archon Books, 1979. Foreword by Daniel J. Crowley.

Rhys, John, ed. *Celtic Folklore: Welsh and Manx.* 2 vols. Oxford University Press, 1901. Reprint. London: Wildwood House, 1980.

Roberts, Leonard W. *South from Hell-fer-Sartin: Kentucky Mountain Folk Tales.* Lexington: University of Kentucky Press, 1955.

Rowling, Marjorie. *The Folklore of the Lake District.* The Folklore of the British Isles. Totowa, New Jersey: Rowman and Littlefield, 1976.

Sabar, Yona, ed. and trans. *The Folk Literature of the Kurdistani Jews: An Anthology.* New Haven: Yale University Press, 1982.

Sampson, John, ed. *Gypsy Folk Tales.* Salem, New Hampshire: Salem House, 1984.

Saucier, Corinne L. *Folk Tales from French Louisiana.* New York: Exposition Press, 1962. Foreword by Irene Wagner.

Schwartz, Howard. *Elijah's Violin and Other Jewish Fairy Tales.* New York: Harper Colophon Books, 1985.

Simpson, Jacqueline, ed. *Icelandic Folktales and Legends.* Berkeley: University of California Press, 1972.

Simpson, Jacqueline. *The Folklore of Sussex.* The Folklore of the British Isles. London: B. T. Batsford, 1973.

Simpson, Jacqueline. *The Folklore of the Welsh Border.* The Folklore of the British Isles. Totowa, New Jersey: Rowman and Littlefield, 1976.

Storer, Edward, trans. *The Facetiae of Poggio and other Medieval Story-Tellers.* Broadway Translations. London: George Routledge and Sons, [1928].

Straparola, Giovanni Francesco. *The Facetious Nights of Straparola.* 4 vols. London: Privately printed for members of the Society of Bibliophiles, ca. 1901.

Theal, George McCall. *Kaffir Folk-Lore: A Selection from the Traditional Tales Current among the People Living on the Eastern Border of the Cape Colony.* London: S. Sonnenschein, Le Bas and Lowrey, 1886. Reprint. Westport, Connecticut: Negro Universities Press, 1970.

Thomas, Rosemary Hyde. *It's Good to Tell You: French Folktales from Missouri.* Columbia: University of Missouri Press, 1981.

Thompson, Stith, ed. *One Hundred Favorite Folktales.* Bloomington: Indiana University Press, 1974.

*Thousand and One Nights. See* Dawood, N. J.; Lang, Andrew; and Mathers, Powys.

Thundy, Zacharias P., ed. *South Indian Folktales of Kadar.* Meerut, India: Folklore Institute, 1983.

Tolstoy, Leo. *Fables and Fairy Tales,* translated by Ann Dunnigan. New York: New American Library, 1962. Foreword by Raymond Rosenthal.

Villa, Susie Hoogasian. *100 Armenian Tales.* Detroit: Wayne State University Press, 1966.

Walker, Barbara K. and Warren S., eds. *Nigerian Folk Tales, as Told by Olawale Idewu and Omotayo Adu,* 2nd edition. Hamden, Connecticut: Archon Books, 1980.

Walker, Warren S., and Uysal, Ahmet E., eds. and trans. *Tales Alive in Turkey.* Cambridge: Harvard University Press, 1966.

Welsch, Roger. *Shingling the Fog and Other Plains Lies.* Lincoln: University of Nebraska Press, 1972.

Whitlock, Ralph. *The Folklore of Devon.* The Folklore of the British Isles. Totowa, New Jersey: Rowman and Littlefield, 1977.

Whitlock, Ralph. *The Folklore of Wiltshire.* The Folklore of the British Isles. Totowa, New Jersey: Rowman and Littlefield, 1976.

Wolkstein, Diane. *The Magic Orange Tree and Other Haitian Folktales.* New York: Alfred A. Knopf, 1978.

Yeats, W. B., ed. *Fairy and Folk Tales of Ireland.* New York: Macmillan Publishing Company, 1983. Contains *Fairy and Folk Tales of the Irish Peasantry,* first published 1888, and *Irish Fairy Tales,* first published 1892. Foreword by Benedict Kiely.

# Index

---

## About the Author

D. L. ASHLIMAN is Associate Professor of German at the University of Pittsburgh. His numerous articles on popular culture and German literature have appeared in such publications as the *Journal of Popular Culture, Modern Austrian Literature, Utah Historical Quarterly,* and *Unterrichtspraxis,* as well as European literary journals.